EIGHT
EXPRESSIONIST PLAYS

EIGHT EXPRESSIONIST PLAYS

by

AUGUST STRINDBERG 1849 - 1912

Translated and with prefaces to
The Pilgrimage Plays by A R V I D P A U L S O N

Introduction and with a preface to
The Ghost Sonata by J O H N G A S S N E R

NEW YORK UNIVERSITY PRESS

NEW YORK

7.00

Contents

Translator's Foreword

In translating the pilgrimage dramas of August Strindberg I have throughout scrupulously tried to adhere to the intent and purpose of the author and have made no attempt at adapting the play or the dialogue, nor have I omitted any part of it. Wherever ambiguities, errata or seeming inconsistencies appear in the printed Swedish editions, I have had the valuable assistance of Professor Walter A. Berendsohn, who generously and unselfishly has devoted much time to comparing the text with that of the available original manuscripts in Sweden. At all times have I attempted to make sensible the innermost meaning inherent in words, idioms, phrases and sentences, taking only the most urgent liberties in the way of adding or deleting a word here and there—and then only for the sake of elucidating, clarifying and making the dialogue not only readable but, principally, speakable. In brief, I have in no way trespassed upon Strindberg's often obscure and mystical phrasings and passages; on the contrary, I trust I have succeeded in penetrating to the core of his thinking, which—particularly in the *To Damascus* trilogy and *A Dream Play*—has offered almost insuperable obstacles and been a persistent challenge to translators. The blending of a variety of moods—mundane, psychological, philosophical, spiritual, mystical and poetical—in these dramas, which are among his most significant works, is but one of the many reasons for my having approached the task with a feeling of the utmost responsibility, not to say reverence.

In the original verse parts of *The Keys of Heaven*, Strindberg uses a poetic form in which anapests are frequently intermingled with iambic or trochaic verse feet. Throughout the play the meter often changes abruptly, according to the mood of the character who is speaking or of the scene, the iambic accent quite playfully being employed by Strindberg where the scene or situation is of a satirical nature. In a few rare instances I have—for the sake of rhyme and rhythm—found it necessary to make slight changes in the poetic speeches; but these changes have been exceedingly few and do not in any measure intrude upon or affect the author's intentions. They are, in fact, merely manifestations of a conscientious effort to recreate the original work in a language that will be authentic, lucid and spontaneous so that it can be spoken by actors on the stage as well as read.

For the purpose of conforming to the American stage custom, I have reversed the author's directions—Right and Left —to their opposites. Thus they are given here from the viewpoint of the actor on the stage. In places where Strindberg has employed inverted sentences (e.g., *The Great Highway*, Scene 7: "Från alpens rena luft jag steg hit ned") , I have transposed each sentence into forthright, everyday language. I have further added casts of characters (not infrequently omitted by Strindberg in his manuscripts) and have inserted additional stage directions wherever urgently needed—details that Strindberg, in his feverish and impassioned absorption in the fundamental labor of the play itself, often neglected or left to the discretion of the publisher and the stage director.

Such changes have been necessary when, for example, no equivalent English word could be found to take the place of the Swedish one, when the equivalent word in English would have offended the ear of an audience, or when it might have presented difficulties to an actor. The lyrical passages, in particular, would have suffered if such obstacles of language had not been circumvented.

When, in 1945, I translated *The Great Highway*, I consulted Latin, Greek and Japanese scholars on the texts in these languages. I learned that the Japanese poem quoted by Strindberg in Scene 4 of that play had been misprinted in all published Swedish editions from the time of its publication in 1909. The poem, by an unknown Japanese poet, is included in the famous *Kokinshū* collection. It is reprinted here as it appears in that anthology. A few other errors in Swedish editions, not previously discovered by Strindberg authorities, have also been corrected. Strindberg did not always proofread his books, and no doubt these errors can be ascribed chiefly to the printers' and proofreaders' unfamiliarity with Japanese and other foreign languages, and perhaps to an occasional slip of the pen on Strindberg's part. When he wrote his final drama, *The Great Highway*, he was suffering from severe ill health.

I wish to acknowledge with gratitude the constructive criticism and valuable suggestions given me by George Jean Nathan after reading my first version of the play in English. "I find it most interesting," he wrote. "The play deserves a hearing in the American theatre, as do, of course, all of the great author's works."

Note on the Translator

Born and educated in Sweden, Arvid Paulson came to America as a young man. He quickly distinguished himself in the theatre as actor and producer. Mr. Paulson's mastery of both Swedish and English, his close association with the theatre, and his lifelong devotion to Scandinavian literature, qualify him, perhaps better than anyone in the world, for the job of translating Strindberg. Among his previous Strindberg translations are *Letters to Harriet Bosse* and *Seven Plays by August Strindberg*. In 1960 Mr. Paulson's translations of *Miss Julie* and *The Stronger* were presented on television by The Play of the Week. In 1962 he was invited by the Library of Congress to present a Strindberg program consisting of readings from his plays, novels, and letters.

Mr. Paulson has been knighted by the King of Sweden for strengthening the cultural ties between the United States and Sweden, and more especially for his translations of Strindberg.

In 1964 he was awarded the Gold Medal of the Royal Swedish Academy of Letters for his translations of Strindberg and other Scandinavian authors—the first time the medal has been awarded for translations.

Strindberg the Expressionist

BY JOHN GASSNER

It is generally recognized by now that Strindberg is the chief originator of the "modernist" drama, if we mean by this term the drama that represents a renewal of imagination after the triumph of nineteenth-century realism. That renewal is largely a twentieth-century phenomenon, and it follows that, although Strindberg was born as long ago as 1849, he is preeminently a twentieth-century author. Eugene O'Neill in America and numerous playwrights in Europe, especially Central European expressionists, took their cue from Strindberg's efforts to widen the frontiers of consciousness and blaze a trail through the jungle of the subconscious—that source and repository of human experience which the realism of surfaces and dialectics left unexplored and frequently even failed to notice.

"Expressionism" is the general term under which these efforts have been classified. It is a very loose term, for all dramatic art is unavoidably "expressive." What else are the speakers of dialogue doing in plays but *expressing* themselves? Not by any means fully, and, in the realistic theatre, frequently without conspicuous articulateness, but with a certain force without which a play is either defective or stillborn. Expressionism, however, is an allowable term in so far as it denotes a modern subjectivity in rendering reality, in contrast to the nineteenth-century naturalists' avowed aim of complete objectivity in art, actually impossible in practice and often confused with mere photographic reproduction of unattractive surfaces. The term embraces fantasy and symbolism in general, and is especially applicable to works distinguished by upheavals of emotion affecting our inner view of the world, distortions of experience and thought, more or less abstract characters (often bearing general designations such as "the Stranger" or "the Student"), and states of mind comparable to dreams or deliriums in which appearance, time, and space lose cohesion or continuity.

1

Strindberg, who had a unique capacity for combining critical lucidity with his subjectivity, was able to describe his technical innovations quite helpfully himself. His explanation will be found in the miniature preface to *A Dream Play* of the year 1902, a few years after the composition of his first expressionist works, the famous *To Damascus* trilogy, the first two parts of which were written and published in 1898. (Part III was written in the year 1901.) He had endeavored, he wrote, to follow the pattern of dreams in which anything seems possible and even probable, and in which time and space have no reality. The imagination weaves new patterns of existence combining memories, fantasies, absurdities, and improvisations as if they were entirely possible, probable, logical. As in our dreams, characters split, double, or multiply, and they may vanish and reappear, blur and become clear; all that holds these disparate and ever-changing phenomena together is the *ruling consciousness* of the dreamer, who is presumably the author himself.

Strindberg's prefatory explanation, written as an afterthought in 1911 and therefore summarizing his conception of a new form of drama, does not cover all types of expressionism, but it is a just description of his so-called dream plays and, to some extent, of related works such as *The Ghost Sonata*. The preface to *A Dream Play* is, we must realize, a *description,* not a program, although expressionism *became* a program in Central Europe—in literature by the time of his death in 1912 and in art actually as early as 1904. One thinks of the famous Dresden *Brücke* group of Pechstein, Nolde, and others that held its first exhibition in 1906, and of the internationally better known *Blaue Reiter* or Blue Horseman group led by Kandinsky, Franz Marc, and Paul Klee who exhibited in Munich with such members of the French avant-garde as Picasso, Rouault, and Braque. One also thinks of the year 1910 when Kandinsky wrote his influential first book on "the spiritual in art," *Über das Geistige in der Kunst,* when Chagall left Russia for the West, and when Kokoschka left Vienna for Berlin and joined the expressionist art periodical *Der Sturm* (*The Tempest*). Strindberg, we should note here, himself became an expressionist painter about a decade before any of these men!

For Strindberg a novel dramatic style, a certain fluidity of scenes, combined paradoxically with much condensation of reality, and situations and characters abstracted by symbolization and intensified by distortion became an inner necessity. It became necessary for him to represent states of mind which precluded Aristotelian logic and that both undermined and went beyond realism.

It became imperative for Strindberg to discard realistic drama in order to come closer than realism could to reality— the reality of his tensions and insights; and to leave naturalistic drama behind in order to be natural on the non-Euclidean plane, as it were—the plane of depth psychology, on the one hand, and the plane of spiritual experience, on the other. Romanticism would not satisfy his need for the expression of tensions too exacting for a mere romantic flight into the blue or an easy escape into some medieval landscape of elves, magicians, and knight-errants. Mere symbolism would not do either, except as a secondary decorative detail or shorthand for mystic imaginings. Symbolist moods were bound to be too indistinct and mild for his intense temperament; although the attractiveness of Maeterlinck's poetic artistry brought Strindberg to the verge of imitation in some minor pieces, Strindberg would not content his irascible spirit with "Maeterlinckéd sweetness," as one punster, recalling Milton's "linked sweetness long drawn out," called Maeterlinck's mesmeric moodpoetry.

Allegory was not an alien mode of drama for Strindberg; it influenced his early play Lucky Per's Journey. But allegory was too impersonal a form for the expression of "inwardness" and the maneuvering of symbols was too artificial. Spontaneity, the constant overflow of powerful emotions, is the essence of Strindberg's latter-day art, which is compelled, rather than calculated, art. What we call the expressionist phase of his writing is the form of expression that brought him closest to the source of his feelings in an underground of fears and fancies and ambivalences of love and hate. Strindberg plunged into this underground, which some will call his "unconscious" and others his "preconscious"; and by whatever name it is called, it was a fascinating as well as frightening world that he reached. He emerged from it with enough bizarre material to bewilder and entrance a modern public which could match his personal discoveries with those of modern "metapsychology" and could outstrip his grotesque vision of the world with its own experience of the twentieth century since World War I.

It was under strong compulsions then, that Strindberg turned expressionist. Born in Stockholm in 1849, he had had an unhappy childhood during years of poverty in the home of mismated parents (the father had been a gentleman, the mother a barmaid), followed by the untimely death of his mother when he was thirteen and his father's remarriage less than a year later. He had found school a torment and university study a hardship and humiliation as a result of extreme privation. The pursuit of a career as a teacher, actor, journalist, and author was also anything but gratifying in the case of a young man whose temperament was decidedly less than equable. But his early troubles were minor by comparison with those that started brewing in his twenty-sixth year when he fell in love with Siri von Essen, the wife of a Swedish baron, whom she later divorced. Marriage with this ambitious woman who tried to follow a stage career and maintained friendships that infuriated Strindberg became an inferno. The uneven course of this marriage, which led to his becoming an avowed antifeminist and to his writing some of the most misogynistic plays (as well as stories—particularly the second part of the collection titled *Married*) in world literature, was terminated under grotesque and extremely unpleasant circumstances in 1891. The consequences were shattering to the psyche of this multifaceted genius of the theatre; they were reflected in naturalistic plays that won him international renown and in a series of remarkable autobiographical works. (One of these, *The Confession of a Fool*, was written in French and published in unauthorized Swedish and German translations that created a veritable scandal.)

After the divorce proceedings, which he memorialized in one of the most powerful short plays of the modern stage (*The Bond*, 1892), he went to Germany, where he met an Austrian journalist, Frida Uhl. He married her in 1893 and had a child by her, but this second, highly publicized marriage capsized quickly despite efforts to save it, and Strindberg's state of mind was seriously imperiled by this piling up of personal disasters. He sought refuge in Swedenborgian mysticism, to which he had been first attracted by a Balzac novel. According to his early admirer and translator Edwin Björkman, Strindberg renounced the philosophical skepticism and materialism he had shared with many intellectuals and became "a believing mystic, to whom this world seemed a mere transitory state of punishment, a 'hell' created by his own thoughts." At the same time, he became inflamed with a passion for alchemy and was thoroughly convinced that he had discovered the formula for making gold.* His sanity, moreover, was plainly in jeopardy when

* See: *Letters of Strindberg to Harriet Bosse*, Arvid Paulson, Ed., 1961, pp. 160-161. Published by Grosset and Dunlap.

he added paranoid "delusions of persecution" (his enemies were getting at him through the very plumbing of his Paris apartment) to his "delusions of grandeur."

In this desperate situation he entered a sanitarium in southern Sweden owned by an old friend of his. Here he began a gradual recovery in 1896 and was able to resume his writing. So introspective a genius as Strindberg naturally first returned to self-examination, producing two autobiographical books, one of which, *Inferno*, is a clinical report in addition to being a unique piece of literature. Björkman, writing before the avalanche of clinical literature in recent decades, considered *Inferno* "one of the most remarkable studies in abnormal psychology in the world's literature"; and the book remains just that about half a century after Björkman made this claim for Strindberg.

The Inferno, however, was still an objective piece of writing. It was with his drama, *To Damascus* (the first two parts of this trilogy were published in 1898) that Strindberg turned to subjective dramaturgy. In this work, he proceeded to create a virtually new style of dramatic composition, dominated not merely by his memories of the past and his search for inner peace, but by the very configuration of dreams and mystic experiences that are surreal rather than real, or expressionist rather than realistic.

In *To Damascus* Strindberg made an accounting of his personality and course of life and tried to understand the meaning of his existence. A work consisting of many levels of interest, it could be called a work of expiatory recollection, conciliation, and conversion. The road to Damascus is the road to salvation, and the title of the play suggests that Strindberg drew a none-too-modest parallel between his mystical experience and the conversion of St. Paul. The protagonist of the drama comes to the end of his journey of blind error and hatred as Saul, later called Paul, did when he had his mystic vision while on his way to Damascus to persecute the early Christians. The Stranger, who is Strindberg himself, renounces worldly ambitions and satisfactions, fame, and women. Then, free at last of the world, he enters a monastery, where he will lay aside his old name, be rebaptized like a newborn babe, and be forbidden to speak for a year. First, wrapped in a shroud, he will have to lie down in a coffin and appear to die. He will be placed in a grave, and the "Old Adam"—that is, the sinning and suffering man he was —will be buried under three shovelfuls of earth. The Tempter tries to dissuade him: Was life so bitter that he is willing to be lowered into a grave? "Yes," replies the Stranger, Strindberg. The conversion may not be final, and the monastery as well as the religion it represents is rather ambiguous—one would not call it Christian in any strict sense of the term, although it is Christian in spirit. But it is, or it approximates, a long-sought resting point in a struggle of Dostoevskian and satanic intensity.

The spiritual atmosphere of this work, as well as of a number of the plays that follow it, is anticipated and specified in Strindberg's autobiographical work which he aptly called *Inferno*. In this volume, published one year before the first two parts of *To Damascus*, he noted that the fruitful epoch of naturalism was past and that men needed a "religion"—that is, a reconciliation with the spirits, or invisible "powers," that rule life. A "God" seemed to be "developing, growing and revealing himself" even though he was likely to leave the world to itself for intervals, like the farmer who lets the tares and the wheat grow together until the harvest. Every era revealed God "animated with new ideas"; therefore religion will return to the world, "but under new aspects." He concluded: "We do not await an epoch of reaction nor a return to outworn ideals, but an advance toward something new." Swedenborgian mysticism seemed to be the answer, as did a broad humanism often extremely attractive to men of letters and devotees of the liberal arts.

One could not conclude, however, that Strindberg had been completely released from his paranoid anxieties by this new-won faith. A "single word" from the *Visions of Swedenborg* from the year 1744 would "suffice to illuminate my soul, and to scatter my doubts and vain fancies," he wrote. But we can only surmise that his symptoms were persistent when he declares that he needs release from "vain fancies regarding supposed enemies, electrical impulses, black magic, etc. . . ." and describes the symptoms from which he has suffered as "feelings of suffocation (angina pectoris), constrictions of the chest, palpitations, the sensation which I called the electric girdle." He could only conclude "that I, a child of the renowned nineteenth century, am firmly convinced that there is a hell—a hell, however, on earth, and that I have just come out of it."

He still felt sufficiently insecure to wonder whether he would be able to hold on to his faith (he leaned toward Buddhism without becoming a Buddhist and was attracted to Roman Catholicism without undergoing conversion) —whether the "powers" would leave him at rest on the bosom of faith. What did the "spirits" still have in store for him? "When I was young I was sincerely pious, and you made me a freethinker," he said to the "powers" he addressed. "Out of the freethinker you made me an atheist, and out of the atheist a religious man. Inspired by humanitarian principles, I became a herald of socialism. Five years later you have shown me the absurdity of socialism; you have made all my prophecies futile. And suppose I become again religious, I am sure that in another ten years you will reduce my religion to an absurdity. What a game the gods play with us. . . . And therefore in the most tormented moments of life, we too can laugh with self-conscious raillery. How can you want us to take seriously what is nothing but a huge bad joke?"

Everything seemed to produce contradictions. What was one to do? Shall one humble oneself? If one humbles oneself before men, one arouses their pride by making them feel superior. If one humbles oneself before God, is it not outrageous "to degrade the Highest by conceiving of Him as the overseer of a slave plantation"? Shall men pray and presumptuously endeavor to alter God's will by flattery and crawling? He, the repentant and reformed man, finds these doubts simply dreadful and cries out, "I look for God and find the Devil! That is my destiny!"

There is even less comfort in his final conclusion because of its extreme negativism and passiveness that makes him the unintentional father of present-day practitioners of the "theatre of the absurd." If every step we take forward only leads to more sinning, and if Swedenborg was right in declaring that sins are simply punishments inflicted by Heaven for more grievous sins (presumably committed by us in a previous existence), then "we must endure the burden of our wickedness and rejoice at the pangs of conscience which accompany it, as at the payment of fees at a toll-gate." One can only conclude then that our straining to be virtuous amounts to an attempt *to escape punishment.* To support his views, Strindberg draws upon Protestant theology: Had not Martin Luther declared that the souls in Purgatory sin continually because they try to avoid their torments and seek peace? Had not Luther declared that our very good works are themselves deadly sins, for the world *must become guilty before God* and learn that no one is justified in the sight of the Lord except through divine grace. "Let us therefore suffer," Strindberg writes at the end of this disputation with himself that we would nowadays call Kafkaesque, "without hoping for any real joy in life, for, my brothers, we are in hell. Let us rejoice in our torments, as though they were the paying off of so many debts, and let us count it a mercy that we do not know the real reason why we are punished."

A more hopeful attitude prevails in the first two parts of *To Damascus* which follow *Inferno* in 1898 and in the semiexpressionistic comedy *Crimes and Crimes* of the year 1899 (see *Seven Plays by August Strindberg*, translated by Arvid Paulson; Bantam Books, 1960), in which he discovers the possibility of laughing at the game the gods play with poor mortals.

A bright interval at the same time yields the lovely drama of forgiveness, *Easter*, in 1900 (see *Seven Plays by August Strindberg*), and the superb folk drama *The Crown Bride*, and in 1901 the atmospheric fairy-tale *Swanwhite*. But during this period he still returns to the memory of his devastating sex-war with Siri von Essen long enough in 1900 to produce perhaps the most acrid of his naturalistic plays, the two-part drama *The Dance of Death*, and a year later he returns to inviolable pessimism with *A Dream Play* (1901–1902). He focuses grimly on the world of reality, pronounces it a nightmare of futility, dismisses it philosophically as *maya* or "illusion," and presents it as an expressionistic mélange of reality and dream. (Writing with fierce fecundity, he also produced three intense historical plays, *Queen Christina* (1901), *Gustav III* (1902), and *The Nightingale of Wittenberg* (1903), a Martin Luther biography, after having completed his Damascus trilogy in 1901 with the third part of *To Damascus* on which he had begun to work the previous year.)

In 1907, his third marriage (to the young actress Harriet Bosse in 1901) having failed to bring him peace of mind and release from his persecution mania, he wrote another formidable expressionistic drama, *The Ghost Sonata*. In it one of the chief characters, the Student, can only conclude that there must be a curse on all creation—on life itself. There is no cure for this situation except by deliverance from individual existence and consciousness. After *The Ghost Sonata* and a minor play of the same year, *The Pelican* and miscellaneous writing, came Strindberg's final expressionist testament. It is *The Great Highway*, a play completed in 1909 but long unknown to American readers until Arvid Paulson made it available in English with the first of his many authoritative translations.

The Great Highway, written by Strindberg in his sixtieth year, three years before his death in 1912, was his farewell to the theatre. Described by him as a drama of peregrination, or a pilgrimage with seven "stations," an allusion to Christ's Passion, the play was another drama of reminiscence. It may be regarded as a continuation of *To Damascus,* and it seems appropriate that Strindberg should have ended his career as a dramatist with this lyrical drama. It is one more statement of the pilgrimage toward a dimly perceived goal of salvation, desperately sought and somewhat tentatively entertained, that sets Strindberg apart from the majority of playwrights in our time who seem to be content with facile solutions and more or less profitable accommodations to popular taste. *The Great Highway* also concludes his experimentation with imaginative playwriting and "open" dramaturgy—in contrast to "closed," tightly knit and narrowly logical realistic play construction.

Already in *Lucky Per's Journey,* his first important play, written in the years 1881-1882, Strindberg had reached for an imaginative and comprehensive, rather than a "closed" and narrowly realistic, action. The rapidly moving scenes of this play, which has been described as "a Swedish *Peer Gynt,*" afford a kaleidoscopic view of the world, modified by disenchantment. The play, outwardly playful and rather facetious, has the external trappings of romantic fairy-tale comedy, and Strindberg once declared that he had intended it for children only. But the abundance of sardonic imagination in the work contradicts the author's protestation of innocence and shows him to have been striving for the same scattering grapeshot style of dramaturgy that culminates in the fragmented world of *A Dream Play.* By comparison, the naturalistic plays of domestic relations with which he first impressed the world, especially *The Father, Miss Julie,* and *Creditors* toward the end of the 1880's, *contract* the dramatic action in order to intensify it. Yet even in these works we find a comprehensive imagination at work, for the private conflicts become a universal duel of the sexes. In *Miss Julie,* in addition, the war of the sexes is paralleled by a conflict of the classes (the frigid Miss Julie's antagonist is not merely a *man* but her father's *valet*), and this parallel between private and social conflict continues to exercise Strindberg's imagination in the expressionistic plays, even as late as *The Ghost Sonata* in 1907, in which the Cook takes all the nourishment out of the food of the masters of the household.

Even in Strindberg's deadly parlor games of domesticity will be found that striving for largeness of reference that made him distinguish in one of his critical pieces between the "little" naturalism he scorned in hack writings and the "big" naturalism to which he aspired. Moreover, he treated these conflicts early and late as conditions of *being* or existence rather than as individual peccadilloes or perversities. They exemplified the ambiguousness of human relationships and the ambivalent nature of the affections. Ultimately, it was human nature itself that caused the rifts between man and woman, while the misery of mankind implicated the nature of the world rather than merely the perversity of an individual. There was no help for being alive in the world, as his latter-day Buddhist leanings taught him half a century before the vogue of the new avant-garde of Beckett and Ionesco in the 1950's. "Use your head, can't you, use your head, you're on earth, there's no cure for that!" says the protagonist Hamm in Samuel Beckett's *Endgame.* Ultimately, it is the "human condition" that Strindberg found burdensome, and it is the World, Existence or the "illusion" of existence, that he rejected out of hand in *A Dream Play.*

There is just one difference, but an extremely significant one, between Strindberg's despairing view of life and the despair of the mid-twentieth-century dramatists: he did not seek "morbid gain" from his negations; he sought *healing* instead. He was not at all willing to accept defeat for the human spirit. The latter-day plays, with the strong exception of his powerful and monstrous sex-duel drama *The Dance of Death,* represent a search for salvation rather than a wallowing in damnation. Strindberg's heart is full, not frozen. And whatever we may think of the ultimate note of faith in his work, the penultimate one of *longing* for faith is a positive quality in the plays and is based on a premise of hopefulness. It is plainly stated in *The Ghost Sonata* when the Student declares his belief that the Liberator is approaching and he prays that the dying Young Lady will awake into a world in which the sun doesn't burn, where friends are pure, and where love is unflawed.

In this one respect Strindberg remained a nineteenth-century man: he treasured a beam of optimism in the Cimmerian night of his world picture; and this is reflected in his poetry, in verbal embellishments that do not altogether escape a certain degree of Victorian sentimentality and decorativeness. This tendency goes counter to the rationalist temper of our day and the bland detachment or matter-of-fact coolness of expression favored by it. When Joseph Wood Krutch complains in his *"Modernism" in Modern Drama* (1953) that for Strindberg "the essence of man's tragic dilemma is that there is no rational, only an irrational, solution," he is in effect complaining that the latter-day Strindberg is a mystic. This is precisely what he became after undergoing the severe mental crisis of his *Inferno* period. To the rationalist this means, as Mr. Krutch put it, "surrender to the irrational element" as well as recognition of the part that the irrational plays in human life; to the religious, it means conversion to faith which if perhaps less definably Christian than Buddhist nevertheless contains approvable elements of humility, compassion, and piety. It is, however, difficult to believe that Strindberg the creative artist really surrendered to the irrational instead of mastering it (if perhaps incompletely) in such impressive works as the first part of the *To Damascus* trilogy, *A Dream Play, The Ghost Sonata,* and *The Great Highway,* or that he really found a fixed point in religion. In his best work he stands approximately midway between the irrational and the rational, faith and unbelief, hope and despair. He stands between extremes and is often torn apart by their pull. He represents and he *expresses* a state of tension rather than of stabilization, and this makes him a uniquely modern dramatist. Like his successors, among whom we would be quite justified in including Eugene O'Neill and Tennessee Williams, he remains a divided man in the very act of trying to resolve conflicts and reconcile polarities. He is veritably the man who could inspire such opposite estimates as Sean O'Casey's ecstatic tribute that "Strindberg shakes flame from the living planets and the fixed stars" and the views of a psychiatrist (Stanley M. Coleman in *The Psychoanalytic Review,* XXIII [1936], 248–273), who can bring in the cool verdict that Strindberg was "a schizothymic personality who maintained his hold on reality only by reacting to external stress by the mechanism of projection."

Out of this state of disequilibrium appears, finally, the latter-day Strindberg, whose simple imaginativeness is prefigured in *Lucky Per's Journey,* written some sixteen years before the first part of *To Damascus,* and a renewal of poetry in the theatre. The plainest details of common life become images and symbols, and the most ordinary statement or conversation may be charged with significance. A special lyricism pervades the play and displaces the prose of realism; and lyricism turns to rhapsody here and there (toward the close of *A Dream Play,* for example) when the author attempts to give language to his compassionate, "mankind-is-to-be-pitied" view of life and his vision of release from bondage to the earth. And there comes into being in the plays a poetry of visual effect distinctively of the theatre; it is that *poésie de théâtre* to which Cocteau later pointed as a possible substitute for inappropriate verbal poetry or rhetorical embellishments in the modern drama.

A powerful theatrical imagination accompanies Strindberg's

ventures into imaginative dramaturgy; and fortunately it manifested itself just as the theatre under such leaders as Appia, Gordon Craig, Lugné-Poë, Copeau, Meyerhold, and Reinhardt were evolving a new theatrical esthetics to justify subordination of realistic scenery and stage direction to suitably expressive stylization. Strindberg had evinced a strong feeling for theatrical effect while he was still writing realistic plays such as *The Father* and *Miss Julie*. But in the distinctly expressionistic plays, he gave free play to his plastic imagination,[1] calling for a kaleidoscopic succession of outdoor and indoor settings, symbolic structures or props, and scenic transformations like the flower bud on the roof (in *A Dream Play*) that opens into a gigantic chrysanthemum. Music and acoustical effects acquire expressive importance in the dramatic action, and the magic of modern stage lighting is constantly called upon to perform its wonders. Strindberg's expressionist plays, in brief, constitute *total theatre* and represent an essential "retheatricalization" of the theatre after its "detheatricalization" during the vogue of naturalism in the theatre after 1887 under the leadership of Antoine at the Théâtre Libre in Paris and of Otto Brahm at the Freie Bühne of Berlin. Theatre became *theatre* again when Strindberg unleashed the full power of his imagination after having kept it within naturalistic bounds during the decade of the eighteen-eighties when he wrote *Comrades, The Father, Miss Julie,* and *Creditors.*

[1] An unsigned article, "A Touch of the Artist," in the publication *Industria International* (1962) calls attention to a little-known fact about Strindberg's multifaceted genius. He became a highly original painter during the *Inferno* period, in the mid-1890's. (He had started painting as early as 1872.) He made strenuous efforts to move beyond the world of appearances and to express an inner reality. "How well he succeeded was recently demonstrated by a traveling exhibition of little-known paintings that had Continental critics wondering whether the claims made for Strindberg as the father of expressionism in the theatre might not be extended to cover abstract art, and even action painting as well. Not only the results, but his methods, were impeccably modern."

"I approach my painting with only a vague idea of what I want to present," he is quoted as saying. "With my spatula, I throw on colors, distributing them and mixing them right on the surface. I am mixing many colors, fourteen, fifteen perhaps, evolving a labyrinth of hues and shapes. Finally, the entire surface is swimming in color. I step back to look at my work and I can't explain what it may mean."

He left it to the viewer to interpret or define the work for himself: "The painting may at first resemble merely a chaos of colors. But gradually, as one looks at them, shapes form themselves, some of them may resemble something familiar, and then again they may not. At last the work opens itself to the spectator." Strindberg was then a so-called *spontanist* half a century before the term gained currency. Pictures should be painted, he declared, in a semi-dark room, "best lit by the glow from a dying fire" and the composition as well as the subject should be "left partly to chance." He was, at the same time, aware that there were disadvantages as well as advantages in this hazardously spontaneous style of art—that it was "impossible to copy," but that it was not going to be "easily sold!"

Lucky Per's Journey

A DRAMA IN FIVE ACTS

❖ ❖ ❖

[1] The dedications are the translator's.

Perhaps the most powerful attribute of the true dramatist is imagination. It furnishes the incentive to penetrate into unknown realms, into the mind, into unexplored areas of thinking and of action, and to project the mind into imaginary lands in search of settings for the ideas and characters the dramatist creates. The greater the dramatist's imagination, the farther away from the beaten path he searches for the heartbeat of the universe, and for the means to express it and make it living in the theatre; in some instances the imagery of the subconscious, properly disciplined by the dramatist, has served him as vividly and realistically as any factual presentation of life itself.

The true form of such drama should contain a core of universality in appeal and meaning. As the mainspring of the dramatist's art, imagination can roam anywhere unfettered and create characters and settings that are stark and challenging, fascinating and believable, in all their exotic and abstract fantasy. This is truly the pinnacle of dramatic creation, especially when the dramatist has the capacity to conjure forth a clash between souls and minds that finds its reflection in the experiences of the audience or the reader.

Many of the world's great epics have contained symbols of restless wandering and pilgrimage. Tales of ages past have been handed down by mouth, from generation to generation, telling of journeys on land and sea, of strange adventures. Fairy tales carry not only children but grown-ups as well into realms of fantasy, imaginary kingdoms, faraway places, over endless seas. Sometimes these tales seem more real to the listener or the reader than those featured in newspapers and novels, on radio and television, not to mention the theatre and motion pictures.

The character of Cartaphilus, Pilate's doorkeeper, said to have told Jesus to walk faster as he came out of the judgment

---

[2] Mr. Paulson's prefatory essays appear in somewhat different form in *The Chronicle*, published by the American Swedish Historical Foundation.

chamber, is one of the wanderers or pilgrims who has frequently appeared in legendary tales throughout the centuries.
When struck by Cartaphilus, Jesus said: "I will go, but you
shall remain waiting till I return." In the sixteenth century
his name changed in German legends to Ahasuerus, and he
became a Jewish shoemaker. He came to be known as "the
wandering Jew" and was doomed, so the legend says, to live
forever, longing and weeping in vain for death to come—a
never-ending pilgrimage in search of atonement and forgiveness for his sin. He appears in two of Strindberg's pilgrimage
plays, *The Keys of Heaven* and *The Great Highway*. The
Hunter (Strindberg) likens himself in the latter play (Scene
6) to Cartaphilus and Ahasuerus. Strindberg seems to have
been fascinated by this dual character. He has repeatedly identified himself with him in both his poetic and his prose works.
(See *Strindbergs dramatik*, Gunnar Ollén, Stockholm, 1961.

The Flying Dutchman too, the skipper who blasphemed God
while sailing round the Cape of Good Hope and as punishment
was condemned to sail the seven seas for eternity, was another
doomed pilgrim whose fate Strindberg compared with his own,
with his own eternal restlessness and quest for happiness. Still
another such ever-searching soul was Goethe's immortalized
Doctor Johannes Faust, whose avidity for knowledge and for
a solution to the riddle of life grew into an insatiable and
inextinguishable passion.

Strindberg wrote his poetic drama *The Hollander* on the
theme of the Flying Dutchman. In *The Nightingale of Wittenberg* he has given Dr. Faust a memorable role—one of the
roles in this play through which Strindberg himself speaks. The
dramatist frequently put his own ideas in the mouth of not
only one character but through several in the same play. Thus,
for instance, he speaks in *The Great Highway* not only through
the Hunter but through the Wanderer and the Japanese.

That Strindberg found much to fascinate and arrest him in
these pilgrimage characters is proven by the fact that at the
turn of the past century he seriously considered bringing them
together in a drama based on the theme of peace among nations. His idea was to place it in the setting of the Hague
Peace Conference of 1899, then about to convene.

When first he found their fate a source of dramatic inspiration, it was the similarity between their forced pilgrimage and
his own continual traveling and restless shifting from country
to country, from city to city, from village to village that attracted him to them. In his last drama, *The Great Highway*,

he touches upon this ceaseless wayfaring in the last scene, when
he cries out with bitter melancholy:

> *A traveler in foreign land*
> *is ever there a lonely stranger.*
> *He goes to city, village, town,*
> *takes lodging, pays, and then continues on,*
> *until his journey's at an end—and he's at home again!*
> *Yet that is not the end. . . .*[3]

But following his so-called Inferno Crisis it became their
condemnation which drew him closer to them and their fate:
it was this judgment upon them that made him feel a kinship
to them, as he himself felt the sting of social ostracism and
condemnation at the hands of the world and his former friends.
Yet, unlike Ahasuerus (Cartaphilus), the Flying Dutchman,
and Faust, he refused to accept his fate in silence. While they
took their banishment without remonstrance, Strindberg fought
against his own punishment as uproariously and rebelliously
as Hagar's son Ishmael once did according to the Bible (Gene-
sis 16, 21, 25). At the end of the final scene in his autobiographical, dramatic confessional, *The Great Highway*, he expresses (as the Hunter) the hope that the Hermit will dig him
a grave "beneath the white and icy blanket, and write, perhaps,
in snow a casual inscription":

> *Here rests one Ishmael,*
> *Son of Hagar—*
> *whom once they gave the name of Israel,*
> *because he'd battled with the Lord*
> *and had not given in till he was felled,*
> *conquered by the bounty of God's almightiness. . . .*

What characterizes Strindberg's pilgrimage dramas is that
they epitomize his own search for the abstruse and the un-
fathomed in the universe, for the essential nature of the reality
of life. The study of occultism and metaphysics had occupied
Strindberg profoundly, as had the supernatural and the subconscious. To him a dream could seem as oppressive or as
exultant as an experience in everyday life and at times seemed
to have the reality of life itself. For what is life but a puzzling, chaotic, enigmatic dream? And does not the subconscious
mind impartially reflect the thoughts and desires of the waking

---

[3] All quotations are in the translation of Arvid Paulson.

mind, without aid or hindrance of human impulses, unfettered by the material senses? It is this dream life we live that Strindberg has captured in the five plays that have been named "the pilgrimage series." In Part I of *To Damascus* Strindberg gives the following appraisal of life as seen and experienced by him: "There are moments when I question that life itself has more of reality than my imagery."

It is this dream life and this constant searching by mankind for the eternal truths, for understanding, for happiness, that Strindberg attempts to interpret in *Lucky Per's Journey* and later, in intensifying measure, in *The Keys of Heaven, To Damascus, A Dream Play,* and *The Great Highway.* In all of these, Strindberg himself is the disguised protagonist, struggling with humanity and even with God for enlightenment and a clear vision of life's mysteries, for the key to heaven on earth.

While Strindberg's original idea for this pilgrimage series may have been derived from his reading of the old medieval mystery and morality plays, Ibsen's influence on him through *Brand* and *Peer Gynt* cannot be overlooked, as Dr. Gunnar Ollén (in his valuable manual *Strindbergs dramatik)* and others have noted. Hans Christian Andersen and Charles Dickens may also have furnished some inspiration; and Dr. John Landquist sees resemblances between Voltaire's *Candide* and this Strindberg drama. Ibsen's influence is especially noticeable in the first play of this series, *Lucky Per's Journey.* The core of the idea for this play is essentially the same as in *Peer Gynt,* although the characters, the plots, and the conflicts are entirely different. The story deals with a lad of fifteen, who from birth has been isolated from people and life in a church tower. On Christmas Eve he is visited by a fairy, who gives him a ring with the power to realize the wearer's every wish. His first wish, for freedom, is granted instantly. Then in succession he gets a taste of how it feels to be rich, to be a reformer, a powerful caliph, and a wanderer in nature. He finds nature to be as cruel and treacherous as it is beautiful. But love, the only thing that can neither be bought nor pursued, Per finds to be the greatest gift of life. It comes to him only after he has realized the vanity and sin of seeking riches and power merely for the sake of personal gain and aggrandizement. He also learns that whatever one does, or attempts to do, one must not lose sight of one's obligations to mankind and society. He is crushed and disillusioned by what he sees and encounters in the world outside, and in the end determines to seek happiness through work, and to dedicate his life to serious and honest effort. In subsequent editions of the play the final scene has been somewhat changed. Dr. John Landquist has voiced the opinion that this may have been done at the urging of theatrical producers. A happy ending has now been substituted for the original one in the published versions. Written partly in the romantic vein, *Lucky Per's Journey* is a deliberate and devastating satire on hypocrisy in society, politics, government, and life in general. In it he also lashes out in unmistakable manner against a well-known poet who was the leading figure in the literary coterie that dominated the cultural scene in Sweden in those days.

Lucky Per's Journey gave rise to one of the greatest ovations known in the annals of the world theatre. When Strindberg arrived in Stockholm from Switzerland on October 20, 1884, to defend himself in court against charges of blasphemy and immorality because of the publication of his famous book *Married (Giftas)*, *Lucky Per's Journey* was to be given for the fifty-ninth time at The New Theatre *(Nya Teatern)*. The author, who had been greeted by overwhelming crowds at the railroad station, was persuaded to be present. Seldom, perhaps never, has an author or a play been received so tumultuously, with such showering of flowers and laurel wreaths, with such rapture and enthusiasm as Strindberg and *Lucky Per's Journey* were that night. Both the audience and the multitude that had assembled outside paid deafening homage to the great man when he, deeply moved, left the theatre.

CHARACTERS

The Old Man in the Tower
Per
Lisa
The Fairy
The Gnome
Nisse } Two rats
Nilla }
The Steward
The Tax Clerk
The Attorney
The Court Attendant
The Petitioner
First Friend
Second Friend
The Female Friend
The Pillory
The Statue
The Wagonmaker
The Shoemaker
The Chiropodist

The Relative
The Streetpaver
The Burgomaster
One of the People
The Master of the Royal
    Household
The Lord High Herald
The Lord High Historian
The Court Chaplain
The Wazir
The Court Singer
The Court Poet
The Bride
Death
The Wise Man
St. Bartholomew
St. Laurentius
The Shadow
The Bier
The Broom

Men and Women, Singers, Dancers, Beasts, and others

THE SETTINGS

Act I. A room in the church tower.
Act II, Scene 1. In the forest.
Act II, Scene 2. The rich man's home.
Act III. The square with the courthouse.
Act IV, Scene 1. The Caliph's palace.
Act IV, Scene 2. The sea beach.
Act V. The country church.

The action takes place
in the Middle Ages.

19

ACT I

A chamber in the church tower. The shutters of the aper-
tures in the rear are open; beyond can be seen the gleaming
stars in the sky, and the rooftops covered with snow. The
gable windows that are visible are brightly lit.

A dilapidated old chair. A brazier with glowing embers;
a table; an image of Mary, in front of which stands a lighted
candle. The room is intersected by square, wooden pillars,
two of which in the center are the width of a broad-shoul-
dered man.

Singing in unison is heard from the church below:

> *A solis ortus cardine*
> *Et usque terrae limitem*
> *Christum canamus principem*
> *Natum Maria Virgini.*

The Old Man comes up the tower stairs. He carries a rat trap,
a sheaf of grain, and a plate of porridge, all of which he
places on the floor.

OLD MAN. Here, little gnome, is your Christmas porridge. You
have certainly deserved it this year. Twice you have waked me
when I fell asleep while watching at the tower aperture, and
once you rang the church bells yourself when there was a fire
in the town. A merry Christmas, dear gnome, and may there
be many happy returns of the day for you! *(He picks up the rat*
trap and sets it.) Now I'll give you your Christmas goodies,
you Satan's rats!

VOICE. Do not curse Christmas!

OLD MAN. I think there are spooks about tonight. . . . Ah!
It's the cold that's getting sharper, and then the beams always
creak—like the beams in an old ship. . . . Here you have your
Christmas feed—and now perhaps you'll stop gnawing off the
bell rope and nibbling at the tallow on the axles, you damnable parasites!

VOICE. Do not curse Christmas!

OLD MAN. Now it's spooking again! Christmas Eve! Yes, yes
. . . well—now they have been fed their share! *(He places the rat*
trap on the floor.) And now to the feathered beasts—they have
to have their turn! . . . They must have a few grains of corn, of
course, so that they can mess up the tin roofing for me! Oh yes,

that's only natural! But it's the church council that pays the piper, so why should I worry? But if I should ask for a small increase in wages—then they have no money for that. They have no eyes for all that I do—but sticking out a sheaf of grain on a pole from the church tower once a year makes them look so very generous! This one looks really quite good—yes, indeed! And to give generously is a virtue! I think we ought to share this with each other—then I would get back my porridge that I just gave to the gnome! (*He shakes the sheaf and gathers the grains in a bowl.*)

VOICE. You are stealing Christmas! You are stealing Christmas!

OLD MAN. Now I am going to put it on this pole—it will make a nice show. For it is done for show as well; it shows something that isn't found inside. (*He pushes the pole through the aperture.*) Oh, you old den of humanity down there! (*He shakes his fist at the town below.*) I spit on you! (*He spits through the aperture; then he goes to that part of the room where the image of Mary is placed and discovers the candle burning before it.*) It must be the boy who has done this. . . . The times are not such that one can afford to burn candles when there is no need for it. (*He blows out the candle and puts it in his pocket.*)

VOICE. Woe! Woe! (*The image of Mary moves its head three times and a vivid ray of light shoots out from her forehead.*)

OLD MAN (*recoils*). Is the devil plying his trade tonight?

VOICE. It is Heaven!

OLD MAN. Per! Per!—Where are you?—My eyes! Bring a light here!—My son! My son!

IMAGE OF MARY. *My* son!

OLD MAN (*feeling his way down the stairs*). My eyes!—They are burning like the coals of hell! (*He stumbles down the stairs.*)

(*The rats, Nisse and Nilla, enter from the left, Nisse leading the way. They are wearing black crepe on their tails.*)

NISSE. I smell fried pork! Don't you?

NILLA. How could I help smelling it?—Watch out, Nisse, I see the trap over there. (*She sits on her haunches.*) It's the same one that trapped our little ones. . . . Oh, oh, oh!

NISSE. I wish we could think of some prank to play on that mean old man—then I would feel really happy in my entrails. Do you see anything he might have left behind—something that he would hate to lose?

NILLA. How about gnawing at the beams here so that the bells fall down on his head?

NISSE. But Nilla—you know I have only a single poor tooth left in my mouth.

NILLA. Yes, but I have two left. And where there is a will . . . you know. . . . But you have no feeling for your children!

NISSE. Now, now—we are not going to start a quarrel on Christmas Eve, are we?

NILLA. Ssh! What's this I see?

NISSE. A bowl of porridge!

NILLA. That the Old Man has left behind. . . .

NISSE. For the gnome! Yes—*there's* someone he's afraid of!

NILLA. Now I know what we will do! We'll eat up his porridge, and then . . .

NISSE. . . . then he'll have the gnome on his neck!

NILLA. And when *he* gets angry, he can make trouble for him, he can! (*They have scampered over to the bowl of porridge, and start to eat.*)

NISSE. Can't you edge over a bit so that I can have room, too?

NILLA. Hush! I hear a patter on the stairs. . . .

NISSE. I am almost at the bottom of the bowl now! I can see the dab of butter there!

NILLA. Help me to lick this corner!

NISSE. There! It's all down! Now let's wipe our mouths and run.   (*They hurry out to the right.*)

GNOME (*climbs down the bell rope. He goes about the room as if he were looking for something*). Where is my Christmas porridge?—Ah! I can smell the fragrance far away! Tonight it will taste especially good in this freezing weather—and I hope he has given me a real big dab of butter this Christmas, since I have been so nice to him! And now—get ready, my dear stomach. (*He loosens his belt by a couple of notches.*) Two holes will be enough, I should think. (*He discovers the bowl.*) Aha! What's this? An empty bowl! What has happened to the old misanthrope? Has he grown stingy and overbearing? Or is he trying to make fun of me, put me to scorn by putting out an empty bowl? There has been porridge in it, and (*He smells the bowl.*) . . . and butter, too! So-o? It hurts me to have to punish you, Old Man—but we gnomes have a mission to perform, as you well know: we punish, and we reward!—I have to sit down and think of just the right Christmas gift for him. (*He seats himself in the chair.*) Let me see! The Old Man has shut himself in up here with his son—whom he wants to protect against the world's evils and enticements. The Old Man has seen much of the world and loathes it. The youngster has never been outside the portals of the church. All he knows of the world is what he has seen from the tower up here. But I know that it holds an attraction for him—simply because he has had a mere bird's-eye view of it. The Old Man has only one real desire in life: to see his son succeed him, and thus be saved from the struggles of life and the evilness of mankind. . . . Very well! What I shall do is to thwart him in this wish of his. It is his only vulnerable spot. Yes—and now I shall call upon his godmother and let her take care of the young Per and show him all the glory of the universe—and then the old man won't be able to restrain him! I know the power of young dreams. . . . So be it! *(He blows a whistle. The Fairy emerges from inside one of the center beams. She is dressed like an old crone in a large brown cloak and carries a stick.)*

FAIRY. Good evening, lad.

GNOME. Good evening, old woman!—Do you think you can entice a youth? Well, well—you mustn't misunderstand me. . . .

FAIRY. That depends. . . .

GNOME. Well—you wouldn't be able to, dressed the way you are now! You see—I am talking about the old man's son here, Per. . . .

FAIRY. Our Per?

GNOME. Just he!—Be silent, woman, and let me speak! The boy is close to my heart; he has been so ever since he was born. We two—you and I—were his godmother and godfather; and therefore we have our duties to him. His upbringing has been neglected. He has never seen the world; and yet today he celebrates his fifteenth birthday. I want him to go out in the world and have a look at it and learn something, so that we can be proud of him. Have you any objection to that?

FAIRY. None whatever! But I am afraid he will meet with hardships out there—hardships we won't be able to save him from, as the sway of our power does not extend beyond the walls of this sanctuary.

GNOME. That is true. I have to ponder and try to think up something else!—I have it! Let us each give him some gift that can be of help to him in all that he may meet with in life. . . .

FAIRY. And what would you give him? Let's hear!

GNOME. Life can often be quite complicated, as you know; and the boy is young. He has neither been brought up with others nor has he had time to learn all the tricks that gain for people what they most desire. Well, there is nothing more that I can ask of life, for I know what it has to offer. Therefore I shall give him my wishing ring. . . . And what will you give him?

FAIRY. Your gift is worthy enough. But once he has been given all that he desires, he will have made his pilgrimage like a man who is blind—and so I shall present him with a gift that will show him the true worth of things. . . . I shall provide him with good companionship on his journey.

GNOME. Female?

FAIRY. Of course!

GNOME. You are a wise woman, you are! Well—from now on, you look after the boy and see that he gets out of here. . . .

FAIRY. But how will I do it? He minds his father and is in fear of him.

GNOME. Never mind! Do your hocus pocus and let him see all the glory and glamour and festivities down there in the houses. You will see it will work wonders.

FAIRY. You think it will?

GNOME. I know the young!—Now, here is my ring—and go to work!

FAIRY. Is it right to play with the fates of our fellow beings, do you think?

GNOME. We do not play with their fates, for they are not ruled by us; we play only with humanity. Sooner or later, the boy has to get out into the world; and he will be equipped as no one before him has ever been. . . . When he has finished his pilgrimage, we can discuss these things further. Are you ready?

FAIRY (goes to the supporting beam from within which she had first appeared). At once!

GNOME. Then I'll blow my whistle. (He whistles and disappears inside the other pillar.)

PER (comes down the stairway leading to the top of the tower). Who is there?

FAIRY (steps from the pillar. She is now dressed as an angel, in white). Your godmother, Per! Don't you recognize me?

PER. Oh! It was you who rescued me in your arms when I fell from the tower that time! What do you wish of me today?

FAIRY. I want to give you a Christmas gift.

PER. A gift? What is a gift?

FAIRY. Something that provides pleasure for someone.

PER. Pleasure? What is pleasure?

FAIRY. The fulfillment of one's desires.

PER. Desires? Now—perhaps—I am beginning to understand. . . .

FAIRY. Haven't you ever had a feeling—when you stand at the ledge of the tower—of being drawn, of being enticed, by what is below you?

PER. Yes—I have . . . I have had that feeling! You see that dark edge over there, where light and darkness meet? During the day it has a different appearance; and when the wind blows, it moves.

FAIRY. It's the woods!

PER. How does it look inside the woods?

FAIRY. It is cool and beautiful in there.

PER. That is good! You see, there is where I am drawn some-times—drawn so violently that I feel like jumping out through one of the openings in the steeple and sailing through the air, as the birds do. . . .

FAIRY. And then—beyond the fringes of the forest—there. . . .

PER. Is there something beyond the forest? What can that be?

FAIRY. Beyond lies the world!

PER. The world? What is that?

FAIRY. Would you like to see it?

PER. Is it a glad world?

FAIRY. Some think so, though most people think it is not. . . . If you will come over here, I will show you some views in this motley panorama that the mortals call life. . . . *(The back-ground, which is transparent, is lighted up, and as the Fairy names the scenes, they become visible.)* Do you see the large house by the square—where every window is lighted? There is where the rich man lives. Now look inside—into the rooms. . . . You see a lighted Christmas tree on a table; it is covered with gifts of every imaginable kind: the golden fruits of the tropics that have been brought by ships from across the seas—the earth's hidden treasures which men worship on their knees, and in whose shimmering raiment the flames of the candles are re-flected. . . . And do you see the candle flames lighting the faces of the little children? That—that, you know—is the sun of earthly life—that is happiness! And that is something you do not know yet, you poor child. . . . But you shall come to know it—for you do want to, don't you?

PER. Who is the good fairy who walks about and distributes the golden fruit to the children?

FAIRY. That is their mother.

PER. The mother? What is a mother?

FAIRY. You, too, have had a mother, but she died not long after you were born.

PER. And that old man sitting in the corner—with the gentle smile on his face?

FAIRY. That is the father. . . . He is reliving his childhood in his memory. . . .

PER. The father! He has such a friendly face!

FAIRY. Yes—because he does not love himself alone.

PER. And the young man who puts his arm round that young

girl's waist, and who now *(He is stirred up.)* . . . who now presses his face against hers—their lips meet. . . . Why does he do that? Is that the way they speak to one another in the world outside?

FAIRY. That is the way love speaks.

PER. Love? It must be glorious to get a chance to see all this!

FAIRY. Wait! Look up there—in that gable window! . . . Where that lone candle is burning—one miserable, solitary candle! *(The scene in the background changes.)*

PER. Poverty! I know what that is! No—show me something that is beautiful!

FAIRY *(regarding him)*. You like the pleasant things in life —you love pleasure! Well, then—keep looking at the window with the lone light! It throws only a faint light—but it burns with a feeling of warmth upon the table of these people, who are poor—but contented.

PER. No—I like to look at something that is beautiful!

FAIRY. So-o? Could anything be more beautiful than. . . . But I'll let you see something else! Look up there—inside the palace—where the King lives! *(The scene shifts to within the palace.)*

PER *(ecstatically)*. Oh!

FAIRY. Do you see all the splendid attire—the sparkling crystal chandeliers? Do you see the walls reflecting the profusion of lighted candles—and all the red roses and the blue lilies that are in full bloom in the midst of winter?

PER. Oh!

FAIRY. And the young maids—their hair hanging down in curls—who pour the red wine into cups of silver . . . ?

PER. There's where I would like to be!

FAIRY. And now the master cooks, all dressed in white, are bringing in the dishes. . . .

PER. Oh!

FAIRY. The heralds sound their staffs against the floor, the trumpets blare. *(A bell is heard striking three times. The room in the tower resumes its previous appearance.)* Alas, the time is up!—Per! Do you wish to go out into life and try living it?

PER. Yes, yes! . . .

FAIRY. For good or evil?

PER. I think I know what is evil. What I want to learn is the good.

FAIRY. You think you know the evil! But you will soon learn that everything that is called good is not good, and that all evil is not evil.

PER. All I want is to get out—out from here!

FAIRY. I will grant you your wish, Per!—But first I shall give you something that will be of help to you on your pilgrimage. You may need it. When you receive it, you will have been given more than other mortals. For that reason, more will be demanded of you some day in the future!

PER. Let me see the gift!

FAIRY. This ring possesses the power to realize for you all your wishes—for your own benefit, yet to the detriment of no one.

PER. That is a rare ring to have! But what will my father say?

FAIRY. He will only receive his just punishment, which he deserves—the punishment for being selfish!

PER. Yes—you are right!—Nevertheless, I shall feel sorry for him. . . .

FAIRY. Do not feel sorry for him—I will watch over him and his sorrow.

PER. His sorrow? Nothing else? He says sorrow is the only pleasure in life! . . . Well—let him sit here and revel in it! I'll give him plenty of occasions to enjoy himself!

FAIRY. And lastly, young lad, would you like to have some wise counsel as food for thought on your journey?

PER. What sort of counsel would that be? Good advice?

FAIRY. Yes!

PER. Oh, I have been stuffed full of that!

FAIRY. Yes, I know! And I know what happens to such advice! —And now, farewell! May life teach you how to live—and when you have finished your pilgrimage—whether you then are great or unimportant, successful or a failure, rich or poor, learned or ignorant—you will be, above all, a human being, a truly *human* being!—Farewell!

(She disappears inside the pillar.)

PER (alone). So-o, Per, you are going out into the world, are you? . . . But you are not the first one to do that! Can it really be so troublous and chaotic out there, I wonder? Of course, I have stood up on the roof and looked down upon humanity and seen how the crowds crawl about in the streets, going hither and thither. One person emerges from one place and enters another one; another person comes from that place and goes somewhere else. . . . It all seems to me to happen so quietly and peacefully, and I have never seen them run into one another although they are swarming like midges. I will admit I have seen dogs and shoemaker apprentices fight occasionally —but never grownups! And the Old Man and I have never come to blows although we pass each other on the stairs ten times a day. I will say that he has struck me—but I have never

struck back! . . . And I can't believe that people can be so
mean as they are said to be! Wasn't there a fire the other day
at the home of a rich merchant—and didn't I see a whole lot
of poor devils come running from all directions, and didn't
they go upstairs in the rich man's house and help to save his
belongings? Why, I saw it myself—I saw them carry out the
silver—all the way from the dining table to away outside the
town—and how they hid it behind some haystacks—just so that
the silver wouldn't melt down! Now wasn't that a neighborly
and kindly thing to do!—Well, we shall see—we shall see!—And
now, my dear Per, now you are going out into the world and
see what you can see and make use of your gifts! *(He regards
the ring.)* Let me see now! What shall I wish for first? *(The Old
Man enters through the wall.)* Oho, the Old Man is here!—I
didn't hear your steps on the stairs. . . . Where did you come
from?

OLD MAN *(seems to be ill at ease).* Did you see me come in?
PER. No.

OLD MAN. Let me look at you! *(He regards Per fixedly.)*
Something has happened here!

PER. No—nothing! Nothing at all!

OLD MAN. My son, soon it will be midnight. . . . Don't you
want to go inside, into your room, and go to bed so that I can
lock the door after you?

PER. You always want to lock me in! Tell me, Father, aren't
you ever going to let me go out into the world? You don't want
me to stay up here forever, and wither away, do you?

OLD MAN. I have experienced life, my son. . . . I know the
poisonous wine of Sodom—and it is from that I wish to protect
you!

PER. But perhaps life is not so bitter as you say it is?

OLD MAN. What do you know about it?

PER. Oh, I can see a thing or two from up here, can't I? Come
over here, and I'll show you. . . .

OLD MAN. What could you show me that I don't know already?

PER *(leads the Old Man over to the apertures).* Oh yes!—
Look here! Do you see the big house over there on the square?
Do you?

OLD MAN. Well—what about it? Hurry up! You must be in
bed before the clock strikes twelve!

PER. Do you see the Christmas tree with its gold and silver?
Do you?

OLD MAN. Nothing but tinsel, my boy!

PER. And all the fruits of the tropics. . . .

OLD MAN. They are worm-eaten. . . .

PER. And the sun of happiness—see how it radiates upon the faces of the children. . . .

OLD MAN. . . . Now and then distorted by envy. . . .

PER. And the old man sitting there—full of contentment and bliss? . . .

OLD MAN. Nothing but a lie! Deep in his heart he trembles, worrying about the rent—which has to be paid on the first day of the new year. . . .

PER. He—the rich man?

OLD MAN. He is hiding his impending ruin.

PER. And these young people? Do you see the young man stretching forth his hand . . . ?

OLD MAN. He counts upon the father to open his money-bags. . . .

PER. For shame!—Now the young man's lips touch the young woman's. . . .

OLD MAN. Out of lust!

PER. And what's that?—Look up there in the gable window, where the lone light is shining. . . .

OLD MAN. Dictated by prudence which demands darkness. . . .

PER. In the glimmer of the peaceful light of contentedness. . . .

OLD MAN. Having stolen the candles at the grocer's, the band of thieves is now sitting scheming their next raid on the town's shops. I know these people all too well, you may be sure!—And up there in the palace, where lights by the thousands are sparkling and being mirrored in the poisonous flow of wine—there they are tumbling about, with empty heads and empty hearts, prating about their concern and their feelings for the welfare of the nation. . . . There they are, rocking back and forth between bottles and wine casks. . . .

PER. Why do you talk so excitedly? Let me say something. . . .

OLD MAN. No—go to bed, Per! Do as I tell you!

PER. No! I want to get away from here! I want to go out into the world! I want to see the faces of children—even if they are sometimes shadowed by envy—I want to taste the fruit of tropical lands, even if worm-eaten—I want to drink of the wine, even if it should be poisonous—I want to put my arm round a maiden's waist, even if she should have an impoverished father sitting in a corner by the stove—I want to possess silver and gold, even if it should turn into nothing but dust in the end! . . .

OLD MAN. By the coals of hell—who has been here?

VOICE. Do not curse Christmas!

PER. What is happening here? Everything that has happened here tonight seems so eerie—so much stranger than usual! Father,

look at me! . . . Heavens! What do I see? He has a different
face! It's not his own!

OLD MAN (*on bended knees*). My son! Listen to your father!
Be obedient to your old father! He has nothing but your good
at heart! Stay here—within these peaceful walls!

PER. It is too late!

OLD MAN (*notices the ring on Per's finger*). What have you
there? That ring! Who gave you that? (*He tries to take it away
from Per.*)

PER. Who are you? You are not my father!

OLD MAN. Your guilty, unfortunate father—who is now under
the spell of the Powers! (*The Old Man is transformed into a
huge black cat.*)

PER (*awestruck and frightened*). Jesus! Mary! Help! (*A powerful ray of light emanates from the image of Mary.*) The troll!
The troll!—Go away, unclean spirit! (*The cat disappears.*) And
now. (*He throws the shutters of the apertures wide open.*) . . .
out into life! (*He keeps shifting the ring on his finger.*) To the
edge of the forest! (*He springs out through the opened shutters.*)

ACT II

SCENE 1. *A snow-covered forest.*

*In the foreground, running diagonally across the stage, a
frozen brook.*

*It is the break of day. The treetops are moving in the
wind.*

PER (*enters*). So this is the edge of the forest to which my
thoughts have flown so often through the clear air! This is the
forest!—And this is snow! Now I'll make a snowball, as I have
seen the schoolboys do. . . . It must be an awful lot of fun! (*He
throws several snowballs.*) Oh well . . . h'm . . . I can't say
this is anything special! I'll throw another one!—Why, I think
it is almost no fun at all!—But what is that playing up there in
the tops of the trees?—The wind! Yes—it sounds quite nice!
Sigh-sigh; sigh-sigh. . . . But I am afraid it will make me sleepy
if I listen to it for long. . . . *Sigh-sigh; sigh-sigh.* . . . It sounds
like the buzzing of mosquitoes on a summer evening!—It's
strange how transient everything in nature is! It grew tedious
being in the tower—and the years seemed so very long! But
what I see out here does not seem so beautiful and pleasant any
longer! (*He notices the brook.*) What is this? Ice?—What fun
can ice give you? Oh, now I remember—one can skate on it!
That is something I must try! (*He steps on the frozen brook.*

The ice gives way and he falls down from fright and remains lying on the edge of the brook.)

LISA *(enters. She runs over to Per).* There he is!—Ah, he is sleeping!—What is this? *(She picks up the ring, which Per dropped when he fell.)* A ring?—He sleeps in the snow! What has happened to him? He has been injured! What am I to do —away out here in the woods and in the snow—where scarcely a human being ever sets foot? . . . But he'll freeze to death if I can't get him away from here! The good fairy sent me to find this young lad—but she didn't tell me that I would find him half dead in a snow drift! Oh, if it at least were summer and the sun were shining on the green grass. *(She thumbs the ring. There is a change of scenery. The landscape is transformed from winter to summer. The icy covering of the brook melts away and the water purls between rocks and stones. A radiant sun illuminates the scenery.)* Oh! What is this? *(She looks around in astonishment.)*

PER *(awakens. He rubs his eyes).* What is this?—I fly out into the air from the tower—come to a forest covered by snow— throw snowballs—slide along on the ice—strike my head against it—lose consciousness—and when I wake up—it is summer! Have I been buried here in the snow for six months? Have I? *(He regards himself in the mirroring brook.)* No—I couldn't possibly—my face is red as a rose. *(He leans down close to the surface of the brook.)* But what is that I see far down in the deep? A blue sky—green trees—white water lilies . . . and in their very midst—a young maid! Just such a maid round whose waist the young man placed his arm at the Christmas party! Her hair is hanging loose—her mouth is like a dream—her eyes are like doves. . . . Oh—she nods to me. . . . I am coming to you—I am coming. *(He is about to dive into the brook, and Lisa gives a cry.)* You are here! And a moment ago you were down there! . . .

LISA. So it appeared! But you mustn't always believe your eyes!

PER. This is a strange world! But I want to make sure you are the same girl. *(He regards her intently.)* Yes—you are one and the same! *(He is about to hasten to her side when he notices that she has his ring.)* What—you have my ring!—You stole it while I lay unconscious! Oh! . . . "Do not always believe your eyes," you said. . . . You are right! Now I have learned my first lesson! I am about to embrace an angel—and what do I find? A thief!

LISA. Do not always believe your eyes, Per! Learn the truth before you judge!

PER. You are right! I shall do so. . . . Who are you, maid?
What is your name?

LISA. My name is Lisa. Who I am, you will not learn until
the time is ripe for it. I came here and found you lying unconscious. I discovered your ring on the ice—but I did not know
its power. . . . (She returns the ring to Per.)

PER. You have saved me from certain death—from freezing
to death. Forgive me, Lisa! You shall be my companion on my
pilgrimage, and you'll see we will have lots of fun. . . .

LISA. You say you are on a pilgrimage? What is the goal of
your journey?

PER. My goal? Why, like everyone else I seek happiness!

LISA. Happiness—is that what you seek? That is an elusive,
fickle thing to seek!

PER. Don't say that! I can have anything I want! In the midst
of winter—haven't we the loveliest summer imaginable? See
how gloriously the sun is shining up there on the pine trees.
. . . You must know that all this is something new for me. . . .
Oh but—what is this? (He picks up a couple of pine cones from
the ground.)

LISA. They are the fruits of the pine trees.

PER. Then one can eat them?

LISA. No—but children play with them.

PER. Play, you say? That's something I have never done. . . .
Shall we play, Lisa?

LISA. Yes, but what shall we play? Shall we play tag?

PER. How do you play tag?

LISA. You play it this way. (She runs and hides behind a
tree; then she throws a cone at Per.) Try and catch me now!

PER (pursues her). Well—that isn't so easy. (He steps on a
cone and hurts his foot.) Those cursed pine cones!

LISA. Do not curse the fruits of a tree!

PER. I can do without fruits like this! I much prefer those
I saw hanging on a Christmas tree! I only wish this pine
tree would bear that kind of fruit! (There is a change of
scenery. The pine tree now bears oranges.) Look! Look! Let
us taste them! (They pluck several oranges and eat them.)

LISA. Well—how do you like it?

PER. Oh yes—they taste good enough—but not as good as
I had thought they would.

LISA. That is the way with everything in life.

PER. How wise you are, you dear little girl!—Lisa! May I
put my arm round your waist? (A bird starts singing softly in
the treetop.)

LISA. Yes, but why do you want to do that?

PER (*putting his arm round her*). Will you let me kiss you, too?

LISA. Yes—I don't see any harm in that. (*They kiss. The bird's song grows louder.*)

PER. The game we played made me very warm, Lisa. . . . Shall we go bathing in the brook?

LISA. Go bathing? (*She covers her eyes with her hands.*)

PER (*pulls off his jacket*). Yes.

LISA (*hides behind a tree. The bird keeps singing*). No—no—no!

PER. What kind of a cry-baby is that up there in the tree?

LISA. It's a bird singing.

PER. What's he singing about?

LISA. Ssh! I understand the twitter of birds. My godmother taught me.

PER. Well, I'd like to hear. (*The bird sings.*)

LISA. "Don't do it! Don't do it!"—that's what he is singing now. (*The bird starts singing again.*) Per, Per! Do you know what he says now?

PER. No.

LISA. "Live innocently! My eye sees you!"

PER. Innocence? What is that?

LISA. I don't know, but—put on your clothes. . . .

PER. How could anyone see us here? All this is nothing but nonsense! (*A cuckoo cries: Oh-yes; oh-yes!*) What does that bird say?

LISA (*imitating the cuckoo*). Oh-yes; oh-yes!

PER. What an awful lot of formality there always must be!

LISA. Why can't you be satisfied with the great and innocent pleasures of nature?

PER. Oh yes—for a few brief moments! Ouch! What was that? (*He pulls off his vest.*)

LISA. An ant.

PER. All these many disagreeable things! (*He swats in all directions with his cap.*) What kind of thing was that which just stung me?—A mosquito?

LISA. Nothing is perfect in this life, Per! Remember that, and take the bad with the good!

PER. The devil may take the bad—I want nothing but the good. There! (*Again he strikes in all directions.*) Now I am tired of this forest! And a fellow can't waste his life playing games! I long for something to do—I want to be out in the world among people!—Lisa, you are such a wise little girl—tell me: what do people value most? For that is what I want to possess!

LISA. Before I answer you, Per, let me give you one piece of common sense: you will find that people are going to be just as disagreeable to you as the mosquitoes—but they will not give you as much pleasure as nature, which remains eternally young.

PER. Nature! Yes—nature is very beautiful, seen from a church tower; but seen close by, it becomes monotonous! Doesn't all in nature remain static? Don't the trees stand just where they stood fifty years ago—and will they not stand there fifty years from now? I am already tired of looking at all this glory—I want to see things that move, and hear excitement. . . . And if people are like mosquitoes, it would be easier to keep them at a distance than these intruders. (*He again wards them off with his cap.*)

LISA. I guess you will find out. You will find out! Experience will be a better teacher than my words.

PER. But tell me, Lisa, what is it that human beings value most in a mortal?

LISA. I am ashamed to say it!

PER. But you must tell me!

LISA. Gold!

PER. Gold? But gold is not a part of the human being! It doesn't belong to the human spirit!

LISA. Well—everybody knows that, of course—but that is the way it is, nevertheless.

PER. What is there about gold that makes it so remarkable, then?

LISA. It has many peculiarities—all sorts, as a matter of fact. It is a cure for everything—and for nothing. It has in it everything that the earth has to offer, for it is the most perfect of all minerals; and no rust can soil it. . . . Yet it can soil people's souls! . . .

PER. And now, Lisa—will you come with me?

LISA. I shall always be with you—at a distance. . . .

PER. At a distance? Why will you not stay at my side? Lisa—I want to put my arm round you once more. (*Lisa tears herself from him. The bird sings.*) Why do you run away from me?

LISA. Ask the bird!

PER. I don't understand his language. . . . You have to tell me what he says.

LISA (*confused*). No—I can't. (*The bird repeats his singing.*)

PER. Will you tell me what he says? Why can't you?

LISA. He is not singing for us now—he is singing to his beloved—and so you must understand what he says.

PER. And you can't tell me? Why?

LISA (*as she runs out*). He says: "I love you—I love you!"

PER. Stay! Why do you run away from me? Lisa—Lisa! . . . She is gone!—Very well! Come here, palace—come, casks and wine—horses and carriages—and servants—and gold—gold! (*There is a change of scenery.*)

SCENE 2. *A magnificent state hall. Servants are carrying in a table laden with food and wine; other servants come carrying a chest filled with gold; still others, a table groaning under an abundant array of golden jugs, vases, goblets, candelabra, etc.*

PER (*goes hither and thither, gazing at the grandeur*). So-o? This is the home of the rich, then! Well—I must say it looks most attractive and promising. . . . Serfs! Bring me my best holiday coat! But it must be of gold! (*Servants bring him a coat of gold cloth; they help him to put it on.*) A chair! (*They place him in a chair of gold in front of the table.*) Now, Per, you are going to enjoy life—and you are entitled to! Haven't you had to rise at four every morning to ring the bells for the early morning service? Haven't you had to sweep out the church every Friday morning and scrub the stairs every Saturday? Haven't you had to live on bread and herring three hundred and sixty-five days in the year and had to swallow it down with cold water? Haven't you slept on dried pea stalks that often were threshed so badly that you could feel the peas in the hollow behind your knees? Yes—you have! And therefore I say: enjoy yourself now! (*Rises to seat himself at the table.*)

STEWARD (*carrying a staff*). Forgive me, Your Grace, but— the table is not yet set.

PER. It isn't set?

STEWARD. The steaks won't be ready for a couple of hours. . . .

PER. I don't care to have any steaks!

STEWARD (*facing him, he stands before Per with his staff*). Sitting down to a table that is not set is something that just is not done, and will not be tolerated!

PER. Who is to forbid me in my own house?

STEWARD. Propriety! Etiquette, Your Grace! It would never permit such a thing—under any circumstances!

PER. Etiquette? What kind of a creature is that?

STEWARD. Your Grace—listen to an old man! Anyone in Your Grace's position who commits a breach of etiquette—is lost!

PER (*scared*). He certainly is a stern old gentleman! Well—I suppose I have to do as he says, even if I am terribly hungry. . . .

But wait! *(He ponders.)* I wonder whether there isn't something that could influence that gentleman? I was told that—gold. *(He walks over to the chest filled with gold and scoops up a handful of ducats.)* I wonder if . . .

STEWARD. Your Grace! I am at the head of the servants. Your Grace is above me, but above us all is—etiquette! Its laws are eternal, for they have their foundation both in reason and what has been called historical prerequisites!

PER. And these historical prerequisites, they are not within reach of—gold?

STEWARD. They are immutable in this case!

PER. What good is all my riches, then, if I can't eat myself full when I am hungry? I am worse off than the poorest sexton! *(The Steward takes a position like a statue at one end of the table. The Tax Clerk and his assistant enter and go from one end of the room to the other taking inventory of its contents.)* Here is another pest! What is it you gentlemen wish to bother me with in my innocence?

TAX CLERK. It's the taxation, Your Grace.

PER. Oh, so it is you who regulate how much people are worth! What is the value of a human being today?

TAX CLERK. Two per cent, Your Grace. Else it is according to . . . to what people have . . .

PER. Tell me, would you object if I retired while you gentlemen are taking inventory? I am both tired and hungry!

TAX CLERK. Impossible! It has to be done in the presence of the property owner.

PER. Oh Lord, what burdens! But you will let me sit down at least, won't you?

TAX CLERK. Certainly! *(To his assistant.)* Two dozen plates with laminated edges—write! Six wine coolers with handles made of a superior yellow metal—write! A sugar bowl with sugar spoon—and two smaller sugar bowls—write! Two dozen knives with handles of mother of pearl—brand new—write!

PER. I wouldn't be surprised if I lost my mind!

TAX CLERK. A dining table of oak with double flap leaves. Write! Six chairs of walnut. *(The Attorney enters.)*

PER. Another one!

ATTORNEY. Your Grace is summoned to appear in court in order to have property deed number 2867 ratified and recorded before twelve o'clock—today.

PER. Summoned to court? A lawsuit! I never want to get involved in a lawsuit, sir!

ATTORNEY. It is not a question of a lawsuit—it is merely to present the facts in the case.

PER. I don't care to present any facts. . . .

ATTORNEY. But let us ponder the matter . . .

PER. I don't care to ponder—I want to eat! Steward, can't I have a sandwich? *(The Steward raises his staff threateningly. The Court Attendant enters.)* Still more coming?

COURT ATTENDANT. Your Grace is summoned to appear before the Magistrates' Court at eleven o'clock tomorrow morning for failure to keep the sidewalk clean.

PER. Do I have to keep the street clean—I who am so rich? Is there anything I am not supposed to do, if I may ask?

COURT ATTENDANT. It is the duty of every property owner to keep the street in front of his house clean.

PER. Etiquette—taxation—pondering of property deeds—keeping the street and backyard clean—going hungry and thirsty. . . . If that is the lot of the rich man, then I would rather be a mere street sweeper! And I haven't even the right to show these gentlemen—who have forced themselves upon me —the way out. . . . And I can't come and go as I please! *(The Petitioner enters, accompanied by a Servant, carrying two baskets filled with documents.)* Mr. Attorney and Mr. Court Attendant, is there no law to protect an unfortunate rich man so that he may have peace in his own home? Or is the law merely for the protection of the poor?

ATTORNEY. Your Grace can no longer be regarded as a private citizen. Whenever anyone, through wealth, rises to the pinnacles of society, he belongs to the public.

PER. And so he is placed outside the law. . . .

ATTORNEY *(smiles; looks around).* Above the law, Your Grace!

PER. Ha!—What is the errand of this latest visitor? What has he in the baskets there—presents?

PETITIONER. Your exalted Grace is—in his capacity as member of the Church Council . . .

PER *(interrupts him).* Summoned to . . .

PETITIONER. Summoned to a meeting the day after tomorrow . . .

PER. . . . at eleven o'clock . . .

PETITIONER. At eleven o'clock—and to be present at the election of the new rector of the parish. But in advance of the meeting, Your Grace must peruse the documents I have brought with me. They will help to show the incompetence of the opposing candidate before the election takes place.

PER. You mean I have to struggle through two baskets full of documents before the day after tomorrow! No—no!

PETITIONER. Perhaps Your Grace would be gracious enough to cast your vote for our candidate?

PER. Without having to wade through all these. . . . Can I do that? Oh, in that case, thank you, my dear, dear friend!—Pen and ink!

PETITIONER *(hands him pen, ink, and a document to sign).* Excellent! I am grateful to Your Grace!

PER *(embraces him).* Oh, it is I who must thank you!

STEWARD *(strikes his staff against the table. Servants enter, bringing wine casks).* Dinner is served.

(All leave except the Steward.)

PER *(seats himself at the table).* At last! . . . *(Soft music begins to play.)* H'm—now they leave when *he* orders them to—but when *I* ask them, they pay no attention.

STEWARD. It is not an order of mine they are obeying, Your Grace; it is the demands of protocol they are following . . . of etiquette. . . .

PER. And they supersede my will?

STEWARD. Laws are an agreement by and between the many, and they take precedence over the will of the private citizen.

PER. He has an answer for everything, hasn't he?—Ah, but now I am really enjoying myself! The wine warms the cockles of my heart, the food warms my stomach—but what good is all this pleasure if you have no one to share it with you?—Mr. Steward, do the laws of etiquette permit me to have someone with me to enjoy these pleasures?

STEWARD. I would almost say that they require something of that sort.

PER. Very well! I would like to have . . .

FIRST FRIEND *(enters briskly and embraces Per).* Oh, my dear, dear friend! That I should see you again after such a long absence! And you haven't changed an iota—a little bit thinner than when I saw you last. . . . And how are things with you now, dear boy?

PER *(regards him fixedly).* Oh, thank you, thank you . . . quite well, as . . . as . . . h'm . . . as you see. . . . Please take a chair and sit down. . . .

FIRST FRIEND. Oh, thanks—I have just had my dinner. . . . I'll go into the drawing room and wait there until you have finished dining.

PER. You are going to do nothing of the kind. Only a moment ago I made the remark that life seemed so barren and lonely when one had to sit and eat alone. Pull up a chair and sit down, please!

FIRST FRIEND. My dear old friend—if you really insist, I shall take a seat at the table beside you while you have your dinner. But I do think it looks as if I had come here just to get a meal.

PER. Even if you had—what does it matter?

FIRST FRIEND (shocked). Oh!

PER. Oh well, I am not saying that's the reason you came.

FIRST FRIEND (seats himself). I see you have come up in the world, as they say. . . . I am glad that you have—glad to see that fate really can be so kind—and it can't help but bring joy to anyone with feelings to see that fortune smiles upon *somebody*. Alas, it isn't everybody who can say a good word for the unpredictable, fickle goddess Luck.

PER. Really? You have no reason to complain, have you?

FIRST FRIEND. I?

PER. Oh well, I don't want to hear anything about anybody's bad luck while I am eating! Won't you please do me a favor and eat a hazel hen?

FIRST FRIEND. You speak of doing you a favor, my friend. . . .

PER. Now, now—you must not keep calling me "my friend"; you must address me by my name.

FIRST FRIEND. When you ask it of me as a favor, Christopher, how can I, poor devil, refuse? (He starts to eat with increasing appetite. Per regards him with growing wonder.)

PER. We must never deny one another anything.

FIRST FRIEND. You express a beautiful thought: one should never deny oneself anything—I mean we should never deny each other anything.

SECOND FRIEND (enters. He goes directly to the table). How do you do, Göran!—You recognize me, don't you? (Per looks at him fixedly.) No, I can see you don't. But I remember you! You see, I never forget my old friends—and whenever I need them, I look them up. Here you sit eating, and I am starving—and so I'll come straight out with what I have to say: Göran, here I am! (He seats himself unceremoniously at the table.)

FIRST FRIEND (to Per). What kind of a cad is that? He swallows his food as if he hadn't had a meal between Christmas and Easter.

PER. Oh—he is a good friend of mine.

SECOND FRIEND (to Per). What sort of beggar is he? He stuffs himself like a wolf in a hard winter.

PER. Oh—he is one of my good friends.

FIRST FRIEND (to Per). Watch out for false friends, Per!

PER. Oh yes, oh yes!

SECOND FRIEND (to Per). Watch out for false friends, Per!

FIRST FRIEND (to Per). Before you know it, you'll see he will want to borrow money from you!

SECOND FRIEND *(to Per)*. If that scamp wants to borrow money from you, tell him *no*. He'll never pay it back!

PER. You don't say! You don't say!—Well, good friends, don't you think the repast is excellent?

SECOND FRIEND. I never flatter!

FIRST FRIEND. No, all you do is eat, my friend! I don't go in for flattery either, but that doesn't mean that I like to shun the truth. And I must confess that I have never partaken of anything comparable to this. It is only someone like Christopher who could have entertained his guests with such a dinner! Skoal, brother Christopher!

PER *(astonished, to himself)*. Christopher?

SECOND FRIEND. I am a plain, everyday being, I am, and I don't know how to sputter grandiose phrases as he does. I detest such things; and coming from a fellow like him, I can only ascribe their intent to a secret desire to borrow money. There you have my straightforward, everyday opinion.

FIRST FRIEND. What impertinence! What impudence!

PER. May I ask that no serious conversation interrupt this delightful gathering, which would be even more enjoyable if it could have been gladdened by the presence of some charming representative of the opposite sex. *(The Female Friend enters.)* Here we have her!

FEMALE FRIEND. So! You couldn't wait for me! That's extremely discourteous, but I forgive you because you are my friend! Here—here is my hand!

PER *(kisses her hand)*. I pray you will forgive me, my beautiful one, but I am afraid I made a mistake in the date. But do sit down! Please make room for the young lady, my friends! Let her sit beside me! *(First and Second Friends move closer to Per.)* Neither one of you will make room? Well—the younger one of my two friends will. *(Neither one moves.)* But perhaps you don't know which of you is the younger. . . . Well, then I'll ask the one who is my best friend to give up his place willingly—and he'll be just as close to my heart as ever if he does. *(Both get up from their places.)* I see that you are both my best friends!

FEMALE FRIEND. And I am your best friend among women! Am I not, Alonzo?

PER. Yes—so you are! And now—when I raise my cup—I wish to drink to Friendship! Friendship is like gold—for it is clean!

FEMALE FRIEND. How beautifully said!

PER. Friendship is like the moon. . . .

THE THREE FRIENDS. Bravo! Bravo!

PER. For it borrows its gold. *(The three regard one another quizzically.)* . . . from the sun! And it loses its luster when the sun disappears. Isn't that so?

THE THREE FRIENDS *(look at one another with sour faces).* Very well put!

PER. But friendship is a fire: it has to be nourished in order to keep burning! You have given me your friendship—and what have I to offer you? *(The three Friends give the room a searching look.)* You are looking at my gold. . . . Oh—my gold is as dust in comparison with your friendship!

FEMALE FRIEND *(prudently).* But that does not mean that we must disdain the material things in life merely because we have our moral and spiritual standards.

FIRST AND SECOND FRIENDS. A splendid observation!

PER. Very well—I wish to reward you for your faithfulness!—Look! I give you all the gold you see here!

THE THREE FRIENDS. Ah! *(They pounce upon the dinner service.)*

PER. But remember what I told you: gold is nothing but dust! *(He covers his mouth with his hand and walks uneasily back and forth.)* Oh, my God, I think I am going to die!

FEMALE FRIEND. What is the matter with you, Alonzo?

PER. I have a toothache! Oh, my teeth! Now you see that the rich man, too, has his troubles in life. *(The three Friends move toward the exits, laden with their acquisitions.)* No—don't leave me alone with my pain—now that I need you most!

FIRST FRIEND. Oh, a little toothache is nothing to worry about. . . . It'll soon disappear. . . .

SECOND FRIEND. Take a swallow of cold water—hold it in your mouth—and you'll soon be rid of the ache. . . .

FEMALE FRIEND. Oh, these men—they are so sensitive to a little pain. You should see how we women take it!

PER. Oh, don't leave me—please! I suffer frightfully!

FIRST FRIEND. I'll never abandon you! *(He has a hold of the door handle.)* I'm running out to get a dentist. . . .

PER. No—stay. . . .

SECOND FRIEND *(near the door).* No—it's up to me as George's oldest friend . . .

PER. You are all leaving me! Don't!—I curse this gold! I curse you all, false friends! *(The objects of gold which the three have removed from the table turn black in their hands.)*

THE THREE FRIENDS. He has deceived us! Look—look! *(All three are attacked by toothache and start moaning from pain.)* Oh-oh-oh-oh!

PER *(who has recovered).* Oh, that's nothing but a little toothache—it'll soon pass. . . . Just take a little cold water in your mouth, old friends, and it will go away! *(The Female Friend faints.)* The idea—a woman fainting from a little pain like that! *(The friends rush out.)* Yes, run to the dentist and let him pull out all your teeth, you foxy creatures—then you won't be able to bite any more sheep. . . .

FEMALE FRIEND *(recovers from her fainting spell)*. Alfred! Your friends left you, but I am staying with you!

PER. Yes—but why should you? I am the poorest of the poor, and soon the tax collector will be here to claim his tax, and then he will take every single stick of furniture as collateral.

FEMALE FRIEND *(steals close to him)*. Then I wish to be at your side and be of help to you. *(She takes hold of his hand and steals his ring from his finger while they talk.)*

PER *(duped)*. You? Is what you say really true?

FEMALE FRIEND. If it is true, you ask?—Look at me!

PER. Alas, I have been told that woman is more faithless than man is. . . .

FEMALE FRIEND. She is wiser than man. *(She pockets the ring.)* That is why she has been called faithless!—Oh, let me sit down—I am so agitated. . . .

PER *(leads her to a chair by the wall)*. Take it easy, my friend! I must have frightened you. . . .

FEMALE FRIEND. Give me a glass of wine—I am so exhausted after all this excitement and emotion. *(Per goes over to the table to pour her a glass of wine. The wall behind the chair opens and The Female Friend, seated on the chair, disappears. She holds up the ring for him to see.)* Hahahahaha!—Little schoolboy! Let this teach you not to believe in a woman whom you have scorned and insulted!

PER *(alone. He runs to the window and looks outside. When he comes away from the window, he has the ears of a donkey)*. Gold and friendship and women—may they all be damned! Now I am alone, abandoned and bereft—with a pair of long ears—and without my magic ring! If I had known that life would be so horrible, I think I would have stayed at home with the troll!—What am I going to do now—with no friends—no money—no home—no roof over my head? Distress and want stand outside the door waiting for me. . . . Am I now really to go out into life and have to work hard in order to realize every wish of mine? . . . Oh, how glad I would be if I were not alone, though!—But why not just as well be alone, as long as there is no such thing as friendship, and everything is false, and all is vanity? . . . Damnation!

LISA *(enters)*. Do not curse, Per!

PER. Lisa!—You have not abandoned me—even though I forgot you in my days of affluence and good fortune?

LISA. It is in days of need that we find our true friends.

PER. Friends! I curse all friendship!

LISA. You must not do that, Per! Just as life can ensnare us with false friends, so it can offer true friendship.

PER. I have already tasted the good in life, and all I found was emptiness and vanity.

LISA. You have tasted life in your own particular way!—However, now you have sowed your first wild oats, and you are on the way to becoming a man! You have searched for happiness in the wrong places! Wouldn't you much rather go out in the world and be of some use, enlighten your fellow beings, and do good? With your sound instincts and your vision you will be able to see past and through the distorted and ignoble that exists in the world!

PER. And become a great man!

LISA. Great or small matters little. You will be useful—you will be a reformer, who will lead humanity forward . . .

PER. Yes, a reformer, who will be honored and worshiped by the people, and whose name will live on the lips of all. . . .

LISA. Oh—how far you have strayed from the truth, Per! You seek human greatness for the sake of honor and glory! You shall have it—and with it, a new experience!

PER. But how? My ring is gone!

LISA. That ring can never be taken away from its rightful owner.

PER (holds up his hand and sees the ring on it). Why—there it is! Now, then—I wish to be a great man—a reformer! And you, Lisa, you shall accompany me!

LISA. Not yet! But I will not be far away from you;
and should you meet with grief, despair, and pain,
and Fortune's sun be hid by clouds in gray—
then I shall come to you, and not in vain!—
Go forth and learn what wrongs are done on earth;
and when you see how flowers are given birth,
rising in beauty through manure,
you'll realize we must both good and bad endure. . . .

ACT III

A square. On the left, the arcade of the courthouse. Above it, an oriel containing seats for the Burgomaster and the Council. On the right, the Shoemaker's house with shop

*windows and shingle; in front of the house, a bench and a
table; beside the bench, a hencoop and a water tub. In the
center of the square, a pillory with two iron collars attached
to chains; surmounting the pillory, a figure holding a birch
rod in its hand. On the left of the pillory, in the center of
the square, a statue of Burgomaster Hans Schulze: a life-size
figure leaning on a pavior's mallet. The Burgomaster's forehead is crowned with a laurel wreath.*

The background shows a view of the town.

PILLORY *(with a bow to the Statue).* Good morning, Statue!
Did you sleep well last night?

STATUE *(with a nod).* Good morning, Pillory! Did you get
any sleep yourself?

PILLORY. Yes, I slept well enough, but I dreamed too. . . .
Can you imagine what I dreamt?

STATUE *(in a surly manner).* How could I?

PILLORY. Well, I'll tell you! I dreamt—can you imagine—I
dreamt a reformer had come to town!

STATUE. A reformer? Did you say a reformer? *(He stamps his
feet.)* Hell—my feet get cold standing here. . . . But what
doesn't one do for the sake of glory and honor!—A reformer,
you say? Well—then I suppose he will want to have a statue,
too?

PILLORY. A statue! Ha! Oh no—he would have to stand like
a statue down here at my feet where I could embrace his neck
with both arms. *(Rattling the iron collars.)* You see, this fellow I dreamt about was a real reformer—not one of those
charlatans like you in your day!

STATUE. Stop your nonsense! You ought to be ashamed of
yourself!

PILLORY. So I should, I suppose—but I am always on the side
of justice. *(He makes a threatening display of the birch rod,
swinging it back and forth.)*

STATUE. What did he specialize in, this reformer of yours,
if I may ask?

PILLORY. Why, he was a reformer in street paving.

STATUE. In street paving! By all that is pestilential and rotten and dastardly! He has the nerve, the audacity to dabble
in my specialty! *(He pounds with the pavior's mallet.)*

PILLORY. Oh no—this fellow knew what he was doing—he
wasn't a faker like you! And if you hadn't been the father-in-
law of our present burgomaster, you wouldn't be standing
where you stand now!

STATUE. Wasn't it I, perhaps, who carried through the new idea of paving the streets with stone? Wasn't it?

PILLORY. So it was, yes—but the idea wasn't a new one. And what did you do? Instead of walking on the soft sand as we used to, we now have to balance ourselves on sharp and uneven cobblestones that do damage both to our feet and shoes —except on the street leading from your house to the public house! There you paved the road with flagstones!

STATUE. And now, you say, this reformer, this charlatan wants to improve upon my creation. . . .

PILLORY. He wants to tear up what you have put down, and pave all the streets with burgomaster flagstones, so that there will be no discrimination.

STATUE. So-o—the fellow is one of those rabid radicals—a revolutionist!

PILLORY. Yes, that's just what he is—and he is a nonpartisan, too! You had the Wagonmaker, the Shoemaker, the Chiropodist, and the Burgomaster on your side—and that is why you could put across your scheme!

STATUE. He had better watch out! Every stone he pulls up will be cast at him—and God help him if he touches my memorial!

PILLORY. I only hope he will expose you, you old rascal! Do you remember how you came to be such a great man after your death? First the priest extolled your virtues for twenty ducats; then the Streetpaver—who made a fortune out of the street business you gave him—read a speech in praise of your honor; then the Chiropodist—whose bunion practice was increased by your beautiful cobblestones—had a commemorative medal struck in your honor; then the Wagonmaker—whose business profited by repairs—named a carriage for you; and finally the Shoemaker arranged an annual memorial service for you! That did the trick! Your son-in-law, the Burgomaster, sent out a petition, inviting everybody to subscribe to a statue —and nobody dared say no! And that is why you are now standing where you stand!

STATUE. So I do, yes . . . and now you are envious! And today the Schulze Society is coming here with wreaths, and they are going to sing the memorial cantata that my son-in-law has ordered. I can imagine how it will hurt you to have to stand there and listen to it!

PILLORY. I won't say it won't! Just the same, I wonder whether my dream will not come true in the end. . . .

STATUE. Shut your mouth—here comes the Society. . . .

PILLORY. I have to pinch myself in order not to break out

into laughter! *(In a mocking voice.)* "Here comes the Society!"
—Three persons! That's the Society! Last year there were six.
You are going downhill, Schulze! Soon you will see they'll move
you out to the ox paddock. . . .

SHOEMAKER *(comes out of his house and opens his shop window)*. I believe it has rained during the night. . . . Brother
Schulze looks a little damp and shining! I only hope it won't
rain when the Singing Society arrives. *(He calls into the shop.)*
Hans!

HANS *(in the window)*. Yes, master!

SHOEMAKER. Sit down in the window and do your work
there. . . . I am going out to perform a civic duty.

HANS. Yes, master.

SHOEMAKER. But if you don't do your work, I'll have the
strap do a dance on your backside! You hear that, you rascal!

WAGONMAKER *(enters, carrying a standard)*. Good morning,
Shoemaker!

SHOEMAKER. Good morning, Wagonmaker!

CHIROPODIST *(enters with a laurel wreath)*. Good morning,
good morning! Do you think we ought to wait for the Burgomaster? You know—I think we ought to hurry—we are going
to have rain again, I'm afraid.

SHOEMAKER. That's exactly what I said to myself early this
morning and that's why I was wise enough to take along my
raincoat.

WAGONMAKER. It seems to me it is time for the crowds to
be forming behind us to serve as background. But I don't see
as much as a cat! Mr. Shoemaker, didn't you tell the printer
that we were observing the day with festivities?

SHOEMAKER. Why, certainly . . . certainly . . .

WAGONMAKER. Will you gentlemen form a semicircle round
Schulze's pedestal? *(The celebrants move together in a cres-
cent.)* That's the way—yes. . . .

CHIROPODIST. I think we may as well commence with the
cantata—then the people will begin to assemble, I am sure.

WAGONMAKER. I can't understand why the Burgomaster
hasn't shown up. He always used to provide us with glögg in
past years. . . .

SHOEMAKER. If we only start the singing he'll wake up, in
case he has overslept. . . . Have you the pitch, gentlemen?
C—F sharp—G—

WAGONMAKER. I'll begin, then. . . . But watch out when it
comes to the trio, so that the ensemble sounds truly monstrous. *(He sings a solo recitative.)*

Hail, you benefactor!
Hail, you burgomaster!
All is perishable in this earthly vale of tears;
but in our memory you have not any peers.
Your deeds shall live eternally despite intrigue and envy!

SHOEMAKER. You whistled that splendidly, Wagonmaker!—
I don't see any sign of the glögg!

WAGONMAKER. Let's continue, Shoemaker! Now comes the aria. It has to be taken very idealistically—then you'll see the Burgomaster will wake up!

SHOEMAKER *(sings the aria)*. The breath of roses and the fragrance of the carnation buds
    amidst the fates of miracle flowers!
    With treacherous heart,
    like the silvery brine,
    She swept her flowing hair about him.
    There murmurs the bracing sea its song. . . .
And lily so white and lily so red
ponder with intimacy life and death!

CHIROPODIST. That's a precious piece of poetry—but I don't see that it has any connection with the object of our veneration, or with conditions of today. Where did you get it from?

SHOEMAKER. Well—you see I have a young apprentice in my shop who is one of that kind that has ideals—and he manufactures verses of this sort when he is free on Sunday.

WAGONMAKER. If I may be permitted to express my opinion, I would say it's terribly hard to know just what the essence of the verses is.

SHOEMAKER. Well, you see that is exactly what makes it so peculiarly distinctive! Oh heavens—I believe it's beginning to rain again! *(He puts on his raincoat.)*

WAGONMAKER. What do you think, gentlemen—do you think we should stand out here in the rain and get wet just for the sake of the old fogy?

SHOEMAKER. Since we are being paid for our vocalizing, the least we can do is to sing the trio before we leave; and when we really get going—all of us together—then not even the devil himself should be able to sleep! As far as the memorial speech is concerned—let's forget about that! And besides, our audience is much too small for such a big speech.—But let us take the trio now! C—F sharp—G—B . . . It hasn't the perfection or beauty that the aria has—but I will say this, that it bespeaks a more positive foothold on a more positive understanding of the concrete conditions. *(The rain falls in torrents and the wind is increasing.)*

CHIROPODIST. I'll be damned if I am going to stay here any longer and catch cold for the sake of that old charlatan! Getting paid for our singing, eh? Six farthings each! I can do just as well without it!

WAGONMAKER. That's what I say!

SHOEMAKER. Weren't you among the subscribers to the statue, eh? Weren't you instrumental in proclaiming him a great man, awarding him a medal, eh? Weren't you?

WAGONMAKER. Well—what else could we do? If we hadn't done it, we would have been subjected to humiliation. . . .

SHOEMAKER. Yes—but it shows ingratitude not to honor his memory. . . . Well—I'll sing the trio by myself, then. . . .

CHIROPODIST. Yes—you can do it! You have your raincoat. . . . I am going home and have my breakfast. (He throws the wreath at the base of the statue and rushes out.)

WAGONMAKER. This is the last time I let myself be used for a spectacle like this! Good-bye! (He, too, hastens out.)

SHOEMAKER (alone). Now I am going to the Burgomaster—at least I'll get myself a glass of glögg there! But before I go, I'll deliver my oration for the old fellow—then I'll have a clear conscience. (He addresses the statue.) You imagine, Schulze—you old fool—that it is for *your* sake we are doing our singing, for *your* sake we are making speeches, don't you? Can't you get it into your head that we need someone like you to be a bigwig—someone we can push to the front when the rest of us are not considered big enough? We need someone we can quote when nobody believes what *we* say. Our little town needed a statue in order to become a big town; your impoverished relatives needed a statue so that they could get a new footing in the community and repair their fortunes —and that's the reason, you see, why you are now placed so high above us, you who were nothing but a cipher before! If you have never heard the truth before, you rascal, you hear it now—perhaps the first and the last time you will ever hear it. (He suddenly looks around, frightened.) I hope to heavens nobody heard what I said!—Ha, here comes a relative of the great man. . . .

RELATIVE. Good morning, Shoemaker! Have you heard—have you heard about the horrible outrage that has been perpetrated? . . .

SHOEMAKER. What's that you say? What has happened, Mr. Relative?

RELATIVE. A reformer has come to town! Haven't you seen his placards and posters?

SHOEMAKER. N-no, n-no!

RELATIVE. Oh! This is terrible. This is unheard of! Look—read for yourself! *(Shows him a poster.)*

SHOEMAKER. I am too agitated—I can't read it! You read it to me!

RELATIVE. Well—just listen to what the blackguard writes! *(He reads.)* "Scarcely a quarter of a century has elapsed since Burgomaster Schulze brought to this community an important improvement with relation to its paving problem: the replacing of the then sandy ground with uneven cobblestones." Did you hear? Did you hear?

SHOEMAKER. Yes, I heard it! But I don't think there is anything so terrible about that!

RELATIVE. Nothing terrible? Doesn't he call him Burgomaster Schulze, doesn't he? A burgomaster isn't called a burgomaster when he is dead—he is spoken of as "that great man!" And doesn't the blackguard use the words "uneven cobblestones," doesn't he? Isn't that proof enough that he means to belittle the great man's service to the community? Isn't it? Eh?

SHOEMAKER. But you can't call it an outrage, can you, just because he says that cobblestones are uneven—for that's what cobblestones are: uneven!

RELATIVE. Yes—they are uneven—but why do you have to talk about it—they have been put there by a great man, haven't they! Watch out, Master Shoemaker—I can see you have your doubts! Watch out—you know what will happen to you. . . .

SHOEMAKER. For heaven's sake, I am not a disbeliever at all! Haven't I just stood here and idealized Brother Schulze in song? Haven't I?

RELATIVE. Brother Schulze, ha! If you fraternized with him when he was alive, just remember that all brotherly skoaling ceases with death! Are you willing to acknowledge that this reformer has made an attempt on his life, or are you not?

SHOEMAKER. Certainly—of course I'm willing! I haven't said anything else, have I? Can you prove that I have said anything else?

RELATIVE. Well—h'm. . . . But take care in the future! We are holding a general court session here in the square at nine o'clock, and that's when this reformer is going to have to defend his case. Do you know what he proposes?

SHOEMAKER. No.

RELATIVE. Can you imagine—he wants to repave all the streets with flat stones!

SHOEMAKER *(spontaneously)*. Why—that's a very good idea!

RELATIVE *(with a bitter laugh)*. A good idea! Yes, a very good idea! What, for example—only to mention your own trade—what would happen to the glorious shoemaker business if people no longer should wear out their shoes?

SHOEMAKER. What did you say? What's that you are saying? —You are right, my friend! Forgive me! . . . I am not thinking of myself, of course—I am thinking of all the poor apprentices and journeymen who will lose their livelihood—and of their poor wives and children!

HANS (*makes a grimace where he sits in the shoe shop window*). Poor, unfortunate apprentices, yes!

RELATIVE. There you see! There you see! (*Pointing to the statue.*) He was friend of the poor, he was! And he was a man who knew what he was doing!

SHOEMAKER. I can assure you that both the Wagonmaker and the Chiropodist will be of the same opinion as I!

RELATIVE. Can I rely on that?

SHOEMAKER. As sure as I live!

RELATIVE. Fortunate is indeed the nation that reveres its great men! (*He hastens out.*)

(*People begin to pour into the square. The Relative is seen talking with the Wagonmaker and the Chiropodist. The clock on the courthouse strikes nine. Two Trumpeters and a Drummer enter and start playing. When the music is over, Per comes in. The Streetpaver joins him.*)

PER. Good morning, Master Streetpaver! How do you think my case will turn out for me?

STREETPAVER. Badly! Very badly!

PER. Don't the people here want to make some progress?

STREETPAVER. There is no question about that! The point is that they are jealous of the reputation of their great man— and you have attacked that!

PER. I have attacked him? (*It has now stopped raining.*)

STREETPAVER. You have called him Burgomaster—and that is a word that has come to be looked upon as a foul and insulting nickname in this town! You have said that his cobblestones are rough on the feet and uneven! In a word, you have given voice to the general opinion of the man—and that is why they have pounced on you. You are done for!

PER. I must say we live in a strange world!

STREETPAVER. The world has its good sides and its bad sides, and it has its little peculiarities. But don't try to make it any better, my dear man, for if you do, you'll be on your way to hell!

PER. The people here are dissatisfied—and when you try to do away with the cause of their dissatisfaction, they stone you!

(*A boy distributes leaflets among the people. He hands one each to Per and The Streetpaver. Per gazes at the sheet and reads it.)* Oh, this is shameless! We have been caricatured—both of us! Have I a nose like that? Have I?

STREETPAVER. The likeness isn't bad at all! But have I ears like that? Have I?

PER. But I can't understand this at all! Yesterday the printer was keen about my idea—and today he insults me!

STREETPAVER. Public opinion, you understand! He told me he was in favor of the project but was afraid to break with public opinion.

PER. A curious way to champion an idea! What—and who—in his opinion represents public opinion?

STREETPAVER. First of all, the consumers—then the Burgomaster—and the ones who have money—and power. . . .

PER. But why has he caricatured you?

STREETPAVER. Because I was aiding and abetting you in your scheme. And I did it, of course, because I saw I could make a fortune! And today he is making hay by selling five hundred copies of this sort of poetizing! *(The trumpets and the drum are sounded. The Burgomaster, Members of the Council and Clerks are seen in the oriel.)*

BURGOMASTER. Well, my children, I presume you have heard that an impostor, a swindler, has come to our town. . . .

ONE OF THE PEOPLE. He is not a swindler—he is a reformer.

BURGOMASTER. Well—that's the same thing. But you should keep your mouth shut, my lad—you can't vote yet!

PER. Mr. Burgomaster, I should like to request that my proposition be brought before this honorable assembly in its original and unadulterated form.

BURGOMASTER. Just listen to him! We are fully aware of your proposal, and it merely remains for us to make a pronouncement. I therefore remit it without any further ado to the insane asylum. Can you imagine what this fellow wants, my children? He wants everybody to walk on flat stones! But since Our Lord has created us all different, then the stones in the street should be different, too. Is there anybody who has anything to add to this?

ONE OF THE PEOPLE. That's not true. God did not make human beings different. . . .

BURGOMASTER. Who gave you permission to bray?

ONE OF THE PEOPLE. As long as we are not allowed to vote, we might at least be permitted to bray!

BURGOMASTER. Go ahead and bray then, if you like—and I'll have you locked up! I take it for granted that you have nothing to add to that!

RELATIVE. Mr. Burgomaster! As a man of honor, I just feel I have to protest against this dastardly attempt upon a man's honor that has been perpetrated here.

PER. I challenge the relative as noncompetent!

BURGOMASTER. On the contrary—I attach much greater importance to his utterance because of his relationship to the great man; that is invariably the best guarantee that society has! . . . Thus we shall consider the propounded suggestion null and void. (*He emphasizes his decision with a bang of the gavel.*)

ROOSTER (*in the hencoop outside the Shoemaker's shop*). Cock-a-doodle-doo!

BURGOMASTER. Who is making all this hellish noise?

ONE OF THE PEOPLE. It's someone with a right to vote! Let him crow!

ROOSTER. Cock-a-doodle-doo!

ONE OF THE PEOPLE. Arrest him! (*There is an outbreak of bedlam and noisy laughter.*)

PER. Mr. Burgomaster. . . .

BURGOMASTER. Keep quiet there!—Now to the second point! The aforementioned adventurer has expressed himself in a nefarious manner about this town's late lamented burgomaster. We wish to hear several impartial burghers. . . . What punishment does he deserve for this in your estimation, Mr. Shoemaker?

SHOEMAKER. I vote with the Council!

BURGOMASTER. That's right! We shall remember you with our good will for that!—What have you to say in this matter, Mr. Chiropodist?

CHIROPODIST. I am in agreement!

BURGOMASTER. And you, Mr. Wagonmaker?

WAGONMAKER. I have the honor to concur with the previous speaker!

ONE OF THE PEOPLE. The ones who have a right to speak say nothing!

BURGOMASTER. Quiet over there!—In view of what has been brought out and supported by conclusive proof, the adventurer, whose name is Per—and without any surname—is herewith, because of profligate language used against the Council, sentenced to be put in the stocks and exposed to ridicule for two hours; and afterward to be exiled from the town that he may be gripped by abject fear, and as a warning to others.

PER. Mr. Burgomaster—you have produced no testimony! No proof!

BURGOMASTER. There is no need for any! Axiomatic or self-

evident truths neither can nor need be proved! Take him outside for the time being! *(Per is led outside.)* Point number
three! In consideration of the unfortunate as well as unex-
pected circumstance that the dogs in our town have been mani-
festing an improper expression of their innate feeling for the
beautiful around the pedestal of the statue to our late lamented
altruist and benefactor Hans Schulze, it is requested that an
appropriation be made for the erection of an iron railing for
its protection! I take it for granted that there is no one here
who will refuse such a deserving man this insignificant tribute
of respect.

CHORUS OF QUALIFIED VOTERS. No!

ONE OF THE PEOPLE. This is the first time anyone has heard
those entitled to vote say no!

BURGOMASTER. Put him behind bars, Constable!—The question is consequently decided in the affirmative.

CHORUS OF QUALIFIED VOTERS. Yes!

ONE OF THE PEOPLE *(bleating like a sheep)*. Baa-aa! *(There
is a moment of laughter and noise.)*

BURGOMASTER. The general court session is adjourned!
(Trumpets and a drum are heard. Then silence.)

RELATIVE *(to the Shoemaker)*. He is an extraordinarily competent and expeditious fellow, that burgomaster, isn't he?

SHOEMAKER. He ought to be in the cabinet—then the public
interest would be served so much swifter!

*(The Burgomaster, the Council Members, and the Clerk go
inside the courthouse. People continue to circulate in the
square. The Shoemaker, the Chiropodist, the Wagonmaker
and the Relative linger. The Streetpaver remains by himself,
apart from the others.)*

SHOEMAKER *(to his three cronies)*. Wouldn't you gentlemen
like to come over to my house and have a glass of ale?

CHIROPODIST, WAGONMAKER, RELATIVE *(in unison)*. We thank
you!

SHOEMAKER *(gives an order to Hans through the door to
bring out some ale)*. Well, Mr. Relative, you did not choose
to be present at your distinguished relative's memorial service
this morning?

RELATIVE. No—I don't see why I should be standing out
there in the rain! But you were there with the Society, weren't
you?

SHOEMAKER. Every single one of us—all three!

RELATIVE. Did you sing?

CHIROPODIST. Yes—somewhat.

RELATIVE *(with a laugh)*. Did you have a big crowd?

WAGONMAKER. Not a soul!

RELATIVE. How about the Burgomaster?

SHOEMAKER. He overslept!

RELATIVE (laughs). Did you read the *Morning Rooster?*

ALL. No.

RELATIVE (takes a leaflet from his pocket). Do you want me
to read what it says? . . . "PAYING TRIBUTE. The customary
memorial tribute that the Schulze Society pays each year to that
highly deserving citizen whose monument is erected in the town
square took place early this morning. An enormous crowd was
present and greeted the musical and vocal contributions in
honor of the departed great man's memory with animated
applause. The songs were rendered by the immense chorus with
its customary accuracy and excellent ensemble. The festival
oration was delivered with vibrant voice by the meritorious
Master of Shoemakers, Pumpenblock. Among the distinguished
personages who were present we noted the town's burgomaster, the relative of the deceased, and others. (All laugh.)
Precious, isn't it?

ALL. Truly precious! You wrote it yourself, didn't you?

RELATIVE. Oh—but did you see the reformer's and the Streetpaver's pictures? That is really something to look at!

SHOEMAKER. But don't you think it was going a little too far
to caricature them like that?

RELATIVE. Well, nobody with common sense would have
anything against their proposal—but why should it have to fall
into their hands!—Silence! Here he comes!

(Per is brought in by a guard and is placed in a pillory, with
an iron collar round his neck. The People crowd around him
and point fingers at him. The Shoemaker's cronies appear
to be somewhat embarrassed. A man playing a stringed instrument and an old Blind Woman enter. The Blind Woman
displays a painted picture on a pole.)

BLIND WOMAN (sings and points to the picture, which is
painted in six separate fields: one for each verse).

> There was a poor nice youngster
> who set out to do good. . . .
> In the square the town's great leaders
> drank their ale in solitude.
>
> The youth said to the people:
> "I'll make your path so smooth!"
> The town's great men reflected:
> "He'll give us grief forsooth!"

The great men sat there drinking
their foaming mugs of ale;
they drank to the people's welfare,
they drank to the public weal.

They pilloried the youngster,
'round his neck they looped a chain . . .
when, as once from Caiphas' palace,
came a rooster's shrill refrain. . . .

These worthy men revere
authority and the law;
fence in their proud memorials,
left prey to sleet and thaw. . . .

But the people have long been fettered—
the darkness keeps them in chain . . .
They wait for the cock to be crowing
its third—and final—refrain!

*(The Shoemaker and his cronies have been making sour
faces and appear not to have been listening. The crowd,
however, seems interested and put a few coins in the Woman's
collection box. The women in the crowd are seemingly affected and some of them wipe their eyes now and then.)*

RELATIVE *(to the Shoemaker)*. Well . . . do you get many
orders nowadays?

SHOEMAKER. Oh—so-so. . . .

BLIND WOMAN *(comes up to the table)*. Please give the blind
woman something!

CHIROPODIST. Begging is forbidden—don't you know that?

ONE OF THE PEOPLE. She is not begging—she requests a grant.

SHOEMAKER. What sort of gibberish is he talking!

ONE OF THE PEOPLE. The Schulze Society has been given
a grant for singing at the statue over there—but the members
put the money in their own pockets and don't show up! This
morning only three of them were there!

SHOEMAKER *(to his cronies)*. Can you imagine—they keep
track of everything, these rascals!

BLIND WOMAN. Please give the blind woman a coin!

RELATIVE. Must we pay, too, to listen to her raucous noise!

ONE OF THE PEOPLE. She sings better than the Shoemaker
sang this morning when we listened to him from behind the
corner! She may not sing about carnations and blooming roses

and fanciful romantics and idealism; but a word of truth at
the right time can be called idealistic too.

RELATIVE. If you don't get away from here, you old crone,
you'll land in the hoosegow! *(It starts to thunder and rain, and
the wind is blowing. There is great excitement and confusion.)*

SHOEMAKER. There—there we have the rain again! . . . Step
inside with me, gentlemen. . . . *(They break up from the
table.)*

BLIND WOMAN. Are you going to let that poor fellow in the
pillory stand there in the rain?

RELATIVE. If my relative, who is such a great man, can stay
outside, I guess that one can stay where he stands, too!

SHOEMAKER. A little cold water on his head will help to cool
off a reformer like him! *(He stumbles and stubs his toe on the
cobblestones.)* Those damned cobblestones! *(He hops into the
house on one foot. Per and the Blind Woman are left alone
on the stage.)*

BLIND WOMAN *(removes her mask and is discovered to be
Lisa).* Well, Per, you have now become a renowned man. Your
name is on the lips of everyone; your image is being paraded
about the streets and squares; and the people praise you as a
reformer. Are you now satisfied?

PER. You know, Lisa—I think I have had enough of being
a reformer!

LISA. You intend to leave your work half done?

PER. Yes, heaven be praised—if I can only get away from
this business without a scratch!

LISA. You were covetous of honor and fame. . . .

PER. Well—isn't that what everybody is?

LISA. Not everybody!—And you had the good will of the
people!

PER. Of the people? What have they to say?

LISA. What you wanted was the good will of the mighty—
those that have the power! Well, now you can really be
ashamed of yourself!—You didn't even believe in the cause
that you fought for!

PER. To tell the truth, I think it matters little whether we
walk on cobblestones or stones that are flat. . . .

LISA. Yes, if you are wearing heavy boots—but not if you
walk in your bare feet!

PER. Anyhow, the community isn't worth as much as this!
(He snaps his fingers.) The whole world is nothing but lies—
all of it! The public good—the public good! That's all people
talk about! What is the public good? It seems to me it is noth-

ing but the merged interests of the few—it's collusion, that's
what it is!

LISA. Society should be for the welfare of all, but it isn't.
Someone fired by inspiration might accomplish it—but it won't
be done by someone like you!

PER. I want to— I want to do it—but I lack the power—you
know that!

LISA. Then see that you get it, Per, and then we'll find out
if I have been mistaken in you!

PER (bursts his chains and the iron collar round his neck,
and goes to Lisa). You will see, Lisa, that I will do something
great, once I have the power!

LISA. Why something great? Something good is worth still
more!

PER. But you must always remain by my side!—Lisa, what
was it that the bird in the forest sang?

LISA. That I shall tell you next time. . . .

PER. No—now!

LISA. He said: "I love you!"

PER. Won't you love me, Lisa?

LISA. Yes—when you love me!

PER. I do now. . . .

LISA. No—you do not . . . you love only yourself! Go out
again into the world, Per, and learn! You have only a few
wishes left that you can ask for. . . . The greatest and most
treacherous wish still remains. . . . The highest gift a weak
mortal can be given is power—and woe be to him who abuses
it! He is the earth's greatest bane—its greatest criminal—for he
creates a false image of our God! Farewell, Sovereign! Your
crown awaits you!   (She disappears.)

PER. And my queen!

ACT IV

SCENE 1. *The interior of a palace in oriental style. On the
left, a throne. In front of it, a table, on which are placed
the regalia. On the right, a divan with pillows placed about
it in a semicircle on the floor.*

*The Lord High Herald is lying on the floor, writing on a
scroll of parchment.*

MASTER OF THE ROYAL HOUSEHOLD (enters). Is this the
genealogical table of the young caliph?

LORD HIGH HERALD. Yes, Your Grace.

MASTER OF THE ROYAL HOUSEHOLD. It looks quite impressive!
—Whom have you given him as his first ancestor?

LORD HIGH HERALD. The Caliph Omar, naturally!

MASTER OF THE ROYAL HOUSEHOLD. It seems to me that
Harun-al-Rashid would have been more fitting.

LORD HIGH HERALD. It is true that Caliph Harun was more
popular; but then our gracious lord and master would not
have been related to the ancient House.

MASTER OF THE ROYAL HOUSEHOLD. You are quite right! Will
you soon have finished? We are expecting him any moment.

LORD HIGH HERALD. Has Your Grace met the new caliph yet?

MASTER OF THE ROYAL HOUSEHOLD. Yes, he looks exactly like
the rest . . . and the only thing that distinguishes him from us
is his pedigree.

LORD HIGH HERALD. Yes—the genealogical table!

MASTER OF THE ROYAL HOUSEHOLD *(looks over the scroll
anew)*. You have broadened it tremendously, it seems to me!

LORD HIGH HERALD. I had to establish a collateral branch.
It makes the table look more impressive and imparts a sem-
blance of strength to the line. That gives it a flattering appeal.

MASTER OF THE ROYAL HOUSEHOLD *(laughs)*. What will the
Caliph Omar say about that?

COURT CHAPLAIN. *Allah, ekbar barai!* How is your health?

MASTER OF THE ROYAL HOUSEHOLD. *Allah Eloim!* Thank you,
splendid!

COURT CHAPLAIN. Have the two copies of the abdication act
been completed?

MASTER OF THE ROYAL HOUSEHOLD. Yes, Your Eminence,
both copies! — Will Your Eminence be kind enough to collate
them, then all he will have to do is to sign them?

COURT CHAPLAIN. If we have time to do that now, I think
that would be best, yes.

MASTER OF THE ROYAL HOUSEHOLD *(takes two documents
from the table in front of the throne and hands one of them
to the Court Chaplain)*. "We, Omar XXVII, herewith solemnly
foreswear our present Roman Catholic religion and accept the
Mohammedan religion, as taught and determined in the Al-
coran and the Holy Scriptures. Datum, et cetera. Omar."
Correct?

COURT CHAPLAIN. Correct!

*(Per enters, accompanied by a retinue. The Lord High
Herald jumps to his feet with the genealogical table. The Lord
High Historian, who has entered with Per and the Wazir,
stands silent, annotating in a book all that passes)*.

WAZIR. Does it please Your Highness to examine this genealogical chart that the Herald of the Realm has laid down, giving Your Highness's lofty ancestry?

PER. My genealogical chart? — I don't know of any other ancestor than my father, the old bell-ringer.

WAZIR (*makes believe he has not heard what Per said*). It originates with a great and glorious name, the Caliph Omar . . .

PER. The Caliph Omar? What kind of a gander was he?

WAZIR (*sternly*). He wasn't any gander. He was a great and glorious regent!

PER. Well, that may be—but I was born in wedlock and don't belong to any collateral branch line, my good gentlemen. . . .

WAZIR. It is not a regent's prerogative to be selfish. A regent must always sacrifice his personal interests and likings for the good of his people!

PER. That's all very well! But does the welfare of the people demand that I be illegitimate?

WAZIR. Yes!

PER. Well—give me that paper! (*The Lord High Herald hands Per the genealogical chart and a pen*). It begins with a lie, and I suppose will end with theft! . . . (*He writes.*)

WAZIR. There remains a slight formality. Will Your Highness graciously sign this document? (*The Court Chaplain hands Per the act pertaining to the renunciation of his old faith.*)

PER. What's this?

WAZIR. Your Highness need not bother to read it; it is only a formality . . .

PER (*reads*). Forswear the faith of my fathers! Why—that's nothing short of an outrage—it's an insult!

WAZIR. Political considerations—the welfare of the People and the State. . . .

PER. I have to turn into a Mohammedan—and not be able to drink even a glass of wine?

WAZIR. In all political matters, there are substitutes. . . .

PER. What, for instance?

WAZIR. Compromises, readjustments, modifications. . . .

PER. Roundabout ways, eh?

WAZIR. Will Your Highness be so gracious as to sign?

PER. But I shall come to despise myself if I should start with a shameful act! And the People will have even greater cause for looking down on me!

WAZIR. The nation demands that the Regent sacrifice all personal considerations for its welfare!

PER. Its well-being should be built on a lie and a criminal act, I suppose?

WAZIR (*goes over to the window*). Your Highness! The Peo-

ple are waiting to greet their sovereign! The People are always
ready and willing to offer their blood and sweat for their
sovereign; therefore they have the right to demand that their
sovereign make *his* sacrifices!

PER. Is what you say really true? Oh well—give me the paper!
(*The document is handed to him; he hesitates.*) The church
tower—the church bells—the hymn singing—the lights and the
candles—Christmas—it all passes before my eyes! No more
Christmas Eves! How cruel life can be! It has nothing but
demands! It never gives anything in return!

WAZIR. Your Highness, the People are getting impatient!
They are waiting to see their new sovereign in the regalia of
the ancient caliphs! The crown and the scepter are waiting
to be worn again by a descendant of the glorious, famed
family tree!

PER (*catches sight of the crown and scepter*). Ah! . . .
Wazir! Who can compel me to forswear my faith?

WAZIR. The laws!

PER. Who made the laws?

WAZIR. Our ancestors!

PER. They were weak mortals like ourselves! Very well, I
shall change the laws!

WAZIR. Your Highness cannot change the laws! Our constitution does not empower the Caliph to legislate.

PER. What form of constitution exists in this land?

WAZIR. We have a constitutional dictatorship!

PER. Answer my question: Am I the Caliph, or am I not?

WAZIR. Not until Your Highness has put his signature on
this document!

PER. Give me the pen! (*He signs the document. The coronation ceremony takes place. Courtiers appear. Dancing and
other forms of entertainment.*)

THE PEOPLE (*outside*). Long live Omar XXVII! Allah! Allah!
Allah!

WAZIR. Does it please Your Highness to ascend the throne
and inaugurate Your reign?

PER. That will be quite a diversion! Let in the People!

WAZIR. The People? The People have nothing to do with
the government!

PER. Yes—but I suppose I should have somebody to rule
over, shouldn't I?

WAZIR. That is done by proclamation! (*He brings out a
number of documents.*)

PER. Proceed, then!

WAZIR. In order to spare Your Highness the drudgery of the

heavy government tasks on Your first day on the throne, we have tabled all affairs of state, with the exception of one; and that one can be decided very expeditiously.

PER. That was a stupid thing to do—but it can't be helped now! Let's hear!

WAZIR. Achmed Sheik salutes with a salaam and prays from the bottom of his heart that he will be permitted to become a Sunnite.

PER. What is a Sunnite?

WAZIR. The Sunnites are a sect—a dangerous sect!

PER. In which respect do their teachings differ from the—h'm—from the true faith?

WAZIR. A true Moslem greets Allah in this manner. (*He folds his arms across his breast.*) But a nonconformist does it in this way. (*With a snap of the fingers, he touches his nose and puts his fingers in his ears.*)

PER (*laughs*). Well—if a man wants to put his fingers in his ears, let him!

WAZIR. No! The laws of the land do not permit it!

PER. Then there is no freedom of religion here?

WAZIR. Yes—for the true faith.

PER. But what about the others?

WAZIR. There must not be any others.

PER. Then I shall give them the right to worship as they please!

WAZIR. Your Highness can't do that!

PER. Can't I? Who can, then?

WAZIR. The government—and only the government!

PER. Who is the government? (*The Wazir and the others present cover their mouths with their fingers.*) It is a secret, is it?

WAZIR. It is the secret of the constitutional dictatorship.

PER. But didn't I have the freedom to change my religion?

WAZIR. That's a different matter—that is politics. . . .

PER. Then—may God save us all from politics! Would you want me to begin my reign by refusing such a reasonable request?

WAZIR. Your Highness could make no better beginning than by securing the laws of the land. . . .

PER. But I shall never put my signature to such a thing as that!

WAZIR. That isn't necessary! That can be done by the government! The Cabinet Council is adjourned! Does Your Highness deign to divest himself of his coronation robe and regalia and return to privacy with its casual diversions? . . . Master of the Household, attend His Highness! (*Leaves.*)

(The Master of the Royal Household removes the coronation robe, the crown and scepter, and leads Per to the divan. Female dancers and singers enter. The Court Poet follows them in. The dancing begins.)

PER. What sort of gathering is this?

MASTER OF THE ROYAL HOUSEHOLD. This is the Court!

PER. Why are their costumes so abbreviated? They don't appeal to me!

MASTER OF THE ROYAL HOUSEHOLD. It is the custom of the land, Your Highness.

PER. Then it isn't just politics, at least!

MASTER OF THE ROYAL HOUSEHOLD. The First Court Singer requests that she be permitted to entertain Your Highness with an idealistic song composed by the renowned Court Poet Timur-I-Leng.

PER. By all means, go ahead and entertain me!

COURT SINGER *(sings, accompanying herself on a lute)*. Say farewell then to Horaire, the caravan is breaking up, But have you the strength, poor man, to speak a solemn farewell?

PER. Where are the rhymes?

MASTER OF THE ROYAL HOUSEHOLD. There are no rhymes in this poesy!

PER. That's bad! Continue!

LORD HIGH HERALD *(aside to the Lord High Historian)*. He won't last long here!

COURT SINGER. Your Highness will excuse me, I am indisposed today.

PER. Master of the Household! Is there anything in the Constitution that is called bastinado, or bastinade? *(General panic.)*

MASTER OF THE ROYAL HOUSEHOLD. Why yes—but . . .

PER *(to the Court Singer)*. Then let's hear the rest!

COURT SINGER *(sings)*. White her brow is, hair luxurious,
gleaming white her pretty teeth;
like the steed whose hoof is injured,
cautiously she treads the mire.

PER. Mire? I don't care for anything dirty in poetry. Go on!

COURT SINGER *(continues her song)*. Full-fledged breasts—
and midget waist— / rise and fall and rise again /
until after each embrace / she does all
but break in two.

PER. Oh!

COURT SINGER *(sings, emphasizing the implication of the words)*. Blessed the man who, well behaved—

and well scented and perfumed—
in her arms may share her divan
to relieve a moment's boredom. . . .

PER. I've heard enough! Where is the author? The author!

COURT POET. Your Magnificent Highness! I have never been prone to flatter!

PER. Haven't you? What kind of a court poet are you? Harangue your poesy then—and we shall hear if you are lying!

COURT POET. Your Glorious Highness! I don't suppose I could ever . . .

PER. Stop talking! Just go ahead and reel it off!

COURT POET. The soul has lost itself
    after touching the flame of love,
    has not yet awakened to consciousness,
    enchanted by the magic of the eye.
    But my love of hinds I am leaving behind . . .

PER. Excuse me—what did you say?

COURT POET (annoyed). But my love of hinds
    I am leaving behind to praise a sovereign,
    great of heart, noble of birth,
    generous, not soiled by low deeds—
    the sovereign who conquered the mighty
    on earth, whatever the challenge,
    strong in the righteous faith,
    the feared scourge of all heretics!

PER (jumps to his feet). Am I hearing aright? Are you serious or are you jesting?

MASTER OF THE ROYAL HOUSEHOLD. He is quite in earnest. Your Magnificence! How could you think . . .

PER (to the Court Poet). Indeed! You are serious when you praise my base actions . . .

COURT POET. Your Magnificent Highness is so far above anything base as the sun over a mud puddle!

PER. I know you and your cohorts and all your kind, you counterfeiter! You call me—who have forsworn my faith—the defender of the faith! You say that I—the son of a bell-ringer—am of noble birth, that I am generous—I who refused the first request made of me after ascending the throne! . . .

I know you—for your kind is found the world over! You say you live for thoughts and ideas and believe in an eternal life. . . . But you are never about when a new thought or idea is being born; you are never seen when a question that has to do with eternity is to be decided! But in the sunshine of success and power, round heaped-up dishes—there you can be seen swarming like fat meatflies, only to fly away and besmear and blacken those who are ready to die for both freedom of thought and their faith in eternity!

Away with you—away from my eyes, liar! I would have you lose your head, had I not thought there was some reason for your being alive. . . . A poor ruler is forced by "political considerations" to commit so many base deeds that he would die from shame if he did not have someone like you in his service to deaden his conscience continually. . . .

Leave!—I wish to be alone!

MASTER OF THE ROYAL HOUSEHOLD. Your Highness! This just will not do!

PER. It will do! *(All leave except the Lord High Historian).* What are you waiting for? What is it you are doing?

LORD HIGH HISTORIAN. I am writing Your Highness's history.

PER. So—you are the Court Historian, are you?

LORD HIGH HISTORIAN. The Lord High Historian . . .

PER. What's the difference? But what are you planning to write? I have carried on no war!

LORD HIGH HISTORIAN. That's just what I wanted to discuss. All Your Highness has to do is to turn to the Minister of War . . .

PER. . . . and then he'll arrange for one! That is his duty— and for that he is paid twenty thousand sequins!

LORD HIGH HISTORIAN. It's the masses, Your Highness, that . . .

PER. . . . that bear the brunt! The ministers of war create them—and we sit at home and accept the glory . . . we never accept the dishonor!

WAZIR *(enters).* Your Highness's bride is waiting!

PER. My bride? Who . . . where . . . ? What does all this mean?

WAZIR. Your Highness's consort!

PER. Lisa! She still loves me despite all my faults! Bring her here! She will carry with her a fresh breath of air from the woods—into these musty palace halls . . .

WAZIR. Will Your Highness first be gracious enough to place Your signature on the marriage contract?

PER. Always something to sign! Well—this time I don't have to do any reading! *(He signs the contract.)* Well, Lord High Historian, this time you can at least record one action in my life that is not a criminal one!

(The Wazir and the Lord High Historian leave.)
(The Bride is escorted in while the dancing and singing are resumed. She is veiled as is the custom in Eastern lands. Her

retinue leaves as soon as she is in Per's presence. Faint music is heard from without. Per rushes toward her.)

Lisa! Lisa! You always come like a ray of sun when clouds are gathering—a friend in the hour of need!

BRIDE *(turns up her veil)*. My name is not Lisa.

PER. What is the meaning of all this! Not Lisa! This is treachery—treason! Who are you?

BRIDE. Your consort!

PER. My consort?

BRIDE *(coldly)*. The government had three candidates for you —but the Wazir chose me because my father threatened to impose a tariff.

PER. The government's candidate? Tariffs! What does all this mean?

BRIDE. Politics demands that the sovereigns sacrifice all personal considerations for the welfare of their peoples!

PER. Political demands! Does the welfare of the people demand having a sovereign?

BRIDE. I don't know about that! . . . But in any case, that is the way things are. . . . And you are now my bridegroom. Will you please be happy—or you will be unhappy. . . .

PER. Are you happy?

BRIDE. I am nothing.

PER. Do you love me?

BRIDE. Certainly not!—Do you love me?

PER. No!

BRIDE. You love your Lisa, don't you?

PER. And you your . . .

BRIDE. Ali!

PER. Oh, what pain! What misery!

BRIDE. Calm down for a moment! For just a moment—while the wedding guests come in and congratulate us! They are all waiting outside. Silence! They are coming! Place yourself at my side!

PER. Must I play the hypocrite once again?

BRIDE. Do as I say—I am a wise woman! When they have left, I shall tell you my plan. Now they are here! Look happy, my consort, else they will say that I have made you unhappy. . . .

PER. Oh, my dear old father! How right you were! Black is black and will never be anything but black!

(Per and the Bride seat themselves on the divan and look tenderly at each other. Female singers and Dancers come in, also the Master of the Royal Household, the Lord High Herald, the Lord High Historian, and the Wazir.)

SINGERS *(in unison)*. Bliss to the young twain

who've found each other now . . .
Sing, you roses and nightingales!
Joy now reigns in lofty palace halls!
Sing to the blissful two
in the Court of the Caliphs!

(Per hides his emotion, as does the Bride.)

WAZIR. The happy nation that you see gathered here at the foot of Your throne, noble Caliph, rejoices in seeing happiness blazing like a sun from Your eyes, shining upon the white rose which has long searched for a tall oak to lean on! A happy nation, young Princess, rejoices over Your happiness and hopes that Your tree will produce an offshoot with fresh rosebuds which some day will spread joy and happiness, like a spring rain, throughout our whole land!

PER *(springs to his feet with drawn sword. The Bride tries in vain to calm him).* Hellfire and damnation! You Grand Wazir of lies! Are you my People, you disguised adventurers —are these hired maidens with their venal ways my People who pay taxes and bring treasures to us only to have us deny their most reasonable demands and petitions? No! I have never even seen my People! Is this young woman, whom you have placed at my side, my consort who loves me? No! She is a heifer that you have admitted into my stable; she is a graft on my family tree, foisted upon me for the purpose of producing offspring; she is a government candidate who favors her husband with a cus-toms treaty! You call us happy simply because we must appear to be happy! But we are profoundly unhappy—for we stand at the border of a crime—a crime which we, however, shall never commit. . . . I curse you, Palace, which has been dedicated as a temple of lies! Down into the mud and mire with you, you false family tree! *(The genealogical chart falls from the wall and rolls together on the floor.)* Shatter into splinters, spire and crown—symbols of violence, constraint, and compulsion! *(The crown and spire fall to the floor, shattered.)* Crumble throne— seat of unrighteousness! *(The throne comes crashing down. Thunder and storm break out.)* Scatter like chaff, you fortune-hunters and harlots who have placed yourselves between the People and the sovereign! *(The Courtiers and the others scatter and disappear. To the Bride.)* You lamb of sacrifice, be free as I am now!—And now I am on my way out into nature, among my People, to see whether honor and uprightness are not still alive in the world.

(The Bride disappears. Per remains standing, his hands covering his face, until the change of scene has taken place.)

Scene 2. *At the Seashore. In the foreground, a beach with scattered remnants of a wreck. On the right, a punt and fishing tackle; also the hull of a wrecked ship.*

In the background, the open sea. Seagulls are winging over the waves.

On the left, a rocky shore with a copse of spruce trees. At the foot of the rocks, a hut.

Per. Where am I? Here I can breathe more freely—all wicked thoughts have left me! I feel a fragrance as of old fairy tales— I hear a murmuring as of distant streams of water—the ground beneath me is soft as a bed! Ah! I am at the seashore. . . .

Oh, ocean! You, Mother Sea—mother of the earth!
Be greeted by a hardened, untamed heart
that now has come to be swept clean by humid winds,
to be refreshed and chastened, cleansed . . .
come to be healed by bathing in your salty waves—
and find a cure for all the hurts and wounds,
that have been wrought by lies and follies of this world.
Blow, Wind, and fill my breast with breezes
of clean air—instead of poisonous vapors!
Sing, Wave, and let my ear rejoice
from the sonority of your pure sounds
as I stand here among the wreckage on the shore—
a wreck myself the sea has cast upon the sands,
when 'gainst the rocky shore my ship was battered!
Be greeted, Sea, that nurses fresh ideas
and makes the soul reborn within a weakened body
when every spring your billows break their bonds,
and tern and seagull frolic o'er the waves
and bring to life again high spirits, hope, and courage!
    (He sees the hut.)
What do I see? A hut where people live! Not even here
am I allowed a single moment's rest! Damnation!

Voice. Do not curse! (It is growing dark and the sea is becoming restless. Soon after, the waves rise, forcing Per down toward the footlights.)

Per. Who spoke? (He tries to escape through the wing on the right, but is driven back by elks.) I am being attacked by wild animals! (He attempts to flee through the wing on the left, but is driven back by bulls.) They are there, too! Get away from me! (The beasts come on the stage and press toward him.) They are surrounding me! Help! (He runs over to the hut and bangs on the door.) Is there no one here? Help! (He tries to escape into the sea, but snakes and dragons emerge *from the waves.)* Ha! Even you, Nature, are a savage beast that wants to swallow anything you are strong enough to vanquish and master! You—my only remaining friend—you, too, deceive me! . . . Oh, this is horrible—horrible! The sea wants to swallow me! My life is at an end!—Come, Death, and liberate me! *(The sea gradually is becalmed. Death enters and the Wild Beasts disappear.)*

DEATH. Here I am, at your service! What do you want of me?

PER. *(panic-stricken, but quickly regaining his composure).* Ah! . . . Oh—it was nothing of any special importance. . . .

DEATH. You called me!

PER. Oh—did I? Well . . . it was merely a way of speaking; we often say things like that! There is nothing I really want of you. . . .

DEATH. Yes, but I want something of you! Stand up straight now, then I'll strike my blow—and it will be over in a second! *(He raises his scythe.)*

PER. Mercy! Mercy! I don't want to die!

DEATH. Nonsense! What could life possibly have to offer you, who have nothing more to wish for?

PER. Oh, I don't know. . . . Give me a chance to think—then, perhaps . . .

DEATH. Oh—you have had plenty of time to do that! Now it is too late! Straighten up now—and let me see you go down like a regular hater of mankind! *(He raises the scythe again.)*

PER. No—no—for God's sake—wait a while longer. . . .

DEATH. You are a coward! Well—go on and live then . . . if you are in love with life! But don't come to me with any regrets later on! The next time I come around will be a long time from now. *(He starts to leave.)*

PER. No, no, no—don't leave me alone!

DEATH. Alone? Haven't you all of Nature, beautiful Nature about you!

PER. Well—Nature can be nice enough when the weather is pleasant and the sun is shining; but at this time of day . . .

DEATH. You see—no matter what, you can't do without your fellow beings!—Go over to that hut and knock on the door three times—then you'll get company!

(Death disappears.)

(Per knocks at the door of the hut three times. The Wise Man comes outside.)

WISE MAN. Who is it you are seeking?

PER. To be brief—a human being! I am unhappy!

WISE MAN. In that case you should not seek out mortals. They can be of no help to you!

PER. I know they can't—and yet: I neither wish to live nor die. . . . I have suffered all there is to suffer, and yet my heart will not break. . . .

WISE MAN. You are young, and you do not know the human heart. I have been pondering in here what might be the cause of human misery. Would you like to see what that little thing that is called a heart looks like? *(He goes inside and returns with a small casket and a lantern, which he hangs on the branch of a tree.)* Do you see this little triangular muscle that now has ceased to move? Once it throbbed and thumped from rage, beat from joy, crumpled from sorrow, swelled from hope. . . . You can see how it is divided into two large chambers: in one dwells the good, in the other the evil—or, in other words, there is an angel on one side of the dividing wall, and a devil on the other. When the two fail to get along with each other—and that happens frequently enough—there is discord in the human heart, and it seems as though it would break—but it doesn't, for its walls are thick and strong. . . . Yes, yes, look at this heart—there you can see a thousand little scars and pin-pricks. . . . They have not penetrated—but the marks are still there! *(He is silent.)*

PER. Tell me, Wise Man, who has borne this heart?

WISE MAN. The most miserable of human beings!

PER. Who was that?

WISE MAN. It was a man. . . . Do you see the marks from a heel—and from the nails? A woman trampled on this heart for twenty-six years!

PER. And his patience did not give out?

WISE MAN. Yes—he tired of it at last—on a Christmas Eve— and released himself from her. As punishment he fell under the spell of the Powers, and—although his heart has been taken from him—he cannot die. . . .

PER. And can't he ever be free from the enchantment?

WISE MAN. When his son has found a faithful mate and led her to his home as his bride, then the enchantment will be broken! But this can never happen, for his son is gone forever!

PER. What happened to him?

WISE MAN. He went out into the world. . . .

PER. Why can this poor boy never find a bride?

WISE MAN. Because—he loves only himself—can never love anyone else!

PER. You—old man—you are my father! Lisa!—It is you! *(The Wise Man disappears through the floor. The hut vanishes. Per is alone. It is growing light.)* Gone! It was my father! —"He who loves only himself!" Those are the very words Lisa used. . . . But I despise myself, I hate myself after all the base acts I have committed . . . and I love Lisa! I love her—I love her! *(The sun is seen shining above the waves, casting its shimmer on the wood of spruce on the left. The clouds in the sky scatter, and a boat is seen out on the sea. During the following scene it comes closer. When it is quite near, Lisa, seated at the tiller, is discovered. She waves to Per, and the boat glides on.)* You seagulls sailing in the sky, tell her that I do love her! You sunrays, take my message on your fiery arrows and bring it to her!—Where shall I seek you—where? *(The boat is visible at the horizon for a brief moment.)* There she is!— Now, magic ring, fulfill my last wish and lead me to her!—The ring is gone! Oh—what pity—what does all this mean? Is my fairy tale at an end—or is it, perhaps, only just beginning? Lisa—my soul's beloved! *(He rushes to the top of the cliff and waves to her.)* If you hear me, answer. . . . If you see me, give me a sign!—Oh, she is turning and sailing out of the cove. . . . Very well—if storm and sea separate me from my heart's beloved, I shall challenge them to do battle for the highest prize! *(He pushes out a boat, lying on the shore, into the sea.)* Blow up, Wind! Rock and toss, Wave! My brittle keel shall cleave you like a sword! Forward, boat! Even if my goal should escape me, let us fight the battle until we go down into the depths of the sea!

ACT V

The interior of a small, wooden country church with painted ceiling.

In the background is an altar, with crucifix. On the right, a pulpit; also on the right, hung on a pillar in the wing closest to the footlights, an image of St. Bartholomew holding an animal skin in his hand. In the wing on the opposite side of the stage, St. Laurentius with a grill. Leaning against the altar railing, at right, stands a broom; to the left of the altar is seen a bier. Two rows of praying-desks on the right and the left form an aisle from the foreground to the altar. In the first wing to the left, a confessional; on the opposite side, right, an iron door.

The Gnome is seen in one of the church windows; the Fairy in another.

GNOME. It was not the Old Man who ate up the porridge —it was the rats.

FAIRY. Then you didn't send Per out into the world for his

own good! You did it because you wanted to punish his old father!

GNOME. We immortals can make mistakes, too. . . . Let us therefore make amends for the wrong we have done!

FAIRY. If it is not too late!

GNOME. How so?

FAIRY. Per has come to hate all mankind, and he finds no satisfaction in life.

GNOME. Lisa will mend all that; and then the Old Man's hardheartedness will be atoned for! We have to put a patch where hearts have been torn!

FAIRY. I have already made my preparations.

GNOME. Here, you mean?

FAIRY. Here—in this room, whose floor we must not tread. . . .

GNOME. Why? . . . Because this is a place of sanctity, and because we were not allowed to participate in the great reconciliation. Something came between—what, we shall never know. However, that does not prevent the mortals from thinking of us as a power for some good; and they are right in doing that—for there are two sides to that question! — While I am not allowed to be present, I shall nonetheless not be absent; and I shall see to it that this reconciliation is carried out correctly! For even we, doomed souls that we are, can rejoice over the happiness of others! And now—farewell for a while!

FAIRY. Farewell, then!

(The Gnome and the Fairy disappear.)

LISA *(enters)*. Here is where the good fairy promised that I should meet Per—in this quiet little church. . . . I wonder how I shall find him. Has he learned something from life—or is he still the same, selfish youth, looking for the pleasures of life in pursuit of fickle fortune? If he had had the courage to do something that was bad for the sake of a good cause—then, at least, he would have proved that he could make sacrifices for something other than himself! The greatest sacrifice we can make is to give up our own high opinion of ourselves. A higher Power determines that such and such a thing is to be done— it chooses the instruments at will, and no one has the right to refuse the task—even at the risk of death! — My friend Per was not such—and that is why. . . . Quiet! I hear steps! It is he! —No—I do not wish to meet him—not yet. . . . I must collect my thoughts—I think I shall hide here—in the confessional. . . . *(She hides in the confessional. Per enters.)*

PER *(falls down on a praying-desk on the right, close to the footlights)*. She flees from me as I am fleeing from my bad thoughts. . . . Alone—abandoned—what is there now for me

to do in life? I have learned nothing—nothing but how empty
life is—and all that is left me is wicked desires. My soul would
be empty as a shell were it not filled with my thoughts of her!
My life—yes, what has my life been like? *(The bier moves and
stamps its feet on the floor.)* What was that?—Are the ghosts
out in sunlight? That is something I should like to see! *(The
broom makes a similar movement and sound.)* There it is again!
—There is a saying that you can see the ghosts in the light of day
if you peer through a crack in a door; yes—they even say that
you can see—*yourself!* See yourself! If one could do that—how
easy it would be to learn to avoid one's worst faults! I'd like
to try! *(He opens the door on the right and places himself
behind it. His shadow mounts the pulpit. It takes a sip from
the water cup, then fumbles with the hourglass. Per himself
remains standing in the doorway, his back toward the audience.)*

SHADOW. My beloved congregation—and you, Per, standing
behind the door there. . . . My sermon is not going to be long,
since the time is short and it really is to this so-called Lucky
Per that I wish to address a few words. Yes, you Per, you have
been leaping through life like a fool, pursuing luck and fortune. You have had all your wishes come true—except one . . .
and none of them has brought you any happiness. Listen to me
now, where you stand behind the door! You have made no
great stride through life. One does not go leaping through life
with any phenomenal speed. Everything you have thought you
have lived through has been nothing but a dream. Believe me,
one realizes no wishes by the use of magic rings here in this
world: nothing is gained here without hard work! Do you
know what work is? No, you don't! It is something heavy and
dreary—it is drudgery! But work should be hard—for it makes
rest so much the sweeter. . . . Work, Per, and be an honest
man—but don't turn into a saint, for then you'll become overbearing. It is not our virtues that make us into human beings—
it is our faults! Listen to me, Per, as you stand there behind
the door! Life is not what it seemed to be in your youthful
dreams: it is a desert, that's true, but a desert is not without
its flowers; it is a stormy sea, but it has its havens, too, close
by greening islands. Pay attention, Per, to what I say now. If
you want to go out into life and if you want to be a man—then
do so in earnest. But you will never be a real man without a
woman! Find her! . . . And now, Per—now I shall let Brother
Laurentius speak, after having dismissed you and your dreams
of youth with the wise man's eternally young—and eternally old

—exhortation: Know yourself! I will now let Brother Laurentius speak.   *(The Shadow vanishes.)*

ST. LAURENTIUS *(showing his grill)*. I am the Holy Laurentius
with the grill, who at the command of Emperor Decius was
flogged with rods day after day for seven days and then roasted
alive on this grill at slow fire. No other being has suffered so
frightfully as I have!

ST. BARTHOLOMEW. Is that anything to speak of! I am the
Holy Bartholomew with the skin, who at the command of
Emperor Pamphilius was flayed alive all the way down to my
knees. And all the miracles that took place after my death!
And haven't you heard of the many mysterious happenings—
or about the devil appearing in the shape of a woman—or the
presaging of the erupting of the volcano?

ST. LAURENTIUS. Is that anything to talk about in comparison
with me! I have six predictions to my credit: the beam in the
temple—the crystal chalice—the dead body of the nun . . .

BIER *(rising on its hind legs)*. Oh—you don't have to boast
so loudly about what you have been through! I am only a bier
—but for fifty years I have carried so many corpses on my back
and witnessed so much misery, so many crushed hopes, so much
disconsolate longing for loved ones who were lost, so many
broken hearts that had to suffer in silence, forgotten, condemned to oblivion, and never remembered with a golden
image! And if you had seen only the half of it, I would keep
quiet if I were you! Alas, life is so black, so black!

BROOM *(angrily stamping on the floor and shaking its twigs)*.
Why should you be chattering about life, you old bier? You—
who have never seen anything but death! Life is black on one
side, and white on the other! I am only a broom today, but
yesterday I lived in the woods—stood up there so slender and
straight—and had hopes of becoming something great—just as
everybody wants to be great. . . . And now you see what happened. . . . Therefore I am thinking like this: whatever happens, happens for the best. And if you are not allowed to grow
big, you have to be something else; there is so much to choose
from. One can be useful, for instance; and if the worst comes
to the worst, one can always find satisfaction in being good!
And not having been given two legs to stand on, one has to be
content nevertheless and skip around on one! *(The Broom
skips about and then comes to rest against the altar railing.
Per comes out from behind the door. He rushes violently over
to the font of holy water near the confessional, dips the Broom*

*in the font and sprinkles the water about the church with
the Broom.)*

PER. Away! Away, you ghosts and evil spirits! *(When he puts
the Broom back against the altar railing, he hears a sound from
inside the confessional.)* Somebody is inside! Reverend Father,
hear me and receive the plaint of a crushed heart!

LISA *(her voice, disguised, is heard from within).* Speak,
my son!

PER. How can I leave my dreams behind me?

LISA. Oh, you have been dreaming long enough—and now
you are no longer a mere youth! Contemplate your missteps—
you have made missteps, haven't you?

PER. Yes, I have been pursuing luck, and sacrificed honor
and conscience merely for the sake of gaining glory and power!
And now I can't bear misfortune, and I hate myself!

LISA. Then you have ceased to love yourself above all else?

PER. Yes—I would like to free myself from myself—if I were
able. . . .

LISA. You mean, then, Per, that you could love someone
besides yourself?

PER. Yes, yes—but where shall I find her?

LISA *(coming outside).* Here, Per. *(They embrace.)*

PER. You will never again leave me, will you?

LISA. No, Per, for now I believe you really love me!

PER. But what good fairy sent you my way?

LISA. You still believe in good fairies! You know that when
a baby boy is born into the world, a baby girl is also born
somewhere else—and they keep seeking until they find each
other. . . . Sometimes they do not find the right mate—and
then unhappiness sets in; again there are times when they never
find each other—and then there is much sorrow and anguish;
but when they do meet, there is joy—and that is the greatest
of joys that life has to offer!

PER. That is paradise regained!

SEXTON *(the Old Man from the tower, with his staff enters).*
The church is being closed!

LISA. Oh—he is driving us out of paradise!

PER. He can't do that! We take it with us and anchor it
like the verdant island out in the stormy sea . . .

SEXTON *(puts away his staff).* . . . or the quiet haven, where
the waves break up and go to rest!

PER *and* LISA. Father! Father!

*(The Fairy and the Gnome appear at the windows, one at
right, the other at the left.)*

The Keys of Heaven

A FANTASY IN FIVE ACTS

❧ ❧ ❧

At the time Strindberg wrote *The Keys of Heaven* he was beset by debt and hounded by creditors. He had just been through the harrowing ordeal of the divorce from his first wife (Siri von Essen) with the attendant trial. His three children had been taken from him and he was in a spiritual abyss. It was his overwrought love for them that prompted and inspired him to write the drama; it helped him to unburden his sick heart.

This interesting play is a rich and sometimes moving drama. Its principal theme is a father's love for his children, but it has its share of love and hatred of woman, as most Strindberg plays have. It also contains impulses of classical and poetic motives, as Dr. Gunnar Ollén points out. St. Peter has lost the keys to heaven and comes to the Smith to obtain a new set shortly after the Smith's three little children have died of the plague. But without the lock, the Smith cannot reproduce the keys, and the lock is fastened to the gate of heaven. So the question arises: how and where to find heaven? The incidents in the play are motivated by the searching of the grieving father and St. Peter, whose memory is failing, the world over for the keys of heaven. Their pilgrimage leads only to disappointment and despair; it exhausts St. Peter, who dies from fatigue. Finally the good Physician, who had valiantly tried to save the children from death, comes to the rescue. Finding themselves in the interior of the ruins of the Tower of Babel, the Physician tries to keep the sorrowing father from ascending the Jacob's ladder that allegorically leads to heaven. He cautions the Smith to keep his feet on earth, even though heaven beckons; and he places the children's fairy-tale books and toys in his hands, as the little ones appear in a niche above the ladder. The Smith gives his departed loved ones the cherished memories of their brief stay on earth. Then the Physician leaves the Smith alone with the vision of his three children imploring him to

> Build now again a heaven of your own on earth,
> but trust not all who rattle with its keys;
> and when your dreams to actuality give birth,
> erect no Babel's tower that will fall like screes.

The implication seems to be that the memory of the children will sustain the father and give him strength to carry on until they meet again. It also suggests Strindberg's favorite theme in the later plays of this series: that the way to heaven is through suffering, and that we must live life to its end, even though it is hard to bear and often bitter.

There is much in this beguiling and original drama that may well have served as an inspiration to many Scandinavian and other European authors and dramatists of a later generation, notably perhaps in the case of Pär Lagerkvist.

PERFORMANCE NOTES

Although written in 1890-1892, *The Keys of Heaven* first had its stage première in 1962 at Uppsala in Sweden. But it was given on radio on October 17, 1929, in Sweden. The radio production was directed by August Falck, Strindberg's former associate at the Intimate Theatre. The Smith was played by Ragnar Widestedt, the Physician by Gabriel Alw. The play was given another radio production in Sweden (1945) with Anders de Wahl as the Smith.

❖

CHARACTERS

The Smith	Romeo
The Physician	Juliet
St. Peter	Bluebeard
Thersites	Lady Macbeth
Don Quixote	Hamlet
Sancho Panza	Ophelia
Tom Thumb	Othello
Cinderella	Desdemona
The Wandering Jew	Montague
The Old Man of	Capulet
Ho Mountain	Narcissus
The Courtesan	The King
The Parson	The Queen

Nymphs, Oreads, Naiads, Men and Women, Children, Frogs, Horses, and others

❖

THE SETTINGS

Act I, Scene 1. The smithy.
Act I, Scene 2. The tarn, with woods in the background.
Act II. The inn.
Act III. The parsonage and the mountain, with the valley, the lake, and the church.
Act IV. Schlaraffenland.
Act V, Scene 1. A chapel in St. Peter's Dome in Rome.
Act V, Scene 2. The shrine at the crossroads.

ACT I

SCENE 1. *A room inside a smithy, separated from the latter by a wooden partition with a large opening in the center. Through this the smithy, which also serves as a trade shop and has a large, open window toward the thoroughfare outside, is visible.*

In the center of the floor of the chamber there is an anvil with a sledge hammer resting on it. By the right wall stand three empty beds; on a bench nearby, playthings; by the bedside, children's apparel, and underneath, several pairs of tiny shoes. By the left wall, a stove of green glazed tile with a built-in bench. The walls of the room are hung with woven hangings, painted with scenes from the Bible: the road to Calvary and Christ's descent into the grave. On the ledges of the panel work, jugs of earthenware, beakers, and containers of silver and pewter.

In the smithy, a long table in the center, covered with articles of wrought iron: tools, sign braces, keys, locks, arms and armor. To the left, the pull handle for the bellows is seen hanging on the partition wall. Through the open windows at the back of the smithy can be seen a street of medieval times.

The Physician, dressed in a doctor's black habit, sits immovable on the stove bench, his back toward the audience. He appears to be reading in a book.

The Smith, dressed in mourning, enters. He seems unstrung, and his eyes are red with weeping.

SMITH. You see! What good, you wondrous doctor, did your skill accomplish?
To what avail were balm and mixtures
against the plague that has laid waste my home?
What do you read there in the book, you learned man in black,
concerning salts and acids
and treacle—and the wise men's stone
that's seated in the belly of the crayfish?
Say, can you read life again into my children
that just were laid below the earth?
I came too late to kiss them a farewell,
too late to follow them, to bear them to the ditch,
where all that is most dear and precious to us

is to be buried, but to turn to dust.
Oh dear God! My hearth is empty now;
and empty stand three little beds!
Here slept my Katarina! Oh, she was my first-born. . . .
There's still an indentation in the snow-white pillow,
where her lovely head lay. . . .
She was the closest to me since her mother died—
and I her dearest friend. . . .
She mothered the two younger ones;
she was so wise, so serious of mind, and tender.
. . . She saw the light of day while times were hard for me
and brought me luck again,
good times and blessings to my home. . . .
My angel, blessed be your memory!

And here's my Margaretha's bed. . . .
You blooming rose, you birdlike little one,
who spread about a fragrance; your chirping
gladdened all within our home. . . .
With open heart and open hand,
it was your greatest joy to give, to share. . . .
Here stand your little shoes. . . .
Now I shall place a coin in them
that you, on waking . . . On waking? Waking when?
Yes—the shoe is here, but where's the little foot,
the chubby little foot
that sped with such agility across the fields?
She lacked the heart to trample on an ant,
would give a muted cry "Forgive me, God!"
Her full heart, being touched so easily,
just could not bear to hurt a living thing. . . .
You little shoe. . . .
Sleep well, my dear, dear Margaretha!

And you, my son, my child of pain
but not of sorrow!
My Benjamin!
You gave your mother's image back to me,
when in the cradle your large, clear eyes
smiled on me as once did hers.
You were so dear to me! How dear
I have not words to say. One thing I know—
that when you died, I died.
Your little body—oh, so frail,

you bore erect with manly will;
your fair-haired, handsome head,
imbued so richly with the seeds of potent thought
gave you no peace and kept you back from playful games. . . .
And in your slender breast a noble heart dwelled:
you took your sister's scoldings on yourself.
Think of it, black doctor,
he took the sins of others on himself. . . .
Yes, he was like the Christ child!
His dearest comrade was the lamb.
You see, the lamb—so innocent and pure—
it had to sleep upon his arm
and eat out of his hand! . . .
My little innocent lamb, farewell,
farewell, my own beloved Johannes!
  (*He seats himself by the children's beds.*)
  PHYSICIAN (*rises*). Is there no ebbing to your sorrow, friend?—
  SMITH. How can there be an end to such a sorrow,
what remedy for it? . . .
Yes—give me back my children;
then I shall recover!
  PHYSICIAN. Then listen to me, and meditate on what I say:
The remedy's not always like the affliction,
for poisonous burn is soothed by cooling salve;
you know that they who've lost their sense of sight
must learn to see with ear and hand;
you know that when your helpmeet died,
you soon forgot her for the children. . . .
  SMITH. And now the children, too, are dead. . . .
  PHYSICIAN. Have patience! I can't bring back to life
those who have gone to the beyond!
I knew your children; and lovelier ones
I have not ever seen. . . .
And that they loved you—that I know.
I saw them in the hours of their pain
and heard how they with tear-filled voices
cried for their father: "Oh, dearest father!
Father, come! Come to us—we're dying!"
  SMITH. You say—they cried for me to come to them?
What else—tell me what else they said!
And did they suffer much? How did they look?
Who was the bravest one?
Pray tell me all! each tiny little detail
that brings them back into my grieving mind.

PHYSICIAN. When in their last delirium they suffocated—
SMITH. Stop, for the devil's sake! You say they suffocated? . . .
Oh God! You did this to my children!
I hate you! . . .
PHYSICIAN.—they kissed and kissed my hand repeatedly—
and called me father. . . .
The first time I had ever heard myself so called!
And when I felt their hot and feverish breaths
upon my hand—uncouth and used to carving human flesh—
I felt for once your bliss—and, too, your grief. . . .
SMITH. You are a man of sensitiveness, Doctor!
PHYSICIAN. To some degree. . . .
However . . . then the thought occurred to me—
for thinking is my strongest side—
well, then I thought:
what bliss to die when one is young—
before the evilness of life has touched us. . . .
SMITH. A thought long-held and it is not a bad thought!
PHYSICIAN. You are sagacious, you are, Smith.
SMITH. To some degree. . . .
PHYSICIAN. But it is also said that you by nature
are a happy man. They say so in your guild.
SMITH. 'Twas true at one time, but no longer is.
My happiness is now at end. . . .
The tree, once it has lost its roots,
soon withers.
PHYSICIAN. But if its twigs are placed in water,
fresh roots appear.
There's something else that I have heard:
that you had an unceasing thirst for knowledge,
and that you knew far more than others of your craft.
SMITH. Indeed! But, without boasting, it is true
that when my comrades spent their time in taverns,
I sat at home and taught myself to read;
and when I'd learned, I taught my older children—
my Katarina. . . .
PHYSICIAN. What did you most enjoy to read?
SMITH. Of court life, princes, castles, forts,
of great men's wars, of armies, battles
in ages past, long years ago;
intrigues, and statesmen, founders of religions,
of foreign lands, of Turks and Persians,
crusaders, Saracens,

and—strange to say—the more I read,
the more I yearned to know still more!

PHYSICIAN. And have you never yearned to roam afar, to
travel?

SMITH. To travel—yes! To see the great and wondrous world,
and not alone to hear it spoken of!
Who has not dreamed such dreams of childhood?
Who has not felt that hope of youthful days?

(*During the preceding scene and the subsequent one, the
following action takes place: first the children's shoes disappear, then their playthings, and finally their garments.
All this occurs step by step.*)

PHYSICIAN. You shall see the world!

SMITH. But how? With whom? And by what means?

PHYSICIAN. With me!

SMITH. I have heard it said that, centuries ago,
the Saviour made a pilgrimage on earth
and brought mankind much happiness;
but never had I thought
that in our day and age
of general enlightenment and heresy and disbelief,
a miracle like this could happen.

PHYSICIAN. Oh yes—such miracles take place continually,
and will until the world comes to an end.
When you can see the ocean rise up toward the sky,
the sky descend close to the earth;
and if the seed, embedded in the soil, can grow into a plant;
if lightning can cleave trees, and sun can melt the ice;
as long as tongues speak words, and brains give birth to
thoughts—
there will be miracles, even this day and every day.

SMITH. Pray tell me, Doctor, can you conjure?

PHYSICIAN. Why, yes—I can, and so can you!
If you should see a maid, and she were ugly, foul as sin
and evil as is venom, sharp as poison—
and if you saw her as a beauty,
as an angel, pure and lovely,
then you would conjure!
Just now, when in the hideouts of your memory
you woke your dear little dead,
distinguishing plainly each of them,
giving a living picture of each one,
I did not only see them, but I heard their voices!
Thus you brought back to life the dead—

And you gave proof that you could conjure. . . .
(He produces a human skull from his pocket.)
Look. Here is the magic capsule, given us by Nature!
In this container lay not long ago
a grayish mass containing phosphorous fat;
through these round holes and cavities
the light-rays penetrated
and the sound waves also;
and then came smell and taste—
and, when they met inside,
each left its special imprint—
on some more sharply, and on others less.
Then they were coupled up, connected, disunited,
and multiplied, if there were fecundation. . . .
And there you have an outline of the thought mechanics,
abbreviated greatly, in conformity with audience demand.
(The children's beds disappear. St. Peter approaches from between the tiled stove and the wall. He is very aged and wears a mossy beard. He is dressed in accordance with the biblical tradition; in his left hand he carries a fish. A large key ring, with no keys, hangs from his girdle.)
And here you have a customer this Friday evening.

SMITH. Which path did he come by?

PHYSICIAN. The narrow path.

SMITH. You're selling fish?

ST. PETER *(sullenly)*. That's not a fish. It is a symbol.

PHYSICIAN. You can tell by the smell that it is a symbol.

ST. PETER. Will you be good enough to speak like an ordinary human being, so that I can understand what you say?

PHYSICIAN. I presume that you come on some sort of errand, since you entered through the stove. But let us hear it speedily, because the Smith and I are going traveling.

ST. PETER. My errand? Let me think—yes! My memory is not what it used to be. I am getting old. . . .

PHYSICIAN. Yes, you do look less youthful than you used to. But you know how old you are, don't you?

ST. PETER. Let me try to think when I was baptized. . . .

PHYSICIAN. Are you baptized, too?

ST. PETER *(with indignation)*. You ask if I am baptized!

PHYSICIAN. Judging by your nose, you look circumcised. And are you confirmed, too?

ST. PETER. I don't know what that is.

PHYSICIAN. Were you ever wedded?

St. Peter. No, I never was, but I was married. What was her name now? The Fathers of the Church call her Constantia—but her name was Perpetua, because she was persevering—she was so tenacious.

Physician. Why—could you by any chance be . . . Your name could not be Peter, or something like it. Could it?

St. Peter. Quite right—although, while I am out wandering about like this, I use the more familiar St. Peter.

Smith. This is getting to be like the fairy-tale books in which St. Peter is on his pilgrimage of the earth.

How many times did I not read
that tale by the hearth for my children. . . .

Physician. Stop your rambling, Smith, and pack your knapsack!

Smith. Apostle! Saint!

You who can wake the dead,
bring back my children to me!

St. Peter. I was no saint, believe me; and I can't bring back the dead. If you have lost your children, you must have patience. We shall all meet in heaven.

Smith. All?

St. Peter. All! *(Sanctimoniously)*. For the kingdom of hell has been crushed by Him who came into the world to abolish its laws, or, as the apostle says: O death, where is thy sting? O grave, where is thy victory?—Yes, that's the way it is. . . . But what was it I wanted to say now, anyhow?

Physician. You were to speak a word of consolation to the grieving father. . . .

St. Peter. A word of consolation—yes. . . . That's what everybody is looking for, but no one wants to hear a word of warning! Do you know why the Lord gave and the Lord hath taken away? Well, it was for the sake of your selfishness and your sins.

Physician. The Smith was never a selfish man, and he sinned less than those who have been permitted to keep their children.

St. Peter. Well, that's something I'm not able to judge!

Physician. Then stop judging!

St. Peter. But I can always give you a word of consolation. *(He produces a batch of pamphlets from his pocket and hands one of them to the Smith.)* Here you are. There is no charge.

Physician. He is asking for an egg, and is given a stone. Are you through with your packing yet, Smith?

St. Peter. In heaven's name! The Smith! Why, it was for him I was looking!

SMITH. It's too late for that now! We haven't time.

ST. PETER. One brief moment only. . . . You see—the trouble is this. . . . Well, now I suppose you think I'm inventing some sort of flimsy falsehood. . . .

PHYSICIAN. Most assuredly!

ST. PETER. Well, I don't know myself if it is true what they say. . . . They say here on earth that I am supposed to be some kind of porter or gatekeeper of heaven . . . and I have a faint recollection that when I stood outside the cathedral in Cologne one time I had a key in this hand—I always carried the fish, of course, in my left hand—but now the key is gone . . . and no matter what happens, a fellow always has a desire to be completely equipped. In a word, Mr. Smith, you may feel I deserve nothing but disdain—but would you please make me a new key!

PHYSICIAN. This is, indeed, a generous order, Smith!

SMITH. You want me to make a key to heaven, do you? Don't you think that's a little too much to ask of a smith?

ST. PETER. Well, it may seem so—but that's what I am in need of just the same. And we all have to help each other, don't we?

SMITH. If I should really be able to do it—what will I receive for it?

ST. PETER. Receive? Why—anything! Everything!

SMITH. That's quite generous! But what is everything?

ST. PETER. Forgiveness for your sins!

SMITH. I've never sinned.

ST. PETER (sanctimoniously). Mind what you say!

SMITH. Well—I have never had more than one God, have never breached the Sabbath, never stolen, never told a lie—well, perhaps a little one—never killed anyone, never dishonored my parents, never been profligate—well, I may have taken a drink now and then . . . in brief, I have been a fairly decent human being, and—in order to do a deed to spare—I'll make your key for you! But where is the lock?

ST. PETER (absent-mindedly). The lock?

SMITH. Yes—the lock! I have to take an impression first, of course.

ST. PETER. The lock is on the gate—where else would it be?

SMITH. Did you bring the gate with you, then?

ST. PETER (cogitates). The gate is affixed to heaven, isn't it?

PHYSICIAN. And where is heaven?

ST. PETER (caustically). That's something only the spiritually impoverished, the less endowed, know, Mr. Doctor!

PHYSICIAN. And as you seem to fit that description, you ought to know!

ST. PETER. Yes—at my age now—being an old man . . . but there was a time when . . .

PHYSICIAN. That must have been ages ago! Now—if you will show us the way, we shall all go together.

ST. PETER. The path is narrow, the portals wide. . . .

PHYSICIAN. No, no—you are not quoting rightly, old man!
(To the Smith.) I think the old man is decrepit!
His speech is plain and smells of mildew.
His memory misses now and then,
and he seems not too sure who he is:
one moment thinks he's he, the next a shadow,
gets history and the Bible tangled up with fairy tales . . .
He's lived a thousand years too long;
the storehouse of his memory has started to decay.

SMITH. Stop rambling, Doctor, and let's be on our way.

PHYSICIAN. Well, shall we take the old man with us, do you think?

SMITH. It wouldn't hurt to have someone come along whom we can have a little fun with, and even if he shouldn't find the way to heaven, no damage will be done. Let's try to talk some sense into him and see if he'll give up those notions of his.

PHYSICIAN. I frankly doubt that it would be possible to impart any sense to this Pharaoh mummy, but his inexperience, his conceit and his uncleanliness will give added zest to the journey. I always feel at home in bad company.

SMITH *(to St. Peter)*. Apostle, are you ready for the journey?

ST. PETER. What did you say?

SMITH. Oho, he's deaf besides. . . .

PHYSICIAN. Now—for the last time, Smith, are you prepared to start upon the journey into life?—
Break with the past and balance up your books,
and—once you've turned your back—have no regrets
when you've made up your mind!
(He emits a whistle on a pipe. There is a change in setting: a drapery descends, covering the opening between the chamber and the smithy. While the scene in the rear is being changed, the stove disappears into the wall, etc.)

SMITH. What is afoot? Has Mother Earth
gone off her hooks? The floor is shaking,
the sturdy walls are pushed aside!
I think the ceiling's falling down!
O God, my children. . . .

PHYSICIAN. You know full well they are not here . . .
and when you see them once again
it will not be upon this earth.
Yet you shall carry their unfading memory with you—
much like a compass on a stormy sea,
a flower pressed within your book of memories,
reminding you of all the best,
the loveliest that life bestowed . . .
perchance the one thing that was good—
that had a true reality!

> *(The Smith, having gone to look for the children's beds,
> now rejoins the Physician.)*

SMITH. Who are you? Are you a sorcerer who can distort
my vision?

PHYSICIAN. I am a master of the art of magic,
but my enchantment is quite rational.
It's nothing but a setting that you see;
its mechanism is a trifle complicated,
and must be mastered thoroughly:
its common name is "change of scene." Let's go!

> *(The change of setting is accomplished.)*

SCENE 2. *The setting is now a wood with a tarn covered with
water lilies.*

> *Thersites, incomparably ugly, fat, large of body, and with
> a narrow forehead, sottish eyes, and bloated puffy cheeks,
> is seated in a punt.*
>
> *He is throwing stones and pebbles in the water in order to
> muddy Narcissus's image in it. St. Peter is at first seen walk-
> ing about, gazing curiously in all directions. Then he puts
> on his spectacles, finds a fishing rod and sits down by the
> side of the tarn and starts to fish.*

SMITH. The journey has a good beginning! A small adventure in the woods!
This is exactly to my taste;
now I'll have something to relate
when once I have come home again.
But, first of all, who is that beauteous youth
who stands there lost in daydreams?

PHYSICIAN. That is Narcissus!

SMITH. Narcissus! Ah—the vain, conceited fool
who never tires in his admiration of his image!

PHYSICIAN. That is precisely what that ugly beast there says—
the one who's seated in the punt there,
and who keeps muddying the water.

Look at that giant slaughterhouse—just take a look!
He calls himself Thersites,
is said to have participated in the Trojan War,
and then—one of the heroes in the service of supplies—
he was as loud-mouthed as his belly's big now. . . .
He was by far the ugliest, to boot,
He thinks himself a devastating singer,
and gladly shows himself upon the stage.
He has no doubt whatever of his beauty—
yet he bears envy toward Narcissus,
and thus keeps muddying his image
with dirt he scrapes up with his nails. . . .
Now listen while I go and flatter him—
If asked or unasked, he'll burst out in song. . . .
My dear Thersites, sing a little for us!
 THERSITES (*rises and makes a bow*).
With utmost, greatest pleasure!
I'm not reluctant like the others! Hm!
What Nature's lavished upon me,
I give right back with open hand.
Singers!
 (*Six bullfrogs rise up out of the water and recite, while
 Thersites conducts.*)
 FROGS. *Croak croak— croak croak croak— croak croak croak
croak croak—croak croak croak—croak croak—croak!*
 THERSITES (*sings*). I am a little singing bird
who sings all day and night.
And though I never learned to sing,
my singing's a delight.
 (*He struts about, self-satisfied. The Frogs applaud.*)
I am a little flower
with scent so pure and sweet.
And though I never learned to smell,
I don't have to compete.
 (*He struts again. The Frogs applaud.*)
I am a little butterfly
out on a flying lark.
And though I never learned to fly,
I fly—like an ostrich, or a shark. (*He dances.*)
 FROGS (*applaud. Then they recite*). *Croak croak—croak croak
croak—croak croak croak croak croak—croak croak croak—croak
croak—croak.*
 PHYSICIAN. You sing, indeed, just like Narcissus,
and if King Midas had not spoiled the style,

you could undoubtedly have challenged e'en Apollo!
   THERSITES. You don't say, Master Doctor!
I can't deny that I have thought about the matter,
but must confess a certain modesty
has kept me from admitting it.
    PHYSICIAN. Why don't you try to match Narcissus in a
       contest—
'twould be a triumph for you—though not very great.
    THERSITES. That vain, conceited fool!
    (An Oread from the wooded hills enters; Dryads, hidden be-
    hind the trees, surround her. Out of the tarn emerge Naiads.)
    OREAD. Thersites, stop! And learn before you babble
about such things you do not understand!
You read a fairy tale as though you were a child,
and find it all so simple;
but your bedimmed and clouded eyes fail to perceive
the underlying thought, the moral of the story.
This is the true tale of Narcissus' fate.
    (She recites or sings.)
This tale is a tale of Pan,
the god of the soughing forests;
he wooed once a fair, sprightly nymph
who'd been given the name of Echo.
But Echo did not love god Pan—
she already loved another
whose name was Narcissus—but he . . .
he found his love in this wisdom:
    Gnoti Seavton.
NYMPHS. And that means: Learn to know yourself!
OREAD. See, there he stands still in reflection
regarding his watery image
and pondering what is beneath,
at the core of his innermost being.
But rowing upon the water
a fool eyes the mirror-like surface
and fancies the image he sees in the deep
is that of a deep-thinking thinker.
    Gnoti Seavton!
   NYMPHS. And that means: Learn to know yourself!
   THERSITES. *Gnoti Seavton!* Bah! And who's the fool, pray?
Are you implying I am one?
Yet notwithstanding this, I'll prove to you
that I can penetrate to depths, if need be,
though, frankly, I see only mud and mire down there.

(He leans over the side of the punt.)

OREAD. No doubt, no doubt, Thersites,
but that's because you merely skim the surface.

THERSITES *(leaning further over the side of the punt).*
But I see heaven mirrored down below here. . . .

OREAD. You still see but the surface. Deeper down, Thersites!
(The boat overturns. Thersites falls in.)

THERSITES. I'm sinking! Help! I can't find bottom!

OREAD. It was too deep for you—
that's why the water went above your head!

NYMPHS. *Gnoti Seavton!*
And that means: Learn to know yourself!

*(Thersites sinks to the bottom. The Frogs jump in after him
and disappear. The Nymphs withdraw into the woods. Narcissus vanishes inside a tree trunk. The tarn is covered by
a carpet of grass. St. Peter, who has been fishing without
luck during the past scene and has not observed what has
been going on, now becomes conscious of the change in the
surroundings.)*

PHYSICIAN. Well, Smith, what do you think of our adventure?

SMITH. Oh, I find it good. It teaches one a lot—
perhaps for me, as well, a trifle deep:
philosophy is not my special forte.

PHYSICIAN. Yes, yes, I gather so. For first we live,
observe, and hear—and then we add it up,
subtract, extract the square root, find the average:
that's the way it goes.
Before you learn to know yourself,
you must know life unto the finger tips.
Thus—up on your feet again, toward unknown paths. . . .
How is our comrade, the apostle?
Has he yet harnessed up his horses?

ST. PETER *(who has cast his angling line onto the grassy
space).* By heaven, I think the lake is gone!

PHYSICIAN. You're fishing in the dry, you ancient fisherman!
Come, let's instead go hook some humans, Peter. . . .

ST. PETER *(pricks up his ears).* I heard that word once on a
time,
a very long, long time ago. . . .
My sickly memory is failing me—
but still I see, as in a mist,
a man—so fair, so gentle,
with bleeding wounds in hands and breast. . . .
He read no books; he only wandered, wandered lonely

among the woods, and in the mountains also,
through towns and villages. . . . **Oh,** now my memory fails
  me. . . .
However—let's go and hook some **humans, Doctor!**
*(He throws away the fishing rod. **They leave.**)*

ACT II

*An inn with a wing on either side, each built at right angles
to the inn and enclosing a courtyard.*

*In the center of the courtyard is a well. The rear of the
inn consists of a wall with a large entrance gate. On the
left, the building houses a barroom; on the right are stables
and barns, carriage sheds, etc.*

Outside the barroom stand two long tables with benches.

*The Smith and the Physician are seated at one of the
tables. On it are an inkstand, also a diary which the Smith
has before him.*

SMITH *(writing).* And there's my name, my character, et
  cetera. . . .
It's your turn now to take the pen.
  PHYSICIAN. It matters little *who* writes. You write for me!
  SMITH. What is your name?
  PHYSICIAN. Anonymous!
  SMITH. A curious name! Your character?
  PHYSICIAN. My character? I've several. . . .
Put down doctor.
  SMITH. From where?
  PHYSICIAN. From my mother's womb.
  SMITH. Your destination?
  PHYSICIAN. The grave.
  SMITH. Ever mysterious!
Who are you, you strange man, in whose hands I've placed
my fate? What do you want of me?
  PHYSICIAN. That you'll know later—when the time is ripe!
  SMITH. When will the time be ripe, pray?
  PHYSICIAN. When you—as I—
have learned to know yourself.
  SMITH. Always one's self!
What is this *self* that you forever preach?
  PHYSICIAN. It is the basic point that Archimedes searched for,
from which he thought that he could move the earth;

it is the self within you—yours and no one else's:
the central point on your horizon.

SMITH. Who am I, then?

PHYSICIAN. A lad of forty years
for the present—with ore and clinkers in admixture;
as quickly moved, by sorrow as by joy, as any child!
And still, no doubt, the simple pleasures of this earth
    entice you:
a table set with food, a brimful glass,
a dance with maidens in the green outdoors. . . .

INNKEEPER'S WIFE (*enters with a bottle of wine and two
    glasses*). It was for you, sirs, wasn't it?   (*She leaves.*)

PHYSICIAN (*pours a drink for the Smith*).
Not exactly—but it doesn't matter. . . . Drink, Smith!

SMITH. And you?

PHYSICIAN. I do not drink.

SMITH. On principle?

PHYSICIAN. By no means; No! I drank so freely in my
    younger days
that wine has no effect on me.

SMITH. Then I shall drink!

PHYSICIAN. And now I leave you;
for he who does not drink becomes a bore. . . .
Now mind yourself! Here come people,
and you'll have company around your jug—
at least while there is something in it!
But if you should be drawn into a wrangle
and suddenly wish to see the doctor—
then merely call; I'll promptly come to you.
        (*He leaves through the large entrance gate.*)

SMITH (*alone*). Philosophy! Bah! Horizon! Archimedes!
What do I care whether the earth goes 'round or if she
plods along on hands and feet!

COURTESAN (*enters. She is bareheaded*). Oh help! Oh help
    me, noble master!

SMITH. What is the matter, beauteous maid?

COURTESAN. I am a poor and lonely woman
who's just been robbed upon the open highway.

SMITH. By whom? But say! Say but one word
and I am ready to defend you instantly,
as it behooves all men who have some honor.
If anyone has breached your modesty and virtue,
I'll have the scoundrels hanged, each one of them!
Speak out, speak out! Who are you?

Where did it happen, and who is the culprit?

COURTESAN. If you're of noble birth, as seemingly you are,
you will not ask me what my name is!

SMITH. I do not ask; I merely inquire . . .

COURTESAN. Pose any question that you like,
but do believe my honesty,
my virtue, and my unjust sufferings in the past.

SMITH. I've faith in you, both for your virtue and your
    beauty,
which I can plainly see with my own eyes—
such beauty as I've never seen before.

COURTESAN. I was convinced you were a noble man. . . .
.Then hear . . . my father wants to force me into marriage!

SMITH. Ha! Now I understand! And you—
you love another!

COURTESAN. No!—But this is my own secret.
You must not ask again—just promise
that you will let me be your sister,
and that as such I'll have your kind protection.

SMITH. My sister! All too gladly, gentle maiden,
if you don't think your charm and noble ways
put me too deeply in the shadow
and make the kinship seem incongruous.

COURTESAN. Oh, speak not of beauty—least of all of mine!
Beauty's but a guise, a cloak. . . .

SMITH. A guise? It is a shining light that warms like sun-
    beams!

COURTESAN. Like the fire of the trolls on marshy heath.

SMITH. That is not true—no, no, it cannot be,
for only beauty is a sign of goodness
as when it's speaking through your lovely eyes;
I can't conceive that any evil word
could pass such lips as yours! Nor that this fair brow
was ever wrinkled from vile anger;
and neither can this little hand be lifted
except to shake a hand, and to forgive. . . .
Will you not come with me—but not as sister?

COURTESAN. How many have not asked the same, yet changed
    their mind!
You do not know me, you have no idea
how poor I am, and how oppressed! . . .

SMITH. So much the better! They get on best who are alike.

COURTESAN. . . . how sick I am. . . .

SMITH. I will forever care for you. . . .

COURTESAN. . . . how terrible my temper is . . .

SMITH. Another virtue! It shows strength.

COURTESAN. Suppose I beat and scold you?

SMITH. 'Twill help to soften up my wretched disposition.

COURTESAN. In truth, this indicates a deep and honest love!
Confess, man, can you love a woman,
no matter what?—No, do not touch me!
But tell me, could you—if I lost my beauty
through grief, old age, or sickness—
still love me just as dearly, just as deeply?

SMITH. Once having looked upon your countenance
I never could forget its beauty.
The memory of it would ever hide,
much like a mask, the ravages of age—
yes, even if the plague should place its imprint on it;
if fire scorched your pure white cheeks,
and if your eyes turned into boils,
I still would see you as before!
The image that I carry in my heart
is dear to me—I see it everywhere.

COURTESAN. Then look—look at a leper and abide the test!
(She removes a mask and shows a leper's ravaged face.)

SMITH (somewhat taken aback at first, but collecting himself). I sorrow, as in snowy winter
one grieves the summer's withered blossoms. . . .
But sorrow is the snow of love,
and underneath the snow the rose is forced. . . .
I love you as before—
yes, even more!
I love you as I love the memory
of one I loved! Beloved!
I give you as my pledge my pristine kiss. . . .
(He is about to embrace her.)

COURTESAN. Do not touch me! Upon my lips I bear
the sting of death!

SMITH. Alas, then let us die together—
and then we never will be parted. . . .
No strife, no passion, and no trivial worries,
no calumny, no envy . . . and we can die
in bliss—as they do who are young!

COURTESAN. O God, I never dreamed there could be such a
love!

SMITH. That's why you should not put your faith in dreams!

ST. PETER (who, in the preceding scene, has been visible in-

termittently in the background, comes forward). Now I think we have found the heavenly kingdom, for a love like this is the love of angels!

SMITH. Ah, there you are, old Peter! Tell me, will you lead us to the altar?

ST. PETER. Why, gladly—if I were only allowed to.

SMITH. Whatever could prevent you?

ST. PETER. You see, I don't know whether I have been ordained or not. Besides, I fear I would risk losing the cloth, if I should wed—a leper.

SMITH. You are a coward, Peter.

ST. PETER. You may call me that—for observing the laws and constitutions.

(Don Quixote enters on horseback through the large entrance gate. He is attired in the traditional armor, but seems excessively obese.)

COURTESAN. Come, let us leave this place before more people arrive!—Ah, there is that abominable Don Quixote. *(She covers her face with a veil.)*

DON QUIXOTE. Greetings, good people!

SMITH. Whom are you seeking, if I may ask?

DON QUIXOTE. I am the knight-errant Don Quixote of La Mancha, and I have been invited to attend the silver wedding of Romeo and Juliet here at the Golden Horse Inn. . . . I haven't come to the wrong place, have I?

SMITH. No, you have come to the Golden Horse, true enough —but if Romeo and Juliet contemplate celebrating their silver wedding here—that's something I know nothing about. So much the less as I have never read in any of the history books that the two were ever married.

DON QUIXOTE. The history books! Don't speak about the history books to me, who has been so belied and vilified by them!—Come here, Sancho Panza!

SANCHO PANZA *(appears, emaciated as a jockey; he takes Don Quixote's horse and leads it into the stable).* At your service, my stern knight-errant!

DON QUIXOTE. Lead my thoroughbred to the oats!

SMITH. Upon my word—I think Rocinante has grown as fat as Sancho has become emaciated!

DON QUIXOTE. Times change, and so do we! And I, too, have learned something from life. I have recaptured my reason, have learned to control myself, and am now a sensible man. . . . Yes, I am damnably sensible!

SMITH. Could it be that the knight, so to speak, has chosen

some sort of career or profession and joined us common folk in our meager, modest circumstances?

DON QUIXOTE. I am breeding trotting-horses, and am engaged in visiting horse auctions. May I leave my address? *(He hands St. Peter a prospectus. In return, St. Peter gives him one of his tracts.)*

ST. PETER. I thank you, noble knight, but I don't need any other horses.

DON QUIXOTE. Any other horses than which?

ST. PETER *(slaps his thighs)*. These.

DON QUIXOTE. Ha ha! You are an old jokester! You manage to ride about pretty well on those nags of yours, don't you?

ST. PETER *(offended)*. At least I manage to stay away from windmills!

DON QUIXOTE. Don't be impudent!

(The wedding party enters from out of the well. Preceded by musicians, Montague and Capulet emerge arm in arm; then come the bridesmaids and groomsmen; Hamlet and Ophelia; Othello and Desdemona; the knight Bluebeard and his wife, Lady Macbeth; then Romeo and Juliet, considerably older and accompanied by their five children—some fullgrown; others half-grown. Men and women. The Innkeeper receives the guests at the top of the steps.)

DON QUIXOTE. In my position as host at this silver-wedding celebration I have the honor to extend a greeting of welcome to all the guests on behalf of the bridal couple. Old Montague and Capulet, it pleases me to see you arm in arm after these many years of enmity and feuding, the moral firmness of which, in the past, can only be compared with the firmness and steadfastness of your friendship today—although the close, friendly ties of the ancient silk house of Montague and Capulet really date from the conversion of the City of Milan's three per cent loan. Next it is my precious task to call attention to the presence of the bridal couple, Mr. Romeo—head of the house of Romeo and Sons—and his dear spouse Juliet. I have no desire to make the reunion painful or to disturb in any way this delightful family gathering. . . . Yet I cannot refrain from offering some kind of reflective remarks on seeing said couple's two deaf-and-dumb children. Allow me therefore merely to make this remark: this marriage would have gained by not having been consummated. . . . And the moral is, if I may add: this is what happens when disobedient, naughty children have their own way. *(There is a murmur of indignation.)* Again among the wedding guests it is with pleasure I note that the knight Bluebeard has abandoned his pernicious, destructive instincts and turned into a complete monogamist through a relatively happy marriage with Lady Macbeth. By working commendably for the abolishment of capital punishment, she has succeeded in leading him away from diabolical thoughts. I greet you. *(Again there is a ripple of indignation.)* It is with similar satisfaction I again see one of my old friends, Othello of Venice. After suffering hardships and adversities, and having gathered incontrovertible proof that his wife, Desdemona, actually had deceived both him and the unpromoted noncommissioned officer Iago in favor of a certain lieutenant Cassio, he determined to seek reconciliation—and now lives an unhappy married life with the jealous Desdemona, who is forever gnawed by a fear that the Moor will avenge himself. I congratulate you—but especially Othello! *(The guests again utter their disapproval.)* Finally let me congratulate Prince Hamlet and Lady Ophelia Polonius upon their exchanging of rings, and their engagement. What the outcome will be for these romantic dreamers, I can't imagine; but I have an idea that they started a trifle too airily—and that they thus may end lower than they expected. In any case, here is to your happiness!—And now let us ponder the festivities! That they will not prove to be particularly joyous in a company such as this, goes without saying; and I must warn the participants not to entertain any illusions . . . above all, no illusions! And in order to spare myself the most disagreeable of all things, unpaid bills, I—being the one who has arranged this affair—beg you to pay your respective fees at the door before entering. Hamlet, being an actor, is of course lacking in ready money—and, besides, he doesn't eat much—so Romeo will pay for him. Now you may enter—but don't forget to pay! Be sure that you pay!

MONTAGUE *(to Capulet).* Now, Capulet, I could almost swear that he has gone completely mad.

DON QUIXOTE. That's what you say, yes! When I believed in windmills, dairy maids, bedpans, unpaid bills, and emaciated mares—then I was mad! And when I didn't believe in dairy maids, unpaid bills, bedpans, and windmills—then I was crazy, too! Go on inside, rabble! Plug yourselves full with food and drink—and chatter about love; but don't call it being in heat . . . sing about Dulcinea, but don't call her a barmaid; do honor to Knight Bluebeard, but don't mention a word about his polygamous instincts; praise Romeo—but don't say anything about his having been engaged once before; put Desdemona on a pinnacle, but don't give the slightest hint that she was a flirtatious hussy!—Go on, rabble! And stuff each other full of lies—so full that you have to go behind the stables and take a look to see how you appear inside! *(The wedding party enters the inn.)*

ST. PETER. Forgive me, noble knight, but you seem to be a man who has lost the most valuable thing in life. . . .

DON QUIXOTE. How so? What is it I have lost?

ST. PETER. Your ideals, noble knight!

DON QUIXOTE. My ideals! In which chapter and verse of Holy Writ is the word *ideal* mentioned? *(St. Peter searches his mind.)* Ponder until doomsday and you won't find it, for it isn't there. What you have in mind, however, is perhaps my illusions? With them I am familiar—I know what they are!

ST. PETER. What are they?

DON QUIXOTE. Windmills, dairy maids, bedpans . . .

ST. PETER. One moment!—You see that man there? *(He points to the Smith.)*

DON QUIXOTE. What about him? He looks as if he was even more stupid than Othello—who allowed himself to be fooled by Desdemona! Who is the woman with him?

ST. PETER. She is his bride.

DON QUIXOTE. That's nice! Why don't they get married?

ST. PETER. It'll come! It'll come! You see, she is sickly: she is suffering from leprosy. But despite her affliction he loves her.

DON QUIXOTE. The man must be crazy, out of his mind! Put *him* in an asylum and send *her* to a hospital.

ST. PETER. No, noble knight! It's love, don't you know. . . .

DON QUIXOTE. That's merely a different name for insanity. Let me have a look at the woman. *(He tears off the veil from her face.)* Ha! *(To the Smith.)* And you are thinking of marrying a woman like that?

SMITH. Most fervently I hope to, if she will deign to have me.

DON QUIXOTE. Say that once more!

SMITH. Upon my faith and honor!

DON QUIXOTE. That she is a leper, you can see for yourself! But that she is a loose woman, a wanton, who has been incarcerated for whoring—that will be news to you, won't it?

SMITH. You lie!

DON QUIXOTE. Come outside—on the hill—and let's fight it out!

COURTESAN. I won't have you sacrifice your lives for one like me! You mustn't lay hands on each other!

SMITH (*to the Courtesan*). Is it true what this man says? Is it true?

COURTESAN. It is true. . . .

SMITH. Oh Lord, help me! Help me, God! . . . Then you lied when you told me you were a pure woman?

COURTESAN. I lied. . . .

DON QUIXOTE. A leprous, lying harlot! . . . What God has joined together, no man shall put asunder. . . .

SMITH. Oh, but lie once more, then—lie, for heaven's sake, and say that you lied just now!

COURTESAN. I could never lie again, having seen the infinite measure of your love!

SMITH. I've faith in you—and follow you
with wounded heart, now not less cankered
than the so lovely features you possessed not long ago. . . .
If you are leprous, so am I as well;
if you have trespassed, I have erred.
I'll bear your fetters and shall bless them,
not condemn them; for the agony of love
endures still longer than its joys—
and I shall love eternally!

ST. PETER. What say you, Mr. Knight?

DON QUIXOTE. Well, I'll be damned!

ST. PETER. This is, indeed, true love—true love, and faithful!

DON QUIXOTE. Well, I'll be damned!

ST. PETER. And have you ever seen its like?

DON QUIXOTE. Well, I'll be—I'll be damned!

ST. PETER. But you don't have to swear so much!

DON QUIXOTE. Sancho! Bring my nag to me!

SANCHO PANZA (*enters, leading the horse*). Master Knight!

DON QUIXOTE. Did you pay for the oats?

SANCHO PANZA. In toto, Mr. Knight!

DON QUIXOTE. But how much have you pilfered? Now, don't harbor any illusions that you will be able to deceive me.

SANCHO PANZA. What's life without illusions, Master? . . .

DON QUIXOTE. What's happened to you? Have you lost your practical insight into things—you, who used to be able to extricate yourself from so many perplexities when I was beset by harassment and difficulties?

SANCHO PANZA. My noble knight-errant, you remember when we—when we were taking our famous excursions and roaming about everywhere, you always used to whip me because I was lacking in wings? You remember, don't you? Well, you pummeled me and whipped me—and at last the wings began to sprout! And that's the reason I won't conceal—no matter how painful and unwise it may be to speak the truth—that I have taken heed of your wise teachings . . . and *I* have begun to have illusions.

Don Quixote. What the hell are you saying?

Sancho Panza. Bold knight-errant, I can't deny that my base origin, my low birth—not to mention my meager earnings —used to place me in the painful situation of feeling more oppressed by the discomforts and annoyances of life than I should have been . . .

Don Quixote. Come to the point!

Sancho Panza . . . and—so—I came to realize the advantage of, so to speak, what is it they call it now . . . of—of stretching a point or two, if necessary. *(Don Quixote pulls his ear.)* Bold knight, it is not out of the realm of possibility that you might still live to experience the adventure of saddling a horse— yes, in your lifetime—yes; perhaps even *my* horse!

Don Quixote. What's that you are saying?

Sancho Panza. Yes—and I may even be given a chance to give you a licking!

Don Quixote. Sancho! You are speaking words of truth!— Nothing is impossible, and there is no doubt that I, through the combined circumstances of fate, may happen into the position of being forced to saddle your hack—in the event that you, as is not impossible, should beguile a rich, young lady— for the power of illusion is mighty. . . . But let me tell you there is one thing I could never do: I could never steal your oats!

Sancho Panza. You could never steal my oats, you say!— You certainly are having crazy dreams!

Don Quixote. Ah! I have been bringing up a viper in my bosom! Sancho! Let us be friends!

Sancho Panza. Friends! Friendship! By heaven, I think the illusions have taken hold of you again! *(The bridal party is gradually emerging from the inside.)*

Physician. Ah, here are my traveling companions! And the knight-errant Don Quixote of La Mancha! An interesting and learned person! You will come with us, won't you?

Don Quixote. If I am not mistaken, you are Doctor Know-it-all. To be sure, I do know a great deal about matters and things, owing to my dearly bought experiences—which are neither to be mentioned nor forgotten—but I do not know everything. And if you gentlemen have no particular object in mind on your journey, I should like to sally forth with you.

PHYSICIAN. The purpose of our journey is to search for the key to heaven, which St. Peter has been careless enough to lose.

DON QUIXOTE. Splendid! Although, to tell the truth, I have lost all illusions of finding a heaven on this earth, having come to the conclusion that it's hell to live. Nevertheless, I shall accompany you. . . .

PHYSICIAN. Mr. Knight-Errant, I wonder whether your deeply rooted displeasure with life is not to be found in the fact that you have left your ideals behind you.

DON QUIXOTE. Bang! There is that word again! Just what are ideals? Look at the Smith there—he has discovered his ideal in a leprous female, once put behind bars for being a loose woman, and whose principal virtue consists in confessing that she has been lying about her past! Is the Smith a happy man?

PHYSICIAN. Probably—for he revels in his misery.

DON QUIXOTE. But suppose he were happy—really happy. . . . Suppose that . . . By heaven, I think I'll come along with you and try to regain my lost ideals, for I am really in need of a little luck after having seen the whole refuse heap of youthful ideals lying about in a mess. Just look at that fat swine Romeo, who keeps smoking twists and is flirting with another man's fiancée; look at Bluebeard, who has joined the league for morality and taken Lady Macbeth for his wife, and she—she is now the presiding officer of the society for the abolishment of capital punishment. Fie, fie, fie! I would like to put them all in one heap of dung, spray them with tar, and then set fire to the manure.

PHYSICIAN. You shadow creatures! I called you forth from earth / to clothe your thoughts in visual form and image—
return below from where you came!
. . . And turn again to will-o'-the-wisps
in dried-up well of putrid vapors!
Be off! Be off at once!

(The wedding party disappears into the well. The Physician slams down the cover, locks it, and throws away the key. When the Courtesan—who is the last one in the procession —is about to descend, the Smith rushes forward and struggles to accompany her; but the Physician prevents him from leaving with her. The Courtesan waves a sad farewell to the Smith. Soon after, little old men with lanterns are seen above the well cover.)

SMITH. She left—and oh, I'm left alone!

PHYSICIAN. You'll meet again! Now don't disturb my work!

SMITH. What will become of me, unfortunate man?

PHYSICIAN. That is for you to say—for you to choose!
What do you wish to be?

SMITH. What I would wish to be?
What am I? . . . Oh, I feel so very aged,
so wicked, now that my beloved illusions
have been taken from me!
It is like walking on a crumbling floor:
one has the fear that one's legs may penetrate
and that one will be caught as in a fox trap.
Ugh! Life stinks, and humans turn my stomach—
the more one learns, the less one's faith holds up;
and he who thinks he knows the most
knows nothing—scarcely that much!
Ah, if I were but a giant and could bear the Alps
upon my broad and mighty shoulders,
I'd stoop and let the entire burden fall
upon the earth and let it crash to bits!
I want to grow, be strong, be stronger than the rest
and trample this great universe asunder,
that I—when all else perishes—
shall be the only one enjoying
the thought that *I* fell by my own hand . . .
while all the others fell by someone else's!

PHYSICIAN. I do not think that a desire could be spoken
in terser, plainer words! And so:
turn giant! Jolt old Mother Earth,
but swing the ancient peg-top carefully
lest she should bump when you are lashing her!

ACT III

*On the left is the veranda of a rectory. It is decorated with
leaves and flowers. In the center of the courtyard, a lone
lime tree, and underneath it a table.*

*On the right, a mountain ridge, seated on which is the
the Old Man of Ho Mountain. A path winds its way past
the giant's feet.*

*In the background is seen a valley with a lake. Nearby
stands the little country church.*

OLD MAN OF HO MOUNTAIN. I am so mighty big, though

not exactly fair;
there's no one upon earth who's bigger—so beware!
I can see wide afar, much further than the human clan;
I've grown into a giant on a rugged mountain peak,
the clouds wash clean my face, my mirror is the creek;
the snow's my overcoat, green mosses hide my cheek;
I take my fill of sun and air, and wind, when'er I can.

There lives an aged priest in the valley below,
and inland stands his church, framed in alder.
The people flock to hear him in weal and in woe
and to worship their new God, the white Balder.

But no one loves the giant, who stands firm in sleet and snow—
though *I* am stronger than them all together.
I save them from the storm when it rages down below
and twist the flash of lightning in my hair into a bow;
the sun's beneficent rays I deflect to make things grow
in pasture land—and gather in the rain in rainy weather.

Deep down in the valley there lives a wretched breed!
Bells tinkle and bells toll, people cross themselves, give heed
to that old tale, dished up no end, with ever different gloss,
of that white god—god Balder, who met his bane by mistletoe;
yet they've no faith in *me*, despite the stones I cast from Ho—
instead of being struck by those that dwarfs toss.

The sun dropped in the lake now; soon night begins to fall—
and all the human beings start for bed;
the church bells, striking three, frighten spirits come to call—
and all crawl 'neath the covers and they pray, big and small;
for the faithful are all fearful of the dark and the dead.
   (*Twilight is setting in. The church bells strike three times.*)
But the giant loves the dark, and the lonely stillness also.
There is silence in the darkness; there's where thoughts
      of greatness grow,
and the midges dance only in the sunshine.
   (*An owl comes flying and alights on his shoulders.*)
Here is my bird, my own, my friend that Night begat:
two eyes upon two wings, and claws just like a cat. . . .
They say you worship with the Devil at his shrine.
Sing, little bird, sing on your weird nocturnal flute—
you know the dark side of the world, and still you sing . . .
   OWL. Hoot! Hoot!

OLD MAN OF HO MOUNTAIN . . . and whisper wisdom deep
into my ear.
When the mountain breeds rodents, you fill your craw within;
when the hare breeds too many, you weed the litter thin. . . .
Not a man dare come the giant and his bird too near!

DWARFS *(enter, carrying pickaxes, crowbars, and shovels.
They start digging and breaking stone at the foot of the mountain beneath the giant. They recite or sing).*

> We pick and we break,
> we knick and we take
> the mountain troll's nest.
> We curry and carry,
> we harrow and harry,
> we give him no rest!
> > No rest!

(The last words are given with emphasis, and held.)

OLD MAN OF HO MOUNTAIN. What are you imps doing down
there?

DWARFS. We grig and we dig,
> we grope and we hope
> to topple the giant.
> We pick and we hack,
> we nick and we knack
> to put him aslant.
> > Aslant!

(They hold on to the last word, as previously.)

OLD MAN OF HO MOUNTAIN. If you imps don't stop hurting
the mountain, the giant will cast stones on you.

ONE OF THE DWARFS. Go ahead and cast!

OLD MAN OF HO MOUNTAIN. Now, now! You had better take
care! Run along!

SECOND DWARF. Did you hear what he said?—He said: Run
along! He must think we are cats! *(The Dwarfs laugh.)*

OLD MAN OF HO MOUNTAIN. So-o! You don't think I am
serious about it! All I have to do is to sneeze, and you'll see
it rain pebbles. Look out down there! *(He sneezes, and a
shower of pebbles comes hurtling down from the mountain.)*

FIRST DWARF. I really think he casts stones! *(He picks up a
stone and aims it at the giant.)*

OLD MAN OF HO MOUNTAIN. Look out now. I am going to
cough this time! *(He coughs. Stones begin to roll down the
side of the mountain, and the First Dwarf falls dead.)*

DWARFS. The King of the Dwarfs is dead. Long live the King
of the Dwarfs!

SECOND DWARF. Now I am the King!

DWARFS. No, not he! Not he!

SECOND DWARF. Who then?

DWARFS. I! I!

SECOND DWARF. We can't all be kings, can we? And I am the oldest—therefore I am the logical one!

THIRD DWARF. Now he is the oldest! But when the oldest one sat on the throne, then he was too old to reign. Then the accent was on youth!

SECOND DWARF. That was when Lasse was alive. But he is dead now, and things are different. But if you want to hold an election, I have nothing against it—on one condition. . . .

DWARFS. What is the condition?

SECOND DWARF. That I can veto the election and that my vote is the deciding one! *(The Dwarfs engage in a noisy brawl, and shriek, yell, and pummel each other.)*

OLD MAN OF HO MOUNTAIN. When the thieves start to fight with each other, the farmer gets back his cow. . . . You little devils! To start a fight on a Saturday night! By my soul and body, you are not a whit better than the big humans! *(Stones hurtle down, killing the Second Dwarf.)*

DWARFS. The King of the Dwarfs is dead! Long live the King!

TOM THUMB *(enters in seven-league boots, escorting Cinderella, riding in a slipper drawn by a rat)*. No! I am the King!

THIRD DWARF. Who are you?

TOM THUMB. I am Tom Thumb, and here is my queen, Cinderella.

THIRD DWARF. On what grounds, may I ask, do you lay claim to this vacant throne?

TOM THUMB. For the reason that I am the littlest one among the little; and he that humbles himself shall be exalted. . . . And you know, of course, that my wife has a tinier foot than anyone.

THIRD DWARF. Such a characteristic may be a recommendation for a queen, but for a king—even of the little people— there are other qualities that are required besides being little. My dear sir, will you be good enough to take off your boots and let us see how you look in your stocking feet?

TOM THUMB. Don't you mean you want to see me in my shirt sleeves?

THIRD DWARF. No, I mean in your stocking feet! For I never fight with a person wearing seven-league boots!

CINDERELLA. Oh, don't start a fight! Don't fight! You must not!

TOM THUMB (*takes off his boots*). A noble knight always fights and never argues, my queen!

CINDERELLA. Oh, I'll faint! I'll swoon! Help! (*Tom Thumb comes to her aid.*)

THIRD DWARF (*snatches Tom Thumb's seven-league boots*). Now, however, *I* refuse to fight, my little sovereign King!

TOM THUMB. Oh, what a deceitful little scoundrel! What a false little thieving midget! (*He weeps and bites his thumb.*)

THIRD DWARF. Pay homage to me now, you rabble! A king like me you have never had before!—And be quick about it—or I'll have your heads taken off! (*There is general confusion, screaming, and battling. Another heap of stones comes rolling from the top of the mountain, and Tom Thumb and Cinderella are buried underneath it, dead.*) I smell Christian blood! (*The Dwarfs disappear.*)

(ST. PETER *enters. He seats himself underneath the lime tree.*)

OLD MAN OF HO MOUNTAIN. Art thou there, St. Peter?

ST. PETER. The voice is the Smith's—but . . . Yes, I am here! But where art thou yourself?

OLD MAN OF HO MOUNTAIN. Up here!

ST. PETER (*suddenly becomes aware of the Old Man of Ho Mountain*). How you have grown, Smith!

OLD MAN OF HO MOUNTAIN. Well, I should think so! How are things with you, old Peter?

ST. PETER. I really don't know what to say. This Doctor Know-it-all doesn't seem to know quite as much as he would have you believe he does. I have an idea he is leading us astray.

OLD MAN OF HO MOUNTAIN. Yes, I shouldn't be surprised if that was his intention, and—to tell the truth—I would like nothing better than to tear myself loose from him.

ST. PETER. I believe he is no other than the devil himself; but you have grown to be so big and strong—you ought to be able to do away with him. . . .

OLD MAN OF HO MOUNTAIN. You just get him within sneezing distance—try to fool him into coming near me—and I'll let him have a shower of stones.

ST. PETER (*suddenly seeing Tom Thumb and Cinderella*). What is this? I believe it is no one else but Tom Thumb. . . . Who has done this? (*He lifts him up into his lap.*)

OLD MAN OF HO MOUNTAIN. I killed him!

ST. PETER. Must you strike down a midget, you big monster?

OLD MAN OF HO MOUNTAIN. Yes, that's what I do when they try to undermine my position as giant!

ST. PETER. Whosoever shall offend one of these little ones . . .

OLD MAN OF HO MOUNTAIN. Well, you see it was they who provoked me! But you have always been partial to the little ones. . . .

ST. PETER. And here lies poor little Cinderella!

OLD MAN OF HO MOUNTAIN . . . whose prime attribute was her small feet. . . .

ST. PETER. And you had the heart to kill these two little ones? Oh!

OLD MAN OF HO MOUNTAIN. If I hadn't, they would have killed me; and there is no law against self-defense. Anyhow, you should have seen how they quarreled and fought with one another, how they cheated and scratched—exactly as the big humans do. Do you think that they felt so much compassion that they were sorry when the King of the Dwarfs had been slain? No, not in the slightest! They tore at each other that same moment, arguing about who was to wear the kingly crown —and let the corpses lie. Beware of the dwarfs who come into possession of the world and rule it! They spend their time inside the mountain hunting for the gold for which humanity will sell both honor and faith—and then they forge the swords with which mankind will destroy itself!

ST. PETER. All this is slander, calumny! And if I could bring these little ones back to life, you would see how grateful they would be, and how gladly they would follow me on my long pilgrimage. . . .

TOM THUMB (awakens). Good morning, grandfather!

ST. PETER. Behold! He lives! And I thought the day of miracles had passed! How are you, you little urchin?

TOM THUMB. Oh, I just made believe I was dead so that I wouldn't be given a beating by the dwarfs.

ST. PETER. Better to flee than to put up a bad fight! Well, you were always a sensible little rascal!—But how about our little Cinderella?

(Tom Thumb starts walking about, notices St. Peter's fish lying on the table. He picks it up and puts it in his pocket.)

CINDERELLA (opens her eyes). Oh, I merely swooned. I learned the trick from my stepmother. If I hadn't fainted, Tom Thumb would have started a fight!

ST. PETER. So little, and yet so wise! Ah, if you only knew how much a tiny chicken brain like hers can hold, you mighty giant up there.

OLD MAN OF HO MOUNTAIN. And how much do you think the breast pocket of a Tom Thumb can hold?

ST. PETER. What is it you are saying up there?

(Cinderella steals over to the table and takes St. Peter's spectacles, which he has placed there.)

OLD MAN OF HO MOUNTAIN. Oh, I just haven't the ambition to repeat it—but if two pairs of eyes see farther than one pair, you can't see any farther than your nose!

ST. PETER. This sounds a little deep to me—and I'm afraid I have to ponder it first. . . . Let me see. . . . Where are my spectacles? *(He searches for them.)*

(Tom Thumb and Cinderella steal out, right.)

ST. PETER. And my symbol! Where is my symbol?

OLD MAN OF HO MOUNTAIN. If you are talking about your fish, it went the same way as your spectacles! Well, now, St. Peter—now you have been given something else to occupy yourself with; and if you have been careless enough to lose your spectacles, I fear you will never find the keys of heaven!

ST. PETER. Well, but I laid them here on the table. . . .

OLD MAN OF HO MOUNTAIN. You did—but Tom Thumb put them in his breast pocket!

ST. PETER. What a rascal! Upon my soul, I'll . . .

OLD MAN OF HO MOUNTAIN. What will you do?

ST. PETER. I'll give him a good thrashing, that's what I'll do!

OLD MAN OF HO MOUNTAIN. One of these little ones? For shame, Peter!—But wait a moment! Don't leave, but stay and keep me company. . . .

ST. PETER *(hesitates)*. I don't know about that—I don't feel quite at home here!

OLD MAN OF HO MOUNTAIN. Oh, won't you! I am so lonely, and I long for friendship!

ST. PETER. Friendship can only exist between persons of somewhat the same—corpulence. You are too huge for me, Smith! Entirely too big!

OLD MAN OF HO MOUNTAIN. And Tom Thumb was too small. . . . How big must one be in order to be accepted, I wonder?

ST. PETER. Oh—about my size. . . .

OLD MAN OF HO MOUNTAIN. Democrat!

ST. PETER. Despot!—Farewell!

(The Parson, the Parson's Wife, their son and daughter-in-law, their granddaughter and her fiancé, and another granddaughter, eight years old, enter from the veranda, two by two: the first pair arm in arm; the second pair with their

arms around each other's waist; the third pair hand in hand; the child follows the second pair.)

PARSON. A lovely evening of a lovely day—
and thank you for it, children—and my children's children!
I now have reached my eightieth year,
and thus am entering life's late twilight.
My thanks to you for giving me a cloudless sunset—
you, who to me have been the essence of this life,
for I have never put my foot beyond this valley;
and life for me had truly its beginning
when here I built my home with my beloved wife. . . .
I don't know why, but on this blessed evening
so many memories come back from long ago. . . .

CHILD *(frightened).* Grandfather! Look! The Mountain Man
is moving!

PARSON. Such superstition, child! This is a mountain—
and mountains do not move—no, never!
A tale is told—you understand, a fairy tale—
about the Mountain Man—that he's a giant
made into a troll once by a bishop,
and that the giant cannot gain redemption
until he's won a woman's heart.
Thus you may be quite certain, my dear child,
that Old Man Mountain is not spooking.

SON. Well, that may be the truth, or not the whole truth,
however, there's been talk about a railroad,
said to be planned to go right through the old man!

PARSON. That's something that I did not know. . . .
It pleases me, and hurts me, too:
this valley's been so dear to me,
so quiet, humble—far from all the worldly din. . . .

CHILD. The lime tree's swaying, Grandpa—
Yet no wind is blowing!

PARSON. You'll find it's blowing up there in its crown,
though we don't feel it here below, my angel!

FIANCÉ *(to his betrothed).* Perhaps it is from pain the lime
tree quivers. . . .
We slashed the bark this morning, carving our names in it.

ELDER GRANDDAUGHTER. I saw the tears of pain it wept; and
why
should it not suffer o'er our pleasure-loving—
for all our joys are founded on the grief of others!

PASTOR'S WIFE. This year the aged lime tree blossomed
gaily,

and we shall have much honey in our hive.

SON'S WIFE. You always think about your household, dear old mother. . . .

PASTOR'S WIFE. Who would be thinking of it, if not I?
When one is seventy or more
one does not carve one's name upon the lime tree;
the old ones then prefer to pluck the blossoms,
preserving them to use for tea
when hacking coughs are chiseling their coffins!

CHILD. Come, Grandpa, let us leave before the darkness falls. . . .
I am afraid when there's no sun. . . .

PARSON. Indeed, my child! We'll go, as we decided, to the church,
where I have something to attend to in the vestry—
in preparation for tomorrow's service. . . . Come!

(The Parson and his wife go out, left.)

DAUGHTER-IN-LAW *(to the Son)*. What blessing, having relatives get on so well—
I never saw a kinship closer bound by love!
Blest be the day—the day I came here, and through you
had the good fortune to be linked into this chain!

SON. Alone 'mongst women, you have not felt it weigh on you!

DAUGHTER-IN-LAW. You jester! Give me a kiss—but not in jest!

(They leave.)

FIANCÉ. And thus my youthful faith that happiness
does not thrive only in the palace is not a mere sham. . . .
I'd rather be a lamb than be a savage beast
That tranquil dale has captured innocence within its frame.

(The Owl hoots.)

ELDER GRANDDAUGHTER. Oh, that nasty, awful owl!

(They leave.)

(Don Quixote enters, without his horse. He removes his helmet and wipes his forehead.)

OLD MAN OF HO MOUNTAIN. Heigh-ho, you old knight-errant!

DON QUIXOTE *(looking up toward the mountain)*. Is that you, Smith? You have turned giant?

OLD MAN OF HO MOUNTAIN. Yes, and a real giant—without any windmill wings on my shoulder blades.

DON QUIXOTE. Ah, keep quiet and don't bring that up! *(He sits down.)*

OLD MAN OF HO MOUNTAIN. Are you downcast, Knight?

DON QUIXOTE. Yes, I am!

OLD MAN OF HO MOUNTAIN. What's the matter now?—And where is your old nag?

DON QUIXOTE. Don't speak about it! *(He gets up.)* Have you any idea what's wrong with a man who can't eat?

OLD MAN OF HO MOUNTAIN. I suppose he has nothing to eat for!

DON QUIXOTE. Faugh!—Do you know what is wrong with a person who can't sleep?

OLD MAN OF HO MOUNTAIN. He has probably napped too long after eating.

DON QUIXOTE. Faugh! What base thoughts you have!

OLD MAN OF HO MOUNTAIN. I believe the knight-errant is beginning to pick himself up again? How do you feel?

DON QUIXOTE. Do you know why I have sold my mare?

OLD MAN OF HO MOUNTAIN. You needed money?

DON QUIXOTE. Materialist! Money? Ha! What is paltry gold compared with—with the golden tresses of a woman. . . .

OLD MAN OF HO MOUNTAIN. Ha ha! The knight-errant has fallen in love!

DON QUIXOTE. Stop using such a banal expression about such sacred emotion!—I love!

OLD MAN OF HO MOUNTAIN. By the Creator! Yes, yes—when we get silver in the hair, we want gold!

DON QUIXOTE. I love! I love purely, innocently, recklessly, and—absolutely monogamously!

OLD MAN OF HO MOUNTAIN. In other words, you want to be alone.

DON QUIXOTE. Have you no sense of shame, Giant—or Smith, or whatever, whoever you are!

OLD MAN OF HO MOUNTAIN. And your holy flame is being returned—recklessly, absolutely monogamously, is it?

DON QUIXOTE. Well, now . . . that's something I don't know —but that's where the charm lies. . . .

OLD MAN OF HO MOUNTAIN. Or the excitement! And how about Rocinante?

DON QUIXOTE. She couldn't stand the smell of horses, and so . . .

OLD MAN OF HO MOUNTAIN. Well, but what does it look like—I mean the object—the object of your desire?

DON QUIXOTE. I have never seen it! But I have heard it— and I have even heard it described!

OLD MAN OF HO MOUNTAIN. Is it a thing of beauty?

DON QUIXOTE. That's none of your business!

OLD MAN OF HO MOUNTAIN. It seems to me that you express yourself in an uncouth manner. Mr. Knight-Errant, and if it pleases you, let's take to the lances.

DON QUIXOTE. There was, forsooth, a time when I fought with giants, but I am now of the opinion that I have outgrown it. And if you have no objection, let us part right now.

OLD MAN OF HO MOUNTAIN. So you refuse to give me satisfaction, do you?

DON QUIXOTE. Yes—and I won't have anything to do with you—nothing at all! You are too big for me! Farewell!—Sancho!

OLD MAN OF HO MOUNTAIN. I'm too big for him, too! *(Sancho Panza enters.)*

DON QUIXOTE. How much did you receive for the mare, Sancho?

SANCHO PANZA. Thirty-six silver pieces, austere master!

DON QUIXOTE. Give them to me! *(Sancho Panza searches his pockets.)* You have squandered the money!

SANCHO PANZA. I have disposed of it. . . .

DON QUIXOTE. Show me the certificate of disposition! *(Sancho Panza again searches his pockets.)* You have no certificate, and you never did have! Yes, yes, you are a wicked human being, Sancho, but there is a certain honesty in your cheating that I value—and therefore I forgive you—and because I love you, too. Come with me now and let us continue the pilgrimage. But let us get out of this sunken valley and up to the heights, Sancho! The heights!

SANCHO PANZA. Oh, so now we are going toward the heights again? And sometimes you want to be in the valleys. . . .

DON QUIXOTE. All movement forward is like a wave—undulating—first up, and then down. And—as the wise Confucius says—it is through change and variation that we attain a true stability.

SANCHO PANZA. He certainly is a wise one! Yes, I have wobbled my way through life—yet I have never reached any true stability. . . .

DON QUIXOTE. You are coming, Sancho, aren't you? Then, come!

SANCHO PANZA. Very well, let's wobble on!—Will it please Your Lordship to precede?

(They depart.)

OLD MAN OF HO MOUNTAIN. It's dreary, dismal, to sit here, and be a giant;

all shun me openly; and what is worse—
the children can be scared by any wet-nurse,
and then they lose all faith in me and turn defiant!
(The Courtesan enters.)
Aha! Here comes the courtesan who ignominiously
    went away. . . .
Now I'll impress her, awe her if I can,
and she'll be mine without delay!

Give heed, my beauty, wandering in the dale:
I am the greatest one upon this earth!
Pray, will you be my own? Will you accept the crown
of gold and sit upon my throne within my mountain hall?
    COURTESAN. Your coronet, Giant, does not suit my head;
your mountain castle is too grand for me!
    OLD MAN OF HO MOUNTAIN. Ha! You are proud, you little
        hoyden,
and you disdain the giant for his ugliness!
    COURTESAN. That's not the reason; but because you bully—
when others pray, as for a grace, a favor. . . .
    OLD MAN OF HO MOUNTAIN. My one great pride is that I
        do not beg;
and I collect all claims of mine in full!
    COURTESAN. What can you give me, who desire nothing?
And love is not among the treasures you possess.
    OLD MAN OF HO MOUNTAIN. Then go to hell, you insolent
        whore,
whom I pulled up once from the mire!
I see now you're rotten to the core
and know your body can be had for hire! *
    *(There is a frightening din and rumbling. The mountain
    collapses, burying the church, the parsonage and the valley.
    The Old Man of Ho Mountain is removed to the center of
    the stage, where he sits alone on the ruins under which the
    Courtesan has been buried.)*
    PHYSICIAN *(enters)*. Well, Giant, tell me what you have been
        doing
and how you find yourself in your position?
    OLD MAN OF HO MOUNTAIN. Oh, its disgusting sitting upon
        ruins
and to be staring at one's fate alone!
    PHYSICIAN. You say so now—and feel it gruesome
now that you've toppled everything, destroyed it. . . .

---

* May love be turned into the blackest hate,
    and let this sad romance now end your tragic fate!

Out of the valley, once so green, you've made a barren
wilderness,
and you've created havoc among those
who found their pleasure in the small and simple things.
OLD MAN OF HO MOUNTAIN. Go on and prattle! I just
wonder whether not the dwarf
would have behaved exactly in the manner I have.
Yes, even you yourself, if you'd been there on high. . . .
PHYSICIAN. I'm there already—yes, much higher. . . .
You seem to have forgot it's through my power
you sit where you are sitting!
OLD MAN OF HO MOUNTAIN. It won't take long to see!—
Fall, mountain, fall!
(There is a rumbling inside the mountain, but it remains
intact.)
PHYSICIAN. Keep rumbling! It has no effect on me.
Your power, Giant, has completely waned!
But if you'll speak with nicety, then we can talk
as formerly and be good friends!
OLD MAN OF HO MOUNTAIN. Well, rather than to sit here
until doomsday,
I now surrender, asking your forgiveness!
(The Physician picks up a pellet and strikes the Old Man
of Ho Mountain with it. There is a sharp flash of lightning
and the Old Man loses his shape; the Smith instead appears.)
PHYSICIAN. Well now, you wretch, are you quite satisfied,
having been elevated to the heights
and seen how puny it is down below?
Have you now found the thread within life's tangled skein?
Are you content with what you've learned?
I see you're not—that you found everything awry,
and therefore I shall lead you to the land
where there is nothing but perfection. . . . Are you ready?
SMITH. Yes, lead me, please, O Master, from this universe
of seamy sides and flaws—but on condition
that I no longer walk alone!
PHYSICIAN. You have my company, the knight and the
apostle. . . .
SMITH. Yes, yes! But man is nevertheless alone
if he has not a woman. . . .
PHYSICIAN. Oho! 'Tis but a moment since you stoned her
unto death yourself—
when you discovered she was of the lowest.
SMITH. I feel regret—if that will help me!

She was the best among the very best,
so proud, so free from any calculation;
she craved no power, and could not be bought with gold. . . .
    PHYSICIAN. You now look on it this way—when she's dead;
but were she to come back, you'd crow a different tune!
    SMITH. But try, please try, and I will vow repentance. . . .
    PHYSICIAN. I'll try, I will, once more. . . .
Now let us wander to the blessed land
where no one lives unto himself but solely for others,
where summer reigns eternal, with the homes uncrowded;
where milk and honey flow in rivers,
where there's no lack of sparrows for the table,
where life will pass like one long song and dance:
this land is named Schlaraffenland . . .
it opens to us now its blest embrace!

ACT IV

*The scene represents a landscape in Schlaraffenland. In the
trees hang all manner of food and fruits. Small streams flow
from the background; one of milk, the other two of honey
and syrup.*

*People dressed in the light and motley-colored habit of
savage tribes lie lazily on their backs, some sleeping, others
half asleep.*

*In the center of the stage a low, Roman dining table with
sleeping couches around it. On the left is a pump, which is
locked and capped by a royal crown.*

Tom Thumb and Cinderella are lying by the syrup stream.

SANCHO PANZA *(enters)*. What a blessed land! What a happy
people! I've been here a full eight days already, and not a
word of disgruntlement have I heard—no opposition, no taxes,
no police! The day is as long as the night, the sun shines
during the day and the moon at night. Fried sparrows fly into
one's mouth, and milk and honey flow in streams.

Oh, it's so perfect—everything—that one could go crazy! A
hail storm, a thunderclap, or a couple of floods would put life
into this sleeping nation! A dull and sluggish nation, full of
bedsores—and gastritis!

If I could only discover one little seed of discontent, no
matter how small, that I could sow in their sleepy brains!

The knight-errant Don Quixote, who at last has come face
to face with his ideals and his ideal state, has now become

prime minister, while in the past, and elsewhere, he has always belonged to the fundamental opposition. And now he has, of course, become a heated opponent of any change! Awake, Nation! *(The Nation shows slight signs of stirring.)* Isn't there a single one of you who has any reason whatever for feeling discontented?

ONE OF THE NATION. What would we be discontented with?

SANCHO PANZA. Some trifling thing!—Everything!—The established order of things!

ONE OF THE NATION. Well, it's a little monotonous, of course. . . .

SANCHO PANZA. You see! The food is good! The climate is fine, and you sleep excellently! Perhaps what you lack is work?

THE NATION. Yes . . . work. . . .

SANCHO PANZA. Fine! A little labor question to begin with! —Isn't there some other little shortcoming or defect in the government or administration that, surely, it's impossible to adjust, but that—for that very reason—can be of permanent value! Tom Thumb, you who are full of mischief, can't you hit upon something?

TOM THUMB. Mr. Partisan, my unimportance and my simple birth . . .

SANCHO PANZA. Bravo! You qualify yourself immediately as a possibility for a cabinet post!

TOM THUMB . . . and my utter lack of knowledge of government affairs have given me cause to wonder whether we live in a privileged society or not, and this owing to a particular condition that long ago should have attracted and caused general discontent.

SANCHO PANZA. What is it? Speak up, angel!

TOM THUMB. Hasn't the Nation noticed that the pump is locked—and, to boot, disfigured by a royal crown?

SANCHO PANZA. Ha! There is a cabinet question that could end in a ministerial crisis!—What has the Nation to say about this violation of the sacredness of the constitution? *(The Nation seems to be waking.)* The Nation is being awakened! The opposition is at hand, and I shall present the interpellation to the Prime Minister!

DON QUIXOTE *(enters).* Don't you think this is the *ideal* state, Sancho? Now you see that ideals can be realized on this earth—something that you always questioned. . . . Oh, blessed land, oh blessed people!—If I now could only see *my* ideal— my love's ideal—then, Sancho, I would gladly, and with my gray hairs, step down into my grave!

SANCHO PANZA. I should think that would be the wisest thing Your Lordship could do, for one ought never to survive one's ideals!

DON QUIXOTE. Very true, Sancho!—But what has taken place here during my brief absence? The Nation is no longer asleep!

SANCHO PANZA. No, for the Nation has waked up!

DON QUIXOTE. Who has waked the Nation from its sweet, delectable sleep?

SANCHO PANZA. The spirit of the times, class consciousness, and—I!

DON QUIXOTE. Why have you done this to us? For he who sleeps commits no sin; and in sleep come the nicest dreams!— What is it that the Nation desires?

SANCHO PANZA. As leader of the opposition I have the painful duty to present the demands of the people to their enlightened servant!

DON QUIXOTE. What do the people desire?

SANCHO PANZA. Work!

DON QUIXOTE. Work? Where will I find work?

SANCHO PANZA. Well now, if we only knew that, then the question would be solved!

DON QUIXOTE. And I have no intention of solving it! Rogue!

SANCHO PANZA. Furthermore, a general displeasure has been noticed concerning the privileged pump, which is being kept locked, and which, besides, contrary to the realm's valid constitutional laws, is decorated with a royal crown.

DON QUIXOTE. Good! Anything else?

SANCHO PANZA. Not for the moment.

DON QUIXOTE. Good! These great questions shall be resolved without delay, and I shall introduce the matter before His Royal Majesty! (He leaves.)

ST. PETER (enters). Oh, what a blessed kingdom! Is it possible that at last I have reached the goal of my pilgrimage and that this can be heaven?—But, come to think of it, I didn't see any gate!

SANCHO PANZA. You didn't? Why, it was standing wide open. . . .

ST. PETER. Oh, so it's you—that nasty Sancho Panza! Well, if you are here, then it can't be the heavenly kingdom!

SANCHO PANZA. So you don't believe in the penitent thief? Come here, Tom Thumb, and bring the fish and the spectacles with you so that the prophet will be convinced that he's in good company here! Come on, Tom Thumb!

Tom Thumb *(to Sancho Panza)*. I'll pay you back for this! *(To St. Peter, to whom he returns the fish and the spectacles.)* Here is the junk. I found it on a table underneath a lime tree.

St. Peter. Ah, my symbol!

Sancho Panza. Are you talking about the spectacles?

St. Peter. And my glasses!

Sancho Panza. You must learn to call each thing by its right name, Peter!

St. Peter *(regards the scenery through his spectacles)*. Hm! It seems to me everything looks so mundane, so worldly here. . . . And the people's countenances are not an answer to my expectations! No, no! This is certainly no heaven!

Sancho Panza *(to Tom Thumb)*. The old man has forgotten both you and your filching! I congratulate you!

(The King [the Smith] and the Queen [the Courtesan] enter.)

King *(to the Queen)*. Yes, this is heaven, and I see it mir- rored
so pure, so blue in your adoring eyes!

Queen. It's not the light of heaven that's reflected,
it is the sparkle from your loving eyes! . . .

King . . . that lighted up beside the fireplace,
for all your virtues, and your beauty . . .

Queen . . . in turn born by your gentle majesty
and nourished by your goodness, noble King!

Don Quixote *(enters)*. Your Majesty ought to make up his mind, for the spirit of rebellion is growing and threatens to assume dimensions.

King. Large or small? You have a habit of magnifying, of exaggerating everything, Don Quixote. Now what was it all about? Oh, yes, the Nation demands work, and the Nation demands a change in the pump! And you feel that you can't resolve these questions immediately?

Don Quixote. No, Your Majesty!

King *(to the Queen)*. Forgive me, my Queen, but I have to do a little governing in order to tickle my appetite for the dinner! *(To the people.)* Is there anyone here who is able to crack this nut without hesitation? If there is, I'll make him prime minister! *(Sancho Panza raises his hand.)* Sancho! Very well, you may speak, but speak wisely, and above all, briefly!

Sancho Panza. I have an idea, something like this: nothing for nothing, and something for something. . . . The dis- gruntled give up their demands for work, and the pump is opened for the use of everybody!

KING. Very good! This is what is generally called a compromise. . . .

DON QUIXOTE. But what guarantee has our Mr. Partisan that the discontented will accept the compromise?

SANCHO PANZA. What guarantees? One simply invites the opposition to a corruption dinner and offers its leader a portfolio.

DON QUIXOTE. In that case I beg to relinquish my mandate! I resign . . .

SANCHO PANZA. Without the victory, however!

KING *(removes the crown from the pump and gives the key to Sancho Panza).* Here is the key to the dung well. Go ahead and pump now, good people! But don't spill it on yourselves!

THE NATION. Ugh!

KING. Now that the cause of the discontent has been removed, I hope that you, Sancho, will reign wisely and stave off future dissensions from the country!

SANCHO PANZA. Your Majesty! Since all causes of discontent have now been removed, the Nation may again abandon itself to the selfsame dreams of blissfulness from which it recently was awakened so rudely and disturbingly! Sleep, Nation! *(He gestures with his hands, as if he were hypnotizing the crowd.)*

KING. What a statesman he is, that Sancho Panza! What a statesman! *(He and the Queen leave.)*

DON QUIXOTE. You are a scoundrel, Sancho!

SANCHO PANZA. The king used the word *statesman* in an entirely different sense!

DON QUIXOTE. Now you are satisfied, aren't you?

SANCHO PANZA. I am satisfied!

DON QUIXOTE. And that's why you think everybody else should be satisfied?

SANCHO PANZA. I hope they already are! I know that they are! *(Having meantime been addressed by Tom Thumb, the crowd starts to clamor.)* What are you whimpering for, Nation?

TOM THUMB. The general discontent, the class consciousness, the spirit of the times—and I—have joined hands in a desire to . . .

SANCHO PANZA. What are you discontented with?

TOM THUMB. Everything! The established order of things, the present, and the future!

SANCHO PANZA. It is remarkable, I must say, that there must always be strife and quarreling and discontent. If you would only obey me and do as I say, there would be a heaven on earth! It grieves me, Tom Thumb, grieves me grievously that you should come with your exaggerated demands. Now that the Nation has it so good, why should you bring it all this unhappiness? *(The Nation gives vent to its dissatisfaction.)*

DON QUIXOTE. You'll come to grief for your doings, villain!

SANCHO PANZA *(to Tom Thumb)*. But what is it that the people want? Enter into details! I want the details!

TOM THUMB. Well, there are some who want the pump to be locked. . . .

SANCHO PANZA. And a minute ago they wanted it to be open!

TOM THUMB. Yes, yes—and now there are still others who want it to be open!

SANCHO PANZA. This is truly hell! Oh, you little great big rascal! I yield to the mastermind who brought party politics into being.

TOM THUMB. Divide and conquer!

KING *(enters with the Queen)*. What's wrong now?

SANCHO PANZA. A ministerial crisis! The spirit of partisanship is abroad!

KING. Do what both parties want!

SANCHO PANZA. But you can't please both parties at the same time, can you?

KING. No, that's right, you can't!—Is it the pump that's causing trouble again?—Now I think I know what to do, good people! I'm going to say good-by to you, that's what I'll do!

QUEEN. No, you must stay!

KING. Must I? Do you know what you are saying?

QUEEN. What language you use! And what a tone!

KING. Perhaps you want to remind me of my simple birth and that I was once a smith? If that is what you have in mind, I'll remind you what you were—what you are! *(He works himself up into a rising anger.)* Wench, hussy! *(He strikes his fist against the palm of his hand.)*

QUEEN *(falling dead)*. That's how much you loved me!

ST. PETER. I think I've come straight into hell! *(He leaves. It grows dark.)*

KING *(kneels by the Queen's dead body)*. She's dead, she's dead! Oh, God in heaven, she is dead! You precious angel, who so brightened life for me. . . .

SANCHO PANZA. It's getting to be a little mawkish here! And now I am tripping off—then I won't have to resign!

(He leaves.)

DON QUIXOTE. I am beginning to think that what has never been is the best. Dulcinea! . . . Dulcinea! . . . *(He departs.)*

TOM THUMB *(to Cinderella)*. You know what, Cinderella?

You are a nice little crony—for when I heap abuse on you, you don't swoon as these queens do!

CINDERELLA. No, because I give tit for tat!

TOM THUMB. With gifts, and gifts in return, love lasts longest!—Let us leave now! Come! I don't care for such scenes as these!—No matter what, this was a good land, but the inhabitants were abominable. This country deserved a better government! *(They leave arm in arm.)*

KING *(kneeling by the dead Queen)*. Oh, miserable life! Oh cruel death!

PHYSICIAN *(enters)*. Have you been causing mischief again?

SMITH. Yes—what have I done? But can I help that she can't stand being spoken to?

PHYSICIAN. You know, Smith, I think it best that she is gone —for that's when you like her most. And we become angels only after we are dead!

KING. Yes, I'm afraid it is so. . . . But if she could only come back once more, then I would try to keep myself in check!

PHYSICIAN. Once more! No—never again!

ST. PETER. Listen now, good friends . . . speaking sincerely, I am beginning to get tired of this pilgrimage—and when I see the Smith doing nothing but making a nuisance of himself and playing practical jokes, I fear we are forgetting our great goal. . . .

PHYSICIAN. Our goal? Yes, of course—it was heaven. . . . We'll get there eventually, but first we must pass through purgatory. Tell me, Smith, are you, too, tiring of this earthly pilgrimage? Are you?

KING. Oh, am I tired? I was so from the very start, and when I gazed into the eyes of life and human beings, it nauseated me—yes, everything!
The great was not sufficiently the great,
the little was to me entirely too little;
and having gone in bankruptcy down here,
one longs, one yearns for what's above, beyond. . . .

PHYSICIAN. Once the devil has grown old, he turns to monk! Now could it be the Church has an enticement for you?

KING. There is some truth in that, for even as a little child I felt a leaning toward the sacred priesthood!

PHYSICIAN. Well, then, we'll catch two flies with but a single smack,
and then St. Peter shall receive the keys to heaven,
kept by the Holy Father down in Rome—
and given him, as an inheritance, by him who founded

the Church upon the rock—I can't recall its name now—
to unify and to set free.
So, for the last time, let's cross the final ditch
and march direct to Rome—and to our heaven!
(The change of setting commences.)

ACT V

SCENE 1. *A chapel in St. Peter's Dome in Rome. Music and singing from offstage. On the right, a bronze statue of St. Peter.*

SMITH *(enters, accompanied by St. Peter. They both bare their heads)*. This is awfully beautiful, gorgeous! And how high it is to the ceiling!

ST. PETER. Yes, it makes me feel almost shy!

SMITH. But what are we going to say now when the Holy Father comes? I think you had best do the talking!

ST. PETER. Quiet! I think it's he coming there! No, it was somebody else!

SMITH *(pointing to the statue)*. Heavens, I wonder who that's supposed to be? Let's see what it says at the base . . . P-E-T-R-U-S . . . Petrus! Why, that's you!

ST. PETER. What in the world! Have they done me in bronze, too! Ha, ha! Ha, ha! But I don't look like that, do I?

SMITH. Oh, I don't know! But they could have given you a little more hair, I think. . . . He is here now . . . kneel. . . .

(The Smith and St. Peter fall on their knees. The Pope enters.)

POPE *(stops)*. Whom have we here?

SMITH *(to St. Peter)*. You answer! I am frightened!

ST. PETER. A lowly servant of the Lord. . . .

POPE. Your name, old man?

ST. PETER. Peter.

POPE. You have another name. . . .

ST. PETER. Simon.

POPE. Rise! *(St. Peter rises.)* Simon Peter! How remarkable! —And your father was named . . . ?

ST. PETER. Jonah, fisherman of Capernaum. . . .

POPE. *Tu es Petrus!* *(He makes the sign of the cross.)* You have been in this city before, haven't you?

ST. PETER. Never. I have been standing outside the dome in

Cologne for eight hundred years, but I have never been in Rome before. . . .

POPE. Your memory fails you! Here, on this spot, you suffered the death of a martyr, and in remembrance and commemoration thereof, this temple was erected.

ST. PETER. I've never died the death of a martyr. . . .

POPE. The Church Fathers say so!

ST. PETER. I am older than the Church Fathers, and I ought to know more about that than they do. . . .

POPE. And the decretals. . . .

ST. PETER. I don't know anything about them. . . .

POPE. But your letters, written in a most excellent style . . .

ST. PETER. I haven't written any letters. . . .

POPE . . . in Greek, in Novum Testamentum. . . .

ST. PETER. As a Hebrew I never learned Greek, especially as I was a poor man without any learning, who had to support myself by fishing. . . .

POPE. Are you Peter, or are you not?

ST. PETER. I am Peter, the selfsame Peter whom Your Holiness is talking about.

POPE. The rock on which the Church was built, and whose heir I am?

ST. PETER. I wasn't any rock, I was merely a frail reed that was frightened that night—you remember—into denying my Master . . . and it is in punishment for that that I am wandering about the earth without being able to find peace.

POPE. And it is on such a foundation the Church is built?

ST. PETER. Yes, I'm afraid I was never too steadfast. . . .

POPE. That you are a heretic—that I can hear, and I would excommunicate and banish you forever, if I didn't suspect you to be an escaped lunatic!—Who is the fellow there with you?

ST. PETER. It's only the Smith. . . .

POPE. Which smith? What are you doing here?

SMITH. Well, it may sound like a fairy tale—but St. Peter came here to take a look at the keys of heaven. . . .

POPE (summons a Sbirro). Sbirro! (The Sbirro enters). Drive out this rabble from the church!   (He goes out.)

SBIRRO. Out!

SMITH. He called you rabble, Peter!

SBIRRO. Out with you!

SMITH. Nicely, nicely now! The Sbirro doesn't know whom he has the honor to drive away!

SBIRRO. Out with you, rabble!

ST. PETER. Can you imagine how they have lied about me! And then they have gone and read my letters, which I have never written. . . . But let us be humble, Smith, let's be humble!

SMITH. Oh, you don't have to be so humble, having your bust in the temple!

ST. PETER. Yes, I feel that way! I'm ashamed! I'm ashamed!

SMITH. I don't blame you, and don't think that I don't feel the same way! I don't care to stay here and be embraced by any bailiffs. . . .

ST. PETER. It seems to me I was never farther from heaven than this very moment. . . .

SBIRRO. Get out!

ST. PETER. This is what you get for being humble and for telling the truth! (*To the Sbirro.*) Out, did you say? Yes—out again. Smith, and wander, ramble, and roam about, without any rest, without any peace! Do you know what it is that we are lacking in, since we never seem to reach our destination?

SMITH. No!

ST. PETER. Faith—that's what we lack! And it just comes back to me now that the way to heaven is by way of the Cross! Let's seek the Cross!

SMITH. You mean through suffering?

ST. PETER. I mean through suffering. . . .

SMITH. Well, I believe that no one suffers more than he who believes in nothing—and yet he is farthest from the Cross!

ST. PETER. Crawl to the Cross, Smith, and then we'll see. . . .

(*They depart.*)

SCENE 2. *Change of setting: A crossroad, with an open shrine; on a base of stone, Christ is seen between the two thieves on crosses. The figures, however, have their backs toward the audience.*

Don Quixote is seated at the foot of the Cross.

The Wandering Jew [the Physician in disguise] enters. He carries a box filled with small wares on a strap round his neck.

WANDERING JEW. Buy something from the Wandering Jew, austere knight. . . .

DON QUIXOTE. What have you to sell, now that you have sold your Master?

WANDERING JEW. I have cuff links and scarf pins, pocket combs and mirrors, pencils and notebooks. . . .

DON QUIXOTE. Give me a mirror!

WANDERING JEW. Here you are, sir, please. . . .

DON QUIXOTE. How much?

WANDERING JEW. One mark.

DON QUIXOTE. Can you give change for thirty silver pieces?

WANDERING JEW. Yes, I can.

DON QUIXOTE. You fail to grasp the sarcasm, Jew. . . .

WANDERING JEW. Oh, no! I understand—but how about the knight-errant himself? *(He spits on the coin and puts it in his pocket.)*

DON QUIXOTE. You spat on the coin?

WANDERING JEW. Yes, exactly as you, Mr. Knight-Errant, does at the Jew. He spits at him, but uses him!

DON QUIXOTE. You have an uncommon sense of humor for one with such a bad conscience!

WANDERING JEW. How so?

DON QUIXOTE. You were one of those who crucified . . .

WANDERING JEW. No—you are thinking of Pilate, the Roman, and his soldiers. . . . He washed his hands because they were unclean—that's why I don't have to wash mine, for they are clean. *(He sits down.)*

DON QUIXOTE. Stand up! And keep walking! Walk, walk as long as the earth exists—you, who refused to let the Master rest when He took His last steps!

WANDERING JEW. Fairy tales, Lord Knight! Besides, if I do as the penitent thief did, and beg for forgiveness, isn't paradise open to me, too?

DON QUIXOTE. Have you prayed for forgiveness, then?

WANDERING JEW. I have done more than that. I have suffered my punishment, and now I am weary.

DON QUIXOTE. Seat yourself here, you poor Jew, and the shadow of the Cross shall refresh you. . . .

WANDERING JEW. Do you know, Mr. Knight-Errant, why Judas cast away the thirty pieces of silver and hanged himself?

DON QUIXOTE. No. . . .

WANDERING JEW. Because they were counterfeit!

DON QUIXOTE. Your thoughts are still concerned with money and mundane things, and you are yet a long way from the Cross. . . .

WANDERING JEW. I am not going to argue with you, Mr. Knight-Errant. I find it much more profitable to share your views—then we are of the same persuasion, at least basically.

ST. PETER *(enters, followed by the Smith).* I see that weary
    wanderers have gathered here,
and that the knight has found the seat of honor.

DON QUIXOTE. Here at the crossroads we all meet;
but only meet to part again!

ST. PETER. You seem to have grown weary, Knight.

DON QUIXOTE. Not only have I wearied, I have fallen!
My life—even if but a fairy tale—
will be relived by generations
as long as heaven still exists, the earth spins round,
and people keep pursuing visions;
as long as nothing has been learned and nothing is forgotten
shall Don Quixote live,
true to the follies of all youth, the wisdom of all manhood!
Farewell, you universe of blest illusions—and of cruel ones!
(He collapses and falls to the ground.)

ST. PETER. The noble knight is dead!

WANDERING JEW. Yet lives—and will live on!
And he himself spoke the ideal funeral oration—
the best that could have been delivered over him!
But see. . . . I think St. Peter's done for:
already he is leaning toward the final rest. . . .

ST. PETER. I'm weary, yes, of toil and search,
and leave the world without regrets;
for here on earth I found no heaven . . .
its portal only—and its name is death. . . .
*(He dies. The Wandering Jew sheds his disguise and appears
again as the Physician.)*

PHYSICIAN *(to the Smith, who is about to seat himself).* No—
for you there is no rest as yet;
your life is only halfway past. . . .

SMITH. So, it is you?— Then we shall part,
and I should like to rest here in the shade—
for I can't follow your peculiar ways and paths. . . .

PHYSICIAN. It is not wise to sleep beneath some certain trees—
and to let others bear the cross that *you* should bear.
It is convenient, but carries with it no reward or purpose.
Stand up, and bear your own until the very end!

SMITH. So I have done . . . and here's the final end!

PHYSICIAN. No—it is—*here!*
*(There is a change in scenery. The scene is now inside the
ruins of the Tower of Babel, with its galleries and passages.
In the background there is a large niche. On the left, a
ladder extending halfway up the wall. In the center, a table,
covered with a handsome tablecloth; underneath the table,
a basket.)*

SMITH. Where am I now? In the infernal regions?

PHYSICIAN. You're now inside the Tower of Babel, underground!

You will recall, from tales told in your youth,
how mankind's children—presumptuous in their aspirations
to climb with boldness up to heaven—
contrived a stairway, spiraled like a tower. . . .
The gods, however *(Catches himself.)*—hm—but God refused to
    suffer this abuse,
and, thus, he smote the tower into ruins. . . .
    SMITH. But why not build it to its height again
in our days, when thunder can be aped
and one can sail up to the skies,
descend into the depths of oceans,
and speak through air to all the corners of the earth?
    PHYSICIAN. You vain intruder of celestial paradise,
your animation and your spirit still persists!
I show you here in imagery your ancient lineage!
    (Phantasmagoria: shown against a white background in the
    niche, rear center. Icarus appears.)
You here see Icarus, who made himself wings
to fly up to the solar planet;
but the hot sun soon melted the waxen contraption,
and the deep of the sea was the end of the flyer!
    (Prometheus appears.)
You here see Prometheus, a real cock-a-hoop
among invaders of celestial spheres. . . .
He is, besides, related to the giant,
whom you recall, but rather would forget!
    (Jacob wrestles with Jehovah.)
And here you see the patriarch Jacob,
who tried to wrestle with his God—
with consequences that you know from reading. . . .
If you would care for more, just say the word!
    SMITH. I've seen enough, and understand!
    PHYSICIAN. You are content, then, with your flight to heaven?
Good! We return then to the earth.
    SMITH. Just one more word! That ladder there?
    PHYSICIAN. Yes—that's the famous Jacob's ladder!
    SMITH. On which the angels once ascended . . .
    PHYSICIAN . . . and soon descended. . . .
Upon my soul, I think the ladder tempts you,
and that the thought of heaven still persists!
    SMITH. Yes, it persists like sin itself. . . .
    PHYSICIAN. That's not so strange! It's grown and multiplied
upon the very tree where sin grows!

Go on, climb up and try the ladder;
but if it should not lead to heaven,
it still will lead you back to earth!
Now let us part, but ere you go,
I leave a small collection of some memories
from him who led you into fairy lands
to while away a dreary evening.
When rain wept tears in competition with the tears of the
        Smith,
I took some playthings in my roomy knapsack—
the best that I could find within the toyshop —
and played the game as is the wizard's wont.
        (*He removes, one by one, the following toys and fairy-tale
        books from the basket, which he has placed on the table.*)
Here is the giant, frightful to behold,
who swallows little ones and who casts stones.
And here is little Tom Thumb,
who devours giants—when he gets the chance,
and faithful Cinderella, who was married to him.
And here you have some fairy tales, with handsome pictures:
about Knight Bluebeard and his many wives,
about St. Peter, wandering over earth,
despite the fact that he's been dead for ages;
Jerusalem's old cobbler—and Schlaraffenland. . . .
It's all for you—to give your dear little ones. . . .
        SMITH. Is this a mockery, more cruel than your many games?
        PHYSICIAN. The only true words I have spoken!—
Ascend the Jacob's ladder there
and you shall see—though *I* shall not.
You'll see there, to begin with,
a smithy and a chamber;
a chamber with three tiny beds. . . .
        SMITH. I never want to see that room again!
        PHYSICIAN. And in the chamber you'll see faces that you
            know!
But do not think that heaven has fall'n down
or that its angels walk on ladders!
        (*The Smith's children can now be seen in the niche above
        the ladder.*)
        SMITH. My children! Oh, my children!
        PHYSICIAN. Now I shall leave . . .
for I can't conjure any more.
Build now again a heaven of your own on earth,

but trust not them who rattle with its keys;
and when your dreams to actuality give birth,
erect no Babel's Tower that will fall like screes.

To Damascus I

A DRAMA IN FIVE ACTS

❖ ❖ ❖

This play is of tremendous importance, not alone for dramatic writing but for the technique of acting, stage designing, and every aspect of the theatre craft to which it gave birth. It is chiefly built upon the more significant and tragically fantastic happenings during the dramatist's Inferno period (1894-97). Each episode and experience is a step on the road of suffering that life imposes on the Stranger, a famous author, in his visionary search for an answer to his soul's doubts about life and its meaning, about his destiny on earth. The Stranger is a disbeliever, whose ideas and ideals generally have clashed with the accepted standards of society and authority. Step by step his querulousness, arrogance and ambition, his sensitiveness, pride, and other human failings are overcome. Fresh doubts as to his own integrity, intellectual power, and superiority take the place of his former self-reliance and highly individual convictions. Through his sufferings he begins to learn the errors of his past life, and in the end he realizes that what he has suffered on this earth has been meted out by a divine power as punishment for his sins.

Before Strindberg wrote *The Keys of Heaven* he had already become obsessed with the notion that we are born to suffer and that only through suffering can we find the gate to heaven. In a letter dated May 31, 1891, he preaches the gospel of doubt and suffering to his friend Birger Mörner. He had suffered in his home at the hands of his stern father, and his mother's predilection for his older brothers hurt him deeply. In school he was often treated harshly. During his struggle for existence and for recognition as a writer, in his marital relations, and in trying to support his family he found the road hard and dismal. And not least did he suffer from the violent and often vicious attacks made upon him and his literary gifts from many quarters by self-appointed moralists in newspapers, periodicals, and pamphlets. Added to this was the suspicion that some of his literary friends, with whom he had freeheartedly discussed some of his ideas for future efforts, had stolen these ideas and made use of them. No publisher or theatre would accept his works. Finding himself, as so often before, in dire economic difficulties, he was aided by his friend and benefactor Torsten Hedlund and by the family of his second wife, Frida Uhl. He went to live at Dornach in Austria at the invitation of his wife's relatives. Thus dependent upon others he fell into a state of melancholia and depression that shattered his nerves and brought him to the brink of mental unbalance and psychopathy. His inspiration to write was gone. When Frida Uhl bore him a daughter, he felt compelled to exert himself to provide for his wife and child, but his exertions were in vain. He departed for Paris, where his reputation as an author was soaring, mainly through the successful productions of *Miss Julie* (at Antoine's Théâtre Libre, January 16, 1893), and *Creditors* (at Lugné-Poë's Théâtre de l'Oeuvre, June 21, 1894). These were followed by the celebrated presentation of *The Father* by Lugné-Poë on December 13, 1894, which brought him additional fame. Despite these happy circumstances he remained untouched by the glory heaped on him. He became increasingly morose and hectically turned to experiments in chemistry, physics, astronomy, and other sciences. He wrote a wide variety of articles, papers, and treatises on these subjects which now absorbed him, in a burning desire to uncover new and unexplored areas of learning and knowledge. He was invited to become a member of outstanding scientific societies and to pursue his experiments at the faculty laboratories of the Sorbonne. He hungered and froze, but continued his experiments with mad determination. He delved into alchemy and thought he had discovered gold, and that this would put an end to his economic insecurity. But tests of his process by some scientists disproved his theories, although others had upheld his claims. Finally he fled in despair to his friend Dr. Anders Eliasson in the city of Ystad in southern Sweden. Benefited by the stay there, he went to Austria to see his little daughter, now two and a half years old, while his wife was in Vienna seeking a divorce. His reading of Swedenborg's spiritual experiences and the works of others, not afflicted with an aberrant psychosis, who had had abstruse and supernatural experiences similar to his own, did much to free him of anxiety. Searching for an explanation of his encounters with "the spirits," he found in such writers the comfort and assurance that he needed. Gradually he recovered. He became critical and skeptical of his own doubts, and after writing *Inferno* and *Legends* he was once again in command of his own self. But the intensity with which he had lived and with which he had interpreted life, was now balanced by a deeper insight into his own character, his faults and errors of the past. His violent, sometimes fanatical sentiments, too, had been mellowed by the feeling of resignation, which had manifested itself after the Inferno crisis. It is the agonizing ordeal of these years that Strindberg has dramatized so eloquently, so movingly in the *To Damascus* trilogy.

In his authoritative work *The Final Years of Strindberg's Life (Strindbergs sista levnadsår)*, Professor Walter A. Berendsohn notes that "the pilgrimage dramas have not only the loosely-knitted sequence of episodes with the continuous introduction of new subordinate characters in common, but also the fact that, from beginning to end, the characters playing opposite the protagonist are not the same. . . . In *To Damascus I-III*, it is God himself who invisibly plays opposite the protagonist. . . . The center of the stage is generally held by a character with whom Strindberg to a considerable degree identifies himself. . . . The sum and substance [of the many different lessons the Stranger learns during his pilgrimage] is the emptiness and vanity, imperfection and misery of human existence."

To Damascus I describes how the Stranger, having believed his fate to be directed by a benevolent higher power, gradually loses his faith after having been humbled and humiliated, embarrassed and debased by a sequence of distressing events. Finally he is forced to accept the charity offered by his wife's family and relatives. When he seeks to flee from his misery and throw off the shackles of his humiliating position and enchainment, he falls from a cliff. Seriously injured he is brought to a nearby monastery, where he has time to contemplate his past. He feels remorse and his conscience belabors him mercilessly for having lived a life of sin and debauchery, and for all the wrongs he has committed. The conviction grips him that his life has been a wretched and fraudulent one and that his sufferings have been meted out by Providence to cleanse him of his sinfulness. Anguished, he thinks he is about to leave this world, but after several episodes he is again brought together with the woman he loves. He voices his gratitude to the God he has disbelieved in the past. Yet he is not convinced that the Church is the symbol of *his* God, when the Lady goes to light a candle to her patron saint. He finds it difficult to believe in dogmas.

The scenes with the Physician can be traced to Strindberg's rest cure at the home of Dr. Anders Eliasson in Ystad, to whom he fled in order to escape "the spirits" that haunted him and to seek aid for his hands. During his chemical experiments

in Paris they had become badly burned and infected, causing
him excruciating pain.

In *To Damascus I* the highroad, the narrow entrance to
the mountain pass, the kitchen and the "rose chamber" in
the forester's lodge have their counterpart in the home of his
second wife (Frida Uhl) near Dornach, Austria. The monastery
scene contains impressions of the St. Louis Hospital in Paris,
where Strindberg had been a patient. Strindberg himself is the
prototype of the Stranger, the Beggar, and, in part, of the
Physician, who in the main represents Baron Wrangel, Siri von
Essen's first husband. The Lady is Frida Uhl, with touches of
his first wife, Siri von Essen, and of his third wife, Harriet
Bosse, in the last part of the trilogy. His Austrian mother-in-
law is portrayed in the Mother, and the Old Man is her aged
father.

In *To Damascus I* the scenes progress from the church
scene at the beginning of the play up to a certain point (the
asylum scene), then, in reverse order, go back to the original
scene—much as the ebb and flow of the tide. "Bringing the
reader and the audience back to the same environment where
the action began strengthens one's feeling of having experienced a dream sequence from the time of going to sleep until
the awakening," Strindberg wrote in a letter to Gustaf af
Geijerstam concerning Part I of *To Damascus*. This technique was first used by Strindberg in *Lucky Per's Journey*,
which began and ended with a scene in a church. *To Damascus
I* begins and ends with a street-corner scene, where a church
is the dominant feature. In his other pilgrimage plays, Strindberg did not carry through this idea.

To Damascus I is a tapestry of mundane and spiritual experiences against a background of religious mood and feeling,
woven with threads of pagan, Buddhistic, Christian, and modern philosophical influences, mainly of von Hartmann and
Schopenhauer. Swedenborg's influence also looms large, and
here and there can be discerned the spell of Kierkegaard and
of the stern Old Testament prophets and patriarchs.

The shadowy texture of *To Damascus I* and the somber
effects and misty colors that envelop this remarkable drama of
allegory and symbolism, dream, and reality are deftly and mag-
nificently woven into a sublime, transcendent pattern of mystical beauty. Some of the scenes are like a Rembrandt painting come to life. It is a haunting and unforgettable drama
which marks a new epoch in the world theatre.

PERFORMANCE NOTES ON THE TRILOGY, *To Damascus*

To Damascus I had its original première on November 19, 1900, at the Royal Theatre in Stockholm. While it was in many respects a noteworthy production as directed by Emil Grandinson with Harriet Bosse as the Lady and August Palme as the Stranger (or the Unknown), the technical resources of the Swedish theatre at that time were insufficiently developed for Strindberg's scenic requirements. The play was produced again in 1910 in Strindberg's own little theatre, The Intimate Theatre, but with little success. The work was played next in the provinces of Sweden in 1912 and 1913 by touring companies; the producer of the 1913 production was Arvid Englind, who was responsible for O'Neill's introduction upon the Swedish stage. Another Swedish production followed in 1915 at the Grand Theatre in Gothenburg by Einar Fröberg, with Victor Seaström playing the Stranger.

After several productions abroad, *To Damascus I* had a significant revival in Stockholm at the Royal Theatre on February 27, 1937, in a production staged by Olof Molander with Lars Hanson in the role of the Stranger. This time the resources of modern stage technique resulted in a remarkably rich mixture of realism and fantasy. Next, the Malmö Civic Theatre gave a production in 1951, the Uppsala Civic Theatre in 1956, and the Stockholm Royal Theatre in 1960. Radio productions in Sweden were given in 1927, 1931, 1936, and 1948.

In Finland, Harriet Bosse, Strindberg's third wife, appeared in 1904, in Part I, as guest performer at the Swedish Theatre in Helsinki in the role of the Lady. The Finnish National Theatre presented the play in 1954 with Jan Sibelius' daughter, Ruth Snellman, in the role of the Lady. The Royal Theatre of Stockholm made guest appearances in Helsinki with the play in 1937, and the Finnish radio broadcast it in Swedish in 1947.

In Germany *To Damascus I* had its première on April 27, 1914, at the Lessing Theatre in Berlin with Friedrich Kayssler and Lina Lossen in the two leading roles.

In 1919, Parts I and II were given at the Volksbühne in Berlin in a laudable production; and also in 1919, Parts I-III were produced at the National Theatre in Mannheim, and in 1922 in Hamburg at the Kammerspiele Theatre. During Hit-

ler's regime in Germany, however, Strindberg's works were
banned, and it was not until 1949 that a performance of the
play was given again in Germany; this performance was given
on radio. A condensation of all three parts of *To Damascus* was
next produced in 1953 at the Tübingen Landestheater; and
another three-hour condensation of the three parts of the
trilogy was given at the Kammerspiele Theater in Munich
in 1956.

The play is said to have had its first performance in America
in 1914-15; and a production was given at the Experimental
Theatre of Vassar College—in a condensed version of the
trilogy in 1958. The first production in England was in 1937
under the title of *The Road to Damascus* at the intimate West-
minster Theatre in London. In 1953, all three parts were given
on radio by the British Broadcasting Company.

In Austria an adaptation of the trilogy under the German
title of *Nach Damaskus* was given at the Landestheater in
Salzburg in the spring of 1952. In Switzerland, the trilogy was
presented in condensed form by Willi Reich at the Civic
Theatre in Lucerne in 1959, and the Schauspielhaus in Zurich
presented this version in 1961. *To Damascus* was presented in
Italy on radio under the title of *Verso Damasco* in the spring
of 1952. A noteworthy French production came in May 1949
when the play was presented at the Théâtre du Vieux Colom-
bier in Paris with Sacha Pitoëff as the Stranger.

Part II, along with Part III, was presented in a German
adaptation in June 1916 by Friedrich Kayssler at the Kammerspiele in Munich. Parts II and III were produced in the
spring of 1918 at the Lessing Theatre in Berlin with the famous
Albert Bassermann as the Stranger while Lina Lossen and
Emilie Unda portrayed the Lady in her separate incarnations.

In Sweden, Part II alone was given at the Lorensberg
Theatre in Gothenburg on December 9, 1924. Parts II and III
were given in slightly condensed form at the Royal Theatre in
Stockholm by Olof Molander in 1944.

Part III had its Swedish première at the Lorensberg Theatre
on November 16, 1922. As staged by Knut Ström, it turned out
to be a deeply moving experience. John Ekman as the Stranger,
Elsa Widborg as the Lady, Gabriel Alw as the Tempter, and
Olof Sandborg as the Confessor gave superior performances.
Per Lindberg produced the play in 1926 at the Concert House
with Olof Sandborg as the Stranger playing opposite Harriet
Bosse as the Lady. In 1938 the Gothenburg Civic Theatre
gave Part III in another production by Knut Ström. In the

fall of 1933, Per Lindberg staged all three parts of *To Damascus* in a condensed version at the National Theatre in Oslo.

The court scene from Part III was given in 1925 in Italian at a small theatre in Rome. It was staged by the distinguished director Bragaglia.

CHARACTERS

THE STRANGER	THE WAITER
THE LADY	THE BLACKSMITH
THE BEGGAR	THE MILLER'S WIFE
THE PHYSICIAN	THE SIX PALLBEARERS
THE SISTER	MOURNERS
THE OLD MAN	THE CAFÉ PROPRIETOR
THE MOTHER	CAESAR THE MADMAN
THE ABBESS	SERVANTS, INMATES, *and others*
THE CONFESSOR	

THE SETTINGS

Act I, Scene 1. A street corner.
Act I, Scene 2. At the Physician's: the courtyard.

Act II, Scene 1. A room in a hotel.
Act II, Scene 2. By the sea.
Act II, Scene 3. On the highway.
Act. II, Scene 4. A narrow entrance to a mountain pass.
Act. II, Scene 5. The kitchen.

Act III, Scene 1. The Rose Chamber.
Act III, Scene 2. The asylum.
Act III, Scene 3. The Rose Chamber.
Act III, Scene 4. The kitchen.

Act IV, Scene 1. Inside the mountain pass.
Act IV, Scene 2. On the highway.
Act IV, Scene 3. By the sea.
Act IV, Scene 4. A room in a hotel.

Act V, Scene 1. At the Physician's: the courtyard.
Act V, Scene 2. A street corner.

ACT 1

SCENE 1. *A street corner. A bench underneath a tree. The side doors of a small Gothic church are visible, also a post office and a café with chairs and tables outside. The café and the post office are closed.*

The strains of a funeral march, indicating an approaching procession, are heard and die out gradually.

The Stranger is standing at the edge of the sidewalk, seemingly at a loss to know in which direction to go. The clock in the church tower strikes: first four times, in a high pitch, the quarter hours; then the hour, three times, in a lower pitch.

The Lady enters. She greets the Stranger and is about to move on, but stops.

STRANGER. Well—there you are. I was almost certain you would come.

LADY. You wanted me to come, didn't you? Yes—I could feel it. But why are you standing here on the street corner?

STRANGER. I don't know. . . . I have to stand somewhere while I am waiting.

LADY. What are you waiting for?

STRANGER. If I only knew. . . . For forty years I have been waiting for something—I think they call it happiness . . . or it may be for nothing but the end of unhappiness. . . . Listen—listen again to this dismal music! Don't leave me, don't leave me, I beg of you. . . . I shall be in dread if you go. . . .

LADY. My friend! We met yesterday for the first time, and we spoke—we two, alone—for four hours. You awakened my sympathy . . . but that does not entitle you to take advantage of my kindness.

STRANGER. You are right. . . . I must not. But I beg—I pray of you: Do not leave me alone! I am a stranger in this city—have not a single friend here—and the few acquaintances I have seem to me even more remote than strangers—I could well call them enemies.

LADY. Enemies everywhere—alone everywhere! Why did you leave your wife and children?

STRANGER. If I only knew!—If I even knew why I was born—why I should be standing here—where to go—what to do! Do you believe that we can be doomed already here on earth?

LADY. No, I don't believe that.

STRANGER. Look at me!

LADY. Have you then never felt any happiness in this life?

STRANGER. No—and when I thought I had found happiness, it was only a trap to lure me into a greater misery. . . . Whenever the golden apple fell into my hand, it was either poisoned or rotten at the core.

LADY. What religion do you profess, if you will forgive my asking? . . .

STRANGER. This is my religion: When my cup has run over, I shall take my leave.

LADY. And go where?

STRANGER. To perdition. The very fact that I hold death in my hand—gives me an unbelievable feeling of strength. . . .

LADY. Oh, my God, you are playing with death!

STRANGER . . . as I have been playing with life—wasn't I a poet? Despite being born with a morbid and melancholy turn of mind, I have never been able to take anything quite seriously—not even my own deep sorrows. . . . And there are moments when I doubt that life is more real than my poetic fancies. (*The funeral procession is coming closer, and the strains of "De Profundis" are heard.*) Here they are again! I can't understand why they should be marching around here in the streets!

LADY. Is it of them you are afraid?

STRANGER. No, but it annoys me. . . . It seems like witchery! . . . I have no fear of death. It is loneliness I am afraid of—for the loneliness of life is peopled. . . . I don't know whether it is someone else or myself I sense—but in loneliness one is never alone. The air becomes dense, the atmosphere thickens, and spirits that are invisible and yet have life can be perceived, hovering about. . . .

LADY. You have felt that?

STRANGER. Yes—for some time I have been intensely aware of such things. . . . But not the way I saw them in the past—as mere things and happenings, shapes and colors. . . . Now I see thoughts and motives. Life—which previously was a meaningless nothing—has taken on purpose, and I observe an intention where I formerly saw only aimlessness, chance. Therefore, when I met you yesterday, the idea occurred to me that you were sent to me either to save me or to destroy me.

LADY. Why should I destroy you?

STRANGER. Because that was your mission in life.

LADY. I have no such intention whatever—and you make me

feel compassion for you most of all, because—well, I have never met a human being . . . never in my life have I met a human being whose very sight makes me feel so like weeping. . . . Tell me what is gnawing at your conscience? Have you committed some vile act that has remained unknown to others and gone unpunished?

STRANGER. You are indeed justified in asking that! I have no more crimes on my conscience than other men who have gone free. . . . Yes—one: I rebelled against being a fool, being at the mercy of life.

LADY. In order to live, one has to be willing to be more or less of a fool, or a dupe.

STRANGER. It seems to be almost a duty, and one I wouldn't want to shirk. Or else, there is a mystery in my past, of which I am not aware. . . . Do you know there is a legend in my family that I am a changeling?

LADY. What is a changeling?

STRANGER. A changeling is a child that has been exchanged by the elves for the child that was born.

LADY. Do you believe such things?

STRANGER. No, but I think it is a parable that has a certain meaning. As a child I cried continuously and seemed to be ill at ease with life. I hated my parents as much as they hated me. I could stand no coercion, no conventions, no rules and regulations. . . . And my only longing was for the woods and the sea.

LADY. Have you ever had any visions?

STRANGER. Never! But I have often seemed to notice that my fate is being ruled by two different forces, one giving me all that I ask for, the other standing beside me tainting the gift, so that when I receive it, it is so worthless that I don't want to touch it. Yet it is true that I have been given everything I wished for of life . . . but I have found all of it to be idle, useless. . . .

LADY. You have been given everything, and yet you are dissatisfied.

STRANGER. That is what I call my curse. . . .

LADY. Don't curse!—But why, then, have you not projected your desires beyond this life—to the land where nothing exists that is unclean?

STRANGER. Because I have doubted the existence of all life beyond that on earth.

LADY. But what about the elves?

STRANGER. Well, that was nothing but a fairy tale!—But shouldn't we sit down on the bench there?

LADY. Why, yes—but what is it you are waiting for?

STRANGER. I am really waiting for the post-office to open. There is a letter for me that has been following me about without catching up with me. *(They sit down on the bench.)* Tell me now a little about yourself!

LADY *(busies herself with her needlework)*. I have nothing special to tell.

STRANGER. It is strange—but I would rather prefer to think of you impersonally—as one without any name. . . . I have only a vague idea of your name. . . . I would like to give you a name myself. Let me see—what name should I give you? . . . Yes— your name shall be Eve. *(He makes a gesture in the direction of offstage.)* Fanfares. *(The funeral march is again heard.)* There is that funeral march again!—Now I shall give you your age— for I have no idea how old you are. . . . From now on you are thirty-four years old—thus you were born in 1864. And now we come to your character. I am in ignorance on that score, too. I shall give you a very good character, for your voice has a ring like my late mother's. . . . When I say mother I use it in an abstract sense—and I pronounce it M-O-T-H-E-R. . . . For my mother never fondled me, but I remember that she used to beat me. Yes—and so, you see, I have been reared in hate. Hate! Hate against hate! An eye for an eye! Look at the scar here on my forehead! It is from an ax—and my brother held it! I had cast a stone at him, and it broke off his front tooth. I refused to attend my father's funeral because he had me thrown out at my sister's wedding. I was born illegitimate while bankruptcy proceedings were going on, and while the family was in mourning for an uncle who committed suicide. Now you know the family! The apple doesn't fall far from the tree. By luck I have escaped fourteen years of hard labor—and therefore I have every reason to be thankful to the elves, though not especially happy. . . .

LADY. I enjoy hearing you speak, but you must not say anything bad about the elves. . . . It hurts me—hurts me deeply!

STRANGER. Frankly, I do not believe in them. . . . Yet they always keep coming back. Are not the elves doomed spirits who have not yet earned their forgiveness? Aren't they? In that case, I am also a child of trolls. At one time I believed reconciliation was close at hand—through a woman. But no delusion could have been greater—for it was the beginning of a seventh hell!

LADY. Oh, how can you say things like that? Yes—you are a doomed soul. . . . But you shall not remain one.

STRANGER. You mean that holy water and church bells would bring me peace. . . . I have tried it, but it had the opposite effect. It affected me as it does the devil when he sees the sign of the Cross. Let us talk about you now. . . .

LADY. There is no need for that!—Have you ever been accused of having wasted your gifts?

STRANGER. I have been accused of everything! No one in my city was so hated as I, no one so detested. Alone I had to tread my way, coming and going alone. If I went into a public place, people moved five yards away from me. If I came to rent a room, it was already rented. The clergy read their anathemas over me from their pulpits, the teachers denounced me from their desks and platforms, and the parents in the homes. Once the ecclesiastical council wanted to take my children away from me. That time I forgot myself and raised my clenched fist against—Heaven. . . .

LADY. Why are you so hated?

STRANGER. I just don't know!—Yes—I could not bear to see humanity suffer. . . . I said so . . . and I wrote: Set yourselves free! I shall help you! . . . And to the poor I said: Do not let the rich squeeze you and suck your blood . . . and to the woman: Let not the man dominate you! . . . Then to the children, and this was no doubt the very worst: Do not obey your parents when they are unjust! The consequences—well, they are entirely incomprehensible . . . for instantly rich and poor, men and women, parents and children, turned against me. . . . And added to this came sickness and poverty, the dishonor of being forced to beg, divorce, lawsuits, exile, loneliness—and now, at the very last—do you think I am insane?

LADY. No, I do not. . . .

STRANGER. Then I believe you are the only one who does not think so—and that makes you the more precious to me.

LADY *(rises)*. Now I must leave you. . . .

STRANGER. You, too!

LADY. But you must not remain here.

STRANGER. Where, then, shall I go?

LADY. You must go home and work.

STRANGER. I am not a laborer—I am a poet. . . .

LADY. I don't wish to hurt your feelings—and you are right: poetry is a grace given to us. . . . But it can be reclaimed. Do not forfeit it!

STRANGER. Where are you going?

LADY. Merely on an errand. . . .

STRANGER. Are you religious?

LADY. I am nothing.

STRANGER. So much the better; then you shall be something. Oh, I wish I were your blind old father, whom you used to lead to the market places to sing. . . . But my misfortune is that I cannot grow old. . . . It is the same with the children of the elves. They do not grow up, only their heads enlarge, and they keep crying. . . . I wish I were someone's dog and that I had someone I could follow, so that I would never be alone. . . . A little food now and then, a kick sometimes, a little petting, a whipping or two. . . .

LADY. Now I must go! Good-by! *(She leaves.)*

STRANGER *(his thoughts wandering).* Good-by! *(He remains seated on the bench, removes his hat and wipes his brow. Then he begins to draw figures in the sand with his stick. The Beggar enters. He has a weird face. He pokes about in the gutter.)* What are you poking about for, beggar?

BEGGAR. First of all: Why do you ask? And secondly, I am no beggar. Have I asked you for anything?

STRANGER. I beg your pardon, but it is a little difficult to judge people by their exterior.

BEGGAR. You are certainly right there. For example, have you any idea who I am?

STRANGER. No, I neither have, nor do I care. It does not interest me.

BEGGAR. Who can tell about that? The interest generally comes afterward—when it is too late. *Virtus post nummos!*

STRANGER. What's this! You are acquainted with the language of the Romans?

BEGGAR. There you see! Your interest is coming to life. *Omne tulit punctum qui miscuit utile dulci.* It is I who have succeeded in whatever I have undertaken—for the reason that I have never done anything. I would like to call myself Polycrates —he with the ring. Do you know that I have received everything that I have wished for from life? But I have never asked for anything; and tired of success, I threw away the ring. Now that I am old and gray, I regret it and keep seeking the ring in the gutter. . . . But as the search might drag out indefinitely, I don't begrudge myself a few discarded cigar butts for lack of the golden ring.

STRANGER. It is not quite clear to me whether you are being cynical—or whether your mind is somewhat disconnected.

BEGGAR. Well, you see that's just what I don't know myself.

STRANGER. But do you know who I am?

BEGGAR. Haven't the faintest idea, and it doesn't interest me.

STRANGER. The interest generally comes afterward. . . . What nonsense is this! Here you let me fool myself into putting your words in my mouth. That's very like picking other people's cigar butts. Phew!

BEGGAR *(tipping his hat).* And you refuse to smoke after me?

STRANGER. How did you get that scar on your forehead?

BEGGAR. An intimate relative gave it to me.

STRANGER. Oh no! Now you frighten me! Let me feel if you are made of flesh and blood! *(He feels the Beggar's arm.)* Yes, he is really a human being!—You wouldn't deign to accept a small amount of money, would you, in return for your promise to seek Polycrates' ring in a more remote part of the city? *(He holds up a coin.) Post nummos virtus. . . .* Why, this is ridiculous! Here I am rechewing his words again! Go away! Go away!

BEGGAR *(accepting the coin).* I'll go—but this is altogether too much. Let me return three-fourths. Then we don't owe each other anything but a friendly gift. . . .

STRANGER. A friendly gift? Am I your friend?

BEGGAR. At least I am yours. And if one stands alone in the world, one can't be too particular when it comes to human beings.

STRANGER. Allow me—as a farewell greeting—to toss the brief word *behave* after you!

BEGGAR. With pleasure, with pleasure! But next time we meet, I shall have a word of greeting ready that will not be as brief. . . . *(He leaves.)*

STRANGER *(seats himself and again starts to make figures with his stick).* Sunday afternoon! The interminable, murky, dreary Sunday afternoon when every family in town eats pot roast and sauerkraut with peeled potatoes. Just now the old people are taking their dinner nap, the young people are playing chess and smoking tobacco, the servants have gone to vesper service, and the shops are closed. Oh, this long, dreary, killing afternoon! The day of rest, when the soul ceases to function—when it is as impossible to run across a familiar face as it is to get into a barroom. *(The Lady returns. She is now wearing a flower on her bodice.)* There! It is strange that I cannot open my mouth and say something without being immediately contradicted.

LADY. Are you still sitting here?

STRANGER. Yes. If I sit here, writing in the sand, or somewhere else—what does it matter, as long as I write in the sand. . . .

LADY. What are you writing? Let me see. . . .

STRANGER. I think I wrote: Eve, 1864. . . . Oh no—don't walk on it!

LADY. What will happen if I do?

STRANGER. Then misfortune will befall you—and me also.

LADY. How can you know?

STRANGER. I do! And I know also that the Christmas rose you carry at your breast is a mandragora. According to symbolism it is the flower of malice and calumny—but in medicine it was once used as a cure for insanity. Won't you give it to me?

LADY (hesitates). As a medicine?

STRANGER. Yes!—Have you read my books?

LADY. Certainly. You know that I have read them . . . that I have you to thank for my education in freedom, and my faith in human rights and human values. . . .

STRANGER. Then you have not read my last books? . . .

LADY. No—and if they are different from your previous works, I don't care to know about them. . . .

STRANGER. I am glad of that! And will you give me your promise never to open another book of mine?

LADY. Let me think that over first. . . . Yes, I promise.

STRANGER. Good! But do not break your promise! Keep in mind Bluebeard's wife, when her curiosity got the best of her and she was tempted to open the forbidden chamber. . . .

LADY. Do you realize that your demands already are those of a Bluebeard? And are you not aware that you have already, for some time, forgotten that I am married, that my husband is a physician, and that he is an admirer of yours—and that his home is open to you whenever you choose to be welcomed?

STRANGER. I have made every effort to forget it—and I have so erased it from my memory that for me it has ceased to be reality.

LADY. That being so, will you accompany me to my home this evening?

STRANGER. No. But would you care to come with me?

LADY. Where?

STRANGER. Out into the world—wherever you choose. I have no home—all I have is my traveling bag. I have no money—except once in a while; in other words, rarely. Money is the only thing life has been obstinate enough to refuse me—perhaps because I have not demanded it with sufficient boldness.

LADY. Hm!

STRANGER. Well—what are you thinking about?

LADY. I am surprised that I do not feel offended by your jesting.

STRANGER. Jest or seriousness—it is all the same to me. . . . There—the organ is playing. . . . It won't be long now before the bar is open.

LADY. Is it true that you do a good deal of drinking?

STRANGER. A good deal, yes! The wine frees my soul from my body—I fly into the ether—I see what no one ever divined— hear what no one ever heard. . . .

LADY. And the day after? . . .

STRANGER. I have the joy of feeling the beautiful pangs of conscience—experience the saving sensation of guilt and re- morse—revel in the sufferings of my body while my soul hovers like mist round my brow. . . . It is as if swaying betwixt life and death—when the spirit feels its wings lifted in flight and can soar into space at will.

LADY. Come to church with me—if only for a moment. . . . You will not have to listen to any preaching—only the beau- tiful vesper music. . . .

STRANGER. No—not to church! It merely gives me a feeling of pain and depression . . . makes me conscious of not belong- ing there—of being a doomed soul, who will never again be one of the fold—no more than I could become a child again.

LADY. You really think such thoughts?

STRANGER. That is how far gone I am! And I almost feel as if I were lying carved up in Medea's caldron, simmering and seething, boiling eternally. If I don't turn into soap, I shall rise up rejuvenated out of my own brine. It all depends upon Medea's skill.

LADY. This sounds like the language of the oracles. Now let us see if you can't become a child again.

STRANGER. In that case it would have to begin with the cradle —and with the right child in it.

LADY. Exactly!—But wait for me here while I go into the chapel of St. Elisabeth! If the café were open, I would ask you nicely not to drink anything—but fortunately it is closed.

(*The Stranger seats himself again and starts to draw in the sand. Six pallbearers, dressed in brown, enter together with some mourners. One of the men carries a standard with the insignia of the carpenters' guild draped with brown crepe; another one an enormous broadax with a garland of spruce twigs; a third one carries a cushion with a speaker's gavel. They halt outside the café, waiting.*)

STRANGER. Forgive me, but who is the dead man?

FIRST GUEST. He was a carpenter. *(He makes a ticking sound, like that of a clock.)*

STRANGER. A real carpenter or one of those carpenter insects that sit in wooden walls and tick?

SECOND GUEST. Both. But most of all, one of the kind that sits in the walls and ticks. . . . What is it they call it now?

STRANGER *(to himself)*. The rascal! He wants to entice me into saying the death tick, but I shall give him a different answer just to annoy him. You mean a goldsmith, don't you?

SECOND GUEST. No—I don't mean a goldsmith. *(The ticking sound is heard again.)*

STRANGER. Is it your intention to frighten me, or is the dead man performing miracles? For, in that case, I shall have to inform you that I am not afraid—and I do not believe in miracles. However, I find it a little strange that the guests show their grief in brown. Why not in black, which is inexpensive, attractive, and practical?

THIRD GUEST. To us in our simple-minded innocence it is black; but if Your Grace so commands, let it be called brown.

STRANGER. I cannot deny that I find this gathering utterly strange, and I feel an uneasiness, which I am inclined to ascribe to yesterday's intoxication from Mosel wine. But if I should say that the broadax is wound with twigs of spruce, I suppose I'd be told that it is. . . . Well—what is it?

FIRST GUEST. It is a grape vine.

STRANGER. I had a curious feeling it wasn't spruce! Well—now—at last! The barroom is open! *(The café is opened. The Stranger seats himself at one of the tables and is served a bottle of wine. The mourners occupy some of the other vacant tables.)* I can see the corpse must have been a happy soul, since you intoxicate yourselves the moment the funeral is over.

FIRST GUEST. Yes, he was a good-for-nothing who never could learn to take life seriously.

STRANGER. And he probably imbibed excessively?

SECOND GUEST. That's exactly what he did.

THIRD GUEST. And he let others take care of his wife and children and feed them.

STRANGER. Not very nice of him! But I suppose that is why he is being given such a nice funeral oration by his friends. . . . *(One of the Guests gets up and knocks against the Stranger's table.)* Would you please stop bumping against my table while I am having my drink?

FIRST GUEST. When I drink, I have the right to . . .

STRANGER. When you drink, yes. . . . For there is, of course, a great difference between you and me. *(The Guests start to demur. The Beggar enters.)* Why, there is the beggar again—the fellow who picks about in the gutters.

BEGGAR *(seats himself at an unoccupied table and orders some wine)*. Wine! Mosel!

CAFÉ PROPRIETOR *(comes out, exhibiting an official placard)*. You will be good enough to leave! We can't serve you anything because you have not paid your taxes and obligations to the state. Here—here you see the decision of the municipal court—and here you'll find your name, your age and your character. . . .

BEGGAR. *Omnia serviliter pro dominatione!* I am a free man with an academic education and refuse to pay taxes because I haven't the slightest desire to run for any office. *(To the Waiter.)* Mosel!

CAFÉ PROPRIETOR. If you don't leave this very minute, you will be given free transportation to the community poor-house! . . .

STRANGER. Couldn't you two gentlemen settle this affair somewhere else? . . . You are disturbing your guests here. . . .

CAFÉ PROPRIETOR. Very well—but I call on you to witness that I am in the right!

STRANGER. Not at all! I think this business is altogether too painful. . . . Simply because a man doesn't pay his taxes—that is no reason why he shouldn't be allowed to enjoy some of the trivial little pleasures that life can offer.

CAFÉ PROPRIETOR. Oh so! You are one of those who go about freeing people of their obligations and responsibilities!

STRANGER. Oh no! This is going a bit too far!—Do you realize that I am a famous man? *(The Café Proprietor and the Guests laugh loudly.)*

CAFÉ PROPRIETOR. You mean notorious, don't you! Just a second—let me look at the placard again and see if that description doesn't fit you. . . . Thirty-eight years old—brown hair—mustache—blue eyes—no permanent occupation—livelihood questionable—married, but left his wife and children—known for his subversive opinions on social questions—and gives the impression of lacking the full use of his mental aculties. . . . Does the description fit, eh?

STRANGER *(rises, pale and crushed)*. Oh! What is this!

CAFÉ PROPRIETOR. By my soul, I believe it fits!

BEGGAR. Perhaps he is the man, then, and not I!

CAFÉ PROPRIETOR. It seems so, doesn't it! And now I think

you two gentlemen can take each other by the arm and go for a walk. . . .

BEGGAR *(to the Stranger)*. Come, let us go!

STRANGER. Us?—This is beginning to seem like a conspiracy! *(The bells in the church tower peal; the sun breaks forth, lighting up the colored, ornamented rose window over the portal, which opens, showing the interior of the church. Organ music is heard, and the singing of "Ave Maris Stella.")*

LADY *(comes from the church)*. Where are you? What are you doing? Why did you call me again? You just have to hang on to a woman's skirts, like a little child, don't you!

STRANGER. Yes—this time I am really afraid. . . . Things are happening—things that cannot be explained by ordinary logic. . . .

LADY. I thought you weren't afraid of anything—not even death. . . .

STRANGER. No—I have no fear of death! But I am afraid of —the other . . . the unknown!

LADY. Come—give me your hand, my friend—then I shall lead you to the doctor . . . for you are ill. . . . Come!

STRANGER. Perhaps I am. But first—tell me one thing. . . . Is this a carnival—or what is it? Is it—as it should be?

LADY. It is no doubt as it should be . . . nothing wrong with these people. . . .

STRANGER. But how about that beggar? I have a feeling he is an abominable person. Is it true that he resembles me?

LADY. Well—if you keep on drinking, you will be like him. But now you must go to the post office and get your letter. . . . Then you will come with me.

STRANGER. No, I am not going to the post office. The letter would only contain court proceedings, legal papers, I am sure.

LADY. But suppose it did not?

STRANGER. Even so, it would only be something unpleasant.

LADY. Do as you please. . . . No one escapes his fate. And at this moment I feel as if a higher power were debating our fate and had come to a decision.

STRANGER. You feel that, too! Do you know that just now I heard the sound of the gavel, the chairs pushed back, and process servers sent out. . . . Oh, this anguish! . . . No—I am not coming with you!

LADY. I don't know what you have done to me! . . . In there, in the chapel, I could find no spiritual comfort—a candle went out on the altar—and a chill wind swept across my face . . . and at that moment I heard you call to me.

STRANGER. I did not call—I merely yearned for you. . . .

LADY. You are not the weakling child you make yourself out to be. You have powers that are enormous. I am afraid of you. . . .

STRANGER. When I am alone, I am powerless as a paralytic. But the moment I find a human being to hold on to, I become strong! That is why I attach myself to you!

LADY. Yes, do—then perhaps you can free me from the werewolf!

STRANGER. Is he really a werewolf?

LADY. It's a name I have given him!

STRANGER. Very well! Then I am with you! To battle with trolls and evil spirits—liberate princesses—slay werewolves—that is to live life!

LADY. Come, my liberator! (*She covers her face with her veil. Then she kisses him impulsively on the lips and hastens out.*)

(*The Stranger stands for a moment in astonishment, stunned. The loud sound of women singing in mixed chorus resembling a scream is heard from within the church. The lighted rose window is suddenly darkened. The tree by the bench shakes; the funeral guests arise from their seats, staring at the sky as if they were witnessing something awesome and fearful.*

The Stranger hastens after the Lady.)

SCENE 2. *At the Physician's. A courtyard, enclosed by three houses joined into one. The houses are one-story frame houses with a tiled brick roof. The windows are, throughout, small and of the same appearance and size. On the left, French windows and a veranda. Outside the windows, at right, a hedge of rose bushes, also beehives. In the center of the courtyard, fire logs are piled up in the shape of an oriental cupola. Close by is a well. Rising above the center house is seen the top of a walnut tree. In the corner, at the extreme left, is a gate leading to the garden. Near the well is seen a large turtle. At left, steps leading to the wine cellar below. An icebox; a barrel for refuse. Outside the veranda, tables and chairs.*

SISTER (*comes from the veranda with a telegram*). Today misfortune is coming to this house, Brother.

PHYSICIAN. It would not be the first time, Sister.

SISTER. But this time. . . . Oh! . . . Ingeborg is returning, bringing with her—can you imagine whom? . . .

PHYSICIAN. Wait a moment! Yes, I know—I have long suspected it—and I have waited for the moment anxiously—he is the author I have most admired—whom I have learned from—and always wanted to know. And now you say he is coming here. . . . Where did Ingeborg meet him?

SISTER. In the city, it seems—in her literary circle, I presume.

PHYSICIAN. I have often wondered whether this man could be the same fellow with whom I went to school and who had a name similar to his. I almost wish he were not—for that fellow had something fatalistic about him. . . . and in a generation his fatal tendencies could have grown and intensified.

SISTER. Don't let him come to this house!—Give some excuse —go away—plead a sick call. . . .

PHYSICIAN. No—it would be of no use—we cannot escape our fate. . . .

SISTER. You—who have never been intimidated by anything, you cringe before this phantasm you call fate!

PHYSICIAN. Life has taught me a few things, and I have spent time and strength battling the inevitable. . . .

SISTER. Why do you allow your wife to go gallivanting around, compromising both her and you?

PHYSICIAN. You know why! Because when I released her from her engagement, I held out to her a life of freedom instead of the restraint she was living under. And besides, I could never have loved her if she had submitted to my will or could have been ordered about.

SISTER. And so you are a friend of your enemy. . . .

PHYSICIAN. Now, now!

SISTER. And now you permit her to drag the very man who will be your undoing into your home. Oh, if you knew how boundlessly I hate that man!

PHYSICIAN. I know, I know! His latest book is really horrible. . . . And at the same time it reveals a mental disturbance.

SISTER. That is just why they should have put him in an asylum. . . .

PHYSICIAN. There are those who have suggested it. But I can't see that he has crossed the borderline. . . .

SISTER. That's because you yourself are an eccentric, and because you have a wife who is stark mad.

PHYSICIAN. I won't deny that maniacal persons have always had a powerful fascination for me. . . . And really, you can't say that there is anything shallow or superficial about originality. . . . (*The sound of a steamboat whistle is heard.*) What was that? I heard somebody scream!

SISTER. Your nerves are strained, my brother. . . . It was only the steamboat. And now I plead with you again: Go away!

PHYSICIAN. I am almost tempted to—but I feel as if I were nailed down. . . . Do you know—when I stand here, I can see his portrait in my study—and the sun casts a shadow over it that disfigures his whole body so that he resembles. . . . Why, it's horrible! . . . Do you see whom he resembles?

SISTER. He looks exactly like the devil!—Again I say: Flee!

PHYSICIAN. I can't!

SISTER. But you can at least defend yourself. . . .

PHYSICIAN. I usually do! But this time I feel as if a storm was in the offing. How often haven't I wanted to move, without being able to. It is as if I were standing on a foundation of iron ore and I were a magnetic needle. . . . If misfortune should strike, it would not be of my choosing. . . , I heard someone come in through the entrance gate now. . . .

SISTER. I didn't hear anything.

PHYSICIAN. But I did! And now I see, too! I see my childhood comrade! . . . He once played a prank in school—and I was given the blame for it and was punished. . . . His nickname was Caesar. Why he got that name, I don't know. . . .

SISTER. And this man. . . .

PHYSICIAN. Yes—life is like that!—Caesar!

LADY (entering). How are you, my husband! I am bringing precious company with me.

PHYSICIAN. So I heard. I wish him welcome.

LADY. He is in the guest room. He is changing his collar.

PHYSICIAN. Are you satisfied with your conquest?

LADY. He is undoubtedly the most unhappy human being I have ever met.

PHYSICIAN. That is saying a good deal!

LADY. Yes—and that takes in all of them, for good measure.

PHYSICIAN. I don't doubt that. Sister, will you go out and show him the way?   (The Sister goes out.)

PHYSICIAN. You have had an interesting trip?

LADY. Yes—I have met many unusual persons. . . . Have you had many patients?

PHYSICIAN. No—the waiting room was empty this morning. My practice seems to be on the downgrade.

LADY (in a kindly tone). My poor husband!—Don't you think the fire wood ought to be brought inside soon? It will get wet with damp where it is.

PHYSICIAN (without any sign of reproach in his voice). Why,

of course, it should be. And the bees should be slaughtered, and the fruit in the garden should be picked—but I just can't get things done. . . .

LADY. You are tired, my husband. . . .

PHYSICIAN. Tired of it all, yes.

LADY (*without any bitterness in her voice*). And you have a good-for-nothing wife who is of no help to you!

PHYSICIAN (*with gentleness*). You must not talk like that. Besides, I don't agree with you.

LADY (*looking in the direction of the veranda*). There! (*The Stranger, dressed more youthfully than in Scene 1, comes from the veranda with a forced abandon and nonchalance. He appears to recognize the Physician, shrinks and stumbles forward, but regains his composure.*)

PHYSICIAN. Welcome to my home!

STRANGER. Thank you, Doctor!

PHYSICIAN. You bring good weather with you, which is something we need. . . . It has been raining here for six weeks.

STRANGER. Not seven! Ordinarily it rains for seven weeks following a rain on Deep-sleepers' Day . . . but—come to think of it—we haven't had Deep-sleepers' Day yet. How stupid of me!

PHYSICIAN. To you—who are accustomed to the attractions of big cities—I am afraid life in our simple little community will seem monotonous.

STRANGER. Oh no! I am no more at home here than there. . . . Forgive me if I ask you a rather blunt question. . . . Haven't we seen each other before? When we were young?

PHYSICIAN. Never. (*The Lady has seated herself by the table and busies herself with her needlework.*)

STRANGER. Are you sure?

PHYSICIAN. Absolutely! I have followed your literary career from its very beginning and, I know my wife must have told you, with the greatest interest. If we had known each other earlier, I would certainly have remembered it—at least the name. However, now you see how a country doctor lives. . . .

STRANGER. If you could only imagine how a so-called liberator lived, you would not envy him.

PHYSICIAN. I can well imagine—having seen how people adore being fettered. But perhaps that is the way it *should* be, since that is the way it *is*.

STRANGER (*listening as if to sounds from outside*). That's strange. . . . Who can that be playing in the house next door?

PHYSICIAN. I don't know who it can be. Do you, Ingeborg?

LADY. No. . . .

STRANGER. It's Mendelssohn's funeral march—that forever haunts me. . . . I don't know whether I hear it in my ear, or . . .

PHYSICIAN. Are you subject to hearing things?

STRANGER. No, I don't suffer from hallucinations, but I seem to be annoyed by petty little incidents that keep pursuing me repeatedly. . . . Don't you hear someone playing?

PHYSICIAN *and* LADY. Yes, someone *is* playing. . . .

STRANGER. And it is Mendelssohn, isn't it? . . .

PHYSICIAN. Yes . . . but Mendelssohn is being played a good deal today. He is quite popular. . . .

STRANGER. I know he is—but that this piece should be played here, at this very moment . . . *(He gets up.)*

PHYSICIAN. Just to put you at ease, I shall ask my sister. . . .

(He goes inside the veranda.)

STRANGER *(to the Lady)*. I suffocate here! I won't sleep a wink beneath this roof! Your husband looks like a werewolf . . . and you turn into a pillar of salt as soon as he appears. These premises have seen murder—there are ghosts here—and I am leaving as soon as I can find an excuse.

PHYSICIAN *(returns)*. Why yes, it's the lady from the post office who is playing the piano. . . .

STRANGER *(nervously)*. Good! Then there is nothing to worry about!—You have a unique place here, Doctor. Everything is so unusual. . . . That pile of logs, for instance. . . .

PHYSICIAN. Yes!—Twice it's been struck by lightning. . . .

STRANGER. How ghastly! And still you leave it there?

PHYSICIAN. Yes—for that very reason. . . . And this year I have made it still higher. But there is another reason: It gives shade in the summer. It's my Jonah's gourd. . . . When fall comes, it is stacked away in the woodbin.

STRANGER *(looking around)*. And here you have Christmas roses. . . . Where did you get them? And blooming at this time of the year. . . . Everything seems to be upside down here. . . .

PHYSICIAN. Oh, those. . . . Well, I have a patient staying here as a guest—he is slightly demented. . . .

STRANGER. Here in this house?

PHYSICIAN. Yes, but he is of a quiet nature. He just broods over the futility of life. He thinks it stupid to let the hellebores stand and freeze in the snow, so he puts them away in the cellar and brings them out again in the spring.

STRANGER. You keep an insane man in the house? This is most disagreeable, I must say!

PHYSICIAN. Oh, but he is so gentle.

STRANGER. How did he lose his wits?

PHYSICIAN. Well, answer that, if you can. . . . It is a disease of the mind, not a bodily ill, you understand.

STRANGER. Just one question! Is he here? I mean—close by?

PHYSICIAN. The lunatic? Oh yes, he potters around in the garden, arranging the blooms of Creation. . . . But if his presence is disturbing, we can lock him up in the cellar.

STRANGER. Why aren't such poor devils put out of their misery once for all?

PHYSICIAN. One can never be certain when they are quite ready. . . .

STRANGER. Ready for what?

PHYSICIAN. For the hereafter!

STRANGER. You don't really think that there is such a thing, do you? *(There is a silence.)*

PHYSICIAN. Who knows?

STRANGER. I don't know—but there is something uncanny, something sinister, about this house. . . . Perhaps there are even a few corpses lying about?

PHYSICIAN. Yes, indeed! Here in the icebox I have a couple of stumps I am sending to the medical board. *(He brings out an arm and a bone.)* Here—see!

STRANGER. Heavens! One would think you were Bluebeard himself. . . .

PHYSICIAN *(with a biting voice).* What do you mean by that? *(He gives the Lady a sharp glance.)* Are you implying I do away with my wives?

STRANGER. Why, certainly not! I can see that you don't, can't I?—But you have spooks here, haven't you?

PHYSICIAN. Do we have spooks! Ask my wife! *(The Physician withdraws behind the wood pile, so that he becomes invisible to the Lady and the Stranger.)*

LADY *(to the Stranger).* You might speak a little louder. . . . My husband is hard of hearing. But he can read your lips. . . .

STRANGER. Then let me tell you, while he is out of sight, that a more miserable half hour I have never experienced in my life. Here we have been standing, prattling the most stupid nonsense, because none of us has the courage to say what he really thinks. A moment ago I suffered so frightfully that I almost took out my knife to open my pulse, in order to bring down my blood pressure. . . . But now I feel a burning desire to speak straight out and seal his doom! Shall we tell him straight to his face that we are planning to run away? That we have had enough of his idiotic nonsense?

LADY. If you keep talking like that, I shall hate you. No matter what, one has to behave with decency.

STRANGER. You are a thoroughbred, I must say! *(The Physician appears again in view of the others, who continue their conversation.)* Will you flee with me before the sun sets?

LADY. My dear sir . . .

STRANGER. Tell me why you kissed me yesterday?

LADY. Sir . . .

STRANGER. Just imagine if he should hear what we are saying. . . . He has such an untrustworthy face. . . .

PHYSICIAN. What shall we do to amuse our guest?

LADY. Our guest has no great expectations as far as pleasures are concerned. His life has not been a very happy one.

PHYSICIAN *(blows a whistle. Caesar, the mental patient, appears in the garden. On his brow he wears a laurel wreath, and is otherwise dressed in a strange manner).* Caesar! Come here!

STRANGER *(unpleasantly touched).* Is his name Caesar?

PHYSICIAN. No, it's a nickname I gave him in remembrance of a schoolmate I once had.

STRANGER *(uneasily).* What is the meaning of this? . . .

PHYSICIAN. Well, it has to do with a strange incident—for which I received the blame.

LADY *(to the Stranger).* Have you ever heard of a child being so vile? *(The Stranger looks pained. Caesar enters.)*

PHYSICIAN. Come here and pay your respects to the great author, Caesar.

CAESAR. Is he the Great One?

LADY *(to the Physician).* Why do you have that lunatic come in here? You know it makes our guest uncomfortable.

PHYSICIAN. You must behave and be polite, Caesar, or I'll have to use the whip.

CAESAR. He may be Caesar—but he is not great! He doesn't even know which came first: the hen or the egg. . . . But I know. . . .

STRANGER *(to the Lady).* I am leaving! I don't know whether you have enticed me into a trap, or what to think. . . . In another minute I presume he'll try to amuse me by setting the bees loose. . . .

LADY. No matter how bad things may seem, I ask you to

have complete confidence in me. . . . And don't speak so loudly. . . .

STRANGER. But we shall never be rid of him, the awful were-wolf. . . . Never!

PHYSICIAN (glancing at his watch). I hope you will forgive me, but I must absent myself for about an hour. Have to make a sick call. I hope you won't find the time too long.

STRANGER. I am used to waiting for what never comes. . . .

PHYSICIAN (to Caesar). Caesar, you rascal, come here! I am going to lock you up in the cellar! . . .

(He goes out with Caesar.)

STRANGER (to the Lady). What is this? Who is persecuting me? You assure me that your husband is kindly disposed toward me. I believe he is; and still he never opens his mouth without wounding me. Every word he spoke went through me like an awl . . . and now that funeral march is being played. . . . And I find the Christmas rose here again. . . . Why does everything come back to one—corpses and beggars and lunatics, and human fates and childhood memories. . . . Come away from here! Out! Anywhere! Let me be your liberator—take you away from this hell!

LADY. That is why I brought you here—and also . . . so that no one would be able to say that you had stolen another man's wife. But there is one thing I must ask you! Can I depend upon you?

STRANGER. Are you referring to my feelings? . . .

LADY. We are not speaking of them—we took that part for granted. . . . They last as long as they last. . . .

STRANGER. Then you are talking about my means of support! —Well, I have considerable money outstanding, and I need only write or telegraph. . . .

LADY. Then I can rely on you. . . . Very well! (She places her needlework in her pocket.) Go straight through that gate there—this minute—then follow the lilac hedge, and you'll come to a gate in the fence. Open the gate—and you are on the highway. . . . We will meet in the next village!

STRANGER (hesitates). The gate in the fence does not appeal to me. I would much have preferred to have battled him right here in the courtyard. . . .

LADY (with a gesture). Hurry!

STRANGER. I'd rather you came along with me now!

LADY. That is what I shall do! But I must be the first one to leave. (She turns round and throws a kiss toward the veranda.) My poor werewolf!

ACT II

SCENE 1. *A room in a hotel.*

STRANGER *(with a traveling bag in his hand).* You have no other room, then?

WAITER. Not a single one.

STRANGER. But I will not sleep in this room! . . .

LADY. As long as there is no other room to be had, my friend, and all the other hotels are filled. . . .

STRANGER *(to the Waiter).* Leave us! *(The Waiter leaves. The Lady sinks down in a chair without removing either hat or cloak.)* Is there anything you would like?

LADY. Yes—one thing—that you kill me!

STRANGER. I can well understand! Hunted by the police—chased out of the hotels because of not being married—we finally land in this one—where I least of all wanted to stay! And in this room—number eight. . . . Someone is waging a battle against me—there is someone. . . .

LADY. Are we in number eight?

STRANGER. You have been here before?

LADY. And so have you, haven't you?

STRANGER. Yes.

LADY. Let us get away from here—out in the street—to the woods—anywhere. . . .

STRANGER. Gladly! But I am as tired as you are after this wild chase! Believe it or not, I had a feeling that our path would lead us here. . . . I fought against it and struggled to go in a different direction. . . . But the trains were not on time—we missed our connections—we were doomed to come here—and to this very room. . . . It is the devil himself I am challenging—and this time we shall grapple unto death, he and I.

LADY. I feel as if we were never again going to have peace in this world. . . .

STRANGER. Just think, how familiar everything is here. . . . There is that ever-wilting Christmas rose. . . . Look—do you see? . . . And here is a picture of the Hotel Breuer in Montreux. . . . I have stayed there, too. . . .

LADY. Did you go to the post office?

STRANGER. I knew you would ask me that. . . . Yes, I was there. . . . And in reply to five letters and three telegrams, I found only one telegram—informing me that my publisher was away on a trip for fourteen days.

LADY. Then we are utterly lost. . . .

STRANGER. Not far from it!

LADY. And in five minutes the waiter will be here to inspect our passports. . . . And then the proprietor will appear, demanding that we leave. . . .

STRANGER. And then there will be only one way out for us. . . .

LADY. Two!

STRANGER. But the second choice is impossible.

LADY. What is the second choice?

STRANGER. To go to your parents in the country.

LADY. You are reading my thoughts. . . .

STRANGER. We can have no secrets from each other from now on.

LADY. And so our long dream is at an end.

STRANGER. Perhaps. . . .

LADY. You must send another telegram!

STRANGER. I ought to do it, yes—but I find myself unable to move. . . . I have no faith any longer in anything I do. . . . Someone has paralyzed me.

LADY. And me, too!—We decided not to speak about the past . . . yet we keep dragging it along with us. Look at the wallpaper here—can you see the portrait that the flowers have shaped?

STRANGER. Yes—it's he—he is everywhere—everywhere! How many hundred times. . . . But I see someone else's face in the pattern of the tablecloth there. . . . Do these things come about naturally? No—they are mere illusions. . . . I expect at any moment to hear my funeral march—and when I hear that, the picture will be complete! *(He listens.)* There it is!

LADY. I don't hear anything. . . .

STRANGER. Then—I am—on the way to . . .

LADY. Shall we go to my home?

STRANGER. The last hope—and the worst! To come as adventurers, beggars!—No, that I could never do. . . .

LADY. It is really . . . no, that would be too much! To come with shame and disgrace, to bring sorrow to the old people . . . and to see you placed in a humiliating position— as you will see me humiliated. . . . We would never be able to have any regard for each other after that.

STRANGER. You are right. It would be worse than death. But can you imagine—I feel it approaching—inevitably approaching . . . and I am beginning to long for the moment—to pass through the ordeal—the sooner the better—since it must come. . . .

LADY *(takes out her needlework).* But I have no desire to be insulted in your presence. . . . There must be some other way out of it. If we were only married! And that shouldn't take long, for my marriage is actually invalid—according to the laws of the country where we were married. . . . All we need to do is go back there and be wedded by the same clergyman who . . . Oh, but that would be humiliating for you. . . .

STRANGER. That fits in perfectly with all the rest . . . since this wedding trip is turning out to be a pilgrimage—or a trial by fire. . . .

LADY. You are right—and in five minutes the proprietor will be here to drive us out! Therefore—and in order to put an end to all these humiliations—we have only one choice: We must swallow this last humiliation. . . . Ssh! I hear someone coming. . . .

STRANGER. I can feel it—and I am prepared. . . . After all this, I am prepared for anything! Even if I can't fight against the invisible One, I will show you how much I can endure. . . . Pawn your jewels, and I'll redeem them as soon as my publisher returns—unless he has drowned while swimming, or been killed in a train collision. . . . If one is ambitious for honor as I am, one must be prepared to offer one's honor first of all!

LADY. Since we are now agreed, don't you think it would be better if we left this place of our own free will? . . . O God! He is coming—the proprietor!

STRANGER. Let us go! . . . Running the gauntlet between waiters, chambermaids, bootblacks, and porters—blushing with shame and turning pale from anger. . . . The beasts of the forest can hide in their lairs—but we are forced to exhibit our shame. . . . Cover your face with your veil, at least!

LADY. This is freedom!

STRANGER. And here you see the liberator!   *(They leave.)*

SCENE 2. *By the sea. A cottage at the top of a mountain crest by the seashore. Tables and chairs outside. The Stranger and the Lady, dressed in light colors appear more youthful than in the preceding scene. The Lady is crocheting.*

STRANGER. After three days of tranquillity and bliss by the side of my wife, the old anxiety and restlessness are back again. . . .

LADY. What is it you fear?

STRANGER. I have a fear that this will not last!

LADY. What makes you think so?

STRANGER. I don't know. . . . I just can't help feeling it will come to an end—suddenly—horribly! There seems to be something unreal about even the sunshine and the calm wind. . . . I have a feeling that happiness will never be my fate in life.

LADY. But everything has been adjusted, hasn't it? My parents have shown patience and understanding, my husband has written in a spirit of friendliness and understanding. . . .

STRANGER. What good does that do? How can it possibly help? . . . Fate spins its intrigues—I can again hear the gavel fall and the chairs pushed back from the table—the judgment has been pronounced. . . . But it must have been made before I was born—for already in my youth I began to serve my punishment. . . . There is not a single thing in my life that I can look back on with a feeling of joy. . . .

LADY. And yet you have been given everything you wished from life, you poor man. . . .

STRANGER. Everything! The only thing I forgot to ask for was riches.

LADY. Now you are harping on that again!

STRANGER. Do you wonder at that?

LADY. Hush!

STRANGER. What is it you are crocheting? Like one of the three Fates of old, you sit passing the yarn between your fingers. . . . But don't stop. . . . The most beautiful thing I know is a woman busy with her work or her child. What is it you are crocheting?

LADY. It is . . . it is nothing but a piece of needlework. . . .

STRANGER. It looks like a network of knots and nerves, in which your thoughts are being woven. I imagine that is how the inside of your brain looks. . . .

LADY. I only wish I possessed half as much as you seem to think I have! But my mental power is nil.

STRANGER. Perhaps that is why I feel so at home with you—feel that you are perfection—and therefore cannot think of life without you!—Now the cloud has disappeared! Now the sky is clear again, the air is mild. . . . Can't you feel it stroking your cheek? This is what I call living—yes, now I am living—in this very moment! And I can feel my ego swell—stretch itself—become rarefied—and take on infinity. . . . I am everywhere; in the sea, which is my blood—in the mountain ridge, which is my skeleton—in the trees—in the flowers . . . and my head reaches up into the heavens—I can look out over the universe, which is I—and I sense the full power of the Creator within me—*I am the Creator!* I feel an urge to take the whole giant mass in my hand and knead it over into something more perfect, more lasting, more beautiful. . . . I would like to see the whole of Creation and all creatures of mankind imbued with happiness . . . to be born without pain, to live without sorrow, to die in peaceful joy!—Eve, will you die with me— now—this very instant . . . for in another moment we shall again be racked by pain. . . .

LADY. No—I am not ready to die yet!

STRANGER. Why?

LADY. I feel I still have something to do here. I may not have suffered sufficiently yet. . . .

STRANGER. Then you think we are put here on earth to suffer?

LADY. So it seems! . . . But now I want to ask you to do me one favor. . . .

STRANGER. And that is . . .

LADY. Do not profane Heaven—as you did a moment ago. And do not liken yourself to the Creator . . . for when you do that, you remind me of Caesar at home. . . .

STRANGER (*agitated*). Of Caesar! How can you know . . . how can you say such a thing?

LADY. Did I say something to offend you? If I did, I didn't mean to! It was a stupid remark that just fell from my lips. . . . I shouldn't have said "at home." . . . Forgive me!

STRANGER. You were thinking of the blasphemies? And in your opinion they identify me with—with Caesar?

LADY. I was thinking only of them. . . .

STRANGER. Strange—I believe what you say—that you had no thought of offending me. . . . Yet, despite that, you do offend me . . . you, like all the rest, with whom I come in contact. Why is that?

LADY. It's because you are hypersensitive. . . .

STRANGER. There you are again! Do you mean that I possess some secret, vulnerable weakness?

LADY. No—I swear by all that's holy I did not mean that!— Oh, now the spirits of dissension and suspicion have come between us! Drive them away! Before it is too late!

STRANGER. You have no cause to say that I blaspheme because I adhere to the ancient maxim: Behold, we are gods!

LADY. If that were true, why can't you come to your own rescue—rescue us both?

STRANGER. You think I can't? Wait! So far we have seen only the beginning. . . .

LADY. If the end is to be like the beginning, then Heaven help us!

STRANGER. I know what you are afraid of—I had a happy surprise in store for you. . . . I wasn't going to tell you just yet. . . . But now I don't want to torment you any longer. *(He produces an unopened registered letter.)* Here—you see. . . .

LADY. The money has come!

STRANGER. This morning!—Who can destroy me now?

LADY. Don't speak like that! You know who can destroy us!

STRANGER. Whom do you mean?

LADY. He who punishes the arrogance of men!

STRANGER. And the courage of men! Especially their courage! This was forever my Achilles heel! I have steadfastly borne everything—except this fatal lack of money—which always strikes me when most in need.

LADY. Forgive me for asking, but how much did you receive?

STRANGER. I don't know—I haven't opened the letter yet. But I know approximately what I have coming to me. Let me look and see! *(He opens the letter.)* What is this? No money—only a royalty statement—informing me that no money is due me. . . . Can this be right?

LADY. I begin to think it is . . . as you say. . . .

STRANGER. That I am a doomed soul, yes! But I catch the curse with two fingers and fling it back on the magnanimous giver *(Flinging the letter in the air.)* . . . followed by my curse!

LADY. Don't, don't! I am afraid of you!

STRANGER. Be afraid—but you must not despise me. . . . The gauntlet has been thrown, and now you shall see grappling between giants! *(Unbuttoning his coat and waistcoat, with a challenging glance at the sky.)* Now—come! Strike me with your lightning and your thunder, if you dare! Frighten me with your storm, if you have the power!

LADY. No—not that! No!

STRANGER. Yes—just that! Who dares disturb me in my dream of love? Who snatches the cup from my lips and the woman from my arms? The envious, be they gods or devils! Paltry bourgeois saints—who parry a sword thrust with pin pricks from behind . . . who don't meet you face to face but retaliate with an unpaid bill, sent by way of the kitchen door— in order to humiliate the master of the house before his servants. . . . No striking down—no thrust of blade—but put to

scorn, derided and mocked. . . . For shame, you mighty powers, you great dominions, you empires! For shame!

LADY. I pray that Heaven will not punish you. . . .

STRANGER. The heavens are still just as blue and silent—the
sea just as blue and still. . . . Quiet! I feel a poetic inspiration. . . . That is what I call it, when an idea comes to life
in my brain. . . . I hear the rhythm first—this time it comes
like horses at a trot—with the clinking of spurs—the clanging
of arms . . . but there is a flapping, too—like the lashing of
sails . . . it is the flags and banners. . . .

LADY. It is only the wind! You hear it moaning in the
treetops. . . .

STRANGER. Hush! Now they are riding over a bridge—it is
a wooden bridge—and there is no water in the river—nothing
but stones and pebbles. . . . Wait! Now I can hear the rosary
being recited by men and women—the "Ave Maria" . . . and
now I see—can you imagine *where* I see it—in your needlework:
a huge, white kitchen, with calcimined walls—it has three small,
grated windows, with potted flowers on the deep window
sill. . . . In the right corner stands the stove—in the left corner
the dining table, with benches of pine—and on the wall by the
table hangs a black crucifix—underneath burns a lamp—and the
ceiling has soot-brown beams. . . . On the walls are also hung
some twigs of mistletoe—they are beginning to wither. . . .

LADY *(alarmed)*. Where do you see all this—where?

STRANGER. In your needlework. . . .

LADY. Do you see any people there?

STRANGER. I see an elderly, a very old man. . . . He is seated
at the table and has a game bag beside him. . . . His hands
are clasped in prayer—and kneeling on the floor is an elderly
woman. . . . Now I can hear again—as from out beyond—
from outside a veranda—the "Ave Maria." . . . But the two in
the kitchen look as if they were made of white wax or honey
. . . and the scene is as if covered by a veil. . . . Oh no, this
is no figment of the imagination! *(He awakens from his
dreams.)* This is something else!

LADY. It is as real as it can be! It is the kitchen in my parents' home, where you have never been. . . . The old man
you saw was my grandfather, the forester, and the woman was
my mother. . . . She was praying for us! It is now six o'clock—
the hour that the rosary is recited by the servants out on the
porch. . . .

STRANGER. This is awesome! I am beginning to have visions.
. . . But what a beautiful thing to see—this room—so snowy

white—and flowers and mistletoe. . . . But why are they praying for us?

LADY. Yes—why? Have we done something wrong?

STRANGER. What—is—wrong?

LADY. I have read that there is no such thing; nevertheless
. . . I have a boundless longing to see my mother—but not my
father, for he has disowned me—just as he cast aside my
mother. . . .

STRANGER. Why did he abandon your mother? . . .

LADY. Who knows? The children least of all.—But let us go
to my home—I have an irrepressible longing. . . .

STRANGER. Lion dens and snake pits—one more or less matters little. I shall go with you—for your sake . . . but not like
the prodigal son—no, no. . . . You will see that for your sake
I can go through fire and water. . . .

LADY. Are you so certain?

STRANGER. I can generally divine. . . .

LADY. Do you also divine that the road is very hard? The
old people live in the mountains where no carriage can pass.

STRANGER. It sounds like a fairy tale—yet I seem to have read
or dreamed something akin to it. . . .

LADY. It is possible; but all that you will see is quite natural
and real. A little out of the ordinary, perhaps—even the people
are not ordinary people. . . . Are you prepared to come with
me?

STRANGER. Entirely prepared—for whatever may happen!

LADY (*kisses him on the forehead and makes the sign of the
cross, simply, humbly and without affectation*). Come!

SCENE 3. *On the highway. A hilly landscape. A chapel on a
hilltop at the extreme left. The highway winds its way toward the rear, its sides lined with fruit trees. Between the
trees are seen shrines, miniature expiation chapels, and
crosses in commemoration of some accident or disaster. In
the foreground there is a signpost with the following notice
attached to it: "Begging Forbidden in This Community."*

LADY. You are tired, my poor husband. . . .

STRANGER. I won't deny it. But I feel it a disgrace to be
hungry because my money has come to an end. I never thought
that would happen to me.

LADY. It seems to me as if we really had to be prepared for
anything. We have fallen out of grace, I think. Do you see that
the leather of my boot has cracked? I am ready to weep—having
to drag along like this—and looking like beggars.

STRANGER (*points to the signpost*). And begging is forbidden in this community. But just why must it be posted here in huge letters?

LADY. That sign has been there as long as I can remember. Can you imagine that I haven't been here since I was a child? At that age, the way seemed short. The hills over there seemed not so high, the trees were smaller, and the birds were always singing, it seemed to me.

STRANGER. The birds sang to you the year round! Oh, you child! Now they sing only in the spring . . . and we are approaching fall. . . . But as a child you danced along this endless Calvary road, plucking flowers at the foot of the crosses. . . . *(In the distance is heard the sound of a hunting horn.)* What is that?

LADY. Oh, that—that is Grandfather returning from the hunt. My dear, dear old grandfather! Let us hurry on so that we reach home before it gets dark.

STRANGER. Are we still far from your home?

LADY. Not very. We have only the mountains—and then the river—to cross.

STRANGER. Then it is the river I hear?

LADY. Yes—it is the great water near which I was born and raised. I was eighteen years old before I came over to this shore—to see what existed in faraway lands. . . . Now I have seen it. . . .

STRANGER. You are weeping. . . .

LADY. Oh, my dear old grandfather. . . . When I was about to step into the boat, he said: Beyond lies the world, my child. When you have seen enough of it, return to your mountains. . . . The mountains know how to keep a secret. Well—I have seen enough! Enough!

STRANGER. Let us go! The road is long, and it is getting dark. . . .   *(They pick up their traveling effects and leave.)*

SCENE 4. *A narrow entrance to a mountain pass between steep crags and precipices. A wood of spruce crowns the mountainous landscape. In the foreground is seen a shelter, or shed. A broom leans against the door, a buck horn hanging from the handle. On the right there is a smithy; the door stands open, emitting a red glare. On the left stands a flour mill.*

In the rear, the mountain pass with a mill brook and footbridge. The mountain formations resemble profiles of giants.

When the curtain rises, the Smith is seen in the doorway of the smithy. The Miller's Wife stands in the doorway of the mill. As the Lady enters, they gesticulate to each other and disappear hastily, each one in a different direction. The Lady's and the Stranger's clothes are torn and disheveled. The Lady enters. She walks toward the smithy, and is followed by the Stranger.

STRANGER. They are hiding—probably because of us.

LADY. I don't think so.

STRANGER. How strange nature is here—as though it had all been created to excite awe. Why are the broom and the horn of anointment standing there? Probably because it is their customary place—yet it makes me think of witches. . . . Why is the smithy black and the mill white? Because the one is sooty and the other one mealy. . . . When I saw the blacksmith standing in the glimmer of the fire, facing the white woman by the mill, I thought of an old poem. . . . But do you see the giants up there? . . . No—I can't endure this any longer. . . . Don't you see your werewolf, from whose clutches I saved you? . . . Why—it's his profile!—Look—there!

LADY. So it is, yes . . . but it's of stone. . . .

STRANGER. It is of stone—and yet it is he!

LADY. Spare me from having to say why we see him!

STRANGER. You mean—our conscience, which comes to life when we have not had enough to eat and when we are worn out from fatigue—but goes to sleep when we are well fed and rested. . . . Isn't it a curse that we have to come to your home like a couple of wretched beggars? Don't you see how torn and tattered we are after the journey in the mountain between the hawthorn bushes? . . . I have a feeling that someone is waging war on me. . . .

LADY. Isn't it you who are the challenger?

STRANGER. Yes—I am aching for a battle in the open! I don't want a contest with unpaid bills and an empty purse. Even if I did—here goes my last farthing. . . . May the water-sprites take it—if there are such things. . . . *(He flings a coin into the brook.)*

LADY. God help us! We were to have used it to take the boat across the river! Now we shall have to speak about money the moment we enter my home. . . .

STRANGER. Has there ever been a time when we talked about anything else?

LADY. No doubt because you always had contempt for money. . . .

STRANGER. As for everything else. . . .

LADY. But not everything is to be disdained. . . . There are good things in life, too. . . .

STRANGER. I have never met with them. . . .

LADY. Come with me, and you shall see. . . .

STRANGER. I will—come. (*He hesitates when he is about to pass the smithy.*)

LADY (*who has preceded him*). Are you afraid of the flames and the fire?

STRANGER. No—but . . .

(*The hunting horn is again heard in the distance. He rushes past the smithy and follows her.*)

SCENE 5. *A roomy kitchen with white calcimined walls. In the left corner are three windows: two in the rear, one in the left wall. The windows are small, with deep niches in which are placed potted flowers. The ceiling is sooted brown; the beams are visible. In the right corner, a large kitchen range with cooking utensils of copper, tin, and iron, wooden jugs and pots and pans. On the wall, in the left corner, hang a crucifix and a vigil light; underneath is a square table with built-in benches. Here and there are hung twigs of mistletoe. There is a door in the rear wall. Beyond is seen the poorhouse, and through the rear windows, the church. There is a sleeping place for dogs by the kitchen range; also a table for beggars.*

The Old Man sits at the table, beneath the crucifix, with clasped hands. In front of him lies a game bag. He is in his early eighties, has white hair and beard, and is powerfully built. He is dressed in the uniform of a chief forester. The Mother is kneeling in the center of the floor. She is about fifty. Her hair is gray, and she is dressed in black, with touches of white.

From outside can plainly be heard the last words of the "Ave Maria": "Holy Mary, Mother of God, pray for us sinners now and at the hour of our death. Amen." The words are spoken in unison by men, women, and children.

OLD MAN *and* MOTHER. Amen!

MOTHER. And now I must tell you something, Father. . . . Two vagrants have been seen down by the river. They were tattered and unkempt and looked as if they had been drenched. When the ferryman came to collect the fare on the boat, they didn't have a single farthing in their pockets. . . . They are now sitting in the waiting room at the ferry station drying their clothes. . . .

OLD MAN. Let them sit there!

MOTHER. You must never refuse to take a beggar into your house. . . . A beggar may turn out to be an angel!

OLD MAN. You are right!—Let them come. . . .

MOTHER. I'll put some food for them here on the beggars' table, if it won't disturb you. . . .

OLD MAN. Not in the least!

MOTHER. Shall I let them have some of the apple juice?

OLD MAN. Yes, give them some. And have a fire ready for them, too, if they should be frozen.

MOTHER. It is a little late to start a fire—but if you wish it, Father. . . .

OLD MAN (looks out through the window). Oh yes—start a fire. . . .

MOTHER. What are you looking at, Father?

OLD MAN. I am watching the river . . . it is rising. . . . And I am wondering—as I have wondered for seventy-five years now—when shall I ever see the ocean. . . .

MOTHER. You are in a sad mood tonight, Father, aren't you?

OLD MAN . . . et introibo ad altare Dei: ad Deum qui laetificat juventutem meam. Yes, I am sad. . . . Deus, Deus meus: quare tristis es anima mea, et quare conturbas me.

MOTHER. Spera in Deo. . . .

(The Maid enters. She gives a sign to the Mother, who goes to her. They whisper. The Maid goes out.)

OLD MAN. I heard what you said! . . . Oh, my God! I must bear even this!

MOTHER. You don't have to meet them—you can go upstairs to your room. . . .

OLD MAN. No—I shall accept it as a penitence. But why do they come like this—like a couple of vagrants?

MOTHER. They probably lost their way and met with some mishap. . . . Do you think that . . .

OLD MAN. But that she would bring her—her man with her here—that is nothing short of indecent. . . .

MOTHER. You know how strange Ingeborg is. . . . She thinks that whatever she does is proper, not to say right and correct. Have you ever seen her ashamed of anything she ever did—or seen her hurt or offended by a reprimand? I never have. Yet she is really not immodest. On the contrary. No matter what she does or says—it may be ever so lacking in what you and I consider good taste—it seems appropriate to her.

OLD MAN. Yes, and I have often been surprised that I can't be angry with her. . . . She always feels as if she had no responsibility for anything. She doesn't even feel the sting of an offending remark. One would almost think she was lacking in self-consciousness—or that she had a dual nature: one doing everything that was bad, and the other one giving absolution. . . . But as for this man—there is no one I have ever detested from afar as I have him! He sees nothing but evil in the world —and I have never heard so many bad things said about anyone as I have of him!

MOTHER. What you say is quite true, Father. . . . But isn't it possible that Ingeborg may have some special mission in this man's life—and he in hers? Could it be that they must torment each other until they obtain salvation? . . .

OLD MAN. It may be as you say—nevertheless it goes against me to be an accomplice in an act that to me seems disgraceful. . . . And to have this man under my roof! But I have to bear it—as I have to bear all else that my sins have brought on me. . . .

MOTHER. In God's name, then. . . . *(The Lady and the Stranger enter.)* Welcome home!

LADY. Thank you, Mother! *(She approaches the two. The Old Man rises. He regards the Stranger.)* God's peace to you, Grandfather! This is my husband. Give him your hand.

OLD MAN. I want to take a look at him first. *(He approaches the Stranger, places his hands on his shoulders, and looks him straight in the eyes.)* With what intentions do you enter this house?

STRANGER *(with simplicity)*. My intentions are none other than to keep my wife company—and at her earnest and urgent request.

OLD MAN. If what you say is true, you are welcome! I have behind me a long and stormy life. Here in the loneliness I have at last found a certain peace. I beg of you not to disturb that peace. . . .

STRANGER. I have not come to ask for favors; and when I leave I shall take nothing with me. . . .

OLD MAN. Your answer does not please me. . . . We all need each other—perhaps even I shall need you—we never know about such things, young man.

LADY. Grandfather!

OLD MAN. Yes, my child! Happiness I cannot wish you, for it does not exist. . . . But strength to bear your fate—that I wish you. Now I shall leave you for a few moments—your mother will see to your needs. . . .   *(He goes out.)*

LADY *(to the Mother)*. Is the table set for *us*, Mother?

MOTHER. You mean the beggars' table? No, that—you must know—was a misunderstanding, of course. . . .

LADY. Well—we look rather miserable after having taken the wrong road through the mountains. . . . And if Grandfather hadn't signaled with his hunting horn. . . .

MOTHER. Grandfather has long ago stopped going hunting. . . .

LADY. Then it must have been someone else who blew. . . . But now, Mother, I am going up to the Rose Chamber and put things in order. . . .

MOTHER. Yes, do that, my child. I'll be up soon. (*The Lady seems about to say something, but hesitates; she leaves.*)

STRANGER (*to the Mother*). I have seen this room before. . . .

MOTHER. And I have seen you before. . . . I have almost been expecting you. . . .

STRANGER. As one expects a misfortune. . . .

MOTHER. Why do you say that?

STRANGER. Because I usually bring disaster with me. But as I have to be somewhere, and can't change my fate, I have no scruples. . . .

MOTHER. In that respect you are like my daughter. . . . She has neither scruples nor conscience.

STRANGER. What do you mean?

MOTHER. Don't think I mean anything bad! How could I say anything bad about my own child? It was only because I took it for granted that you, too, were sensible of her characteristics that I made the comparison.

STRANGER. I have never noticed that Eve possesses the characteristics you ascribe to her. . . .

MOTHER. Why do you call Ingeborg Eve?

STRANGER. By giving her a name of my own invention, I made her mine—just as I intend to remold her according to my desires. . . .

MOTHER. In your image, you mean! (*She smiles.*) I have heard it said that the wizards among the peasants carve an effigy of the one they try to bewitch. And then they baptize it with the name of the person they are trying to destroy. It is in the same manner you have figured out that you, through the Eve of your own creation, will destroy her whole sex.

STRANGER (*regards the Mother with astonishment*). Well, I'll be damned! Forgive me! You are my mother-in-law—but you are also deeply religious: how can you harbor such thoughts?

MOTHER. They are your thoughts.

STRANGER. This is beginning to be interesting! I had been

under the impression I was to encounter an idyl in the loneliness of a forest . . . and—I find myself in a witch's
kitchen. . . .

MOTHER. Not precisely—but you forget—or you didn't know
—that I am a woman who was infamously abandoned by a man
. . . and that you are a man who shamelessly abandoned a
woman.

STRANGER. You certainly speak plainly—straight out: and now
I know where I am.

MOTHER. And now I would like to know where I stand: can
you take care of two families?

STRANGER. Yes—if things go as they should. . . .

MOTHER. Things don't always go the way you wish them to
go here in life—money can dwindle and be lost. . . .

STRANGER. My talent is a capital that is not likely to be
lost. . . .

MOTHER. I must say that sounds strange! Haven't some of
the greatest talents suddenly ceased to exist—or dwindled little
by little?

STRANGER. Never in my life have I met a man or a woman
who could so rob one of courage. . . .

MOTHER. Your arrogance must be subjugated! Your latest
book was a step backward. . . .

STRANGER. You have read that one, too?

MOTHER. Yes—and that is why I know all your secrets. So
it's no use trying to do any acting. If you keep that in mind,
you'll be well received. And now to a little matter that casts
an unfortunate reflection on this house: Why did you not pay
the ferryman?

STRANGER. Now you have touched my Achilles' heel!—I'll
explain why. . . . I threw away my last coin. . . . But is
there nothing you can speak about in this house except money?

MOTHER. Indeed there is . . . but in this house we have,
first of all, the habit of living up to our duties, and afterwards
we can amuse ourselves.—I can only conclude, then, that you
have traveled here by foot for lack of money.

STRANGER. Y-e-s!

MOTHER. And perhaps you haven't eaten anything either?

STRANGER. N-o-o!

MOTHER. Listen to me! You are nothing but a boy, a reckless
scamp. . . .

STRANGER. I have had many experiences in my days—but
never before have I been in a situation like this. . . .

MOTHER. I almost feel sorry for you. And I would be inclined to laugh at your pitiful predicament, if I didn't know that you will be shedding tears before long—and not only you, but some others. But now that you have had your way, hold on to her who loves you. For if you abandon her—well, then you shall never be happy again . . . and you will soon forget what real happiness is. . . .

STRANGER. Is this a threat?

MOTHER. No—a warning. . . . Go and eat your supper now. . . .

STRANGER (*pointing to the beggars' table*). At this table here?

MOTHER. This mean trick is a prank of your own doing. But it can turn out to be stark seriousness. Such things have happened before.

STRANGER. I believe there is no limit to what may happen now—for this is the worst that has happened to me yet. . . .

MOTHER. Oh no! It could be much worse. . . . Just wait and see!

STRANGER (*depressed*). Yes—now I can expect anything. . . .

(*He goes out.*)

(*The Mother is alone. Soon after, the Old Man enters.*)

OLD MAN. Well—it didn't turn out to be an angel, did it?

MOTHER. At any rate, no angel of light!

OLD MAN. No, that he is not!—You know how superstitious the people here are. Well, when I went down to the river, I overheard some of them talking. One man said that his horse had shied at the sight of "him"; another one that his dogs had made such a racket that he had to tie them up; the ferryman swore that the ferry lightened the moment he boarded it. . . . All this is, of course, mere superstition—yet . . . yet . . .

MOTHER. Yet . . .

OLD MAN. Well . . . it was only that I saw a magpie fly in through the window—the closed window—through the glass pane in their room. But perhaps I didn't see right. . . .

MOTHER. Probably—but why does one see wrong sometimes—and in the right place. . . .

OLD MAN. The mere presence of this man makes me ill. And I get a pain in the chest when he looks at me.

MOTHER. We must try to get him to leave—though I am almost certain he will not feel at home here for very long.

OLD MAN. I, too, have a feeling he won't remain here very long. . . . You see—I received a letter this evening, warning me about this man. Among other things—he is being sought by court officers. . . .

MOTHER. Court officers? Here in your house?

OLD MAN. Yes . . . financial matters. . . . But I beg you . . . the laws of hospitality—even toward a beggar . . . or even an enemy—are sacred. Leave him in peace for a few days until he has recovered after this wild chase. . . . You can plainly see that Providence has caught up with him, and that his soul has to be ground to grist in the mill before he is put through the sieve. . . .

MOTHER. I already feel an irresistible call to act as an instrument of Providence in his case. . . .

OLD MAN. But take care that you do not confuse a revengeful spirit with a call from on high. . . .

MOTHER. I shall try to—if I can. . . .

OLD MAN. Good night now!

MOTHER. Do you think that Ingeborg has read his latest book?

OLD MAN. I have no idea! It doesn't seem probable. How could she possibly have become attached to a man who holds such opinions? . . .

MOTHER. You are right! She hasn't read it—but now she is going to. . . .

ACT III

SCENE 1. *In the Rose Chamber, a plain room, furnished tastefully and in a homelike manner, at the Forester's. The walls are plastered a rosy red; the curtains are of the same shade and of thin muslin. In the small, grated windows are potted flowers on the sill. On the left, a writing table and a bookcase. On the right, an ottoman, over which is hung a canopy, in the same shade as the curtains at the windows. Chairs and tables in antique German style. There is a door, rear. Outside is seen a landscape with the poorhouse, a dreary, dilapidated building with black window holes without curtains. The sun is shining brightly.*

The Lady is seated on the ottoman, crocheting. The Mother is standing before her, a book with red covers in her hand.

MOTHER. You will not read your own husband's book?

LADY. No—not that book! I have given him my promise not to:

MOTHER. You do not care to know the man to whom you have entrusted your fate?

LADY. No! What good will it do? We are satisfied the way we have it.

MOTHER. You don't demand much of life, do you?

LADY. What would be the use? Our demands are never fulfilled anyhow.

MOTHER. I don't know whether you were born with all the wisdom of the universe—or whether you are merely innocent, or foolish.

LADY. Well, I know little or nothing about myself. . . .

MOTHER. As long as the sun shines and you have enough to eat for the day, you are satisfied.

LADY. Yes! And if the sun doesn't shine, I say to myself: Well, I suppose that's the way it's meant to be. . . .

MOTHER. Now . . . let us speak about something else. Do you know that your husband is being harried by court officers for some kind of financial obligation?

LADY. Yes, I know that . . . but so are all poets. . . .

MOTHER. Tell me!—Is your husband a lunatic or a rogue?

LADY. Oh—now, Mother! He is neither, of course! He is a little eccentric; and there is one thing I find rather tiresome: I can never mention anything that he doesn't already know. As a consequence we say very little to each other—but he is happy merely to have me near him . . . and I feel the same way about him!

MOTHER. So! You have already come to a deadlock! Then you are not far from the rapids. But don't you think you will have something to talk about when you have read what he has written?

LADY. Perhaps! Leave the book here, if you like. . . .

MOTHER. Take it—and hide it! It will be a surprise to him to hear you recite something from his masterwork.

LADY (*hiding the book in her pocket*). He is coming! It is almost as if he could hear at a distance when he is being spoken of. . . .

MOTHER. If he could only *feel* at a distance when others suffer for his sake. . . . (*She goes out.*)

(*The Lady is alone for a moment. She reads here and there in the book and is taken aback. She hides it again in her pocket.*)

STRANGER (*entering*). Your mother was here just now. You spoke about me, of course. I still seem to hear the vibration of her angry words. I can feel their lashing in the air—I can see them darken the sun rays—I seem to notice the impression of her body in the atmosphere of this room—and she has left an odor after her as of a dead snake.

LADY. Oh, how nervous and excited you are today!

STRANGER. Frightfully nervous! Some bungler has tuned over my nerves and put them out of tune—and now he is playing on them with a bow of horsehair, bringing forth a squeak like the clucking of a partridge. . . . You have no idea what it is like. . . . Here is someone who is stronger than I am—someone who pursues me with a searchlight, taking aim at me wherever I go. Tell me—do people use magic in these parts of the land?

LADY. Don't turn your back to the sunshine . . . look at the lovely landscape, and it will calm you.

STRANGER. No—I can't bear to look at the poorhouse out there—it seems to be built especially for me. And there is a crazy female over there, who is forever waving in this direction. . . .

LADY. Do you feel you are being treated badly here?

STRANGER. I wouldn't say that exactly—no! But I am being glutted with delicacies as if I were being readied for slaughter; yet nothing seems to have any taste—because it is being offered grudgingly—and I can feel the hate like an icy cellar exuding a damp cold. Can you imagine, I feel a cold wind everywhere—despite the dead calm and the frightful heat. And that damnable mill—I hear it continually. . . .

LADY. Well—but it isn't grinding now. . . .

STRANGER. Yes—it keeps grinding—grinding. . . .

LADY. But my dear husband. . . . There is no hate here. . . . They may feel compassion—but nothing else. . . .

STRANGER. And then another thing. . . . Why do people cross themselves whenever they see me on the highway? . . .

LADY. That's merely a habit of theirs. They do that when they trudge along on the road reciting their silent prayers. . . . You received a disagreeable letter this morning, didn't you?

STRANGER. Yes—and such a letter! It made the hairs stand up on my head! I felt like spitting my fate in the face! Think of it, I have money being owed to me, but I can't get it. . . . And now I am being harassed by—by my children's guardians, for not contributing to their support. . . . Have you ever seen any human being in such a humiliating predicament? And yet I am without blame. I am in a position to take care of my obligations—want to do the right thing—yet I am hindered

from doing so. Am I then to be blamed, do you think? No—
but the shame—the shame is mine! This is an unnatural state
of things. . . . It is the doings of the devil!

LADY. But why should it be so?

STRANGER. Exactly! There is the rub! Why are we born so
ignorant of laws, customs, conventions, and formalities against
which we breach—from ignorance—and for which we are
scourged? Why do we grow into youths with all sorts of noble
intentions and ideals, which we hope to realize? And why are
we driven into all manner of despicable misery that we abhor
and despise? Why—why?

LADY (*unobserved, has been glancing in the book, absent-
mindedly*). I presume there is some meaning to it, although
we are not aware of it. . . .

STRANGER. If it is intended to make us humble—as they say
it is—then it is not the right way. In my case it only serves to
make me more arrogant. . . . Eve!

LADY. You must not call me by that name!

STRANGER (*startled*). Why not?

LADY. I don't like it. No more than you would like being
called Caesar. . . .

STRANGER. So we are back again where we started. . . .

LADY. Where? What?

STRANGER. Did you have any veiled implication in mind
when you called me by that name?

LADY. Caesar? No—I did not. But now I insist that you tell
me the whole thing.

STRANGER. Very well! May I have the honor of falling by my
own hand: I am Caesar—the schoolboy who perpetrated a
prank for which another boy was given the blame. This other
boy was your husband—the werewolf! That is how fate amuses
itself, twisting, plaiting thongs for eternity. . . . A noble pleasure, eh? (*The Lady hesitates; remains silent.*) Say something!

LADY. I can't!

STRANGER. Say that he turned into a werewolf because of
having lost his faith in a divine justice as a child when he was
innocently punished for another's misdeed. . . . Say *that*—and
then I shall tell you how I suffered tenfold more from remorse
and pangs of conscience . . . and how I came out of the religious crisis, that followed as a consequence, so chastened that
I could never do anything like it again.

LADY. It isn't that! It is not that!

STRANGER. What is it, then?—You mean that you no longer
can have any respect for me?

LADY. That isn't it, either!

STRANGER. Then it is that you want me to acknowledge my shame to you—to humiliate me! If so, everything is over be tween us.

LADY. No!

STRANGER. Eve!

LADY. No, not that—you will only bring to life evil thoughts. . . .

STRANGER. You have broken your promise! You have been reading my book!

LADY. Yes.

STRANGER. That was wicked of you!

LADY. My intention was good—entirely good!

STRANGER (with sarcasm). The result seems to have been tarnished by your good intentions. . . . Now I am blown sky high—and I have supplied the gunpowder myself. To think that everything has to come back to us—everything: childish pranks and villainous misdeeds! That we have to reap evil where we have sown evil—that is fair play. . . . But I only wish I would see a good act rewarded at least once! However, that is something I will never see! He who keeps a record of all his sins and mistakes, small as well as great, is put to shame. . . . And how many of us do it? We human beings may forgive—but the gods never do. . . .

LADY. Don't speak things like that!—Don't! But say that you can forgive!

STRANGER. I am neither mean nor petty, as you well know— but what have I to forgive you?

LADY. Oh—so much! There is so much that I have not the courage to tell you. . . .

STRANGER. Then tell me—and we are rid of it!

LADY. Well—he and I used to read the curse from Deuteronomy over you—you . . . who destroyed his life. . . .

STRANGER. What is this curse?

LADY. It is in the Book of Moses—which the priests chant in unison at the beginning of Lent. . . .

STRANGER. I don't remember it. . . . But what does it matter—one more or less?

LADY. Yes—for in our family there is an old saying that anyone we place a curse on, will be struck down! . . .

STRANGER. I put no faith in such things. . . . But that evil exudes from this house, I have no doubt. May it fall upon their own heads! That is my prayer!

And now—according to the custom of this land—I ought to go out and shoot myself—but I can't do that while I still have duties to fulfill. . . . Imagine, I am not even permitted to die—and thus have lost the last vestige of what I called my religion. . . . How cleverly calculated! I have heard it said that man can wrestle with God, and not without profit. But battling with Satan—that is something not even Job could do!—Shouldn't we talk a little about you now?

LADY. Not yet—a little later perhaps. . . . After becoming acquainted with your terrible book—I have merely glanced through it; only read a few lines here and there—I feel as if I had eaten of the tree of knowledge: My eyes have been opened and now I know what evil is—and what good is!—I didn't before. . . . And now I see how wicked you are! Now I know why you gave me the name of Eve! Yet if sin came into the world through her, the mother of the world, another woman—who was also a mother—brought expiation and atonement into it! If our first mother brought on damnation, blessing came through the other one! Through me you shall not destroy the race. . . . My mission in your life is an entirely different one! We shall see. . . .

STRANGER. So you have eaten of the tree of knowledge. . . . Farewell!

LADY. You are thinking of leaving?

STRANGER. What else can I do? How can I remain here?

LADY. Don't go!

STRANGER. I must—in order to unravel my tangled affairs. I am going to bid good-by to the old people. . . . Then I'll return to you!—And so—for a few moments. . . . (He goes out.)

LADY (remains standing as if turned to stone. Then she advances toward the door and stands gazing outside). Oh—he is gone—he is gone! (She takes refuge within herself and falls on her knees.)

SCENE 2. The asylum. The refectory of an ancient cloister, resembling a simple, white Norman or Romanesque church with round arches. The plastered walls are covered with spots of dampness which have formed into bizarre figures. There are dining tables with bowls. At one end of one of the tables is a stand for the lector. In the rear, a door to the chapel. Lighted candles on the tables. On the wall to the right, a painting, representing Michael slaying Satan.

Seated alone with his bowl at a long table on the right

is the Stranger. He wears the white garb of a hospital pa-
tient. At the table on the left sit the Brownclad Mourners
from Act I; the Beggar; a Woman in Mourning, with two
children; a Woman, resembling the Lady, but who is not
the Lady—and who is knitting instead of eating; a Man, who
resembles the Physician but is not the Physician; Caesar's
Image; the Images of the Old Man and the Mother; the
Image of the Brother; the Parents of the Lost Son; and oth-
ers. All are dressed in white, over which they wear habits of
crepe in different colors. Their faces have a waxen, death-
like pallor. They all look and move like ghosts.

When the curtain rises, all—except the Stranger—are speak-
ing the last words of a paternoster.

STRANGER *(rises, goes over to the Abbess, who is standing by*
the serving table). Mother, let me speak to you a moment.

ABBESS *(in the black-and-white dress of the Augustinian or-*
der). Yes, my son. *(They walk downstage.)*

STRANGER. Let me first ask you where I am.

ABBESS. In the cloister of "Good Help." You were found in
the mountains above the pass—with a cross you had broken off
from the shrine. You were threatening someone you imagined
you saw up in the clouds. You had a fever, and you fell down a
precipice. You were not hurt, but you were delirious. They
brought you here to the hospital, and we put you to bed. You
have been delirious ever since, and you've been complaining
of pain in your hips. But the doctors have been unable to
discover any injury.

STRANGER. What did I say when I was delirious?

ABBESS. The usual fantasies of a sick and fevered mind. . . .
You reproached yourself for all sorts of things and had visions
of your victims, as you called them.

STRANGER. What else?

ABBESS. Well, you talked a great deal about money. You said
you wanted to pay for your keep here in the hospital . . . and
I tried to quiet you by telling you that we don't do things for
money here. . . . What we do, we do for love.

STRANGER. I want no charity—I don't need it!

ABBESS. It is more blessed to give than to receive. . . . But
it requires a great spirit to be able to receive, and to be grateful.

STRANGER. I need nothing, and I ask for nothing. . . . I
have no desire to be coerced into feeling grateful.

ABBESS. Hmm. Hmm.

STRANGER. But will you tell me why none of these people want to sit at the same table with me? They immediately get up, and avoid me. . . .

ABBESS. I presume they are afraid of you.

STRANGER. Why?

ABBESS. You—look—so . . .

STRANGER. I—look—so . . . But that group over there—how do they look? Are they real people?

ABBESS. If you mean real . . . then they present a ghastly reality. That you look at them in a peculiar way might be due to your fever, which is still with you . . . unless there is some other reason.

STRANGER. But I feel as if I knew them all—all of them! It is almost as if I were looking at them in a mirror . . . and as if they were making believe that they are eating. . . . Is this some sort of drama that is being acted out? . . . There I see a couple that look like my parents—in a vague way. . . . I have never had a fear of anything before, because I was indifferent to life—but now I am beginning to be frightened.

ABBESS. If you don't think these people are real, we'll ask the confessor to introduce them to us. . . . (*She gestures to the Confessor, who comes over to them.*)

CONFESSOR (*dressed in the Dominican black-and-white habit*). Sister!

ABBESS. Will you tell this poor suffering man who the people are, sitting at the table there?

CONFESSOR. That won't be difficult. . . .

STRANGER. Allow me to ask you first: Haven't we seen each other before?

CONFESSOR. Yes—I sat at your bedside while you were ill with fever . . . and you asked me to hear your confession. . . .

STRANGER. My confession, did you say?

CONFESSOR. Yes . . . but I was unable to give you absolution because I felt that, in your fever, you did not know what you were saying. . . .

STRANGER. Why?

CONFESSOR. Because there was scarcely a crime or a sin that you did not take upon yourself. . . . And besides, they were of such a horrible nature that the sinner customarily would be required to subject himself to severe penitence before asking for absolution. Now that you have regained your senses, I feel I should ask you whether there was any ground for your self-accusations. . . . (*The Abbess leaves them.*)

STRANGER. Is it your duty to inquire into such things?

CONFESSOR. No—you are right, it is not. . . . However—you wanted to know in whose company you are here. . . . Well, it is not the happiest company. There we have, for example, a lunatic called Caesar. . . . He went insane from reading a certain author, whose notoriety far surpassed his fame. . . . And there we have the Beggar, who refuses to acknowledge that he is a beggar . . . because he has studied Latin, and found freedom! And then there is the Physician—or, as he is commonly called, the werewolf—whose story is well known . . . and then a couple of parents, who worried themselves to death over their depraved son—who had raised his hand against them—who had refused to accompany his father's remains to the graveyard—and who, in a drunken stupor, profaned his mother's grave. . . . Well—that is something he himself will have to answer for! And there sits his poor sister, whom he drove outside into the snowy winter—according to his own statement, with good intentions. . . . There you see an abandoned wife with two children who are unprovided for . . . and there is another—the one who is knitting. So you see, they are all old acquaintances—every one of them. . . . Go over and speak with them. . . .

(During the final part of the Confessor's recitation, the Stranger has turned his back to the assemblage. Now he goes over to the table on the right and sits down, his back still to the company. As he lifts his head, he sees the painting of Michael and he turns his eyes toward the floor. The Confessor goes to the Stranger and places himself behind him. At that moment a Catholic requiem, played on the organ, is heard from the chapel. The Confessor, standing, speaks with the Stranger in a subdued voice, while the music plays softly.)

Quantus tremor est futurus
Quando judex est venturus
Cuncta stricte discussurus,
Tuba mirum spargens sonum
Per sepulchra regionum
Coget omnes ante thronum.
Mors stupebit et natura,
Cum resurget creatura
Judicanti responsura.
Liber scriptus proferetur
In quo totum continetur

Unde mundus judicetur.
Judex ergo cum sedebit
Quidquid latet apparebit
Nil inultum remanebit.
(*The Confessor goes over to the stand at the table, left. He opens his breviary. The music subsides.*)
Let us continue the reading: But it shall come to pass, if you will not hear the voice of the Lord, your God, to keep and to do all his commands and precepts—that all these curses shall come upon you and overtake you.

Cursed shall you be in the city, and cursed shall you be in the field.

Cursed shall be your barn, and cursed your stores.

Cursed shall you be when you come in, and cursed going out!

CONGREGATION (*in subdued voice*). Cursed!

CONFESSOR. The Lord shall send upon you famine and hunger, and a rebuke upon all the works which you shall do: until He consume and destroy you quickly, for your most wicked inventions, by which you have forsaken Him.

CONGREGATION (*aloud*). Cursed!

CONFESSOR. The Lord make you to fall down before your enemies: one way may you go out against them, and flee seven ways, and be scattered throughout all the kingdoms of the earth.

And be your carcass meat for all the fowls of the air, and the beasts of the earth, and be there none to drive them away!

The Lord will smite you with the ulcer of Egypt, and the part of your body, by which the dung is cast out, with the scab, and with the itch: so that you cannot be healed.

The Lord shall strike you with madness and blindness and fury of mind; and you shall grope at midday as the blind are wont to grope in the dark, and not make straight your ways. And you shall at all times suffer wrong, and be oppressed with violence, and you shall have no one to deliver you!

You shall take a wife, and another sleep with her; you shall build a house, and not dwell therein; you shall plant a vineyard and not gather the vintage thereof.

May your sons and daughters be given to another people, your eyes looking on, and languishing at the sight of them all the day, and may there be no strength in your hand. . . .

Neither shall you be quiet, nor shall there be any rest for the sole of your foot; for the Lord will give you a fearful heart, and languishing eyes, and a soul consumed with pensiveness: And your life shall be as it were hanging before you. You shall fear night and day. . . . In the morning you shall say: Who will grant me evening? And at evening: Who will grant me morning? . . . And because you did not serve the Lord your God with joy and gladness of heart, for the abundance of all things:

You shall serve your enemy, whom the Lord will send upon you, in hunger and thirst, and nakedness, and in want of all things: and he shall put an iron yoke upon your neck, till he consume you.

CONGREGATION. Amen!

(The Confessor has read the words speedily and in a loud voice, without any allusion by glance or gesture to the Stranger. All those present—with the exception of the Lady, who has been knitting—have listened and joined in the anathemas without seeming to notice the Stranger, who throughout has sat with his back turned to the Congregation, in quiet contemplation. The Stranger rises and is about to leave. The Confessor goes toward him.)

STRANGER. What was the text you read?

CONFESSOR. It was from Deuteronomy.

STRANGER. Oh, yes. . . . But I seem to recall that there is a blessing in it as well.

CONFESSOR. Yes—for those who keep His commandments.

STRANGER. Oh!—I won't deny that for a moment I felt a little shaken . . . but I don't know whether this is a trial that has to be withstood, or a warning that has to be heeded. . . . However, now I am certain that my fever has taken hold of me again, and I am going to seek a competent physician.

CONFESSOR. Well—but what about the *real* physician?

STRANGER. Yes, of course, of course!

CONFESSOR. He who cures the "beautiful pangs of conscience." . . .

ABBESS. If you should ever be in need of charity, you know where to go. . . .

STRANGER. No—I don't. . . .

ABBESS *(almost inaudibly)*. Well—then I shall tell you! In a rosy red room—by a broad, flowing river. . . .

STRANGER. You are right! In a rosy red room. . . . Let me think—how long have I been lying sick here?

ABBESS. It is exactly three months today. . . .

STRANGER. A quarter of a year! Oh! Have I been sleeping, or where have I been? *(He glances outside through the win-*

dow.) Why, it is already fall. The trees are barren, and the clouds have a frigid look. . . . Now my memory is coming back. . . . Can you hear a mill grinding away? A hunting horn —blowing dulcet tones? A rushing river—a whispering forest— and . . . a woman, who is weeping? Yes—you are right—only *there* is charity! Farewell!   (*He hastens out.*)

CONFESSOR (*to the Abbess*). That lunatic! That lunatic!

SCENE 3. *The Rose Chamber. The curtains have been removed. The windows are gaping like black holes against the darkness outside. The furniture is covered with brown linen covers, and has been placed in the middle of the room. The flowers are gone; a large black parlor stove is lighted. The Mother is busy ironing white curtains by the light of a single candle.*

There is a knock at the door.

MOTHER. Come in!

STRANGER (*entering*). Good evening!—Where is my wife?

MOTHER. It's you!—Where did you come from?

STRANGER. I would say from hell!—But where is my wife?

MOTHER. Which one of them?

STRANGER. You might well ask me that. . . . There is justification for everything—except myself!

MOTHER. There may be good reason for that. That you realize it is a good sign. But where have you been?

STRANGER. I don't know whether it was a poorhouse, a lunatic asylum, or an ordinary hospital—but I would like to think it was all a delirious nightmare. I have been ill—out of my mind —and I can't believe that three months have passed. . . . But where is my wife?

MOTHER. I ought to ask you that same question. When you abandoned her, she left—to search for you. Whether she tired of it and gave up, I don't know. . . .

STRANGER. It looks ghastly in here!—Where is the Old Man?

MOTHER. Where he is now, there is no more grief. . . .

STRANGER. You mean—he is dead!

MOTHER. Yes—he is dead. . . .

STRANGER. You say it, as if I were the cause of it. . . .

MOTHER. Perhaps I had a right to think that.

STRANGER. He didn't seem so very sensitive. He was certainly capable of hating. . . .

MOTHER. No, he hated only what was evil—in himself and in others.

STRANGER. Then I am wrong in that, too! *(There is a silence.)*

MOTHER. What have you come for?

STRANGER. Charity!

MOTHER. At last!—How did you fare at the hospital? Sit down and tell me. . . .

STRANGER *(seating himself).* That is something I do not care to remember! I do not even know that it was a hospital. . . .

MOTHER. Strange! But what happened after you left us here?

STRANGER. I fell down a precipice and injured my hip, and lost consciousness. . . . If you speak gently to me, I'll tell you the whole story.

MOTHER. I shall speak gently.

STRANGER. Very well. . . . I woke up in a bed, made of red steel bars, and saw three men pulling at a cord that ran through two blocks. . . . Each time they pulled, I felt as if I had been stretched two yards—and . . .

MOTHER. Something was out of joint, and they had to pull it back into place. . . .

STRANGER. Yes, of course, I never thought of that. . . . And afterward I . . . well, as I lay there, I saw my entire life pass before me—from the days of my childhood, through my youth, until that hour. . . . And when the cavalcade had passed, it started all over again—and all through it I heard the grinding of a mill. . . . I hear it now. . . . Yes, the sound follows me here, too!

MOTHER. It was not a pretty picture you saw, was it?

STRANGER. No! And I finally came to the conclusion that I was a loathsome creature. . . .

MOTHER. Why do you say such a thing?

STRANGER. I understand very well that you would prefer to have me use the expression "a wayward human being." . . . But somehow I feel that anyone using that expression is a braggart. And, besides, the term implies a confidence in judgment that I have not yet acquired.

MOTHER. You are still the doubter!

STRANGER. Yes! About some things—about many things. . . . But there is one thing that is beginning to be clear. . . .

MOTHER. What is that?

STRANGER. That there are powers—that there are forces . . . in which . . . I put no faith before. . . .

MOTHER. Have you also noticed that it is neither you nor any other human being who rules your remarkable fate?

STRANGER. Yes—I sensed that. . . .

MOTHER. Well—then you are on the right road. . . .

STRANGER. But I am also—bankrupt. . . . I have lost my poetic inspiration—and I can't sleep nights. . . .

MOTHER. Why not?

STRANGER. I have nightmares . . . and—what is worse—I have a fear of dying—for I am no longer convinced that our misery ends with death—once it comes!

MOTHER. Really?

STRANGER. But the worst of all is that I have come to detest myself to such a degree that I should like to put an end to myself—but I am not free to do that. If I were a Christian, I would not be able to live up to the first commandment, to love my neighbor as myself; for then I would hate my neighbor. . . . And that's what I undoubtedly do. . . . It is probably true that I am a wretch and a scoundrel. I have long suspected that I was. But because I always refused to be duped by life, I kept an eye on my fellow beings. And having discovered that they were no better than myself, I was angered when they tried to subjugate and muzzle me.

MOTHER. That is all very well—but you are looking at these things in the wrong way. You seem to think that it is a matter between you and your fellow beings—but it is a matter entirely between you and Him. . . .

STRANGER. Him?

MOTHER. The Invisible One, who rules your fate.

STRANGER. If I could only meet Him!

MOTHER. You will be dying when you do!

STRANGER. Oh no!

MOTHER. Where do you get this fiendish spirit of rebellion from? Will you never humble yourself as others do? If you will not, then you shall be broken like a reed!

STRANGER. I don't know from where I get this hellish obstinacy and defiance. . . . It is true—I tremble when I can't pay a bill; but if I were to ascend Mount Sinai and I should come fact to face with the Eternal One, I would meet Him with my face uncovered!

MOTHER. Jesus! Mary!—When you speak like that, I believe you are an offspring of the devil!

STRANGER. That seems to be the general opinion here! But I have heard it said that they who are close to the devil usually have honors, gold, and riches heaped upon them—especially gold! Does it seem to you that I justify the suspicion!

MOTHER. You will bring a curse upon my house!

STRANGER. In that case I shall leave your house. . . .

MOTHER. In the dark of night! No, no—where would you go?

STRANGER. I shall go and seek the only one I do not hate. . . .

MOTHER. Are you so certain she will welcome you?

STRANGER. Absolutely certain!

MOTHER. I am not!

STRANGER. But I am!

MOTHER. Then I must make you feel less confident.

STRANGER. You can't shake my confidence!

MOTHER. Yes—I can!

STRANGER. You lie!

MOTHER. We are no longer speaking calmly, and so let us stop. Do you think you can sleep up in the attic room?

STRANGER. Anywhere! I'll get no sleep anyway!

MOTHER. Then I shall say good night . . . whether you think I mean it sincerely or not!

STRANGER. I hope there are no rats up there! I am not afraid of ghosts—but rats are disgusting.

MOTHER. I am glad you are not afraid of ghosts, for—no one has ever slept out the night up there. . . . What the reason may be, I don't know. . . .

STRANGER (tarries a moment; then says). You are the meanest human being I ever met in my life! But that's because you are religious!

MOTHER. Good night!

SCENE 4. *The kitchen. It is dark, but the moon outside casts shadows of the grated windows upon the floor. The shadows move when the storm clouds drift by. In the corner to the left—underneath the crucifix, where the Old Man used to sit—the wall is now covered with hunting horns, shotguns, and game bags. A stuffed bird of prey stands on the table. The windows are open, and the curtains are flapping; kitchen and scouring rags, aprons and towels, hung on a line in front of the range, move in the wind. The soughing of the wind is heard. From the distance, the roaring sound of a waterfall. Occasionally there is the sound of a knock from the wooden floor.*

STRANGER (enters, half dressed, a candle in his hand). Is someone there?—Not a soul! (He advances, light in hand; the light reduces the shadow play.) What is that on the floor that's moving?—Is someone here? (He goes over to the table, but

seeing the bird of prey, he remains standing as if petrified.)
Christ in heaven!

MOTHER *(comes in, dressed, carrying a candle in her hand).*
Are you still up?

STRANGER Yes—I could not sleep.

MOTHER *(gently).* Why not, my son?

STRANGER. I heard someone tramping above me. . . .

MOTHER. That's impossible—there is no floor above you.

STRANGER. That's just what made me feel uneasy. . . . What
is that crawling on the floor like snakes? . . .

MOTHER. It's the moonbeams!

STRANGER. Yes—it's the moonlight! And this is a stuffed
bird—and there are some kitchen rags. . . . Everything is as
simple and natural as that—and that's the very thing that dis-
turbs me. . . . Who is it who keeps knocking in the night? Has
someone been locked out?

MOTHER. No—it is just one of the horses in the stable,
stamping his hoofs.

STRANGER. I have never heard that horses . . .

MOTHER. Oh yes, horses suffer from nightmares, too.

STRANGER. What is a nightmare ?

MOTHER. Well—who knows. . . .

STRANGER. Let me sit down for a moment. . . .

MOTHER. Sit down and let us have a serious talk. I was
unkind last evening, and for that I beg you to forgive me. But,
you see, just because I am so terribly sinful, I use my religion
as I do the hair shirt and the stone floor. In order not to
offend you, I shall put the question to myself: What is a
nightmare?—It is my own evil conscience. . . . Whether it is
I myself or someone else who punishes me, I do not know
. . . and I do not think I have any right to pry into that!
—Now tell me what happened to you upstairs. . . .

STRANGER. Really . . . I don't know . . . I didn't see anything—but when I came into the room, I could feel that
somebody was there. I looked round with the candle, but
saw no one. Then I went to bed. Suddenly somebody started
walking about with heavy steps, directly over my head. . . .
Do you believe in ghosts, or in people coming back? . . .

MOTHER. No—and my religion forbids me to have such
notions. . . . But I believe in the power of our sense of justice
to create its own means of punishment. . . .

STRANGER. And then . . . after a while an icy chill settled
across my chest. It moved about and focused on my heart. . . .

My heart turned cold as stone—and I jumped out of bed. . . .

MOTHER. And what happened then?

STRANGER. I felt myself riveted to the floor and had to watch the whole panorama of my life roll by—everything, everything . . . and that was the very hardest of all. . . .

MOTHER. Yes! I know—I know it all . . . I have been through it myself. . . . The illness has no name—and there is only one cure. . . .

STRANGER. And—what is it?

MOTHER. You know!—You know what children have to do when they have misbehaved!

STRANGER. What do they have to do?

MOTHER. First they must ask forgiveness . . .

STRANGER. And then?

MOTHER. Then they try to make up for their misdeeds.

STRANGER. You mean it is not enough to have to suffer one's deserts?

MOTHER. No, that would be nothing but revenge!

STRANGER. Well, what else?

MOTHER. Can you yourself make good a life you have destroyed? Can you undo an act of evil? Undo it?

STRANGER. No—you are right! But I was forced to use evil means in self-defense—to achieve justice, when it was denied me. And shame on him who forced me! Woe to him! (With his hand on his heart.) Oh, now he is here—in this room—and he is tearing the heart out of my breast! Oh!

MOTHER. Humble yourself!

STRANGER. I cannot!

MOTHER. Down on your knees!

STRANGER. No—I will not!

MOTHER. O Christ, have mercy! Lord, be compassionate! . . . (To the Stranger.) Get on your knees before the One who was crucified! He—and He alone—can undo what you have done!

STRANGER. No—I will not bend a knee before Him! Not before Him!—And if I am coerced into doing it, I will recant and disavow Him afterward!

MOTHER. Down on your knees, my son!

STRANGER. I cannot—I cannot!—Oh, help me, Eternal God! Help me! (There is a silence.)

MOTHER (fervently mumbles a prayer, then asks). Do you feel better?

STRANGER (seeming to recover). Yes. . . . But do you know what it was? . . . It was not death—it was annihilation. . . .

MOTHER. The annihilation of the divine . . . what we call spiritual death.

STRANGER (soberly, with no sign of irony). You mean to say . . . yes, now I am beginning to understand. . . .

MOTHER. My son! You have taken leave of Jerusalem, and you are now on the road to Damascus. . . . Continue on the same road that you have traveled to come here—and plant a cross at every station you come to; but halt at the seventh . . . you do not have to suffer the fourteen that He had to. . . .

STRANGER. You speak in riddles. . . .

MOTHER. Never mind!—Go and seek all those to whom you have something to say . . . first of all, your wife. . . .

STRANGER. Where?

MOTHER. Seek her—but do not forget to look in on him whom you call the werewolf. . . .

STRANGER. Never!

MOTHER. That is what I am told you said when you were about to come here—and you remember I told you I expected you. . . .

STRANGER. What made you expect me?

MOTHER. I had no tangible reason. . . .

STRANGER. Perhaps much as I have seen this kitchen before —in a sort of vision . . . if I may call it that.

MOTHER. That is why I now regret that I tried to separate you from Ingeborg—for it was meant that you were to meet. . . . However, go and seek her now. . . . If you find her, all is well again; if you don't—then perhaps that is the way it was meant to be. . . . But the day is dawning. . . . Morning is here—and night is over.

STRANGER. And what a night!

MOTHER. It is a night that you must never forget!

STRANGER. I am not anxious to remember all it has brought —but I shall keep some of it in my memory!

MOTHER (looking out through the window, speaking as though to herself). You beautiful morning star—how could you so stray from your heaven? (There is silence.)

STRANGER. Have you ever noticed that before the sun rises, we humans shiver and shudder? Can it be that we are children of darkness, since we tremble when we face the light?

MOTHER. Don't you ever tire of asking questions?

STRANGER. No—never! You see—I long for the light!

MOTHER. Then go and seek it! And peace be with you!

ACT IV

SCENE 1. *Inside the mountain pass. It is now autumn, however, and the trees have lost their leaves. One hears the sound of a sledge hammer from the smithy, and the grinding of the mill.*

The Blacksmith is standing in the doorway, right; the Miller's Wife stands at the left of the stage. The Lady is dressed for traveling in a short jacket and wears a patent leather hat. Her dress indicates she is in mourning. The Stranger is wearing an Alpine suit, Bavarian in style: shooting jacket, knee breeches, Alpine boots, alpenstock, and a green hunting cap with a black cock feather. Over this he wears a cape with fur collar and hood.

LADY *(enters; she seems weary and distressed).* Has a gentleman, dressed for traveling, passed by here? *(The Blacksmith shakes his head, as does the Miller's Wife.)* Could you possibly put me up for the night? *(The Blacksmith again shakes his head; so does the Miller's wife. To the Blacksmith.)* Would you let me stand in the door there and warm myself? *(The Blacksmith pushes her aside.)* May God reward you as you deserve. *(She goes away and soon after disappears over the footbridge.)*

STRANGER *(entering).* Has a lady, dressed for traveling, gone across the river? *(The Blacksmith shakes his head; the Miller's Wife does likewise. To the Miller's Wife.)* Could I buy a loaf of bread from you? Here's the money. *(The Miller's Wife makes a gesture of refusal.)* No compassion. . . .

ECHO *(in the distance).* No compassion. . . . *(The Blacksmith and the Miller's Wife burst out into a long, loud laughter, answered by the echo.)*

STRANGER. This is what I like: an eye for an eye, a tooth for a tooth! This helps to lighten my conscience somewhat! *(He goes into the pass.)*

SCENE 2. *On the highway. It is now fall. The Beggar is sitting by the shrine, holding a lime twig and a bird cage that houses a starling.*

STRANGER *(entering, dressed as in the preceding scene).* My dear beggar, have you seen a lady, dressed for traveling, pass by here?

BEGGAR. I have seen five hundred ladies in traveling dress

pass here. But I must seriously ask you not to refer to me as a beggar. . . . I have now found something to do.

STRANGER. Oh—so it is you!

BEGGAR. *Ille ego qui quondam.* . . .

STRANGER. What sort of work are you doing?

BEGGAR. I have a starling who whistles and talks. . . .

STRANGER. In other words, it is the starling who works?

BEGGAR. Yes, I have become my own employer. . . .

STRANGER. So you catch birds, too, do you?

BEGGAR. Oh, you mean the lime twig? No—that's only for display.

STRANGER. So you go in for appearances, do you?

BEGGAR. Why, certainly! What else is there to judge by? The inside is nothing but empty—trash!

STRANGER. So that is the sum of your philosophy?

BEGGAR. The whole metaphysical substance! My viewpoint may be considered somewhat obsolete; still . . .

STRANGER. Won't you tell me—seriously—just one thing! Tell me something about your past. . . .

BEGGAR. Ugh! What good does it do to rake up old rubbish! —Keep on reeling and winding, my dear sir, just keep on winding! Do you think I am always as silly as you see me now? No—it's only when I meet you—for you are excruciatingly funny.

STRANGER. How can you keep smiling with your whole life gone to splinters?

BEGGAR. Now, now—now he is getting to be impertinent!— When you no longer can laugh at misery—not even at other people's—then life is nothing but idle nonsense! Listen carefully to me! If you follow that wheel track in the mud of the road, you will come to the water—and there the road ends. . . . Sit down and rest there—and you will soon take a different view of life! Here there are so many mementos of tragedy— so many religious objects and unhappy memories that prevent your thoughts from going to the Rose Chamber. . . . But just follow the track closely—only the track! If you get a little soiled or dusty now and then, just spread your wings and fly aloft!

. . . And speaking of wings—I once heard a bird sing something about Polycrates' ring—and that he had been given all the glory of the world . . . but didn't know what to do with it. And so he prated east and west about the great emptiness of the universe, which he helped to create out of nothing. . . . I would not say it was you—if I didn't believe it so firmly that I could swear to it . . . and I remember that I once asked you if you knew who I was, and you replied that it did not interest you. . . . In return I offered you my friendship—but you refused it with these words: For shame!—However, I am neither super-sensitive nor do I hold a grudge! Therefore I shall give you some good advice to chew on on the way: Follow the track!

STRANGER *(backing away)*. Oh no, you won't deceive me again!

BEGGAR. My dear sir! You think nothing but bad thoughts. That is why nothing good comes your way! Try my advice!

STRANGER. I—shall—try. . . . But if you deceive me—then I shall be justified in . . .

BEGGAR. You will never be justified in that!

STRANGER *(as if to himself)*. Who reads my secret thoughts—who turns my soul inside out—who persecutes me? Why are you following me?

BEGGAR. Why are you following me, Saul? *(The Stranger goes out with a haunted expression. The strains from the dirge can be heard as before. The Lady enters.)*

LADY. Have you seen a gentleman dressed for traveling go by here?

BEGGAR. Yes—there was a poor devil here a moment ago. . . . He hobbled by. . . .

LADY. The person I am seeking does not limp.

BEGGAR. This fellow didn't limp either, but he seemed to be suffering from a hip ailment. . . . His walk was a little un-steady. No, I mustn't be mean! Look there in the mud—on the road. . . .

LADY. Where?

BEGGAR *(pointing)*. There! There—where you see the wheel track . . . and right beside it you'll see the imprint of a hiking boot—someone with a heavy trudge. . . .

LADY *(goes over to investigate)*. Yes, it is he—with his heavy step. . . . But will I be able to catch up with him?

BEGGAR. Follow the track!

LADY *(takes his hand, kissing it)*. Thank you, my friend.
(She leaves.)

SCENE 3. *By the sea. It is now winter. The sea is blue-black, and clouds are piled aloft in the shape of gigantic heads. In the distance can be seen the naked masts of a shipwrecked vessel, resembling three white crosses. The table and the bench beneath the tree still remain, but the chairs have been removed. The ground is covered by snow. Now and then a bell buoy emits its sound of warning.*

The Stranger enters from the right. He pauses for a moment and glances out over the sea. Then he disappears, left, behind the cottage. The Lady enters from the right. She seems to be tracing the footprints that the Stranger has left in the snow. She goes out, left, past the cottage. The Stranger comes from the left. He crosses to the right, and discovers the Lady's footprints. He stops and glances over his shoulder, toward the left. The Lady returns.

LADY *(throws herself in the Stranger's arms, then recoils).* You thrust me aside?

STRANGER. No—but someone seemed to stand between us!

LADY. You may be right!—But what a reunion!

STRANGER. Yes. . . . It is winter—as you see. . . .

LADY. Yes—I can feel the chill on you!

STRANGER. Over there in the mountains, I was chilled to the marrow. . . .

LADY. Don't you believe there will be another spring?

STRANGER. Not for us! Driven from Paradise, we shall wander among stones and thistles. . . . And when our feet are rent, and our hands are torn and pricked, we will have to sprinkle salt on each other's wounds. And so the eternal mill grinds on—ceaselessly . . . for the water that drives it flows on without end.

LADY. I think you may be right.

STRANGER. Yes—but I don't want to yield to the inevitable— I wouldn't like to see us tear each other apart—and therefore I shall carve myself to pieces—as an offering to the gods. . . . I shall take the guilt upon myself—shall say that it was I who persuaded you to throw off the shackles—that it was I who enticed you—and . . . you are free to blame me for everything: the curse itself and all its consequences. . . .

LADY. It would be more than you could bear!

STRANGER. Oh no! There are moments when I feel myself carrying all the sins and sorrows, the filth and shame of the universe! There are times when I believe that the evil act, the crime itself, is a punishment inflicted upon us! Do you know that recently, when I lay sick with fever, so much happened to me. . . . Among other things, I dreamt that I saw a crucifix— but without the Crucified One . . . and when I asked the Dominican—there was a Dominican there among the others— when I asked what it could mean—and he answered: You do not wish Him to suffer for your sake—therefore suffer yourself! . . . And that is why mankind has become so sensitive to its own sufferings!

LADY. And that is why our conscience becomes so heavy when no one will help to carry our burden. . . .

STRANGER. Have you also come to that crossroad?

LADY. Not yet—but I am on my way there!

STRANGER. Put your hand in mine and let us leave this place together. . . .

LADY. Where shall we go?

STRANGER. Let us return the same way we came! Are you tired?

LADY. No longer!

STRANGER. I have been on the point of succumbing several times. . . . And then I met a curious beggar—perhaps you remember him. . . . I have heard people say he resembles me somewhat—and he asked me to trý to think kindly of his intentions, merely to make the effort. . . . I did try, simply as a test, and . . .

LADY. And . . .

STRANGER . . . and he proved to be right!—And ever since I have felt strong enough to continue. . . .

LADY. Let us be on our way!

STRANGER (facing the sea). Yes—it is growing dark—the clouds are gathering. . . .

LADY. Turn away from the clouds. . . .

STRANGER. But underneath the clouds—what is that I see?

LADY. It is only a sunken ship.

STRANGER (in a whisper). A trinity of crosses!—What new Golgotha can be awaiting us now?

LADY. But they are white! That is an omen for good!

STRANGER. Can anything good be in store for us ever?

LADY. Yes—but not this very moment. . . .

STRANGER. Let us go!

SCENE 4. *A room in a hotel. The Lady is seated beside the Stranger. She is knitting.*

LADY. Say something!

STRANGER. No—I have nothing to talk about except unpleasant things, since we came back to this room.

LADY. Then why did you have no rest until you could move into this horrible room?

STRANGER. I just don't know! There is nothing I could have wished for less!—I felt I had to come here in order to suffer! That's the reason!

LADY. And you have suffered. . . .

STRANGER. Yes. . . . No longer do I h‹ ar anything to inspire me—I see nothing of beauty. . . . In the daytime I hear the mill grinding and see the vast panorama which has enlarged into a cosmorama . . . and during the night . . .

LADY. Yes—why did you scream in your sleep?

STRANGER. I had a dream. . . .

LADY. A true dream? . . .

STRANGER . . . so horribly real. . . . Now you can see the curse coming true: I feel a compulsion to tell someone . . . and to whom if not you? But I can't—for then I would open the door to the forbidden room. . . .

LADY. The past, you mean?

STRANGER. Yes!

LADY (artlessly). There must be something wicked in your past?

STRANGER. There might well be. (There is a silence.)

LADY. Tell me!

STRANGER. I am afraid I must!—Well, I dreamed that I saw—your former husband—married to—my former wife. . . . My children, consequently, would have him—as their father. . . .

LADY. No one but you could have invented such a thing!

STRANGER. Oh! If it were only a dream!—But I saw him mistreat them. (He rises.) And then I strangled him, of course. . . . No, I can't go on! . . . I shall have no peace until I have reassured myself—and to do that, I shall have to seek him out—in his own home! . . .

LADY. It has come to this!

STRANGER. It has been brewing for some time—and now there is no turning back. . . . I have to see him!

LADY. And if he refuses to see you?

STRANGER. Then I must go to him as a patient and tell him about my sickness. . . .

LADY (frightened). Don't tell him about your sickness—whatever you do!

STRANGER. I see what you mean. . . . You mean he might feel compelled to shut me up as demented. . . . Well, I have to take that risk. . . . I feel that I have to risk everything—life, liberty, and all that goes with it! I feel the need for an emotion, an excitement so powerful that my own self is shaken up and brought to see the light again! I revel in torturing myself until the balance in our relationship is restored—so that I won't have to lurk about like a man in debt. . . . And so: down into the snake pit—and the sooner the better!

LADY. If you would only let me go along with you. . . .

STRANGER. There is no need for that! I shall suffer for us both!

LADY. Then you will be my liberator . . . and the curse that I once called down upon you shall be turned into a blessing! You see—it is spring again!

STRANGER. I see it by the Christmas rose there—it is beginning to wither.

LADY. But can't you feel it in the air?

STRANGER. Yes, I feel the chill in my breast going away. . . .

LADY. Perhaps the werewolf can cure you completely?

STRANGER. We shall see. He may not be so dangerous after all.

LADY. He certainly couldn't be as cruel as you are.

STRANGER. But my dream!—Imagine. . . .

LADY . . . if it turned out to be nothing but a dream!—Well, now I have no more yarn left—but my worthless needlework is finished! And look how soiled it is!

STRANGER. It can be washed.

LADY. Or dyed.

STRANGER. A rosy red.

LADY. Oh, no!

STRANGER. It resembles a scroll of parchment . . .

LADY . . . holding the saga of our lives . . .

STRANGER . . . written in the dust and grime of the highroad— in blood and tears. . . .

LADY. Yes—soon our tale will be told. . . . Go and complete the final chapter!

STRANGER. And then we shall meet at the seventh station— from where we started. . . .

ACT V

SCENE 1. *At the Physician's. The setting is nearly the same as earlier. The woodpile, however, is only half its former size; and on the veranda is seen a bench, on which lie a number of surgical instruments: knives, lancets, saws, pincers, etc. The Physician is engaged in cleaning the instruments.*

SISTER *(coming from the veranda).* There is a patient waiting for you.

PHYSICIAN. Do you know him?

SISTER. I didn't see him—but here is his card.

PHYSICIAN (*taking the card and glancing at it*). Why! This surpasses anything I have ever heard of. . . .

SISTER. It isn't he, is it?

PHYSICIAN. It is! While I do not belittle courage, I can't help finding this sort of forwardness a little cynical. I feel myself challenged! But, never mind, let him come in.

SISTER. Are you serious?

PHYSICIAN. Of course I am! But you might engage him in a casual conversation to begin with, if you wish—you know how to do it.

SISTER. That is what I intended. . . .

PHYSICIAN. Good! You start in with the preliminaries, and I'll put on the finishing touches. . . .

SISTER. Don't worry! I'll tell him everything that your good heart forbids you to say.

PHYSICIAN. Never mind about my heart. And hurry up before I lose my temper. . . . And lock the doors!

(*The Sister leaves.*)

What are you doing there again by the trash barrel, Caesar? (*Caesar steps forward.*) Tell me, Caesar—if your enemy came to you and put his head in your lap . . . what would you do?

CAESAR. I'd chop off his head!

PHYSICIAN. That's not what I have taught you!

CAESAR. No—you told me to heap hot coals on his head . . . but I think that's cruel!

PHYSICIAN. I think so, too, as a matter of fact! It is more cruel, and more crafty and treacherous. Don't you think it would be better to take a less harsh revenge, so that the other fellow could be rehabilitated and feel that he has made up for his errors, so to speak? . . .

CAESAR. Since you understand such things better than I— why do you ask me?

PHYSICIAN. Be quiet, Caesar! I am not talking to you! And so—let us take off his head—and then we'll see what to do next. . . .

CAESAR. Depending upon how he behaves. . . .

PHYSICIAN. Exactly!—How he behaves. . . . Now be still! And go away! . . .

STRANGER (*comes from the veranda. He is agitated, but he collects himself with an air of resignation*). Doctor!

PHYSICIAN. Oh yes!

STRANGER. You are surprised to see me here, aren't you?

PHYSICIAN (*with a solemn expression*). I ceased to be surprised years ago; but I see I have to begin all over again.

STRANGER. Will you let me have a private talk with you?

PHYSICIAN. On any subject fit to be discussed between cultivated persons, yes! Are you sick?

STRANGER (*hesitating*). Yes!

PHYSICIAN. Why do you come especially to me?

STRANGER. You should be able to guess why. . . .

PHYSICIAN. I don't care to. . . . What is troubling you?

STRANGER (*hesitatingly*). I can't sleep.

PHYSICIAN. That isn't an illness. It is a symptom. Have you been to any other physician?

STRANGER. I have been lying sick in—in an institution—with fever. . . . But it was no ordinary fever. . . .

PHYSICIAN. What was strange about it?

STRANGER. May I first ask you one question: Is it possible that one can walk about in a delirium?

PHYSICIAN Yes—if one is deranged—but only in such cases. (*The Stranger rises; then he seats himself again.*) What was the name of the institution?

STRANGER. Its name was the Good Help. . . .

PHYSICIAN. There is no hospital of that name.

STRANGER. Is it a cloister, then?

PHYSICIAN. No—it is an insane asylum! (*The Stranger rises. The Physician gets up also, calling out.*) Sister! Lock the door to the street! And the back gate—to the highway! (*To the Stranger.*) Won't you please sit down!—I have to lock the doors because we've had tramps in the neighborhood recently. . . .

STRANGER (*quieting down*). Doctor, tell me frankly: do you think I am mentally disturbed?

PHYSICIAN. It is not customary to give a frank answer to such a question—you know that. And no one suffering from such a malady ever believes what he is told. Therefore it matters little what my opinion is. If, on the other hand, you feel that your soul is afflicted, then—go to your spiritual adviser. . . .

STRANGER. Wouldn't you care to assume that task yourself for the moment?

PHYSICIAN. No—I do not feel myself capable of that.

STRANGER. Even if . . .

PHYSICIAN (*interrupting*). Besides, I haven't the time, for we are preparing for a wedding. . . .

STRANGER. My dream! . . .

PHYSICIAN. I thought it would give you a little peace to know

that I have overcome my sorrow—consoled myself, as it is called
. . . and that it would even make you happy . . . that's what
usually happens. . . . But instead I see you suffer even more.
. . . There must be a reason for that! I have to get to the bottom
of it little by little. . . . How can my marrying a widow
possibly upset you?

STRANGER. With two children?

PHYSICIAN. Let me see! Let me see!—Now I have it! An
infernal thought like that is indeed worthy of you! Listen carefully! If there were a hell, you would be its sovereign lord, for
—when it comes to punishments—your power of invention surpasses my boldest fabrications—and yet I have been named the
werewolf!

STRANGER. It might seem . . .

PHYSICIAN (interrupting). For a long time I bore a hatred for
you, as you perhaps know . . . because you—by an unforgivable
act—brought me an undeservedly bad reputation. . . . But as
I grew older and more understanding I realized that if my
punishment at that time seemed unjust, I nevertheless deserved
it for other pranks that had remained undiscovered. . . . And,
besides, you were the sort of child with a conscience that would
make you suffer—so that shouldn't worry you, either! Was this
the subject you wanted to discuss?

STRANGER. Yes!

PHYSICIAN. Are you satisfied now, if I let you leave without
hindrance? (The Stranger looks at the Physician quizzically.)
Or did you, perhaps, think that I intended to lock you up—
or saw you in two with my instruments there? (He points to a
case with surgical instruments.) Perhaps kill you? Such poor
wretches should be done away with, of course, shouldn't they?
(The Stranger looks at his watch.) You have time to catch the
boat.

STRANGER. Will you give me your hand?

PHYSICIAN. No—that is something I can't do! I would be a
traitor to myself! What good would it do, anyhow, if I did forgive you—when you haven't the strength to forgive yourself.
. . . There are things that can only be helped by being undone. What you have done is irreparable!

STRANGER. The Good Help . . .

PHYSICIAN. That was of some help, yes!—You challenged fate,
and were defeated. . . . There is no shame in an honest battle!
I did the same—but as you see, I have done away with part of
my woodpile: I don't care to invite the lightning indoors—and
I have given up playing with fire. . . .

STRANGER. One more station—and I have reached my goal. . . .

PHYSICIAN. We never reach our goal, my dear sir!

STRANGER. Farewell!

SCENE 2. *On the street corner. The Stranger is seated on the bench underneath the tree. He is drawing in the sand. The Lady enters.*

LADY. What are you doing?

STRANGER. I am still writing in the sand. . . .

LADY. You have found nothing to inspire you?

STRANGER *(pointing toward the church)*. Yes—but from in there. . . . In there is someone I have wronged without knowing it. . . .

LADY. I thought the pilgrimage was coming to its end, since we happened to come back here. . . .

STRANGER. Where we started from . . . in the street—between the barroom, the church, and—the post office. . . . The post office. Post . . . tell me—didn't I leave a registered letter uncalled for there—at the general delivery? . . .

LADY. Yes—because it was full of maliciousness, you said. . . .

STRANGER . . . or legal court proceedings. *(He strikes his forehead.)* . . . It's still lying there.

LADY. Go inside with the thought that it brings good news. . . .

STRANGER *(with irony)*. Good news!

LADY. Think it! Believe it!

STRANGER *(goes into the post office)*. I shall try! *(The Lady, waiting on the sidewalk, walks back and forth. The Stranger comes out from the post office with a letter in his hand.)*

LADY. Well?

STRANGER. I am ashamed of myself!—It's the money!

LADY. You see!—And all these sorrows—these many tears—all in vain. . . .

STRANGER. Not in vain!—It may seem like a game of evil, but it probably isn't. . . . I wronged the Invisible One when I doubted. . . .

LADY. Ssh! Not that! No excuses!

STRANGER. No—it was my own stupidity—my own weakness and evildoing. . . . I hated to be the dupe of life—that is why I became its victim!—But the elves. . . .

LADY. They have made the exchange!—Let us leave. . . .

STRANGER. Yes, let us go and hide ourselves in the mountains —with all our misery. . . .

LADY. Yes—the mountains hide—and they protect. . . . But

first I must go inside and light a candle to my good Saint Elisabeth. *(The Stranger shakes his head.)* Come!

STRANGER. Oh well! I'll go with you inside—it can't hurt me —but I won't stay long!

LADY. You never know. . . . Come! In there you will receive fresh inspiration. . . .

STRANGER *(follows her to the portals of the church).* Perhaps. . . .

LADY. Come!

To Damascus II

A DRAMA IN FOUR ACTS

❖ ❖ ❖

Parts II and III of *To Damascus* contain chiefly variations of the *Damascus I* theme. The searching for the key to life and the hereafter continues unabated in these sequences. The core of the theme is expressed by the Lady in Act II of Part I, when she tells the Stranger, "I may not have suffered sufficiently yet," and he answers, "Then you think we are put on earth to suffer?"

In Part II of *To Damascus* the Stranger's former arrogance flashes up anew. As in the early scenes of Part I, he magnifies now and then his personal power, intellectual gifts, and resentments. He lets his ambition lead him away from his good intentions and resolutions. The Confessor's spiritual advice that he accept his trials as a grace from God does not always remain with him. He meets with phantom figures conjured forth by his conscience at the thought of past misdeeds and injuries he has caused to others. There is Caesar, the madman (first met with in Part I), who lost his mind reading "a certain author"; the Physician, with whose wife he had eloped; his parents, to whom he had not always been a dutiful and respectful son; a sister, whom he once drove out into the wintry cold; and others to whom Strindberg owed restitution, or who he felt needed or deserved chastisement. He still thinks, as the Beggar exclaims, praying that the Stranger may be saved from going mad, "all evil to be truth, and all good to be lies." His trials continue: he sees his three little children and they seem to recognize him, but turn away from him. Conscience-stricken he falls to the ground, wrestling with his human feelings and temptations that prevent him from salvaging his soul. When he has risen he is faced with the sight of the mad Caesar springing to his death from the footbridge across the gorge, followed by the Physician, who also seems to be torn by a suicidal impulse. Seeking her brother (the Physician) comes the Sister, agonized and homeless, now that her brother's mind has been deranged; and the Stranger realizes at last his wickedness, feels remorse and anguish. He bemoans the fact that pangs of conscience usually come when it is too late to feel regrets and to make amends. He weakly asks the Beggar if he cannot take the Sister's sufferings upon himself, but the Beggar firmly replies that he cannot assume the burden, implying that no being can atone for another in the matter of personal guilt or grief. Aided by the Beggar he finds his way to the Lady. In her home the Beggar appears in the guise of the Confessor, much to the astonishment of the Stranger. The Lady commends him to the care of the Confessor with the words: "Nothing is left for this unhappy man but to leave the world behind and take refuge in a monastery." Although the rebel in the Stranger has not left him entirely, he follows the Confessor. As they reach the door, he turns to the priest and warns him not to linger, fearing that he, the Stranger, might change his mind and return to the earthly fold.

The Stranger now enters the pastures of divine contemplation. He has torn himself free from earthly pleasures and temptations, from the life that he had found wanting and nothing but illusion.

CHARACTERS

THE STRANGER
THE LADY
THE MOTHER
THE FATHER
THE CONFESSOR
THE BEGGAR
THE DOMINICAN
THE PHYSICIAN

CAESAR
THE MIDWIFE
THE WET NURSE
SISTERS OF CHARITY
THE WOMAN BARTENDER
THE POLICEMAN
THE PROFESSOR
MUSICIANS and others

THE SETTINGS

Act I. Outside the house.

Act II, Scene 1. The laboratory.
Act II, Scene 2. The Rose Chamber.

Act III, Scene 1. The banquet hall.
Act III, Scene 2. The prison.
Act III, Scene 3. The Rose Chamber.

Act IV, Scene 1. The barroom (the banquet hall).
Act IV, Scene 2. Inside the mountain pass.
Act IV, Scene 3. The Rose Chamber.

ACT I

Outside the house. On the left, a terrace on which a dwelling is situated. Below is seen the high road, running toward the back, where a dense pine forest is growing on slopes whose lines intersect one another. On the right, the shore of a river is indicated without its being actually visible.

The house is white, with small windows that are set in frames of limestone and provided with gratings. The wall is covered with vines and rambler rose. Outside the house, upon the terrace, there is a well; at the edge of the terrace grow pumpkins whose leaves and large yellow blossoms hang down over the edge. The road is lined with fruit trees; there is also a cross as a memorial to someone who lost his life in an accident on the road. Steps lead from the terrace to the road, and on a balustrade on each side are flower pots. Below the steps, a bench.

The road runs from the left in the foreground and winds past the terrace, which shoots out into a point and then continues toward the rear of the stage. Bright sunshine from the right. The Mother is sitting on the bench at the foot of the steps. The Dominican stands facing her.

DOMINICAN. You have summoned me in regard to a family matter of vital importance, madam. Let me hear!

MOTHER. Father Confessor, I am a woman who has been hard-tried by life. And I do not know wherein I have sinned that I should fall into disgrace with Providence.

DOMINICAN. It is a grace to be subjected to suffering by the Eternal One. Whoever survives the battle, his shall be the triumph!

MOTHER. There have been times when I have thought so—but there is a limit to what one can suffer. . . .

DOMINICAN. There is no limit to suffering! Suffering is boundless—as is His grace!

MOTHER. First my husband leaves me—abandons me for another woman . . .

DOMINICAN. Let him go—he will come back to you—and on bended knees!

MOTHER. And you know, Father Confessor, that my only daughter was married to a physician. Now she has abandoned him, and she comes here with a stranger and introduces him as her new husband.

DOMINICAN. That is something I cannot understand; our Church does not permit divorce.

MOTHER. No—but they traveled to another country where the laws are different. And he, who belongs to the Old Catholic Church and does not believe in dogmas, got an ecclesiastic to marry them.

DOMINICAN. That is not a true marriage; and it cannot be dissolved, for the simple reason that it has never existed. But it can be declared invalid. Who is this present son-in-law?

MOTHER. Quite frankly, I wish I knew! But one thing I do know, and that is enough to fill my cup of sorrow; he is a divorced man—and his wife and children have scarcely enough to live on.

DOMINICAN. This is a serious case; but I believe we shall be able to cope with it. What exactly does he do?

MOTHER. He is a poet, and he is said to be famous in his own country.

DOMINICAN. And, of course, he is godless?

MOTHER. Well, he used to be, at least. But after this second marriage of his, he hasn't had a moment of happiness in his soul; fate, as he calls it, took hold of him with cruel hand and drove him here with its iron rod, like a destitute beggar. Time after time he was struck by misfortune until I was moved to compassion—and at that very moment he fled from this house. Wandering about in the forest, he was found there and mercifully brought to an asylum; and there he lay ill for three months without knowing where he was!

DOMINICAN. Wait a moment! Last year a man was admitted to the cloister of the Good Help under just such circumstances as you now mention. I am the confessor there. While in a state of fever, he opened his heart to me, and there was scarcely a crime or transgression he did not take upon himself. When he came out of the delirium, he insisted he had no recollection of anything. In order to test him and to get at the truth, I availed myself of the apostolic power that has been given to us and pronounced upon him the preliminary ban of excommunication of the Church. You know, when a secret crime has been committed, the curse of Deuteronomy is read over the suspect. If he is innocent, he will come out of the ordeal—but if his culpability seems unquestionable, then—as St. Paul says—his body will be left to be plagued and tormented by Satan, in order that the culprit's soul may seek repentence and better itself, and the man be saved.

MOTHER. Oh God! It is he!

DOMINICAN. Yes, it is he—your son-in-law! Strange, indeed, are the ways of Providence. But has he been sufficiently scorched by a consciousness of guilt?

MOTHER. Yes—and he . . . He slept here last night but was awakened by an inexplicable power, and he said, his heart was cold as ice.

DOMINICAN. And he had horrible visions, didn't he?

MOTHER. Yes!

DOMINICAN. And he was haunted by anxiety such as Job speaks of: "When I say: My bed shall comfort me, my couch shall ease my complaint; then you sear me with dreams, and terrify me through visions; so that my soul chooses strangling, and death rather than my life!"—That is exactly as it should be! But did this help to open his eyes?

MOTHER. Yes, but only to have his vision distorted; for when the misfortunes began to heap up and he no longer could explain them, and when no physician was able to cure him, he commenced to realize that he was struggling against higher, conscious powers.

DOMINICAN. Which were intent upon doing him harm, and therefore were evil. That is what usually happens. . . . And afterward . . .

MOTHER. Then he got hold of some books that taught him that these evil powers could be fought off and overcome.

DOMINICAN. So-o, he has come to that: he is delving in the occult, the mysteries of life, which are meant to be hidden? Well, has he succeeded in casting a spell upon these spirits of punishment? Has he?

MOTHER. He says he has. And he now seems to be finding peace at night.

DOMINICAN. Yes, so he thinks. But you see, madam, because he has not accepted love as truth, God will send in his path a fearful snare—in the form of a deception and delusion—that he may believe a lie to be the truth.

MOTHER. And then he will have to put up with the consequences. But he has changed my daughter's views also. Although she was neither warm nor cold, good nor bad, before, she is now on the way to becoming evil!

DOMINICAN. How do the two get along together?

MOTHER. Half the day they get along like angels, and the rest of the day they torture each other like demons.

DOMINICAN. That is the way they will keep torturing each other until they have found their way to the Cross.

MOTHER. Unless they should leave each other.

DOMINICAN. So soon?

MOTHER. They have left each other four times—each one in his turn— and each time they have returned. It seems as if they were chained to each other—and if they were, it would be a good thing, for a child is now on the way.

DOMINICAN. Let the child come, by all means. Children have a habit of bringing with them a new spirit that helps to invigorate musty souls.

MOTHER. I wish it were so! But that again seems to be something for them to feud about. They are already quarreling about what to name the child, and whether or not it is to be baptized. And the mother is now jealous of her husband's children by his first wife: he refuses to promise her that he will love his new child as much as his first ones; and my daughter insists that he give her that promise without evasion. There is no end to this abysmal life!

DOMINICAN. Oh yes—you just wait! Once he has entered into relations with the Powers, then we have him cornered. And he will not be able to resist our prayers, madam: they are just as effective as they are mysterious and invisible! *(The Stranger can be seen on the terrace. He is dressed in a hunting coat and a British-Indian topee. He carries an alpenstock.)* Is that he—up there?

MOTHER. Yes—that is my present son-in-law.

DOMINICAN. It is strange how much he resembles her former husband!—But do you notice how he is acting. . . . He has not yet seen me, but I feel he senses that I am here. *(The Dominican makes the sign of the cross in the air.)* Do you see how restless he becomes—and now he is inflexible as an icicle. . . . Watch! He is soon going to burst into a shriek!

STRANGER *(has stopped short and stands motionless. His hand goes to his heart. He calls out).* Who is down there?

MOTHER. It is I.

STRANGER. But you are not alone.

MOTHER. No—I have someone with me.

DOMINICAN *(crosses himself).* Now is the time to silence him and fell him to the ground like a tree hewed down! *(The Stranger crumples up and sinks to the ground.)* Now I am going! For if he should see me here he would have a nervous breakdown. But I shall soon be back. You see now he is in good hands. Good-by—and peace be with you!   *(He departs.)*

STRANGER (*gets up and walks down the steps*). Who was here?

MOTHER. A wanderer. . . . Sit down—you look so pale.

STRANGER. I had an attack of dizziness. . . .

MOTHER. You always come with new names; yet they don't give the key to what is wrong with you. Sit down here on the bench!

STRANGER. No—I don't like sitting there. People are continuously passing here.

MOTHER. And I have been sitting here since I was a child and have watched life pass—just as the river below. Here I have seen people walking by on the road: at play, haggling, begging, cursing and swearing, dancing. . . . I love this bench, and I love the river down there, despite the fact that it causes damage every year and gnaws and eats away our land. Last spring it destroyed all our hay fields so that we were forced to sell all our cattle. During the last few years the property has deteriorated until it is now worth only half of what it used to be worth; and now that the lowering of the lake up in the mountains will soon be completed, and the water from the bogs let out into the river, it will rise so high that it will wash away the house. We have carried on a lawsuit for ten years, and we have lost in every instance—and so we are doomed to go under! It is as unavoidable as fate.

STRANGER. Fate is not unavoidable!

MOTHER. Take care—if you think you can fight against it!

STRANGER. I am fighting it now!

MOTHER. Oh, oh! Now you are starting all over again! You have learned nothing from the chastisement that Providence metes out to us!

STRANGER. Yes—I have learned to hate. Can one love evil—all that causes evil, and makes one suffer?

MOTHER. I have much to learn, as you know, but yesterday I read in an encyclopedia that the meaning of the word "Eumenides" is "the gracious, or the benevolent."

STRANGER. That is true—but it is not true that they *are* benevolent or gracious. I know only one gracious fury—and she is mine!

MOTHER. You call Ingeborg a fury?

STRANGER. Yes—for she is a fury; and as such she is great. Her inventive ability for torturing me exceeds my most infernal devices; and if I escape from her alive, I shall emerge as pure as gold from the fire.

MOTHER. You have been given what you deserve. You were

to recreate her according to your desire, you said—and you have succeeded!

STRANGER. Perfectly!—But where is my fury?

MOTHER. She went down the road a moment ago. *(She points.)*

STRANGER. In that direction?—Then I am on my way to destruction! *(He goes toward the rear.)*

MOTHER. How can you still be jesting?—You just wait! *(The Stranger goes out of sight. The Mother is alone for a moment, until the Lady enters from the left. She is dressed in summery clothes and carries a mail pouch. In her hand are seen several opened letters.)*

LADY. Are you alone, Mother?

MOTHER. Yes, now I am.

LADY. Here is the mail—and it is all for Job!

MOTHER. You open his letters?

LADY. I open all his letters because I want to know with whom I have joined my fate, and I suppress all communications that are likely to inflate his pride and his overbearing attitude. In brief, I isolate him so that he will keep the electricity within him . . . and be in fear of blowing up.

MOTHER. You have learned a lot, haven't you?

LADY. Yes—since he is careless enough to confide to me almost everything, I shall soon hold his fate in my hand! Imagine, he is now experimenting with electricity and he says he is going to tame thunder and lightning so that it will give him light and heat and motive power. All that may be well enough, but today I find through one of these letters that he is corresponding with alchemists.

MOTHER. He wants to make gold now? Can this man be sane?

LADY. That is the big question. The lesser one is: Is he a charlatan?

MOTHER. Do you suspect that he is?

LADY. I think of him as being everything that is evil—and in the next moment, everything that is good.

MOTHER. What other news have you?

LADY. This—that my divorced husband—whose plans to remarry have been thwarted—has now begun to brood. He has abandoned his practice and is roving about on the highways.

MOTHER. Oh—what a pity!—After all, he was once my son-in-law. And underneath the rude, irascible surface, he had nevertheless a good heart.

LADY. Yes—that is true! And the name of werewolf that I

gave him was only given him in his capacity as my husband and master! As long as I felt assured that his mind was at peace and that he would be able to get over the shock of my leaving him, I was untroubled. . . . Now he will be haunting me like a bad conscience.

MOTHER. Have you a conscience?

LADY. I hadn't in the past, but after having read my husband's writings, my eyes have been opened and I can now see the difference between good and evil.

MOTHER. He had forbidden you to read his books, and he hadn't taken into account that you would disobey him.

LADY. Who can calculate all the consequences of one's acts?

MOTHER. What other unpleasant news have you in your box, Pandora?

LADY. The very worst! Oh! . . . Can you imagine, mother, that his divorced wife is on the verge of being married again?

MOTHER. But that ought to be good news to you as well as to him.

LADY. But don't you know that what he fears most is that his former wife will do just that, and that his children then will have a stepfather?

MOTHER. If he can bear that, by himself, then I will think him a remarkable man.

LADY. Do you think he is as sensitive as that? Hasn't he said himself that a cultured gentleman of the late nineteenth century never allows himself to be taken unawares!

MOTHER. People say so many things, but when it comes to the point . . .

LADY. But at the bottom of my Pandora's box lay a gift that was anything but sad! Look here, Mother! This is a picture of his six-year-old son!

MOTHER (regarding the portrait). He is an angel of a child!

LADY. He is so beautiful in every way that one feels permeated by goodness just looking at him!—Tell me, do you think my child will be as beautiful? Do you? Answer me, or I shall be unhappy! I can't help loving this little child, but I feel I would hate him if my child were not to be as beautiful as he! Yes, I am already jealous!

MOTHER. I had hoped that when you came here after your wretched, weary honeymoon, things would be more harmonious. But now I see it was only the preface to what is to come.

LADY. I, too, am now prepared for everything; and I do not believe this tangle can ever be unraveled. It has to be cut.

MOTHER. However, by suppressing his mail the way you are, you are only making more trouble for yourself.

LADY. In the past, when I went through life like a sleep-walker, I was able to remedy everything simply by blowing on the hurt. But now that he has awakened my mind, I am beginning to waver. Ssh! I hear him coming! *(She quickly hides the letters in her pocket.)* Ssh!

MOTHER. Another thing! Why do you let him make a spectacle of himself by wearing your former husband's summer suit?

LADY. It amuses me to torture and humiliate him. I have made him think it is becoming to him and that it was my father's suit. Seeing him in the apparel of the werewolf gives me the feeling that I have them both in my clutches.

MOTHER. May the Lord help us! How vicious you have become!

LADY. Perhaps that was meant to be my function—that is, if I had a function to perform in this man's life.

MOTHER. There are times when I wish the river would rise and wash us all away while we are asleep at night! And if it were to sweep and swash and splash for a thousand years, then perhaps the sin upon which this house was built could be cleansed away.

LADY. So it is true, that my grandfather, the notary, did illegally appropriate property that belonged to others? I have heard it said that this house was built with the inheritances of widows and orphans, with money gained by levying a distress upon people who were bankrupt, by pouncing upon property left by deceased men and women, with bribes taken from litigants suing one another. . . .

MOTHER. Let us not talk about it, please. The tears of their children and children's children have grown into a lake; and people say it is this lake that is now being drained and that will make the river rise and wash us away.

LADY. But isn't there some way to stop it—through some legal action? Is there no longer any justice in this world?

MOTHER. Not in this world—but in heaven there is. And it is the justice of heaven that is about to drown us—the heirs of the evildoers!   *(She goes up the steps.)*

LADY. So it is not enough that we have to be weighed down by our own tears. We inherit the tears of others as well. . . .

STRANGER *(enters again)*. Did you call me?

LADY. No—I only persuaded you—I had no real desire to see you.

STRANGER. I could feel that you were busying yourself with my fate in a manner that made me uneasy. Before long you will have acquired my cunning.

LADY. And many other things besides.

STRANGER. But one thing I ask: Do not touch my fate with clumsy hands. For you see, I am Cain, and I am under the ban of the Powers. And the Powers permit no mortal to interfere with their acts of vengeance. (*He raises his hat.*) Do you see the mark of Cain on my forehead? It means "The Lord says: Mine is the revenge."

LADY. Does your hat weigh heavily on your brow? . . .

STRANGER. No, but it burns—like a stigma—and so does my coat! And if it hadn't been for you, I would have cast them both into the river. But I always try to please you. . . . Do you know that whenever I walk about the countryside here, people call me "the Doctor." I assume they think I am your former husband, the werewolf. I am pursued by bad luck. If I ask who planted this tree or that, the answer is inevitably: The Doctor did. If I ask who is the owner of that green fish-chest, the answer is the same: The Doctor. And anything that doesn't belong to the Doctor, belongs to his wife—meaning you! This matter of being continuously confused with someone else is making my visit here unbearable . . . and I would like to go away. . . .

LADY. Haven't you tried to leave half a dozen times? And each time you have failed.

STRANGER. So I have—but I shall succeed the seventh.

LADY. Try, then!

STRANGER. You say this as though you were convinced that I would fail.

LADY. And I am!

STRANGER. Torture me in some other way, my dear fury.

LADY. Don't worry, I can!

STRANGER. In some new way! Try to say something malicious that "the other one" has not said already.

LADY. The other one—that's your first wife! How tactful of you to remind me of her!

STRANGER. Everything that lives and moves—everything that is dead and rigid and motionless reminds me of the past. . . .

LADY. Until that little somebody arrives who will blot out the dark past and bring us light.

STRANGER. You mean the little one we are expecting?

LADY. Our child, yes!

STRANGER. Do you love it?

LADY. From this day I shall love it.

STRANGER. From this day? What has happened, then? Five months ago you wanted to go to an attorney and get a divorce from me because I refused to take you to a quack and have him destroy the unborn child.

LADY. That was then! Today things are different.

STRANGER. Today—different? (*He looks about as if he had a premonition of something.*) Today?—Has the mail come?

LADY. You are craftier than I am—as yet! But before too long the pupil will surpass her master.

STRANGER. Were there any letters for me?

LADY. No.

STRANGER. Then let me have the other mail.

LADY. How did you know?

STRANGER. Give me, then, the rest of the mail, since your conscience makes such a fine distinction between letters and other mail.

LADY (*produces the mail bag which she had hidden behind the bench*). Here you are! (*The Stranger takes out the photograph from the mail bag, gazes at it intently, and puts it in his breast pocket.*) What was that you had?

STRANGER. The past!

LADY. Was it something lovely from the past?

STRANGER. Yes—something more beautiful than the future can ever be.

LADY (*with darkened brow*). That you ought not to have said!

STRANGER. No. I admit I should not. And now I suffer pangs for it. . . .

LADY. You mean you can suffer?

STRANGER. Today I suffer doubly—for when you suffer, I suffer, too. And if I, in self-defense wound you—it is I who suffer the fever of the wound.

LADY. In other words, you are at my mercy?

STRANGER. Yes—and still more so now that you have the protection of the innocent being you carry under your heart.

LADY. The child shall be my avenger.

STRANGER. Or mine!

LADY (*with tears in her voice*). Poor little child! Born in sin and shame—born to avenge, through hate.

STRANGER. It's a long time since I heard you speak in that tone!

LADY. No doubt.

STRANGER. That was the voice that once trapped me, because it was like a mother's when she speaks to her child.

LADY. When you speak the word "mother" I am incapable of thinking anything but good of you. But a moment later, I think: This is merely another way of deceiving me.

STRANGER. What harm have I really done you? *(The Lady does not know what to answer.)* Answer me! What harm have I ever done you?

LADY. I don't know.

STRANGER. Try to think of something! Say something like this: I hate you because I can't deceive you!

LADY. Can't I?—I feel sorry for you.

STRANGER. Then you must have some poison hidden in your pocket.

LADY. So I have—yes.

STRANGER. What can it be?—Who is that I see coming down the road?

LADY. It's a bird of ill omen.

STRANGER. Is it a human being of flesh and blood, or is it a ghost?

LADY. It's a ghost from the past.

STRANGER. He is wearing a tailcoat and a laurel wreath—but is barefoot.

LADY. It is Caesar!

STRANGER *(confused)*. Caesar? Why, that was my nickname at school.

LADY. Well—but it is also a name given to the lunatic who was a patient of my—of my first husband—if you will forgive me for using that expression.

STRANGER. Is this madman going about loose?

LADY. So it seems.

(Caesar enters from the rear. He is wearing a tailcoat, a stiff-bosomed shirt without collar, and on his head a laurel wreath. He is barefoot. Everything about his appearance is bizarre. He speaks to the Stranger.)

CAESAR. Why don't you greet me? . . .You should say *Ave Caesar*—as I am now the master! For let me tell you that the werewolf has lost his mind—after the Great Genius took off with his wife, whom he himself had snatched from her first lover—or fiancé—or whatever you care to call it.

STRANGER *(to the Lady)*. That was enough poison to kill off two grown-up people! *(To Caesar.)* Where is your master—or slave—or alienist—or keeper? Where is he?

CAESAR. He'll soon be here. But you don't have to be afraid of him—he is not going to use either knife or poison on you. All he has to do is to show himself—and all living things will

bolt and run out of sight—the trees will shed their leaves—
and the dust of the highway will whirl about—much as the
pillar of a cloud did before the children of Israel. . . .

STRANGER. Tell me—

CAESAR. Keep quiet when I am speaking. . . . And sometimes he imagines he is a werewolf, and threatens to devour a
little unborn child that he says is his, because he is the real
father. . . .　　　　*(He moves toward the exit and leaves.)*

LADY *(to the Stranger)*. Can you drive out this demon?
Can you?

STRANGER. I can't get the upper hand of demons who brave
the sunshine!

LADY. You let fall a few boasting words the other morning.
You said: "To come creeping in the dark of night, when they
cannot be seen, and attack you, is odious. If they want to come,
let them come during the day, when the sun is shining!" Now
they have come!

STRANGER. And that makes you glad?

LADY. Yes—almost!

STRANGER. What a pity I can't get the same feeling when
you are being beset by ordeals! Let us take our places on the
bench—the bench of the accused. . . . There will no doubt be
others.

LADY. No, let us rather go!

STRANGER. No. I want to see how much I can stand. Furthermore, at every lash from the scourge I feel as if a guilt or debt
had been erased from my blackboard.

LADY. But I can't endure much more!—Do you see? There
he comes!—Oh God—this is the man I once thought I loved!

STRANGER. Thought? Yes—because all of it is nothing but delusion. Still—delusions are not to be laughed at.—By all means,
go! I'll make it my duty to remain—alone. . . . *(The Lady
goes up the steps. Before she reaches the last step, the Physician
is seen coming from the rear. His long hair is gray and hangs
down to the nape of his neck. He wears a hunting coat, similar
to the Stranger's, and a British-Indian topee. He seats himself
on a rock on the other side of the highway, opposite the
Stranger, who is seated on the bench. He takes off his topee
and wipes the perspiration from his brow. The Stranger, meanwhile, has grown impatient.)* What is it you want?

PHYSICIAN. All I want is to see the house where once I found
happiness—and where my roses blossomed. . . .

STRANGER. Any man of the world who had any common sense
would have chosen a different time for such a pursuit. He would

have come when the present occupants were away on a short trip, for example. He should have done this for his own sake, in order not to appear ludicrous.

PHYSICIAN. Ludicrous? 1 just wonder which one of us is the more ludicrous.

STRANGER. For the moment, it is probably I.

PHYSICIAN. Yes. Yet I doubt you are conscious of the full extent of your miserable position.

STRANGER. What are you driving at?

PHYSICIAN. Simply this: that you wish to own what was once mine.

STRANGER. Go on! Go on!

PHYSICIAN. Have you noticed that we are dressed alike?— Very well! And do you know why? I'll tell you! It is because you are wearing my clothes—the clothes I forgot to take with me when the disaster came. And, you see—that is what no man of the world at the end of the nineteenth century, having any intelligence whatsoever, should lay himself open to.

STRANGER (casting off his hat and coat). Accursed woman!

PHYSICIAN. Don't be ashamed—help yourself! Cast-off men's clothing has always been an omen of death, ever since the well-remembered shirt of Nessus. Go inside now and change. I'll sit out here and look on! I want to hear how you settle this matter with that damnable woman when you two are alone.—Don't forget your stick! (The Lady, hurrying toward the house, trips and falls at the foot of the steps. The Stranger stands bewildered.) The stick! The stick!

STRANGER. I ask no mercy for the woman—but for the sake of the child, I do!

PHYSICIAN (savagely). Oh—so there is a child, too! Our house, our roses, our clothes—not forgetting the bedclothes—and our child! You have me in your house—I sit at your table—lie in your bed! I am in your blood—your lungs—your brain—I am everywhere—but you can't lay your hands on me. When the pendulum strikes at the hour of midnight, I shall blow my cold breath on your heart—and it will stop like a run-down clock! When you sit working, I shall come with a poppy that you cannot see, and it shall put your thoughts to sleep; it shall bring disorder and confusion to your mind and make you see visions that you will be unable to distinguish from reality! I shall lie like a rock on your path, and you will stumble—I shall be the thorn that pricks your hand as it is about to pluck the rose; my soul shall stretch and fasten itself like the web of a spider across your soul—and through the woman you stole from me, I shall lead you like a bullock; your child shall be mine, and I shall speak through its mouth—in its eyes you shall read my gaze; and so you will push the child away from you as if it were an enemy. And now farewell, you little house! Farewell, you Rose Chamber! No happiness shall bloom within your walls—no happiness that I would envy!

(He leaves. Meanwhile the Stranger has been sitting on the bench and listening to the Physician without finding words to answer him.)

ACT II

SCENE 1. The Laboratory. *A garden pavilion in rococo style, with French windows. In the middle of the floor stands a large writing table on which are placed diverse chemical and physical apparatuses. Two copper wires, hanging from the ceiling, are attached to an electroscope that stands in the center of the table. To this electroscope are attached small bells whose purpose is to record the tension of atmospheric electricity. On a table at the left is a big, old-fashioned friction machine with glass disks, brass conductors, and Leyden batteries, for producing static electricity. The posts are lacquered red and black. On the right is a large, old-fashioned open fireplace with tripods, crucibles, tongs, bellows, etc. Through the French windows in the rear can be seen the countryside in the distance. The sky is overcast, the weather is gloomy; occasionally, however, the reddish rays of the sun cast their glow into the pavilion.*

A brown cloak, with cape and hood, hangs by the fireplace. Close by, a traveling bag and an alpenstock.

The Stranger and the Mother are seen in the pavilion.

STRANGER. Where is—Ingeborg?

MOTHER. You should know that better than I.

STRANGER. Very well—she is with the attorney. She is seeking a divorce.

MOTHER. Why?

STRANGER. Because . . . No, it is all so incredible that you would think I was lying.

MOTHER. Do tell me!

STRANGER. Why, she wants a divorce because I didn't give her demented husband a beating! She calls me a coward. . . .

MOTHER. I don't believe you.

STRANGER. There—you see! You only believe what you choose to believe—everything else is a lie. Well—does it suit you to believe that she has stolen some of my letters?

MOTHER. I know nothing about that.

STRANGER. I didn't ask you whether you knew—I asked you whether you believed it.

MOTHER (changing the subject). What is it you are occupying yourself with here?

STRANGER. I am experimenting with atmospheric electricity.

MOTHER. And—isn't that a lightning rod that you have on the writing table?

STRANGER. Yes, but there is no danger—for the moment there is a disturbance in the air, the bells will ring.

MOTHER. This is blasphemy—it's black magic! Take care!— And what have you in the fireplace? What are you doing there?

STRANGER. I am trying to make gold.

MOTHER. And do you think you can?

STRANGER. You take it for granted that I am a charlatan, don't you? I can't blame you for that. But don't be too hasty in your judgment. I may have my formula confirmed any day now, with a certified analysis.

MOTHER. That's all very well—but what do you plan to do if Ingeborg should not return?

STRANGER. She will return—this time also. But later—after the child has been born—she may leave me again. . . .

MOTHER. You seem so very sure that she will.

STRANGER. As I just said: I am still convinced she will. . . . It's a feeling one has—so long as the tie is still unbroken. But once broken, one is gripped by a disagreeable sensation.

MOTHER. But once you are free of each other, you may still both be bound to the child. That is something you cannot take account of beforehand.

STRANGER. I have safeguarded myself against that eventuality by providing myself with a special interest which I hope will fill my empty life.

MOTHER. The gold, you mean, and the honor that would come with it?

STRANGER. Precisely! The most enduring illusions a man can have!

MOTHER. So you are still building your life upon illusions?

STRANGER. What else should I be building upon, when everything on earth is illusion?

MOTHER. Once you awaken from your dreams, you will discover realities that you could never have dreamed of.

STRANGER. Then I shall wait until that day comes.

MOTHER. Yes, you wait!—Now I am going to close the windows before the thunderstorm breaks.

STRANGER *(walks toward the rear)*. That will be interesting. *(A hunting horn can be heard in the distance.)* Who can that be?

MOTHER. No one knows—but it is not a good omen. . . .

(She leaves. The Stranger busies himself with the electroscope, turning his back to the open French window. Then he takes up a book and reads aloud from it.)

STRANGER. "When Adam's mighty generations had multiplied so that they felt themselves sufficient in number to risk an attack upon those above them, they began to build a tower whose top was to reach unto heaven. Those who were in authority were then seized with fear; and in order to protect themselves, they broke up the conspiracy by so confounding the language, and by making their minds so confused that when two people met, they could not understand each other— even when they spoke the same tongue. Ever since, those in authority rule through dissension: divide and rule. And dissension is kept alive by making people believe that truth has been discovered. But whenever one of their prophets is believed by some, he is called a false prophet by others. On the other hand, if some mortal should happen to uncover the secret of those who are highly placed, he will be struck with madness lest anyone believe him—and so that no one ever shall. From that time on, mortals have been more or less demented: the ones who have been considered wise men more so than others. The mentally deranged are the only ones who could be called sane. They can feel what is obscure and intangible—they can see the invisible—can hear what has no sound. Yet they cannot impart their experiences to others." So speaks Zohar, the greatest of all the books of wisdom—and that is why no one believes it. I don't intend to build a Tower of Babel—but I shall tempt the Powers into my mousetrap—and then I shall dispatch them to the Powers in the underworld to be neutralized. It is these powerful Schedim who have come between mortals and the Lord of Sabaoth—and that is the reason why peace and joy and happiness have disappeared from this earth.

LADY *(enters, throws herself at the feet of the Stranger, grasping them with her arms, her forehead touching the ground.)* Help me! Help me! And forgive me!

STRANGER. In God's name—get up! Get up! Don't do anything like this! What has happened?

LADY. Oh! I have done something foolish—out of anger! And now I have been caught in my own trap!

STRANGER (raises her up). Stand up, you foolish child—and tell me what is wrong!

LADY. I went to see the public prosecutor, and . . .

STRANGER. . . . and applied for a divorce.

LADY. That was what I intended to do—but instead when I arrived there, I brought information against the werewolf for invasion of privacy and attempted murder.

STRANGER. But he did neither!

LADY. No, but I accused him of both. And while I am there, he himself comes in, and he makes a charge against me for falsely accusing him. Then I went to the attorney, and he said I can expect to be sentenced to prison for at least one month! Think of it—my child born in a prison!—How will I get out of it? Oh, help me! You can, if you will! Help me! Say that you will!

STRANGER. Yes—I can help you. But don't take revenge on me afterward if I do help you!

LADY. How you misjudge me! But there is no time for delay! Tell me if you will do it!

STRANGER. Well—I have to take the blame for it upon myself —say that I sent you.

LADY. Oh, what a dear you are!—Why, then I'll be free of the whole affair!

STRANGER. Dry your tears, my child, and don't worry. But tell me—and it has nothing to do with this—did you leave that purse here? (The Lady is embarrassed.) Tell me!

LADY. Have you had any such experience before?

STRANGER. Yes. My other wife tried to use the same trick in order to find out whether I was a thief. And the same scheme was used once before in the past. That time I cried—for it happened when I was a child.

LADY. No—really?

STRANGER. At this moment you are to me the most abominable creature on earth!

LADY. Is that why you love me?

STRANGER. No, that is not the reason!—And you have stolen my letters, haven't you? Answer yes! It is for that reason you wanted to make me out to be a thief also by leaving that purse there.

LADY. What have you there on the table?

STRANGER. Lightning! *(There is a flash of lightning, without thunder.)*

LADY. You are afraid!

STRANGER. Occasionally, yes—but I am not afraid of what you fear. *(The Physician's face is seen in the window, his features twisted and contorted.)*

LADY. Is there a cat in here? I feel uncomfortable.

STRANGER. No, I don't think there is. But I, too, have a feeling as if someone were here. . . .

LADY *(turns and sees the Physician's face pressed against the window pane. She screams and dashes toward the Stranger for protection).* Oh! It is he!

STRANGER. Who? Where? *(The Physician's face disappears.)*

LADY. There—at the window—it is he!

STRANGER. I don't see anyone. You must be mistaken!

LADY. No! I saw him—the werewolf! Can't you get rid of him?

STRANGER. Yes—I suppose we could do away with him—but that wouldn't help us; for his soul is immortal, and it is bound to yours.

LADY. Why didn't I realize that before?

STRANGER. I think you will find it in your catechism!

LADY. Then let us die!

STRANGER. That was my religion at one time—but now that I no longer believe death to be the end, nothing remains for us but to endure to the end whatever may come—and to struggle —and suffer!

LADY. How long must we suffer?

STRANGER. So long as *he* suffers and our conscience keeps flogging us. . . .

LADY. We shall have to try to vindicate ourselves to our conscience—find some sort of justification for our reckless actions. Let us try to put our finger on some of his imperfections and shortcomings.

STRANGER. Try!

LADY. That is easier said than done! Knowing how unhappy he is, I can see only his good side—and you lose by comparison.

STRANGER. You see how wisely everything is planned. His sufferings sanctify him, while mine make me ludicrous and abhorrent! This is like being in the presence of something for which there is no help! We have destroyed a soul—therefore we are murderers.

LADY. Who is to blame?

STRANGER. He who has so bungled mankind's fate. (*There is a flash of lightning. The electric bells ring.*)

LADY. Jesus! Mary! What is that?

STRANGER. Our question was answered.

LADY. Have you placed the lightning rod here—in the pavilion?

STRANGER. The priest of Baal tries to bring down the lightning from heaven. . . .

LADY. Now I am in fear—I am frightened of you—you fill me with terror!

STRANGER. Now you see!

LADY. Who are you to dare defy Heaven and play with the destinies of men?

STRANGER. Get up and gather your senses!—If you will listen to me, have faith in me, and give me the respect I deserve, I shall raise us both high above this frog marsh in which we are now stuck! I shall blow on your sick conscience and make it heal like any other wound. Who I am? I am a man who has done what no other man has ever done. I shall overthrow the Golden Calf and knock the tables of the money-changers to the ground. I hold the fate of the world in my crucible—and a week from now the richest of the rich will be poor. Gold, the false measuring rod of wealth, will have ceased to be the ruler—we shall all be poor—and the children of mankind will be crawling about like ants when their anthill has been trampled upon!

LADY. What good will that do us?

STRANGER. Do you think I have been making gold for the purpose of enriching ourselves and others? Oh no! I have done it in the hope that the present world order may be done away with—may be destroyed! Don't you see? I am the devastator, the disintegrator, the one who sets the universe afire! And when the earth lies in ashes, I shall roam hungering through the ruins and rejoice at the thought that this is my handiwork —mine—and that I have written the final chapter in the history of the universe—and that this is its conclusion. (*The face of the Dominican appears at the open window. He is unseen by those on the stage.*)

LADY. What you have just said was what you said in your last book! So it was not mere imagery, was it?

STRANGER. No! But in order to accomplish it, I had to take on a duality: I had to link my own self with that of another being, so that he could relieve me of and absorb all that which holds my soul captive in its grip—so that my spirit might re-

cover its pure, fiery breath and rise upward into the ether—
eluding the Powers and reaching the throne of the Eternal
One and there lay at His feet the complaints of mankind. . . .
*(The Dominican makes the sign of the cross in the air and
vanishes.)* Who is here? Who is the Awesome One who keeps
pursuing me and who cripples my thoughts?—Do you see
anyone?

LADY. No—I see no one.

STRANGER. But I can feel that he is here. *(His hand goes to
his heart.)* Can you hear—do you hear—far in the distance—
far, far away—the Ave Maria being recited? Do you hear?

LADY. Yes, I hear. But it is not the Ave Maria—it is the
curse of Deuteronomy. Woe unto us!

STRANGER. Then it must be in the cloister of the Good
Help. . . .

LADY. Woe unto us!

STRANGER. Beloved! What troubles you?

LADY. Say that word again—*beloved!*

STRANGER. Are you ill?

LADY. No—but I am suffering—and at the same time I am
happy. . . . Go and ask my mother to make up my bed. . . .
But first give me your blessing!

STRANGER. You want me to . . .

LADY. Say you forgive me. . . . When the little one comes,
it may mean my life! Tell me that you love me!

STRANGER. It is strange—but I can't get that word across my
lips!

LADY. Then you don't love me?

STRANGER. When you say it, it seems so. It is horrible—but
I think I hate you.

LADY. You can at least offer me your hand—as you would
give it to anyone in distress. . . .

STRANGER. I want to—but I can't. There is another nature
within me which revels in your suffering—but it is not I—it is
not myself, for I would like to carry you in my arms and take
your suffering upon myself! Yet there is something that forbids me! Therefore I cannot!

LADY. You are hard as rock!

STRANGER *(restraining his emotion)*. Perhaps not! Perhaps
not!

LADY. Come to me!

STRANGER. I am unable to move from the spot. It is as if
someone had taken possession of my soul! I would like to take
my own life and thus kill off that other one!

LADY. Think of your child with joy. . . .

STRANGER. I can't even do that, for it will bind me to the earth.

LADY. If we have sinned, we have already been punished! God in heaven! Is there no end to this!

STRANGER. Perhaps some day there will be . . . but not yet.

LADY *(sinks down)*. Oh, help me! Have mercy on me! I am dying!

(The Stranger gives her his hand as though he had just come out of a state of hypnosis or catalepsy. The Lady kisses his hand. The Stranger lifts her up and leads her toward the door.)

SCENE 2. The Rose Chamber. *A room with rose-colored walls, small windows with iron gratings, and potted flowers. The curtains are rose-red; the furniture is white and red. In the rear, a door leads to a bedroom in white; when opened, a large bed with canopy and white curtains is seen. On the left, a door leads out of doors. On the right, a coal stove with a fire in it. In front of the stove, a bathtub covered with a cloth, and a cradle in white, rose-red, and pale blue colors. Baby clothes are scattered about the room. A green dress hangs on the wall, left. Four Sisters of Charity, their faces toward the rear, are kneeling. They wear the black-and-white garb of Augustinian nuns. The Midwife, dressed in black, stands by the stove. The Wet Nurse, wearing the black-and-white peasant dress of Brittany, waits nearby. The Mother stands at the door at the rear, listening. The Stranger is seated in a chair on the left; he is reading a book. Close by him hangs a brown cloak, with cape and hood, and a hat. A small traveling bag stands on the floor.*

SISTERS OF CHARITY *(singing a hymn, in which the others join from time to time)*.

Salve, Regina, mater misericordiae;
Vita dulcedo, et spes nostra, salve.
Ad te clamamus, exules filii Evae:
Ad te suspiramus gementes et flentes
In hac lacrymarum valle.

(The Stranger gets up and goes to the Mother.)

MOTHER. Stay where you are!—A human being is coming into this life—while another one passes out of it. And you are indifferent to it all.

STRANGER. Who knows. . . . When I want to go inside, you

won't let me. And when I don't want to, you tell me I have to. I would like to go inside now.

MOTHER. She doesn't wish to see you. Besides, your presence here is not necessary. The child is the more important thing just now.

STRANGER. For you, yes—but I am still the most important person as far as I am concerned.

MOTHER. The doctor has forbidden anyone to go inside to her—whoever it may be—because of the danger to her life.

STRANGER. Which doctor?

MOTHER. I see your thoughts are there again. . . .

STRANGER. Yes, and it is you who lead them there! An hour ago you tried to make me believe the child was not mine! By saying that, you stigmatized your daughter as a whore! But such a thing means nothing to you—so long as you can stab me in the heart! You are very nearly the most contemptible creature I know!

MOTHER (to the Sisters of Charity). Sisters! Pray for this unhappy man!

STRANGER. Step aside and let me go in!—For the last time—step aside!

MOTHER. Leave this room—and get out of this house!

STRANGER. If I were to do what you tell me to do, you would be sending the sheriff after me within ten minutes, accusing me of having abandoned my wife and child!

MOTHER. If I should send for the sheriff, it would only be to have him take you to the asylum you already know.

MAID (enters from the rear; she turns to the Stranger). Your wife wishes you to do something for her.

STRANGER. Speak up!

MAID. There is a letter in her dress hanging in this room.

STRANGER (looks around and discovers the green dress hanging on the wall, left. He takes a letter from the pocket). This letter is addressed to me. It was opened two days ago. Consequently it was stolen! A nice state of affairs!

MOTHER. You have to have forgiveness for your wife. She is ill.

STRANGER. She was not ill two days ago!

MOTHER. No, but she is now.

STRANGER. But she was not two days ago! (He reads the letter.) However—I can now forgive her—with the magnanimity of one who has won a victory.

MOTHER. A victory?

STRANGER. Yes—a victory! For I have done what no other man has ever done.

MOTHER. You mean—the gold? . . .

STRANGER. Here is the document certifying to the correctness of my formula—from the greatest of living authorities. Now I shall go and see him in person.

MOTHER. You are leaving—now?

STRANGER. As you have suggested so insistently!

MAID (to the Stranger). The Lady asks if you will come in now. . . .

MOTHER. You hear!

STRANGER. No—now I don't wish to! You have made my wife —who is your daughter—into a whore! And you have given my unborn child the name of bastard. Now you can keep them both! You have destroyed my honor! And so I have only one recourse: to find redress elsewhere!

MOTHER. You have no forgiveness in you!

STRANGER. Yes—I forgive you—and then—I leave! (He puts on the brown cloak and his hat, picks up the traveling bag and his stick.) For if I should stay, I would soon be worse than I really am. The innocent child, which was to be an ennobling influence and bring about a change in our warped relationship, you have tainted and made unclean in your womb! It would be a constant source of wrangling and discontent—and a seed of punishment and revengefulness! Why, then, should I remain here and let myself be torn to pieces?

MOTHER. For you, the word duty does not exist!

STRANGER. It does, indeed—and my first duty is to protect myself from going under completely. . . . Farewell!

ACT III

SCENE 1. A banquet hall. Long tables are decorated with flowers and candelabra. Platters with peacock and pheasant, complete with feathers; boar's head; whole lobster; also oysters, salmon, asparagus, melons, and grapes.

In the left corner rear, eight musicians are seated on a balcony. At the table of honor sits the Stranger, dressed in formal evening clothes. Next to him, a man in civil uniform, wearing his decorations; a man in professorial evening dress; for the rest, ordinary formal evening clothes, with ribbons of orders and medals, more or less distinctive and brilliant. Seated at the adjoining table, a few formal dress coats among

*black cutaways. At the third table, neat, everyday suits; at the
fourth table, soiled, ragged figures with strange countenances.
The tables are so arranged that the first table stands farthest
away to the right, and the fourth one, at the far left side,
is so placed that the people seated at it can not be seen by
the Stranger. At the fourth table, seated close to the footlights, are the Physician and Caesar. Both are shabbily
dressed.*

*The dessert has just been served, and each guest has a
goblet of gold in front of him. When the curtain rises, the
Musicians are in the middle of Mendelssohn's Funeral
March, played pianissimo. The guests are conversing with
one another in subdued tones.*

PHYSICIAN *(to Caesar)*. The atmosphere is a little depressing,
and the dessert came a bit too soon.

CAESAR. The whole thing appears to me to be some sort of
humbug, if I may say so. I am sure he couldn't have made
gold. It's a lie—like everything else.

PHYSICIAN. I don't know—but that's what they say. In these
enlightened times we can expect anything to happen.

CAESAR. There is a professor sitting on the dais. He must
be an authority on such things, I imagine—but exactly what
is he professor of?

PHYSICIAN. I have no idea—but I presume it must be metal-
lurgy and applied chemistry.

CAESAR. Do you recognize the decoration he is wearing?

PHYSICIAN. No—I don't know that one. . . . I imagine it
is some insignificant foreign order.

CAESAR. Well, at a subscription dinner such as this, the
company is always somewhat mixed.

PHYSICIAN. Hm.

CAESAR. You mean that we . . . Hm—yes, we are not dressed
so very elegantly—but as far as intelligence goes . . .

PHYSICIAN. Listen, Caesar—you are a lunatic—and you are
under my supervision . . . therefore you must avoid as much
as you can talking about intelligence.

CAESAR. That is the greatest impertinence I have heard in
a long time! Don't you know that I was appointed to watch
over you after you lost your reason?

PROFESSOR *(clinking his goblet with his spoon)*. Gentlemen!

CAESAR. Hear, hear!

PROFESSOR. Gentlemen!—Our little community has today been
honored by the presence of the great man whom we now have

here as our guest of honor; and as the board of governors . . .

CAESAR *(to the Physician)*. He means the government, you know. . . .

PROFESSOR *(continuing)* . . . and as the board of governors has. asked me to give voice to the feelings that animate its members, I was at first in doubt as to whether I ought to accept that honor. But when I compared my own incapacity with that of some others, I arrived at the conclusion that neither of us really lost by the comparison.

VOICES. Bravo!

PROFESSOR. Gentlemen! The century of great inventions is coming to a close with the mightiest, the most devastating of all inventions—an invention divined by the followers of Pythagoras, forecast and nurtured by Albertus and Paracelsus—and now finally achieved by our guest of honor. May I be permitted to present to you on behalf of our Society this feeble token of our admiration for the greatest man of this great century: the laurel wreath! *(He places a laurel wreath on the Stranger's head.)* And, on behalf of the board of governors of our Society —this. *(He hangs the brilliant insignia of the Society's medal round the Stranger's neck.)* Gentlemen! Long live the great producer of gold!

ALL *(except the Stranger)*. Hurrah! Hurrah! Hurrah!

(The orchestra plays a few chords from Mendelssohn's Funeral March. During the final part of the preceding speech, servants have exchanged the goblets of gold for dull ones of tin, and they now start to remove the peacocks, pheasants, etc. The Musicians play softly. General conversation.)

CAESAR. Don't you think we should have a chance to taste some of those things before they are taken away?

PHYSICIAN. This whole thing seems to be nothing but humbug—all except the gold-making.

STRANGER. *(clinking his goblet)*. Gentlemen! To me it has always been a cause for pride that I am not easily deceived . . .

CAESAR. Hear, hear!

STRANGER . . . and neither am I an easy prey to enthusiasm. . . . But the sincerity which your magnificent tribute to me bespeaks has touched me . . . and when I say that I have been touched, I mean it!

CAESAR. Bravo!

STRANGER. We always find skeptics—and in the life of every man there are moments when doubt takes hold of even the strongest. And I have to confess that even I myself have been a doubter. But having been the object of such a sincere tribute, emanating from the heart, as I have witnessed at this royal celebration—for royal it is!—and, finally, as the government itself—

VOICE. The board! The board of governors!

STRANGER.—as the board of governors, if you like, has given such a glowing acknowledgment of my inconspicuous services, which the future alone will be able to judge, I no longer am a doubter: I believe! *(The man in the civil uniform steals out.)* Yes, gentlemen—this is the greatest moment in my life— the most beautiful moment—for it has given me back the most precious possession a human being can have: faith in himself!

CAESAR. Marvelous! Bravo!

STRANGER. My thanks to you all! To your health! *(He raises his goblet. The Professor rises. The guests follow suit and begin to mingle with one another. All the Musicians, except two, go out.)*

GUEST *(to the Stranger).* Quite a delightful gathering! Quite delightful!

STRANGER. Superb! *(All those wearing formal evening dress steal out. The Father, an elderly dandy of military bearing and wearing a monocle, goes up to the Physician and greets him.)*

FATHER. Why, how do you! So you are here, too?

PHYSICIAN. Yes, Father-in-Law, I am here, too. Wherever he goes, I go.

FATHER. You must not call me Father-in-Law any more. I am now *his* father-in-law, you know.

PHYSICIAN. Has he met you yet?

FATHER. No, he hasn't had that honor—and I am here incognito—so please don't betray me!—Is it really true that he has made gold?

PHYSICIAN. So they say. But there is one thing that is true: that he left his wife while she was having a child.

FATHER. That sounds as if I could expect a new son-in-law soon, doesn't it? Yes, my boy, it is not a very nice state of affairs—this sort of thing. And the uncertainty that goes with it gives me a distaste for being a father-in-law. Well, well—I have nothing to say about such matters. . . . After all . . .

(By this time, the tables have been cleared, and tablecloths and candelabra removed so that only boards or tabletops on trestles remain. A large bowl of earthenware is brought in, and small, very plain earthenware mugs are placed on the table of honor. Caesar loudly raps for silence: the shabby-looking, ragged people seat themselves on the dais with the

Stranger, and the Father places himself astride a chair, staring at the Stranger.)

CAESAR. Gentlemen! This has been called a royal banquet—not because the repast has been so royally sumptuous—for on the contrary it has been miserably bad—but because the man to whom we have paid homage is a king—a king in the realm of the Spirit and the Intellect—and I am the only one who is qualified to judge that. *(There is laughter from One of the Ragged.)* Keep quiet, you ill-bred vulgarian!—But he is more than a king; he is a friend of the people, the common man, the oppressed—he is the guardian of lunatics—he brings joy and happiness to fools and simpletons. It does not matter to me whether he has made gold or not—I don't care about that—and, besides, I don't think I believe it anyhow. *(A murmur goes through the assemblage. Two Policemen enter and take seats near the entrance door; the Musicians come down and seat themselves at the tables.)* But suppose he has made gold—suppose he has—then he has solved all the questions that the daily press has in vain been trying to solve for the last fifty years. . . . However—this is merely a supposition—that's all. . . .

STRANGER. Gentlemen!

ONE OF THE RAGGED. No—don't interrupt him!

CAESAR. This is merely a supposition, of course, without any real basis, and it could be that the analysis is wrong!

ANOTHER ONE OF THE RAGGED. Stop talking nonsense!

STRANGER. In my capacity as guest of honor, it should not be without interest for those present to hear on what principles my discovery is based—and the evidence in support of it. . . .

CAESAR. No! We don't care to hear! We don't care!

FATHER. Wait a moment! It seems to me it is no more than just that the accused should have an opportunity to explain what he has in mind. Wouldn't our guest of honor, therefore, be good enough to tell us his secret in a few words?

STRANGER. The discovery being my own, I cannot surrender its secret formula. Furthermore, I cannot understand why this should be necessary, since I have submitted my results to authoritative quarters, under oath.

CAESAR. Then the whole thing is nothing but hocus-pocus; and we don't believe anything the authorities say, anyhow, for we are free-thinkers!—Did you ever hear of anything so brazen? The idea—that we, in good faith, should honor a man who keeps his secrets to himself—an impostor, a charlatan!

FATHER. Just a moment, good people!

(During this scene a partition screen with palm trees and

*birds of paradise has been removed, and now can be seen
a row of dilapidated shelves for bottles and glasses, and a
serving bar, behind which stands the Woman Bartender,
dispensing drinks. Figures of the Night and disagreeable-
looking women go up to the bar and start boozing.)*

STRANGER. Did you invite me here in order to insult me?

FATHER. Far from it! Our friend Caesar may be a little garrulous, but so far he hasn't said anything insulting.

STRANGER. Don't you think it is an insult to be called a
charlatan?

FATHER. That was not meant to be taken seriously.

STRANGER. Even if said in jest, I think the word "impostor"
is an affront of the worst kind!

FATHER. He didn't use that word.

STRANGER. What? I appeal to all who are present: didn't
he call me an impostor?

ALL. No! He did not!

STRANGER. Why! Where am I? What kind of company have
I got into?

ONE OF THE RAGGED. Do you find any fault with it, do you?
*(The Guests start murmuring. The Beggar, on crutches, steps
forward; he strikes the table with one of his crutches with
such force that several of the mugs are broken.)*

BEGGAR. Mr. Chairman!—I would like to say a few words.
(He breaks some more of the earthenware on the table.)
Throughout my life, gentlemen, I have never allowed myself
to be easily taken in. But this time I have been caught! My
friend, however, seated here in the seat of honor, has now convinced me that I have been thoroughly deceived as regards his
good judgment and common sense—so much so that I feel
veritably touched. There is a limit to pity, and a limit also to
cruelty. It hurts me to see real merit being dragged into the
mire—and this man deserves a better fate than his folly has
led him to.

STRANGER. What is the meaning of all this?
*(The Father and the Physician have stolen out while the
Beggar was speaking. The shabby-looking ragged people
now occupy all the seats on the dais. The derelicts standing
at the bar collect in groups and glare at the Stranger.)*

BEGGAR. This is what I mean! You, who consider yourself
to be the man of the century—you accept an invitation from
a society of alcoholics to have yourself feted as a man of
science! . . .

STRANGER *(rises)*. But the board of governors—

BEGGAR. Yes—the board of governors of the Society of Alcoholics conferred on you its highest degree by that insignia, which you will have to pay for yourself.

STRANGER. But how about the Professor?

BEGGAR. He is only called that—he isn't one. I think he teaches something or other. And that uniform, which must have impressed you no end, was nothing but that of a lackey at the Royal Chancellery.

STRANGER (tears off his laurel wreath and the ribbon with the insignia). So!—But who was the old gentleman with the monocle?

BEGGAR. That was your father-in-law.

STRANGER. Who is responsible for this levity, this farce?

BEGGAR. This is no jesting—it is absolute seriousness. The Professor came to you on behalf of humanitarianism—for they call themselves a humanitarian society—and asked if you would accept the honor—and you answered "yes"—and so it became an actuality! (Two unpleasant, shabby women carry in a dust barrel on a wooden pole and place it on the table on the dais.)

FIRST WOMAN. Are you the fellow who makes gold, eh? Then treat us to a drink, why don't you?

STRANGER. What is the meaning of this?

BEGGAR. This is the last phase of the reception, and it means, figuratively, that gold is nothing but—dust!

STRANGER. If that were true, then dust could be exchanged for gold.

BEGGAR. Oh well, that is merely the philosophy of our society —and you have to adopt the philosophy of wherever you are.

SECOND WOMAN (sits down next to the Stranger). Do you recognize me?

STRANGER. No!

SECOND WOMAN. Oh yes, you do! At this late hour of the night, you needn't be embarrassed!

STRANGER. I suppose you would like to pretend you were one of my victims? Perhaps I was one out of the first hundred who seduced you?

SECOND WOMAN. No—that isn't what you mean to say. But at the time I was about to be confirmed I came across a pamphlet which exhorted the young not to allow their sexual instincts to be suppressed.

STRANGER (rising). Now, perhaps, I may go?

WOMAN BARTENDER (comes up to him with a bill). You may —after you have paid your bill.

STRANGER. My bill? I have ordered nothing!

WOMAN BARTENDER. I know nothing about that, but you are the last one of the company to eat.

STRANGER *(to the Beggar)*. Is this part of the reception also?

BEGGAR. Certainly. And as you well know: everything has to be paid for—even honor. . . .

STRANGER *(takes out a visiting card and hands it to the Woman Bartender)*. Here is my card. The bill will be paid tomorrow.

WOMAN BARTENDER *(drops the card into the dust barrel)*. Hm! Your name is not familiar to me; and this is not the first visiting card that has landed in the dust barrel. What I want is money. *(A policeman enters.)*

BEGGAR. Now listen, madam—I give you my word of honor that this man will pay. . . .

WOMAN BARTENDER. So-o? You have the audacity to jest with me, too, have you?—Officer! Come here a moment!

POLICEMAN. What's the trouble? The bill, I can imagine. Come along with me; then we'll settle the matter at the police station. *(He makes an annotation in his notebook.)*

STRANGER. I prefer that to standing here arguing. *(To the Beggar.)* I don't mind a little jesting—but I had never expected a reality as cruel as this.

BEGGAR. You have to be prepared for anything, after having challenged such powerful interests as you have! And, between ourselves, let me tell you something: Be prepared for something still worse! For the very worst!

STRANGER. To think that I could let myself be so deceived—so—

BEGGAR. Feasts of Belshazzar invariably end in this way: one hand is stretched out, writing a bill, and another hand is placed on the shoulder of the customer and removes him to the police station. But it should be done with dignity—with royal dignity!

POLICEMAN. I think the discussion has gone on long enough now! *(He places a hand on the Stranger's shoulder.)*

THE WOMEN *and* THE RAGGED. The alchemist! The fellow who knows how to make gold can't pay! Hurrah! He is being put behind iron bars! He is being put behind bars!

SECOND WOMAN. Yes—but I feel sorry for him!

STRANGER. You feel compassion for me? For that I thank you —even if I don't precisely deserve it! And *you* feel compassion!

SECOND WOMAN. Yes—and that is something I also have learned from you!

(Without the curtain being lowered, the scene is changed.

The stage is darkened and a conglomeration of scenery, representing landscapes, palaces, and interiors is lowered and moved forward while people and furniture disappear—all except the Stranger, who stands rigid, as if seized with catalepsy. He seems to be asleep. Finally he also is obliterated, and out of the confusion there emerges a prison cell.)

SCENE 2. The Prison. *A door on the left, and above it a grated aperture in the wall, through which the sun casts a beam forming a white spot on the wall, right. A large crucifix hangs on that wall.*

The Stranger, wearing a brown cloak and a hat, sits at the table, regarding the patch of sunlight. The door opens, and the Beggar is admitted.

BEGGAR. What are you cogitating upon?

STRANGER. I am pondering why I am here, and wondering where I was last evening.

BEGGAR. And where do you think you were?

STRANGER. I was either in hell, I think—or I must have been dreaming.

BEGGAR. Then wake up—for we are coming back to reality.

STRANGER. Let it come! It is only ghosts that frighten me.

BEGGAR *(takes a newspaper from his pocket).* First of all, the eminent authority has changed his mind and withdrawn his endorsement of your formula for making gold. It says so here in the newspaper. He states that he was swindled by you. As a result, the newspaper calls you a charlatan.

STRANGER. Hell and damnation!—Who or what is it I am fighting?

BEGGAR. You are fighting against unwieldy forces—like many another—

STRANGER. No—this is something else . . .

BEGGAR. —against your own gullibility, your self-delusions.

STRANGER. No—I am not gullible, and I know I am right.

BEGGAR. What's the good of that, if no one else knows it?

STRANGER. If you will just let me get out of here, I'll clear up this matter.

BEGGAR. The charges have been withdrawn since payment has been made. . . .

STRANGER. Who paid?

BEGGAR. Probably the Society, or the board of drunken governors.

STRANGER. Then I can go?

BEGGAR. Yes—but there is one thing more. . . .

STRANGER. What is that?

BEGGAR. Don't forget that an enlightened man of the world must not allow himself to be caught by surprise.

STRANGER. I am beginning to suspect that.

BEGGAR. You will find the advertisement on the front page.

STRANGER. That means—she is already married again, and my children now have a stepfather. Who is he?

BEGGAR. Whoever he may be—don't murder him! For whoever takes a forsaken woman for his wife is not a sinner.

STRANGER. My children!—Lord Jesus! My children!

BEGGAR. I see you did not expect that to happen, did you? But why not be a little cautious—especially being as old as you are—and a man of the world so enlightened!

STRANGER (beside himself). Oh Lord Jesus! My children!

BEGGAR. Enlightened gentlemen don't cry! But listen to me now, my boy! When a gentleman receives a blow such as this one, he usually—either . . . well, what does he do?

STRANGER. Shoots himself!

BEGGAR. Or . . . ?

STRANGER. Oh no—no! Not that!

BEGGAR. Yes, my dear boy—that is exactly what he does! He puts out a sheet-anchor and takes his chances.

STRANGER. This is hopeless! Hopeless!

BEGGAR. You are right—so it is! Absolutely hopeless! And you may have to live out still another generation, and then you will have a chance to contemplate your villainy and your knavish tricks in peace and quiet.

STRANGER. Shame on you!

BEGGAR. I say the same to you!

STRANGER. Have you ever seen a human fate like mine?

BEGGAR. Look at mine!

STRANGER. I know nothing of your fate!

BEGGAR. Nor has it ever occurred to you during all the years we have known each other to inquire about my circumstances. You once scorned the friendship I offered you, and instead you fell headlong into the arms of your alcoholic friends. And now you are welcome to it! And—good-by, until we see each other again!

STRANGER. Don't go!

BEGGAR. Perhaps you would like to have someone accompany you when you get out of here?

STRANGER. Why not?

BEGGAR. It hasn't occurred to you that I might not care to be seen with you, has it?

STRANGER. No, you are quite right, it hasn't.

BEGGAR. But such is the case. Do you think I would like to be suspected of having been present at that immortal alchemy banquet which is described in this morning's newspaper? Do you?

STRANGER. So you refuse to be seen in my company?

BEGGAR. Even a beggar has little vanities, and a fear of ridicule!

STRANGER. You don't wish to be seen with me!—Am I then so utterly vile and worthless?

BEGGAR. That is a question you must ask yourself; and only you can answer it! (*A sad cradle song is heard. It sounds as if it came from faraway.*)

STRANGER. What is that?

BEGGAR. It is a mother singing at her baby's cradle.

STRANGER. Why must I be reminded of that just now?

BEGGAR. Presumably so that you may be conscious of all that you have left behind for the sake of a vain and horrible illusion.

STRANGER. Could it be possible that I have made such a mistake? If I have, then it is plainly a delusion foisted on me by the devil, and I lay down my arms and surrender.

BEGGAR. The sooner you do that, the better!

STRANGER. No—not yet! (*An Ave Maria is heard intoned in the distance.*) What is that? (*A long-drawn-out note from a hunting horn is sounded.*) That is the mysterious huntsman! (*The chords from Mendelssohn's Funeral March are heard.*) Where am I? (*He remains standing as if in a hypnotic sleep.*)

BEGGAR. Humble yourself and surrender, or you will come to your end!

STRANGER. I cannot humble myself!

BEGGAR. Then you have sealed your doom!

(*The Stranger collapses. There is the same manner of conglomerated scenic effects as at the end of the banquet scene.*)

SCENE 3. The Rose Chamber. *The setting is the same as in Act II, Scene 2. The Sisters of Charity are kneeling, reading from their breviaries:* "... Exules filii Evae, ad te suspiramus gementes et flentes in hac lacrymarum valle." *The Mother is by the door, rear; the Father by the door, left.*

MOTHER (*approaching the Father*). So-o? You have come back?

FATHER (*humbly*). Yes.

MOTHER. Your beloved has left you, hasn't she?

FATHER. Don't be more cruel than you have to be!

MOTHER. And you say that—you who gave away my wedding presents to your mistress—you who were cad enough to ask me to choose gifts for your concubine—who wanted me to teach you about clothes and colors! What do you want here?

FATHER. I heard that my daughter . . .

MOTHER. Your daughter is hovering between life and death; and you know her feelings for you are anything but friendly. So I must ask you to leave before she finds out you are here.

FATHER. You are right—and I have nothing to say. But let me sit in the kitchen for a moment. . . . I am so tired—so very tired.

MOTHER. Where were you last evening?

FATHER. I was at the club. But let me ask you one question: Is her husband here?

MOTHER. Must I stand here and expose all our miseries? Don't you know the tragedy that has befallen our daughter?

FATHER. Yes, yes—I know. . . . And a man like him . . . a man such as *he* . . .

MOTHER. Such as all men!—Go down and sleep off your tippling!

FATHER. The sins of the fathers . . .

MOTHER. You sound as if you were delirious.

FATHER. Well, I am not speaking of my own sins, of course —I am speaking of the sins of our parents. Do you know—they say that the lake up in the mountains is to be drained. . . . Then the river will be rising. . . .

MOTHER (*pushing him out of the door*). Don't speak about it! Misfortune will catch up with us soon enough! You don't have to urge it upon us!

MAID (*enters from the rear. To the Stranger*). The Lady would like to see the master.

MOTHER (*to the Father*). She means her husband.

MAID. Yes, the master of the house—the Lady's husband.

MOTHER. He has gone out. He left a little while ago.

STRANGER (*enters*). Has the child come yet?

MOTHER. No. Not yet.

STRANGER (*running his hand over his forehead*). Can that be possible?—Can it take so long?

MOTHER. So long? What do you mean?

STRANGER (*looking around*). I have no idea what I mean. . . . Well, but—how is the mother doing?

MOTHER. Her condition is as before. . . .

STRANGER. As before?

MOTHER. Why don't you go back to your gold-making?

STRANGER. Now I am at my wit's end—I understand nothing any more! But I have one hope left: that my worst dream was only a dream. . . .

MOTHER. Yes—you do look as if you were talking in your sleep.

STRANGER. Do I? Oh—I wish I were asleep. There is only one thing I have been afraid of—and I would then no longer have to fear it.

MOTHER. He who guides your destiny seems to be aware of your vulnerable spots.

STRANGER. When finally only one such spot was left, he found that, too—but fortunately it was only a dream. Blind Powers! Impotent Powers!

MAID (*comes in again*). The Lady asks if you will please come and help her.

STRANGER. She lies in there like an electric eel, communicating her shocks from a distance. What kind of friendly assistance does she now want?

MAID. There is a letter in the pocket of her green dress.

STRANGER. Oh Lord! It is a letter bringing bad news! (*He takes the letter out of the pocket of the dress which is hanging next to her gown by the stove. He reads the letter.*) Now I am done for! I had dreamed this before—but now it has really happened!—My children have a stepfather!

MOTHER. Whom can you blame for that?

STRANGER. I blame myself! I blame no one else!—I have lost my children!

MOTHER. You will soon have another one.

STRANGER. But think—if he should be cruel to them! Oh!

MOTHER. Then you will have their suffering upon your conscience—if you still have one.

STRANGER. He might even beat them!

MOTHER. Do you know what I would do, if I were you?

STRANGER. Yes, I know what you would do! But at this moment I don't know what I am doing!

MOTHER (*to the Sisters of Charity*). Pray for this man!

STRANGER. No! Not that! Not that! It will be of no help, and I don't believe in prayer. . . .

MOTHER. But you believe in your gold?

STRANGER. No—nor in gold! It is the end! All is at an end!

MIDWIFE (*enters from the bedroom, rear*). A child has been born! Praise be to God!

MOTHER *and* SISTERS OF CHARITY. The Lord be praised!

MIDWIFE *(to the Stranger).* Your wife has given you a daughter.

MOTHER *(to the Stranger).* Wouldn't you like to see your child?

STRANGER. No! I no longer want to tie myself to anything on this earth. I am afraid I would come to love her. And then you would tear the heart out of my body. Let me get away from this atmosphere which is too pure for me. I don't want this innocent little child to come near me, for I am a lost soul, damned and doomed, and for me there is no joy, no peace, no grace!

MOTHER. My son! You are now speaking words of wisdom! Frankly, and without malice, I bless your decision. There is no place for you here, and you would suffer unbearably among us women. Therefore—leave in peace!

STRANGER. I am afraid I shall have no more peace—but I must be on my way. . . . Good-by!

MOTHER. *Exules filii Evae*—on earth you shall have no home, and you shall be an outcast. . . .

STRANGER. Because I slew my brother!

ACT IV

SCENE 1. The Banquet Hall. *The scene is the same as in Act III, Scene 1. However, the banquet hall is now dilapidated, with rough, unpainted wooden tables and benches. Crippled men are seated here and there, drinking by the light of tallow candles; for the rest—beggars, nightwalkers, and prostitutes.*

The Stranger and the Second Woman are seated together at the table, drinking. Before them stands a decanter of corn brandy. The Stranger is drinking heavily.

SECOND WOMAN. You must not drink so much.

STRANGER. Aha! You preach morality also!

SECOND WOMAN. No, but I don't like to see a man for whom I have respect degrade himself.

STRANGER. But it was for that very reason I came here: to lower myself, to take a mud bath that would harden my skin against the pinpricks of life, and to find support that was not too much on the moral side among those about me. And I chose your company because you have always been the most despised among women—yet you have always retained a spark of humanity. You felt compassion for me when no one else did—not even myself. Why did you have pity for me?

SECOND WOMAN. How does one know?

STRANGER. But do you know—there are moments when you look almost beautiful.

SECOND WOMAN. Oh, how can you say . . .

STRANGER. Yes, yes—and then you look like someone who once was very dear to me.

SECOND WOMAN. Thank you for saying that.

WOMAN BARTENDER. Don't speak so loud! There is someone lying sick inside!

STRANGER *(to the Second Woman)*. Tell me— have you ever been in love?

SECOND WOMAN. We don't use that word—but I understand what you mean. . . . Yes—I had a lover once; and we had a child.

STRANGER. That was careless.

SECOND WOMAN. Yes, I imagine I thought so, too. . . . But he said the time for liberation was at hand, and then all chains would be severed, all barriers done away with—and then . . .

STRANGER *(in anguish)*. And then . . .

SECOND WOMAN . . . then he left me. . . .

STRANGER. In short, he was a blackguard! *(He drinks.)*

SECOND WOMAN *(looking at him intently)*. Is that what you think of him?

STRANGER. Yes—I most certainly do!

SECOND WOMAN. Now you are a little severe, aren't you?

STRANGER *(drinks)*. Am I?

SECOND WOMAN. Don't drink so much! I want to see you at the top—high above me . . . or you won't be able to raise me up. . . .

STRANGER. What illusions you have, my dear child! I lift you up—I, who am away down at the bottom? Oh but—I am not—and it is not I who am sitting here—for I am dead. . . . I know that my soul is somewhere else—far, far away—far away. *(He stares into space, absent-mindedly.)* . . . where a great body of water flows, like molten gold, in the sunshine— where roses blossom among vines by a wall—where a little white baby carriage stands in the shade of acacias. . . . But the child is asleep—the mother sits beside it, crocheting— crocheting a long, long strip which comes out of her mouth and on which is written—let me think: "Blessed are they who grieve, for they shall be comforted." But I don't think that is true! I shall never be comforted! . . . Tell me, isn't there thunder in the air? It seems so close, so oppressively warm. . . .

SECOND WOMAN (*looking out of the window*). No—I don't see any clouds in the sky. . . .

STRANGER. That's strange . . . now I see lightning. . . .

SECOND WOMAN. No—you are mistaken.

STRANGER. One—two—three—four—five. . . . Now there should be a clap of thunder! But it doesn't come. I have never been afraid of thunder until today—I meant to say, until tonight. . . . Well, but—is it day, or is it night?

SECOND WOMAN. Why, it's night, my dear.

STRANGER. Yes—it is night! Night!

(*During this scene, the Physician has come in and seated himself behind the Stranger, without being seen by him.*)

WOMAN BARTENDER. Don't talk so loud! There is someone lying sick inside!

STRANGER (*to Second Woman*). Give me your hand!

SECOND WOMAN (*wiping her hand on her apron*). Oh! Why . . . !

STRANGER. You have a lovely hand—so white. . . . But—look at my hand—it's all black! Can't you see it is?

SECOND WOMAN. Why, yes—so it is.

STRANGER. Already turned black—perhaps even moldered. . . . I must feel if my heart has stopped. (*He lays his hand on his heart.*) Yes—it has stopped! So I must be dead—and I know when I died! How strange—that one can be dead and still be moving about. . . . But where am I? Are all these people here dead too? They look as if they had risen from the sewers, or as if they had been dragged out of a prison, or a poorhouse, or an insane asylum. Nightwalkers—suffering, groaning, cursing, fighting—they all torture one another, cast insults at one another, and envy one another—as though they possessed something that was worth being envied! The fire of sleep spreads through their veins, their tongues stick to the roofs of their mouths which have become dry from cursing and yelling—and then they put out the fire with water—firewater—which creates fresh thirst—the firewater, which itself burns with a blue flame and devours the soul like peat-moss afire, leaving nothing but the red sand. (*He drinks.*) Fire burn! Put out the fire! Fire burn! Put out the fire! But there is one thing that will not burn—and that, sad to say, is—the memory—of—the past! What is there that will burn out that memory?

WOMAN BARTENDER. Will you be good enough not to talk

so loud! There is a man lying sick inside! Yes—and he is so sick he has already asked to be given the last sacrament.

STRANGER. Let him depart for hell, then, as quickly as possible! *(All utter a murmur of disapproval.)*

WOMAN BARTENDER. Take care! Take care!

SECOND WOMAN *(to the Stranger).* Do you know that man who has been sitting behind you, staring at you all the time?

STRANGER *(turns. He and the Physician stare at each other for a moment without uttering a word).* Yes, I used to know him.

SECOND WOMAN. He looks as if he would eat you whole. *(The Physician takes a seat opposite the Stranger and stares at him.)*

STRANGER. What are you staring at?

PHYSICIAN. I am looking at your gray hairs.

STRANGER *(to the Second Woman).* Has my hair turned gray?

SECOND WOMAN. Why, of course, it is gray!

PHYSICIAN. I am looking at your fair lady, too! Sometimes you have good taste; other times not.

STRANGER. And sometimes it has been your misfortune to have the same taste as I.

PHYSICIAN. That was not kind of you to say. But twice in the past you have robbed me of my life—so keep it up!

STRANGER. *(to the Second Woman).* Let us get away from here!

PHYSICIAN. You sense when I am near you. You feel my presence from afar! But even if you hid yourself in the depths of the sea, or far down in the earth—like a bolt of lightning I would find you! Try to lose me if you can!

STRANGER *(to the Second Woman).* Come—let us go! Lead me—I can't see. . . .

SECOND WOMAN. No, I don't want to go yet—and I don't care to be bored!

PHYSICIAN. You have the right idea, you maid of easy virtue! Life is hard enough without having to worry about the pain and suffering others have brought upon themselves. But that man—he refuses to carry his own burden; he makes his wife carry his burden for him.

STRANGER. What's that you say? Let me tell you—she accused you falsely of invasion of privacy and attempt at murder!

PHYSICIAN. And now he is throwing the blame on her! *(The Stranger drops his head in his hands and lets it sink onto the table. From the back can be heard music played on violin and guitar. To the Second Woman.)* Is he sick?

SECOND WOMAN. I think he is mad. He says he is dead. *(From*

*afar comes the beating of drums for reveille, which soon after
is faintly heard being sounded by a bugler.)*

STRANGER. Is it morning? Night has passed—the sun is rising—
and the ghosts go back to their graves again to sleep. Now I
must go. Come!

SECOND WOMAN *(moving closer to the Physician).* I told
you before—no!

STRANGER. You, too—my only remaining friend! Am I then
such a horrible wretch that I can't even get a prostitute to keep
me company for pay?

PHYSICIAN. I guess you must be!

STRANGER. I can't believe it—even though they all say so!
I believe nothing, as a matter of fact; for whenever I have
believed in anything, I have been deceived. But tell me one
thing: hasn't the sun risen yet? I heard a cock crow and a dog
bark a moment ago, and now they are ringing the Angelus
Bell. . . . Have they put out the lights? It is so dark.

PHYSICIAN *(to the Second Woman).* He has gone blind. . . .

SECOND WOMAN. Upon my soul—I believe he has!

STRANGER. I can see you—but I can't see the lights. . . .

PHYSICIAN. Darkness is setting in for you. . . . You have
played with the lightning and thunder and gazed too steadfastly into the sun—and that is not healthy—it is not good. . . .

STRANGER. We are born with an urge to do it—but we are
told not to. It is out of sheer envy. . . .

PHYSICIAN. What do you possess that could induce envy?

STRANGER. I am the possessor of what you will never understand and what only I can value.

PHYSICIAN. You mean the child? . . .

STRANGER. You know that was not what was in my mind;
for if I had meant the child, I would have expressed myself
in this way: I have what you were never able to have. . . .

PHYSICIAN. So you are back to that again! Then let me express myself just as plainly: you took what I had discarded!

SECOND WOMAN. Shame on you! Oh, oh! I refuse to have
anything to do with two such swine as you! *(She gets up and
moves to another seat.)*

STRANGER. You can't deny that we have sunk very low—but
on the other hand, the deeper I sink, the closer I will come
to my goal: the end!

WOMAN BARTENDER. Don't talk so loud! There is a man lying
on his deathbed inside.

STRANGER. I thought I had been smelling a corpse!

PHYSICIAN. Perhaps it is we ourselves.

STRANGER. Can we be dead without knowing it?

PHYSICIAN. The dead say no one knows the difference.

STRANGER. You frighten me! Could it really be so? And all these shadow-figures whose faces I seem to recognize . . . memories from my youth, from school, from the swimming pool, from the gymnasium. (*His hand goes to his heart.*) Oh! Oh! Now he is coming nearer to me—he, the Terrible One, who sucks my heart out of my breast. . . . He is coming, the Invisible One, who has pursued me these many years. He is upon me—he is here!

(*He is beside himself. The doors are swung open. A Choirboy, carrying a lantern with blue glass panes, enters. The lantern throws a blue light upon the guests. The Choirboy rings a silver bell, and all start to howl like savage beasts. The Dominican enters with the sacrament, the Woman Bartender and the Second Woman throw themselves on their knees, the others keep on howling. The Dominican raises the monstrance, and all fall to their knees. The Choirboy and the Dominican go into the room on the right.*)

BEGGAR (*enters. He goes toward the Stranger*). Come away from here! You are sick. And court officers are looking for you to serve you with a summons.

STRANGER. A summons? From whom?

BEGGAR. Your wife.

PHYSICIAN. The electric eel delivers a shock a considerable distance away! She once started proceedings against me for defamation of character because I would not allow her to stay away nights.

STRANGER. Stay away nights?

PHYSICIAN. Exactly! Aren't you aware of to whom you have been married?

STRANGER. I have heard it said that she had been engaged before she married—before she married you.

PHYSICIAN. Yes, it was called an engagement—but as a matter of fact, she was the mistress of a married man, whom she later brought suit against for rape. She had forced herself upon him in his studio after posing for him in the nude.

STRANGER. And this was the woman you married!

PHYSICIAN. Yes. She started a lawsuit against me for breach of promise after having seduced me—and so I had to marry her; and for fear that I might leave her, she had me watched by two detectives. And this was the woman you took for your wife!

STRANGER. I married her because early in life I had found that all women were alike; and for that reason I thought it useless to go to the trouble of making a choice.

BEGGAR. Come away from here! If you don't, you will regret it!

STRANGER *(to the Physician)*. Was she always religious—this woman?

PHYSICIAN. Always.

STRANGER. And tender, good-hearted, self-sacrificing? . . .

PHYSICIAN. With a vengeance!

STRANGER. How can one make her out?

PHYSICIAN. You can't—but you can lose your mind worrying about her. That is why one had to take her as she was: a charming, intoxicating woman!

STRANGER. Precisely! But, you see, that is why one is defenseless against one's feeling of compassion; and that is why I don't want to have anything to do with lawsuits. I can't put up a defense without making accusations—and I refuse to make them.

PHYSICIAN. You have been married before. . . . How did you like that experience?

STRANGER. No difference.

PHYSICIAN. This thing called love—it affects you like henbane. You see suns where there are none, and stars where there are no stars. But it gives you a pleasant feeling while it lasts.

STRANGER. But then comes the day after? Oh, the day after!

BEGGAR. Come away, you unfortunate man! . . . He is sitting there poisoning you, and you don't realize it. Come away!

STRANGER *(gets up)*. Poisoning me? You think he is not telling the truth?

BEGGAR. Everything he has told you is a lie!

STRANGER. I don't believe it!

BEGGAR. No. You believe only lies. It serves you right!

STRANGER. Has he really been lying? Has he?

BEGGAR. You can't believe an enemy, can you?

STRANGER. But he must be my friend, or he would not have told me the bitter, unvarnished truth.

BEGGAR. Eternal Powers—save his reason! He believes all evil to be truth, and all good to be lies. Come away, or you will be lost!

PHYSICIAN. He is lost already—lost like a poached egg! But now he will be whipped into froth, dissolved into atoms, and be an ingredient in the great pancake. And now—set off to hell! *(He turns to the rest of those present.)* Let us hear a howl from hell—a howl from the victims! *(The Guests howl.)*

And no more womanly compassion! Howl, woman! *(The Woman makes a gesture signifying disapproval.)*

STRANGER *(to the Beggar).* That man is not a liar!

SCENE 2. *Inside the mountain pass. A mountain pass with a stream running through the center. The stream is spanned by a footbridge. In the foreground, a smithy and a mill, both in ruins. Several trees have fallen across the stream. In the background a starlit sky forms a panoply over a forest of spruce. The constellation of Orion is clearly visible. The foreground is covered with snow; the background is in the green of summer.*

The Stranger and the Beggar enter.

STRANGER. I feel afraid! The stars seem to be hanging so low tonight—it is almost as if they were about to fall down on me, like molten silver. . . . Where are we?

BEGGAR. We are inside the ravine—by the stream. That will tell you where we are.

STRANGER. Oh, oh! You ask me if I know them! You ask if I know them! Don't I know them from my honeymoon journey?— But where is the smithy? And the mill?

BEGGAR. Both in ruins! In ruins! The Lake of Tears was drained eight days ago. The stream swelled—the river rose— and everything was laid waste: arable and pasture land, gardens—everything!

STRANGER. And the silent, peaceful house?

BEGGAR. It was swept clean of the old sin—but the walls are still standing.

STRANGER. And those who lived there?

BEGGAR. They have gone to the colonies. And that is the end of that story.

STRANGER. And mine is at an end, too, and so thoroughly that there isn't a single memory of happiness that remains. The last one was defiled by that poisoner. . . .

BEGGAR. For whom you had mixed the poison! Why don't you give up the battle and surrender, then?

STRANGER. Yes—now I give up!

BEGGAR. Then the day of settlement will soon be at hand.

STRANGER. I dare say the settlement has already been made— for if I have sinned, I have also been punished.

BEGGAR. But on the other hand, the others don't think so.

STRANGER. Ever since I found that the Powers who guide the fate of mankind do not tolerate any helper, I have ceased to trouble myself about others. And the crime of my life has been that I have felt a compulsion to be a liberator . . .

BEGGAR . . . a liberator of mankind, freeing men from their duties, and culprits from their sense of guilt, until they became completely conscienceless. You are neither the first nor the last one to dabble in the devil's profession, Lucifer *a non lucendo*. But when the sly fox gets to be old, he turns monk— for that is how wisely it has been contrived—and then he has to divide himself against himself and drive out Beelzebub with his own Baalish penance.

STRANGER. And it is to that I am to be driven?

BEGGAR. Yes—where you wanted least to go! You will preach against yourself from roofs and chimneys; you will rip apart the very warp and woof of your life, thread by thread; you will flay yourself alive at every street corner and show how you look within! But it takes courage to do that—yet anyone who has played with lightning and thunder should have no fear! Oh well, occasionally—when night has fallen and the Invisible Ones, who can only be seen in the dark, begin to ride astride his chest—then he will be in terror! Yes—he will even be in terror of the stars, but most of all of the awesome mill of sins that unceasingly keeps grinding the past—grinding it over and over again! But you will remember what one of the seven and seventy wise men has said: that the victory over one's own self is the greatest victory of all! But that is something that the foolish human beings do not believe; and so they are deceived—for they believe only what the nine and ninety foolish prophets have said thousands of times.

STRANGER. You have said enough!—Tell me only one thing: Isn't that snow I see here on the ground?

BEGGAR. So it is— we have winter here.

STRANGER. And over there it is green.

BEGGAR. There it is summer.

STRANGER. And it is growing light over there! *(A bright beam of light illuminates the footbridge.)*

BEGGAR. Yes—there it is light—and here darkness.

STRANGER. And who is that coming over there? *(Three Children in summery clothes, two girls and a towheaded boy, are seen on the bridge, coming from the left. He calls to them.)* My children! My children! *(The Children prick up their ears in attention and stare at the Stranger without any sign of recognizing him. The Stranger cries out to them.)* Gerda! Erik! Thyra! It is I—your father! *(The Children act as if they recognize him, but turn away from him, toward the left.)* They know me no longer! They don't care to know me! *(The Hus-band and his Wife come from the left; the Children scamper off to the right and disappear. The Stranger falls on his face on the ground.)*

BEGGAR. That was to be expected! Things often happen like that! Up on your feet again!

STRANGER *(struggling to his feet)*. Where am I? Where have I been? Is it spring—or winter—or summer? What century am I living in—where in the universe am I? Am I a child or an old man—am I man or woman—god or demon? Who are you? Are you *you*—or are you *I?* Are these my entrails that I see about me—do I have stars or clusters of nerves in my eyes— or is it water—or tears? There! Now I am pressing onward in time—a thousand years—I am beginning to shrink—to solidify— to assume definite form! Wait now! Soon I shall be recreated— and out of the murky waters of Chaos the lotus flower will stretch its head into the sun and say: This is I! . . . I must have been sleeping more than a thousand years—I dreamed I was blown to atoms and that I turned into ether . . . no longer could I feel anything—I suffered no longer—I felt no joy—I had entered into a state of peacefulness and perfect serenity! But now . . . oh, now I suffer as if I were the whole of man-kind. . . . I suffer—and I have no right to complain. . . .

BEGGAR. By all means, suffer—and your suffering will be over the sooner. . . .

STRANGER. No—what I am suffering is the anguish and pain of eternity. . . .

BEGGAR. And so far only a minute has passed. . . .

STRANGER. I can't endure it!

BEGGAR. Well—then you must accept help.

STRANGER. What's this coming now? Is there no end to it? *(It grows light over the bridge. Caesar rushes in and throws himself into the stream from the footbridge. He is followed by the Physician, who enters from the left; he is bareheaded, has a wild look in his eyes, and acts as if he also were about to jump into the stream.)* He has already revenged himself so thoroughly that he couldn't make me conscience-stricken. *(The Physician disappears, right. The Sister comes from the left, act-ing as though she were searching for someone.)* Who is that?

BEGGAR. That is the Physician's unmarried sister. She is not provided for and she is now in anguish, for she has no home, now that her brother has lost his mind from grieving and gone to ruin.

STRANGER. That is much too hard a fate! Poor woman! But

what can one do to help her? Even if I were to take her suffering upon myself—would that help her?

BEGGAR. No—it wouldn't!

STRANGER. Why do pangs of conscience come after an act, and not before?—Can you answer that?

BEGGAR. No—and no one else can! Let us go on!

STRANGER. Where to?

BEGGAR. Come along with me!

SCENE 3. The Rose Chamber. *The Lady, dressed in white, is sitting beside the cradle. She is crocheting. The green dress is hanging by the door, left. The Stranger enters and looks about in astonishment.*

LADY *(simply and gently, with no trace of astonishment).* Come over here, but make no sound, and you will see a beautiful sight!

STRANGER. Where am I?

LADY. Ssh! Look at the little stranger who arrived while you were away.

STRANGER. I was told that the river had risen and swallowed up everything.

LADY. Why must you believe everything you hear? Yes—the river did inundate us—but this little being has someone who protects not only her but hers. . . . Wouldn't you like to see your daughter? *(The Stranger comes over toward the cradle. The Lady lifts the hood of the cradle.)* You see how beautiful she is? Isn't she lovely? *(The Stranger's face darkens.)* Please look at her!

STRANGER. Everything is poisoned! Everything!

LADY. You think it is? Perhaps.

STRANGER. Do you know that your former husband has lost his mind and is now wandering about in this vicinity, pursued by his sister who is trying to find him? And that is not all— he is destitute, and has taken to drink. . . .

LADY. Oh, my God! My God!

STRANGER. By all means, put the blame on me!

LADY. You will be reproaching yourself—let that be enough. Then I would rather give you some good advice: Go to the cloister of the Good Help—there you will find a man who will rid you of the evil that you fear.

STRANGER. Go to that cloister where they damn you and enchain you? . . .

LADY. But where they also redeem you!

STRANGER. To be quite frank, I believe you are trying to deceive me. I put no faith in what you say any more.

LADY. Neither do I believe you! Therefore you may consider this your farewell visit.

STRANGER. I dare say that is what I had intended it to be. But first I wanted to find out if we could come to an agreement. . . .

LADY. You can plainly see that we cannot build our happiness upon the sufferings of others. And therefore we must part. There is no other way to alleviate this torment. I have my child—she will fill up my life for me; and you have your ambitions and aspirations with their great and glorious goal. . . .

STRANGER. Are you still ridiculing me?

LADY. Why, no! What do you mean? Haven't you solved the great enigma?

STRANGER. Don't speak of it! Not another word about that subject, even if you do think I have solved it!

LADY. But if everybody else thinks you have . . .

STRANGER. Nobody does.

LADY. Why, gold has been made in England—and it has been confirmed! It says so in today's newspaper.

STRANGER. You have been misinformed. . . .

LADY. No!—Oh God! He refuses to believe his own good fortune!

STRANGER. I put no faith in anything any longer!

LADY. The newspaper is in the pocket of my dress there. Go over and get it!

STRANGER. That green witch's dress that put a spell upon me one Sunday afternoon between the barroom and the church! That will bring me nothing good!

LADY (gets up to fetch the newspaper herself. She also brings back a large envelope). See for yourself!

STRANGER (tears the newspaper to pieces). There is no need for me to look!

LADY. He doesn't believe it! He will not believe it! Yet the chemical fraternity has arranged a banquet in your honor for next Saturday. . . .

STRANGER. You don't say! Does it say that in the newspaper, too?

LADY (hands him the large envelope). And here is the citation of honor. Why don't you read it, man?

STRANGER (tears up the envelope). Perhaps there is a decoration that the government has conferred on me as well?

LADY. He whom the gods would destroy, they smite with

blindness. You had no good purpose in mind with your discovery; that is why you were not permitted to be the only one to make it.

STRANGER. Now I shall go, for I don't care to stay here and face the shame of my failure. I have turned into a laughing-stock; that is why I want to go and hide myself, bury myself alive—for I haven't the courage to seek death!

LADY. Then go, my dear! We are off to the colonies in a few days.

STRANGER. That, at least, turned out to have some truth in it! —Now we are coming closer to a solution.

LADY. A solution of the riddle of why we had to meet. . . .

STRANGER. Why was it meant that we should?

LADY. So that we could torment each other.

STRANGER. For no other purpose?

LADY. You were to save me from a werewolf, who was not a werewolf, and instead you turned into one yourself; and then I was to deliver you from your evilness by taking upon myself all your evil—and I did so. . . . But the consequence was that you became still more evil. My poor liberator, now you are bound hand and foot, and no one can set you free—not even a wizard!

STRANGER. Farewell—and thank you for everything!

LADY. Farewell—and thank you for this! *(She indicates the child in the cradle.)*

STRANGER *(going toward the rear).* Perhaps I ought to say good-by in there, too, before I go. *(He points to the door, rear.)*

LADY. Yes, do that, my dear. *(The Stranger goes out through the door, rear. The Lady goes to the door on the left and admits the Dominican [The Beggar]).*

CONFESSOR. Is he prepared now?

LADY. Nothing is left for this unhappy man but to leave the world behind and take refuge in a monastery.

CONFESSOR. So he still does not believe he is the great genius that he actually is?

LADY. No, he believes nothing that is good of anyone—not even of himself. . . .

CONFESSOR. Yes—that is the divine punishment that was meted out to him: that he believes lies to be the truth, because he refused to accept the truth.

LADY. But try to ease his burden of guilt a little! Try to make it lighter for him—if you can!

CONFESSOR. No—for then he would at once become arrogant

and accuse God of being cruel and unjust. For this man is a demon, and he must be put under restraint and be confined. He belongs to the dangerous category of nonconformists and rebels, and he would misuse his gifts by doing evil. And there is no limit to what human beings will do when they are evil.

LADY. Will you not—for the sake of the devotion you have shown for me in the past—make it a little easier for him to carry his burden of guilt—where it weighs heaviest upon him —where his transgression seems less serious?

CONFESSOR. That is something you must do so that he may leave you in the belief that there is something of good within you and that you are not such as your first husband has pictured you to be. If he then believes you, I shall in time set him free, just as I once bound him when he lay ill in the cloister of Good Help and made his confession to me.

LADY (goes to the rear and opens the door there). So be it, Father!

STRANGER (enters). There is the Terrible One! How did he get in here?—Why, it is the beggar, isn't it?

CONFESSOR. Yes—I am your terrible friend. I have come to fetch you.

STRANGER. You mean—I have—

CONFESSOR. Yes. Once in the past you forswore your soul to me—at the time you lay ill and felt that you were on the verge of losing your mind. It was then you promised to serve the Powers of Good. But when you had recovered your health, you broke your vow; and that is why you were beset by anxiety and restlessness and why you have been roaming about like an outcast, plagued and tortured by your conscience.

STRANGER. Who are you? Who are you—who dare tamper with my fate?

CONFESSOR. Ask her.

LADY. I was once betrothed to this man. But I abandoned him—and since then he has devoted his life to the service of the Lord. . . .

STRANGER. Even if it were so . . .

LADY. Therefore you need not feel so badly about your own offense, as it was through you that my faithlessness and the other one's lack of conscience received their punishment.

STRANGER. His evildoing cannot justify mine. Moreover—like everything else—I suppose it is a lie. You say it merely to comfort me.

CONFESSOR. He is a lost soul!

STRANGER. Doomed and damned!

CONFESSOR. No! *(To the Lady.)* Say something good about him!

LADY. If I should say something good about him, he would not believe it. He believes only what is evil!

CONFESSOR. Then I shall have to speak a good word for him. At one time a beggar came and asked for a drink of water; but instead of water, he was given wine—and he was invited to sit at his table. Do you remember?

STRANGER. No—I never remember such trivial matters. . . .

CONFESSOR. Pride! False pride!

STRANGER. Pride is a higher courage—the last vestige of our divine origin. Let us be off—before darkness falls. . . .

CONFESSOR. "Over all the earth shone a bright, clear light, and men labored without hindrance, doing their work. Over them, night spread its thick blackness—a foreboding of the darkness that was to set in over them; for they themselves were harder upon one another than the darkness."

LADY. Try not to inflict any pain upon him!

STRANGER *(passionately, vehemently)*. Think of it! How beautifully she can speak—and yet she is so malicious! Look at those eyes of hers! They cannot weep—but they can be softly caressing, they can sting you, they can lie! And still she says: "Try not to inflict any pain upon him." See—now she is afraid that I shall wake the child—the little nuisance that is sending me away from her! Come, priest, before I change my mind!

To Damascus III

A DRAMA IN FOUR ACTS

❖ ❖ ❖

The reconciliation with mankind through woman began when the Lady begged the Confessor to lead the Stranger to the monastery. The Stranger is at last nearing the end of his journey. From the foot of the mountain he sights the white, massive monastery building at its pinnacle, lighted by the shining sun. But there were still obstacles to be overcome. Having said farewell to his daughter, he starts the climb toward his goal. He sees a sight that fills him with horror, pain, and remorse: a tarn exuding sulphur vapors, seated around which is a motley host of syphilis victims, their hands a bloody crimson. His conscience drives a spike into his heart: these wretched beings owe their fearful plight to his carelessly uttered words, his incitements to break with oldfashioned notions of morality. He continues his way. In a vision he sees his wife; but before he can reach her, she is transfigured into his mother—the mother for whose love he had yearned as a child. But she, too, is out of his reach, for she disappears in a misty cloud. Still bound by a desire for human love, he descends to the mundane world again and remarries (his third wife: Harriet Bosse) —but the inevitable happens: they soon part. In the final scene he has reached his goal: the nondenominational monastery, which has beckoned him, and he resigns himself to selfless devotion. After a brief ritual, in which his former self is buried, the pilgrim is at home, at peace with himself and the good Creator. He has discovered the unknown quantity in his heart with the help of God's grace.

Despite a lessening of the awesome pessimism of Parts I and II, Part III lacks neither spirit nor drama. The theme follows, in substance, the same lines as in the first two dramas of the trilogy. The scenes in the home of the newlyweds and in the monastery have many fascinating and poetic nuances, many delightful situations; and Strindberg's dialogue is ever brilliant and masterly. It is particularly stimulating in the scenes with the Tempter in Part III. Yet neither Part II nor Part III reaches the dramatic stature of Part I, whose grandeur and nobility place it in the vanguard of world dramas. The shifting scenes of futility and sanguinity, the fathomless imagination of the author juggling with occult and subliminal riddles, states of consciousness, and the awesome atmosphere engendered by the dramatist's gigantic genius for creating phantom worlds and characters of a dream life, set within the confines of the theatre, will be a lasting inspiration and a challenge not only to actors, stage directors, and producers, but, indeed, to all mankind. Repentance, remorse, and penance are the watchwords of Strindberg in this mighty drama.

In the final scene of Part III, which is written in a lighter vein than the preceding parts, the Tempter asks the Stranger whether he never felt any joy in life, and he answers, "Yes, much joy—but oh, so brief—and it seemed as if it only existed to make the grief over losing it so much the deeper!" "Could one not, conversely, say that sorrow existed for the purpose of bringing out joy, and emphasizing it?" asks the Tempter; and the Stranger bluntly replies, "One can say whatever one likes." A little later the Tempter, pointing to a passing bridal couple, remarks, "And there you see the sweetest —the bitterest—Adam and Eve in their paradise . . . which after a week or so will be a hell—and in fourteen days a paradise again. . . ." The Stranger meditates. "The sweetest! The brightest! The first—the only—the last . . . that which gave meaning to life. I, too, had my day in the sun once. . . . It was a day in spring—on a veranda—beneath the first tree to bear leaves—a tiny coronet crowned her head—a white veil, like a gentle mist, covered her countenance, which was not of this world. . . . And then came the darkness. . . ." The Tempter slyly asks: "From where?" and the Stranger answers, "From the light itself! . . . That is all I know!" And to this the Tempter makes the reply: "It could not have been anything but a shadow; for without light there can be no shadow—but where there is darkness, there can be no light." The Stranger admonishes him to cease, fearing that there will be no end to the discussion. At this point the Confessor and the Chapter enter in procession, and the Tempter quickly disappears. The Stranger takes his place in the coffin, in simulation of the renunciation of his old self, and the Confessor covers him with the funeral pall, while intoning, "May the Lord give him eternal rest!" The choir chants, "And may perpetual light shine upon him!"—"May he rest in peace!" intones the Confessor. The choir sings, "Amen!"—and the Stranger has left his former life behind him and entered a new one behind the cloistered walls. Yet he has not compromised with his conscience by subscribing to any dogmas; he is still seeking the solution to the enigma of life and death, although his mind and spirit have now been liberated from past doubts of the omnipotence and wisdom of the Creator.

Throughout the three parts the reader follows the dramatist's passionate yearning for the liberation of his soul from the material and the earthly. Based on the sufferings that had been heaped upon him throughout his turbulent life, and what he had endured during his *Inferno* crisis in the 1890's, *To Damascus* represents his periods of poverty and loneliness, his nervous breakdown, his physical and mental exhaustion, not to say hysteria, his broken ties with home, wife, and children, the depressive reaction following the sensational court proceedings because of his book *Married (Giftas I,* 1884) and, despite his acquittal, the hesitancy of publishers to accept his writings for fear of being drawn into controversy or legal entanglements. Strindberg became a lonely nomad, an expatriate. When his second marriage, to Frida Uhl, had broken up, he was haunted by imaginary spirits and fled again, fearful of losing his mind. He thought of himself as having been chosen as a scapegoat on whom all the sufferings of mankind were being loaded. This became a fixed idea with him. His defiance of God and man in his younger years, his arrogance and past behavior drove him to chastise himself in the belief that he could attain salvation only through atonement and expiation, through crawling on his knees to the cross for forgiveness. But even this humbling of himself before the Cross was not according to the rule of strait-laced, dogmatic acquiescence and ritual. What he confessed to and was dominated by was rather an expansion and a deepening of his earlier spiritual tenets and beliefs, augmented by the teachings of a variety of creeds and philosophies, wherein pessimism played a significant role.

The core and basis of *To Damascus* is the soul-searching process through which the Stranger, after having passed his "Inferno" crisis, finally reverts to his earlier communion with the life beyond. The essence and mainspring of the elements that combine to bring about his conversion from a life of arrogance and egotism is suffering: and this he finally recognizes as having been visited upon him by the Almighty. Thus, humbled and ready to forsake the joys and pleasures of the world, he enters the nondenominational monastery, where he hopes to find time to devote himself to contemplation and to be given peace of soul.

By dramatizing the subconscious, laying bare the conflicts of a soul, and by weaving the experiences of a wayward, self-sufficient and arrogant sinner on the road to Damascus by way of remorse and penitence, into a pattern of vivid and often profoundly stirring scenes, Strindberg the dramatist has built a lasting monument to himself in the history.

CHARACTERS

THE STRANGER
THE LADY
THE CONFESSOR
THE TEMPTER
SYLVIA, the Stranger's daughter
OLD MAIA
THE HOSTESS
FIRST WORSHIPER, one of the Stranger's daughters
SECOND WORSHIPER, (the Stranger's son Erik)
A PILGRIM (CAESAR)
THE SHERIFF
THE ACCUSED MAN
THE BAILIFF

THE FATHER OF THE DEAD WOMAN
THE WOMAN (the Stranger's first wife)
EVE
THE SERPENT
THE PRIOR
FATHER ISIDOR (THE PHYSICIAN)
FATHER URIEL (blind)
FATHER CLEMENS
FATHER MELCHER
MEN *and* WOMEN of all ages, CHILDREN, SPECTATORS, and others

THE SETTINGS

Act I.   On the shore of a large river.

Act II. A crossway in the mountains.

Act III, Scene 1. A terrace on the Monastery Mountain.
Act III, Scene 2. Higher up in the mountains.
Act III, Scene 3. A dining room in a dwelling.
Act III, Scene 4. The same.

Act IV, Scene 1. The interior of a chapter house in Gothic style.
Act IV, Scene 2. A gallery of paintings in the chapter house.

The scene is laid in Austria in the late nineteenth century.

ACT I

The foreground represents the shore of a large river (the Danube). On the left the shore juts out into a point covered with willow trees. The background represents the opposite shore line: a steep mountainside crowned with forest trees. Above the leafy treetops rises a huge four-cornered edifice: the monastery. It is entirely white and has two rows·of tiny windows. The straight lin.: of the façade is broken by the monastery chapel, which, in Jesuit style, is flanked by towers. The chapel portals stand open so that at a given moment the monstrance on the altar may be seen in the light of the sun.

Between the two shore lines can be seen the river, silently flowing past. On the low, sandy shore in the foreground grow purple and golden loosestrife. A flat-bottomed boat is moored there. On the right, the ferryman has his shack.

It is an evening in early summer and the sun is about to set. The foreground and the river, as well as the lower part of the background, lie in the shadow. The foliage on the opposite shore sways gently in the breeze. Only the monastery is illuminated by the sun's rays.

The Stranger and the Confessor enter from the left. The Stranger is dressed as añ alpine climber; he wears a brown cloak with cape and hood, and carries an alpenstock and knapsack. He limps slightly. The Confessor wears the black-and-white habit of the Dominicans. They stop before a willow tree which hides the monastery from view.

STRANGER. Why are you leading me on this uphill, roundabout way which never comes to an end?

CONFESSOR. The way here *is* like that, my friend! But now we shall soon be there. (*He leads the Stranger downstage. The Stranger suddenly sees the monastery and is entranced by the view of it. He removes his hat, puts down his knapsack and the alpenstock.*) Well . . . ?

STRANGER. I have never seen anything so white on this unclean earth—except in my dreams!—Yes, this has been the dream of my youth: a house and home where peace and purity would dwell! . . . You pure abode, I welcome you with open arms! . . . Now I feel I have at last found my home!

CONFESSOR. So be it—but first we must await the pilgrims on

this shore, which is called the shore of farewells—because it is here they say their farewells before the ferryman takes them across.

STRANGER. Have I not said farewell often enough? Has not my whole life been one long, thorny path of farewells? At roadside inns, at landing piers, at railroad stations—with the waving of tear-drenched handkerchiefs?

CONFESSOR. And still your voice trembles with the pain of what you have lost—and missed!

STRANGER. I miss nothing—and wish to recapture nothing!

CONFESSOR. Not even your youth?

STRANGER. Least of all my youth! Why should I wish to be given back youth and have to feel the suffering so much the more.

CONFESSOR. What about its pleasures?

STRANGER. I have never had any enjoyment. . . . I was born with a thorn in my flesh: every time I reached out to snatch it, to capture a pleasure, my hand was pricked, and Satan slapped me in the face. . . .

CONFESSOR. Your pleasures were empty, vile, and foul. . . .

STRANGER. Not so empty, not so vile. . . . I had a home of my own, a wife, children. . . . I had my duties, my obligations to others. . . . No—I was born in disgrace—a stepchild of life—hounded and hunted—in short, I was cursed!

CONFESSOR. Because you did not obey the commandments of God. . . .

STRANGER. Commandments that no one can live up to, according to St. Paul. But what no one else can do—I am forever expected to be able to do! Why should I be the only one? Because they wanted me to be a scamp and a scapegrace! And more was demanded of me than of others! *(With a cry of agony.)* And I was treated unjustly!

CONFESSOR. Are you reverting to that again, you rebellious man?

STRANGER. Yes—again. . . . I cannot get away from it!—Let us cross the river!

CONFESSOR. Do you think that you can climb aloft and reach that white house without being prepared?

STRANGER. I am prepared. Put me to the test!

CONFESSOR. Very well!—The first of the monastic vows is humility!

STRANGER. And the second is obedience! Neither was ever an innate virtue of mine; and so, for that very reason, I am willing to make the effort. . . .

CONFESSOR. And to display your pride and arrogance by way of your humility!

STRANGER. Be that as it may, I am indifferent to everything. . . .

CONFESSOR. Everything? The world and its best gifts—the innocent joy of little children—the pleasant warmth of a home —the recognition of fellow men—the satisfaction derived from fulfilling one's duties—do none of these things matter to you?

STRANGER. No—because I was born insensible to joy and happiness. . . . There have been times when I have been an object of envy—but I have never been able to understand what it was that they envied me for—whether my sufferings in times of misfortune, or my anxiety in times of success, when I was afraid it would not last.

CONFESSOR. It is true—life gave you everything you wished for—toward the end even a small share of gold. And I seem to remember that a sculpture of you was erected, too.

STRANGER. Yes—a bust was made. . . .

CONFESSOR. Do such things impress you? Do they?

STRANGER. Not in the least! But, at any rate, such a tribute gives evidence of undoubted recognition that neither envy nor lack of understanding can shake.

CONFESSOR. You don't say? I seem to have noticed that human greatness is dependent upon public opinion. And when public opinion changes, greatness can speedily be reduced and dwindle into less than nothing.

STRANGER. I have never permitted the opinion of others to influence my own.

CONFESSOR. Really? You don't say!

STRANGER. And no one has been so severe with himself as I have been! And no one has been so humble! They have all demanded that I show them respect—while they trampled on me and spat at me. . . . Finally, when I realized that I had a duty to the immortal soul given in my care, I began to demand respect for this immortal soul of mine—and then was branded as the vainest of the vain! But by whom? By the very vainest of all: the vainest among the humble and the lowly!

CONFESSOR. I think you are getting tangled up in contradictions.

STRANGER. So do I! Life is nothing but one long chain of contradictions: the rich are the spiritually impoverished; the majority, the common people, hold the power; and the exalted take advantage of the many who are poor. And never have I met with such arrogance as among the so-called humble! I have never met an uneducated person who did not think himself competent to sit in judgment on culture and education, or who felt he had any use for it himself. It is among the so-called saintly that I have come across the vilest of mortal sins —I mean self-righteousness. I was one of the saintly myself in my youth—and never have I been so unclean as I was then. The better I thought I was, the worse I became. . . .

CONFESSOR. Then—what is it you seek here?

STRANGER. I have already told you; but I will add this: I am seeking death without having to die!

CONFESSOR. The death of the carnal appetites in you, the death of your old self! . . . So be it! Hold your peace—here come the pilgrims on their log rafts to celebrate the festival of Corpus Christi.

STRANGER (with a glance of astonishment toward the left). Who are these?

CONFESSOR. They are people who have faith. . . .

STRANGER. Then help me in my unbelief! (The sun is now illuminating the monstrance in the chapel above. It gleams like a windowpane in the setting sun.) Has the sun itself come into the church, or . . .

CONFESSOR. The sun has come into the church! . . . (The first raft has now landed from the left. Children dressed in white, wearing wreaths around their heads and carrying lighted candles in their hands, are standing round a flower-bedecked altar, which supports a staff with a standard depicting a golden lily on a field of white. As the raft slowly glides past, they sing.)

CHILDREN. Blessèd he who fears the Lord,
Beati Omnes, qui timent Dominum,
who walks in His ways.
Qui ambulant in viis ejus.
You shall feed yourself by the toil of your hands.
Labores manuum tuarum quia manducabis:
Blessèd be you, and Godspeed!
Beatus es et bene tibi erit!
(The raft disappears. Another raft comes into view. On one side it carries young men; on the other sit young maidens. Its standard has a rose on its field.)

YOUNG MEN and MAIDENS. Your wife shall be like a fruitful vine
Uxor tua sicut vitis abundans
in the bosom of your house.
In lateribus domus tuae.

(The raft glides out of sight. A third raft with men and their wives glides in. It carries a standard having a center of fruits: figs, grapes, pomegranates, melons and ears of grain, etc.)

MEN and WIVES. *Filii tui sicut novellae olivarum,*

Your children—like olive branches around your table.

In circuitu mensae tuae.

(The raft floats away. A fourth raft carrying aged men and women has a standard with a spruce tree, sprinkled with snow, in its center.)

OLD MEN and WOMEN. Behold the blessings to the man,

Ecce sic benedicetur homo,

who fears the Lord.

Qui timet Dominum.

(The raft disappears.)

STRANGER. What was it they sang?

CONFESSOR. It was a pilgrimage song.

STRANGER. Who wrote it?

CONFESSOR. A royal personage. . . .

STRANGER. Who is here, you mean? What is his name? Has he written anything else?

CONFESSOR. He has written at least fifty songs, and his name is David, the son of Jesse. But he did not always write psalms. . . . When he was young, he occupied himself with other things. . . . Yes, yes—that is the way it goes!

STRANGER. May we cross now?

CONFESSOR. In a moment—but first I have a few things to say to you. . . .

STRANGER. Speak!

CONFESSOR. Very well—but you must not let it distress you, and you must not be angry. . . .

STRANGER. Why, of course not!

CONFESSOR. Well—you see, on this side of the river you are a well-known not to say famous man—but over there on the other side you are completely unknown to the brothers; consequently you are nothing more and nothing less than a plain, ordinary human being.

STRANGER. O-oh! Don't they read anything over there in the monastery?

CONFESSOR. Not about the vain things of this world—only serious books.

STRANGER. But don't they read any newspapers?

CONFESSOR. Not the kind that write about you.

STRANGER. And so—my life's work does not exist on the other side of this body of water?

CONFESSOR. Which work?

STRANGER. Oh—very well! Should we go now?

CONFESSOR. In just a moment. Have you no one you would like to say good-by to?

STRANGER *(after a pause).* Yes—but it is beyond the realms of possibility.

CONFESSOR. Have you ever known anything to be impossible? Have you?

STRANGER. As a matter of fact, no—not after seeing my own fate!

CONFESSOR. Well, then—who is it you would like to meet?

STRANGER. I once had a daughter—I called her Sylvia because she sang all the day long like a willow warbler. It is some years since I saw her. She should now be a girl of sixteen. But I have a fear that life would again take on interest for me if we were to meet. . . .

CONFESSOR. You fear nothing else, do you?

STRANGER. What, for instance?

CONFESSOR. That she might have changed!

STRANGER. That would only have been to her advantage.

CONFESSOR. Are you so certain?

STRANGER. I am!

CONFESSOR. She shall come to you. *(He goes down toward the river's edge and beckons to the left.)*

STRANGER. Hold on! . . . I wonder whether this is a wise thing to do. . . .

CONFESSOR. I can see no harm in it.

(Again he beckons. A boat, being rowed by a young girl of sixteen, is seen on the river. The girl is dressed in summer clothes; she is bareheaded and her blonde hair is hanging loose. When the boat is behind the willow tree she gets out. The Confessor withdraws out of her sight toward the ferryman's shack but remains within view of the audience. The Stranger waves to the girl. She returns his greeting and rushes into the Stranger's arms and kisses him.)

SYLVIA. Father! My dear father!

STRANGER. Sylvia! My beloved child!

SYLVIA. How in all the world do you happen to be roaming about up here in the mountains?

STRANGER. And how about yourself? How do you happen to be up here? I thought I had succeeded in stowing myself out of sight!

SYLVIA. Why should you want to hide?

STRANGER. Ask as few questions as possible! . . . You have grown into a big girl . . . and I have turned gray.

SYLVIA. Why no, you are not gray! . . . You are as young as you were when last we were together.

STRANGER. When last we were together . . .

SYLVIA. When you left us. *(The Stranger remains silent.)* Are you not glad to see me again?

STRANGER *(in a faint voice)*. Yes. . . .

SYLVIA. Oh, but show it, then!

STRANGER. How can I be glad when this is the last time we shall see each other in this life?

SYLVIA. Why? Where are you thinking of going?

STRANGER *(makes a gesture in the direction of the monastery)*. Up there!

SYLVIA *(with a knowing expression)*. The monastery?—Yes, now that I think of it—that may be the best place for you.

STRANGER. You mean that?

SYLVIA *(with pity, but well-intentioned)*. I mean—since you have misspent your life. *(Caressingly.)* Oh—now I hurt your feelings!—Tell me something. . . .

STRANGER. Tell *me* something—something that has been worrying me more than anything else. . . . You have a stepfather now? . . .

SYLVIA. Yes.

STRANGER. And how does he . . . ?

SYLVIA. He is really a fine man. . . .

STRANGER. Who possesses all the virtues I lack . . . ?

SYLVIA. Doesn't it make you happy that we are now in better hands?

STRANGER. Good—better—best. . . . How is it that you go about bareheaded?

SYLVIA. George is carrying my hat.

STRANGER. Who is George? And where is he?

SYLVIA. George is my sweetheart, and he is waiting for me down at the river bank.

STRANGER. Are you two engaged?

SYLVIA. No, certainly not!

STRANGER. Are you planning to be married?

SYLVIA. Never!

STRANGER. I can see it by your spotted cheeks—they are like the cheeks of a child that has matured too soon; I hear it by your voice which no longer resembles the willow warbler's but reminds me of the jay's; I could feel it when you kissed me—your kisses had a cold burning in them like the sun's rays in the month of May; the cold, fixed look in your eyes tells me you are carrying a secret of which you are ashamed, but of which you would like to boast. . . . And what about your sisters and your brother?

SYLVIA. Oh, they are well, thank you.

STRANGER. Have we anything else to say to each other?

SYLVIA (coldly). Perhaps not. . . .

STRANGER. How you resemble your mother now!

SYLVIA. How do you know? You—who never were able to see her as she was!

STRANGER. And young as you are you have understood that!

SYLVIA. I have come to understand it—thanks to you. I only wish you could understand yourself.

STRANGER. Is there anything else you would like to teach me?

SYLVIA. There may be. But when you were young that would have been considered improper.

STRANGER. My days are gone and no longer exist—just as Sylvia no longer exists: she is merely a name, a memory. (He takes a travel guide out of his pocket.) Take a look at this travel guide! You see the tiny spots there—marks made by little fingers . . . and here you see the marks of damp little children's lips? Do you see? They are marks made by you when you were five years old, while we were traveling on a train. You were sitting in my lap—it was the first time we saw the Alps. . . . You thought that what you saw was heaven . . . and when I told you that the pinnacle was the Jungfrau, you begged me to let you kiss the name where it was printed in the book. . . .

SYLVIA. I don't remember that. . . .

STRANGER. Our beautiful memories so often fade away and are lost, but the ugly ones remain with us. Have you no memories of me?

SYLVIA. Why, yes!

STRANGER. Don't speak! I know what you are going to say! . . . One night . . . yes. . . . Oh—oh, that dreadful, dreadful night! . . . Sylvia, my child—when I shut my eyes I see a pale little angel who slept in my arms when she was sick—who thanked me whenever I brought her a gift. . . . Where is she—where is she, for whom I long so desperately and who no longer exists—and yet she is not dead? . . . You who stand here before me—you are a stranger to me—one whom I never seem to have known, and whom I could never long to see again! Oh, if only Sylvia lay dead in her grave—then there would at

least be a graveyard where I could leave some flowers. . . .
How strange it all is. . . . She is neither among the dead nor
among the living upon this earth! Can it be that she has never
existed—that it has all been a dream—like everything else? . . .

SYLVIA (caressingly). My dear, dear father!

STRANGER. It is she! (There is a silence.) No—it was only her
voice I heard! . . . (There is another silence.) You mean to
say that my life has been useless, wasted?

SYLVIA. Yes—but now . . . let us speak of it no more. . . .

STRANGER. Yes. Because I now remember that I once saved
your life. . . . You lay ill with typhoid fever for a month and
suffered with pain. Your mother—who had a mind of her own
—pleaded with the doctor to deliver you from your torture by
some death-dealing drug—but I stepped between and—so I
saved you from dying, and your mother from going to
prison. . . .

SYLVIA. I don't believe you!

STRANGER. But a fact is a fact—even if you do not believe it.

SYLVIA. It is something you have dreamed. . . .

STRANGER. Who knows if I have not dreamed it all, from
beginning to end, and if I am not dreaming now? Oh, if it
were only so!

SYLVIA. I must be going now, Father dear.

STRANGER. Well, then—farewell!

SYLVIA. May I not write to you?

STRANGER. The dead write to the dead? No—no letters will
reach me any more. . . . And visitors are not allowed. But I
am glad that we met once more, for there is nothing that
binds me to earth any longer. (While he goes toward the right.)
Farewell now, maiden or mistress, whatever you be. . . . And
there is no need for weeping!

SYLVIA. That had not occurred to me—although, perhaps,
propriety might have demanded something of that sort. And
now—farewell!   (She goes toward the left.)

STRANGER (to the Confessor, who comes out of his hiding).
I came out of that very well, Confessor! To be able to part
with mutual satisfaction is a grace from heaven. But man
makes rapid progress, and our self-control increases in propor-
tion to the diminishing of our tears. I have seen so many tears
in my life that I almost feel disappointed at this lack of them.
She is certainly a strong-willed child—exactly the way I once
wanted to be. . . . And this was the most sublime thing that
life had to offer: the child, the angel, as she lay in her cradle
swaddled in white gauze, and—when she was sleeping—with a

blue canopy over her—blue, and arched like the heavenly sky. . . . That was the best of all things!—Now what will the worst be like?

CONFESSOR. You must not let yourself be disturbed! On the contrary, you must be of good cheer. . . . But first you must get rid of that stupid travel guide, since this is to be our last journey!

STRANGER *(holding up the travel guide)*. You mean this one? —Very well! *(He opens the book and imprints a kiss inside the cover, then flings it into the river.)* Anything else?

CONFESSOR. Yes—if you have anything of gold or silver on you, you must give it to the poor.

STRANGER. I have a watch of silver. I could never afford one of gold.

CONFESSOR. Give it to the ferryman, and he will give you a glass of wine in return.

STRANGER. The last drink! This is like an execution!—Perhaps you want to shave off my hair, too?

CONFESSOR. Yes. That comes later. *(He takes the watch and walks over to the ferryman's shack, where he whispers a few words inside the door. He returns with a bottle of wine and a glass which he places on the table.)*

STRANGER *(fills the glass but does not drink)*. Will I get no wine up there?

CONFESSOR. You will get no wine and will see no women. You will have singing—but it will not be the kind of songs that go with wine and women.

STRANGER. I have had enough of women; they hold no temptation for me any more.

CONFESSOR. Are you so certain?

STRANGER. Quite certain. But tell me one thing: What is your opinion of woman, since she is not even allowed to set foot inside your consecrated walls?

CONFESSOR. Are you still inquisitive?

STRANGER. And why may not an abbess hear confession, or preach, or conduct mass? . . .

CONFESSOR. I am not going to answer that question.

STRANGER. Because your answer would be the same as what I think on the subject.

CONFESSOR. If we were really to be agreed on one point, it would not be a calamity, would it?

STRANGER. On the contrary!

CONFESSOR. Empty your glass now!

STRANGER. No—I want to take a last glance at the wine.
. . . It is beautiful to look at!

CONFESSOR. Don't become engrossed in contemplation—at
the bottom of the cup lie memories of the past.

STRANGER. And forgetfulness, oblivion—poetic flight—and
power, imaginary power—and for that reason all the more
intense. . . .

CONFESSOR. If you will wait here, I shall go and arrange for
the crossing. . . .

STRANGER. Hush! I hear a poem singing in my mind—and
I see it now. . . . For a moment I saw a vision as of a banner
unfurling in a gust of wind, only to fold again and hang
limply like a rag on the flagstaff—and that is all that can be
seen—a tattered rag. . . . In one brief flash I saw my whole
life—with its joys and sorrows, its beauty and its wretched-
ness—pass before me . . . and now—it is all gone. . . .

CONFESSOR (goes toward the right). Wait here a moment
while I go over and arrange for the crossing!

(The Stranger comes downstage so that the rays of the setting sun, which sift through the foliage of the willow trees
on the left, cast his shadow across the ground and the river's
surface. The Lady enters from the left, so that her shadow
gradually falls in front of the Stranger.)

STRANGER (who at first is intently observing only his own
shadow). Ha! The sun! The sun that creates a bloodless image out of me—a giant who walks upon the flowing water,
climbs the mountain, stalks across the roof of the monastery
chapel . . . and now—now ascends into space—heavenward, to
the stars . . . yes, now I am up among the stars. (He suddenly
notices the Lady's shadow in front of his own.) But who is
that pursuing me? Who is that disturbing my ascension?—trying to climb up over my shoulder? (He abruptly swings round.)
You! . . .

LADY. Yes—I. . . .

STRANGER. All in black! Black and cruel!

LADY. No longer cruel. . . . My grief. . . .

STRANGER. Your grief? For whom?

LADY. Our Mitzi. . . .

STRANGER. My daughter! (The Lady stretches forth her arms
as if about to throw herself in his embrace, but he evades her.)
I am happy for the dead little child! For you I am sorry! I
myself feel nothing. . . .

LADY. You must console me!

STRANGER. A nice thought! I am to comfort my avenging

spirit, weep with my executioner, drive away the cares of my tormentor, am I?

LADY. Are you completely lacking in feelings?

STRANGER. Completely! Whatever I had of feelings, I squandered on you and others.

LADY. You are right. . . . Reproach me for it!

STRANGER. No—I have neither the time nor the inclination to do that. Where are you bound for?

LADY. I am going across with the ferry.

STRANGER. Hard luck for me—I am going the same way. *(The Lady weeps in her handkerchief. The Stranger takes it from her and wipes away her tears.)* Wipe away your tears, child, and be your own self! Be as hard and as unfeeling as you are by nature! *(The Lady tries to put her arm round his neck. The Stranger gently raps her hand.)* No—do not touch me! When you failed to get what you wanted by pleas and looks, you would always try to get it by pawing and appealing to my passions. Forgive me for asking a trite question: are you hungry?

LADY. No, thank you!

STRANGER. You are tired. . . . Sit down! *(The Lady seats herself at the table. The Stranger flings the bottle and the glass into the river.)* And now—what is to be your life from now on?

LADY *(sadly)*. I don't know.

STRANGER. Where will you go?

LADY *(sobbing)*. I don't know. . . .

STRANGER. You are in complete despair, are you not? You see no meaning in life, and no end to our misery, do you? There is the bond between us! What a pity that there are no retreats for both women and men—then we could be together. . . . Is the werewolf still living?

LADY. Do you mean . . . ?

STRANGER. Your first husband.

LADY. He will never die!

STRANGER. Just like a certain worm! . . . And now that we are far away from the world and its emptiness and trivialities, tell me this: why did you leave him that time and come with me? Why?

LADY. Because I loved you!

STRANGER. And how long did your love last?

LADY. Until I read your book and the child came.

STRANGER. And then . . .

LADY. Then I came to hate you! By that I mean—I wanted

to rid myself of all the evil you had imbued me with—but I could not!

STRANGER. It may well have been so—but we will never know the real truth.

LADY. Have you noticed that one rarely learns the real truth about anything? That we can live with someone—live with our parents, brothers and sisters—for a score of years without really knowing them . . . ?

STRANGER. So you, too, have discovered that?—Since you seem to discern things so keenly, tell me—tell me how you came to love me. . . .

LADY. I don't know . . . but I shall try to refresh my memory. (There is a silence.) Well—you had the masculine courage to be rude to a lady! What you looked for in me was the companionship of a human being rather than the woman. I considered this a compliment both to me and to you.

STRANGER. And now I would like to ask you: Did you ever find me to be a misogynist?

LADY. A woman-hater, in other words? That is something every healthy man is deep down in his heart, and it is the abnormal male who worships and adores woman.

STRANGER. Is this intended as a compliment? Is it?

LADY. Any woman who flatters a man is of unsound mind.

STRANGER. I can tell you have done a good deal of thinking.

LADY. That is the least I have done. The less I thought, the more I seemed to understand. Moreover, what I just told you may be mere improvisation, as you like to call it, and need not have an iota of truth in it.

STRANGER. Yes, but as long as it tallies with what I have generally found to be true, it makes it highly probable. (The Lady weeps in her handkerchief.) Now you are weeping again! . . .

LADY. I am thinking of Mitzi . . . the most beautiful thing in our life is gone. . . .

STRANGER. No—the most beautiful of all is my memory of you: the time you sat up all night, watching over our child. . . . You had taken her into bed with you because her cradle was too cold. (Three loud raps are heard on the ferryman's door.) Hush!

LADY. What was that?

STRANGER. It is my companion waiting for me!

LADY. I never thought that life could offer anything so lovely as a child!

STRANGER. And at the same time anything so bitter. . . .

LADY. Why do you say bitter?

STRANGER. Haven't you yourself been a child? Then you will remember how we, just after our marriage, came to your mother's home, ragged, dirty, and without money. I recall she did not find us so very appealing.

LADY. That is true.

STRANGER. And I . . . well, only a moment ago I met my daughter Sylvia. . . . I had hoped to see that all that was good and beautiful in her when she was a child had opened up and flowered into full bloom in the young maiden. . . .

LADY. And what did you . . .

STRANGER. I found a faded rose that seemed to have opened too soon. . . . Her breasts were fallen, her hair untidy, like that of a neglected child, and her teeth seemed to be worm-eaten. . . .

LADY. Ugh!

STRANGER. Therefore I say: Do not grieve for our little one! You might have had to grieve for her when she was older—as I have had to do for my Sylvia!

LADY. Then—life is like this. . . .

STRANGER. Yes—that is how life is. And that is why I go to bury myself alive!

LADY. Where?

STRANGER (with a gesture toward the monastery). Up there!

LADY. In the monastery? . . . No—do not leave me—stay with me! I am so alone in the world, and so poor, so poor! When the child died, my mother turned me out of her home, and after that I shared an attic room with a seamstress. In the beginning she was kind and decent; but after a while the long evenings grew lonely for her—and she went out in search of other company. And so we parted. Now I am walking the highways, with nothing but the clothes on my back, and the sorrow in my heart. . . . My sorrow I eat and drink—it nourishes me and puts me to sleep. . . . I would not be without it for anything in the world! (The Stranger weeps.) You are weeping—you . . . !—Let me kiss your eyelids!

STRANGER. All this you have suffered for my sake?

LADY. Not for your sake! No, no! And you have never done anything to hurt me. . . . But my taunts have driven you from house and home and child!

STRANGER. I do not recall that you ever did . . . but to think that you should speak of it!—Can it be that you still love me?

LADY. I may—I do not know. . . .

STRANGER. And that you would like to start all over again?

LADY. Start all over again? The quarrels and dissensions?—
No, we must not. . . .

STRANGER. You are right—the strife would only begin all over!
And yet—to part—would be so hard. . . .

LADY. To part? The sound of the word alone is awesome!

STRANGER. Then—what shall we do?

LADY. I don't know. . . .

STRANGER. No—we know nothing—and hardly that—and that
is why from now on I am going to *believe*. . . .

LADY. How can you be certain that you will be able to
believe? Belief is a gift of grace.

STRANGER. We can receive the gift if we pray. . . .

LADY. Oh! If I could only pray! But I have never been able
to go begging for anything.

STRANGER. I have had to learn to do it—why should not you?

LADY. One must first humble oneself. . . .

STRANGER. Life takes ample care of that.

LADY. Mitzi—Mitzi—Mitzi! (*She has taken the shawl that she
was carrying on her arm and rolled it up so that it resembles
a baby in swaddling clothes, and now she places it on her lap.*)
Hushaby, sleep—hushaby, sleep! . . . Oh—I see my baby. . . .
Look, look—she is smiling at me—but she is wrapped in black
—perhaps she, too, is in mourning! How foolish I am—it is
because her mother is in mourning. . . . And she still has her
two little teeth below, and they are white—her milk teeth—
it was never meant that she was to have any more. . . . Oh,
but, can't you see her, when *I* can? I am not seeing a vision—it
is Mitzi I see!

CONFESSOR (*comes out of the ferryman's shack. He speaks to
the Stranger in a stern tone*). Come! Everything is in readiness.

STRANGER. No—I can't come just yet. . . . I must first set
my house in order—I must take care of my wife's needs—this
woman was once my wife. . . .

CONFESSOR. So-o? Now you want to stay?

STRANGER. No—I don't want to stay—but I do not wish to
leave any unfulfilled obligations behind me. This woman is
left without home, without money—is abandoned on the highways!

CONFESSOR. That is of no concern to us, is it? Let the dead
bury their dead!

STRANGER. Is that what you teach?

CONFESSOR. No—that is what you have been teaching! . . .
My tenets, on the contrary, bid me to send down a Sister of

Charity to look after this unfortunate woman who—who . . .
She will soon be here. . . .

STRANGER. I take your word for it. *(The Confessor takes the Stranger by the hand and forces him to come with him.)*

CONFESSOR. Come along now!

STRANGER *(in agony)*. Lord Jesus Christ! Help us, help us all!

CONFESSOR. Amen!

(The Lady has averted her eyes from the Confessor and the Stranger. Suddenly she looks up and gazes after the Stranger as if she were about to rush after him and prevent him from leaving; but the thought of the imaginary infant which she nestles at her bosom holds her back.)

ACT II

A crossway up in the mountains. On the left, several huts; on the right, a tarn. Sitting around it are men and women invalids, dressed in blue garments. Their hands are red, the color of cinnabar. Now and then blue vapor and small, flickering, blue flames rise from the tarn. Whenever this happens, the sick stretch out their hands and cough. The mountain in the background is covered by a spruce forest whose treetops are obscured by a gray, lingering mist.

The Stranger is seated at a table outside one of the huts. The Confessor enters from the left, rear.

STRANGER. At last!

CONFESSOR. Why do you say "at last"?

STRANGER. You left me here more than a week ago and you said: Wait here until I come back!

CONFESSOR. Well—did I not warn you that the way leading to the white house up there was a long and hard one?

STRANGER. I cannot deny that it is!—How far have we come now?

CONFESSOR. About fifteen hundred feet. We still have more than three-fourths of the way left.

STRANGER. But where is the sun?

CONFESSOR. Up there—beyond the clouds. . . .

STRANGER. Then we shall have to go through the clouds?

CONFESSOR. Precisely!

STRANGER. But all these sick people? What kind of companions are they anyhow? And why are their hands so red?

CONFESSOR. I don't wish to contaminate either you or myself

by using unclean words—and so I shall speak in palatable riddles, which you—being a poet—should be able to understand.

STRANGER. Yes, by all means, speak beautifully—there is so much here that is ugly. . . .

CONFESSOR. You have undoubtedly observed that the signs of the planets correspond with the symbols given to certain metals, haven't you? Very well! Then you must have noticed that Venus is represented by a mirror. This mirror was in time immemorial made of copper, and this metal was called Venus and bore the Venus sign. But nowadays the back of the mirror of Venus is coated with quicksilver, or mercury.

STRANGER. Mercury on the other side of Venus!—Horrible!

CONFESSOR. Consequently, quicksilver is Venus's wrong side. The quicksilver is by nature shiny, much like a calm sea, like a lake in the height of summer. . . . But when Mercury and firestone, or flint, get together, Mercury gets burned and blushes; he turns red like freshly drawn blood, like the scarlet carpet on the executioner's scaffold, like the lips of the whore —the cinnabar-painted lips of the whore. . . . Do you begin to understand now?

STRANGER. Hold on! Cinnabar is sulfur and mercury. . . .

CONFESSOR. So it is, yes. And Mercury has to go through fire once he has come too close to Venus! . . . Have we talked enough about this now?

STRANGER. Then there are sulfur springs here, evidently?

CONFESSOR. Yes. And the sulfur flames either purify or destroy all that is rotten and decayed. Therefore, when the wellspring of life has beeen tainted, the victim is sent to the sulfur springs.

STRANGER. How does one's wellspring of life become tainted?

CONFESSOR. When Aphrodite, born from out of the virgin bosom of the sea, welters in the mire of the earth! . . . When the celestial Aphrodite Urania debases herself and turns into a Pandemos, a venal creature.

STRANGER. What brought our desires into being?

CONFESSOR. Our pure desires are created within us to be gratified; our unclean desires to be suppressed and stifled. . . .

STRANGER. What is pure, and what is not pure?

CONFESSOR. Are you coming back to that again?

STRANGER. Ask these men. . . .

CONFESSOR. Take care! (*He gazes fixedly at the Stranger, who shrinks before his gaze.*)

STRANGER. You are suffocating me. . . . I feel it here. *(He strikes his chest.)*

CONFESSOR. Yes—I shall take your breath away from you—take away the air you breathe when you use it for rebellious blather, for your stinking quarrelsomeness. . . . Now sit down here until I come back. . . . Until you have learned to be patient and you have passed all the tests! But keep in mind that—wherever I am—I can hear and see you—and I know everything you do!

STRANGER. So I am being tested, am I? I am glad to know that!

CONFESSOR. And you must not speak to any of the Venus-worshipers!

(Old Maia appears, rear. She is an old woman.)

STRANGER *(gets up, horror-stricken)*. Who is it I meet here—at long last! Who . . .

CONFESSOR. Of whom are you speaking?

STRANGER. Of that woman—that old woman there!

CONFESSOR. Well—who is she?

STRANGER *(calls out)*. Maia!—Maia!—Don't you hear me? *(Old Maia vanishes. The Stranger hastens after her.)* Maia, my friend—listen to me! . . . She disappeared!

CONFESSOR. Who is Maia?

STRANGER *(seats himself)*. Oh God! Now that I have found her at last, she disappears. . . . For seven long years I have searched for her, advertised, written letters. . . .

CONFESSOR. And why?

STRANGER. This is how our fates are linked. *(There is a silence.)* Maia was my first child's nursemaid. . . . It was during the years that were the hardest for me. . . . I was battling the Invisible Powers who refused to give their blessing to my work! I kept writing until my brain and nerves started to disintegrate like grease in alcohol . . . but all my efforts were not enough! I was one of those whose earnings are never sufficient. . . . And there came a day when I was unable to pay our servants their wages. . . . It was a terrible experience! I became a servant to my servants and they became my masters. Finally—in order to save my soul, if nothing else, I fled before the overpowering odds—fled into the wilderness; and there, in the solitude, I again recovered my broken spirit. The thing that was uppermost in my mind was—my indebtedness! For seven years I searched in vain for Maia! For seven years I saw her ghost—saw it from train windows—from the decks of steamers—in foreign cities—in distant lands

—yet never was I able to get hold of her. For seven years I dreamed of her—for seven years I felt myself humiliated—and whenever I downed a glass of wine I blushed for shame, thinking of Old Maia who perhaps had nothing to drink but water in a poorhouse! I tried to ease my conscience by giving what I owed to her to the poor; but it was no use. . . . And now—now that I suddenly find her—she disappears at the same moment. (*He gets up and walks to the rear, vainly looking for her.*) How can you explain this? I am anxious to pay my debt, now that I am able to—yet I cannot. . . .

CONFESSOR. You are a fool! You must yield to the inexplicable—to what seems beyond understanding. Everything will be revealed and made clear later. You will see!—Farewell!

STRANGER. Later?—Everything comes later!

CONFESSOR. Everything that does not happen now. (*He leaves. The Lady enters. She is deep in thought and she seats herself opposite the Stranger at his table.*)

STRANGER. Oh, it is you—back again! . . . You—yet so unlike yourself! . . . You have grown so beautiful—as beautiful as you were when first I saw you—the day I asked you to let me be your friend, your slave. . . .

LADY. That you see beauty in me, which I do not possess, proves that your eye has regained its mirror of beauty. . . . The werewolf never saw anything beautiful in me—he had nothing beautiful in him to see with. . . .

STRANGER. But why did you kiss me that time? Why did you?

LADY. You have asked me that question time and time again, and I have never been able to answer you—because I don't know why I did it! Now—now that I have been away from you—and after having come up here on the way to the Alpine heights, where the air is purer and one is closer to the sun. . . . No, don't speak—now—now I see you in my mind's eye sitting there that Sunday afternoon, helpless, brokenhearted, like a rejected child, grappling with your own fate. . . . And it was then that a feeling that had been dormant—and compassion, compassion and pity for a human soul—filled my heart—and I forgot. . . .

STRANGER. I am ashamed. . . . And now I know why. . . .

LADY. But you—you took it in a different way. . . . You thought that . . .

STRANGER. Don't say it!—I am ashamed!

LADY. How could you think of me in such a low way?—Didn't you notice that I dropped a veil between us—as the knight of old used to place his sword between himself and his bride on their bridal night?

STRANGER. I am ashamed of myself! It was my own thoughts that were tainted—not yours! Ingeborg—you were far better than I. . . . I am ashamed!

LADY. At this moment you look sublime—truly sublime!

STRANGER. No—no—not I! But you *are!*

LADY *(with ecstasy)*. No—no! You! . . . Now I have had a glimpse of what is behind the mask you wear—and your disguised features! . . . Now I see the man you have tried to hide from me—the man I believed you to be—and whom I was forever seeking—seeking. . . . There were times when I thought you were a hypocrite. But we are not hypocrites—no, no, no—we could never descend to that level. . . .

STRANGER. Ingeborg—now that we are on the other side of the river and have left life behind us, and beneath us—how different everything seems. . . . Now I can see your soul—the primary image, the angel, which—because of sin—was condemned to be imprisoned in the flesh. . . . There must be something higher, something beyond us, beyond the infinite end. . . . The beginning was not when we were born, nor is it the end when we die. Life is a mere fragment; it has no beginning and no end. . . . That is why it is so hard to fathom!

LADY *(gently)*. So hard—so very hard! Can you tell me, for example—now that we no longer are concerned as to who is guilty or not guilty—how did you come to hate woman?

STRANGER. Let me think! . . . How I came to hate woman? Hate? I have never hated woman. That has been my misfortune! . . . From the time I was eight years old, I have always had some sort of romantic attachment, generally of an innocent nature. And three times I have loved like a volcano in eruption! But let me say this: I have always had the feeling that women hate me. They have always tormented me. . . .

LADY. How strange!

STRANGER. Let me think now. . . . I may have been jealous of my own personal integrity and character. My first love tried to make herself into both governess and nursemaid to me. And you know, there are men who do not like to be ruled by children, just as there are men who refuse to be ruled by women.

LADY *(amicably)*. But you have accused woman of being an enemy of man. Do you really believe that?

STRANGER. Of course I mean it, seeing that I wrote it. And

what I wrote was based on actual experience—not mere speculation. I sought to discover in woman an angel—on whose wings I could soar—and instead I fell into the arms of an earth spirit who blanketed me with bedding stuffed with feathers from her wings—until I could not breathe. I had gone in search of an Ariel—and I found a Caliban. . . . When I aimed for the heights—she pulled me down; and it always ended in our falling into sin. . . .

LADY *(gently)*. Do you recall what Solomon—who knew women as few ever have—had to say? "And I find more bitter than death the woman whose heart is snares and nets, and her hands as bands: who so pleases God shall escape from her; but the sinner shall be taken by her."

STRANGER. And I was never pleasing in the sight of God! Could it therefore have been my punishment? Perhaps so. . . . But I was never pleasing to anyone—was never given a kind word! Did I never do anyone a good deed? Could any human being fail to do at least one good deed in his life? It is heart-rending never to receive a kind word!

LADY. You have been given praise, but whenever you have been, you have thrust it aside, as though it gave you pain.

STRANGER. Yes, so I did—you are right. . . . I recall it now. . . . But why did I do it? Can you explain?

LADY. Why?—You never cease to ask for an answer to the unfathomable. "I applied my heart to know wisdom, and to understand the distraction that is upon earth . . . and I understood that man can find no reason of all those works of God that are done under the sun; and the more he shall labor to seek, so much the less shall he find: yes, even though the wise man should say that he knows it, he shall not be able to find it."

STRANGER. Who said these words?

LADY *(takes out a doll from her pocket)*. The Preacher, in Ecclesiastes. This is little Mitzi's doll. . . . Can you see that she is longing for her little mistress? Can you? You see how pale she is? And she seems to know where Mitzi is for she is forever gazing up to heaven, no matter how I hold her. See—her eyes follow the stars—they are like a compass needle—she is my compass, this little doll—she shows me where to find heaven. . . . She should, of course, be dressed in black because we are in mourning—but we are so poor! Do you know why we were always without money? Because God was wroth with us—because of our sins. "The righteous shall not want any good thing."

STRANGER. Where did you learn that?

LADY. In the book where everything is written. Everything!
(She puts the doll inside her cloak.) You can see that she is
beginning to get cold—it is because of the clouds in the sky. . . .

STRANGER. How do you dare to wander about in the mountains by yourself?

LADY. The Lord is with me—what have I then to fear from
mortals?

STRANGER. Doesn't the sight of the diseased at the tarn sicken
you?

LADY. I do not see them. I no longer see what is ugly and
horrible.

STRANGER. Ingeborg! It was I who made your heart evil—and
now you are on the way to make mine good. And now I will
tell you—it was my dream to find reconciliation—through a
woman. . . . Perhaps you will not believe it—but it is true!
Just as it is true that in days gone by nothing whatever was
of any worth to me if I could not lay it at a woman's feet! But
only as an offering to what she possessed of goodness and loveliness—not as a tribute to the woman in her that thirsted for
power! . . . It was a joy to me to give; but she wanted to take
—not accept . . . and that is why I hated her! When I grew
desperate and my helplessness reached its breaking point, I
thought the end was near and I became obsessed by a yearning to be cradled to sleep in a mother's lap, burying my weary
head in her ample bosom and drinking in the tenderness I
had never been given. . . .

LADY. Had you no mother?

STRANGER. Briefly. . . . And I have never felt myself related
to either my father or my brothers and sisters. . . . Ingeborg
—I was the son of the servant girl of whom it is written: "Cast
out this bondwoman and her son: for the son of this bondwoman shall not be heir with my son."

LADY. Do you know why Ishmael was driven out? It is mentioned shortly before. . . . Because he was a scoffer. And then
it says: "He will be a wild man; his hand will be against every
man, and every man's hand against him; and he shall dwell in
the presence of all his brethren."

STRANGER. Does it say that, too?

LADY. Yes, my child—it is all there.

STRANGER. All?

LADY. Yes—all! There you will find the answer to all your
questions—even the most searching questions!

STRANGER. Let me be your child—then I shall adore you. . . .
And when I adore somebody—then I can be her servant—I can
obey any command—take any ill-treatment—endure any suffering—I can bear anything.

LADY. You must not adore me—only your Creator. . . .

STRANGER. He is against me—as my father was!

LADY. He is Love—all Love. And you—you are Hate personified!

STRANGER. You are His daughter—and I am His prodigal
son! . . .

LADY (caressingly). Be still—be still! You . . .

STRANGER. If you only knew what I have suffered these last
eight days!—I don't know what kind of place I have come to?

LADY. How is that?

STRANGER. The woman in charge of these cabins. . . . She
stares at me as if I had come to rob her of her last farthing.
. . . What is worse, she never speaks to me—and as soon as
she sees me, she seems to mumble some sort of prayer.

LADY. What sort of prayer?

STRANGER. The kind that are said backward for those who
have the evil eye and who bring bad luck with them.

LADY. How strange!—Have you ever heard of people who
can distort another person's vision?

STRANGER. Yes—I have. But who would ever do such a thing?

HOSTESS (comes over to their table). Well, what do I see!—
I dare say the lady is your sister.

STRANGER. Well—yes, she is—now, we might say. . . .

HOSTESS (to the Lady). I am glad to meet someone at last
to whom I can open my heart! This gentleman, you see, is so
taciturn that you feel you must show him some respect, especially as I imagine he carries some sort of burden, some sorrow. . . . But you being his sister, I can tell you, and I don't
mind if he hears it. From the moment he came into this house,
blessings began to pour down on me. I had had nothing but
misfortunes: I had no one lodging with me—my only cow had
died—my husband was in a home for alcoholics—and my children were without anything to eat. I prayed to God that He
would send me help from heaven—for from those on earth I
hoped for nothing. And then came this gentleman. . . . Not
only did he pay me double what I asked, he brought me luck!
My house was blessed!—May God bless you, my dear sir!

STRANGER (gets up, visibly agitated). Be silent, woman, you
are speaking blasphemy!

LADY. He does not believe what you say! Oh God! He does

not believe it!—Look at me! *(Her eyes and the Stranger's meet.)*

STRANGER. Now that I look at you, I believe. . . . She gives me her blessing! . . . And I—who am among the damned—I have brought a blessing upon her! Is it really true? Can it be true that I—I . . . ? *(He collapses at the table and weeps in his hands.)*

LADY. He is weeping—weeping tears—rain from heaven that will remove the heavy weight from his stone-hard heart. . . . Oh fall, tears! He is weeping. . . .

HOSTESS. He—with his heart of gold—he who has been so good to my children! He who is so generous!

LADY. Do you hear what she says? Do you?

HOSTESS. There is only one thing about him I cannot understand—but it is nothing really bad, and so I . . .

LADY. And what is that?

HOSTESS. Well, it is only a small matter—and yet . . .

LADY. Do tell me!

HOSTESS. He cannot bear my dogs.

LADY. I cannot blame him for his dislike for an unclean dog. I abhor everything that is bestial in myself and in others. That does not mean that I hate animals. I hate nothing that has been created.

STRANGER. Thank you for that, Ingeborg!

LADY. You see! I do not overlook your merits, even though you think I do!—Here comes the Confessor. *(The Confessor enters.)*

HOSTESS. Then I shall leave you, for the Confessor has no love for me.

LADY. The Confessor has love for all mankind.

CONFESSOR *(comes forward and turns to the Lady)*. And most for you, my child, for you are the essence of goodness. Whether you are beautiful to look at, I cannot see, but I feel that you are—because you are good. Yes—you were the bride of my youth, and my spouse in spirit. And you shall always remain so, for you gave me what others would not be able to receive. I have lived your life in the spirit, I have borne your sufferings, but have not shared your joys, for you have had but one—your child. . . . The beauty of your soul I alone could see; our friend here divined it—that is why he was attracted to you. . . . But the evil in him was too overpowering—and in order to free him of it, you had to ingest his evil and bear it. . . . You had to go through all the tortures of hell, bearing his evil, suffering for his sake, to obtain expiation. Now your work is done. Go in peace now!

LADY. Where?

CONFESSOR. Up there—where the sun is forever shining. . . .

LADY (rises). Then there is a home waiting for me there also?

CONFESSOR. There is a home for everyone there. I will show you the way. (*He leads her upstage. The Stranger makes a motion as if restless and impatient.*) You are impatient, aren't you?—Do not be impatient! (*Goes out.*)

(*The Stranger remains seated. He is alone. Suddenly the Worshipers of Venus rise and walk toward the Stranger. They encircle him.*)

STRANGER. What do you want of me?

WORSHIPERS OF VENUS (*in chorus*). Hail, Father!

STRANGER (*in utter anguish*). Why do you call me "Father"?

FIRST WORSHIPER. Because we are your children—your dear children, your minions!

STRANGER (*tries to escape but they prevent him by surrounding him*). Go away from me! Let me go!

SECOND WORSHIPER (*a pale youth*). Don't you recognize me, Father?

TEMPTER (*appears in the background near the right branch of the crossways*). Ha ha!

STRANGER (*to the Second Worshiper*). Who are you? You seem familiar to me.

SECOND WORSHIPER. I am Erik—your son Erik!

STRANGER. Erik?—And you are here?

SECOND WORSHIPER. Yes—I am here!

STRANGER. May God have mercy! And forgive me, forgive me, my son!

SECOND WORSHIPER. No—never! You showed us the way that ended in the sulfur pit! Is it far to the lake? (*The Stranger collapses.*)

TEMPTER. Ha ha! *Jubilate temptatores!*

WORSHIPERS OF VENUS (*in chorus*). Sulfur! Sulfur! Sulfur! And Mercury!

TEMPTER (*comes forward, goes to the Stranger and touches him with his foot*). This miserable creature! (*To the Worshipers of Venus.*) You can make him believe anything you like! And that comes from his monstrous conceit and vanity! Has he not always acted as if the universe pivoted round him, as if he were the source and origin of all evil? The stupid fool has the fixed idea *he* was the one who taught youth to go in search of Venus! Ha! As if youth did not know about such things long before he was born! His arrogance and conceit are insufferable, and he has been presumptuous enough to encroach upon and dabble in my profession. Give him another raking over, deceitful Erik! *(Second Worshiper [the pale youth] bends over the Stranger and whispers in his ear.)* Originally there were seven deadly sins—now there are eight. The eighth is my own invention. It is called despair. For to have no faith in the power of goodness and to have no hope of forgiveness is the same as to say that *(Here he hesitates, loath to speak the word "God"—which, when he does speak it, he utters as if it burned his lips.)* . . . that God—is wicked. That is nothing short of slander—it is a denial of Him—it is blasphemy. . . . Look—look how he writhes and wriggles!

STRANGER *(gets up in haste and looks the Tempter in the face).* Who are you?

TEMPTER. Your brother! Don't we look like brothers! You have certain characteristics, it seems to me, that I recognize in myself.

STRANGER. Where have I seen a portrait of you?

TEMPTER. Oh—almost everywhere. . . . You see me frequently in the churches—though not among the saints. . . .

STRANGER. I do not recall. . . .

TEMPTER. Then it must have been a long time since you went to church. Oh yes—I am usually portrayed there in company with St. George. *(The Stranger trembles from head to foot. He gives the impression of wanting to vanish, but he cannot move.)* Michael and I are also seen together sometimes in a group. It is true, I am not represented there to my best advantage—but that can be changed with time. Everything can be changed—so that one day the last may be the first. And so with you, too! Just now things are not going too well with you —but there can come a change—if you would only have enough sense to choose better company. . . . You have been around too many skirts, my boy! Skirts raise dust—and dust settles over the eyes and on the chest. . . . Come over here and sit down, young man, and let us have a little talk. *(He jestingly takes the Stranger by the ear and leads him to the table.)* Now you can sit here and tremble—sit down and tremble, young man! *(They seat themselves.)* And now—what would you like to have? A little wine—and a pretty woman? No? Well—that is too ancient an expedient—as old as Dr. Faustus! Good! We moderns are in search of unusual mental dissipations. . . . And now—now you are on your way up there—to the holy men, who believe that, once you are asleep, you are free from temptation . . . up to those who have lost their spirit and have turned their backs on life merely because they have met with defeat a few times . . . to those who bind souls instead of setting them free. . . . And speaking of setting free—has any holy man ever freed you of the burden of sin? Has he?—No! . . . Do you know why your sins have been so oppressive, so heavy to bear lately? I will tell you. It is because you—through abstinence and mortification and penance—have grown so weak that anyone can pounce on your soul and take possession of it. Indeed, they could even do it from a distance. You have, in fact, so erased your own personality that you see with the eyes of others, hear with ears not your own, and think the thoughts of others. . . . In a word, you have committed murder on your own soul. Did I not hear you just now speaking well of the enemies of mankind—of woman who turned paradise into a hell? Didn't I? There is no need for you to answer —I can read your answer in your eyes—I hear it on your lips. . . . And you talk of having a pure unsullied love for woman! It is nothing but lust, my boy—the lust for any woman you meet—and for which we have to pay so dearly. You will say that you do not desire her. Then why do you always yearn to be near her? Why?—You would like to have a friend?—Well, take a male friend, as many as you like!—You have let them persuade you that you are not a woman-hater. But the little woman gave you the right answer to that: Every healthy man is a woman-hater—yet he cannot survive if he does not ally himself with his enemy and bring about strife. All deviates and effeminate perverts among men have an adoration for women!—How do you feel now? Oh yes, you saw the sick here, and at once you thought you were to blame for their misery. But believe me, they are hardy fellows—and in a few days they will be discharged and able to go back to their occupations. Yes, yes, yes —that deceitful Erik is a sly dog! And you—you are so far gone that you cannot tell your own children from others! I am glad to be rid of this whole mess! What do you say?—Now you see that I know how to solve things, don't you? Even though I am not a holy man!—Now we shall call Old Maia. (*He puts his fingers into his mouth and whistles. Old Maia enters.*) Ah, there you are!—Well, what are you wandering about here for? You have no quarrel with this young man, have you?

OLD MAIA. Oh no! He is such a good man—and he always was! But he had a mean wife. . . .

TEMPTER (*to the Stranger*). Do you hear what she says? You never heard anyone say that before, did you? But no doubt the opposite! She, the good angel whose life you have blighted—

we have all heard the story. . . . Now, Old Maia, what is this story he has been telling everybody? For seven years he has been going about with a bad conscience because he owed you some money.

OLD MAIA. He did owe me a small sum once—but he gave it back to me, and with generous interest, too. Yes, far more than the savings bank would have paid. Yes, he certainly is both honest and generous!

STRANGER (*springs up from his seat*). What is this you say? Can it be possible that I have forgotten?

TEMPTER. Have you the receipt on you, Old Maia? If you do, let me have it!

OLD MAIA. The receipt the gentleman must have—but I have the savings-bank book with me. And there it says he deposited the money in my name. (*She produces a savings-bank book and hands it to the Stranger, who glances in it.*)

STRANGER. Yes—she is right—and now it comes back to me. . . . Then why these seven years of torment, of feeling guilty and disgraced? Those endless reproaches during sleepless nights? Why—why—why?

TEMPTER. You may go now, Old Maia. . . . But before you go, say something nice about this self-tormentor. Can't you remember some human quality in this wild beast who has excited people's passions and been baited by people all these years? . . .

STRANGER (*to Old Maia*). Hold your tongue—say nothing! (*He covers his ears with his hands.*)

TEMPTER. Well, Maia?

OLD MAIA. Oh yes—I know very well what they say about him—but that has to do with what he writes in his books. And I don't read what they say—because I can't read. And nobody has to read it if they don't want to. Just the same, this gentleman was always so nice. . . . Look, he puts his hands over his ears! Yes, I don't like flattery either—but I can tell this to you, that . . . (*She tells him in a whisper.*)

TEMPTER. Yes, yes—all people who are highly emotional are set upon like wild beasts! That is the common practice, yes!— Good-by now, Old Maia!

OLD MAIA. Good-by, good gentlemen! . . . (*She departs.*)

STRANGER. Why did I have to suffer for seven years when I was innocent of doing anything wrong?

TEMPTER (*with a gesture in the direction of the mountain-top*). Ask up there!

STRANGER. Where I was never given an answer! . . .

TEMPTER. Oh well, that is what happens. . . . Do you think I have a sympathetic face?

STRANGER. I wouldn't say that!

TEMPTER. Your own face has a goodly portion of meanness in it, too. Do you know why we look alike?

STRANGER. No. . . .

TEMPTER. Because the hate and wickedness of our fellow creatures has fastened itself on us. You know—up there you will find true saints who have never done anything sinful themselves, but who suffer for the sins of others, for kin and family who have committed unexpiated crimes. These spiritual beings, who have taken the evilness of others upon themselves, in the end come to look like highwaymen. What have you to say to that?

STRANGER. I have no idea who you are—but you are the first man who has given me answers to my questions—answers that might reconcile me to life. . . . You are . . .

TEMPTER. Go ahead and say it!

STRANGER. You are the deliverer!

TEMPTER. And that is why . . .

STRANGER. That is why you were given a vulture!—But tell me, has it never occurred to you that there is as much reason for this as for everything else? Let us suppose that this earth is a prison where dangerous criminals are being shut in. If so, is it advisable to set them free? Would you say it would be right?

TEMPTER. What is that you say?—Come to think of it, I have never given that a thought. Hm! Hm!

STRANGER. And have you ever thought of this: that we may be born with sin?

TEMPTER. That is no concern of mine. What interests me is the present.

STRANGER. And so—don't you think we sometimes are punished wrongly and that we, as a consequence, fail to recognize the logical connection, although it may exist?

TEMPTER. There is no lack of logic in that—but the whole of life is so full of errors and transgressions, offenses, and defects. And no matter how trivial they may be in relation to human weakness, we are nevertheless being punished by the most consistent revenge. Everything is revenged—even things we do thoughtlessly, imprudently. And who forgives us? The man who is generous and high-minded? Sometimes, yes! But divine justice—never! *(A Pilgrim appears, rear.)* Ah, here we have a penitent! I am curious to know what he has done. Let us ask him! *(He goes up to the Pilgrim.)* Welcome, peaceful wanderer, to our tranquil regions! And sit down here at the frugal table of the ascetics—where you will find nothing to tempt you!

PILGRIM. I thank you, fellow wanderer in this vale of tears. . . .

TEMPTER. What are *your* troubles?

PILGRIM. Oh, none to speak of—on the contrary, my hour of liberation is at hand, and now I am on my way up there to be given absolution.

STRANGER. Look here—haven't we met each other before?

PILGRIM. We have, indeed!

STRANGER. Caesar! Why, it's Caesar!

PILGRIM. *Was* Caesar—I no longer am!

TEMPTER. Ha ha! Imperial acquaintances, I hear!—Well, well, well!—But let us hear!

PILGRIM. Now that my penance is at an end and I may speak —now you shall know my story. . . . When we met at the house of a certain doctor, I was confined there as being insane. It was said that I suffered from the delusion that I was Caesar. At last the Stranger will now learn the truth. I had no illusion that I was Caesar, but I was forced from scruples of conscience to make the best of it, and to say nothing. . . . A friend—a treacherous friend—had written proof in his possession that I was the victim of a misunderstanding, but he did not speak up when he should have—and I took this omission as an appeal to me not to say anything either, and to suffer in silence. Why did I keep silent and suffer? I shall tell you. . . . In my youth I was once in great need. I was received as a guest in the home of a man who lived on an island far out to sea. Despite the fact that he was uncommonly gifted, his rare gifts had failed to win promotion for him in his branch of service—and this because of a fantastic arrogance. In his lonely existence and from constant brooding this man had come to hold a quite extraordinary view of himself. I noticed it and kept quiet. One day, however, his wife confided to me that there were times when her husband acted abnormally and thought himself to be Julius Caesar. For years I kept her confidence conscientiously— for I am by nature not ungrateful. But life plays pranks on us, and a number of years later this Caesar began to interfere in my most intimate affairs. Enraged, I revealed the secret of his Caesar mania; and my former benefactor became a general laughingstock so that life grew to be unbearable to him. And now let me show you how Nemesis deals out her vengeance.

A year later I wrote a book. I must tell you, by the way, that I am an author who has not yet made a name for myself. In this book I casually described some incidents of my family life: how I used to play with my daughter, who was named Julia, like Caesar's daughter, and with my wife—whom we simply called Caesar's wife because no one ever referred to her by her name. And for this foolhardy indiscretion, in which my mother-in-law joined, I was to pay dearly. . . . When I read the proofs of the book, I sensed the danger, and I said to myself: "This will be your downfall!"—I intended to delete these passages . . . but, believe it or not, the pen refused to do its work, and a voice inside me kept saying: "Let it stand! Let it stand!"—I did let it stand—and it brought about my fall!

STRANGER. But why did you not ask your friend to make public the letter he wrote? That would have explained everything.

PILGRIM. Because when the blow came, I felt it to be the hand of God at work—that it was His will that I suffer—suffer for my ingratitude. . . .

STRANGER. And so you bore the burden?

PILGRIM. Not in the least! I just laughed up my sleeve and tried to make the best of my predicament. And because I accepted my punishment in silence and humility, God lightened my burden. . . . I never felt the sting of ridicule. . . .

TEMPTER. That is indeed a rare story—but that is the way things sometimes happen. . . . Don't you think we ought to be on our way now? We shall all go together—now that we have been through the storms of life. Pull yourselves up now by the roots—and then we shall climb to the lofty heights!

STRANGER. The Confessor told me to wait for him. . . .

TEMPTER. Oh, he will have no difficulty finding you. . . . And up there in the village they are holding court today; a particularly interesting case is to be tried—and I, can you imagine it!—I am to be a witness in the case! Come now—come, let us go!

STRANGER. Well—I can't see that it makes much difference where I sit—whether up here, or up there!

PILGRIM (to the Stranger). Who is that fellow?

STRANGER. I have no idea! He looks like an anarchist!

PILGRIM. He has an interesting face, at any rate!

STRANGER. He is a skeptical gentleman—who has seen life. . . .

TEMPTER. Come now, children—and then I will tell you some stories on the way. . . . Come now—come, come along now! *(They go toward the rear.)*

ACT III

SCENE 1. *A terrace on top of the mountain on which the monastery is built. On the left, a shelf projecting from the rock; a similar projection on the right. In the distance, the background depicts a bird's-eye view of a river landscape with towns and villages, cultivated land and clumps of trees. Beyond can be glimpsed the sea. Downstage, in the center, stands an apple tree with ripe fruit. Underneath the tree is a long table. At one end of it, a chair; at the sides, benches. On the left, downstage, a corner of the village courthouse. A cloud hangs directly over the village.*

The Sheriff, acting as judge, sits at one end of the table; his Deputies are seated on the benches alongside the table. The Accused Man stands before the Sheriff, to the left of the table. The Witnesses—among whom is the Tempter—on the right side. The Spectators—among them the Pilgrim and the Stranger—are grouped about the Judge and the table.

SHERIFF. Is the defendant present?

ACCUSED MAN. Present.

SHERIFF. This is an extremely sad story that has brought both shame and grief to our little community. Florian Reicher, age twenty-three, is accused of having shot and killed the fiancée of Fritz Schlipitska—shot and killed with the full intention of murdering her. We have before us a case of clearly premeditated murder; and the provisions of the law are clear and unmistakable. Have you, Florian, anything to say in your defense—or are there extenuating circumstances you wish to bring to light?

ACCUSED MAN. No.

TEMPTER. One moment!

SHERIFF. Who are you?

TEMPTER. The attorney for the Accused.

SHERIFF. I admit that the Accused is entitled to the services of counsel; but in a clear case such as the one before the court, I think public opinion has already been so well established by the facts heretofore presented that the murderer hardly has a chance to regain sympathy. Or what do you say?

THE PEOPLE. He has already been condemned!

TEMPTER. By whom?

THE PEOPLE. By the law—and because of the crime he committed!

TEMPTER. Hold on there!—In my capacity of counselor for the accused I am taking his place and am speaking for him. I therefore take the accusation upon myself. I ask the Court's permission to speak.

SHERIFF. I can't say no to that.

THE PEOPLE. Florian has been condemned already!

TEMPTER. He has to be heard first!—I had reached my eighteenth year—it is Florian who is speaking now. . . . My mother had brought me up and under her watchful eye my spirit and mind had remained clean and pure; and there was no deceit or guile in my heart—not even the slightest—for I had never either seen nor had any contact with any wickedness. . . . Then a young girl happened to cross my path—remember, it is Florian who is speaking. . . . This girl was in my eyes the most beautiful of all things I had seen on this wicked earth. She was goodness itself. I offered her my hand, my heart, and my future. . . . She accepted—and vowed she would be true to me forever. For five years I slaved for my Rachel—and slave I did, gathering straw by straw for the little nest that we planned to build. . . . My whole life was centered round my love for this woman; and as I myself was true to her, I never doubted her faithfulness to me. . . . By the fifth year—after I had built our little home and furnished it—I suddenly discovered that she had been false to me and that she had carried on affairs with at least three men. . . .

SHERIFF. Have you any witnesses?

BAILIFF. Three—all acceptable. I am one of them.

SHERIFF. The bailiff alone will suffice.

TEMPTER. And then I shot her—not out of revenge, but to free myself of the unhealthy thoughts her faithlessness had engendered in me. For no matter how hard I tried to erase her image from my heart, the images of her lovers kept ever coming before me, and crept into my blood—until at last I felt myself to be living in an illicit relationship with three men—through the wiles of a woman!

SHERIFF. You were jealous, in other words.

ACCUSED MAN. Yes—I was jealous.

TEMPTER. Yes—jealousy! That passion for purity that protests against the heart's being contaminated by carnal or unnatural relationships with outsiders. . . . If I had shut my eyes—or if I had not been jealous—I would have stepped into a vicious circle . . . and that I did not want. That is why she had to die her death so that my thoughts would be cleansed of that mortal sin which by itself should be punished with perdition. I have finished.

THE PEOPLE. The dead woman is guilty! She brought it upon herself!

SHERIFF. The dead woman is guilty! She brought it upon herself!

FATHER OF THE DEAD WOMAN (comes forward). Your Honor, judge of my dead child—and you, my friends and neighbors— I would like to speak. . . .

SHERIFF. The Father of the Dead Woman may speak!

FATHER OF THE DEAD WOMAN. You have slandered and accused my dead daughter—therefore I must give answer!—Maria, my child, was undoubtedly guilty of a crime and is responsible for the crime this man committed. There is no doubt of that. . . .

THE PEOPLE. No—no doubt! She is the guilty one!

FATHER OF THE DEAD WOMAN. Let me just add a word or two to help you understand her undoing, even if I cannot defend her. (There is an undercurrent of curiosity and suspense among the people; a murmur goes through the crowd.) When Maria was fifteen she met a man who seemed to have made it his aim in life to trick and entice young girls—much as a bird-catcher sets traps for birds. . . . He was no ordinary seducer, for he took pleasure in fettering their minds and their senses and feelings, only to cast them away and gloat over their agony when he had broken their hearts and scorched their wings —an agony worse than any other! For three years Maria was cared for in an institution for mental cases, and when she was released from there she was broken down; her mind was disjointed. One could say she had a dual personality. She was good as an angel in one side of her personality, and feared God— but her other personality was a demon, and it reviled all that was holy. I have seen her go from dancing and intoxication to meet her beloved Florian. . . . I have seen her, when they were together, suddenly take on a different expression, heard her speak in a tone so different that I could have sworn she was not the same person. Yet, to me, she seemed equally sincere, no matter which character she took on. Is she to blame— or is her seducer?

THE PEOPLE. The blame is not hers! Who is her seducer?

FATHER OF THE DEAD WOMAN. There he stands! (He points to the Tempter.)

TEMPTER. Yes—it was I!

THE PEOPLE. Stone him!

SHERIFF. The law must be adhered to. We must hear what he has to say!

TEMPTER. Very well—listen to what I have to say, Argives! . . . I was born of poor but fairly honorable parents. It was my fate to be born one of those strange birds who in their youth go in search of their Creator—but without finding him, of course. . . . As you know, it is more usual that old cuckoos seek him when they begin to grow old and decrepit—and for good reason! However—this pursuit was coupled with a purity of heart and a modesty that evoked laughter even in my nurse-maids . . . yes, you may well laugh when I tell you that as a child I could only bring myself to change underclothes in the dark of a closet! But even though the coarseness and crudities of life have completely corrupted us, we can not help finding something appealing, and—as we get older—even something touching in such behavior! But the way we are constituted today, we just ridicule and laugh at the innocence of the little child!—So, by all means, let us hear your scornful laughter—all of you here!

SHERIFF *(with a serious mien).* You underestimate your listeners!

TEMPTER. In that case I stand here with my shame! *(After a moment he continues.)* Well—and then I grew up—I, Florian —grew into a youth, and it was not long before I met with tricks and schemings—all conspiring to rob me of my inno-cence! Steeped in sin as I am, even I have to blush. *(He doffs his hat.)* Yes, look at me!—I blush when I think of the taste I got of this world of Potiphar-wives that kept surrounding me! I did not find a single woman who . . . forgive me—yes, I must confess I am ashamed on behalf of humanity and the female sex! . . . There were times when I did not believe my eyes, and I thought some demon had distorted my vision. . . . The holiest of bonds. *(He pinches his tongue.)* No, I must not say any more! Mankind would feel it was being slandered! . . . Anyhow, I kept up the contest until I was twenty-five and did not succumb, neither to ridicule nor to . . . Yes—I was named Joseph; and I was Joseph!—I was jealous of my virtue: the ogling of an unchaste wanton woman wounded me. . . . But finally I fell—seduced in a cunning way . . . and from then on I became a slave of my passions! I would sit at Omphale's and spin and spin, and I sank into the very deepest depravity and suffered, suffered, suffered! But it was really only my body that was debased—my soul lived its life apart, I might say a life of its own, in purity. And I dreamed innocently of young, unsullied maidens—and they, no doubt, sensed in turn the sympathetic feeling that drew us together. For, without boasting, I can say they were attracted to me. Yet I did not want to transgress and cross the borderline—but they did; and when I fled the danger, they told me their hearts were broken. In short, I swear I have never seduced an innocent girl. . . . Am I then to be blamed for this young woman's heartsickness—for her mental suffering? Should I not instead be commended, held in esteem, for shrinking back from bringing about her fall?— Who will cast the first stone at me?—Nobody! Then I have misjudged my listeners—for I thought I would be held up as a laughingstock, standing here pleading in defense of my manly innocence! And now I feel young again; and I wouldn't mind offering a slight apology to mankind—if it were not for the fact that I see a cynical smile on the lips of the woman who seduced me when I was young. Step forward, woman, and take a look at your work of destruction—see what the seed brought forth. . . .

WOMAN (steps forward. She is modest and dignified). Yes— it was I! Allow me to tell my simple story—of how I was seduced when I was a girl. . . . And, as luck would have it, my seducer is here among you. . . .

SHERIFF. My good friends! I must break off the proceedings —else we shall get back to Eve in paradise. . . .

TEMPTER. Who was the one who seduced Adam in his youth! It was exactly her we wanted to get back to: Eve—Eve! (He swings his cape in the air. At once the tree trunk takes on transparency and Eve is seen. Her hair is wound about her body, and round her loins she wears a girdle.) And now, Mother Eve, it was you who seduced our father. What have you to say in your defense?

EVE (simply, with dignity). The Serpent put temptation in my way!

TEMPTER. Well answered! Eve has won her freedom! Bring in the Serpent! The Serpent! (Eve vanishes.) Bring in the Serpent! (The Serpent is seen within the tree trunk.) Here you see the seducer of us all! Well, Serpent, who led you astray?

ALL (in horror). Silence, blasphemer!

TEMPTER. Answer me, Serpent! (There is a clap of thunder, accompanied by lightning. All flee except the Tempter, who *has fallen to the ground, and the Pilgrim, the Stranger, and the Lady.) Causa finalis,* or the final cause—that is something we shall never know! . . . However—since the Serpent has been given the blame—we are relatively innocent of guilt. But that is something people must not be told!—At any rate, the accused seems to have come out of his predicament; and the court has vanished, gone up in smoke, so to speak!—Yes, yes—you shall not judge, you shall not judge, you judges!

LADY *(to the Stranger).* Come—come with me!

STRANGER. But I would like to listen to this man. . . .

LADY. Why? He is like a little child: he asks questions about all the things for which there is no answer. Don't you know how inquisitive small children are?—"Papa, why does the sun rise in the east?"—Can you answer that question, can you?

STRANGER. Hm.

LADY. Or this one: "Mama, who created God?"—You think of that as something profound!—Come with me!

STRANGER *(struggling with his admiration for the Tempter).* Yes—but that about Eve—that was something new!

LADY. Oh, nothing of the sort. I read it in my Bible history when I was eight years old. And that we inherit the debts of our fathers—*that* you find written in the law of the land.

TEMPTER *(rises, stretches his limbs; then, limping, he climbs to the top of the precipice, left).* Come—and I shall show you the world that you think you know, but don't.

LADY *(who is climbing the precipice on the right. To the Stranger).* Come over here, my child, and I shall show you God's beautiful Creation as I have come to see it after the tears of sorrow washed the dust from my eyes!—Come to me! *(The Stranger stands hesitant as to whom to heed.)*

TEMPTER. And how did the world appear through your tears? Like the willows on the shore, mirrored in troubled, turbulent waters! A chaos of curved lines—with the trees seen standing on their heads. . . . No, my child, with my farseeing field glasses, dried at the fire of hate, with my terrestrial telescope I can see things in their true perspective—in sharp, perfect focus, exactly as they are!

LADY. What do you know of things as they are, my child? It is not the thing itself you see with your eye; it is its image. And an image is merely an illusion—not the thing itself. So you are arguing about nothing but images and illusions.

TEMPTER. Well, what do you think of that! A little philosopher in skirts! By Zeus, a disputation like that in this giant amphitheatre of the mountains calls for a suitable audience.

LADY. I have my audience with me: my friend, my husband, my child! If he cares to listen to me, then I am satisfied— and all will be well with him and with me!—Come over here, my dear, for here you will find the road! This is Mount Gerizim, where you will be given a blessing. And over there is Mount Ebal, where you are cursed.

TEMPTER. Yes—this is Mount Ebal, where they curse: "Cursed be the earth for your sake, woman; in sorrow shall you bring forth children, and you shall be under your husband's power, and he shall have dominion over you." And to the man: "Cursed is the earth for your sake; thorns and thistles shall it bring forth to you; and in the sweat of your face shall you eat bread."

Thus spoke the Lord—not I!

LADY. "And God blessed the first man and woman; and God blessed the seventh day after He had ended His work, which He had made, and it was good." But you . . . but we—we have made it into something evil—and that is why . . . that is why. . . . But he who lives up to the commandments of the Lord, he belongs upon Mount Gerizim, where blessings are still being given. Thus the Lord says: "Blessed shall you be in the city, and blessed in the field. Blessed shall be the fruit of your womb, and the fruit on your ground. Blessed shall you be coming in and going out. The Lord will open his excellent treasure, the heaven, that it may give rain in due season, and He will bless all the works of your hands; and your offspring and issue will thrive. And you shall lend to many nations, and shall not borrow of anyone. And you shall be above all people and under none. And I set before you a blessing that will follow you in all that you do, if you will obey the commandments of the Lord your God. . . ." So come, my friend, and lay your hand in mine! (Clasping her hands, she kneels.) By the love that once united us—by the memory of the child that held us together—by the power of a mother's love—a mother's, a mother's, a mother's: for that is how I have loved you, you lost, strayed child whom I have tried to find in the dark hiding places of the forest—and whom I again found at last, hungry, worn, languishing for want of love—I beg you to come back to me! Come, my child of sorrow, and hide your tired head next to my heart, where you rested before you saw the light of the sun! (While she has been speaking, the Lady has

gradually changed into a full-bosomed, motherly-looking wom-
an with hair hanging loose. She has shed her original clothing
and now appears in white garb.)

STRANGER. Mother!

LADY. Yes, my child, your mother! In life it was denied me
to caress you—the will of higher powers refused to grant my
desire. . . . Why? I dare not ask. . . .

STRANGER. My mother? But my mother is dead!

LADY. Your mother *was* dead—but the dead are not dead.
Don't you know that a mother's love can conquer death?—
Come, my child, and I shall make amends for the wrong I once
did you . . . upon my knee I shall cradle you to sleep—I shall
wash you clean of the hate and sin that . . . *(She omits the*
word she cannot bring herself to speak.) I shall untangle your
hair, matted with the sweat of anguish, and warm a white
linen night shirt for you before the fireplace of our home—
the home you never came to have, you homeless outcast, son of
Hagar the handmaid, who was born of a slave, and against
whom every man's hand was raised. The plowmen plowed their
furrows on your back and they made the grooves deep. . . .
Come—and let me heal your wounds—let me take the pain of
your sufferings upon me! . . . Come!

STRANGER *(weeping hysterically, shaking from head to foot.*
He walks to the cliff on the right, where the Mother stands
waiting for him with open arms.) I am coming. . . .

TEMPTER. I see I can do nothing here any more. But we
shall meet again—some day! *(He disappears behind the cliff.)*

SCENE 2. *Higher up in the mountains. A rocky landscape,*
surrounded by marsh and framed by clouds.

STRANGER. Oh, Mother! Mother! Why do you leave me? Just
when my beautiful dream was about to come true!

TEMPTER. What was your dream? Tell me!

STRANGER. My most fervent hope, my most secret desire, my
final prayer . . . to be reconciled to mankind through woman. . . .

TEMPTER. Through woman—who taught you to hate. . . .

STRANGER. Just because of that—because she bound me to
earth—like the iron ball which the slave has to drag after him,
chained to his ankle, to keep him from escaping.

TEMPTER. Ha! Woman! Always woman!

STRANGER. Yes, woman! She is the beginning and the end—
for us men, at any rate. In and by themselves, they are nothing.

TEMPTER. Consequently they amount to nothing by them-selves but mean everything to us, and are everything through us. They are our honor and our shame; our greatest joy, our deepest pain and distress; our redemption and our fall; our reward and our punishment; our strength and our weakness.

STRANGER. You put your finger on it! Our shame! You who are a wise man, can you solve this riddle for me? Whenever I was seen in public with a woman—my own lovely wife, whom I adored—leaning on my arm, I felt ashamed, as of a weak-ness! Answer that riddle, if you can!

TEMPTER. You were ashamed? . . . No—I don't know the answer!

STRANGER. You have no answer? You!

TEMPTER. No. I don't know the answer. But whenever *I* was out among people with my wife, I felt she was being defiled by people's glances; and through her, I also.

STRANGER. And when she committed some shameful act, her behavior reflected on you. Why?

TEMPTER. The Eve of the Greeks was called Pandora, and she was created by Zeus out of malice and spitefulness in order to torment the men and subjugate them. As a wedding gift she was given a box, in which were encased all the misfortunes of the world. Perhaps this riddle of the sphinx could be more easily solved by looking at it from the heights of Olympus, rather than from the Garden of Eden!—In any case, it will never be solved completely! And I am no closer to a solution than you are. But while I am pondering this subject, I can still take delight in the most beautiful of created things!—Why don't you do the same?

STRANGER. The most beautiful of the devil's illusions is what you mean! For she—who to me seems most beautiful—may seem ugly to someone else. But even to me she can appear uglier than any other woman when she is in a rage. So—what is beauty?

TEMPTER. Merely an illusion, the reflection of your own good heart. (*He covers his mouth with his hand.*) Now—what the devil! There it slipped out—and now—now the devil is loose!

STRANGER. The devil? Yes! But how can the devil make me want to be virtuous and good? How can *she*—if she is a devil? For that was what I experienced with number one. I saw her beauty and was gripped by a desire to be like her and thus become worthy of her. I first went in for the externals: by taking baths and exercises, by using cosmetics and wearing fine clothes. But I only made myself ridiculous. Then I began from within: I made it my habit to think wholesome, beautiful thoughts, to speak only what was good, to act and behave nobly. And, behold, one day—when the outer image had stamped itself upon the soul, then—so she said—then I had turned into the very image of her!—And it was she who first spoke those sublime, bewitching words "I love you" to me. How can a devil ennoble us—how can a spirit of hell inspire goodness within us? How can . . . No, she was no devil; she was an angel! True, she was a fallen angel—and her love a broken ray from that glorious light that gives warmth and love—love —love! . . .

TEMPTER. Now listen, old boy, are we to stand here like a couple of youngsters and grapple with the conundrum of love?

CONFESSOR. What is it that that garrulous fellow is saying? All his life he has done nothing but talk! That is why he has never found time to accomplish anything!

TEMPTER. I was to have been a priest—but the vocation was denied me!

CONFESSOR. While you are waiting for it, you might help me to find a drunkard who has gone and drowned himself here in the marsh. His body can't be very far from here, for I have trailed him as far as this.

TEMPTER. Then it must be he who is lying in that thicket over there.

CONFESSOR (removes some of the branches. The fully clothed body of a man with a youthful face and the pallor of death on it is seen). Yes—it is he! (He regards the dead man pensively.)

TEMPTER. Who is the dead man?

CONFESSOR. This is remarkable! Remarkable!

TEMPTER. He was a handsome man—almost a youth!

CONFESSOR. No, good friends. He was fifty-four years old. And when I saw him a week ago, he looked like sixty-four. His eyes were a grayish-yellow—like the slime of a garden snail— and were inflamed and bloodshot from drunkenness, but also from shedding tears of blood over his iniquities and his misery. His face was bloated and puffed up like a piece of liver on a butcher's chopping block, and it had the color of liver; and in his shame he hid himself from the eyes of men. . . . Even to the last, he seems to have been ashamed of the shattered mirror of his soul—and that is why he must have hidden his face underneath the shrubbery. I witnessed how he fought to conquer his weaknesses—saw him pray on bended knee to God for deliverance after he had been dismissed from his teaching post. . . . But—well, now he has been set free! And now—do you see how all the evilness has taken flight, and how all that was good and beautiful in him remains! That is the way he looked at nineteen. . . . It is our sins, inflicted upon us as a punishment, that stamp us with ugliness. . . . Why? That we are not told. "He who hates the righteous shall be desolate"—so, approximately it is written. . . . Or—I knew him when he was young—and I now recall that he was always extremely contemptuous of those who did not imbibe. He sat in judgment, and he condemned, and always set his cult of the grape upon the altar of earthly joys!—Now he has been delivered— he is free of sin—free from shame—free from all ugliness! Yes— he is beautiful in death—and death sets us free!—Do you hear that, you liberator—who could not even rid an alcoholic of his abominable craving for drink!

TEMPTER. Crime as a punishment? Yes—not a bad idea! It is rather a profound thought!

CONFESSOR. Why, I should think so! There you have a new subject for discussion!

TEMPTER. Now I shall take leave of you gentlemen for a while. We shall meet again before long. . . .   (*He leaves.*)

CONFESSOR. I saw you a moment ago in the company of a woman. . . . So you are still being beset by temptation, are you?

STRANGER. Not of the kind you have in mind!

CONFESSOR. What kind, then?

STRANGER. To be sure, I still think it possible to bring about a reconciliation between mankind and woman through a woman. And what is more, through the woman who was once my wife and who now—cleansed and exalted through want and sorrow—has grown into the woman I once thought her to be. But . . .

CONFESSOR. But . . . ?

STRANGER. But experience has taught us that the closer we are to our goal, the further away we are; and the further we are from one another, the nearer we may be.

CONFESSOR. That is something I learned in infancy. And Dante—who possessed the soul of Beatrice throughout his life —knew it; and Beethoven—though separated by distance—became one in spirit—with Therese von Brunswick, who was the wife of another!

STRANGER. And still—we find happiness only when we are near a woman.

CONFESSOR. Then be near her!

STRANGER. You forget one thing: we are divorced.

CONFESSOR. Very well—then begin a wholly new marriage, and one that is more promising, now that you are two entirely new human beings.

STRANGER. Do you think anybody would consent to marry us?

CONFESSOR. You mean—would I? That is asking a little too much!

STRANGER. I had forgotten! But we'll find someone, no doubt. The more difficult question will be to get settled—to get a home.

CONFESSOR. There are times when luck is on your side— even though you refuse to recognize it. Down there by the river is a little house. It is newly built, and the owner has not even seen it yet. He is an Englishman who was about to be married—but at the last moment she jilted him. It was built by his attorney, and neither the Englishman nor his intended wife have set eyes on it. So it is in perfect condition, you see.

STRANGER. And it is for rent?

CONFESSOR. Yes.

STRANGER. Good. Then I shall take the risk and try to start life over again.

CONFESSOR. And so you are going down—instead of up?

STRANGER. Coming down from the clouds! Down there the sun is still shining; up here the air is a little thin.

CONFESSOR. Good! Then we shall part again—for a time.

STRANGER. Where are you going?

CONFESSOR. Upward.

STRANGER. And I go down—down to the earth—our Mother Earth with the soft bosom and the warm lap. . . .

CONFESSOR. Until you once again feel a longing for the bleak, and the stark, steadfast rock—and what is pure. . . . Farewell! My greetings to the world below!

SCENE 3. *A handsome wainscoted dining room with a stove, faced with tiled majolica. In the center of the room, a dining table overflowing with flowers in vases; also two lighted candles. On the right, a large, carved buffet. On the left, two windows. At the rear are two doors: the right door stands open and shows the Lady's drawing room, furnished in pale green and mahogany. A lighted floor lamp of brass*

*has a large, lemon-colored shade. The door on the left is
closed. There is an entrance from the hall on the right,
behind the buffet.*

*The Stranger and the Lady enter from the right. The
Stranger is dressed as a bridegroom, and the Lady, radiating
youth and beauty, as a bride.*

STRANGER. Welcome to my house, beloved—to your home
and mine, my bride—to your house and home, my wife!

LADY. I thank you, dear heart! It is like a fairy tale, isn't it?

STRANGER. Yes, a fairy tale! A whole collection of fairy tales,
my child, which I have conceived and fathered. *(They seat
themselves at the table, facing each other.)*

LADY. Is it all real? It seems too wonderful to be true!

STRANGER. I have never seen you look so young, so beautiful!

LADY. Your eyes deceive you. . . .

STRANGER. My eyes have learned to see! And it was your
goodness that was their teacher . . .

LADY . . . and who in turn had it taught to her through
sorrow. . . .

STRANGER. Ingeborg!

LADY. This is the first time you have called me by my name!

STRANGER. The first time? I have never met Ingeborg before
—I have never known you before—you who are sitting here
now—in our home. What a precious word: home! What a thing
of beauty and loveliness—that I have never possessed in the
past! A home and a wife! You are my first wife, my only wife—
for what lies in the past no longer exists—no more than the
moments that just lapsed!

LADY. Orpheus! With your words you have sung life and
beauty into these dead stones! Sing life into me also!

STRANGER. Eurydice—whom I recovered from the underworld! I shall love life into being in you—I shall breathe
life into you with my words of imagery—and this time we shall
know what real happiness is, for we are now aware of the
dangers that must be shunned!

LADY. The dangers, yes. . . . How wonderful it is in here!
It is as if the rooms were filled with invisible guests bidding
us welcome—kindly spirits come to bless us and our home!

STRANGER. The candle flames stand still in silent devotion—
the flowers are deep in thought and meditation. . . . Yes. . . .

LADY. Hush! Outside, the summer night is sleeping, dark and
feverish—the stars hang large upon the trees, large and tearful,
like candles on a Christmas tree. . . . This is what I call happiness! Let it not escape us!

STRANGER *(pensively).* And yet . . .

LADY. Hush!

STRANGER *(rising).* I feel a poem being born in me. . . . It is for you!

LADY. You must not speak it! I can read it in your eyes. . . .

STRANGER. Yes, and I read it in yours! . . . Besides, I cannot speak it, for it has no words—but it has color—and fragrance. . . . And at the sound of my voice, it would die. The unborn is always more beautiful—the lost and the ungained dearer to us!

LADY. Hush! Or our guests will leave us! *(There is a silence.)*

STRANGER. This is happiness—but I cannot capture it—hold it!

LADY. Let it remain in your vision—breathe it—for it cannot be grasped.

STRANGER. You are looking at your little room, I see. . . .

LADY. It is as light and green as a meadow at midsummer! And there is someone in there—there is more than one in there. . . .

STRANGER. My thoughts are there!

LADY. Your good thoughts, your beautiful thoughts . . .

STRANGER. Which you have given me. . . .

LADY. Do you think I had anything to give you?

STRANGER. You had everything to give me! But in those days I was not free to accept—my hands were not clean enough to caress your little heart. . . .

LADY. Now, my beloved, the reconciliation is drawing near!

STRANGER. To mankind and to woman—through woman? Yes—it has already come about—and so, may you be blessed among women! *(The lamp and candles go out, and the dining room is in darkness, except for a faint glow of light from the yellow brass lamp in the Lady's room.)*

LADY. Oh! What makes it so dark?

STRANGER. Where are you, beloved? Give me your hand! I am afraid!

LADY. Here is my hand, my dear!

STRANGER. Your little hand that you held out to me in the darkness—that guided me over rocks and thorns—that soft, dear little hand! Lead me into the light—into your bright, warm room—green and light like hope. . . .

LADY *(leads him toward the pale green room).* Are you afraid?

STRANGER. My white little dove—it is with you the frightened eagle takes refuge when the thunder of heaven spreads its murky blanket beneath the sky; for the dove is unruffled and has no fear. . . . The dove has not provoked the thunder by vexing heaven!

(As they are about to enter the inner room, the curtain falls.)

SCENE 4. *The setting is the same as in the previous scene, but the table has now been cleared. The Lady sits at the table without occupying herself with anything. She gives the impression of being bored. On the left in the foreground, close to the footlights, a window is open. Silence.*

STRANGER *(enters with a sheet of paper in his hand).* Now you shall hear!

LADY *(preoccupied, resigned).* Have you already finished?

STRANGER. Already? Are you serious? I have spent seven days writing this one little poem. *(Silence.)* Perhaps you will be bored if you listen to it?

LADY *(dryly.)* No, of course not. *(The Stranger seats himself at the table and keeps regarding the Lady.)* Why do you keep looking at me?

STRANGER. I want to read your thoughts!

LADY. But you have heard them, haven't you?

STRANGER. That means nothing—I want to see them! *(There is a silence.)* For what people say is usually nothing but idle talk. *(Again there is silence.)* May I read to you?—No, I see you don't want to hear! You don't care to have anything more to do with me! *(The Lady seems to be about to say something.)* This is what the expression on your face tells me: "I have had enough! You have sucked the marrow out of me, eaten me hollow, killed everything within me—my very self, my personality!" . . . In answer to that I say, "How, my beloved? You say I have killed your very self—I who would have given you everything—who let you skim the pith and substance from my cups, filled with experiences from my long life, from forays through the deserts and groves of the arts and literature."

LADY. I don't deny that. But those were not my own experiences—something I myself had lived—something I could call my own.

STRANGER. Your own? What is your own? What is yours is merely what you have taken from others!

LADY. And what you call yours, *you* have taken from others!

STRANGER. No—what I have lived and experienced is mine and no one else's! What I have absorbed by reading has become mine because I first had to break it down and shatter it—like glass—and then melt it down; and out of the molten mass I created other commodities of new and different shapes and patterns.

LADY. That is all very well—but I could never be yours. . . .

STRANGER. I have become yours!

LADY. What have I ever given you?

STRANGER. And you ask that?

LADY. And yet—although you do not show it, I nevertheless have a feeling that you do feel so: you would like to see me far away from you!

STRANGER. I must have you at a distance in order to be able to see you. Now you are out of focus, and I can only see you dimly.

LADY. The nearer, the farther away!

STRANGER. Exactly!—But when we are away from each other, we long for each other, and when we are together again, we ache to be apart.

LADY. Do you really think we love each other?

STRANGER. Yes—but not like other people. Ours is not an ordinary love. We are like two drops of water that are in fear of coming too close to each other lest they should cease to be two and turn into one.

LADY. This time we were aware of the dangers and hoped to stay clear of them. However, it seems as if they could not be averted.

STRANGER. Perhaps they really were not dangerous—merely harsh necessities imposed by the laws of the powers-that-be among the Immortals. (Silence.) To me your love always felt like hate. And when you brought me happiness, you envied me the happiness you gave me. But when you saw me unhappy —then you loved me!

LADY. Do you want me to leave you?

STRANGER. If you do, I shall die!

LADY. And if I stay, then I shall die!

STRANGER. Then let us die together and live for our love in a higher life, for our love does not seem to be of this world —let us soar to another sphere where distance and nearness do not exist, where two are one, where numerals and speech, and time and space, are other than here. . . .

LADY. I longed for death—yet I do not wish to die! I think I already am dead!

STRANGER. The atmosphere up here is overpowering.

LADY. If you speak like that, you cannot love me!

STRANGER. Quite frankly, there are moments when you don't

exist for me. But then again, there are times when I literally feel your hatred as though it were fumes suffocating me.

LADY. And when you are angry with me, I feel as if my heart were creeping out of me!

STRANGER. And so—we hate each other!

LADY. And love each other!

STRANGER. We hate each other because we love each other; we hate each other because we are bound to each other; we hate the bond; we hate love; we hate the loveliest which is the bitterest—the best that life has to offer us. We have reached the end!

LADY. Yes.

STRANGER. What buffoonery—if one takes life seriously! And how depressing if one takes it as a jest, lightly, flippantly!— You were to take me by the hand and lead me into the light; your less harsh fate was to make it more tolerable for my own fate; I was to lift you high above the bogs and mire and quicksands—but you felt yourself drawn back to earth and tried to convince me that it was the higher regions. Is it possible, I keep asking myself, that you drew upon yourself all that was evil in me when I was set free of it; and that all that was good in you was transferred into me? Therefore, if it is I who have made you evil, I beg you to forgive me, and I kiss your little hand—which could both caress me and scratch me —your little hand that guided me in the darkness—that led me on the long journey to Damascus. . . .

LADY. Does this mean good-by? (Silence.) It is your good-by, then? (Silence. She leaves. The Stranger collapses on a chair by the table. The Tempter puts his head through the open window, leaning upon his elbows and puffing a cigarette.)

TEMPTER. Yes, yes!—C'est l'amour! The most mystifying of all mysteries, the most inexplicable of all that is inexplicable, the most perplexing of all perplexities.

STRANGER. So you are back again.

TEMPTER. Always on the spot whenever I scent anything that might spell disaster. And wherever love is involved, there is always disaster.

STRANGER. Always?

TEMPTER. Always! I was a guest at a silver-wedding anniversary yesterday. Twenty-five years of married life is not to be shrugged off—and all these years they had been feuding. Their love-life for a quarter of a century had been nothing but one long quarrel, with many petty ones in between. And still they loved each other, and expressed thanks for all their blessings through the years! All that was painful and bitter was forgotten; for a single moment of happiness can make up for ten days of hell with all its many stings and lashings. Yes—whoever refuses to accept his share of pain and misery will never receive the good things of life. The rind is bitter—yes, it can be very bitter—but the tiny seed within may be sweet!

STRANGER. Yes—but there is awfully little of it!

TEMPTER. My dear friend, there isn't much of it—but what there is, is good! . . . But tell me, why did your madonna run away?—You can't answer that question, because you don't know. Now we will have a vacancy to be filled in the hotel! —Here is a sign—I'll hang it out: For rent. One person comes, another one goes! C'est la vie, quoi! Rooms for transients.

STRANGER. Have you ever been married?

TEMPTER. Yes, to be sure, I have.

STRANGER. Why did it come to an end?

TEMPTER. Primarily because—and this may be a peculiarity of mine—primarily because . . . Well, you know, of course, that a man usually marries in order to have a home of his own; and a woman, to get out of one. She wanted to get out; and I wanted to stay in. I was so constituted that I could not accompany her when she went out among people, for I felt she was made unclean by the glances given her by some men. And in the company of others my wonderful, glorious wife became a little grimacing shrew whom I couldn't even bear to look at! And so—well, I found it best to stay at home; and she—she stayed away from home. And when I met her again, she was a different person. She—my unblemished white sheet of paper had been scribbled full of pothooks and scrawls; her lovely, clean-cut features had come to resemble a satyr's, due to her association with her strange men friends; in her eyes I saw pictured bullfighters and guardsmen in miniature; I heard the strange intonations of strange men in her voice; she now would play only cheap melodies by strange men on our grand piano, where before only the great among composers had been heard; and on our table there now was found only the favorite reading matter of strange men. In short, my whole existence was being perverted into a spiritual concubinage with strange men—and this went against my nature, which has always felt the need of woman! And—I scarcely need to add—the tastes of these strange men were always in direct conflict with what I liked. She developed into a veritable genius in her efforts to discover things that were objectionable and abhorrent to me! This, she maintained, was done "to protect her own personality." Can you comprehend this?

STRANGER. I understand—but I am not going to attempt to explain it.

TEMPTER. Despite all that, this woman insisted that she loved me, and that I did not love her. And yet, I loved her so intensely that I could not bring myself to speak to anyone else; for I felt I would be unfaithful to her if I were to find enjoyment in being with others—even with my men acquaintances. I had married because I felt the need of a woman, and in order to make the most of our relationship, I gave up my friends. I had married in order to find a companion; instead I found utter loneliness. And I had to keep up house and home—all for the sake of providing strange men with a female companion. *C'est l'amour*, my dear friend!

STRANGER. One ought never to talk about one's wife!

TEMPTER. No—for if one speaks well of her, people merely laugh; and if one has nothing good to say about her, everybody will sympathize with her. And—as I said before—if people should laugh and you ask them why, you will get no answer.

STRANGER. You are right. One never knows whom one is married to! One can never take hold of her—it is as though she had no fixed personality!—What is woman? What is she?

TEMPTER. Who knows! Perhaps some sort of larva, or pupa, out of whose somnambulist life a man will be created. She is like a child, yet is not one; she is a sort of child, but is not like one. When the man pulls upward, she drags downward; when the man drags downward, she pulls upward!

STRANGER. She always voices an opinion contrary to her husband's; and what he abhors, she has sympathy for. She is crudeness personified underneath a silken surface, and she hides her maliciousness beneath all that is best in her. And in spite of all this—I have always become better, been enriched and inspired whenever I have been in love.

TEMPTER. You have, yes—but how about her?

STRANGER. She? All through the growing-years of our love she has been developing backward! At the same time, she has grown more and more malicious and coarse!

TEMPTER. How would you explain that?

STRANGER. I can't. But there was a time when I was trying to solve that riddle, in the assumption that I was the one who was in the wrong. I came to the conclusion that she was absorbing what was evil in me; and I, what was good in her.

TEMPTER. Do you think women are more false than men?

STRANGER. Yes—and no. The fact that she tries to conceal her weaknesses merely indicates that she is ambitious, and also that she has a sense of shame. The whore, on the other hand, is frank and straightforward, and that is what gives her her cynical attitude.

TEMPTER. Tell me some more nice things about woman!

STRANGER. I once had a girl friend. . . . She soon made the observation that when I drank I became uglier than usual; and so she pleaded with me not to drink. I can recall one evening—after we had spent a great many hours together in a café talking with each other. When it was close to ten in the evening, she begged me to go home and go to bed, and to drink no more. After saying good night, we left each other. Some days later I learned that after we had said good night, she had gone to a large party where she had been drinking all night until the next morning. As I at that time was constantly in search of all that was good in woman, I said to myself: "Well—she meant well by me, yet she had to sully herself for reasons of business."

TEMPTER. It is nice of you to think of it that way, and your intentions are well justified. She wanted to see you better than herself, higher and purer, so that she could look up to you. You can't very well explain that away just as glibly, can you? A woman is forever spiteful to her husband, and discontented; and the husband always kindly and grateful. He does everything he can to make her happy, and she everything to torment him.

STRANGER. That is not true!—It may, of course, appear so at times. But I once had a woman friend who unloaded all her faults upon me. She was, for example, utterly in love with herself—and so she called me the most egotistical man she had ever met; she drank excessively—and so she accused me of being a drunkard; she changed linen only infrequently—and so she called me dirty; she was jealous, even of my men friends—and so she likened me to Othello; she was domineering and had a craving for power and so she said I was a Nero; she was miserly—and therefore gave me the name of Harpagon!

TEMPTER. Why didn't you pay her back in her own coin?

STRANGER. You know very well why I didn't. If I had told her my opinion of her, I would instantly have lost her—we would no longer have been on speaking terms. And I wanted to remain in her good graces. . . .

TEMPTER. No matter what the cost! Yes—there you have the source of our degradation! You got into the habit of not speaking up, and ended by finding yourself caught in a tissue of falsehoods.

STRANGER. Wait a moment! Don't you think that a married couple can fuse their personalities to such a degree that they can't tell the difference between what is hers or his; that they can't make a distinction between each other's personalties; that they can't tell their own faults from their mates'. My jealous woman friend who called me an Othello confounded me with herself, identified me with herself. . . .

TEMPTER. It sounds rational enough!

STRANGER. Well—there you see! By not asking whose fault it is, one is more likely to get closer to a solution. Thus, when a husband and wife find it difficult to get along with each other, it is actually a house divided against itself—and that is the worst of all disharmony.

TEMPTER. There are moments when I think a woman is incapable of loving a man.

STRANGER. You may be right. "To love" is an active verb, and "woman" is a passive noun. He loves—she is loved; he interrogates—she merely answers!

TEMPTER. What is a woman's love, then?

STRANGER. The man's! . . .

TEMPTER. Well answered!—And therefore, when the man ceases to love her, she detaches herself from him.

STRANGER. Then, yes—but even—

TEMPTER. Ssh! Someone is coming this way. . . . A prospective tenant!

STRANGER. A man or a woman?

TEMPTER. A woman—and a man! But the man stops at the door—he turns—and sets off to the woods!—This is interesting!

STRANGER. Who are they?,

TEMPTER. See for yourself!

STRANGER (looking out of the window). It is she! My first wife —my first love!

TEMPTER. Who evidently has left her second husband— and now arrives here with husband number three; and he— judging by certain movements of his back and legs—seems to be slinking off, no doubt after a somewhat stormy scene. . . . Yes, yes. . . . But she is not aware of his sly intentions. Most interesting!—Now I'll go and find a place where I can listen! (He disappears. The Woman knocks.)

STRANGER. Come in! *(The Woman enters. There is a silence.)*

WOMAN *(emotionally upset)*. I came here to see about the house. . . .

STRANGER. I am at your service.

WOMAN *(hesitatingly)*. If I had known who was renting it, I wouldn't have come here!

STRANGER. Does that matter?

WOMAN. May I sit down for a moment? I am tired.

STRANGER. By all means! *(They seat themselves on opposite sides of the table, as in the scene between the Stranger and the Lady in Scene 1.)* It is a long time since we sat like this.

WOMAN. With flowers and candles on the table—of an evening. . . .

STRANGER. When I was dressed as a bridegroom and you as a bride. . . .

WOMAN. And the candle flames stood still in silent devotion, and the flowers in meditation. . . .

STRANGER. Is your husband outside?

WOMAN. No.

STRANGER. And you are still seeking—what does not exist?

WOMAN. Doesn't it?

STRANGER. No! And I have always told you so; yet you would not believe me. You wanted to find out for yourself!—Have you learned your lesson now?

WOMAN. Not yet.

STRANGER. Why did you leave your husband? *(There is a silence.)* Did he beat you?

WOMAN. Yes.

STRANGER. How could he forget himself so far?

WOMAN. He was in a rage.

STRANGER. What made him enraged?

WOMAN. He had no reason to be.

STRANGER. Why should he fly into a rage for no reason?

WOMAN *(getting up)*. Oh no, thank you! I am not going to sit here and be lectured!—Where is your wife?

STRANGER. She has just left me.

WOMAN. Why?

STRANGER. Why did you leave me?

WOMAN. Because I sensed that you were thinking of leaving me; and so I left you instead—having no desire to be deserted!

STRANGER. That is no doubt how it was. But how could you know what was in my mind?

WOMAN *(sits down again)*. How, do you ask? We didn't have to speak in order to reveal our thoughts.

STRANGER. We made a mistake in our married life, however, when we accused each other of our wicked thoughts before they had actually been put into action. Instead of really living, we lived a life of concealed and suppressed thoughts and desires. To give an example: I once saw you joyfully accept the shameless ogling of a stranger, and I berated you for being unfaithful to me.

WOMAN. You were in the wrong that time—yet you were right, for I had sin in my heart.

STRANGER. Don't you think that my habit of reading your thoughts prevented you from giving in to the temptation?

WOMAN. Let me think! Yes—you are right! But I was vexed at having you constantly spying into the innermost recesses of my mind, which was mine, and mine only.

STRANGER. But it was not yours only; it was ours.

WOMAN. Well—but I considered it to be mine and felt that you had no right to delve into it. When you nevertheless did so, I hated you; and in self-defense I said you had a morbidly suspicious nature!—And now I can tell you something quite frankly: your suspicions were never wrong! They proved how sharp-witted, how intuitive, you really are!

STRANGER. Oh!—You know that when we had gone to bed and said good night and fallen asleep as friends, I would nevertheless wake up and feel your hatred spitting its poison over me; I almost had to get out of bed in order not to suffocate. One night I awakened and felt as if something were pressing on my brain. . . . I saw you lying fully awake with your hand close to my mouth—and the thought occurred to me that you were having me inhale some poisonous vapor from a vial—and to make certain of it I clutched you by the hand!

WOMAN. Yes, I recall.

STRANGER. And what did you do, then?

WOMAN. Nothing. I only hated you.

STRANGER. Why did you hate me?

WOMAN. Because you were my husband—because I ate your bread!

STRANGER. Do you think it is always that way?

WOMAN. I don't know—but I imagine it is.

STRANGER. But there were times when you also looked down upon me?

WOMAN. Yes—when you were ludicrous! A man who is in love always provokes laughter. Do you know what a jackanapes is? That is what a man in love is! A crowing, love-sick rooster!

STRANGER. If you find every man who is in love with you ridiculous—how can you return his love?

WOMAN. We don't! We merely tolerate him—and go in search of another man who does not love us!

STRANGER. And if he, too, should start to love you—then you look for a third man, do you?

WOMAN. Perhaps we do.

STRANGER. This is fantastic! *(Silence.)* I remember you long had a wild infatuation for some nonentity you used to call the Toreador—and whom I translated into horse-butcher! Well —you finally got your Toreador—but he gave you no children and no bread—nothing but beatings! Toreadors always like to beat and butcher! *(Silence.)* At one time I was fool enough to let myself be enticed into competing with that man. I took up bicycling and sports and fencing, and things of that sort. But all it brought me from you was disgust and contempt! So I concluded that what is proper for the lover is not always proper for the husband!—After that you began to exhibit a predilection for page boys! That one, for instance, who used to squat on the Brussels carpet and read bad poetry! My good poems were not good enough for you! Is it that page boy you have caught this time?

WOMAN. Yes—but his poems are not bad!

STRANGER. Oh yes, my dear, they are! I know him only too well! He has appropriated my rhymes and rhythms and adapted them to his own ends for the hurdy-gurdy.

WOMAN *(gets up and walks toward the door)*. Shame on you!

TEMPTER *(comes in by the door, holding a letter in his hand)*. A letter for Mrs. . . . *(He hands the Woman the letter. She reads it and collapses on a chair.)* A little farewell note! Yes, yes—when it comes to love, the beginning is always the hardest! And if one hasn't the patience to surmount the initial difficulties—then one will surely lose the golden fruits! And page boys are by habit always impatient! Young stranger—have you had enough now?

STRANGER *(gets up, takes his hat)*. My poor Anna!

WOMAN. Do not leave me!

STRANGER. Yes, my dear—I must!

WOMAN. Don't leave me! In spite of everything, you were my best husband!

TEMPTER. Perhaps you would even like to start all over again? That would be a sure way to put an end to it. For as soon as two lovers tie up with each other, they lose each other!

After all, what is love? And now—before we go our own separate ways—say something clever!

WOMAN. I don't know what love is. The most sublime and beautiful that has to be dragged down into the mire and turned into the lowest and ugliest of things!

STRANGER. Into a caricature of divine love.

TEMPTER. A one-year plant that blossoms during the engagement period, goes to seed in marriage, and then droops toward the earth to wither and die.

WOMAN. The flowers that are most beautiful have no seed. The rose is the flower of love.

STRANGER. The lily is the flower of innocence. If it wanted to, it could produce seeds; but its white chalice never opens up except for a kiss.

TEMPTER. And through buds procreates itself, forming new lilies—much as chaste Athena sprang full grown from the head of Zeus, and not from his royal loins. Yes, yes, my children, there is much I have understood, but not this: what the beloved of my soul has to do with . . . (He hesitates.)

STRANGER. Speak out!

TEMPTER. What love, which is so potent a force—which is the marriage of two souls—has to do with procreation.

STRANGER and The WOMAN. There! He said it!

TEMPTER. I have never been able to understand how a kiss —which is an unborn word, a speech without sound, the silent language of the soul—can, through a consecrated act, be bartered for a surgical operation—which invariably ends in weeping and gnashing of teeth. And I have never understood why the first night, that consecrated night, when two souls embrace in a kiss of love—why it must always end in strife and hate, in mutual contempt, in the shedding of blood—and in bandages! (He covers his mouth.)

STRANGER. Think of it—if the story of the fall of man were true! In pain shall you bring forth children. . . .

TEMPTER. Well—then one could understand. . . .

WOMAN (to Stranger). Who is this man who is saying these things?

TEMPTER. Only a wanderer on the drifting sands of life. (The Woman gets up.) All set to go! Who will be the first one?

STRANGER. I will!

TEMPTER. And where will you go?

STRANGER. Still higher! And you?

TEMPTER. I shall stay down here—between heaven and earth. . . .

ACT IV

SCENE 1. *The spacious interior of a chapter house, in Gothic style. In the background a long, arched gallery whose archways open onto the cloisters and the monastery courtyard. In the center of the courtyard is a fountain with a statue of the Mother of Christ, surrounded by long-stemmed white roses. The walls of the chapter house have built-in oaken choir stalls. The Prior's stall is to the left of the center; it is somewhat higher than the others. In the middle of the room stands an enormously large crucifix. The sun illuminates the statue of Mary in the courtyard.*

The Stranger enters from the rear. He is wearing the coarse black garb of a monk, with a rope round his waist and sandals on his feet. He stops in the doorway, gazing at the chapter house; then he goes over to the crucifix and stands in front of it. The final strain of a chant is heard from the other side of the courtyard.

The Confessor enters from the rear. He wears black-and-white garb; his hair and beard are long and the crown of his head is slightly, almost imperceptibly, shaven.

CONFESSOR. Peace be with you!
STRANGER. And with you!
CONFESSOR. How does the white house seem to you?
STRANGER. Thus far I see nothing but black. . . .
CONFESSOR. You yourself are still black, but you will be white in time—so very white. . . . Did you sleep well last night?
STRANGER. Like a tired child—without any dreams. . . . But tell me—why are there so many locked doors here?
CONFESSOR. You will learn to open them in time.
STRANGER. Is this a very large establishment?
CONFESSOR. There is no end to it. It dates from the time of Charlemagne; and through gifts and the beneficence of the devout it has continually been enlarged. Its growth has been untouched by the spiritual changes and eruptions during various epochs, and it stands on the mountain heights as a monument to Western culture; that is, Christian faith—in addition to the learning of Hellas and Rome.
STRANGER. Then it is not exclusively devoted to religion?
CONFESSOR. The sciences and the fine arts are nourished here as well; it has libraries and museums and laboratories, and an

observatory—as you will see later. Horticulture and agriculture are also studied and carried on here; and a hospital for outsiders, with its own sulfur springs, is operated by the monastery.

STRANGER. One other question before the Chapter meets: Who is the Prior here?

CONFESSOR *(with a smile)*. He is the Prior!—He is without peer. He stands alone on the summits of human knowledge and —well, you will soon be seeing him.

STRANGER. Is it true that he is so very old?

CONFESSOR. He has reached an unusually great age; he was born early in this century, which soon will be coming to an end.

STRANGER. And has he always belonged to a monastic order?

CONFESSOR. He has not always been a monk; however, he has always been a priest. Once he was in the diplomatic service of the Church—that was seventy years ago; twice he has been a university chancellor; once, an archbishop. . . . Ssh! Mass is over. . . .

STRANGER. I hope he is not one of those sanctimonious priests who act as though they were full of shortcomings, yet haven't any?

CONFESSOR. Far from it! But he has seen life and knows humanity, and he is more human being than priest.

STRANGER. And what about the reverend fathers?

CONFESSOR. They are all wise men whose lives have been out of the ordinary—each one unlike any of the others.

STRANGER. But who have never lived life. . . .

CONFESSOR. They all have—many times over. They have been shipwrecked and then started all over from the beginning; they have sunk down to the very bottom and come up again. . . . Wait and you will see!

STRANGER. It is the Prior himself, however, who is to interrogate me, isn't it? But you must not think I intend to agree with him in everything. . . .

CONFESSOR. On the contrary, you must be true to your own self and defend your opinions to the utmost.

STRANGER. You mean that contradicting is tolerated here?

CONFESSOR. Here, you say?—You are a child who has been living in a child's world, where you have been playing with thoughts and words. You have labored under the fallacious belief that anything so mundane as language could be a cloak for anything so subtle as feelings and thoughts. We, who have discovered this delusion, therefore give voice to our thoughts as infrequently as possible; for we apprehend and perceive one another's innermost thoughts. Through spiritual exercises we have developed our perception to such a degree that we each have become like a link in a single chain. And whenever we find ourselves in complete accord, we derive a feeling of utter joy and oneness. The Prior, whose development is on a higher plane than ours, can sense it the moment anyone's thoughts deviate from their proper course. In certain respects he is like —and note that I say *like*—the galvanometer of the telegraph engineer, which indicates when and where there is an interruption on the line. And so we can keep no secrets from one another; consequently, we have no need of confession. Remember this carefully when you face the Prior and his searching, scrutinizing eye!

STRANGER. Is it his intention to examine me?

CONFESSOR. Oh no! He will merely put a few questions to you —none of any profound significance—merely preliminaries to the pragmatic examinations. . . . Ssh! They are coming!

(He withdraws to one side. The Prior enters from the rear; he is wearing a white garb and a white hood, which is turned up. He is a man of large build, his long hair and flowing beard are white, and his head resembles that of Zeus. His unwrinkled face is full, but pale. He has large eyes, darkly shadowed, and extremely heavy eyebrows. A tranquil, majestic calm characterizes his whole being. He is accompanied by twelve priestly fathers dressed in black and white. They also have their hoods, which are black, turned up. All pass in front of the crucifix, before which they genuflect and then go to their respective seats.)

PRIOR *(after having regarded the Stranger for a moment).* What have you come in search of up here? *(The Stranger is confused. He tries to find an answer but cannot. The Prior, gently, imperiously, indulgently.)* You have come to find peace, haven't you? *(The Stranger nods affirmatively.)* But the whole of life being one long struggle—how do you expect to find peace among the living? *(The Stranger stands speechless.)* You wish to turn your back on life because you feel you have been shorn of your illusions, perhaps even defrauded and wronged?

STRANGER *(weakly).* Yes.

PRIOR. You have been unjustly treated—the victim of wrongs, you say. And these injustices began at an early age, in your childhood; therefore it seemed incredible to you, an innocent child, that you could have committed a crime that deserved to be punished! Well—you once were accused of having stolen some fruit; and you kept tormenting yourself until you took the guilt upon yourself. You tortured yourself into making a false confession and asking for forgiveness for an offense you had not committed. Isn't that correct?

STRANGER (*with firmness*). Yes, it is.

PRIOR. So it is. And you have never been able to get over it! Never! Tell me now—you have a good memory, I know—do you remember *The Swiss Family Robinson?* Do you?

STRANGER (*shrinks*). The Swiss—*The Swiss Family Robinson?*

PRIOR. Yes. Your tortures began in the year 1857; but at Christmas time the year before, consequently 1856, you mutilated the pages of that book—and out of fear of being punished, you hid it underneath a wardrobe in the kitchen entrance. (*The Stranger is overcome with astonishment.*) The wardrobe was stained in oak, and in the upper part of it hung clothes, in the lower part were kept shoes. That wardrobe seemed to you enormously large, for you were a mere child; and it never occurred to you that it could ever be moved. However, during a house-cleaning at Easter time, the hidden book was discovered! Out of fear of the consequences, you put the blame on one of your comrades—and he had to endure the stigma of guilt, because appearances were against him, and because you had the reputation of being truthful and trustworthy. It was following this incident that your own suffering began, as a logical consequence. Do you agree with this reasoning?

STRANGER. Yes! I am prepared to take my punishment!

PRIOR. No, I am not here to punish you. I myself offended in similar ways—when *I* was a child. But will you—from now on and forever—promise me to forget your own sufferings and never allude to them again?

STRANGER. I promise! If only he whom I wronged could forgive me!

PRIOR. He has already forgiven you. Haven't you, Father Isidor?

FATHER ISIDOR (*the Physician*). With all my heart!

STRANGER. You—Father Isidor?

FATHER ISIDOR. It is I, yes!

PRIOR (*to Father Isidor*). Father Isidor, say a few words to him—just a word or two. . . .

FATHER ISIDOR. It was in the year of 1856 that I suffered my torture; but already in 1854 one of my brothers had endured the same kind of false accusation, which I had made against him. *(To the Stranger.)* So you see, we are all sinners, and not one of us is perfect or without fault; and I am almost certain that he to whom I caused suffering could not have had a clear conscience himself. *(He sits down.)*

PRIOR. Let us now have done with casting stones at one another—and, above all, at eternal justice! For we are all born with sin and are heirs of Adam!—However . . . *(To the Stranger.)* You wished to ask a question, didn't you?

STRANGER. I would like to know what life really means— its innermost meaning. . . .

PRIOR. Its very deepest meaning? In other words, you would like to know what no one will ever know!—Father Uriel! *(The blind Father Uriel rises. The Prior turns to the Stranger.)* Look at óur blind father here! We have named him in memory of Uriel Acosta whom you, perhaps, are acquainted with? *(The Stranger makes a negative gesture.)* Oh? All young people ought to know Uriel Acosta. He was a Portuguese of Hebraic ancestry who had been brought up in the Christian faith. At a fairly young age he began to question and to probe as to whether or not Christ were actually God; and as a consequence he was converted to the Jewish faith. He then commenced to study the Mosaic scriptures and to inquire into the immortality of the soul. This led to his being handed over by the rabbis to the Christian hierarchy for punishment. After a time he went back to the synagogue and Judaism again. But there was no end to his thirst for knowledge, and he continued to delve until he found himself confronted by the silence of absolute nothingness and vacuity—and in despair over having been unable to penetrate the deepest, most unfathomable of all secrets, he took his own life with a pistol shot. And now look at our own good Father Uriel here. There was a time when he was very young, and eager to learn and to know. He always wanted to be in the vanguard of every modern movement, and was always discovering new philosophies. I may mention, by the way, that he has been a friend of mine since boyhood and is very nearly as old as I am. However, about 1820 he stumbled upon the so-called natural philosophy, which had already been buried and laid to rest twenty years before. With this philosophy as a master key all locks were to be opened, all questions resolved, and all opponents silenced, done away with. It was all so very simple and clear and concise. Our friend Uriel was at that time decidedly opposed to all religions. He made the mesmerists—as the hypnotists of that day were called—his particular target. In 1830 he became—somewhat belatedly—a Hegelian. And then he turned to God again—but to God in Nature and in man; and he discovered he was a little god himself. But, to his misfortune, there were two sides to Hegel, just as there are to Voltaire; and one side of Hegel—which I might call the conservative Hegel—had evolved his all-Godhead into a compromise with Christianity. And so Father Uriel—who never liked to be behind the times—became a rationalistic Christian, who was given the thankless task of waging war on both rationalism and himself. Out of consideration for Father Uriel I shall abbreviate the long, painful story. In 1850 he again turned to materialism and resumed his enmity to Christianity. In 1870 he became a hypnotist, in 1880, a theosophist, and in 1890 he was on the verge of committing suicide. It was then I came upon him in Berlin—sitting on a bench in Unter den Linden. He was blind. Uriel means "God is my light." And this Uriel—blind; he who for nearly a century had carried the torch of enlightenment at the head of every one of the movements of our time! *(To the Stranger.)* You see, he was eager to learn—but he was denied understanding! That is why he now *believes* instead. Is there anything else you would like to know?

STRANGER. I merely wish to ask one more question. . . .

PRIOR. Speak out!

STRANGER. If Father Uriel had adhered to the faith he originally held in 1810, people would have called him a conservative, or old-fashioned; but since he became a follower of the progressive movements of his time and consequently gave up the religious faith of his youth, they will say that he was an apostate, a traitor to the Church. In short, no matter what he did, people will treat him with contempt.

PRIOR. Do you pay attention to what people say?—Father Clemens, do you object if I tell how little you let people's opinions affect you? *(Father Clemens rises and makes an approving gesture.)* Father Clemens is our greatest figure painter. To the world he is known by another name—a very famous name. In 1830 Father Clemens was a young man who felt he had a talent for painting and devoted himself to it with heart and soul. When he was twenty he exhibited his paintings; but the public, the critics, his teachers, and his parents were uniformly of the opinion that he had chosen the wrong profession. Young Clemens was sensitive to what was said about him and his efforts, and so he gave up his painting and took up a trade. He became a printer. When he had reached fifty and his life was in the past, a stranger happened upon his youthful efforts—and they were acclaimed by the public and the critics, by teachers and relatives, who recognized them as masterpieces. But by that time it was too late! And when Father Clemens complained of the unrighteousness of the world, the world answered with a heartless grin: "Why did you let yourself be cheated!" This so mortified Father Clemens that he came here to us. But now he no longer feels any grief. Or do you, Father Clemens?

FATHER CLEMENS. No. But that is not the end of the story. My paintings of 1830 hung in a museum until 1880 and were admired. That year taste abruptly changed, and one day a newspaper of high standing carried an article in which my paintings were criticized as a blot upon the museum. And so my paintings were relegated to the attic!

PRIOR (to the Stranger). That is a meaningful story, isn't it?

FATHER CLEMENS. But this is still not the end of the story. By 1890 taste had changed back again, and then a certain professor at the Academy of Art wrote that it was a disgrace to the nation that my masterpieces should be consigned to the attic. And so the paintings were brought down; and they are momentarily being looked upon as the works of a master. But I wonder for how long?—There you see, young man, how little worldly fame really means. *Vanitas vanitatum omnia vanitas!*

STRANGER. Is life worth living, then?

PRIOR. Ask Father Melcher! He has been through the trials of not only this world of delusions but through that of misunderstanding, lies, and contradictions as well. Go with him— he will show you the gallery of paintings, and he will tell you stories about them.

STRANGER. I'll gladly go with anyone who can teach me something!

(Father Melcher takes the Stranger
by the hand and they leave.)

SCENE 2. A gallery of paintings at the monastery. The gallery contains principally portraits, and all have two heads.

FATHER MELCHER. So—here we have first a small landscape— by an unknown master; it is called "The Two Towers." Perhaps you have traveled in Switzerland and have seen it in actuality?

STRANGER. I have been in Switzerland.

FATHER MELCHER. Well, then you have seen a tower called Zwing-Uri at the station of Amsteg on the St. Gothard railway, haven't you? It has been commemorated by Schiller in his *Wilhelm Tell*. It stands there as a reminder of the cruel oppression of which the inhabitants of Uri were victims under the German emperors. Very well! On the other side of St. Gothard, toward Italy, lies the station of Bellinzona, as you know. There you will find many towers, and the most remarkable of all these is Castel d'Uri. This tower has been erected as a reminder of the cruel oppression that the Italian cantons suffered under the inhabitants of Uri! Are you beginning to understand?

STRANGER. You mean to imply that freedom is also synonymous with freedom to oppress? That is something new!

FATHER MELCHER. Then let us go to the portrait collection without any further ado. The first number in the catalogue is the two-headed Boccaccio. All our portraits have at least two heads. His history is well known. This great man began his career by writing profligate and godless stories which he dedicated to Queen Joanna of Naples, who had seduced the son of St. Bridget. Boccaccio ended as a saint in a monastery. There he had to deliver lectures on Dante's hell and the demons— the demons that he in his youth had thought he could drive out in a most amazing manner! I am sure you will observe how the two faces seem to be at variance as they gaze at each other!

STRANGER. Oh yes—but I don't see the slightest trace of humor in either face! Certainly one could expect a man with such knowledge of himself as our friend Boccaccio to reveal a little humor!

FATHER MELCHER. Number two in the catalogue. Yes—that is our two-headed Dr. Luther. In his youth a champion of tolerance; and in his later days a partisan of intolerance. Is this sufficient?

STRANGER. Quite sufficient!

FATHER MELCHER. Number three in the catalogue: the great Gustavus Adolphus accepting Catholic subsidies from Cardinal Richelieu for the purpose of fighting for Protestantism, in return for observing neutrality toward the Catholic League!

STRANGER. How can the Protestants explain away this triple contradiction?

FATHER MELCHER. They say it is untrue. Number four in the catalogue: Schiller, the author of *The Robbers*. In 1792 he was made an honorary citizen of Paris by the leaders of the French Revolution. Yet in 1790 he had been appointed a Court

Councillor of the Duchy of Saxe-Meiningen, and in 1791 was awarded a royal stipend by the King of Denmark. This painting depicts the Royal Councillor—a friend of His Excellency Johann Wolfgang von Goethe—as he, years later, in 1798, personally receives the scroll conferring the honorary citizenship upon him from the leaders of the French Revolution. Imagine it! The scroll of the Reign of Terror—in the year of 1798, when the French Revolution had come to an end and the Directory with its Committee of Five was at the helm of the state! How I would have liked to have seen the Court Councillor then! But all that matters little, for the following year, i.e., 1799, he expresses his thanks for the honor in *The Song of the Bell* and pleads with the Revolutionaries to take it easy. Yes, such is life! But what does it matter! We are civilized human beings, and we love both *The Robbers* and *The Song of the Bell;* Schiller as well as Goethe!

STRANGER. The master goes to his oblivion, but his work lives on!

FATHER MELCHER. Goethe, yes!—Number five in the catalogue. His first literary efforts were *The Cathedral of Strassburg* and *Götz von Berlichingen*—in which he struck a blow in defense of Gothic Germanic art as against Grecian and Roman art. During the latter part of his life, however, he fought against Germanism and became a champion of classicism. Goethe against Goethe! There you can see the traditional Elysian tranquillity, harmony, et cetera, in utter disharmonious conflict with itself. But dejection turns into pain when the young romantic school suddenly emerges and makes war on the Goethe of *Iphigenia* with his very own theories from *Götz von Berlichingen.* That the "great heathen" concludes by converting Faust in Part II by letting him be saved by the Virgin Mary and the angels is commonly overlooked by his admirers. So is the fact that this man of crystal-clear vision toward the end of his life began to find everything so remarkable, so wonderful, so strange—even the simplest of things which he had long before fully perceived and grasped to the core. His very last wish and hope was for a more enlightened world! Yes, yes! But what does it matter? We are fond of our Goethe in spite of everything, for are we not broad-minded and civilized?

STRANGER. And you have good reason to appreciate him!

FATHER MELCHER. Number six in the catalogue: Voltaire! he had more heads than two—he, the atheist who devoted his whole life to the defense of God! Voltaire—the scoffer who was

himself scoffed at because he "believed in God like a child"—
he, the author of the cynical *Candide,* who wrote:
Gratifying sensual passions
was the pastime of my youth. . . .
Soon I learned 'twas all delusion;
what seemed sweet had now turned bitter.
In my winter's age I see
life is only vanity!
Dr. Know-it-all—who once thought he had comprehended all
that is between heaven and earth by means of science and common sense—sings this tune when he is at the end of the road
of life:
Egged by pride I was allured
to pursue all spheres of learning,
and, with eyes that see not, questioned
heaven's boundless infiniteness!—
All I've learned has only hurt me. . . .
Knowledge is but vanity!
But what does it matter? Voltaire can serve so many different
ends. The Jews use him against the Christians, and the Christians use him against the Jews because he was an anti-Semite
—as Luther was. Chateaubriand made use of him to vindicate
the Roman Catholic Church; and even in our day Protestants
quote Voltaire in support of their attacks on Catholicism. He
was, indeed, unstintingly useful!

STRANGER. And what is your own opinion of him, then?

FATHER MELCHER. We have no opinions here; we have faith,
as I told you before. And that is why we have only one head—
and that is placed exactly above the heart!—However, let us
proceed to number seven in the catalogue. Yes—here we have
Napoleon! Himself a creature of the French Revolution, he
became the Emperor of the People—the Nero of Liberty—the
Suppressor of Equality—and the "big brother" of Fraternity!
But of all the two-headed he is the craftiest, for he knew how
to laugh at himself: he could surmount and master any rifts
and dissensions in the camp, could change his skin, could turn
his soul inside out—yet, with every change he would have a
clear idea of his new incarnation—he would have unmistakable
and convincing control of himself.

There is only one other human being who can be compared
to him in this respect: that is Denmark's Kierkegaard. He was
from the very first conscious of this parthenogenesis of the
soul; in other words, its faculty for renewing and regenerating
itself in this life, without conceiving, by means of spontaneous

generation or other modes of rebirth. For this reason—and in order not to be made a fool of by life—he used a variety of pseudonyms when he wrote *Stadia on Life's Way*—each one representing a step on the road of life. But can you imagine—despite all his precautionary measures—the Lord and Master of Life made a fool of him. Kierkegaard—who all through his life battled against the hierarchy of the State Church and against professional preachers—was toward the end of his life driven by necessity to become a salaried preacher himself!—Yes, yes! That is the way things go sometimes. . . .

STRANGER. The Powers play their tricks. . . .

FATHER MELCHER. The Powers play tricks on tricksters and ridicule the arrogant—especially those who insist that they alone possess truth and knowledge. . . . Number eight in the catalogue: Victor Hugo. He divided himself into innumerable parts. He was a French nobleman by birth, a grandee of Spain, a friend of kings, and the socialistic author of *Les Misérables*. He was, of course, called an apostate, a renegade, by his compeers, while the socialists hailed him as a reformer. . . . Number nine. Count Friedrich Leopold von Stolberg. He wrote a fanatical book in praise of Protestantism—and soon after he was converted to Catholicism! How can you explain an act like that by a man in his right senses? Would you call it a miracle? Or perhaps—a little journey to Damascus? . . . Number ten. Lafayette: the hero of the war for freedom—the revolutionary . . . who was forced to leave France—where he was looked upon as a reactionary because he came to the aid of Louis XVI! When he was captured by the Austrians, he was imprisoned at Olmütz as a revolutionary! Was he a reactionary or a revolutionary?

STRANGER. He was both.

FATHER MELCHER. Yes—he had a dual personality—and two halves make a whole—a complete man. Number eleven: Bismarck—the paradox! The honest statesman who once stated he had made the discovery that telling the absolute truth was the height of craftiness and deceit. And during the last six years of his life he was forced—I presume by the Powers—to expose himself as a self-admitted liar. . . . I see you are getting tired of all this! Then we shall stop.

STRANGER. Yes, my friend—if one's thoughts and ideas constantly go in the same groove—if one's opinions never change throughout life, one grows antiquated, according to the laws of nature. Then one will be called conservative, old-fashioned, stagnant. And if one adheres to the laws of progress and

marches forward with the times and is rejuvenated by ever
new, fresh impulses and by the spirit of one's age, one is
heckled as being vacillating and a renegade.

FATHER MELCHER. That is a thought that is as old as the
world, no doubt. But what does a sensible man care what he
is called? A man will be what he is meant to be.

STRANGER. But who formulates the periodic, ever-changing
opinions and the spirit of the times?

FATHER MELCHER. You really have to answer that question
yourself, and you should answer it this way: the spirit of the
times is promulgated by the Powers themselves, and develops
in what appears to be cycles. Hegel, the philosopher of contemporary times, was dimorphic; and—because one can cite
either a left Hegel or a right Hegel—he has most successfully
solved the contradictions of life and history and the spirit with
his magic formula: thesis—affirmation; antithesis—negation;
synthesis—summarization! Young man—well, you are relatively
young—you started out in life by endorsing everything; then
you turned about and began to disavow and repudiate everything on principle. Now end your life by summarizing! In
brief, be no longer one-sided! Do not say: either-or, but: both-
and! In short: humanity and resignation!

SCENE 3. *The sanctuary of the chapel. An open coffin with
funeral pall. Two lighted candles. The Confessor enters. He
leads the Stranger, now dressed in the white linen robe of a
novice, by the hand.*

CONFESSOR. And so you have carefully considered the step
you are now about to take?

STRANGER. I have—carefully!

CONFESSOR. And have no more questions you wish to ask?

STRANGER. Questions to ask? . . . No!

CONFESSOR. Then remain here while I go to call together
the Chapter, the fathers and the brothers, so that we can begin
the ceremony.

STRANGER. Very well! So be it! (*The Confessor leaves. The
Stranger is alone. He stands meditating. The Tempter enters.
He goes to the Stranger.*)

TEMPTER. Are you ready?

STRANGER. So ready that I have no words left to answer you
with.

TEMPTER. At the brink of the grave. . . . I understand. You
are to lie in that coffin and make believe you are dying; three
shovels of earth are to be heaped on the old being, and then

De Profundis is to be sung. With that you are raised from the dead—you will have shed your old name—and you will be baptized again like a newborn infant. . . . What will be your new name, do you know? *(The Stranger does not answer.)* There it is written: John—Brother John—because you had been preaching in the wilderness and—

STRANGER. Let me be!

TEMPTER. Say a few words to me first, before you enter upon the long silence . . . after this, you know, you will not be permitted to speak for a whole year!

STRANGER. So much the better! Toward the end, speaking became a vice, just like drinking! And why speak—when your words fail to convey what you think?

TEMPTER. Now that you stand at the brink of the grave—did you find life so very bitter?

STRANGER. *My* life—yes!

TEMPTER. Did you never know any joy?

STRANGER. Yes, much joy—but oh, so brief—and it seemed as if it only existed to make the grief over losing it so much the deeper!

TEMPTER. Could not one, conversely, say that sorrow existed for the purpose of bringing out joy, and emphasizing it?

STRANGER. One can say whatever one likes. *(A Woman, carrying an infant in a baptismal robe, passes across the stage.)*

TEMPTER. There you see a little mortal about to be consecrated to suffering!

STRANGER. Poor child!

TEMPTER. The beginning of a human tale. *(A Bride and Bridegroom walk across the stage. The Tempter points to them.)* And there you see—the sweetest—the bitterest—Adam and Eve in their paradise . . . which after a week or so will be a hell—and in fourteen days a paradise again. . . .

STRANGER. The sweetest! The brightest! The first—the only —the last . . . that which gave meaning to life. I, too, had my day in the sun once. . . . It was a day in spring—on a veranda —beneath the first tree to bear leaves—and a tiny coronet crowned her head—a white veil, like a gentle mist, covered her countenance, which was not of this world. . . . And then came the darkness. . . .

TEMPTER. From where?

STRANGER. From the light itself! . . . That is all I know!

TEMPTER. It could not have been anything but a shadow; for without light there can be no shadow—but where there is darkness, there can be no light.

STRANGER. Stop! Or there will be no end to this! *(The Confessor and the Chapter enter in procession.)*

TEMPTER *(as he disappears)*. Farewell!

CONFESSOR *(with a large black funeral pall)*. May the Lord give him eternal rest!

CHOIR. And may perpetual light shine upon him!

CONFESSOR *(covering the Stranger with the funeral pall)*. May he rest in peace!

CHOIR. Amen!

A Dream Play

❖

This fascinating and brilliant drama is considered Strindberg's finest play by many critics. Indra's Daughter is ordered by her Father to descend from their heaven and to wander about on earth in order to experience what humanity has to endure. Indra wishes to ascertain whether human beings have just cause for their eternal bickering, complaints and dissatisfactions. After sharing their hardships and sorrows, she would return to her celestial Father and give him an accounting of what she has seen and learned of their trials and tribulations during her pilgrimage.

In *A Dream Play* the whole of mankind is placed on trial. Its hopes and longings, joys and sorrows, loves and hates are all there in a nutshell of concentration and completeness. It is a sublime cameo of earthly existence. As the Daughter of Indra wanders about on earth she discovers that no joy or happiness exists there that does not have another side, a dark side of pain and sorrow. By doing someone a good turn, one gives hurt to someone else. Human discontent is most clearly and poignantly illustrated by the Billposter, who all his life has wished for a dip-net in a certain shade of green, and when he finally obtains one, is disappointed and dissatisfied because it is not the shade of green he had set his heart on. On the other hand, the Officer represents the faithful, loyal lover, who year in and year out buoyantly and optimistically waits for his beloved Victoria without ever seeing his yearning realized, his ideal attained. He is hope personified, in the face of constant disappointment. In his preface to *A Dream Play,* Strindberg speaks of the dreamer's imagination "spinning and weaving in new patterns: an intermingling of remembrances, experiences, whims, fancies, ideas, fantastic absurdities and improvisations, and oddly original inventions of the mind." While some of the episodes may be ascribed to actual dreams, it is unquestionably also true, as Professor Martin Lamm suggests, that most of the scenes are based on actual experiences of Strindberg's, which he has enriched by focusing them in the light of dreams. Professor Lamm considers *A Dream Play* the most personal of all of Strindberg's works that followed in the wake of the Inferno crisis. It is undoubtedly the most profound and all-encompassing one. It also gives a truer picture of Strindberg's concern for mankind and is the point of departure

for his chamber plays. The rough drafts he left behind show
that he originally had not intended to write it in the form
of a dream play nor to have the Daughter of Indra as one of
the characters in it. The many drafts also indicate that Strindberg took a long time preparing for the writing of this epoch-
making drama. In one of his drafts the title appears as *The
Prisoner (A Dream Play)*; but the most striking outline is the
one he titled *The Corridor Drama*. The gist of this embryonic
attempt is also found in another sketch called *Waiting*, which
he planned to enlarge into a play written in the style of Hans
Christian Andersen. These two latter outlines served as the
basis of *The Growing Castle*, a title Strindberg changed to
A Dream Play when he had completed the drama at the end
of 1901 or early in 1902.

Throughout his life, Strindberg kept asking the eternal question: "What is life, and what is its meaning?" While this
question cannot be answered, Strindberg nevertheless in *A
Dream Play* fills the vacuum with a dialogue pondering human
existence, good and evil, happiness and sorrow from the beginning of life unto death. In his distinguished analytical work,
Martin Lamm points out that *A Dream Play*, "despite its
seeming whimsicality and vagaries, is poetically logical in its
sequence" and that "notwithstanding its lack of a defined
artistic plot [it is] the most spontaneously poetic work which
Strindberg has achieved following his Inferno crisis."

In his *Strindberg's Dramaturgy*, Dr. Gunnar Ollén points
out that the key to *A Dream Play* may be found in a letter
dated June 28, 1875, which Strindberg wrote to Siri von
Essen. Dr. Ollén quotes from it: "Why is it that we suffer so
when we are oppressed? I believe this emotional process comes
about in this way: First, I am the one who is the victim! Oh,
it is a horrible feeling! But I have only to look to the right
and the left, and I see someone else who is in the same plight.
Then I suffer with him. And the pain is doubled! Then I
see still others, and my blood curdles. In my emotional state
of mind, I begin to think that the whole of the universe is
being tyrannized, and suffering from oppression. My anguish
grows a thousand times greater—I take upon myself, I absorb
within myself, the suffering of all mankind—I become a sort
of Christ—I turn into a mouthpiece for the whole of humanity." This letter epitomizes much of what Strindberg has so
remarkably dramatized in this dream play, in which he also
emphasizes that our expectations in life are never realized;
that life—as he also accentuates in *The Ghost Sonata*—is an
illusion, an emptiness as bare as the space behind the mysteri-

ous door: a nothingness; that our human body is a hindrance for us in our loftier aspirations, a straitjacket, tying our senses to worldly appetites; that we are not brought into the world with evil, but that we are made evil by contamination, by contact with life; that it is through physical love that sin and death have come into being; that those who try to reform the world and make it into a better place to live by delivering us from evil are deprecated and proscribed by the self-righteous as madmen, incarcerated, crucified, or burned at the stake.

What is found behind the mysterious door when it is opened is—nothing. That is the symbolic answer to our knowledge of the mystery of the universe, the mystery of life and death. For "in the beginning," Strindberg says, "God created heaven and earth out of nothing"; and seemingly nothing in life and human nature and behavior has really changed in the world since then. The Daughter of Indra, through her own trials and tribulations on earth, comes to realize that it is not easy to be a creature on earth, that mankind is to be pitied—a phrase that recurs throughout the play. Yet *A Dream Play* is not the embodiment of tragic hopelessness and despair. On the contrary, there are touches of brightness in it, and a feeling of compassion dominates the play as a whole.

The everyday scenes which Strindberg has incorporated in this drama are veiled in a dreamlike atmosphere which is enhanced by the masterly, spirited dialogue. As Martin Lamm so adroitly notes, Strindberg's dialogue is remarkable in its many shifts and nuances. Without ever resorting to academic language, he can with simple means fortify, and make overpowering, scenes of gravity and momentousness. The phrase "Mankind is to be pitied" can, however, easily become laughable in the mouths of unseasoned or uninspired actors because of its frequent repetition in the play. For that reason I have thought it important to vary it somewhat in translating the play.

PERFORMANCE NOTES

A Dream Play had its première at the Swedish Theatre on April 17, 1907, with Harriet Bosse as Indra's Daughter, Ivar Kåge as the Officer, Tore Svennberg as the Attorney, and Ivan Hedqvist as the Poet. Because of the lack of today's technical resources in lighting, projection, and décor, the performance was not entirely satisfactory or successful. But the critics appreciated the extraordinary beauty of the drama and the first-night audience was enthusiastic.

In 1916, when stage technique had greatly improved, the Danish-born stage designer Svend Gade showed in Berlin how Strindberg's dream visions could be realized on the stage. On October 28, 1916, Mauritz Stiller produced the play at the Lorensberg Theatre in Gothenberg, with incidental music by the distinguished composer, Wilhelm Stenhammar. Exactly five years later (1921), Max Reinhardt staged the play at the Royal Theatre of Stockholm and the production, although criticized for its slow tempo—which may have been due to this famous German director's unfamiliarity with the Swedish language—won high praise for its imaginativeness. The scenery was by the Austrian stage designer Alfred Roller.

On October 25, 1935, Olof Molander staged the play at the Royal Theatre in Stockholm with great effect. Lars Hanson played the Officer, Tora Teje the Daughter of Indra, and Ivar Kåge the Poet. Molander has staged the play a number of times since then. In February 1955 he produced it at the Royal Theatre again with Gunn Wållgren as Indra's Daughter and Jarl Kulle as the Officer. In 1959 the Malmö Civic Theatre gave the play with Annika Tretow as Indra's Daughter, Sture Lagerwall as the Officer, and Max von Sydow as the Attorney; Bengt Ekerot staged the production. The play has also been given on the radio in Sweden on several occasions.

A Dream Play had a successful première in German on March 17, 1916, at the Theater in der Königgrätzerstrasse in Berlin under the title of *Ein Traumspiel,* with Svend Gade receiving high praise for his stage settings. The play was shown again in Berlin in 1917, and in 1921 Max Reinhardt presented it at the Deutsches Theater with Helene Thimig as Indra's Daughter, Eugen Klöpfer as the Attorney, and the famous actor Werner Kraus in five different minor roles. The production proved a triumph for Reinhardt.

In Vienna *A Dream Play* made a deep impression at the Raimundtheater in the fall of 1922 and at the Volkstheater in 1957.

The play was also presented in German in 1947 at Cologne and in 1948 at the Civic Theatre in Munich. In 1955 *A Dream Play* was given a notably surrealistic presentation at the Kurfürstendamm Theater in Berlin, with Maria Wimmer as Indra's Daughter and Tilla Durieux as the Portress; unfortunately, important scenes and passages were omitted and the author's intentions were subordinated to the ingenious scenic production. The same company also presented the play in London in 1957. In Germany a brilliant television production was given from Cologne in 1959.

Copenhagen had a production of the play in 1917 at the Dagmar Theatre with settings by Svend Gade, and a noteworthy production in 1940 by Olof Molander presented Anna Borg as Indra's Daughter and Holger Gabrielsen as the Officer. The Danish radio celebrated Strindberg's centenary with a production in 1949.

The play was presented in Paris in 1928 under the title of *Le Songe* at the Théâtre Alfred Jarry in what was described as a distinctly bizarre production.

In Finland the play was given a production at the Swedish Theatre in Helsinki in 1934 and received another production at the Kansallisteatteri in 1959. It was also given on the radio in Finland in 1954 and 1955.

In Switzerland, where Strindberg's influence may be traced today in the work of Friedrich Dürrenmatt and Max Frisch, *A Dream Play* was given most successfully in Zurich in 1947. When produced in 1960 at the Civic Theatre in Bern the play was discussed at the university, and much was made of Strindberg's influence on latter-day European modernists such as Brecht, Cocteau, Sartre, Ionesco, and Samuel Beckett.

A Dream Play was also turned into an opera by Julius Weissman under the title of *Ein Traumspiel,* and the work had its première in the spring of 1925 in Duisburg, Germany. It was presented as a radio play in England in 1948 and 1957. In the United States the play was produced in 1925 by the Provincetown Players in New York, of which organization Eugene O'Neill was one of the founders; another production was given at Theatre East in November 1960. Numerous American colleges and universities have also performed this work, no doubt the best known of Strindberg's expressionist and pilgrimage plays.

As in his previous dream play, *To Damascus,* the author has in *A Dream Play* attempted to reproduce the detached and disunited—although apparently logical—form of dreams. Anything is apt to happen, anything seems possible and probable. Time and space do not exist. On a flimsy foundation of actual happenings, imagination spins and weaves in new patterns: an intermingling of remembrances, experiences, whims, fancies, ideas, fantastic absurdities and improvisations, and original inventions of the mind.

The personalities split, take on duality, multiply, vanish, intensify, diffuse and disperse, and are brought into a focus. There is, however, one single-minded consciousness that exercises a dominance over the characters: the dreamer's. There are for the dreamer no secrets, no inconsequences, no scruples, no laws. He neither pronounces judgment nor exonerates; he merely narrates.

Since dreams most frequently are filled with pain, and less often with joy, a note of melancholy and a compassion for all living things runs through the limping story. Sleep, the liberator, often appears as a tormentor, a torturer, but when the agony is most oppressive the awakening rescues the sufferer and reconciles him to reality. No matter how agonizing reality may be, it will at this moment be welcomed cheerfully as a release from the painful dream.

CHARACTERS

THE VOICE OF INDRA
THE DAUGHTER OF INDRA
THE GLAZIER
THE OFFICER
THE FATHER
THE MOTHER
LINA
THE PORTRESS
THE BILLPOSTER
THE SINGER
A WOMAN'S VOICE (VICTORIA)
THE BALLET GIRL
THE CHORIST
THE PROMPTER
THE POLICEMAN
THE ATTORNEY
KRISTIN
THE QUARANTINE MASTER
THE POET
HE
SHE
THE PENSIONER
THE ELDERLY DANDY
THE OLD FLIRT
HER LOVER (THE MAJOR)

THE THREE SERVANT GIRLS
PLAIN-LOOKING EDITH
EDITH'S MOTHER
ALICE
THE TEACHER
THE NAVAL OFFICER
SEVERAL BOY PUPILS
THE HUSBAND
THE WIFE
THE BLIND MAN
FIRST COAL HEAVER
SECOND COAL HEAVER
THE GENTLEMAN
THE LADY
THE LORD CHANCELLOR
THE DEAN OF THEOLOGY
THE DEAN OF PHILOSOPHY
THE DEAN OF MEDICINE
THE DEAN OF JURISPRUDENCE
THE SHIP'S CREW
MEMBERS OF THE OPERA
  COMPANY
CLERKS, HERALDS, DANCING
  GIRLS, MEN and WOMEN,
  and others

Prologue. The background represents cloud banks shaped like disintegrating slate cliffs, dotted with castles and fortified strongholds.

The constellations Leo, Virgo, and Libra can be discerned in the firmament. In their midst the planet Jupiter is visible, shining with a bright light.

The Daughter of Indra stands on the topmost cloud.

VOICE OF INDRA *(heard from above)*. Where are you Daughter . . . where?

DAUGHTER OF INDRA. Here, Father . . . here!

VOICE OF INDRA. You've lost your way, my child! Take care
—you're sinking. . . .
How did you stray?

DAUGHTER OF INDRA. I followed in the path of lightning
from the ether
and used a cloud as travel coach. . . .
The cloud, however, sank—and now we're falling. . . .
Oh, tell me, lofty Father Indra, to what regions
I have come. And why so sultry here,
so hard to breathe?

VOICE OF INDRA. You've left the second world and come into
the third one—
you've passed the star of morning,
and from Çukra you now enter
the atmosphere of Earth; there you will see
the Scales, the seventh house of planet Sun,
where Çukra stands on guard at the autumnal equinox—
when day and night are equal in duration.

DAUGHTER OF INDRA. You spoke of Earth. . . . Is that the
dreary planet
whose darkness is lit up by Mother Moon?

VOICE OF INDRA. It is the heaviest and densest
of the spheres that sail in space.

DAUGHTER OF INDRA. And do the sun's rays never reach it?

VOICE OF INDRA. Oh yes, it gets some sun, but not at all
times. . . .

DAUGHTER OF INDRA. There is a rift now in the cloud—and
I can see below—

VOICE OF INDRA. What do you see, my child?

DAUGHTER OF INDRA. I see . . . that there is beauty—the
woods are green—

the water's blue—and snowcapped mountains—yellow fields. . . .

VOICE OF INDRA. A beauty such as only Brahma could
create. . . .

yet it has once had even greater beauty
when Time was born, long, long ago. . . . Then something
happened—
its destined orbit was disturbed, or maybe something else;
revolt bred crime that had to be suppressed. . . .

DAUGHTER OF INDRA. Now I can hear sounds from down
below. . . .

What kind of beings live upon that planet?

VOICE OF INDRA. Descend and see. . . . I will not slander
these poor children of Creation;
and what you now can hear is their tongue.

DAUGHTER OF INDRA. It sounds as though. . . . It has a ring
that is not happy.

VOICE OF INDRA. I feared so!—Their mother-tongue is discontent!
Yes—I fear that the people of the Earth
are hard to please, a most ungrateful race. . . .

DAUGHTER OF INDRA. Speak not unkindly. . . . Now I hear
joyous cries—
and shooting—thunder—I see lightning. . . .
Now bells are ringing, fires burning—
and voices—thousands upon thousands—
sing praise and thanks to the celestial. . . .
(There is a silence.)
You judge them much too harshly, Father. . . .

VOICE OF INDRA. Descend, then, and when you have learned,
have seen, and heard,
return and tell me if they've cause to grumble and complain,
to be lamenting and bewailing constantly.

DAUGHTER OF INDRA. I'll go then—down to them . . . but
won't you, Father, come with me?

VOICE OF INDRA. No, no—I cannot breathe down there.

DAUGHTER OF INDRA. The cloud is sinking. . . . Oh, how
close it is. . . . It's stifling here.

This is not air I'm breathing . . . it is smoke and moisture. . . .
It weighs me down—it drags me downward, downward;
I feel a tilting, turning motion—
the third world truly can't be said to be the best. . . .

VOICE OF INDRA. No, it is not the best—yet not the worst;
its name is Dust, it rotates like the rest of them—
that's why the people there are prone to dizziness,

a thing betwixt plain foolishness and madness. . . .
Take courage now, my child, for this is but a test, a trial.

DAUGHTER OF INDRA (*kneels as the cloud descends*). I am
sinking . . .

*Outside the growing garden. The background represents
giant hollyhocks in bloom. The flowers are of various colors:
white, pink, crimson, sulfur-yellow and bluish-purple. Above
their tops is seen the gilded roof of a castle; its apex is a
flower bud resembling a crown. At the foot of the foundation
walls of the castle, hay and straw heaped up in stacks. These
cover litter cast out from the stable.*

*The wings, which remain unchanged throughout the play,
are stylized frescoes: a blending of interior, architecture and
landscape.*

The Glazier and the Daughter of Indra are seen entering.

DAUGHTER OF INDRA. The castle is steadily growing up from
the earth. . . . Can you see how it has grown since last year?

GLAZIER (*to himself*). I have never seen this castle before—
have never heard of a castle that could grow—but . . . (*To
the Daughter of Indra, with sincere conviction.*) Yes—it has
grown six feet. . . . That's because of the manure . . . and if
you take a good look, you will see that a wing has sprouted
on the side where the sun shines.

DAUGHTER OF INDRA. Don't you think it will come out in
bloom soon, now that it is past midsummer?

GLAZIER. You see the flower up there, don't you?

DAUGHTER OF INDRA. Yes—I see it! (*She claps her hands joyfully.*) Tell me, father, why is it that flowers rise up out of
dirt?

GLAZIER (*with piety*). Because they do not thrive in dirt.
That is why they are anxious to reach the light, so that they
may blossom and die.

DAUGHTER OF INDRA. Do you know who lives in the castle?

GLAZIER. I did know once but have forgotten.

DAUGHTER OF INDRA. I believe someone is imprisoned there
. . . he must be waiting for me to set him free.

GLAZIER. And at what cost?

DAUGHTER OF INDRA. One never bargains when it comes to
duty. Let us enter the castle.

GLAZIER. Yes—let us go in.

(*They go toward the rear, which slowly opens, dividing itself*

in two parts that disappear in the wings.)
The scene is now a plain, naked room. A table and a few
chairs are the only furnishings in it.
On one of the chairs is seated the Officer, attired in a
bizarre, yet modern, uniform. He is rocking back and forth
in his chair while striking the table with his saber.

DAUGHTER OF INDRA *(goes over to the Officer and gently*
takes the saber from his hand). You mustn't do that! You
mustn't do that!

OFFICER. Agnes dear, let me keep the saber!

DAUGHTER OF INDRA. No, you will break the table! *(To the*
Glazier.) Go down to the harness room now and put in the
pane. We'll see each other later.   *(The Glazier leaves.)*

DAUGHTER OF INDRA. You are a prisoner in your own house.
I have come to set you free.

OFFICER. I have been waiting for you to come, although I
was never certain you *would* come.

DAUGHTER OF INDRA. The castle is a stronghold—it has seven
walls—but . . . it will be done!—Do you wish to be free, or
don't you?

OFFICER. To tell the truth, I don't know. Whatever I choose,
it will mean suffering. Every joy in life has to be paid for with
double its worth of sorrow. Living here is hard enough, but
if I have to buy back my precious freedom, I shall have to
suffer threefold. . . . Agnes, I'd rather endure life as it is
here, if I may only see you.

DAUGHTER OF INDRA. What do you see in me?

OFFICER. In you I see beauty—which is the harmony of the
universe. Only in the solar system's motion, in the exquisite,
inspiring chords of a stringed instrument, in the vibrations
of light do I find delineated anything resembling the beauty
of your figure. . . . You are a child of celestial spheres—

DAUGHTER OF INDRA. And so are you!

OFFICER. Why, then, must I tend horses, look after stables,
and see that the litter is removed?

DAUGHTER OF INDRA. That you may wish to get away from
it all!

OFFICER. I wish to—but it is so hard to do!

DAUGHTER OF INDRA. But we owe it to ourselves to seek
freedom in light, don't we? It is a duty we have—

OFFICER. Duty? Life has never recognized its duties to me!

DAUGHTER OF INDRA. You feel that life has been unjust to
you, then?

OFFICER. Yes—it has been unjust. . . .

Voices can now be heard behind the screen or partition which is drawn aside in the next moment.
The Officer and the Daughter of Indra glance in that direction. Then they remain motionless in position, gesture, and expression. Seated at a table is the Mother. She is sickly. Before her is a lighted taper. Now and then she prunes the wick with a pair of snuffers. Piled on the table are some shirts which she has just finished making and which she is now marking with quill and ink. On the right stands a dark, wooden wardrobe.

FATHER *(hands her a cape of silk. Then he speaks to her gently).* Don't you want it?

MOTHER. A silken cape for me, my dear? What use would it be to me, when I am going to die soon?

FATHER. Do you really believe what the doctor says?

MOTHER. That, too . . . but most of all I believe the voice inside me. *(Her hand fumbles toward her heart.)*

FATHER *(with sorrow in his voice).* Then you are really seriously—? And first, last, and always you are thinking of your children. . . . ʹ

MOTHER. Haven't they been everything to me—my life, my very reason for living, my happiness, my sorrows?

FATHER. Kristina! Forgive me—for all I have failed in!

MOTHER. Forgive you? For what? . . . But forgive *me*, my dearest! We have both tormented each other—and why? That's something we cannot explain . . . there was no other way out, I suppose! Now here is the children's new linen. . . . Be sure to see that they change twice a week, Wednesdays and Saturdays, and that Louise washes them—their whole bodies. . . . Are you going out?

FATHER. I have to be at the teachers' staff meeting at eleven.

MOTHER. Will you ask Alfred to come in to me, before you leave?

FATHER *(points to the Officer).* But, dearest, he is standing right here!

MOTHER. To think that my eyes should be failing me, too . . . yes, darkness is setting in. *(She snuffs out the taper.)* Alfred, come here! *(The Father disappears through the wall. As he leaves, he nods good-by. The Officer steps over to the Mother.)* Who is that girl there?

OFFICER *(in a whisper).* Why, it's Agnes!

MOTHER *(in a similar tone of voice).* Oh, it's Agnes, is it? Have you heard what they are saying? That she is the daughter of the God Indra, and that she pleaded with him to come down to Earth in order to see how human beings really live and behave. But don't mention this to anyone. .. .

OFFICER. A child of heaven, that's what she is!

MOTHER *(in a louder voice).* Alfred, my darling, I shall soon be leaving you and the rest of the children. But before I go, I want to leave a thought with you, to be remembered all through your life!

OFFICER *(sadly).* Speak, Mother—

MOTHER. Just these words: Never quarrel with God!

OFFICER. What do you mean, Mother?

MOTHER. You must not go about feeling that life has wronged and cheated you.

OFFICER. But when people treat me unjustly . . .

MOTHER. You are alluding to the time when you were unfairly punished for having taken a coin that later was found elsewhere?

OFFICER. Yes! That piece of injustice has distorted the purpose of my life ever since—

MOTHER. Perhaps it has! But go and look in the wardrobe now—

OFFICER *(shamefaced).* So you know, then! It's—is it . . . ?

MOTHER. *The Swiss Family Robinson*—for which—

OFFICER. Don't say it—don't—

MOTHER. —for which your brother was punished . . . and which you had torn the leaves out of—and hidden!

OFFICER. To think that this old wardrobe should still be here—after twenty years. . . . After the many times we have moved! And my mother died ten years ago!

MOTHER. Well, what has that to do with it? You just *have* to ask questions about everything. That's why you ruin for yourself the best that life has to give!—Ah, there is Lina!

LINA *(enters).* I want to thank you ever so much, ma'am, but I can't go to the christening after all.

MOTHER. Why not, my child?

LINA. I have nothing to wear.

MOTHER. I'll lend you my cape here.

LINA. Dear me—no, that wouldn't *do!*

MOTHER. I don't see why not! I shall never again be going to another party.

OFFICER. What would Father say? He gave it to you, didn't he?

MOTHER. Oh, what petty minds.

FATHER *(puts his head inside the door)*. Are you letting the maid use the cape I gave you?

MOTHER. Don't say things like that! Remember that I, too, was a servant girl once. . . . Why do you want to be insulting to an innocent young girl?

FATHER. And why should you offend me, your husband?

MOTHER. Oh, this life of ours! When you do something out of the goodness of your heart there is always someone who finds it ugly and bad. And if you do something good for *one* person, then someone else feels hurt. Oh, this life!

(She trims the taper, so that it goes out. The scene is now in darkness, and the partition is pushed back into its previous position.)

DAUGHTER OF INDRA. Humanity is to be pitied!

OFFICER. Is that what you think?

DAUGHTER OF INDRA. Yes. Life is hard—but love conquers all! Come—and see! *(They walk toward the rear.)*

The alley outside the opera house. The backdrop is now raised. One sees a different background, representing a dilapidated, ancient fireproof wall. In its center is a gate opening onto a path that terminates at a green, sun-lit space, featuring a blue aconite, or monk's hood, of giant proportions.

On the right, close by the gate, sits the Portress. She wears a shawl wrapped round her head and shoulders, and she is busy crocheting a star-studded bedspread.

On the other side of the gate, left, there is a small billboard, which the Billposter is in the throes of cleaning. Nearby stands a dip-net on a pole painted green. Farther to the left is a door with an air-hole shaped like a four-leaf clover.

To the right of the gate stands a dwarfed lime tree. Its trunk is jet-black, and it bears few leaves. These are pale-green in color. Nearby is seen an opening, leading to the basement.

DAUGHTER OF INDRA *(steps over to the Portress)*. You haven't finished the star-covered bedspread, have you?

PORTRESS. No, my dear little friend. Twenty-six years is not a long time for a work like this!

DAUGHTER OF INDRA. And he never came back—your lover?

PORTRESS. No—but that was not *his* fault. He *had* to go away . . . poor man. . . . It's thirty years ago now!

DAUGHTER OF INDRA *(to the Billposter).* She used to be in the ballet, didn't she? In there at the Opera?

BILLPOSTER. She was the best one they had there. . . . But when he went away, it was as if he had taken her dancing feet with him—and it was not long before her career was ended.

DAUGHTER OF INDRA. People do nothing but complain. You see it in their eyes—and the lament is in their voices, too. . . .

BILLPOSTER. I don't think I complain very much. Certainly not now that I have got myself a dip-net and a green fish-chest!

DAUGHTER OF INDRA. And that makes you happy?

BILLPOSTER. Yes, it makes me very happy! I have dreamed of it since I was a lad! And now my dream has come true!—I know I am past fifty, of course. . . .

DAUGHTER OF INDRA. Fifty years for a dip-net and a fish-chest.

BILLPOSTER. A *green* fish-chest—a *green* one. . . .

DAUGHTER OF INDRA *(to the Portress).* If you will let me have your shawl now, I'd like to sit here and watch the human children. . . . But you must stand behind me and help me a little! *(She is given the shawl and takes the Portress' seat by the gate.)*

PORTRESS. Today is the last day of the season, and then the Opera will be closed. Today they will know whether they have been re-engaged.

DAUGHTER OF INDRA. What about those who are not engaged?

PORTRESS. Oh, may God forgive me—I hate to look at them. . . . I cover my face with my shawl—I—

DAUGHTER OF INDRA. Poor human beings!

PORTRESS. Look! Here is one of them! . . . She is not among the chosen!—See how she is crying.

(The Singer enters from the left. She hastens out through the gate, holding a handkerchief to her eyes. She stops momentarily on the path outside the gate and presses her head against the wall. Then she leaves quickly.)

DAUGHTER OF INDRA. Man is to be pitied! . . .

PORTRESS. But here—here you see what a happy human being looks like! *(The Officer enters through the gate. He is dressed in a redingote and top hat; in his hand he carries a bouquet of roses. He radiates joy and buoyant happiness.)* He is engaged to be married to Miss Victoria—

OFFICER *(stands downstage, looks up above and sings).* Victoria!

PORTRESS. Miss Victoria will be here in a moment.

OFFICER. Good! The carriage is waiting—the table is set—the champagne is on ice. . . . I'd like to embrace you ladies. *(He embraces the Daughter of Indra and the Portress. Then he sings out again.)* Victoria!

WOMAN'S VOICE *(sings back from above).* Here I am!

OFFICER *(starts to pace).* Oh well . . . I shall wait!

DAUGHTER OF INDRA. Do you know me?

OFFICER. No—I know only one woman—Victoria! For seven years I have been waiting for her here—waiting—waiting . . . at noon of day when the sun's rays touch the chimney-stacks, and in the evening when the dusk of night sets in. . . . Look —here you can see the imprint of my steps on the walk—the faithful lover's steps. . . . Hurray! She is mine! *(He sings.)* Victoria! *(This time there is no reply.)* Well—she is dressing. *(To the Billposter.)* There is your dip-net, I see! Everybody at the Opera is mad about dip-nets—or I should say, fish! Because the fish are mute—and therefore can't sing. . . . How much does a gadget like that cost?

BILLPOSTER. It's rather expensive.

OFFICER *(sings).* Victoria! *(He shakes the lime tree.)* See! It's getting green again! For the eighth time! *(He sings out.)* Victoria! . . . Now she is arranging her hair. *(To the Daughter of Indra.)* My sweet lady, please let me go upstairs and fetch my bride!

PORTRESS. No one is allowed to go backstage.

OFFICER. For seven years I have been coming here! Seven times three hundred and sixty-five makes two thousand five hundred and fifty-five! *(He halts and pokes at the door with the four-leaf clover.)* And I have looked at this door two thousand five hundred and fifty-five times without being able to figure out where it leads! And that clover leaf, which is supposed to let in light! For whom is it to let in light? Is anybody in there, eh? Does anybody live in there?

PORTRESS. I don't know anything about it! I've never seen it opened.

OFFICER. It looks like a door to a pantry. I saw one like it when I was four and went visting with our maid one Sunday afternoon! She took me from one family to another—to chat with the servants there—but we never went beyond the kitchen. And I had to sit wedged between the water barrel and a keg of salt. I have seen a multitude of kitchens in my days, and the pantry was invariably in the servants' hall outside the kitchen and always had small round holes bored in the door—holes shaped like a four-leaf clover. . . . But why should they have a pantry at the Opera, when they haven't any kitchen there! *(He sings.)* Victoria!—Tell me, my dear lady—she couldn't have gone out any other way, could she?

PORTRESS. No—there is no other way.

OFFICER. Oh well, then I am bound to see her. *(Artists come rushing out. The Officer scrutinizes each and every one.)* Now she simply must be here before much longer! Oh, madam! That blue aconite out there! I've seen that flower there since I was a child. . . . Is it the same flower? . . . I recall being in a parsonage out in the country when I was seven. . . . The aconite has two doves—two blue doves underneath its hood . . . and then a bee came flying and crept into the hood. I thought to myself: now I'll catch you . . . and I cupped my hands round the flower. But the bee stung my hand right through the petals, and I started to cry. Then the pastor's wife came and put some wet earth on it to ease the pain . . . and then we had wild strawberries and cream for supper. . . . I think it's already getting dark. *(To the Billposter.)* Where are you going now?

BILLPOSTER. I am going home for supper.

OFFICER. *(running his hand across his eyes).* Supper? At this time of day?—Oh, please, may I go in and make a brief telephone call to "the growing castle"? May I?

DAUGHTER OF INDRA. What business could you have there?

OFFICER. I want to tell the Glazier to put in the storm windows. Soon we'll have winter—and I suffer so terribly from the cold! *(He goes inside to the Portress.)*

DAUGHTER OF INDRA. Who is Miss Victoria?

PORTRESS. She is his sweetheart.

DAUGHTER OF INDRA. There is truth in your answer. What she is to us and to others, means nothing to him. Only what she is to *him* is what she *really* is! *(There is a sudden, stark darkness.)*

PORTRESS *(lights her lantern).* It is getting dark early today.

DAUGHTER OF INDRA. To the gods the years are as minutes.

PORTRESS. And to us humans a minute may seem like a year!

OFFICER *(comes out again. He is covered with dust, and the roses are withered).* She hasn't come yet?

PORTRESS. No.

OFFICER. But she will, I am sure!—She will come! *(He starts to pace.)* Yes, perhaps I had best cancel the dinner—since it is already a little late. . . . Yes, yes, that's what I'll do! *(He goes inside again to telephone.)*

PORTRESS *(to the Daughter of Indra).* May I have my shawl now?

DAUGHTER OF INDRA. No—you take it easy for a while, my dear. I'll take care of your duties! I want to learn all I can about life and human beings. . . . I want to see if life is really so hard as they say it is.

PORTRESS. But one never gets a moment of rest here. Day and night, one never gets a chance to shut an eye.

DAUGHTER OF INDRA. No sleep—even at night?

PORTRESS. Well, yes—if you can manage it with the bell cord round your wrist . . . for there are watchmen on the stage all through the night—and they are relieved every three hours.

DAUGHTER OF INDRA. But that's torture!

PORTRESS. You may think so, but the rest of us are only too glad to get a position like this. If you only knew how envious people are of me.

DAUGHTER OF INDRA. Envious! They are envious of the tortured!

PORTRESS. Yes. But let me tell you something that is harder to bear than all the night vigil and all the drudgery, harder than the draft and cold and dampness—and that is to have to receive the confidences of all the unfortunates here—as I have to do. . . . They all come to me! Why? Perhaps in the wrinkles of my face they read the runes of past suffering. Perhaps that is what persuades them to confide to me their secrets. . . . That shawl, my dear, holds agonies and disappointments, secrets and confidences—my own and theirs—of the past thirty years!

DAUGHTER OF INDRA. It is heavy, and it burns like nettle.

PORTRESS. Wear it then, if you like. . . . And if you should find it too heavy for you, just call me and I'll come and relieve you.

DAUGHTER OF INDRA. Good-by. What *you* can do, *I* should be able to do.

PORTRESS. We'll see! . . . Only treat my poor young friends kindly—and never lose patience with them when they come with their complaints!   *(She disappears down the walk.)*

The stage grows completely dark. During the darkness, there is a change of season: the lime tree now has lost its leaves; the blue aconite has withered. When daylight has returned, the verdure in the perspective of the walk has changed into autumn brown.

The Officer appears again, coming out when the stage is

lighted. His hair is now gray, likewise his beard. His clothes are shabby, his collar wilted and soiled. All that remains of the bouquet of roses is the forked stems—no leaves, no petals are left. He walks to and fro.

OFFICER. Judging by what I see, summer is gone and fall is near. I can see it by the lime tree there—and the monk's hood! *(He commences his walk again.)* But autumn is spring for me, for that's when the Opera opens again! And that's when she'll be here! Dear madam, will you allow me to sit down for a little while?

DAUGHTER OF INDRA *(gets up from her chair and offers it to the Officer).* Sit here, my friend . . . I'll stand.

OFFICER *(seats himself).* If I could only get a little sleep, too! That would be still better. *(He dozes momentarily, and then suddenly gets up with a start and begins to pace back and forth. He stops before the door with the four-leaf clover and pokes at it.)* This door—it just won't give me any peace! What is behind it? There must be *something!* *(Faint music is heard from above, in dance tempo.)* So! They've started rehearsals again! *(The stage is now lighted by fits and starts, as by a flashing light.)* What's the meaning of this? *(He accentuates the words as the lights go on and off.)* Light and dark; dark and light. . . .

DAUGHTER OF INDRA *(imitates him).* Day and night; night and day. . . . A merciful Providence desires to shorten your waiting. That is why the days fly, ever pursuing the nights!

(It again grows light on the stage. The Billposter enters with his dip-net and billposting material.)

OFFICER. So—it's you—with your dip-net. . . . Did you have a good catch?

BILLPOSTER. Yes, I should say I did! It was a warm summer, and a little long. . . . The net wasn't bad—but not as good as I had expected it to be. . . .

OFFICER *(accentuates the words).* Not as good as I had expected it to be! That is very well put! Nothing is as *I* expected it to be! . . . Because the thought is greater than the deed—higher than anything material. *(He starts to pace again, beating the bouquet against the wall so that the last remaining petals and leaves fall off.)*

BILLPOSTER. Hasn't she come down yet?

OFFICER. No, not yet, but she won't be long now!—Have you any idea what is behind that door?

BILLPOSTER. No, I have never seen that door open.

OFFICER. I am going in to telephone for a locksmith to come and open it. (*He goes inside. The Billposter puts up a bill; then he goes toward the right.*)

DAUGHTER OF INDRA. What was wrong with the dip-net?

BILLPOSTER. What was wrong? Well, there wasn't anything wrong with it exactly—but it wasn't precisely what I had expected it to be. . . . So my first joy turned into disappointment, you might say. . . .

DAUGHTER OF INDRA. What had you expected when you bought the dip-net?

BILLPOSTER. What I'd expected? Why—I don't know. . . .

DAUGHTER OF INDRA. Let me tell you then! You had expected it to be what it turned out *not* to be. You wanted it to be green, but *not*—the green you got!

BILLPOSTER. You put your finger on it, lady! You know everything! That's why they all come to you with their troubles. . . . I wish you would listen to *me*, too, some time. . . .

DAUGHTER OF INDRA. I will be happy to. Come and tell me, pour out your heart to me. (*She goes into her room. The Billposter remains outside and talks to her through the wicket.*)

Again the stage is in complete darkness. Then it grows light, and the lime tree can be seen, its leaves now green; the aconite is blooming again, and the sun shines on the verdure in the space at the end of the walk, in the background.

The Officer comes out. He is now an old, white-haired man. His clothes are in rags, his shoes worn. He still carries the stems that are left of the bouquet of roses. He walks to and fro, moving like a man who has aged considerably. Then he stops and studies the bill that has just been posted. A Ballet Girl comes from the left.

OFFICER. Has Miss Victoria left yet?

BALLET GIRL. No, she has not.

OFFICER. Then I'll wait! No doubt she'll be down soon?

BALLET GIRL (*with a serious expression on her face*). No doubt she will!

OFFICER. Don't go away yet, and you'll see what is behind this door. I've just sent for the locksmith!

BALLET GIRL. It will really be interesting to see that door opened. That door and the growing castle! Do you know the growing castle?

OFFICER. Do I!—Haven't I been a prisoner there!

BALLET GIRL. You don't say? Was that you? But tell me—why did they have so many horses there?

OFFICER. Why—it was a stable castle—

BALLET GIRL (*painfully touched*). How stupid of me! I should have known. . . .

(*A Chorist enters from the left.*)

OFFICER. Has Miss Victoria left yet?

CHORIST (*in a serious voice*). No! She hasn't left! She never leaves!

OFFICER. That's because she loves me! . . . Don't leave now before the locksmith comes to open the door here.

CHORIST. Oh—are they going to open the door? Oh, that will be fun to see!—I just want to ask the Portress a question.

(*The Prompter enters from the left.*)

OFFICER. Has Miss Victoria left yet?

PROMPTER. No, not as far as I know.

OFFICER. There you see! Didn't I say that she would be waiting for me!—But don't go! The door is to be opened.

PROMPTER. Which door?

OFFICER. Is there more than one door?

PROMPTER. Oh, I know. The one with the clover leaf! Then I certainly want to stay! I just want to have a word with the Portress. (*The Ballet Girl, the Chorist, and the Prompter group themselves beside the Billposter outside the Portress' window. They take turns speaking with the Daughter of Indra. The Glazier enters through the gate.*)

OFFICER. Are you the locksmith?

GLAZIER. No, the locksmith couldn't come. But I guess I can do the job, even though I am a glazier.

OFFICER. Certainly—but have you your diamond with you?

GLAZIER. Of course! A glazier without a diamond! What do you think?

OFFICER. Never mind!—Let's get to work! (*He claps his hands. All gather round the door. Chorists dressed as Master-singers, and Ballet Girls, attired as the dancers in Aïda, enter from the left. They join the others.*) Locksmith—or glazier . . . do your duty! (*The Glazier steps to the door with his diamond in his hand.*) A moment like this does not come often in a man's life. For this reason, my good friends, stop to think . . . think carefully. . . .

POLICEMAN (*enters*). In the name of the law, I forbid you to open that door!

OFFICER. Oh heavens, what a fuss there is whenever anybody tries to do something great and new! But we shall take this matter to court! I'll see a lawyer! Then we'll find out what the law says! I'm going to the Attorney!

Without lowering the curtain, the scene changes to an attorney's office. The gate remains in its place, functioning now as the entrance wicket in the railing that extends from left to right, clear across the stage.

The Portress' room serves as the Attorney's private compartment, the front partition having been removed. The lime tree, now barren, serves as a hat and coat rack. The billboard is covered with official and legal notices and court decisions. The door with the clover leaf now hides bookshelves on which documents are piled.

The Attorney, in evening dress with tails and white tie, sits at a writing desk littered with legal papers and documents, right, in back of the railing. His face speaks of untold sufferings. It is chalk-white and wrinkled, with shadows of bluish purple. He is ugly, and his countenance reflects all the crimes and vices with which he has been forced to come in contact.

His two clerks are both infirm: one has lost an arm, the other one is minus an eye.

The ones who collected to view the opening of the door remain on the stage; they now seem to be waiting to gain admittance to the Attorney. They appear to have been waiting forever.

The Daughter of Indra, wearing the Portress' shawl, stands downstage, as does the Officer.

ATTORNEY (*steps forward to the Daughter of Indra*). Tell me, my sister, may I have that shawl? I'll hang it inside until I can make a fire in the stove—then I'll burn it with all its sorrows and miseries. . . .

DAUGHTER OF INDRA. Not yet, my brother! First I want to have it completely filled! And above all, I want it to absorb all your agonies—all the confidences about crime and vice, about revilement and slander, about things wrongly gained. . . .

ATTORNEY. My dear little friend—for that your shawl would not be big enough! Look at these walls. . . . Even the wallpaper seems to have been soiled by every kind of sin! Take a look at these papers, which are filled with stories of wrongs, written by me! Look at *me!*—Among those who come here you will never find a human being with a smile on his face—here you see only vicious glances, clenched fists, and teeth ready to bite! And they all squirt their anger and their envy, and spit their suspicions over me. . . . See. . . . Look at my hands! They are black—and can never be washed clean! You see how cracked and bleeding they are! I can never wear a suit of clothes more than a day or two before it stinks of other people's crimes. . . . Sometimes I have the place fumigated with sulfur—but it doesn't help much. . . . I sleep in the back room, and whenever I dream, I dream about crime. . . . Just now I have a murder case before the court. . . . That's bad enough—but do you know what is worse—the very worst?—Having to separate a married couple!—I feel as if I heard a cry from the bowels of the earth and from the heavens—a voice crying treason—treason against the source of life, against the wellspring of everything that's good, against love itself. . . . And you'll find that after reams and reams of paper have been scribbled full of mutual accusations . . . and then a sympathetic person takes one of them aside for a heart-to-heart talk, and asks—with a pinch of the ear, or with a smile—this simple question: What is it that you really have against your husband?—or your wife, as the case may be—then he—or she—stands mute, can't find an answer, doesn't know the cause of it all! I can remember once when . . . yes, I think the trouble was caused by a salad . . . another time it was caused by a mere word—generally such trouble is caused by nothing but trifles. . . . But the suffering, the torture! That's what I have to bear! Look at my face! Do you think I could ever win a woman's love with a face such as mine—a criminal's face? And do you think anybody would care to be a friend of mine—I, who have to collect debts and accounts and liabilities for everybody in the city?—To be a human being is hard!

DAUGHTER OF INDRA. Man is to be pitied!

ATTORNEY. Indeed, man is! And how people manage to live is a puzzle to me! They marry on an income of two thousand a year—when they need four thousand. . . . And so they have to borrow, of course! They all borrow! And then they muddle along and zigzag through life for the rest of their days until they die. . . . And then it's discovered there is nothing left but debts! Who is it who pays in the end? Well—who knows. . . .

DAUGHTER OF INDRA. He who feeds the birds!

ATTORNEY. Well—but if He who feeds the birds would only come to Earth and see what we poor human creatures have to go through—then, perhaps, He would show compassion. . . .

DAUGHTER OF INDRA. Man is, indeed, to be pitied!

ATTORNEY. Man is, indeed! *(He turns to the Officer.)* What is it you wish?

OFFICER. I simply wish to know whether Miss Victoria has left yet.

ATTORNEY. No, she has not, you can rest assured of that. . . . But why are you poking at my closet there?

OFFICER. Why, the door looks exactly like . . .

ATTORNEY. Oh no—oh no—oh no. . . .

(Church bells are heard ringing.)

OFFICER. Is there a funeral in the city?

ATTORNEY. No, today is university graduation day. They are conferring doctors' degrees. They are conferring the degree of doctor of laws on me today. Wouldn't you, too, like to have a degree conferred on you and receive the laurel wreath?

OFFICER. Why, I have no objection. At least it would be a kind of distraction.

ATTORNEY. Well, then, let's get ready for the solemnity without delay. . . . But you must first go home and dress for the occasion! *(The Officer leaves.)*

The scene is darkened, and the setting is changed into the chancel of a church.

The railing now functions as the balustrade; the billboard serves as an announcement board for the hymns to be sung at the occasion; the Attorney's desk is the pulpit of the presiding functionary; the door with the clover leaf is the entrance to the vestry.

The Chorists from Die Meistersinger *function as heralds with staffs. The Ballet Girls carry laurel wreaths. The others act as spectators.*

The backdrop is raised, baring the new background representing the pipes of a huge organ. The instrument itself with the keyboard is below. On it, above, is the organist's mirror. The music swells from the organ.

On each side are representatives of the four faculties: Philosophy, Theology, Medicine, and Jurisprudence.

The scene is empty for a few moments. The Heralds enter from the left. The Ballet Girls follow, carrying the laurel wreaths, which they hold high before them. Three Conferees enter in turn, one after the other, from the right. Each one is crowned with a wreath; after which they go out, left.

The Attorney steps forward to receive his wreath. The Ballet Girls turn their backs on him, refusing to present him with a wreath, and leave. The Attorney, visibly affected, sup-

ports himself against a temple column. All withdraw, leav-
ing the Attorney alone on the stage. The Daughter of Indra
enters. She wears a white veil over her shoulders and head.

DAUGHTER OF INDRA. Now, you see, I have washed the shawl.
. . . But why are you standing here? Didn't you get your
wreath?

ATTORNEY. No—I was not considered worthy of it.

DAUGHTER OF INDRA. Why not? Because you have been cham-
pioning the poor, spoken a good word for the wicked, lightened
the burden for the guilty, obtained another chance for the condemned? Oh, humanity! . . . Men are no angels—they are to
be pitied!

ATTORNEY. You must not speak badly about human beings.
. . . Isn't it my duty to plead for them?

DAUGHTER OF INDRA *(supports herself against the organ).*
Why do they always abuse their friends?

ATTORNEY. They don't know any better.

DAUGHTER OF INDRA. Then let us show them the light. . . .
Will you help? Shall we—together—

ATTORNEY. They do not care to be enlightened. . . . Oh,
that the gods in heaven would hear the weeping of our sorrow.

DAUGHTER OF INDRA. I shall reach their ears. *(She seats herself*
at the organ.) Do you know what I see in the mirror here? The
world as it *should* be—as it *really is!* Because as it is now, it
is upside down!

ATTORNEY. How did it come to be turned upside down?

DAUGHTER OF INDRA. When the copy was made . . .

ATTORNEY. You put your finger on what is wrong! The copy
. . . I always sensed that the replica was faulty! When I
recalled the original, I became dissatisfied with the world. And
I was called an ingrate, hard to please; I was told I was looking
at things through the devil's eyes, and much more in that vein.

DAUGHTER OF INDRA. Yes, isn't it a mad world! Look at the
four faculties here! The government—whose duty it is to pre-
serve society—pays their salaries, all four of them. Theology,
the science of God, is constantly attacked and ridiculed by
Philosophy, which declares itself to be the cornerstone of all
wisdom. And Medicine, which is forever at odds with Philosophy, contradicts Theology's claim to be a science and calls it
mere superstition. And yet the four are part of the same academic council—whose duty it is to teach respect for the university! Wouldn't you call this madness? And woe be to him
who first recovers his reason and sanity!

ATTORNEY. The first ones to realize it are the theologians. As a preparatory study they take philosophy. Philosophy teaches them that theology is nonsense. Then, when they study theology, they are taught that philosophy is nonsense! Isn't that madness?

DAUGHTER OF INDRA. Then there is jurisprudence—the servant of all, except the toilers—

ATTORNEY. Justice, which—in the name of the law—can mark a man for life! Justice—which so often makes a mockery of justice!

DAUGHTER OF INDRA. What a sorry mess you have made for yourselves, you children of humanity! For that's what you all are—children!—Come here, and I shall give you a wreath— one that will be more appropriate for you! *(She places a wreath of thorns on his head.)* and now I shall play for you. *(She sits down at the keyboard of the organ. But instead of hearing organ music, one hears human voices.)*

VOICES OF CHILDREN. Eternal One! Eternal One! *(The last note is sustained.)*

VOICES OF WOMEN. Be merciful, O God! *(The last note is similarly held.)*

VOICES OF MEN *(tenors)*. Save us, for Your mercy's sake! *(Again the last note is held.)*

VOICES OF MEN *(basses)*. Spare Your children, O Lord, and let not Your wrath descend upon us!

ALL. Be merciful, O God! Hear us! Take pity upon us mortals!—Eternal One, why are You afar from us? We cry out of the depths to You: Have mercy upon us, God Eternal! Make not the burden of Your children too heavy! Hear us! Hear us!

The scene grows dark. The Daughter of Indra rises, goes toward the Attorney. Through effects of lighting, the organ is transformed into Fingal's Cave. The backwash of the sea can be seen against the basalt pillars, and the sounds of waves and wind can be heard in harmonious blending.

ATTORNEY. Where are we, sister?
DAUGHTER OF INDRA. What do you hear?
ATTORNEY. I hear the dripping of water.
DAUGHTER OF INDRA. It is tears . . . the tears of mankind. What else do you hear?
ATTORNEY. I hear sighing. . . . I hear whining and wailing.
DAUGHTER OF INDRA. This is as far as the plaints of mortals

reach . . . and no farther. But why this eternal wailing? Is there nothing in life to rejoice over?

ATTORNEY. Yes—that . . . which is sweeter than anything . . . and yet more bitter than anything: love—a wife and a home: the most sublime and the most hollow!

DAUGHTER OF INDRA. I would like to submit myself to the test.

ATTORNEY. With me?

DAUGHTER OF INDRA. With you!—You know the pitfalls and the stumbling blocks. . . . Let us stay clear of them.

ATTORNEY. I am poor . . .

DAUGHTER OF INDRA. What does it matter? All that matters is that we love each other! A little beauty does not have to be bought.

ATTORNEY. I have dislikes and aversions. They may be your likes and sympathies.

DAUGHTER OF INDRA. We have to modify and compromise, give way to each other.

ATTORNEY. And if we tire of each other?

DAUGHTER OF INDRA. When the child comes, it will bring a joy that will be ever young!

ATTORNEY. And you—you will have me, poor and ugly as I am, scorned and despised, disdained and rejected?

DAUGHTER OF INDRA. Yes. Let us unite our destinies.

ATTORNEY. So be it.

The Attorney's living quarters. A starkly simple room behind the Attorney's office. On the left, a large double bed with curtains around it; close by, a window.

On the right, a parlor stove with cooking utensils. Kristin is busy pasting paper strips, or tape, along the openings between the windows and the casement.

There is a door, rear, leading to the law office. It is open, and beyond it can be seen men and women, all visibly poor, waiting to see the Attorney.

KRISTIN. I paste, I paste!

DAUGHTER OF INDRA (*sits by the stove. She looks pale and worn*). You are shutting out the air! I am stifling!

KRISTIN. I have just one little leaky spot left now . . .

DAUGHTER OF INDRA. Air! Air!—I can't breathe here . . .

KRISTIN. I paste, I paste!

ATTORNEY. That's right, Kristin. . . . Heat costs money!

DAUGHTER OF INDRA. Oh, I feel as if my jaws were glued together.

ATTORNEY (*standing in the doorway, holding a document in his hand*). Is the little one asleep?

DAUGHTER OF INDRA. Yes, at last!

ATTORNEY (*gently*). Its continual crying drives away my clients.

DAUGHTER OF INDRA (*in a mild tone of voice*). What is there we can do about it?

ATTORNEY. Nothing!

DAUGHTER OF INDRA. We must try to find a roomier place to live.

ATTORNEY. We can't afford it.

DAUGHTER OF INDRA. Will you let me open the window? The air here is foul! It suffocates me!

ATTORNEY. Then the heat will escape, and we'll freeze.

DAUGHTER OF INDRA. This is horrible! Will you let us scrub the floor in the office?

ATTORNEY. You are not strong enough to do that! I haven't the strength either! And Kristin must finish the pasting. She has to paste strips throughout the house, from top to bottom—every crack and crevice—in the ceilings, the walls, and the floors.

DAUGHTER OF INDRA. I foresaw that we might be poor, but I was not prepared for this filth and dirt.

ATTORNEY. Poverty is a kin of squalor.

DAUGHTER OF INDRA. This is worse than I had thought!

ATTORNEY. There are others who are worse off. We still have some food in the house.

DAUGHTER OF INDRA. But what kind of food?

ATTORNEY. Cabbage is cheap. And it is nourishing and good.

DAUGHTER OF INDRA. Yes—if you like cabbage! To me it is distasteful!

ATTORNEY. You never complained before.

DAUGHTER OF INDRA. I tried to sacrifice my own preferences out of love for you!

ATTORNEY. Then I must make a sacrifice of what I like, too. We each must sacrifice something.

DAUGHTER OF INDRA. What shall we eat, then? Fish?—But you don't like fish!

ATTORNEY. And it's expensive, too.

DAUGHTER OF INDRA. This is more wretched than I thought it would be.

ATTORNEY (*in a gentle voice*). Now you see how hard it is. . . . And the child was to be the bond between us—our blessing! The child turns out to be our undoing.

DAUGHTER OF INDRA. Beloved! I shall die in here—in this air! All I ever see is the view of the yard in the back! I hear nothing but crying children, and lie without sleep for hours! I hear the people outside, whining without end, bickering with each other, accusing each other. . . . There is nothing left for me but death!

ATTORNEY. My poor little flower, who is without light—without air—

DAUGHTER OF INDRA. And you say there are those who have it worse than we?

ATTORNEY. I am one of the few envied ones in our street.

DAUGHTER OF INDRA. If I could only have some beauty in my home, things might not seem so bad.

ATTORNEY. I know . . . you mean a flower—above all a heliotrope. But that would cost as much as six bottles of milk or half a bushel of potatoes.

DAUGHTER OF INDRA. I'll gladly go without food if I can only have a flower.

ATTORNEY. But there is one kind of beauty one doesn't have to pay for! Its lack in the home is more painful than anything else to a man with a feeling for beauty. . . .

DAUGHTER OF INDRA. What is that?

ATTORNEY. If I should tell you, you'll be angry with me.

DAUGHTER OF INDRA. Haven't we agreed never to get angry?

ATTORNEY. So we have, Everything can be overlooked, Agnes, except a short-tempered, sharp, curt tone of voice. Have you ever heard such a tone of voice? Or haven't you?

DAUGHTER OF INDRA. Such a tone will never be used by either of us.

ATTORNEY. Never as far as I am concerned!

DAUGHTER OF INDRA. You can tell me now!

ATTORNEY. Well—when I come into a room, the first thing I look at is the curtains—to see how they are draped in the sash. (He goes over to the window and adjusts the curtains.) If they hang like a rope or a rag, then I don't remain long in that house. . . . Next I take a glance at the chairs. If they are placed where they should be placed, I stay. (He moves a chair back against the wall.) And finally I look at the candles in their holders. If they are askew—then the whole house is awry. (He puts straight a candle on the bureau.) It is this kind of beauty that cannot be bought, my dearest.

DAUGHTER OF INDRA (with bent head). Don't be short-tempered, Axel—

ATTORNEY. I wasn't short-tempered!

DAUGHTER OF INDRA. Yes, you were.

ATTORNEY. Now, what in hell . . .

DAUGHTER OF INDRA. What kind of language is that?

ATTORNEY. Forgive me, Agnes! But I have suffered as much from your disorderliness as you have suffered from dirt and filth. And I haven't dared offer my help to keep the house in order for fear that you would be angry. You would think I was reproaching you. Ugh! Don't you think we ought to stop bickering?

DAUGHTER OF INDRA. It is a hardship to be married. . . . A greater test than anything else! One has to be an angel. . . .

ATTORNEY. I think you are right.

DAUGHTER OF INDRA. I feel as if I were beginning to hate you!

ATTORNEY. That would be the end for us! Let us never feel hatred for each other! I vow I shall never again remark upon the disorderliness in our home—even though it tortures me!

DAUGHTER OF INDRA. And I shall eat cabbage, even if I suffer agony.

ATTORNEY. A married life of common pain and deprivation! What is pleasure to one is pain to another.

DAUGHTER OF INDRA. Men are to be pitied!

ATTORNEY. You've come to realize it now?

DAUGHTER OF INDRA. I have . . . but in the name of Heaven, let us stay clear of the rocks, now that we know their dangers.

ATTORNEY. Yes, let us try. . . . We are both good, and we are intelligent. We both have forbearance, and have learned to forgive.

DAUGHTER OF INDRA. Why shouldn't we pass over all trifles with a smile?

ATTORNEY. We can! And only we can do it. . . . Let me tell you—I read today in the *Morning* . . . By the way, where is the newspaper?

DAUGHTER OF INDRA (*embarrassed*). Which newspaper?

ATTORNEY (*in a biting tone*). Do I keep more than one? Do I?

DAUGHTER OF INDRA. Smile now, and don't speak harshly. . . . I used it to start the fire with.

ATTORNEY (*bursts out violently*). Hell and damnation!

DAUGHTER OF INDRA. Smile . . . smile! I burned it because it ridiculed what to me is holy!

ATTORNEY. And to me—unholy! Cha! (*He strikes his fist against the palm of his hand, incontrollably.*) I'll keep smiling until my molars show. . . . I'll be lenient and forgiving, and suppress my opinions, and say *yes* to everything and anything, and be a sneak and a hypocrite! So, you have burned my newspaper, eh? *(He rearranges the curtain round the bed.)* Now you see—I am rearranging things again, and that will make you angry. Agnes, this just cannot go on!

DAUGHTER OF INDRA. No, it can't.

ATTORNEY. And yet we must endure it. It isn't our vows and promises that matter so much as our child!

DAUGHTER OF INDRA. You are right! It's the child that matters!—that matters most! . . . Oh! Oh! . . . We must keep going. . . .

ATTORNEY. Now I must go out to my clients. You hear how they chatter, impatient to tear at each other, aching to see the other fellow getting fined and imprisoned! They are lost souls.

DAUGHTER OF INDRA. These poor, poor people. . . . And this incessant pasting! *(She bends her head in silent despair.)*

KRISTIN. I paste . . . I paste. . . .

(The Attorney stands at the door, nervously squeezing and turning the doorknob.)

DAUGHTER OF INDRA. Oh! The screech from that knob! It makes me feel as if you were squeezing my heart . . .

ATTORNEY. I turn and twist, I turn and twist . . .

DAUGHTER OF INDRA. Please—please don't!

ATTORNEY. I turn and twist . . .

DAUGHTER OF INDRA. Don't! . . .

ATTORNEY. I . . .

OFFICER *(turns the knob from within the office).* Allow me . . .

ATTORNEY *(lets go the knob).* Certainly . . . seeing that you have a doctor's degree . . .

OFFICER. Now I have all of life before me! All roads are open to me! I have reached my Parnassus, have won the laurel wreath, gained fame and immortality! The world is mine!

ATTORNEY. And what are you going to live on?

OFFICER. Live on?

ATTORNEY. You must have a place to live in, you must have food, clothes . . .

OFFICER. There is always a way out, so long as you have someone to love you.

ATTORNEY. I can well imagine! I can well . . . Paste, Kristin! Paste until they can't breathe any longer!

(Goes out backward, nodding.)

KRISTIN. I paste, I paste—until they can't breathe. . . .

OFFICER (to the Daughter of Indra). Will you come with me now?

DAUGHTER OF INDRA. This very moment! But where?

OFFICER. To Faircove! Where it is summer, where the sun is shining—where there is youth, where there are children and flowers, singing and dancing, gaiety and exuberant life!

DAUGHTER OF INDRA. Then I would like to go there!

OFFICER. Come, then!

ATTORNEY (enters again). Now I return to my first hell. This was the second—the more terrible one! The sweeter the hell, the more horrible! . . . Now look here—she has dropped hairpins on the floor again! (He picks up the hairpins.)

OFFICER. Imagine, he has discovered the hairpins, too!

ATTORNEY. Too? Look at this one! It has two prongs, yet it is one pin. Two—yet only one! If I straighten it, then it is one; if I bend it, it becomes two—yet without ceasing to be one! That means that the two are one! But if I should break it— like this—then the two are two. (He breaks the hairpin in two and throws away the pieces.)

OFFICER. He has seen all that! But before breaking, the prongs must diverge. If they converge—they will hold.

ATTORNEY. And if they are parallel, they will never meet— and then they will neither break nor hold anything.

OFFICER. The hairpin is the most perfect among created things! A straight line that equals two parallel lines!

ATTORNEY. A lock that shuts while it is open—

OFFICER. —for, while open, it shuts in a braid of hair that remains outside while it is shut in . . .

ATTORNEY. Much like this door! When I close it . . . I open —the way out—for you, Agnes.

(He withdraws, closing the door after him.)

DAUGHTER OF INDRA. And now?

Foulgut. There is a change of scenery. The bed with the curtains is transformed into a tent; the stove remains. The backdrop is raised; and one sees now in the background a beautiful, wooded shore with flags flying from its jetties, to which white sailboats are moored. Some of the boats have their sails hoisted, others have dropped sails. Small Italian villas, pavilions, kiosks, and marble statues can be discerned along the shore, between the treetops.

On the left, downstage, is a hillside, scorched by fire and with patches of red heather; here and there a smoky, black-

ened white tree stub and several pigpens and outhouses, painted red.

Below is an open-air gymnasium for the rehabilitation of physically handicapped and other ailing persons, where patients go through a routine of exercises on apparatuses resembling instruments of torture.

On the right in the foreground are visible some of the open sheds of the quarantine station, supplied with fireplaces, furnaces, and piping conduits.

Between the shore in the background and the landscape in the foreground is a narrow strait.

The Quarantine Master, dressed as a blackamoor, is walking along the shore. The Officer steps up to him. They shake hands.

OFFICER. Well, if it isn't Ordström! So you've landed out here?

QUARANTINE MASTER. So I have, as you see!

OFFICER. Can this be Faircove?

QUARANTINE MASTER. No—Faircove is across the strait. This is Foulgut.

OFFICER. Then we have come to the wrong place!

QUARANTINE MASTER. We?—Won't you introduce me?

OFFICER. No, that wouldn't do! *(In an undertone).* Do you know who she is? She is the Daughter of Indra!

QUARANTINE MASTER. The Daughter of Indra? I thought she was the Daughter of Varuna himself! Well, aren't you surprised to see my face black?

OFFICER. My dear boy! When one has reached fifty, one ceases to be surprised at anything!—I immediately took it for granted that you were going to a masquerade ball this afternoon.

QUARANTINE MASTER. You are quite right. And I hope you will both come with me.

OFFICER. And why not? . . . For I can't say—I can't say that this place seems especially inviting. . . . what kind of people live here anyway?

QUARANTINE MASTER. Here is where the sick live . . . over there are the healthy.

OFFICER. Then you have nothing but poor people here, I suppose?

QUARANTINE MASTER. On the contrary . . . here is where you find the rich! Take a look at that one on the rack there. He has stuffed himself with goose liver and truffles and consumed so much burgundy that his feet have curled into knots.

OFFICER. Into knots?

QUARANTINE MASTER. Yes, he has developed knotted feet. And that one over there—on that guillotine—has swallowed so much brandy that his spine has to be mangled out!

OFFICER. Will that really help?

QUARANTINE MASTER. For the rest, all who have some sort of misery that they wish to hide, live on this side! For instance— do you see the man coming here? (*An Elderly Dandy is pushed on the stage in a wheelchair. He is accompanied by a woman of sixty, an emaciated ugly Old Flirt, dressed in latest fashion. She is being attended by her Lover, a man of about forty.*)

OFFICER. It's the Major! He went to school with us, didn't he?

QUARANTINE MASTER. Yes—Don Juan! You can see, can't you, that he is still in love with that old spook-face next to him! He doesn't even see how she has aged—that she is ugly, faithless, and cruel!

OFFICER. Well—that's what love does! But I never thought that such a fickle fellow as he used to be could fall in love so deeply, so seriously!

QUARANTINE MASTER. You look at things in a very sympathetic way, I must say.

OFFICER. I have been in love myself—with Victoria . . . and I am still waiting—waiting for her to come.

QUARANTINE MASTER. Oh, it's you—it's you who are waiting for her in the passageway.

OFFICER. Yes—I am the fellow. . . .

QUARANTINE MASTER. Tell me—have you got that door opened yet?

OFFICER. No—the matter is still before the court. . . . The billposter is out fishing with his dip-net, of course—and that's what's delaying the testimony. . . . Meantime the Glazier has been putting in the windows in the castle—it has now grown half a story higher. . . . This has been an exceptionally good year—warm and wet.

QUARANTINE MASTER. But you haven't had it as hot as I have had it here, that's certain!

OFFICER. How hot do you keep your ovens, may I ask?

QUARANTINE MASTER. When we fumigate suspected cholera cases, we run it up to 108 degrees Fahrenheit.

OFFICER. Is the cholera rampant again?

QUARANTINE MASTER. Didn't you know?

OFFICER. Yes, of course, I know—but I forget so frequently things I should remember. . . .

QUARANTINE MASTER. I often wish I could forget, too, especially myself. That's one reason why I like to disguise myself and go to masquerade balls and take part in theatricals.

OFFICER. What have you been doing these many years?

QUARANTINE MASTER. If I told anyone, people would say I was boasting. And if I should say nothing, I would be called a hypocrite!

OFFICER. Is that why you have blackened your face?

QUARANTINE MASTER. Yes—I've made myself a little blacker than I really am!

OFFICER. Who is that man coming here?

QUARANTINE MASTER. Oh, he is a poet. . . . He is coming to get his mud bath. . . . *(The Poet enters. His eyes are turned heavenward. He is carrying a bucket of mud.)*

OFFICER. In Heaven's name! Why don't you give him a sun bath—or an air bath—instead?

QUARANTINE MASTER. Oh no—he is forever flitting about in loftier regions—and so gets homesick for the mud occasionally. . . . Wallowing about in the slime and dirt toughens the skin. Look at the pigs! And once he is toughened, he is immune to the stings of the horseflies.

OFFICER. This is a strange world! So full of contradictions!

POET *(ecstatically.)* Out of clay the god Ptah created man, on a potter's wheel, or lathe . . . *(Skeptically.)* out of clay or something else—whatever it was! *(Ecstatically.)* Out of clay the sculptor creates his more or less immortal masterpieces . . . *(Skeptically.)* most of the time nothing but rubbish *(Ecstatically.)* Out of clay are manufactured the wares and utensils— so absolutely necessary in a household—which we commonly call pottery, earthernware, dishes, and so forth . . . *(Skeptically.)* anyhow, what do I care *what* they are called! *(Ecstatically.)* That much for clay! When the clay is oozy, or thin, in liquid form, it's called mud. And that's what I want! *(He calls.)* Lina! *(Lina enters with a bucket.)* Lina, show yourself to Miss Agnes! —She knew you ten years ago when you were a young girl, full of joy—and, we might say, pretty. . . . But take a look at Lina now—after five children, drudgery, baby-cries, lack of nourishment, and cruel treatment! You can see how all that was lovely has vanished—that happiness is gone! And all the while she was trying to exercise her duties—duties which ought to have given her an inner satisfaction that would have shown in her face! Her face would have had a pleasing symmetry, her eyes would have shone with warmth and gentleness . . .

QUARANTINE MASTER *(covers the Poet's mouth with his hand).* Keep your mouth shut! Will you keep your mouth shut!

POET. That's what they all say! And if I keep silent, they say: Why don't you say something? Oh, these unpredictable mortals!

DAUGHTER OF INDRA *(goes over to Lina).* Tell me what troubles you!

LINA. I wouldn't dare! It would only make things worse for me!

DAUGHTER OF INDRA. Who is so cruel to you?

LINA. I wouldn't dare say. . . . I would only suffer for it. . . .

POET. Well, never mind . . . but I shall—even if the black-amoor should threaten to knock all my teeth out! . . . I am not afraid to say that we don't always get justice here!—Agnes, daughter of the gods, do you hear the music and dancing up there on the hillside?—Then listen to what I have to say! It is all for Lina's sister, who has come home from the city, where she went astray—you know what I mean. . . . Now they are killing the fatted calf for her—but Lina, who stayed at home— she has to carry the slops to the swine and feed them!

DAUGHTER OF INDRA. Bear in mind: there is rejoicing in that home not alone because the misguided child has come back to her parents, but all the more because she has abandoned the path of evil!

POET. But why not then give a ball and a banquet every evening in the week for the blameless toiler who never strayed from the straight and narrow path? Why not do that? No— that they would never do! But when Lina has a moment to herself, she has to go to a prayer meeting and hear herself reproached for not being perfect!—Do you call that justice— do you?

DAUGHTER OF INDRA. I find it hard to answer your questions because they—because there are so many unforeseen, so many different angles to take into consideration. . . .

POET. That is just what Harun the Just, the caliph, realized while he sat tranquilly on his throne. There he sat, away on high, without any knowledge of how the mortals fared below. . . . Finally the complaints reached his ear. One day he descended, and in disguise he mingled unrecognized with the crowds. He wanted to find out what sort of justice was being meted out to his subjects.

DAUGHTER OF INDRA. But I am not Harun the Just!

OFFICER. Let us talk about something else. . . . Here come

some visitors. . . . *(A white, dragonlike boat with sails of light blue on a gilded yard and with gilded mast glides slowly into the strait from the right. A rosy red pennant flies from the masthead. "He" and "She" are seated aft by the rudder, their arms entwined around each other.)* There—there you see perfect happiness, boundless bliss, triumphant young love. . . .

(The scene gradually grows light. "He" stands up in the boat and sings.)

HE. Hail, hail, fairest cove
where in youth I spent my springtime . . .
where in rosy colors I dreamt youth's sweet dreams.
Here I come to you again—
though not, as then, alone!
Greet her, you sea and sky,
you bays and groves—
greet her. . . .
My love, my bride,
my life, my sun!

(The flags flowing from the slips and jetties at Faircove are dipped in salute; white handkerchiefs are waved from the cottages and the shore, and soft music from harps and violins is heard.)

POET. Behold the shining light that radiates from them! Hear the music floating over the water!—The god of love . . . Eros!

OFFICER. It's Victoria!

QUARANTINE MASTER. Well—what of it?

OFFICER. It's *his* Victoria! My Victoria is still mine! And I won't let anybody see her. . . . Now—you hoist the quarantine flag, and I shall pull in the net! *(The Quarantine Master waves a yellow flag. The Officer pulls at a rope, causing the boat to turn toward Foulgut.)* Hold on there! *("He" and "She" suddenly become aware of the dread features of the locality and express their horror audibly.)*

QUARANTINE MASTER. Well, well—this takes the wind out of your sails, doesn't it? But they all have to come here—all who come from cholera-infested localities.

POET. Imagine speaking in that manner—doing such a thing to two human beings who are in love! Don't you touch them! Don't soil their great love! It would be a crime—nothing short of high treason! . . . Woe unto us! All that was once beautiful must be dragged down—dragged into the mud and mire! *("He" and "She" step ashore. They now look shamefaced and sad.)*

HE. Why should we have to suffer this grief? What have we done?

QUARANTINE MASTER. You needn't necessarily have done anything, even if you are pricked by life's little barbs.

SHE. That is how long happiness and joy last!

HE. How long do we have to stay here?

QUARANTINE MASTER. Forty days and forty nights.

SHE. Then let us rather die!

HE. To have to live here—among fire-scorched hills and pigsties! Oh!

POET. Love conquers all—even sulfur fumes and carbolic acid!

QUARANTINE OFFICER (makes a fire in the oven. Blue sulfur flames break out). Now I have started the fire and am burning the sulfur. . . . Will you please step inside. . . .

SHE. Oh! My blue dress will be discolored. . . .

QUARANTINE MASTER. It will turn white—and so will your red roses. . . .

HE. And your cheeks, too, before the forty days are over!

SHE (to the Officer). That will make you glad!

OFFICER. No, that's not true! . . . It's true that your happiness became the source of my unhappiness—but . . . that doesn't matter now. I have received my degree and have now a tutoring position across the strait . . . yes, yes—yes, yes—and in the fall I'll be teaching school. . . . I'll be teaching the boys the same lessons I learned in my long childhood, and all through my youth—and now I'll be teaching these same lessons throughout my manhood—and finally, the very same lessons till I am an old man and ready to die: How much is two times two?—How many times two is four? . . . until I'm pensioned off and have nothing to do except to wait around for the meals to be served, and for the newspapers! . . . And at last I am brought to the crematorium and burned to ashes. . . . Is there nobody here who is entitled to a pension? I think it's about the worst next to "two times two is four"! And to start going to school all over again, after being given a doctor's degree—and to have to ask the same questions over and over again until you die! (An aged gentleman, his hands on his back, is seen passing.) See—there you have a pensioner who is waiting for nothing but the end. . . . I think he must be an army captain who couldn't make the grade—or he may have been a clerk of the supreme court who failed to be appointed to a judgeship. Many are called, but few are chosen. . . . He is impatiently waiting for his breakfast. . . .

PENSIONER. No—for the newspaper! The *Morning News!*

OFFICER. And he is only fifty-four years old. . . . He might be waiting for his meals and his newspaper twenty-five years from now! Isn't it frightful?

PENSIONER. What is it that *isn't* frightful? Tell me, tell me, tell me!

OFFICER. Well, let him answer who can! . . . Now I am going to teach boys that two times two is four—and how many times four can be evenly divided by two. (*He scratches his head in desperation.*) And Victoria—whom I loved and therefore wished the greatest happiness in the world. . . . Now she has found her happiness—the greatest for her . . . and I suffer . . . I suffer . . . suffer!

SHE. Do you think I can be happy when I see you suffer? How can you think that? Perhaps it will lessen the pain for you to know that I am being incarcerated here for forty days and forty nights? Does that lighten the pain?

OFFICER. Yes—and no! How can I be happy, while you suffer? Oh . . .

HE. And do you think my happiness can be built on your misery and pain?

OFFICER. We are all to be pitied!

ALL (*they lift their hands toward the sky and utter a dissonant cry of anguish*). Oh! . . .

DAUGHTER OF INDRA. Eternal One, hear their cry! Life is misery! Men are to be pitied!

ALL (*as before*). Oh! . . .

Faircove. For a moment the stage is dark. During this period, those on the stage disappear or change position. When the stage is light again, the shore at Foulgut can be seen dimly in the background. The strait flows between Foulgut and Faircove; the latter is visible in the foreground. The body of water and Faircove are bathed in light. On the left, a corner of the main pavilion or casino. Through its open windows can be seen a couple, dancing. On a wooden crate outside stand three servant maids with their arms round each other's waists. They are watching the dancers inside. On the terrace stand a piano with open keyboard and a bench. Seated on the latter is Plain-looking Edith. She is bareheaded and seems depressed; she has a mass of tousled hair, and sad eyes.

On the right is a yellow frame house. Two children in summer dress are playing ball outside. On the downstage side of the strait is a jetty with sailboats tied up to it. In the rear, flags and pennants fly from the jetty's flagpoles. In the stream is anchored a white navy brig with gunports.

The entire scene is in winter dress, and both the ground and the barren trees are covered with snow.

The Daughter of Indra and the Officer enter.

DAUGHTER OF INDRA. Here is peace and happiness. Here you can relax. Drudgery is banished. Every day is a day of enjoyment. People are dressed as for a holiday. Music and dancing from early morn. *(To the Servant Maids.)* Why don't you go inside and join in the dancing?

ONE OF THE SERVANT MAIDS. We?

OFFICER. Can't you see they are servants?

DAUGHTER OF INDRA. I forgot!—But why is Edith sitting there by herself? Why isn't she dancing? *(Edith buries her face in her hands.)*

OFFICER. You shouldn't have asked her that! She has been sitting there for three hours, and no one has asked her to dance. . . . *(He goes into the yellow house on the right.)*

DAUGHTER OF INDRA. What cruelty there can be in pleasure!

EDITH'S MOTHER *(comes out from the casino. She is dressed in a low-necked dress. She goes directly over to Edith).* Why don't you go inside as I told you!

EDITH. Because—I can't put myself on exhibition! I can't force people to dance with me, can I? I know I am not pretty to look at! That's why nobody wants to dance with me . . . and I wish you would stop reminding me of it. . . *(She starts to play on the piano Johann Sebastian Bach's Toccata con Fuga, No. 10. At first the music from within is heard faintly; then it increases in sound as if it were trying to drown out Bach's Toccata. Edith, however, persists and the dance finally stops. Guests at the casino appear in the doorway, fascinated by her playing. They all stand silent, in rapt attention.)*

NAVAL OFFICER *(puts his arm round the waist of Alice, one of the guests, and leads her down toward the jetty).* Come quickly!

(Edith breaks off her playing abruptly, rises and follows them, agonized, with her eyes. She remains standing as if she had turned into stone.)

(The façade of the yellow house is now removed, revealing a classroom in a school. One sees three rows of benches, seated on which are a number of boy pupils. Among them is the Officer. He seems to be ill at ease, restless, and worried. Facing the pupils stands the Teacher; he is wearing spec-

tacles, and in his hand he has a piece of chalk and a rattan cane.)

TEACHER *(to the Officer).* Well, my boy, can you tell me now what two times two makes? *(The Officer remains seated. He racks his brain without being able to give the answer.)* Stand up when you are asked a question!

OFFICER *(painfully affected, he rises).* Two . . . times two. . . . Let me see . . . it's . . . two two . . .

TEACHER. Oho! You haven't studied your lesson!

OFFICER *(ashamed).* Yes, I have—but . . . I know the answer— but I can't tell you. . . .

TEACHER. You are trying to get out of answering! You know the answer—but you can't tell me! Perhaps you want me to help you! *(He pulls the Officer's hair.)*

OFFICER. Oh, this is terrible—terrible!

TEACHER. Yes, isn't it! A big boy like you—so completely lacking in ambition. . . .

OFFICER *(tortured).* A big boy! Yes—I am big—bigger than the other boys here. . . . I'm a grown man—have been through school. *(He searches his mind; he seems to be recovering his memory.)* I have been given a doctor's degree, haven't I?— Then why am I sitting here? Haven't I been given a degree?

TEACHER. Of course you have . . . but you see, you have to sit here to mature. You have to mature—isn't that so?

OFFICER *(runs his hand over his forehead).* Yes, of course . . . you are right—we have to mature. . . . Two times two—is two . . . and I'll prove it by a demonstration in analogy—the highest form of reasoning that exists. Now listen to me!—One times one is one; isn't it? Therefore two times two is two! For what applies in one case must of necessity apply in another.

TEACHER. Your conclusion is in complete conformity with good logic—but the answer is wrong!

OFFICER. What is right according to logic can't be wrong! Let's put it to the test. One divided by one gives one—and so two divided by two must give two.

TEACHER. Entirely correct according to the conclusion arrived at by analogy. But what does one times three make?

OFFICER. Three!

TEACHER. Consequently two times three should also make three, shouldn't it?

OFFICER *(ponders the question).* No—that can't be right . . . it can't be—unless . . . *(He sits down in despair.)* Yes, I see I am not mature yet!

TEACHER. No—you are not! Not by any means!

OFFICER. But how long will I have to sit here, then?

TEACHER. How long?—Do you believe in the existence of time and space?—Suppose that time does exist—then you should be able to tell me what it is. What is time?

OFFICER. Time? (He reflects.) I can't say exactly what it is—but I know very well what it is. . . . Consequently, why can't I know what two times two makes, without being able to say it? Can you tell me what time is, teacher?

TEACHER. Of course I can!

ALL THE PUPILS (in chorus). Tell us, then!

TEACHER. Time—let me see! (He stands immobile, one finger on his nose.) While we are talking, time flies . . . therefore it is something that flies . . . while I talk . . .

A PUPIL (stands up). Now you are talking, Teacher, and while you are talking, I fly. . . . consequently I am time!

(He runs out.)

TEACHER. Absolutely correct according to the laws of logic!

OFFICER. But in that case the laws of logic are ridiculous—for Nils, who just skipped class, can't possibly be time. . . .

TEACHER. What you say is also quite in accordance with the laws of logic, except that it's silly. . . .

OFFICER. Then all logic must be silly!

TEACHER. It really seems so. . . . But if logic is asinine, then the whole world must be crazy . . . and then the devil himself wouldn't want to stay here and teach you any more idiotic stupidities!—If anybody cares to treat me to a good stiff drink, I wouldn't mind taking you for a swim!

OFFICER. I would call this a *posterus prius,* or—the world turned upside down. I always thought the swim came first and the drink afterward. You old fogy!

TEACHER. I warn you not to get a swelled head, Doctor!

OFFICER. Call me Major, if you please! I am an army officer—and I haven't the faintest idea why I am sitting here taking scoldings like any schoolboy. . . .

TEACHER (pointing his finger at him). We have to learn—to mature!

QUARANTINE MASTER (enters). The quarantine is now in effect!

OFFICER. Oh, there you are! Can you imagine—he made me sit among the young lads in this classroom, despite my degree as a doctor of philosophy!

QUARANTINE MASTER. Well, why didn't you get up and leave?

OFFICER. Leave, you say. . . . Well I don't know. . . . It isn't so easy as you think. . . .

TEACHER. No—you are quite right! You just try!

OFFICER *(to the Quarantine Master)*. Save me! Save me from his staring eyes!

QUARANTINE MASTER. Just come with me!—Come and join in the dance . . . we have to dance before the plague breaks out—we simply must!

OFFICER. Is the brig sailing?

QUARANTINE MASTER. Yes, that's the first thing we must do—get the brig away from here!—There'll be much weeping, of course. . . .

OFFICER. There always is, whenever that brig comes here—and whenever it leaves!—Let us go. . . . *(They go out. The Teacher, in pantomime, continues calmly with his teaching.) (The Servant Maids, who have been standing outside the casino windows, now drag themselves mournfully down to the jetty. Edith, who has remained standing like a statue by the piano, follows them.)*

DAUGHTER OF INDRA *(to the Officer)*. Is there then not one person who is happy in this paradise?

OFFICER. Yes—there is a couple that have just been married. . . . Let's listen to them and watch them. *(The two newly-married enter.)*

HUSBAND *(to his wife)*. My bliss is so boundless that I could die happy this moment. . . .

WIFE. Why should you wish to die?

HUSBAND. Because at the core of happiness lies the seed of unhappiness. . . . Happiness devours itself as fire does! The flame can't burn eternally—it is doomed to die. . . . This foreknowledge of the finality of things annihilates bliss at its very apex.

WIFE. Then let us die together—this very moment!

HUSBAND. Die . . . together. . . . Come! I am frightened of happiness and its treachery! . . .

(They disappear toward the sea.)

DAUGHTER OF INDRA *(to the Officer)*. Life is misery! Man is to be pitied!

OFFICER. Look at this man coming here! He is the most envied of the humans in this community! *(The Blind Man enters. He is being led by another man.)* He is the owner of hundreds of Italian villas here. He owns all these coves and bays, shores and woods, the fish in the water, the birds in the air, and the game in the woods. These, close to a thousand human beings, are his tenants—and the sun rises over his holdings by the sea and sets over his properties inland. . . .

DAUGHTER OF INDRA. And does he complain also?

OFFICER. Yes—and with good reason. . . . He can't see. . . .

QUARANTINE MASTER. He is blind!

DAUGHTER OF INDRA. And he is the most envied of all. . . .

OFFICER. Now he is watching the brig sail away. . . . His son is aboard. . . .

BLIND MAN. I may not see—but I can hear! I can hear the claws of the anchor grappling with the mud at the bottom of the sea . . . exactly as when one extracts a fishhook from a fish and the heart is dragged out at the same time. . . . My son—my only child—is leaving for strange lands across the wide open seas . . . and I can only be with him in my thoughts. . . . Now I hear the cable screech and groan . . . and . . . I hear something flutter and flap in the wind—like wet wash on a clothes line. . . . It might be wet handkerchiefs hung up to dry. . . . And I hear weeping and sobbing—as when people can't control their feelings. . . . I can't tell whether it's the small waves lapping against the seams of the ship, or whether it's the young girls on the shore—the ones who are being abandoned and who are disconsolate. . . . I once asked a little boy why the sea was so salty. . . . The child's father was away on a long voyage. . . . Without a moment's hesitation he answered: The sea is salty because seamen cry so often. Why do seamen cry so much? I asked. Because they always have to leave their homes; that's why they always have to hang their handkerchiefs on the masts to dry! . . . And why do human beings cry when they feel sorrow? I asked again. Why! said he, that's because the windows of the eyes have to be washed now and then so that we can see more clearly. . . .

(*The brig has now set sail and is slowly gliding off. The girls on shore wave their handkerchiefs and some of them wipe their eyes. From the signal rack on the foremast is then hoisted the signal "yes": a red ball on a white field. In answer to it Alice exultantly waves her handkerchief.*)

DAUGHTER OF INDRA (*to the Officer*). What's the meaning of that flag?

OFFICER. It carries the message "yes." It's the lieutenant's way of reaffirming his love—in red—like the crimson blood of a heart—against the sky-blue canvas of heaven. . . .

DAUGHTER OF INDRA. How would they signal the word "no"?

OFFICER. It would be blue as the rancid blood in blue veins. . . . But just see how Alice almost leaps with joy!

DAUGHTER OF INDRA. And Edith is weeping!

BLIND MAN. To meet and to part . . . to part and to meet.
. . . That is life. . . . I met her—his mother. . . . And then
she left me—and I was left our son. . . . Now he has left me. . . .

DAUGHTER OF INDRA. But he will come back. . . .

BLIND MAN. Who is that speaking to me? I have heard that
voice before—in my dreams—in my youth—when the holidays
of summer came—when first I was married—when my child was
brought into the world—whenever life smiled upon me, I heard
that voice—like the soughing of the south wind—like the voice
of harps from ethereal worlds; as I feel the angels would have
sung their greeting on the night of His birth. (*The Attorney
enters. He steps over to the Blind Man and whispers in his ear.*)
You don't say?

ATTORNEY. Yes—believe me! (*He turns to the Daughter of
Indra.*) Now you have seen many things—but you have not met
with the worst. . . .

DAUGHTER OF INDRA. And the worst is . . .

ATTORNEY. To go back, to go over again, to recapitulate! To
have to learn the same lesson over and over again! Come!

DAUGHTER OF INDRA. Where are we going?

ATTORNEY. To your duties!

DAUGHTER OF INDRA. And what are they?

ATTORNEY. Whatever you are in dread of! Whatever you
have no desire to do, yet must do! It means—to deny yourself
things you desire—to sacrifice—to go through hardships and
deprivations—in brief, everything that lacks joy and beauty—
everything that is vile, loathsome, and painful. . . .

DAUGHTER OF INDRA. Are no duties pleasant, then?

ATTORNEY. Yes—when they are done—when they are fulfilled!

DAUGHTER OF INDRA. And then they no longer exist. . . .
Duty, then, is always something odious. . . . Is there nothing
that is joyful and pleasant here?

ATTORNEY. Pleasures are sin.

DAUGHTER OF INDRA. Sin?

ATTORNEY. Something to be punished, yes! If I enjoy myself
day and night, I suffer the agonies of hell and have a bad
conscience the day after.

DAUGHTER OF INDRA. How strange!

ATTORNEY. I wake up in the morning with a headache—
and at once the iteration, the recapitulation begins! But it is
always a perverted recapitulation! What seemed beautiful and
delightful and witty the night before seems to me the next
morning ugly and loathsome and stupid. Pleasure seems de-

cayed; joy disintegrated. What people like to call success invariably turns out to be the cause of their next setback. Every success I have achieved during my life has turned into some failure for me. People have an instinctive fear and envy of seeing others get along. They feel that fate is unjust when it favors someone else; and so they try to restore the balance by placing obstacles in the way of others. To be talented is dangerous to one's life: one runs the risk of starving to death! —But you must return to your duties—or I shall bring suit against you. . . . I'll take it through every court, from the lowest to the highest.

DAUGHTER OF INDRA. I have to go back to the stove and the cooking, the cabbage, and the baby's clothes? . . .

ATTORNEY. Yes, you must! We have a big wash today—all the handkerchiefs have to be washed.

DAUGHTER OF INDRA. Oh, must I do this again . . . again . . .

ATTORNEY. Life is one long stretch of repetitions. . . . Look at the schoolmaster in there! Yesterday he was given a degree, was given the laurel wreath and a salute of guns, reached his Parnassus, and was embraced by the monarch. . . . And today he is back in school again, asking for an answer to what two times two makes . . . and he'll be asking that question until his dying day. . . . But—come back to your home, come back to me!

DAUGHTER OF INDRA. I would rather die!

ATTORNEY. Die? No—you must not think of that! First of all, it is a disgrace—a disgrace so great that your body would be abused and subjected to insults; and secondly, you would find no rest in the hereafter. . . . It is a mortal sin!

DAUGHTER OF INDRA. It is not easy to be a human!

ALL. How true!

DAUGHTER OF INDRA. I will not return with you to humiliation and dirt—I yearn to go back up there, from where I came . . . but . . . first the door must be opened so that I may learn the secret within. . . . It is my will that the door be opened!

ATTORNEY. To learn that secret you must retrace your steps, travel the road back, all the way, and suffer through all the vexations and adversities, repetitions, restraints, and circumlocutions that go with a lawsuit. . . .

DAUGHTER OF INDRA. So be it . . . but first I shall go to some lonely spot out in the wilderness and find my own self again. . . . We shall see each other in the future. (*To the Poet.*) Follow me! (*Cries of anguish and pain are heard distantly:* "O woe! O woe! O woe!") Did you hear that?

ATTORNEY. That came from the lost souls over at Foulgut. . . .

DAUGHTER OF INDRA. Why is their anguish today louder than usual?

ATTORNEY. Because the sun is shining here, because there is youth and dancing here, because there is music in the air. . . . It is then that they feel their pains and afflictions so much more deeply.

DAUGHTER OF INDRA. We must set them free!

ATTORNEY. You may try!—Once there was a man who sought to liberate . . . He was hanged on a cross. . . .

DAUGHTER OF INDRA. Who hanged him?

ATTORNEY. The self-righteous, the sanctimonious! . . .

DAUGHTER OF INDRA. Who are they?

ATTORNEY. Don't you know who the self-righteous are? You will soon learn to know them!

DAUGHTER OF INDRA. Was it they who refused you your degree?

ATTORNEY. Yes!

DAUGHTER OF INDRA. Then I know who they are. . . .

A beach on the Mediterranean. On the right, in the foreground, is a white wall. Protruding above it are orange trees, laden with fruit. In the background are villas and the casino with its terraced approach.

On the left, a big pile of coal and two wheelbarrows.

In the background, to the left, can be discerned a faint and limited view of the blue sea. Two Coal Heavers, naked to the waist and black of body, face, and hands from handling the coal, sit on the wheelbarrows. Their faces show despair and agony.

The Daughter of Indra and the Attorney are visible in the background.

DAUGHTER OF INDRA. This is paradise!

FIRST COAL HEAVER. This is hell!

SECOND COAL HEAVER. Nearly eighty-seven degrees in the shade!

FIRST COAL HEAVER. What do you say about a dip in the sea?

SECOND COAL HEAVER. And get the police on us! Don't you know you can't bathe here?

FIRST COAL HEAVER. How about picking an orange from one of the trees?

SECOND COAL HEAVER. No—we'll have the police on us. . . .

FIRST COAL HEAVER. But I can't work in this heat. . . . I'm quitting right now.

SECOND COAL HEAVER. If you do, the police will be after you. . . . *(There is a silence.)* And furthermore—you wouldn't be able to buy yourself food. . . .

FIRST COAL HEAVER. No food? We, who work harder than anyone else—we get the least to eat! The rich, on the other hand, who do nothing, get all they want! . . . Don't you think one can truthfully say that this is unrighteous and unjust?—I wonder what the Daughter of the Gods has to say about it?

DAUGHTER OF INDRA. I am at a loss for a reply!—But tell me— what have you done to make you so grimy? Why are you having such a hard life?

FIRST COAL HEAVER. What we have done? It was our lot to be born of poor parents—and not too respectable at that. . . . We may have been convicted a couple of times, too. . . .

DAUGHTER OF INDRA. Convicted?

FIRST COAL HEAVER. Yes! The unpunished lounge up there in the casino, feasting on eight-course dinners and wine.

DAUGHTER OF INDRA *(to the Attorney)*. Can this really be true?

ATTORNEY. Broadly speaking, yes. . . .

DAUGHTER OF INDRA. You mean to say that every mortal, if given his just deserts, would—at some time or other—have been condemned to prison?

ATTORNEY. Yes.

DAUGHTER OF INDRA. Even you?

ATTORNEY. Yes—even I!

DAUGHTER OF INDRA. Is it true that the poor cannot go bathing in the sea here?

ATTORNEY. Yes—not even with their clothes on! The only ones who escape being fined are the ones who try to drown themselves. . . . But I have heard that they are given a good thrashing by the police. . . .

DAUGHTER OF INDRA. But isn't there some place on the outskirts of the community, out in the country, where they can go bathing?

ATTORNEY. There is no such facility here—all the properties are fenced in.

DAUGHTER OF INDRA. But I mean—on the free, open shore beyond. . . .

ATTORNEY. Nothing is free here. It all belongs to somebody.

DAUGHTER OF INDRA. Even the sea—the great, open sea? . . .

ATTORNEY. Yes—even the sea! You can't go sailing the sea and put into port without being duly registered and charged for it. A nice state of affairs, isn't it?

DAUGHTER OF INDRA. This is no paradise. . . .

ATTORNEY. No—this is not paradise!

DAUGHTER OF INDRA. Why, then, do people do nothing to improve their lot?

ATTORNEY. People do try, of course! But the ones who do try —the reformers—end in a prison or a madhouse. . . .

DAUGHTER OF INDRA. Who has them put in prison?

ATTORNEY. All the righteous, the respectable people. . . .

DAUGHTER OF INDRA. And who sends them to the madhouse?

ATTORNEY. Their own anguish . . . despair over the hopelessness of their struggle.

DAUGHTER OF INDRA. Has the thought not occurred to anyone that things—for reasons not known—must remain as they are?

ATTORNEY. Yes—to them who are well off! They always think that way!

DAUGHTER OF INDRA. That the world is as it should be? . . .

FIRST COAL HEAVER. Nevertheless—aren't we the very foundations of society?—If we didn't deliver the coal, you would have no fire in the kitchen range, or in the fireplaces in the rest of the house—you would have no coal for your factories. The lights in the streets, in the homes and the shops would go out, you would freeze in darkness! That's why we sweat like hell to see that you get the black coal. . . . And what do you give us in return?

ATTORNEY (to the Daughter of Indra). Help them! (There is a silence.) Things can't be the same for all—I understand that . . . but why should the gap be so great? (The Gentleman and the Lady walk across the stage.)

LADY. Will you come with me and play a game?

GENTLEMAN. No, I have to take a walk—otherwise I'll have no appetite for dinner. . . .

FIRST COAL HEAVER. No appetite for dinner? . . .

SECOND COAL HEAVER. No appetite! . . . (Several Children enter. They scream, frightened when they see the two Coal Heavers.)

FIRST COAL HEAVER. They scream when they see us! They scream. . . .

SECOND COAL HEAVER. Hell and damnation!—I'm afraid we'll have to drag out the scaffolds soon and operate on this carcass. . . .

FIRST COAL HEAVER. Yes, damn it, I say the same! (He spits contemptuously.)

ATTORNEY (to the Daughter of Indra). There is no question— something is wrong. . . . Yet people are not too bad . . . but it's . . .

DAUGHTER OF INDRA. But—what?

ATTORNEY. It's their superiors—those who have the authority. . . .

DAUGHTER OF INDRA (*hides her face*). This is not paradise!
(*She leaves.*)

COAL HEAVERS. No—it's not paradise! It's hell—that's what it is!

Fingal's Cave. Languishing great green waves roll into the cave. In the foreground a red alarm buoy rocks to and fro on the waves; it emits no sound, however, except at such times as indicated in the play. Music of the winds and the waves. The Daughter of Indra and the Poet are visible when the curtain rises.

POET. Where have you brought me?

DAUGHTER OF INDRA. Far from the murmur and moans and laments of the children of humanity, to the farthest end of the seven seas—to this grotto, which has been given the name of Indra's Ear because it is here that the Master of the Heavens is said to listen to the complaints of the mortals. . . .

POET. Here?—How can . . .

DAUGHTER OF INDRA. Can't you see that this grotto is built like a sea shell? You can see it, can't you? And don't you know that your own ear is built like a shell? You know it—but you haven't given thought to it. (*She picks up a sea shell on the shore.*) When you were a child, don't you remember holding a sea shell to your ear, listening—listening to its singing? . . . You heard the ripple of your heart's blood, the hum of your brain thinking, the snapping of thousands of tiny little worn-out fibers inside the tissues of your body, didn't you? All *that* you heard in such a little sea shell. . . . Imagine then what sounds you will hear in this enormous ear!

POET (*listens*). I hear nothing but the whisper of the wind. . . .

DAUGHTER OF INDRA. Then let me interpret what it tells me. . . . Listen to the wailing of the winds. (*She recites to soft music.*)
Born beneath the firmament of heaven,
Indra's flashing lightning soon pursued us
to the earth of dust below. . . .
Litter of pasture fields soiled our feet;
we were forced to endure
the dust of highways,
the smoke of cities,
and evil-smelling breaths,

the odors of wines and cooking. . . .
Finally we fled to the open sea
to take breath and fill our lungs
with fresh air, to flap our wings
and cleanse and bathe our feet.
Indra, Lord of the Heavens,
hear us! . . .
Hear our sighs! . . .
Unclean is the Earth,
life there is miserable;
mankind is not wicked—
yet it can't be called good.
People live as best they can,
for each passing day.
Sons of the Dust, they trudge through dust;
born out of dust,
they return to dust.
Feet they were given to move with,
wings were denied them. . . .
Laden with dust they are. . . .
Are they to be blamed—
or are You?

POET. And then I heard one time . . .

DAUGHTER OF INDRA. Hush! The winds are still singing. (*She continues, to soft music.*)
We, the winds, the sons of Air,
Scatter abroad the wails of humans. . . .
Did you hear us
on autumn nights—
whining in the chimneys,
rattling the stove shutters,
or stealing through leaky windows,
whilst the rain wept tears on the roof tiles? . . .
Or in wintry night,
in snow-clad woods of pine? . . .
Have you heard moaning and bewailing
in sails and rigging
upon the windswept sea? . . .
It is we—we, the winds—
sons of the Air! . . .
And we've learned these sounds of pain
from anguished human breasts,
which we have pierced and invaded—
on sickbeds, on battlefields . . .

but mostly when babes
whimper at childbirth
and utter cries
of painful anguish at being born. . . .
It is we—winds of the Air—
hissing and whining!
Woe! Woe! Woe!

POET. It seems as if I once . . .

DAUGHTER OF INDRA. Hush! The waves are singing. *(She again recites to subdued music.)*
It is we, the billowy waves,
that cradle the winds
to their sleep! . . .
Green are the cradles we rock,
watery are we and salty;
we leap like fiery flames—
watery flames we are. . . .
Burning and quenching,
bathing and cleansing,
begetting, conceiving. . . .
We—the billowy waves
that cradle them, rock them
into sleep!

Treacherous and faithless waves. . . . All on earth that is not burned, falls victim to the sea. . . . Look here. *(She points to a heap of debris.)* Look what the sea has plundered and destroyed. . . . All that remains of the sunken ships is the figurehead—and their name-boards: *Justice, Friendship, Golden Peace,* and *Hope.* . . . This is all that remains of Hope—of inconstant and capricious Hope! Railings and rowlocks and bailers! And look here: a lifebuoy—that saved *itself,* but let men in distress go down!

POET *(searching in the pile of debris).* Here is the nameboard of the good ship *Justice*—the very same ship that sailed from Faircove with the Blind Man's son aboard! It was lost, then! And so is Alice's betrothed, with whom poor Edith was so hopelessly in love.

DAUGHTER OF INDRA. The Blind Man? Faircove? Could I have been dreaming? And Alice's fiancé, ugly Edith, Foulgut with its quarantine, its sulfur and carbolic acid, the university ceremony in the church, the Attorney's office, the Portress's cubicle at the Opera, and Victoria, the growing castle and the Officer . . . I have dreamed it all. . . .

POET. I have lived it in my imagination. . . .

DAUGHTER OF INDRA. You know what poetry and imagination are, then. . . .

POET. I know what dreams are. . . . But what is poetry?

DAUGHTER OF INDRA. It is not reality. . . . It is more than reality. It is not dreaming—but dreams come alive, envisioned. . . .

POET. And the children of humanity think that we poets only like to play, are mere jesters—that we merely fabricate, make believe!

DAUGHTER OF INDRA. And that may be a good thing, my friend. Else the world would lie fallow and be barren for lack of care and cultivation. Everybody would be lying on his back, gazing at the sky; and nobody would touch a hoe or a pick-ax, a shovel or a plow.

POET. And you say this—you, Indra's daughter, who hail from realms above? . . .

DAUGHTER OF INDRA. You reproach me justly. . . . I have dwelt too long down here, wallowing in the mud like you. . . . My thoughts no longer take flight—their wings are weighted down by clay—the mud sticks to their feet! And I myself . . . *(She raises her arms.)* I myself keep sinking . . . sinking . . . Help me, O Father, God of the Heavens! *(There is a silence.)* No longer can I hear His voice! The ether no longer carries the sound from His lips to my ear—the silvery thread has snapped. . . . Woe to me, I am earthbound!

POET. When will you ascend? Is the time near?

DAUGHTER OF INDRA. When I have shed this mortal guise and it has burned to dust . . . for all the water of the sea cannot make me clean. . . . Why do you ask?

POET. Because I have a favor to beseech of you: a prayer, a fervent supplication. . . .

DAUGHTER OF INDRA. What is it you desire?

POET. A prayer of all mankind—to the ruler of the universe—framed in words by a dreamer . . .

DAUGHTER OF INDRA. And by whom do you wish it to be given to Him? . . .

POET. By Indra's daughter!

DAUGHTER OF INDRA. Have you committed it to memory—this petition?

POET. Yes, I know it by heart.

DAUGHTER OF INDRA. Then speak it!

POET. I'd rather you did!

DAUGHTER OF INDRA. Where may I read the words?

POET. In my mind—and also here. *(He hands her a scroll.)*

DAUGHTER OF INDRA *(accepts the scroll, but speaks without glancing at it)*. Then I shall give voice to your prayer. . . .

"Why must you be born in anguish,
child of mankind? Why must mothers
suffer birth pains when you bring her
the most precious of all gifts:
motherhood, life's greatest blessing?
Why must you to life awaken? . . .
Why do you salute the sunlight
with a cry of pain and mean ill-temper?
Why do you not smile on dawning life,
mortal child, since human happiness
has been promised as your birthright?
Why must we be born like beasts—
we, descendants of both gods and mortals?—
Better guise could have been given us than this
wretched body spun of blood and slime . . .
and why must this image of the gods shed teeth?"

Silence, rash one! Blame the image—not the Maker!
No man yet has solved life's riddle!

"Started thus, the pilgrimage begins
over stones and thorns and thistles. . . .
Should it lead across a beaten path,
you will find the road forbidden;
and if you should pluck a flower,
you'd be held for trespass—and for thieving also;
if a field should stop you from advancing
and you take a short cut through it,
you will trample down the farmer's crops;
others do the same to you,
equalizing thus the damage!—
Every moment that gives joy
brings to others only grief;
your own sorrow spreads, however,
not much gladness anywhere:
thus it's sorrow after sorrow! . . .
So the pilgrimage goes on—
even death brings gain to others!"

Is it this way, you—the son of Dust—
mean to come before the Great Almighty? . . .

POET. How could I, the Son of dust,
find such chaste, ethereal words
that they'd soar to realms beyond?
Child of Gods, will you translate
all our sorrows into speech
that will reach immortal ears?

DAUGHTER OF INDRA. I will.

POET *(points to the buoy).* What is that floating there?—
Is it a buoy?

DAUGHTER OF INDRA. Yes.

POET. It looks like a lung with an Adam's apple.

DAUGHTER OF INDRA. It is the watchman of the seas. When
there is danger ahead, it utters a warning.

POET. It looks as if the sea were rising and the waves were
growing restless and ever higher. . . .

DAUGHTER OF INDRA. So it does. . . .

POET. Woe! What do I see? A ship—just outside—close by the
reef. . . .

DAUGHTER OF INDRA. What ship can that be?

POET. I believe it is the eternal ghost ship. . . .

DAUGHTER OF INDRA. The ghost ship? What ship is that?

POET. The Flying Dutchman. . . .

DAUGHTER OF INDRA. Oh, I know. . . . Why is he being
punished so cruelly, and why doesn't he ever put ashore?

POET. Because he had seven unfaithful wives.

DAUGHTER OF INDRA. Why should he be punished for that?

POET. He was condemned by all the righteous-minded. . . .

DAUGHTER OF INDRA. How strange this world is!—But can't
he ever be freed from the curse?

POET. Freed?—One has to be careful not to set people
free. . . .

DAUGHTER OF INDRA. Why?

POET. Because . . . No, it's not the Flying Dutchman! It's
just an ordinary ship in distress!—Why doesn't the buoy cry
out a warning now?—Look, the sea is rising, the waves are
growing higher and higher. . . . Soon we shall be marooned
in the cave!—The ship's bell is clanging now . . . before long
there'll be another figurehead floating on the water. . . . Cry
out your warning, buoy! Do your duty, watchman! *(The buoy
emits a four-tone chord of fifths and sixths, resembling the
sound of a foghorn.)* The crew are signaling and waving to us—
and we ourselves are perishing. . . .

DAUGHTER OF INDRA. Is it not your wish to be set free?

POET. Why, certainly! Of course I wish to be set free . . . but not at this moment—and not through water!

CREW (*singing in quartet*). Christ Kyrie! (*Cries and shouts from the ship.*)

POET. Now they are shouting—and the sea roars—and no one can hear them. . . .

CREW (*singing as before*). Christ Kyrie!

DAUGHTER OF INDRA. Who is that coming there?

POET. Walking on the waters? There is only one who walks on the waters. And it is not Peter the Rock, for he sank like a stone. (*A white light appears on the surface of the water in the distance.*)

CREW. Christ Kyrie!

DAUGHTER OF INDRA. Is that He?

POET. It is He—who was crucified. . . .

DAUGHTER OF INDRA. Why . . . tell me . . . why was He crucified?

POET. Because He wished to set free . . .

DAUGHTER OF INDRA. I have forgotten who . . . who crucified Him.

POET. All the righteous-minded. . . .

DAUGHTER OF INDRA. What a strange world!

POET. The sea is rising! Darkness is coming upon us! The storm is increasing! (*The Crew gives out a scream of terror.*) The men are screaming, horror-stricken at the sight of their Saviour! . . . and now—and now they are jumping overboard out of fear. (*The Crew screams anew with fear.*) They cry from fear of dying! They come into the world crying and go out crying! (*The rolling, surging waves keep increasing in height and volume and threaten to drown the two in the grotto.*)

DAUGHTER OF INDRA. If I were only certain that it is a ship. . . .

POET. To tell the truth . . . I don't believe it is a ship . . . it is a two-story house with trees before it . . . and . . . a telephone tower—a tower reaching to the skies. . . . It is the Babel's Tower of our times sending messages by wire to higher regions—communicating with the dwellers there. . . .

DAUGHTER OF INDRA. My child, the thoughts of mankind need no wires for transmission! The prayers of the pious reach to the far ends of the universe. . . . No—it cannot be a Tower of Babel . . . for if you wish to assail the heavens, you must do so by prayer. . . .

POET. No, it is no house—and no telephone tower. . . . You can see that, can't you?

DAUGHTER OF INDRA. Then what do you see?

POET. I see a vast snow-covered space—a drill ground. . . .
The winter sun is peeking out from behind a church on a
hillside, and its tower casts a long shadow over the snow. . . .
Now I see a company of soldiers marching across the open
field. . . . They march straight to the tower, march up the
spire. . . . Now they have reached the cross, but I have a
foreboding that the first one who steps on the weathercock
at the pinnacle will die. . . . Now they are close to the top—
a corporal is at the head of his men. . . . Aha! A cloud comes
sweeping across the field . . . it blots out the sun . . . now
everything has disappeared . . . the moisture of the cloud
has put out the sun's fire! The sunlight created the shadow
picture of the tower, but the shadow picture of the cloud
disembodied the shadow image of the tower. . . .

*While the preceding dialogue is being spoken, the setting
is being shifted: it now shows again the alley outside the
Opera.*

DAUGHTER OF INDRA *(to the Portress)*. Has the Lord Chancellor arrived yet?

PORTRESS. No.

DAUGHTER OF INDRA. Have the Deans come?

PORTRESS. No.

DAUGHTER OF INDRA. Then please call them at once . . . the
door is about to be opened!

PORTRESS. Is it so important?

DAUGHTER OF INDRA. Yes, it is. People have become excited.
. . . They have a notion that the solution to the riddle of the
world is being hidden in there!—So please call the Lord Chancellor and the Deans of the Faculties at once! *(The Portress
blows a whistle.)* And don't forget the Glazier with his diamond! If he doesn't come, we'll have to call it off!

*(People of the Opera enter from the right, as in the earlier
scenes. The Officer enters from the rear. He is dressed in
a redingote and top hat and carries a bouquet of roses. He
is radiantly happy.)*

OFFICER. Victoria!

PORTRESS. Miss Victoria will be down in a moment!

OFFICER. Splendid! The carriage is waiting, the table is set,
the champagne is on ice. . . . Let me embrace you, madam!
(He embraces the Portress.) Victoria!

WOMAN'S VOICE *(sings out from above)*. Here I am!

OFFICER *(starts to pace)*. Good! I'll be waiting!

POET. It seems to me as if I had experienced all this once before. . . .

DAUGHTER OF INDRA. I also!

POET. Perhaps I have dreamed it!

DAUGHTER OF INDRA. Or lived it in your imagination—in a poem?

POET. Perhaps even that. . . .

DAUGHTER OF INDRA. Now you know what poetry is. . . .

POET. Now I know what dreams are. . . .

DAUGHTER OF INDRA. I feel as if we have spoken these very words once before—but in some other place. . . .

POET. Therefore you can easily conceive what reality is. . . .

DAUGHTER OF INDRA. Or dreams!

POET. Or the imagery of poetry! (*The Lord Chancellor and the Deans of the theological, philosophical, medical, and law faculties enter.*)

LORD CHANCELLOR. It is about that door, of course!—What does the Dean of Theology think about the matter?

DEAN OF THEOLOGY. I don't think. I believe—*credo* . . .

DEAN OF PHILOSOPHY. I hold the view that . . .

DEAN OF MEDICINE. I know . . .

DEAN OF JURISPRUDENCE. I hold a doubt until I have seen the evidence and heard the testimony!

LORD CHANCELLOR. Now they'll start wrangling again! . . . Well, let's first hear what Theology has to say!

DEAN OF THEOLOGY. I believe that this door should not be opened for the reason that it has been placed there to conceal dangerous truths . . .

DEAN OF PHILOSOPHY. Truth is never dangerous!

DEAN OF MEDICINE. What is truth?

DEAN OF JURISPRUDENCE. That which can be proved by two witnesses.

DEAN OF THEOLOGY. A shyster lawyer can prove anything—with two false witnesses!

DEAN OF PHILOSOPHY. Truth is wisdom; and wisdom plus knowledge is philosophy itself. . . . Philosophy is the science of sciences, the supreme knowledge, and all the other sciences are merely its handmaids.

DEAN OF MEDICINE. There is only *one* science: natural science! Philosophy is no science. It's nothing but empty speculation!

DEAN OF THEOLOGY. Bravo!

DEAN OF PHILOSOPHY (*to the Dean of Theology*). You shout bravo! What about yourself? You are the archenemy of all

knowledge. You are the very antithesis of science—you are full
of obscurity and vagueness. . . .

DEAN OF MEDICINE. Bravo!

DEAN OF THEOLOGY *(to the Dean of Medicine).* You shout
bravo—you who can't see any further than your nose, when
you look through your microscope—you, who only put faith
in your deceptive senses: your eye, for example, which may
be farsighted, nearsighted, blind, dim-sighted, cross-eyed, one-
eyed, color-blind, red-blind, green-blind . . .

DEAN OF MEDICINE. Dolt! Idiot!

DEAN OF THEOLOGY. Fool! Ass! *(They fly at each other.)*

LORD CHANCELLOR. Calm yourselves! Are you two crows trying to peck each other's eyes out?

DEAN OF PHILOSOPHY *(to the Chancellor and the Deans of
Jurisprudence and Philosophy).* If I had to choose between
those two, Theology and Medicine, I would choose—neither!

DEAN OF JURISPRUDENCE. And if I had to sit in judgment
over you three, I would—find you all guilty!—You don't seem
to find a single point on which you can agree! Neither now
nor in the past!—But let's get back now to the case in hand!
What is the Lord Chancellor's opinion regarding this door
and its opening?

LORD CHANCELLOR. Opinion? I have no opinions. I have
merely been appointed by the government to make sure that
you don't break each other's arms and legs during Council
meetings—for the edification of the students! My opinion . . .
No, no! I stay away from anything that has to do with opinions. . . . There *was* a time when I had an opinion or two,
but it didn't take long to put an end to them. . . . Opinions
are quickly proved to be erroneous—by one's opponents, of
course!—Could we proceed with the opening of the door now
—even at the risk of discovering some dangerous truths behind it?

DEAN OF JURISPRUDENCE. What is truth? *What is truth?*

DEAN OF THEOLOGY. I am the truth and the life . . .

DEAN OF PHILOSOPHY. I am the core of all knowledge . . .

DEAN OF MEDICINE. I am the exact science . . .

DEAN OF JURISPRUDENCE. I doubt! . . .

(They fly at each other.)

DAUGHTER OF INDRA. Shame on you, you teachers of the
young!

DEAN OF JURISPRUDENCE. Mr. Lord Chancellor! As the representative of the government, as the head of the body of in-
structors in this university, it is your duty to bring this woman

before a court of justice for her offensive demeanor. She has dared to tell you to be ashamed of yourselves! This is an insult! She has—in a scoffing, sneering manner—sarcastically labeled you the teachers of the young. . . . This is nothing short of slander!

DAUGHTER OF INDRA. I pity the young!

DEAN OF JURISPRUDENCE. She feels sorry for the young! Isn't that the same as an accusation against us?—Lord Chancellor, prosecute her without a moment's delay!

DAUGHTER OF INDRA. Yes—I accuse you, all of you, of sowing doubt and dissension in the minds of the young.

DEAN OF JURISPRUDENCE. Listen to her! She is herself casting doubt on our authority, inveigling the young! And what is more, she accuses us of creating doubts! I ask of all the righteous-minded: Is not this a criminal offense?

ALL THE RIGHTEOUS-MINDED. It is indeed a criminal offense!

DEAN OF JURISPRUDENCE. All the righteous-minded have judged you!—Now leave—leave in peace with what you have gained from us—or else . . .

DAUGHTER OF INDRA. What I have gained from you?—Or else —or else what?

DEAN OF JURISPRUDENCE. Or you will be stoned!

POET. Or crucified. . . .

DAUGHTER OF INDRA (to the Poet). I shall go. . . . Follow me, and you shall learn the riddle.

POET. Which riddle?

DAUGHTER OF INDRA. What did he mean when he spoke of my gain?

POET. Probably nothing. What he said was what we call fatuous prattle. He just talked.

DAUGHTER OF INDRA. It was this that hurt me more than anything. . . .

POET. That's probably why he said it. People are like that. . . .

ALL THE RIGHTEOUS-MINDED. Hurrah! The door has been opened!

LORD CHANCELLOR. What was behind it?

GLAZIER. I don't see anything. . . .

LORD CHANCELLOR. You can't see anything? No, of course, you can't! Deans! What was hidden behind the door?

DEAN OF THEOLOGY. Nothing! That is the solution of the riddle of the world. . . . In the beginning God created heaven and earth out of nothing . . .

DEAN OF PHILOSOPHY. Out of nothing comes nothing . . .

DEAN OF MEDICINE. Nothing but nonsense—and that's nothing!

DEAN OF JURISPRUDENCE. I doubt. It is a clear case of fraud. I appeal to all the righteous-minded!

DAUGHTER OF INDRA *(to the Poet)*. Who are the righteous-minded?

POET. Well—tell me that—whoever can! All the righteous-minded are usually only one person. Today it may be I and my followers—tomorrow it may be you and yours. It is a position one is chosen for—or rather, one chooses oneself!

ALL THE RIGHTEOUS-MINDED. We have been deceived, defrauded!

LORD CHANCELLOR. Who has deceived you?

ALL THE RIGHTEOUS-MINDED. The Daughter of Indra!

LORD CHANCELLOR. Will the Daughter of Indra please tell us why she was so anxious to have this door opened?

DAUGHTER OF INDRA. No, my friends. . . . for if I did tell you, you would not believe me. . . .

DEAN OF MEDICINE. But there is nothing in there!

DAUGHTER OF INDRA. You speak the truth—yet you do not understand it.

DEAN OF MEDICINE. She is talking nonsense, rubbish!

ALL. Nonsense! Rubbish!

DAUGHTER OF INDRA *(to the Poet)*. They are to be pitied! . . .

POET. Are you speaking seriously?

DAUGHTER OF INDRA. I am always in earnest.

POET. Do you feel pity for the self-righteous, too?

DAUGHTER OF INDRA. I think I pity them most. . . .

POET. And the four faculties?

DAUGHTER OF INDRA. Yes, and not least them. Four heads, four minds—and all part of one body! Who created this monster?

ALL. She hasn't answered the Lord Chancellor's question. . . .

LORD CHANCELLOR. Then flog her!

DAUGHTER OF INDRA. I have already answered.

LORD CHANCELLOR. Listen—she is answering back! . . .

ALL. Beat her! Flog her! She is answering back. . . .

DAUGHTER OF INDRA. Whether she answers or doesn't answer, strike her, beat her! *(To the Poet.)* Come with me, Seer, and then I shall answer the riddle—but far away from here—out in the wilderness—where no one can hear us, no one can see us. *(The Attorney appears. He takes hold of the Daughter of Indra by the arm.)*

ATTORNEY. Have you forgotten your duties?

DAUGHTER OF INDRA. Oh God! No!—But I have other duties, higher duties, to perform. . . .

ATTORNEY. And your child?

DAUGHTER OF INDRA. My child. What more?

ATTORNEY. Your child is crying for you. . . .

DAUGHTER OF INDRA. My child! Woe to me! I am earth-bound! . . . And this pain in my breast, this dread, this anguish! . . . What is it?

ATTORNEY. And you don't know? . . .

DAUGHTER OF INDRA. No!

ATTORNEY. It is remorse—the pangs of conscience. . . .

DAUGHTER OF INDRA. Alas, is that my grieving conscience?

ATTORNEY. Yes!—Remorse sets in after every duty that has been neglected; after every pleasure indulged in, however innocent—if there *is* such a thing as an innocent pleasure; after every suffering inflicted upon others.

DAUGHTER OF INDRA. And is there no remedy for it?

ATTORNEY. Yes, there is a remedy—and only one! By fulfilling one's duties without hesitation. . . .

DAUGHTER OF INDRA. You look like a demon when you utter the word *duty!*—But I—I have not *one* duty—my duties are twofold—What am I to do?

ATTORNEY. You fulfill one at a time.

DAUGHTER OF INDRA. Then the highest duty first . . . and so: will you look after my child while I fulfill my duty? . . .

ATTORNEY. Your child will miss you, and will suffer. . . . Can you endure knowing that someone will suffer for your sake?

DAUGHTER OF INDRA. Now there is struggle in my soul . . . it seems to be cleaving in two—each part pulling away from the other. . . .

ATTORNEY. It is a mere sample of the disharmony that exists in life! Now you know how it feels! . . .

DAUGHTER OF INDRA. Oh! How it tugs and tears at my heart!

POET. If you knew . . . if you only suspected how much grief and devastation I have caused by fulfilling my calling—and note that I use the word calling, which is a higher, more sublime duty—then you would not touch my hand!

DAUGHTER OF INDRA. What have you done, then?

POET. I was an only son. My father cherished the hope that I would some day take over his business. But I ran away from business school. My father took it so to heart that he died. My mother, who was deeply religious, wanted me to be religious, too. I *could* not. . . . She disowned me. I had a friend who helped me through hard and trying days. This friend behaved like a tyrant toward those whose cause I had taken upon myself. I was compelled to strike down my friend and benefactor in order to save my soul! Ever since, I have had no peace. Now I am called scum, offal, infamous and lacking in honor! —And this despite the fact that my conscience tells me: "You were in the right!" For in the next moment it tells me: "You did wrong!"—That is the way life is. . . .

DAUGHTER OF INDRA. Come away with me—out into the wilderness!

ATTORNEY. What about your child?

DAUGHTER OF INDRA *(indicates all those who are present)*. These are my children! Individually they are good—but as soon as they get together with one another, they quarrel and become demons. . . . Farewell!

Outside the castle. The setting is the same as in the first scene in the early part of the play. Now, however, the ground, facing the foundation walls of the castle, is covered with flowers: blue monk's hood, or aconite.

Topmost on the roof of the castle, on its lantern, is seen a chrysanthemum bud about to open its petals. The castle windows are illuminated with tapers.

The Daughter of Indra and the Poet appear on the stage.

DAUGHTER OF INDRA. The moment for my ascent to the ether is not far off. . . . I shall have the help of fire. . . . It is this severance from Earth that you call death, and that you humans look forward to with fear. . . .

POET. Fear of the unknown . . .

DAUGHTER OF INDRA. That you have within you . . .

POET. Who has? . . .

DAUGHTER OF INDRA. All of you! Why do you put no faith in your prophets?

POET. Prophets have always been disbelieved! Why? . . . And—"if God has spoken, why will not men believe?" . . . Nothing can stand up against His Omnipotence. . . .

DAUGHTER OF INDRA. Have you always doubted?

POET. No—many a time I have felt certainty beyond doubt . . . but then it slipped away . . . like a dream on waking. . . .

DAUGHTER OF INDRA. It is not easy to be a mortal. . . .

POET. You have come to realize—and admit it?

DAUGHTER OF INDRA. I do. . . .

POET. Tell me—did not Indra once send His son down to Earth to probe the plaints and charges of mankind?

DAUGHTER OF INDRA. So He did—yes!—And how was He received?

POET. How did He fulfill His mission?—to answer with another question. . . .

DAUGHTER OF INDRA. And may I answer with still another? —Was not Man helped by His stay on Earth? Answer me truthfully!

POET. Helped?—Yes—in a measure . . . yet very little. . . . But instead of asking questions—will you not explain the riddle to me?

DAUGHTER OF INDRA. Yes—but how can it be of help to you? You will not believe me!

POET. I shall believe you, for I know who you are. . . .

DAUGHTER OF INDRA. Then I shall tell you. . . . In the early morning of Time—before the sun was born—Brahma, the divine force of all living things, allowed himself to be tempted by Maya, the Mother of the Universe, to propagate himself. This meeting of the divine primal force with the earth matter, constituted the fall of heaven into sin. Thus the universe, mankind, existence are merely a phantom, a dream, an illusion . . .

POET (ecstatically). My dream!

DAUGHTER OF INDRA. A dream of truth! . . . But Brahma's offspring seek to free themselves from the earthmatter through self-denial and suffering. . . . Thus suffering becomes the liberator. However, this yearning for suffering comes into conflict with the craving and the desire to find enjoyment—and love! Do you now understand what love is, with its mixture of the greatest in enjoyment and the greatest in suffering, the sweetest and the bitterest? Can you now understand what woman is? Woman—through whom sin and death came into being? . . .

POET. I can. . . . And where is the end?

DAUGHTER OF INDRA. You know the end. . . . The struggle between the pain that follows enjoyment and the pleasure that we take in suffering: between the penitent's torment and torture and the sensualist's dissipations. . . .

POET. And therefore strife?

DAUGHTER OF INDRA. Struggle between opposites produces energy—just as fire and water generate steam.

POET. But peace—and rest?

DAUGHTER OF INDRA. Hush! You must ask no more questions; and I must speak no more! . . . The altar is already adorned for the sacrifice: the flowers stand on guard, the tapers are lighted, white sheets are hung in the windows, twigs of spruce have been spread in the gateway. . . .

POET. You speak as calmly as though suffering did not exist for you!

DAUGHTER OF INDRA. As though it did not exist! . . . I have suffered all your sufferings hundredfold, for my sensibilities are so much more receptive. . . .

POET. Tell me your sorrows!

DAUGHTER OF INDRA. Could you, Poet, lay bare your own, frankly, candidly? Could your words, even once, for a fleeting moment, impart the full and true meaning of your thoughts?

POET. No—you are right! I have always seemed to myself a mere deaf-mute! The crowd always listened admiringly to my outpourings, but I could find them only hollow and empty. And so, you see, I felt ashamed when people acclaimed me and paid me homage. . . .

DAUGHTER OF INDRA. And yet you wish me to . . . Look me in the eye!

POET. I cannot endure your gaze!

DAUGHTER OF INDRA. How would you then be able to endure my words if I were to speak in my celestial tongue?

POET. But before you go, tell me what you suffered most from down here!

DAUGHTER OF INDRA. From being—from living—from feeling one's sight weakened by an eye, one's hearing impaired by an ear, and my thoughts—my luminous, enlightening, ethereal thoughts—bound up in a labyrinth of coiled slime! You have seen a brain, haven't you?—with its crooked, crawling, worming tracks and passages. . . .

POET. I have—and that's what makes all the righteous-minded think so crookedly. . . .

DAUGHTER OF INDRA. Malicious—always malicious! But you are all the same!

POET. How could we be otherwise?

DAUGHTER OF INDRA. Now I shake the dust off my feet—the dust, the earth, the clay. . . . (She removes her shoes and casts them in the fire.)

PORTRESS (enters. She places her shawl on the fire). You don't mind if I burn my shawl, too? (She leaves.)

OFFICER (enters). And here are my roses—with nothing but the thorns left. . . . (He, too, offers them to the flames.)

BILLPOSTER *(enters).* The posters you may have—but the dip-net—never! . . .

(He throws the posters into the fire.)

GLAZIER *(enters).* Take the diamond that opened the door! Farewell!

(He rushes out, after having sacrificed his diamond.)

ATTORNEY *(enters).* And here is the dossier containing the minutes of the great dispute concerning the pope's beard or the diminishing water supply in the sources of the Ganges River.

(He sacrifices the documents to the flames; then he leaves.)

QUARANTINE MASTER *(comes in).* Here is my contribution: the black mask which changed me into a blackamoor against my will. . . .

(He throws the mask into the fire.)

VICTORIA *(enters).* I offer you my beauty—my sorrow!

(She leaves.)

BLIND MAN *(enters. He thrusts his hand into the fire).* Having no eye to sacrifice, I give my hand!

DON JUAN *(enters in his wheelchair. He is followed by "She" and the Lover [the Major]).* Make haste, make haste! Life is short!

(He leaves together with the others.)

POET. I have read somewhere that when the end is near, all of life passes before us in one long cavalcade. . . . Is this the end for you?

DAUGHTER OF INDRA. Yes—it is the end! Farewell!

POET. Then speak a word before we part!

DAUGHTER OF INDRA. No—that I cannot! Could your words, do you think, truly image your thoughts?

DEAN OF THEOLOGY *(enters. He is in a raging temper).* God has disavowed me—I am persecuted by man—the government has deserted me—and I am the scorn of my colleagues! How can I keep my faith, when no one else has faith? How can I defend a God who does not defend his own? . . . It's rubbish —that's all it is!

(He flings a book into the fire and struts out.)

POET *(snatches the book from the flames).* Do you know what he threw into the fire?—A martyrology! A calendar with a martyr for each day of the year. . . .

DAUGHTER OF INDRA. A martyr?

POET. Yes—one who has suffered and been tortured to death for the sake of his faith! And can you tell me why? Do you

believe that all who endure pain, suffer? And that all who
are put to death, feel pain? Isn't it through suffering we gain
redemption from sin—and doesn't death give us deliverance
and set us free?

KRISTEN *(enters, carrying her strips of paper)*. I paste—I paste
—until every nook and cranny has been pasted over. . . .

POET. And if there were a cleft in heaven itself, you would
try to patch it with your tape. . . . Go away!

KRISTIN. Are there no double windows in the castle?

POET. No! That is one place where you won't find any!

KRISTIN *(turns to leave)*. Well, then I'll be going!

DAUGHTER OF INDRA. My life on earth is ending—it is time
to leave. . . .
Farewell, you mortal child, you poet-dreamer,
who—better than the rest—has learned to live. . . .
Borne upon wings, you soar to heights beyond this earth,
yet sometimes fall into the mire,
but don't get caught in it—you merely graze it!

Now that I leave, the loss of what has been,
what I have loved, and the remorse for things left *undone,*
arises in me, as—when parting from one's friends—
one says Godspeed to them, and to the places one holds
dear. . . .
Oh! In this moment I can feel the utter pain of *being,*
of *living,* and of being mortal. . . .
One misses even what was once disdained
and feels a guilt for wrongs that one did never do. . . .
One longs to leave—yet yearns to stay. . . .
Thus in a tug of war the heart is torn in twain
and feelings rent asunder by the beasts
of conflict, indecision, and disharmony. . . .
Farewell! And tell your earth-kin I shall never
forget them where I go—and I shall bring
their plaint to Indra—in your name. . . .
Farewell! . . .

*(She enters the castle. Music is heard. The background is
illuminated by the flames from the burning castle and reveals a wall of human faces—faces that are searching and
inquiring, sorrowful and grief-stricken, tortured by agony
and anguish. As the castle burns, the flower bud on the roof-
top opens into a chrysanthemum of giant proportions.)*

The Great Highway

A DRAMA OF A PILGRIMAGE, WITH SEVEN ROAD STOPS

❖ ❖ ❖

Strindberg has spoken of his last play as his farewell to life and his testament. It is written partly in prose, partly in unrhymed iambic verse. The leading character is the Hunter, the embodiment of Strindberg's own search for happiness, his lifelong pursuit of unattainable ideals, and his tragically passionate longing to find his own true self, his soul. It is divided into seven stations, or roadstops, along the highway of life, and may be symbolical of the Saviour's last seven words on the cross, the seven deadly sins, the seven ages of Man, or other parallels in which the magical seven figures.

Ostracized and alone, after having executed metaphorically himself for the sins of others as well as his own, the Hunter's restless soul is still bound to the earth, when, after struggling to gain ultimate freedom and eternal peace in the realms beyond, he finds himself near the pinnacle of an alpine mountain. While he is hesitating whether to proceed any farther, meditating that he has stayed too long among mankind, pawning his soul, his heart, and his thoughts, he meets the Hermit. He tells him that he loves mankind, loves men too much—and that is why he fears them. The Hermit counsels him to return to earth and live out his life, and adds some sage advice.

The Hunter's melancholy response characteristically portrays Strindberg's own confused and complex self:

I know it all too well. . . . If I could only
remain spectator, sit among the audience,
but I must ever be one of the actors on the stage;
and when I play a part—my memory fades,
and I forget just who I am. . . .

Although a hunter, he speaks of himself as a soldier, as he is constantly fighting to retain his personal integrity and independence. He is at war with evil forces, in order to be able to live as God has taught us to live—thus reaffirming his belief in the Almighty. He is crusading against the world and mankind because he has found them lacking in loyalty to the responsibility of Man's mission on earth, and he castigates men for their failure to hold life sacred. All in all, he has found life more bitter than death itself. He has arrived at the pessimistic conclusion that beauty cannot be made real in life and that all he has believed in has proved to be counterfeit and a de-

ception: that, therefore, he is really not the person he seems to
be, that he has been merely a masquerader.

He finds that the ideals the world professes are never practiced. Having in succession been a preacher, an architect, a
counselor-at-law, and a woodsman, he gave up life, became
socially dead, and continued his life spiritually. "I have belonged to that category of people," he says, "that believes what
a person says—without any doubt of his word." On encounter-
ing the Tempter at the end of the play, he refuses uncom-
promisingly to sell his soul, although promised all manner of
material reward. Instead he sets out to seek again the Land of
the Fulfilled Desires, bidding farewell to the world with these
Old Testament words:

> "And Elijah seated himself under the juniper tree, and he
> longed for death to come, and he said: 'This is enough!
> Take me unto You, O Lord!' "

And so, having had his fill of earthly pleasures and disil-
lusionments, he takes to the highway again, to reach the lofty
heights where the Hermit dwells, hoping that he will give him
"a resting place beneath the white and icy blanket." And turning his back on the world, he ends with a prayer and a
supplication, an appeal to the Almighty, for His blessing upon
mankind and himself, and with a self-confession that, like a
cry from a bleeding heart, sums up the tragedy of his remarkable, unhappy, and tormented life:

O bless me, bless Your humankind
that suffers—suffers from Your gift of life!
Me first, who's suffered most . . .
who's suffered most: from grief, from anguish,
not to be able to be as I wanted to be—
the one I longed to be! . . .

PERFORMANCE NOTES

The Great Highway, written and published in 1909, was
first produced at Strindberg's Intimate Theatre in Stockholm
on February 19, 1910. The production was not particularly
impressive. The play was next presented in 1924, at the Lorensberg Theatre in Gothenburg by Sandro Malmquist, with
Gabriel Alw as the Hunter. The play received a gala production in 1949 in commemoration of the author's centennial. In
this production at the Royal Theatre in Stockholm, Lars
Hanson excelled as the Hunter. On April 7 of the same year

the Swedish Royal Theatre Company gave a radio production of the play and a stage production at the National Theatre in Oslo on May 10. And a dramatic reading was given at the National Museum in Copenhagen in the same year.

Arvid Paulson's translation, the first one to be made into English, was given a public reading in February 1948 at the Rockland Foundation in Nyack, New York, and had its American stage première at the Pasadena Playhouse in Pasadena, California, on March 27, 1952. The production by Bobker Ben Ali won high praise for both producer and translator from the critic on *Variety,* who spoke of it as a brilliant translation "of exceptional verbal beauty." Mr. Paulson also read scenes from his translation on the radio in New York on the occasion of the hundredth anniversary of the dramatist's birth.

In London the play, translated by Elizabeth Sprigge and Lady Low, received a production at the experimental Watergate Theatre in the fall of 1950; the actors won praise for their performances although the play did not find much favor with the London reviewers.

✤

CHARACTERS

The Hunter
The Hermit
The Wanderer
The Miller A.
The Miller E.
The Wife of the Miller A.
The Girl
The Schoolmaster
The Smith
One of the People
A Waitress
The Organ-Grinder
The Photographer
Euphrosyne, his wife
Gotthard, their son
Klara, their daughter
The Japanese
Möller, the murderer
The Child
The Voice in the Dark (The Blind Woman)
The Tempter
Men, Women, and Children

✤

THE SEVEN ROAD STOPS

1. In the Alps.
2. By the windmills.
3. In Donkeyville.
4. A thoroughfare in the city of Tophet.
5. In the arbor outside the crematorium.
6. At the last gate.
7. The dark forest.

During the last road stop, Chopin's Thirteenth Nocturne, Opus 48, No. 1, is played softly in the distance until the fall of the curtain.

409

1. In the Alps. High up in the mountains. A signpost with two arms, one pointing upward, the other down.
    In the background are seen black thunderclouds. During the action of the scene a thunderstorm breaks out.

HUNTER *(enters; reads the sign)*. Where have I come—and
    how far up? . . .
Yes, this road leads me upward, that one down. . . .
It's not hard going down—but I will toward the heights. . . .
However, this guide here puts out his arm
as if to warn against the upward climb—
implying danger, many dangers,
upon the road that's steep and narrow. . . .
It does not frighten me who worships danger—
but first, I think I'll rest a little while,
take breath, relax,
collect myself, my thoughts—
and be myself again . . .
the self that has been stolen. . . .

I stayed too long down there among mankind
and put in pawn my soul,
my heart, and all my thoughts;
and what was left was purloined, too. . . .
They pinioned me with kindliness,
with gifts I never even desired. . . .
True, it was pleasant to be down there,
to go from home to home
and sit at festive tables,
with music, flowers, lights and wine . . .
but soon the warmth of it grew into choking heat. . . .

I tore myself, then, from my moorings,
threw overboard the ballast, all that weighed me down. . . .
What joy it was—for, lo, I rose!
Here I can breathe—the seed-leaves of my heart
can give an airing to my weather-beaten lungs . . .
no dust, no smoke, no breath from other human beings
can poison now my blood. . . .

You clean and pure white snow
of sublimated vapor! Water diamonds!
You, fairest lilies, frozen into stone from cold;
you, flour of the heavens, sifted through the hairnets of
    black clouds. . . .
You, hallowed silence, draw your silken blanket
and cover up the weary wanderer's head
when he with muted breath murmurs his good-night prayer!

What's in the north? A peak of slate,
a cloud that's like an unused blackboard
in a school . . . a rumble! Now the teacher comes—
and there's a hush throughout the class! . . .
All Nature's silent once He speaks—the Great Teacher! . . .
Behold! A flash of lightning, east to west,
now writes its name in ink of fire
on jet-blue cloud! I know You. . . .
Invisible, yet seen—and infinite;
austere—yet all-compassionate! . . .
The pine trees on the mountain bow,
the brooks stand still in deathlike muteness;
the mountain goat, in awe, falls to his knees,
baldheaded vulture, without crown, is crouched aloft
on alpine crest—and Nature trembles. . . .
I called the lord of all creation:
a name in jest of which I am not worthy.
I bow my head in shame, and blush—
the humblest one before the throne of Your omnipotence!

Behold, the cloud burst! The curtain spread—
it's drawn aside. . . . What do I see?
You beauteous Earth! You temptress,
who still attracts me to you. . . .
How you've adorned yourself—
in green of Hope and blue of Faith,
in rosy red of Love.
The stately pine trees, painted by the sunset,
the cypresses of tomb and night;
a crest, crowned with a marble temple—
whether of honor or good fortune must be seen;
a cave, home of some gray old sibyl,
who frights the nymphs within the olive grove. . . .

The sun appears! . . . How it sparkles
from rosy colored stones of frost; the clouds are edged

with silver bands—and blue-black hoods
are hung aloft for airing in the wind. . . .
What is it moves? Who shuts the sun out—
and draws a shadow picture in the snow?
Majestic eagle, golden-breasted chrysaëtos,
knight of the air, in gilded coat of mail,
with knighthood chain around his neck. . . .

What? Are you sinking down into the valley,
when wing has wearied, and the rudder-tail
has no more strength to force the flight aloft?
Yes, he would down! Down—down to rest,
and breathe the warm breath of humanity—
and feel the fragrance of the clover fields,
where summer still holds sway below. . . .
Down there the rain falls from the clouds like pearls—
and here like precious stones, like brilliants;
there the brook purls—here it is struck silent;
here barren snow wastes, with some white flowers—
down there below white daisies bloom . . .
up here, down there! Yes, hither and thither
are humans driven—to what is good, and what is bad. . . .

HERMIT *(enters).* Where are you bound? *Quo vadis,*[1]
    wanderer?
You've come halfway—and yet you look behind.
Excelsior was heretofore your watchword. . . .
    HUNTER. And still it is.
    HERMIT. What do you seek up here?
    HUNTER. Myself—which I've lost sight of down below. . . .
    HERMIT. What you have lost down there,
you don't expect to find again up here?
    HUNTER. Quite right . . .But if I should go back up there,
I'd lose still more—and never find what I am lacking.
    HERMIT. You are afraid to lose that skin of yours. . . .
    HUNTER. No, not my skin—my soul. . . .
    HERMIT. You do not love humanity. . . .
    HUNTER. Yes, much too much—that is why I fear
    humanity. . . .
    HERMIT. To love is to give: *give!*
    HUNTER. But people care not to receive—they take.
Not only take the gift—they take the giver, too.
    HERMIT. The shepherd gave himself for his flock. . . .

[1] *Quo Vadis.* Where are you going?

HUNTER. 'Tis true, dust turns to dust . . . but still the soul
belongs to God.

HERMIT. You fence well with your tongue and ought to take
up writing. . . .

In any case, your life is halfway past;
do not commit abortion: too early birth will not
make you into a man, a human being. . . .
Live out your life: descend once more—there is no danger;
the highway's dust you can brush off again;
the road is lined with ditches—if you fall into them,
climb out again! Where you find gates—
jump over, crawl beneath, or just unhook the latch;
when you meet people, take them close unto you—
they do not bite, but if they should, their bite's not dangerous;
if you get drenched—the water will run off.
Give of your earthly goods—you'll be rewarded. . . .
Up here there is not anything to gain—
for stone is stone, and snow is snow. . . .
But humans—that's another matter.

HUNTER. I know it all too well. . . . If I could only
remain spectator, sit among the audience,
but I must ever be one of the actors on the stage;
and when I play a part—my memory fades,
and I forget just who I am. . . .

HERMIT. Who are you?

HUNTER. Enough! Now let us end it. . . .
Besides, it's getting much too cold for me up here.

HERMIT. And somewhat thin the air—and much too
lonely. . . .
Watch out, I see a stranger coming!

HUNTER. A curious fellow! Comes from up above—
looks rather worn out. . . . Halt a moment, wanderer!

WANDERER. I'm coming from the summit of the Alps;
have bathed in air—but now have finished bathing
and dressed myself, soon to be off again,
with or without companions—preferably with
What is the name of yonder distant land, Hermit?

HERMIT. It's called the Land of Desires.

WANDERER. The Land of Pious Desires?

HERMIT. Of pious and of unrestrained desires,
according to . . .

WANDERER. . . . whatever they may be.
So . . . here I find companions, I can see . . .

with whom have I the honor . . . ?

HUNTER. I am a soldier. . . .

WANDERER. And I a wanderer. . . .
Take my advice: one travels best incognito;
for—while it's safe enough to be acquainted—
it's never wise to get to know a person;
nor does one ever, for that matter—
One only thinks one does. . . . Therefore:
in company, with neither animosity nor friendship,
two steps apart, and not too close—
advance! And downward—to the level highway!
A hillside up, and down a slope—
a bar, a halt, a little drink . . .
but keeping straight to south the course!
*(While the Wanderer has been speaking, the Hermit is seen
continuing his journey upward.)*

HUNTER. With the sun as beacon, we can't stray. . . .
It never dies—and its custodian never sleeps. . . .
(He looks around for the Hermit.)
I believe he's left us, our hermit?

WANDERER. Well, let him go—for he does not belong
down there where we are going.
He's made his choice and taken leave of this world. . . .

HUNTER *(gazing aloft)*. Perhaps he has done right. . . .

WANDERER. Do not look in that direction!
For "earth" and "insanity" rhyme with "mirth" and "vanity,"
just as "thither" rhymes with "hither". . . .
But we are not going thither, but—hither!

2. *By the windmills. The background shows a gloomy sky.
On each side of the stage is seen a windmill: the one named
Adam and the other one Eve.
To the left, a roadhouse or tavern.
The Hunter and the Wanderer are seated at a table, out-
side, each one with a glass before him.*

WANDERER. It's peaceful down here in the valley.

HUNTER. A little too peaceful, thinks the miller . . .

WANDERER. . . . who sleeps, no matter how hard the water
runs . . .

HUNTER. . . . because he is always on the alert for wind and
weather. . . .

WANDERER. . . . which useless pursuit has awakened in me a
certain antipathy to windmills. . .

HUNTER. . . . just as it did in the noble knight Don Quixote of la Mancha . . .

WANDERER. . . . who never, however, became a turncoat because of the way the wind blew . . .

HUNTER. . . . but rather the opposite . . .

WANDERER. . . . which was the reason for his getting into perplexing situations. What are we doing—playing a game?

HUNTER. Mr. Incognito, why do you drink so much?

WANDERER. Because I am forever on the operating table—and so I have to anaesthetize myself.

HUNTER. Then I'll ask no more questions.

WANDERER. Perhaps I have already said too much.

HUNTER. Imagine—I can't guess what you are by profession. . . .

WANDERER. Stop guessing—it is much more fun.

HUNTER. I am inclined to agree with you. It has been a day of gloom, hasn't it? And it looks as if it would be gloomy for the rest of the day.

WANDERER. Just let me get a few drinks inside me, and you'll see how much brighter it gets . . . *(He drinks.)* You know Greek? Do you know what *oinos* means?

HUNTER. *Oinos* is wine.

WANDERER. Yes, it's wine. . . . You have studied, evidently.

HUNTER. *Noli me tangere!* Don't touch me! I have stingers. . . .

WANDERER. Have you noticed that the fruit of the grape vine resembles a bottle, and the tendrils a corkscrew? It is a characteristic signature, isn't it?

HUNTER. But its juice has none of the properties of an anaesthetic . . .

WANDERER. . . . until the fruit has been trampled under foot and has putrefied in dregs and dirt . . .

HUNTER. . . . and so the spirit of the vine has been liberated from its filthy encasement . . .

WANDERER. . . . when it rises to the surface like the foam of the sea . . .

HUNTER. . . . from out of which Aphrodite was born . . .

WANDERER. . . . naked.

HUNTER. Without even a vine leaf for covering . . .

WANDERER. . . . for covering of the body is but a consequence of the fall of man. Are you always so serious as this?

HUNTER. Do you always jest in this manner?

WANDERER. Which one of us is the more curious?

HUNTER. Now you are stretching out your imprisoning tentacles . . .

WANDERER. . . . animated by the common law of attraction . . .

HUNTER. . . . and followed by a mutual feeling of repulsion . . .

WANDERER. . . . because of which it is best to keep a distance of two paces and march ahead in single file . . .

HUNTER. . . . according to agreement as made on this day and date as of above. . . . Period. . . . Here come the actors. . . .

WANDERER. May I borrow your glasses? . . . I don't see very well. (*The Hunter hands his glasses to the Wanderer, who continues to speak.*)
What do I see on the lens? It looks like hoarfrost,
like water crystallized, salt from the sea . . .
a tear that's dried—hot from its source,
it cooled so quickly it turned into rock salt . . .
the steel, of which the rim is made, has rusted:
he often weeps—but ever secretly;
the flowing tears have dug their furrows
from eye to smiling wrinkles of the mouth—
to stifle merriment, keep it from being lit in laughter.
Poor human being!
Your mask is worn to tatters . . .
and when you show your teeth,
one does not know if it's to bite or smile. . . .

HUNTER. And now the play begins! An idyl in a setting of windmills . . .

WANDERER. A pastoral in minor-major; watch it closely now! . . .

MILLER A. Well, neighbor, today we are even, as there isn't a sign of wind—but just the same you are going to move your mill, for you are encroaching on my business.

MILLER E. You mean to say that I take the east wind from you—but since you take the west wind from me, we are just about quits.

MILLER A. But I had my mill here first, and you built yours out of sheer spite. Now that it's going badly for us both, don't you think it would be better if it went well for one of us?

MILLER E. You mean for you?

MILLER A. You mean for you?

MILLER E. Yes, that's just what I mean.

MILLER A. But I meant the one of us—who deserves it most, the one who has the right on his side.

MILLER E. And who is that?

MILLER A. Do you think it is fair for us to judge in such a matter?

MILLER E. I have a better grain-sieve than you have—and my Eve there does the grinding faster, she can make quicker turns, and she has brand-new sails.

MILLER A. But my Adam was built before your Eve, and my millhopper is made of boxwood, and . . .

MILLER E. Hold on! We'll ask the two gentlemen sitting over there . . .

WANDERER. Oho! Now *we'll* be getting into this! . . .

HUNTER. They will want to abduct us as witnesses, and perhaps as judges—and then sit in judgment on our decision. . .

WIFE OF MILLER A (enters). Come and have your dinner now, old man!

MILLER A. Wait a while. . . .

WIFE OF MILLER A. I can't wait.

MILLER A. You have to learn never to be in a hurry.

WIFE OF MILLER A. Never . . . ?

MILLER A. Never—as long as the world exists, and a word is a word.

WIFE OF MILLER A. But the cabbage will get cold. . . .

MILLER A. Have you cabbage today? Well, why didn't you say so? I'll be coming right away. . . .

WIFE OF MILLER A. But then the world will be topsy-turvy, and a word will no longer be worth anything. . . .

MILLER A. Did I say that? Then I take it back. . . .

(Miller A. and his wife go out.)

WANDERER. He sold his birthright . . .

HUNTER. . . . for a dish of cabbage.

WANDERER. And that is as much as it mattered to him.

HUNTER. But now we will get the miller, who owns that Eve there, on us. Look how he circles and zigzags and weaves his way toward us . . . he wants us to do some sort of favor for him—is angling for some information to add to what he already knows. Now he is setting his course straight on us—he scrutinizes us with his eyes, inspects our clothes, shoes, hair and features. The man is a thief. . . .

MILLER E (approaches the Hunter and the Wanderer). Excuse me . . .

WANDERER (in an undertone to the Hunter). He is going to try to entice us into talking. Don't answer him.

MILLER E. From where do you gentlemen come?

WANDERER. That's none of your business.

MILLER E. Strictly speaking, no. . . .

WANDERER. We are strictly restrictive today, so you had better be on your way.

MILLER E. I am not going to steal anything.

WANDERER. No, you wouldn't find it an easy matter. . . .

MILLER E. On the contrary, I was thinking of giving you something. . . .

WANDERER. We don't need anything.

MILLER E. I'll be damned! . . . Indeed, I was thinking of giving you gentlemen something—for which I expect nothing in return—some information! Some valuable information at that! (*There is a pause.*) What I was going to say was that they are about to blow up a rock right behind you (*Pause.*) . . . and one, two, three—we'll have a shower of stones raining on our heads. (*The Wanderer and the Hunter rise.*)

WANDERER. Why didn't you say so in the first place?

MILLER E. You didn't want to listen. . . . But don't be in a hurry, for the blasters will yell out a caution first.

WANDERER. Tell me, is this the road to the Promised Land?

MILLER E. This is the straight road. . . .

WANDERER. How is the weather going to be this afternoon?

MILLER E. We can expect more thunder and rain. The weather is very uncertain round here.

WANDERER. Is it so the year round?

MILLER E. Always undependable—the whole year, year in and year out.

WANDERER. And what is the name of the village beyond?

MILLER E. (*with suddenly changed demeanor*). That's none of your business! I dare say there is more joy in giving than in receiving, but to be robbed is no fun. Thief—where is your passport?

WANDERER. What do I want with a passport?

MILLER E. Oh yes, there have been bandits in the forest, and anybody who doesn't want to give information as to where he comes from, has to be searched.

HUNTER. Oho! Now we are mixed up in something . . .

WANDERER. In something that isn't exactly a mill romance.

MILLER E. I am going to get my neighbor and his farmhands now, and then we'll soon find out if you have an alibi.

WANDERER. This is a peculiar way to . . .

MILLER E. Yes . . . because I am the parish constable and my neighbor is on the jury. . . .   (*He goes out.*)

WANDERER. And now they'll be friends—Herod and Pilate!

HUNTER. I really set out to save my own life; but he who will save his life, he shall lose it. So let us throw ourselves into the tumult again . . .

WANDERER. . . . and risk sinking . . .

HUNTER. . . . without going to the bottom . . .

WANDERER. . . . thanks to a certain life buoy that sensible persons attach to themselves! There—there she is—the woman.

(The Girl enters.)

HUNTER. Close to Adam and Eve—as might be expected . . .

WANDERER. . . . without any prospect of finding a paradise.

HUNTER. Period! Now it begins. . . .

WANDERER. I think the offensive should be more advantageous. What is your name, my lovely child?

GIRL. Guess!

WANDERER. Let me see. . . . Blonde, daughter of a miller, short, round-faced . . . Your name is Amalia!

GIRL. How did you know?

WANDERER. I could tell by your looks!

GIRL. Had I been dark, tall, and lean-faced—what would my name have been as the daughter of a smith?

WANDERER. Jenny, of course.

GIRL. That's right.

WANDERER. Now that I have taught you something—what do I get for it?

GIRL. I'll let you—tell me where you acquired all this wisdom to read people's minds.

WANDERER. Life, experience, certain books, an inherited superior mind, and a goodly portion of acquired keenness of vision. . . . Tell me, why don't you like to marry your neighbor the miller's son?

GIRL. You know that, too . . .?

WANDERER. But you ought to take him—and so the mill question would be settled without litigation; then you can sell one of the mills here and have it moved to the adjoining county, where it is needed.

GIRL. How wise you are—how wise. . . .

WANDERER. But I can see you don't want the miller's son— I have a sneaking suspicion you would rather have one of the brigands in the forest, isn't that so? The one with the black eyes and the large mustache. . . .

GIRL. Now I am getting to be afraid of you. Are you a fortuneteller?

WANDERER. As you can hear. But I can only tell the fortunes of young people.

GIRL. How is that?

WANDERER. Because old people are so crafty.

GIRL *(to the Hunter)*. Is that really true?

WANDERER. Don't speak to him. He does not wish to be brought into this. . . . Speak to me. . . . Give me something in return for all the things you have learned in these brief few moments—otherwise you will remain in my debt. . . . And that you don't want. . . .

GIRL. No. . . . Yes, I will give you something in return, so that you will go away from here rewarded—richer than when you came—laden with knowledge for which I make no charge. . . .

WANDERER. The devil you say!

GIRL. First of all, my name is not Amalia. . . .

WANDERER. It's Jenny—what did I tell you?

GIRL. No, and it is not Jenny, either! Secondly, the two millers here have no son. Thirdly, there are four windmills in the neighboring county, and so the mill question here remains unsettled. Furthermore, I'll throw in a piece of advice, or two, for you. Don't start off by being familiar with a girl you never met before. You can never know with whom you are speaking, no matter how keen visioned you may think you are. And lastly, don't be disloyal to a friend merely because someone else comes along—for when you are alone again and need him, he may not be within reach.

WANDERER. I have not been disloyal. . . .

GIRL. Oh yes, you tried to ridicule him just now in order to gain favor with me—and that wasn't very nice. Now you are on the defensive . . . and if you asked me my name now, I wouldn't answer as you answered the miller a while ago, when he wanted to save you from the brigands in the forest. . . .

HUNTER *(rises)*. Wouldn't the young lady like to sit down?

GIRL. Yes, I am a lady—from the manor house—and not the miller's daughter. *(To the Wanderer.)* Go inside to the miller now and tell him I sent you. He will give you your passport. Go now—just tell him the young lady . . .

WANDERER. But I must know your name. . . .

GIRL *(seats herself)*. I don't give my name to persons I do not know; and if you had any principles, you wouldn't have asked it. . . . There's the way. . . .

(The Wanderer goes out.)

(The Hunter and the Girl are alone.)

GIRL. Life's pleasant, good to you who travel
and meet so many, learn to know so many. . . .
HUNTER. Well, learn to know . . .
GIRL. True—that one doesn't. . . .
But get acquainted. . . .
HUNTER. Scarcely that; but guessing riddles
is a pastime also. . . .
GIRL. For what people say
has not much core or kernel in it!
HUNTER. Ah! It has to be translated;
for every language might be called a strange one—
and strangers are we, and remain unto each other.
We travel all incognito.
GIRL. And to ourselves remain the unknown quantity!
You bear a sorrow—but are not in mourning. . . .
HUNTER. And you are dressed as mill-girl—yet you are a lady!
GIRL. And what about your comrade?
HUNTER. But an acquaintance, yet completely unknown.
GIRL. What is your opinion of that man?
HUNTER. Everything, and nothing.
I have not added him together yet. . . .
GIRL. What did you do up there?
HUNTER. Forgot—and took a breathing spell.
GIRL. But why forget? For without memories
our life would be an empty nothingness . . .
HUNTER. And with them—a cargo that could sink the ship . . .
GIRL. . . . an empty ship is easy prey to winds . . .
HUNTER. . . . and that is why one takes on ballast . . .
GIRL. . . . and hoists in sails . . .
HUNTER. . . . as on a windmill . . .
GIRL. . . . else there is danger that the wings be broken . . .
HUNTER. . . . yet on the heights they spin round best . . .
GIRL. . . . but best of all down in the valleys of the plains . . .
HUNTER. . . . down where the air lies heavy . . .
GIRL. . . . so heavy one can see for miles,
can count the village steeples with the naked eye,
and, in the dark of night, see all the stars. . . .
HUNTER. But not on the horizon. . . .
GIRL. No, but in zenith . . .
and zenith you have everywhere, when you have come
to the horizon. . . .
HUNTER. But will I ever reach it?
GIRL. The place you sought, you now have reached
this very day, this morning. Is it not sweet

to gain the new, when you possess the old already?
    HUNTER. But what about the distant land?
    GIRL. Continue, and you'll reach it . . .
but if you weary, it will disappear. . . .
No mortal's ever had the polar star in zenith—[2]
still they set out to reach it, and turn round,
and others vainly try again, and are repelled. . . .
Do you as they—but learn throughout the struggle!
    HUNTER. One dredges, grapples, with one's nose in nadir. . . .
    GIRL. But now and then the eye in zenith! . . .
    (Signals from a horn are heard.)
    HUNTER *(alertly)*. Listen!
    GIRL. I hear, but don't know what it means. . . .
    HUNTER. I will translate it. . . .
You hear but sounds—while I hear words. . . .
    GIRL. What does the horn speak?
    HUNTER. "Give answer where you are—where are you?"
    (The answer comes from the horn: "Here!")
    GIRL. Someone is calling you. . . .
    (Another signal is heard.)
    HUNTER. "Come here to me, come here to me, come here
        to me! Come here!"
    GIRL. I hear you are a soldier—rather see it . . .
they're calling you. . . . No sooner have we met than we
    must part!
    HUNTER. Not quite so soon, nor without pain. . . .
Come with me on my way a piece—
unto the town beyond!
    GIRL. And your companion?
    HUNTER. Oh, such you find in any barroom.
    GIRL. How cruel you are!
    HUNTER. I'm making war!
In war the word is *forward*—not *to stay behind!*
    GIRL. That's why I, too, go; otherwise—I stay behind!
    HUNTER. And if you leave, you take something away with you.
    GIRL. And if I stay—then you have taken something that
    is mine! . . .
    HUNTER *(gazing into the distance)*. Look there! A quarrel!
In a moment there will be a fight . . .
they're fighting. . . . Now they'll call me as a witness!
But you must go—must not become involved.

[2] *Polar Star in zenith. The Great Highway* was written in 1909 before Peary
reached the North Pole and the news of his and Dr. Cook's claims had been
announced to the world.

GIRL. You can find time to think of me!

HUNTER. Not only of you, for you—
but with you, through you!—And now, farewell!
(She starts to leave.)
An unplucked flower, seen through garden lattice work,
gives by its beauty to the wanderer a moment's joy,
then sends its fragrance out upon the wind
for but a fleeting second—and that is—the end. . . .
And now—now forward!

GIRL. Farewell—and forward then! *(She leaves.)*

HUNTER. Now I am down! . . . In fetters chained,
ensnared in clutches of the legal windmill,
with net of sentimental waste on slender wings,
in an affair that concerns me not. . . .

WANDERER *(enters)*. Are you still here? I thought you had
left. You must be a faithful soul.

HUNTER. Did you get yourself into a fight?

WANDERER. I gave the miller a smack on the jaw because he
had poked fun at me. All that about blasting a rock in the
mountain and about bandits in the forest was a lie. Now we
are both summoned to appear in court in the autumn, I as a defendant and you as witness.

HUNTER. Then you gave them our names?

WANDERER. No, I invented a couple—in the twinkling of an
eye.

HUNTER. How dared you? Now we may be dragged into a
falsification action also. . . . To get mixed up in a business
like this!—Who did you say I was?

WANDERER. I said you were traveling under the name of Incognito. . . . And those fools swallowed it!

HUNTER. And now I am going to testify against you?

WANDERER. In three months, yes. . . . So let us use our
freedom meanwhile and proceed on our journey. . . . I understand they are celebrating a festival in the next village.

HUNTER. What kind of festival?

WANDERER. Some sort of *jeux floraux,* or donkey festival—
where the greatest jackass in the village is crowned with a
gilded coronet of cardboard. . . .

HUNTER. That's precious! What's the name of the village?

WANDERER. They call it Donkeyville. The one in which we
are now is called Prevarication—because all the inhabitants in
it are liars.

HUNTER. *Enteuthen exelaunei* [3]—and from there he marched on. . . .

WANDERER. *Parasangas trêis*—three leagues. . . .

HUNTER. And so they marched. . . .

3. In Donkeyville. [4] *To the right, a smithy; to the left, a bench, on which the Hunter and the Wanderer are seated inconspicuously in the shade.*

HUNTER. Now we have walked together for quite a distance . . .

WANDERER. . . . and not come any closer to each other; not even close enough for me to have any idea who you are.

HUNTER. I am a soldier, I have told you—for I am constantly fighting, fighting to keep my personal independence . .

WANDERER. . . . but not always winning the victory.

HUNTER. That's too much to expect. . . .

WANDERER. Especially since the defeats are the more instructive . . .

HUNTER. . . . for the victor . . .

WANDERER. . . . but the worst of it is that one does not always know who is the victor; for in the last war the victor lost most.

HUNTER. Which war?

WANDERER. By the windmills!

HUNTER. May I borrow your penknife? I lost mine up in the mountains.

WANDERER. We must have no inquisitiveness!—If you, for instance, regard this knife, you'll find it has quite a story to tell. This large blade is almost unused—the owner can't be engaged in any craft consequently. The small blade, on the other hand, shows traces of lead pencil and different colored crayons; so he might be an artist—though he need be nothing more than an amateur. The corkscrew has seen much use—you can feel that; the bottle-opener likewise. But then there is a drill and a saw! Yes—and here is a pick appended . . . that speaks a more eloquent language, though in this case it was only thrown into the bargain, for the price of the knife. So you see, you didn't get much intelligence from the knife!

HUNTER. So . . . this is Donkeyville! And here comes the

[3] *Enteuthen exelaunei.* Literally: thence he marched. A phrase that is recurrent throughout Xenophon's *Anabasis.*

[4] *Donkeyville.* In his *The Blue Books* Strindberg relates how he once during his travels in Denmark came to a village which in reality was an institution for the demented.

schoolmaster. . . . This time we must keep our mouths shut, so we won't get into any trouble.

WANDERER. If that does any good . . .

SCHOOLMASTER[5] *(enters).* Abra-cadabra, abracadabra, ab-ra-ca-dab-ra. *(He gazes at the strangers.)* No! They didn't hear. . . . Once more! Abra-cadabra—abracadabra—abra-cadabra!—No! They must be thoroughbreds, gentlefolk: they have self-control!—Gentlemen, he who keeps silent, assents; now I shall ask if you gentlemen would like to receive a deputation of the foremost intellectuals in the village who will challenge you gentlemen to a duel of words. If I don't get an answer, I'll consider the question decided in the affirmative. . . . One, two, three!

HUNTER *and* WANDERER *(in the same breath).* No!

SCHOOLMASTER. Splendid!

WANDERER. Considering you are from Donkeyville, my dear man, you are not so stupid.

SCHOOLMASTER. I am the only sane man in the village, that's why I must act the part of a fool, otherwise they would lock me up. I have an academic education, I have written a tragedy in five acts, in verse, entitled *Potamogeton*[6]—it is so damnably silly that it should have brought me the prize; but the village blacksmith surpassed me by turning out a memorial poem in honor of *The Devastator of the Nation*—and so I was passed by. Yes, I am one of those who have been left by the wayside. . . . No doubt you gentlemen think I am subjectively inclined because I talk about myself, but there are two reasons for it: firstly, I must introduce myself; secondly, you gentlemen wouldn't like me to talk about you!—Here comes the village smith. I have to disguise myself, or he might think I am sane —and then he would lock me up. *(He puts on a pair of donkey ears.)*

SMITH[7] *(enters).* Abra-ca-dab-ra, abra-cadabra!

SCHOOLMASTER. Greetings, Mr. Sledgehammer-handle!

[5] *Schoolmaster.* In his character Strindberg lampoons a former friend, Axel Klinckowström, whose tragedy *Olof Trätälja* was awarded The Swedish Academy's *grand prix* in 1907. Olof Trätälja was the son of an Uppsala king. He established a kingdom of his own in western Sweden, close to the Norwegian border, and is mentioned in some of the Icelandic sagas.

[6] *Potamogeton.* A genus of aquatic plants of the pondweed family, growing in fresh and brackish water. The word is used satirically by Strindberg as the title of The Schoolmaster's poetic tragedy.

[7] *Smith.* Strindberg caricatures in this rôle Verner von Heidenstam, recipient of the Nobel Prize for Literature in 1916 and author of *Karolinerna* (published in America by The American-Scandinavian Foundation under the title *The Charles Men*). Strindberg and von Heidenstam were close friends for nearly three decades but became estranged in 1909, shortly before this play was written.

SMITH. Is that supposed to be a gibe at me?

SCHOOLMASTER. Yes, life is a struggle. We all have to struggle.

SMITH. Do you refer to the emancipation question, or the free tariff?

SCHOOLMASTER. Two times two is four, and if you add six, it makes eight. You agree . . . ?

SMITH. I reserve the right to all arithmetic, for that's my major subject, next to *quatuor species,* which means the four rules of arithmetic in whole numbers, including fractions—with the exception of ordinary whole fractions and decimal fractions.

SCHOOLMASTER. Sometimes even the good Homer falls asleep . . .

SMITH. But six and four makes eleven, and if you place the comma two spaces to the left, it makes it even as a nail. Isn't that right, gentlemen? Am I not right?

WANDERER. Absolutely correct. Six and four makes eleven, and not eight.

SMITH. Now let us pass on to the lighter constituents, or, as I might say, the conversational subjects. Gentlemen, conversation is not blown out of the nose, if I may so express myself, even though the subject for conversation may be light. A light conversational subject may—on closer inspection—be divided into two equally great parts. First comes the subject—there must be a subject in all conversation—and then follows the conversation as if by itself. Again the subjects can be as numerous as . . . as there are days in the year, or even more —let us say, the drops of water in the sea, or even more—let us say, the sands in the desert . . . while I have never been in a desert, I have a vivid picture of what it looks like; but, on the other hand, I once took a boat trip—it was very expensive, gentlemen . . . I only tell you in case you have never taken one . . . but that wasn't what I wanted to say . . .

SCHOOLMASTER. The Guano islands are situated at 56 degrees longitude, north, and 13 degrees east to east, due south.

SMITH. Is that supposed to be a gibe at me? I don't like gibes. . . .

SCHOOLMASTER. But that's nothing in comparison with Carolus the Great! [8]

---

[8] *Carolus the Great.* Charles XII of Sweden, during whose reign (1697-1718) his country was almost continuously embroiled in war. A great and brave soldier who won many victories in the face of tremendous odds. His defeat by the Russians caused the Swedish nation's impoverishment. He was killed during his invasion of Norway.

SMITH. No, but it's harder to shoe an ambler so he won't wear out his shoes at the edges.

SCHOOLMASTER. Hafiz[9] says for that reason very justly in volume 3, on page 78, as follows: "Eat, man! Eat! You don't know when you'll be back on earth again!"

SMITH. I just want to inform you that the word page is called *pagina* in Latin, just as you say Carolina, China, etcetera. Am I not right, perhaps—it's pronounced *pagee-ina,* isn't it?

SCHOOLMASTER. Yes, yes, yes . . .

SMITH. Right is right—that's my principle. Do you know, Mr. Schoolmaster, when Julius Caesar[10] was born? This time I'll catch you!

SCHOOLMASTER. In the year 99 before Christ!

SMITH. Before Christ was born? That's impossible, because the calendar only begins in the year I—and you can't count backward. Isn't that so?

SCHOOLMASTER. What do you mean—you can't count backward?

SMITH. Watch out, now! Don't start any arguments! Watch out, I say! You are so light in the head that something might happen to you!—Can you tell me, Mr. Schoolmaster, what is the difference between rye and wheat?

SCHOOLMASTER. Julius Caesar was born in 99 and died in 31 . . .

SMITH. Listen now! What kind of sense is that? Are you trying to tell me he lived backward?—The difference between rye and wheat is, first of all, the price of grain, or the market price; secondly, it is the free tariff, because rye is protected by duty, and there is no duty on wheat! Didn't I do that well?

SCHOOLMASTER. Yes, yes, yes . . .

SMITH. But the monetary standard—that's something else again! I am a silver man[11], and I don't deny it; and the stock exchange—that's something else again; and official quotations —that's still something else; and agio is something else again.

SCHOOLMASTER. What is it?

SMITH. What is it? Need I stand here and explain that?

---

[9] *Hafiz.* The most renowned of Persian lyric poets. The year of his birth is unknown; he died approximately 1388.

[10] *Julius Caesar.* Caius Julius Caesar was born 100 B.C.; assassinated in 44 B.C. Strindberg ridicules The Schoolmaster's professed learning by having him give erroneous and absurd answers to The Smith's questions. Similarly he discloses The Smith's mental weakness through the remarks the latter makes throughout the scene in Donkeyville.

[11] *Silver man.* One who advocates the free and unlimited coinage of silver at a ratio with gold of 16 to 1; or, one who supports the advocacy of the free coinage of silver.

Haven't I got other things to do? Haven't I made my contribution to society—am I not a married man? I only ask you! I only ask! If any one has anything to say, I'll speak to him in private—in private! You know what that means—or don't you? Behind the stables. Don't say a word—I won't stand for being answered—don't answer me back, ever. Do you consider all these questions concluded now in my favor, or do you want to come behind the stables with me? I am a very serious-minded man, but I am not one to fool with!—Now, gentlemen, do you know what kind of an ass you have before you— I am not speaking of myself but the Schoolmaster—who thinks we can be born before the chronological beginning of time! But I want you to know exactly what kind of man he is! He is the stupidest ass that ever walked in a pair of shoes. He is so asinine he thinks there are Guano islands—now, how could there ever be Guano islands, I ask you! *(He takes out a flask and gulps down some of its contents.)* He doesn't know the difference between rye and wheat—and he drinks, too. Perhaps you think I too drink, but I only take one as I jog along—and you can't call that boozing, for that's something else.—Gentlemen, knowledge is a virtue, but the Schoolmaster is an ignoramus; he doesn't know a thing—and such a man has been placed in charge of bringing up children . . . but he is a despot, too, a tyrant—a poor wretch who is greedy for power, and always full of fight. Now you know what he is!

WANDERER. Just a moment! I don't exactly mean to answer you, for then you'll want to fight. I don't mean to question you, for then your knowledge would prove itself defective. I don't intend to ask you to have a drink, for that isn't necessary—just as I don't care to argue with you, for you wouldn't understand what I meant, and you would never admit I was right—but I would like to ask you one question.

SMITH. Go ahead and ask—but ask in a nice way!

WANDERER. You are a character, aren't you?

SMITH. I am a true character, a genuine character—in a word, full of character.

WANDERER. And you are a silver man, besides?

SMITH. I am proud to be called a silver man.

WANDERER. You don't acknowledge gold as a standard in the world trade?

SMITH.No! No gold!

WANDERER. Not even for personal use?

SMITH. I have to give that some thought! *(Aside.)* Is he trying to swindle me on the exchange? *(Aloud.)* I won't answer that

one! I won't answer. . . . No one can compel me to answer
—and though my understanding is perfect, I haven't the faintest idea what you are driving at!—In spite of it!

WANDERER. In spite of it! Are you afraid your firmness of
character would not survive in the test?

SMITH. Are you sitting there talking behind my back? Don't
do that, because I am an absolute dictator in this village. I
am a despot! *(The Wanderer laughs.)* Don't you look at me
like that, for I am a dangerous despot.

WANDERER. I wasn't looking at you. I only laughed.

SMITH. Don't laugh! I vote in this district for six thousand
—and that's nothing to laugh at! I have five children, all well
brought up, greatly talented, especially gifted in the head—
two of them are in America, however . . . yes! That's the way
things go . . . and one of them has gone wrong—but he has
made up for that, so that's nothing to speak about, nothing
at all . . .

WANDERER *(aside to the Hunter).* He is precious, isn't he?

HUNTER. But it must have an end! I suffocate!

SMITH. I'll just go and get my manuscript, then the festivities
can commence! But you gentlemen must not leave. I am the
burgomaster here, and my word is law. The Schoolmaster will
read from his tragedy *Potamogeton* in the meantime. It isn't so
bad considering it's by an amateur—but many hounds soon put
an end to the hare, as the saying goes. . . .

SCHOOLMASTER. And the verses run along by themselves, just
like gangling goslings . . .

SMITH. Was that a gibe at me?

SCHOOLMASTER. How could it be? You are a grown man,
aren't you, Mr. Blacksmith?

SMITH. Full-fledged is the word you should use when you
speak about birds. Read nicely now for these gentlemen—I'll
be back immediately. But don't slander me while I am gone.

WANDERER. But he can't very well slander you when you are
present, can he?

SMITH. No, that's true—and having to choose between two
evils, one chooses the best. . . . So—slander me while I am
gone, but not while I am present.   *(He leaves.)*

WANDERER. What kind of village is this? Is it an institution?

SCHOOLMASTER. Yes—they are so mean that they have gone
crazy.

WANDERER. Are you under supervision here?

SCHOOLMASTER. They have placed me under supervision because they suspect me of being sane.

WANDERER. Why don't you escape and come along with us, then?

SCHOOLMASTER. Then they would catch us all three.

WANDERER. It isn't only stupidity, then?

SCHOOLMASTER. Evil is the mother of lunacy—and at the same time its offspring.

WANDERER. Who is this blacksmith?

SCHOOLMASTER. He is the kind of soiled god of whom Isaiah speaks. He is a composite of the others' wickedness, envy, hatred, and lies. The Smith became burgomaster because the baker was the one best fitted for the office; when I had served faithfully for twenty-five years, the day was celebrated with festivities and a banquet for the Smith; and at the last donkey festival the Smith was crowned poet laureate because he had composed the worst poetry.

HUNTER. Better to flee than to put up a bad fight. Here we can't very well fight—so let us flee.

WANDERER. We may well be in danger of our lives . . .

SCHOOLMASTER. . . . but in still greater danger if you flee.

WANDERER. Can't we fool them—since they are inclined to be foolish?

SCHOOLMASTER. But they are sly—like all who are stupid. . . .

WANDERER. Let us try. (He calls.) Mr. Blacksmith! (The Smith enters.) Abra-cadabra, abra-cadabra . . .

SMITH. What's this? . . . Are you gentlemen thinking of leaving? You can't do that! No, you can't do that.

WANDERER. We are only going to the next village to get some requisites for the festival.

SMITH. To get what?

WANDERER. Requisites.

SMITH. That means requisitions, I presume. Requisitions are always welcome, especially if they have to do with supplies for the smithy. . . .

WANDERER. It's for hoof-nails and axle boxes, scythes and spades . . .

SMITH. Excellent!

WANDERER. But we have to have the Schoolmaster come along to help us carry them.

SMITH. He is much too weak, and he is such a simpleton.

WANDERER. But requisitions are nothing but scraps of paper, and he ought to be able to carry them.

SMITH. Very true, very true, but axle boxes are axle boxes— they are heavy. He won't have the strength to . . .

WANDERER. But requisitions for axle boxes are not any heavier than requisitions for nails.

SMITH. Very true, very true. . . . Well, go along then! But be sure you come back. . . .

WANDERER. Can't you understand that if you go, you must come back . . .

SMITH. Wait a moment! What is it that goes and goes, but never returns?

WANDERER. Time, of course, and you can tell that by the clock. But we are not clocks, and therefore we come back.

SMITH. That's good logic, and I can understand that. But wait just a moment; that means that you gentlemen's clocks are *not* coming back?

WANDERER. We have no clocks. We carry watches.

SMITH. Very true . . . and there are some clocks that have alarms—little bells that ring. Watches are something else. But hold on a second! Bells don't go! Therefore . . .

WANDERER. But we are going—and that's the main point!

SMITH. Precisely! That's the main point! And it is good logic! I like to see logic in all conditions of life. The only kind of reasoning I can follow in a conversation is a strictly logical one. . . .

WANDERER. That's the reason you must not follow us, for we are not a logical conversation.

SMITH. Absolutely correct! Therefore I'll stay where I am—and you go on! Go on!

WANDERER. Sing the praises of the donkey, you great rhymester! *(Recites.)*
The sanest of all animals on earth,
your sense of hearing is, indeed, unrivaled;
your cone-shaped ear, long a butt for mirth,
can hear the grass grow underneath a stone;
your eyes can spy with ease, in east and west, an object;
your stiff-legged gait epitomizes character;
your will is law—your master knows that best—
for when you should stand still, you stubbornly may run—
and urged to speed, you may decide to rest.

SMITH. That's really very well said—for the mammal in question has belonged to the misjudged in the world too long, has been in the camp of the dumb, and truly deserves being re—ha—bi—

WANDERER. —litated! But did you ever *hear* a dumb ass?

SMITH. No, but I don't care about that. I care about character, steadfastness of character, and that is why I understand the misunderstood poor animal. I feel a kinship to it—yes, that's how I feel. . . .

WANDERER. You stick to that?

SMITH. I stick to it!

WANDERER. Then we go . . .

SMITH. Just a moment! I stand for what I say, but I don't stand alone. I have public opinion and the party behind me—all the right-thinking, enlightened, and unbiased; in a word —the nation gathers round my standard . . . and as I stand here, I will show you, you are in the wrong . . . for right is right, isn't that logical, eh?

SCHOOLMASTER. The greatest justice is the greatest injustice!

SMITH. And the voice of the people is the voice of eternity! Enter, my people! Assemble, Nation! (*The People enter. They are only a scattered few.*)

WANDERER. The nation it is—but they are so few. . . .

SMITH. They are few—but you don't see the rank and file, the masses, standing behind them.

WANDERER. No, I can't see any masses. . . .

SMITH. You don't see them for the simple reason that they are invisible! That's only logical. Fellow citizens! These learned charlatans maintain that there is such a thing as Guano islands. There are no such islands, are there?

THE PEOPLE (*in unison*). No!

SMITH. These gentlemen are therefore either liars or igno-ramuses!—Can you think of any punishment severe enough for scoundrels such as these, who spread lies?

WANDERER. Yes, there is one that is more cruel than anything else. And that is—exile!

SMITH. Yes, that is not such a bad idea! But we shall first prove completely our case against them. One of them has the temerity to assert that Homer slept!

WANDERER. Occasionally.

SMITH. Occasionally or incessantly or everlastingly—that's nothing but sophistry and quibbling. Do you, fellow citizens, believe that a poet sleeps? Have you ever heard anything so idiotic?

ONE OF THE PEOPLE. But I suppose he slept nights . . .

SMITH. Nights? Is that an answer? Have I permitted anyone to give me answer? Come behind the stables with me, and I'll give you an answer. . . .

ONE OF THE PEOPLE. Is it a question of voting with the party?

SMITH. Of course, we have to be partisans, we human beings —otherwise we might be taken for spineless jellyfish.

SCHOOLMASTER. Won't you read something from your *Carolus the Great,* Mr. Blacksmith, so that we get this argument over with. The visiting gentlemen are in a hurry. *(Aside to the Hunter and the Wanderer.)* His name is not Carolus the Great, but we have to call him that, otherwise we'll be locked up.

SMITH. I heard what you said! And I saw you gentlemen grin—and he who grins, assents.—Lock them up! You know what I mean. Seize them! *(Injured; in a menacing undertone.)* His name is not Carolus the Great, but we call him that, because he was simply great!—Bat them on the jaw and put them behind bars until they get better sense in their heads! *(The Hunter, the Wanderer, and the Schoolmaster are seized and about to be taken away.)*

HUNTER. But we have already been exiled and were going to town to get the requisitions. . . .

SMITH. Quite right, quite right. . . . I'll let you go but on your word of honor that you come back, and with the promise —or rather, in return for the promise—that you will be grateful. For an ungrateful human being is the saddest burden the earth can carry. I have, namely, a wife who conducts a *salon* —yes, that may sound ridiculous, but it is a literary *salon—* and I shall expect you gentlemen to be present at the next meeting. . . .

WANDERER. Free at last! But at what price!

HUNTER. You call that freedom—to be bound by the chains of one's word of honor in the smithy [12] of a literary *salon?*

SMITH. Be off with you! But—the nation remains!

(The Hunter, the Wanderer, and the Schoolmaster depart.)

4. A thoroughfare in the city. An arcade in Tophet. In the foreground, to the right, is seen a fruit- and florist's shop; next to it, rear, a Japanese tea- and perfume shop. To the left is seen a restaurant; adjoining it is a photographic studio, and in the rear, a sea-shell shop.

The Hunter and the Wanderer are seated outside the florist's shop.

WANDERER. You seem so depressed.

HUNTER. Have come down too far. . . .

WANDERER. You have been here in Tophet [13] before. . . .

---

[12] *Smithy.* Strindberg uses the word *anchor smithy.* During the 18th and 19th centuries convicts were employed on work projects at fortifications and other government properties, as well as in prison forges, where anchors for the navy were made, particularly at the Karlskrona naval base and in Stockholm. The word *anchor smithy* therefore came to signify a place of enchainment or forced labor.

[13] *Tophet.* Hebraic word for Hell.

HUNTER. Yes, I lived here once.

WANDERER. I could see it.

HUNTER. I must anaesthetize myself—my wounds are beginning to ache.

WANDERER. *Vinum et circenses!* [14] We'll see a drama here without paying for it, I dare say. This seems to be the city's wastepipe, through which all its filth has to pass. *(He makes a gesture in the direction of the restaurant. The Waitress brings some wine.)* Don't you think they'll recognize you here?

HUNTER. Impossible, for I have shaved off my beard, clipped my hair, and washed my hands this morning. Washing oneself is in itself a disguise in this town.

WANDERER. But the Waitress is staring at you.

HUNTER. Perhaps I remind her of one of her former friends.

WANDERER. Here we'll get a little diversion. *(To the Organ-Grinder* [15] *who has just entered, with a monkey.)* Come over here, you, and we'll redeem our heads with a round sum of money for you.

ORGAN-GRINDER. Your heads?

WANDERER. Well, let's say ears, then. Here—I'll give you this gold coin, if you'll stop playing.

ORGAN-GRINDER. But it's the monkey that's the main attraction. . . .

WANDERER. Then we'll look at him—but without accompaniment.

ORGAN-GRINDER. But there is text that goes with it . . .

WANDERER. Is it true that you here in this town are descended from a monkey?

ORGAN-GRINDER. Is it true . . . ? You'd better watch yourself! . . .

WANDERER. Looking at you closer, I really believe it is true —I am sure it is. . . . I could swear it is! Let me see the text. . . . Yes—but this head of Zeus resembles more a ram. . . .

ORGAN-GRINDER *(regarding it).* Yes, so it does. . . . Well, then I suppose it is.

WANDERER. Do you really believe that that mammal there, dressed up in red tails and shooting with that toy pistol, is the father of mankind?

ORGAN-GRINDER. If the gentleman is a freethinker, the gen-

---

[14] *Vinum et circenses.* Wine and circus (entertainment).

[15] *The Organ-grinder.* In the scene between The Wanderer and The Organ-grinder Strindberg deftly and ironically rebukes the Darwinians for their obdurate attacks on him. They had frequently offended him by making light of his spiritual and religious leanings and expressions.

tleman had better be careful. We here in this town are ortho-
dox, and we are the defenders of the faith.

WANDERER. Which faith?

ORGAN-GRINDER. The one and only true one: the doctrine
of evolution.

HUNTER. Now we may be prosecuted for blasphemy! . . .
What happened to the Schoolmaster?

WANDERER. He disappeared, of course, after having used us
for his own selfish ends.

HUNTER. Shall we continue?

WANDERER. It does not matter much, does it? It does not
matter into whose hands we fall—whether we get entangled
here or somewhere else.

HUNTER. No, for people lie in ambush like highwaymen in
a road ditch, always on the lurk for each other. Look over toward the restaurant window, where the girl stands staring at
you with ogling eyes as though she were begging you to take
her—out of pity, as a favor. She is pretty, and could stir other
feelings in you than compassion! Presume you should consider
liberating her from her tedious, perhaps degrading work in
there . . . presume that you offered her a home in order to
protect her against life's worst jolts—and it would not be long
before she had robbed you of friends, torn you away from
relatives, disrupted relations with superiors and patrons . . .
in other words: swallowed you whole.

WANDERER. And if I objected, she would start suit against me
for having maltreated her.

HUNTER. And for having ruined her youth. . . . But the
worst that could happen would be to become involved with a
family you didn't know . . .

WANDERER. . . . but of which I can form an idea. . . . Just
think—there she stands, sucking in the air . . . stirring up a
whirlpool . . . she is spinning a net that affects one like warm
air. . . . Wait a moment—I am going in to pull it apart . . .

HUNTER. . . . or get caught in it . . . (*The Wanderer goes
into the restaurant.*) (*Alone.*) Man overboard!

PHOTOGRAPHER (*advances with a camera*). May I take a photograph of you, sir?

HUNTER (*with emphasis*). No!

PHOTOGRAPHER. Please do me the favor. I am so poor.

HUNTER. Well . . . but only on the condition that you don't
exhibit me in your show case or put me in a cigarette package
or on a soap wrapper. And if I should turn out to look like a

Hottentot or like the latest wholesale murderer, you'll destroy the negative.

PHOTOGRAPHER. The gentleman is very suspicious . . .

HUNTER. Not at all—I am merely a trifle prudent. . . .

PHOTOGRAPHER (*gestures in the direction of the studio. The Photographer's wife, Euphrosyne, appears*). May I introduce my wife—she helps me with the developing, and the fixing baths. . . . Come here, Euphrosyne—I have promised this gentleman to take a picture of him, even though I am terribly busy. . . . Come, Euphrosyne, and talk to the gentleman while I am working. . . .

EUPHROSYNE (*seats herself*). You were born under a lucky star, my dear sir, to find such an artist as my husband . . . he has the greatest talent I have ever seen—and if the photograph doesn't turn out well, you have every right to say I don't know a thing about art! For that reason you ought to appreciate his work and not act as if you were doing us a favor!

HUNTER. Now, just a moment . . .

EUPHROSYNE. Yes, you don't have to be so arrogant in your behavior—when you ask a person to do you a favor, you should be grateful for it.

HUNTER. Now, just a second . . .

PHOTOGRAPHER (*calls out*). Gotthard!—Come here, you have placed the negatives backward in the plateholder.

GOTTHARD (*comes out from the studio*). I didn't put any negatives in the plateholder. . . .

EUPHROSYNE. Don't talk back to your father—your own father.

GOTTHARD. I don't even know what a plateholder looks like. . . . I only look after the sea shells. . . .

PHOTOGRAPHER. You look after them, yes—but do you sell any? Ask this gentleman if he wants to buy any sea shells. I think he said something a while ago about sea shells. . . .

HUNTER. I haven't said a word about sea shells. I spoke about cigarette packages and soap wrappers. . . .

EUPHROSYNE. Gotthard, bring some cigarettes—don't you hear the gentleman is asking for some?

HUNTER. I asked you not to put my picture in any cigarette packages and on any soap wrappers . . .

GOTTHARD (*seats himself on a chair*). The gentleman is a little difficult to deal with, I can see—but let us discuss the matter, and I think we can get things straightened out. . . .

EUPHROSYNE. You are right, Gotthard, the gentleman has to become acclimatized to our circumstances, then he will understand. . . . Ask Klara to come out. . . .

GOTTHARD *(calls inside).* Klara! *(Klara comes out from the florist's shop.)*

EUPHROSYNE. Try to sell this gentleman a flower—he is so frugal, or I should say stingy, that he won't even buy a sea shell, although Gotthard has the most beautiful I have ever seen.

KLARA *(sits down).* Perhaps he can be made to see reason, although he seems arrogant. Are you a hunter?

EUPHROSYNE. You can see that, can't you?

KLARA. You kill animals—you mustn't do that, for it's a sin . . . but you look cruel, too, like all boozers—yes, for all who drink in the forenoon are boozers. . . .

HUNTER *(to Klara).* What have you done with your husband? *(Klara is frightened.)* it is sinful to kill a human being. . . . Don't you know that?

KLARA. You mean that . . .?

HUNTER. Yes, that is what I mean!

KLARA. You are my witnesses. He means . . .

ALL. Yes, we heard. . . .

HUNTER. Let me say just one word—just one word . . .

GOTTHARD. No-o, why should we . . . ?

HUNTER. I am not going to say what you think, but something entirely different.

EUPHROSYNE *(bursting with curiosity).* Say it, then!

HUNTER. Has Möller been arrested yet? *(All rise in terror.)*

WANDERER *(coming from the restaurant).* What's going on here?

HUNTER. Has Möller been arrested yet? *(All disperse—but are in a threatening mood.)* For the third time!—Has Möller been arrested? . . .   *(All disappear.)*

WANDERER. What's the meaning of all this?

HUNTER. That was the secret of this town. They all know that Möller committed the most recent murder here—but no one dares to testify because they can't prove his guilt. But having tossed my bombshell we shall now be forced to leave. Come!

WANDERER. I can't . . .

HUNTER. Caught?

WANDERER. In a barroom—driblets of liquor in glasses—matches and cigar-ash—relations with young men about town—saturated with smoke and late hours; and despite this—despite all this—I let myself be snared. . . .

HUNTER. Pull yourself out of it. . . .

WANDERER. I can't. . . .

HUNTER. Then let us flee. . . .
WANDERER. I can't. . . .
HUNTER. Very well, then stay. . . .
WANDERER. I can't. . . . I can't do anything. . . .
HUNTER. Then let me say good-by. . . .
WANDERER. We'll meet again. . . .
HUNTER. That happens always—having met once.
WANDERER. Farewell, then. *(He goes into the restaurant.)*
HUNTER *(alone, paces up and down a few times in the thoroughfare; then stops, aimlessly, before the photographer's show case.)* All this was once my own—
long time ago! 'Twas here I strolled
on rainy days beneath the glass roof . . .
when gray-gilt daylight preyed upon my spirits,
the cheerful lights in here helped to change my mood;
and fruits and flowers gave my eye much joy . . .
and sea shells, whispering their tales from out the ocean.
The pictures here on display—of persons known,
and some of unknown—
were company to me in my aloneness:
a glance from them, a mere expression,
sufficed as friendship with the mortals. . . .
They still are there. Here is my very oldest friend;
he must be gray by now—his image,
like leaves in autumn,
has only yellowed. . . .
Here I see relatives, and ex-relations, too—
an in-law who no longer is one—
and here . . . Oh, Saviour of the world, oh, help me . . .
for I am done for . . . my child!
My child—that is not mine . . .
was once—but is not any more! . . .
Another's! And yet mine! . . .
And here's—my favorite café. . . .
That table there was ours . . . many years ago . . .
all this has ceased to be—
but still remains . . . the memory!
A fire, not to be put out,
that burns—but gives no warmth . . .
that burns—but does not burn out. . . .
JAPANESE *(comes out of the tea-shop. He has the appearance of a dying man. The Hunter goes to support him)*. A human being—at last. . . . Where from—and going where?

HUNTER. From the great highway. . . . How can I be of service to you?

JAPANESE. Help me to die. . . .

HUNTER. There is time enough for that. . . .

JAPANESE. Don't say that . . . I can't live any longer . . . have no one to whom I can turn for the last services, for in this town of Tophet there isn't a single person . . .

HUNTER. What services do you mean?

JAPANESE. You will hold my sword while I . . .

HUNTER. No, that is something I cannot do. . . . Why do you wish to die?

JAPANESE. Because I can't live any longer.

HUNTER. Then . . . tell me briefly your life's tale. . . .

JAPANESE. Yes! . . . Yes! . . . I left the country of my birth —because I had been guilty of a low deed. . . . I came here, strongly determined to live an honest life and to adhere strictly to the laws of honor and of conscience . . . I gave good quality at a reasonable price. But the people of this community liked only counterfeit and imitation wares at low prices. I had to choose the only way out—or go under. Instead of distilling the fragrance of the flowers, I used chemicals; instead of the leaves of the tea plant, I gave them leaves from the aloe plant and the cherry tree. My conscience did not rebel at first—I had to live!—But one day I woke up—that's fifteen years ago now. It seemed to me that day as if everything in my life—all that I had ever done—had been written in a book . . . and now the book was opened. Day in and day out, over and over again, I read all the false entries and transactions, all the irregularities throughout its pages. . . . I have struggled to make amends —but in vain. . . . Only death can liberate me, for the worst of evil is in the flesh. . . . My soul has been cleansed through my suffering. . . .

HUNTER. What can I do to help you now?

JAPANESE. I shall tell you. I am about to take a sleeping potion that will put me into a coma . . . as though dead. You shall see that I am placed in a coffin which has been brought to the crematorium.

HUNTER. But if you should awaken?

JAPANESE. That is just what I am hoping for. . . . In that moment I shall feel the atoning and purifying power of the flames. . . . I shall suffer a few moments . . . and then I shall have attained salvation through liberation. . . .

HUNTER. And then? . . .

JAPANESE. Then you will gather the ashes and place them in my costliest vase . . .

HUNTER. . . . and have your name inscribed on it. . . . What is your name?

JAPANESE. One moment! . . . I have used the name of Hiroshima, after the city of my birth, have erred and suffered under that name. But in my country there is a custom that, when a man dies, he sheds the old name that has been soiled and cursed, and is given a new one which is called the name of eternity. Only this name is inscribed on the gravestone, together with a legend or proverb, after a branch of the sakaki tree has first been offered up to the dead one.

HUNTER. Have you these things ready?

JAPANESE. I have. . . . Here they are.

HUNTER. What is the meaning of these words?

JAPANESE. *Harahara to.* It means: rustling as leaves, or silk—but it means also: falling tears.

HUNTER. And the legend?

JAPANESE. *Chiru hana wo*
Nani ka uramin
Yo no naka ni
Waga mi mo tomo ni
Aran mono kawa.

HUNTER. Will you interpret this legend for me?

JAPANESE. The blossoms are falling . . .
Why should I feel aggrieved?
The gods have willed it;
and I, too, must—as the flowers—
turn to dust some day . . .

HUNTER. I shall fulfill this last wish of yours. . . . But have you no one to survive you?

JAPANESE. I had a child once . . . a daughter who came here three years ago when she thought I was going to die. She came to get her inheritance. But when I did not die, she was angered—could not hide her feelings—and went away. From that day she was dead to me.

HUNTER. Where is this to take place—that of which we were speaking?

JAPANESE. Outside the town—at the crematorium.

HUNTER. Shall we go together, or shall we meet there?

JAPANESE. We meet in the bower at the inn—in a little while—when I have shaved and bathed. . . .

HUNTER. We shall see each other there, then. . . .

JAPANESE (*goes toward the shop. He turns his head and gives the Hunter a look of warning).* Here comes the murderer. . . . Be careful!

HUNTER. Is it Möller?

JAPANESE. Be careful! He is the most powerful man in this town. . . . *(The Japanese leaves.)*

MÖLLER *(enters. He is the murderer. He carries himself stiffly and with arrogance; his arms hang limply and somewhat self-consciously at his sides. He stares fixedly at the Hunter).* Aren't you . . . ?

HUNTER. No, I am not.

MÖLLER. Well, then I must be . . .

HUNTER. No—used to be. The one you have in mind, no longer exists. . . .

MÖLLER. So, you have passed out of this life, eh?

HUNTER. Yes. . . . Twelve years ago I committed hara-kiri: I executed my old self. And he whom you see here, you do not know—will never know!

MÖLLER. Yes, I remember you were fool enough to mount the scaffold and—standing there on the blood-red carpet—confess publicly all your defects and weaknesses. . . .

HUNTER. And the whole community reveled in it. They all thought themselves to be superior human beings and felt themselves cleared of any guilt after I had been socially ostracized and condemned. No one voiced a word of either pity or approbation when I confessed my trespasses and shortcomings.

MÖLLER. Why should they?

HUNTER. When I—after ten years of suffering—had atoned for my wrongs and made restitution, it occurred to me that I ought to uncover your sins as well. Then you sang a different tune—all of you. . . .

MÖLLER. I should hope so—what the hell. . . .

HUNTER. You, for example, who have committed murder . . .

MÖLLER. You don't make such accusations—when you haven't any proof. . . .

HUNTER. I know you are the most powerful man in the community, that you tyrannize even the grand duke—and all because of the existence of a secret organization here. . . .

MÖLLER. What's that you say?

HUNTER. You know only too well. A band of evildoers and destroyers—that has nothing to do with things that are sacred. . . .

MÖLLER. What about yourself?

HUNTER. I have never belonged to this clique—but I can identify the members by their deeds. . . .

MÖLLER. Take a look in the book shop—in the window there—then you'll find out who you are!

HUNTER. You mean the caricature there? That isn't a caricature of me—but of you. That's how you all look inwardly. It reveals what you have made of yourselves. It's the image you have created—and you can have it.

MÖLLER. You have a faculty for shaking off your own vermin. . . .

HUNTER. Why don't you do the same? Only don't shake them off on me. Put an end to yourself, as I did—was driven to do, when you made me the scapegoat, on whom you loaded all your sins and transgressions!

MÖLLER. What's that you say?

HUNTER. I'll give you an example. Once upon a time there was a fool who wrote this stupidity—that if he stood alone at the pinnacle of Mount Gauri Sankar [16], and the deluge came and drowned all humanity, no loss would have been suffered, if only he survived. When the next carnival took place, Gauri Sankar was represented in the procession, and at its peak stood I—not the renegade. What have you to say to that? . . . Yet on my birthday anniversary it was he who was honored, not I! When I had invented the new insulators, it was you who was awarded the prize—but when you committed murder . . . then I was accused of it! In the same vein: when sugar rose in price on the exchange, my insulators were blamed for it, despite the fact that you had been credited with the invention. . . . Can you imagine anything more incongruous, anything more ridiculously absurd! To do that you have to stand on your head first, and then turn your backside front.

MÖLLER. Can you produce any proof, since you dare call me a murderer?

HUNTER. Yes, I can! (*Möller is taken aback.*) But I wouldn't dare to use it before a jury of your henchmen, for they would deny the truth of the facts and have me arrested. And now—tell me, who is the girl in there that snared my companion here?

MÖLLER. She is—your daughter!

HUNTER (*clutches at his heart; his face turns white. He puts*

---

[16] *Gauri Sankar.* Sometimes spelled Gaurisankar. In 1904 it was definitely accepted that this Himalayan mountain peak was not identical with Mount Everest, and that the latter peak was by far the higher one. Mount Everest (Chomolungma) is approximately 36 miles from Mount Gauri Sankar.

his handkerchief to his mouth. It is stained red from blood).
This child—that you have brought up—she is my daughter! . . .
Now I must go to the crematorium. . . .   *(He goes out.)*

5. In the arbor outside the crematorium. Outside the colum-
bary. A walk, lined with cypresses, leads to the rear. A bench,
a chair, a table. The stage is in half-light.

HUNTER *(enters, alone).* What do I see? Urns—a whole col-
    lection—
and all alike. . . .
A pharmacy or a museum? Neither!
A columbary—yes, a home for doves;
yet not one dove, no branch of olive—
chaff only, for the kernel grows elsewhere. . . .
Within these urns are ashes—therefore all alike,
as dust resembles dust. . . .
Humanity departed—
now numbered, and supplied with labels reading:
"Here rests . . ."—Yes, I knew you,
but you did never learn to know yourself . . .
and you—you masqueraded all your life,
your long and dreary life;
when I tore off your mask, you died!
Your name was idol-worshiper—[17]
and false your character! You made us deify
your gruesome consort and your loathsome children;
one had to, or was sacrificed,
ripped open with a flint knife every Saturday of undevotion
and flayed to boot in the gazettes on Sundays,
robbed both of bread and honor. . . .
    (Möller comes forward, after having listened to the Hunter
in the background.)
You, Light of Tophet's State, you gathered in the nation
around your bier; then, although dead,
you counted all the wreaths
and threatened your revenge upon the missing one!
    MÖLLER. There is something awesome about a grave, isn't
there?
    HUNTER. This is not a grave—it is a jar filled with rubbish.
No—with a stone. He has turned into stone by now. . . .

[17] *Idol-worshiper.* In the scene outside the crematorium Strindberg lashes out
against Gustaf af Geijerstam. Long a friend of his, Strindberg had pilloried him in
his book *Black Banners* (1907) and again defamed him in *The Great Highway,*
his "last will and testament."

MÖLLER. You mean he died from hardening, . . .

HUNTER. To limestone, yes. . . .

MÖLLER. Tell me a little about yourself. . . .

HUNTER. I did so thirteen years ago, and I know you are tired of it. But in this urn lie the ashes of one I could speak well of—had he not been murdered . . . murdered by you! Your victim never did anything wrongful with malicious intent. His only wrongdoing was done in self-defense; and when he refused to be implicated in your crimes, he was murdered, after you had robbed him of everything.

MÖLLER. You are friendly with that rascal the Japanese.

HUNTER. Are you trying to lay a trap for me now, as the Great Light did?

MÖLLER. Say nothing bad about him who is dead; say "the poor soul."

HUNTER. That's how you always speak about scoundrels who get caught with their fingers in the sugar-box—but never about your victims. . . . Be on your way now! Be quick about it!

MÖLLER. I go when I want to. *(The Hunter takes out his handkerchief, and Möller sees the blood on it. Möller turns away his face and starts to leave.)* I can't stand seeing blood . . . it's a peculiarity of mine . . .

HUNTER. Ever since the fourth of April! [18] *(Möller drags himself out. To the Japanese who enters.)* Are you prepared now for the journey?

JAPANESE. I am—but let's sit down,
Until the fire has come up . . .

HUNTER. With pleasure. *(They seat themselves.)*
Come, tell me, with life lying at your feet now—
like quarry hunted, conquered, shot . . .
how does the journey seem?

JAPANESE *(after a pause).* A stroke with many ups and downs,
such as the picture of the writing
a blotter copies in reverse:
a scrawl, a dash, an up, a down . . .
but in the mirror you can read what's written. . . .

HUNTER. What did you find most hard to bear,
what stone hurt most your foot upon the road?

---

[18] *The fourth of April.* The reason for Strindberg's use of this date is obscure. However, there is a possibility that he had in mind an episode involving a relative by marriage. Strindberg had accused this in-law of his third wife, Harriet Bosse (for whom he wrote several rôles), of having attempted to poison him. It is not unlikely that Strindberg has depicted him in the character of Möller, the murderer.

JAPANESE *(after a moment of reflection)*. I spared one time
    an enemy—
and afterward he struck me down! . . .
You see—to have to feel regretful for the good
one's done, is among the worst of feelings. . . .

Another time I recommended
a man who was oppressed . . . he turned into a foe—
took everything away from me . . .
and I stood there defenseless in an unfair contest,
for he—he had in writing from myself
he was a better man than I was!
But all such things are yet as nothing,
compared with life itself, its stern reality:
the humiliation to appear
a shiny skeleton, dressed up in flesh,
and made to move by sinews, cords,
through one small motor in the engine room
within the bosom, driven by the energy
the belly's coalbin can produce. . . .
And yet the soul, the spirit's in the heart,
imprisoned in the breast, much like a bird
caged in a poultry basket.

You little bird, soon I shall burst the cage,
and you may fly away—unto your land . . .
the islands of the sun and flowers,
where I was born on earth—
but fate denied me death!
Regard . . . my dearest vase, an ancient heirloom,
which now shall hold the dust of my remains—
but in the past adorned,
with flowers filled, the table
at parties where youth's eager eyes
were mirrored, with its cheeks of red,
in gilt-edged tumblers . . .
and to the children tiny hands dealt out
the best the household could provide. . . .

Then you became an urn for tears, dear vase . . .
for all that life gave us of good
was given to be once lamented.

I call to mind—'twas in the spring,
when children celebrate their doll-feast; [19]
all dolls are saved by us from generations past—
a child!
What does exist that is so perfect
a thing as such a little one!
Not man, not woman—
yet both . . . and also neither of them—
humanity in miniature.
Oh, wanderer, I have forgot you
in my own sorrow . . . Say a word
about yourself—and *your* life. . . .
How do you look on life, the present and the past?
What did you find most hard and bitter?

HUNTER. This gave me greater pain than death itself:
to have to take this super-mockery in seriousness—
to sanctify the things I found so brutal. . . .
When I was forced to laugh at the buffoonery, I wept;
when I became contaminated by the savagery,
I suffered in my shame. . . .

And this:
I was a preacher once. . . .
I started out by speaking of mankind with good will,
set forth the loftiest tenets that I knew
and placed my aims in life on highest plane—
they are called ideals commonly—
the shining banners upon flagstaffs
that summon crowds on feast- and holidays. . . .
Alas, how hard! The noble and exalted thoughts I'd thought
and spoken . . . I now have to take back!

The beautiful does not exist in this life,
cannot be made reality down here—
where the ideals are not practiced. . . .

JAPANESE. I know it—but they are a memory,
a hope, a beacon to set sail for. . . .
Thus: with all the colors at the masthead,

[19] *Doll-feast.* The girls' doll festival in Japan is generally celebrated on March 3; the boys' festival on May 5. The latter is actually not a doll festival; the day is celebrated by the hoisting of the image of a fish, made out of cloth, to the top of a pole. In the evening the celebration is concluded with a children's feast given in the homes by the parents. In the entrance hall there is then displayed a miniature armored figure. There is some variance in the date of celebration in certain regions of Japan.

let them fly gaily in the breeze—
their place is at the top, where they can best be seen,
and point the way on high . . . toward the sun!
     HUNTER. The fire now is glowing hot . . .
     JAPANESE. . . . and throws a rosy glimmer—like the sun,
when it breaks forth at dawn in red array—
upon the cypress crowns. . . .
Be greeted, Day! Farewell, you Night,
with your depressing dreams!
This is the last time I undress
and go to rest—and sleep. . . .
And when I wake—I'm with my mother,
my wife, my child, and friends. . . .
Good night to you—poor human being! . . .   *(He goes.)*
     (The stage is growing light, and one sees in the background,
     up in the clouds, an image of the same Alpine mountain
     setting as in Scene 1: The Land of Desires.)

6. *At the last gate. In the background two white gates open*
upon a low sand beach and the blue sea.
     To the right, a forester's cottage or lodge, painted red and
surrounded by a wood of beech; to the left, a hedge of yoke-
elm, enclosing a garden of fruit trees.
     Outside the cottage, right, a small table set for a birthday
celebration.
     Beyond the hedge, a shuttlecock (volant) can be seen being
tossed back and forth.
     A baby carriage with blue folding-top, opened, stands by
the gate.

     HUNTER *(enters; he is lost in thought).*
Yes. . . . Alone! . . . That is the end,
if one's desire is to keep one's life
and take no part in bargaining,
or barter, to attain position;
or face coercion—yet remain oneself,
immutable and incorruptible. . . .

When first my mind awakened,
and I began to realize
I was confined in an insane asylum,
a sanitarium, a penal prison,
I wished that I would lose my sanity and wits,
lest any one divine my inmost thoughts—

"Thelō, thelō manēnai!" [20]
I begged—and do so still—that I go mad. . . .
And wine became my friend. . . .
Intoxication thus became my hiding-cloak—
in jester's garb I was forgotten;
and none remembered my identity. . . .

My guise has changed now. . . .
Oblivion's draught has now become the memory's:
I now remember all . . . all, yes—all! . . .
The seals are broken, and the ledgers opened:
each page takes voice and speaks aloud;
and when I tire hearing them, I see:
I see, see all, all, all. . . .
　　(He awakens from his thoughts.)
Where have I come?—The sea . . .
and woods of beech, a hunting lodge—
and there, a shuttlecock that rises, falls;
a little carriage with a newborn babe:
its hood, like sky-blue heaven's canopy,
is arched above the sleep of innocence. . . .
In the red house, behind green shutters, two beings
conceal themselves from sight,
to hide their happiness!
For happiness exists, there is no doubt,
but brief, like lightning,
like sunshine, or like the convolvulus—
whose flower lives for but a day,
And that's the end.
. . . I see the chimney smoke arising from the kitchen;
a well-stocked larder just beyond it—
and, underneath, a little cellar;
a bright veranda toward the woods. . . .
I know just how it ought to be—
how once it was! . . .

And here's a festive table set
for the little one! . . .
A tiny altar raised to childhood,
to hope, to joyous innocence,
built on its own happiness—

---

[20] *Thelo, thelo manēnai.* Literally: I wish, I wish to go mad. From one of the poems of Anacreon, Greek poet born about 563 B.C., died 478 B.C. He is principally famous for his love lyrics and bacchanalian poems.

and not on others' misery. . . .
And there's the shore—
with sand so white and clean, so warm and soft . . .
with sea shells and with pebble-stones—
and bluish water to go plashing in,
in one's bare feet. . . .
And garlands have been hung, the path is raked—
they must expect some company—a children's party!
The flowers have been watered—
my childhood's flowers:
the blue monkshood adorned with twin doves—
the crown imperial, with diadem,
and orb, and spire—
the passion flower, of suffering,
in white and amethyst, with cross
and lance, and with its spikes—
called on by busy bee that from its cup
can gather honey,
where we find only gall. . . .
And there, most beautiful of all the plants
in this—the children's—paradise! . . .
In dark green frame of leaves appear
the fairest flowers—two and two—
with cheeks of white and red, like ox-heart cherry,
the face of little children—brother, sister . . .
who, amidst play, caress each other, swaying in the wind. . . .
And between branch and trunk a rustic singer
has built his nest:
an unseen singer with a song on wings . . .
Hark! The sand is crunching under little boots. . . .
Here comes the sovereign mistress!

CHILD (enters. She takes hold of the Hunter by the hand and
leads him to the wicker carriage). Come quietly and I'll let you
look at the doll. . . . This is the doll—that's what we call her. . . .
But you must not walk on the path, for it has just been raked.
. . . Ellen has raked it, because we are going to have company.
. . . It's my birthday today. . . . Are you sad?
  HUNTER. What is your name, little child?
  CHILD. My name is Maria.
  HUNTER. Who lives in the house there?
  CHILD. Father and Mother.
  HUNTER. Will you let me see your birthday table?
  CHILD. But we must not touch anything. . . .

HUNTER. No, I won't touch anything. You little child . . .

CHILD. Do you know what we are going to have for dinner today?—We are going to have asparagus, and strawberries! Why are you sad? Have you lost your money? You may take a cracker candy on the table, but you mustn't take the big one, for that's for Stella. Do you know that Stella had bread-crumbs in her bed last night, and she cried, and then it started to thunder, and we were afraid, and Mother shut the window . . . Yes, she was eating a sandwich in bed, and the sandwich broke into pieces—because it was that kind of brittle bread that you buy in the city. . . . Now let's tell a fairy-tale—do you know any fairy-tales?—What is your name?

HUNTER. My name is . . . Cartaphilus. [21]

CHILD. No, that's not your name. . . .

HUNTER. Ahasuerus, then—he who keeps wandering and wandering forever. . . .

CHILD. Now let's talk about something else. . . . Have you ever had trouble with your eyes?

HUNTER. Yes, little child, much trouble, much trouble. . . .

CHILD. You should never read in bed by lamplight. It's bad for the eyes. *(The sound of a hunting-horn is heard.)* That's father coming! *(She runs out.)*

HUNTER. My child! My child! She did not recognize me! What luck—what luck for both of us!

Farewell, you fairest sight!

I must not now obscure the sun

and cast a shadow o'er the garden of these children. . . .

I know the father there, the mother also. . . . .

You lovely parable—a parable

that halts, and yet is beautiful!

A memory, perhaps, or even more:

a hope—a summer's day in woodland

along the sea—a birthday table and a cradle . . .

a ray of sun from eyes of little ones,

an unasked gift from tiny hands—

and now . . . I'm on my way again—out—into the darkness!

The Dark Forest. Within a murky clearing.

HUNTER. Alone!—I've lost my way . . . in the darkness . . .

---

[21] *Cartaphilus (Ahasuerus).* According to legend, a Roman who served as Pilate's doorkeeper and who struck Jesus when he came out from the judgment chamber, and told him to walk faster. Jesus is said to have answered: "I will go, but you shall remain waiting till I come." His name is changed in German legends in the 16th century to Ahasuerus, the wandering Jew, who was doomed to live forever, longing and weeping for death to come.

"And Elijah seated himself under the juniper tree, and he longed for death to come, and he said: 'This is enough! Take me unto You, O Lord!' "

VOICE *(the Woman, speaking in the darkness)*. He who will lose his life, he shall find it.

HUNTER. Who are you who speaks out of the darkness?

WOMAN. Is it dark?

HUNTER. Is it dark?

WOMAN *(enters)*. I am asking because I cannot see—I am blind. . . .

HUNTER. Have you always been blind?

WOMAN. No . . . when my tears ran out, my eyes lost their sense of vision.

HUNTER. It is good to be able to cry.

WOMAN. But I can still hear, and I know your voice. . . . I know who you are . . . I believe in you . . .

HUNTER. You must not believe in me, nor in any one human being. You shall put your faith in God.

WOMAN. I do—I do.

HUNTER. And in God only. Humanity's children are not worthy of your trust. . . .

WOMAN. You were a counselor-at-law once, weren't you?

HUNTER. I was attorney for the one and only True One, against the idol-worshipers. Humanity has always indulged in worship: you have worshiped yourselves, your relatives, your friends . . . but you would never give simple, unadulterated justice. . . .

WOMAN. You would sometimes abandon the case you represented. . . .

HUNTER. Only when I found I had been beguiled into feeling pity for a trespasser, on the pretext that he was a poor human being, did I abandon his iniquitous case. . . .

WOMAN. Once you were an evangelist also, but tired of it. . . .

HUNTER. I did not tire—but when I found that I could not live as I preached, I stopped preaching in order not to be a hypocrite. And when I discovered that there was no actual or practical application of these beautiful teachings, I deferred the realization of them to the land of the Fulfilled Desires.

WOMAN. And now you are dead!

HUNTER. As far as the world is concerned—yes . . . but not spiritually. . . . For as I still carry on my struggle, I live. . . . *I* am not living—only what I have done lives. The good and the evil. The evil I have confessed and suffered for—have tried to atone for it by doing good. . . .

WOMAN. Do you still desire to take on mankind's cause?

HUNTER. Whenever the cause is just—otherwise not. . . . I happened to plead once for a man because of being confused in my mind by the debt of gratitude I owed him. . . . But by so doing I did a profound injustice to the one who was innocent. That's the kind of prank our finest feelings sometimes play on us: they deceive us into committing evil deeds!

WOMAN. You accuse, you prosecutor. . . .

HUNTER. Whom do I accuse?

WOMAN. Those who have the power!

HUNTER. Go away, Satan! Before you excite me to blasphemies!

WOMAN. Satan?

HUNTER. Yes, Satan!

WOMAN. No one was more profligate than you.

HUNTER. Because you blackened me so that I would be like you. But explain this to me: when I confessed my sins, you acted as though you were free from sin and thanked God you were not such as I was, though you were by no means less despicable. When I was a child, I remember witnessing an execution. . . . The mob looked like a pack of sanctimonious rabble. When they returned home they were full of commiseration. Yet afterward they went out into the taverns and spoke ill of the dead man, and felt both holier and more respectable for having done so. . . . But later some of them went back to the scene of the hanging and took some of the dead man's blood— as a cure for epilepsy. They dipped their handkerchiefs in his blood . . . Look! (*He takes out a handkerchief and holds it before the Woman.*) I forget you are blind. . . . Take hold of it, your hand will see for you. (*He hands her the blood-soaked handkerchief.*)

WOMAN. It feels like red—but it's sticky, and has a fragrance like—like a slaughterhouse. Oh, I know now . . . only recently I had a relative who coughed up . . . first his lungs, and finally his heart.

HUNTER, He coughed up his heart?

WOMAN. Yes.

HUNTER (*regarding the handkerchief*). I believe . . . the goat is, as you know, no clean animal. But on the great day of atonement he was chosen to carry all the sins of mankind; and thus loaded down he was driven out into the wilderness to be devoured by wild animals. . . . He was the original scapegoat. . . .

WOMAN. You mean that you have suffered for the sins of others?

HUNTER. For my own and others. . . . Thus for others, too. . . .

WOMAN. Weren't you something else before you turned to law?

HUNTER. Yes, I was an architect. . . . I built many structures. Not all were good—but when I built well, people were displeased because I had done an honest piece of work. And so the contract was given to others—who did not do as well. That was in the city of Tophet—whose theatre I erected.

WOMAN. It is considered beautiful. . . .

HUNTER. Recall it in your mind, then, when I have ceased to be . . . and forget me.

WOMAN. "I am not living—only the good I have done lives." Why did you never show compassion for your fellow creatures?

HUNTER. The question is put wrongly. . . . Did you ever see anyone show pity for me? No!—How, then, could I return feelings that were never felt for me? And, besides, who was it that first preached: "Have pity on mankind!"

(The Woman leaves.)

She disappeared! They always do when one seeks to defend oneself!

TEMPTER *(enters)*. So there you are! Now we'll have a little chat, but it's a shade too dark here, so let us have some brightness *(It grows light.)* . . . so we can see each other. We must, of course, be able to see each other in order to talk reason. . . . I come from the grand duke—he values you for your talents. . . . He offers you the post of court architect, with so and so much salary, together with maintenance, firewood, et cetera . . . you understand. . . .

HUNTER. I desire no post . . .

TEMPTER. Wait a moment . . . but I have to ask that you . . . well—in a word—that you behave like a human being . . . like an ordinary, normal human being. . . .

HUNTER. Go on . . . it would interest me to know how a normal human being behaves.

TEMPTER. Don't you know?—Why do you look so mystified?

HUNTER. I shall answer your last question as briefly as I can. I seem mystified because I am confused. I have belonged to that category of people namely that believes what a person says —without any doubt of his word. Therefore I have been stuffed full of lies. Everything I have believed in has proved to be a fraud. For that reason my whole life has become a lie. I have been going around with false notions and ideas of people and of life, have calculated with false figures, have unknowingly deceived with base counterfeit: thus I am not the one I seem to be. . . . I can't be among other human beings, can't rely on, or quote, or repeat what others have said—can't trust in any-one's word, for fear it may be a lie. In several instances I have entered as an accomplice in the chain smithy that is called society—but when I found myself becoming like the rest, I broke away, took refuge in the woods, and turned huntsman.

TEMPTER. All this is just talk. Now let us get back to the grand duke who requests your services.

HUNTER. He does not desire my work—he demands my soul. . . .

TEMPTER. He demands that you interest yourself in his great project. . . .

HUNTER. I can't do it. . . . Now go away—I have not long to live and wish to be alone to go over my accounts . . .

TEMPTER. Aha! if now the day of reckoning's at hand,
then I shall come with invoices,
with endless bills, and summonses . . .

HUNTER. Then come—come with the agony,
you tempter, who would bribe me to deny,
with cowardice, our good Creator. . . .

(The Tempter leaves.)
I came down from the pure air of the Alps
to mingle yet a while with human beings,
to share with them their trivial little sorrows;
but there was no wide, open roadway—
a narrow, thorny path was all—
and, caught in the brambles, I was rent,
leaving a shred of myself here and there. . . .
Good deeds were but a cloak for selfish purpose—
a gift bestowed: a trick to snare a debtor;
one rendered service but to dominate—
and liberated merely to enslave. . . .
My lone companion lost his way
I met with untold snares repeatedly;
was dragged into a mill wheel—
came out of it the other side;
met there a child whose starry eyes
lit up the road that led me here—
into this darkness.
Now you come forward with your bills . . .
(He turns and finds that the Tempter has left.)
What! Has he, too, disappeared!

And so I am alone!

in night and blackness . . .
where trees are sleeping, and the grass weeps tears
from cold, bereft of sun. . . .
The beasts—not all, though—are on the alert. . . .
The night owl spins its dark intrigues,
the snake is coiled 'neath poisonous toadstool,
nocturnal badger moves about again
after its day of hibernation. . . .
Alone! . . . Why? . . .
A traveler in foreign land
is ever there a lonely stranger.
He goes to city, village, town,
takes lodging, pays, and then continues on,
until his journey's at an end—and he's at home again!
Yet that is not the end. . . .
I hear still: the snapping of a rotted branch—
an iron heel against the mountain rock. . . .
It is the fierce, frightening smith. . . .
I see the idol-worshiper, with knife of flint—
he's seeking me. . . .
The miller and his mill wheel
that dragged me in,
and where I nearly perished. . . .
The people of the thoroughfare . . .
a trap, easy to get into—
but hard to get out of. . . .
And the murderer Möller . . .
with heaps of bills, and summonses—
and alibis and libel threats . . .
abominable beast! . . .

What do I hear now? . . . Music! . . .
I recognize your tones, your gentle hand . . .
but do not yearn to meet you. . . .
The fire warms at comfortable distance,
but not too close—for then it injures!—
And now: a child's voice in the darkness. . . .
You, little child, you last bright memory
that follows me into the gloomy forest
on the last journey to that far-off land—
the Land of the Fulfilled Desires—
that beckoned from the Alpine heights,
but from the valleys seemed obscured
by dust from highway and the smoke from chimneys. . . .

Where are you gone, oh, beautiful sight,
land of longing and of dreams?

If but a dream, I wish again to see you,
from snow-white heights, in crystal-clear air,
at the hermit's; there I shall remain,
to await the liberation! . . .
No doubt he'll offer me a resting place
beneath the white and icy blanket—
and write, perhaps, in snow a casual inscription:
Here rests one Ishmael [22], son of Hagar—
whom once they gave the name of Israel,
because he'd battled with the Lord
and had not given in till he was felled,
conquered by the bounty of God's almightiness. . . .

Eternal One! I won't let go Your hand,
Your strong, firm hand, till You have given me Your blessing!
O bless me, bless Your humankind
that suffers—suffers from Your gift of life!
Me first, who's suffered most . . .
who's suffered most: from grief, from anguish
not to be able to be as I wanted to be—
the one I longed to be! . . .

[22] *Ishmael*. Son of Abraham and Hagar, a concubine and servant maid. It was said of him: "His hand will be against every man, and every man's hand against him." (Gen. XVI. 12.) Hagar and Ishmael were driven out into the desert because of Sarah's (the wife of Abraham) jealousy. There they and their followers became wanderers and lived by hunting. The name Ishmael now generally connotes a social outcast.

The Ghost Sonata

A DRAMA IN THREE SCENES

❖   ❖   ❖

The Ghost Sonata is a unique play even though it shares its expressionistic style with *To Damascus* and other pilgrimage plays—including *A Dream Play*, in which the seeker is the supernatural Indra's Daughter who has come to the earth in order to experience its misery. *The Ghost Sonata* is *not* one of the pilgrimage plays. It is also less poetic, expansive, and romantic than these plays. It is, rather, a masterpiece of condensation and it has admirers who plainly prefer it to *A Dream Play*, the public favorite among the expressionistic dramas.

This is not to say, however, that *The Ghost Sonata* is an unpoetic work in conception and execution, or that it is unrelenting in its assault on evil and its proponents. While taking scornful note of the world's malice and maladies, Strindberg is sympathetic to his protagonist, the Student, who is obviously Strindberg himself; and he adds compassion to his description of the fears and failures of the weak and the innocent. Speaking through his alter ego, the Student, who has endeavored in vain to take the Young Lady out of the prison of her home and bring her to his own as his bride, Strindberg feels nothing but pity for the dying girl—the child of an inconstant world of illusion, sin, suffering, and death. Still Strindberg's sympathy is pale beside the passion of his scorn and anger. He never excoriated humanity so thoroughly as in his portraits of the ubiquitous leech Hummel, the old man who tries to steal the soul of the Student. And Strindberg had previously only occasionally created images of the vileness of the world—that insane asylum, prison, and morgue, the Earth!— as appalling in their concreteness as the weird home of the Young Lady, with its Room of the Trials and Tribulations in which she has lost her will to live, with its closet where the Mummy, the woman who thinks herself a parrot, has spent twenty years bewailing her sin, and where Hummel hangs himself with the rope with which he had (figuratively) strangled one of his victims shortly before—this house, in short, where men and women torment one another and lose their reason and their very desire to live.

A remarkable blending of realism and symbolism results from this phantasmagoria which combines the possible and the impossible and makes free use of extravaganza to point up the absurdities of life—as in the treatment of the sticky Hummel, the eerie Mummy, and the insufferable fat vampire Cook. Closer to the surfaces of life than *A Dream Play*, this expressionist drama is at the same time more bizarre and grim; and it is just as imaginative in the ultra-modern "Kafkaesque" and later "theatre of the absurd" manner of pretended literalness or factualness, while the details of everyday existence are used to imply or symbolize a larger meaning.

The most remarkable feature of the play, however, is the compression of the continuous action, the drive toward a relentless exposure of the sorry state of the life represented on one level and symbolized on another. Strindberg wrote *The Ghost Sonata* as one of five "chamber plays" for his own Intimate Theatre in Stockholm, where it was produced on January 21, 1908, with considerable success. He wrote the play in one full sweep of the imagination, with one swift curve of hauntingly hallucinatory or "surreal" action and revelation, and without diverging from a central idea, which it may be difficult to summarize but which can be felt at every point as a protest against the wastefulness and frustration with which humanity lives in its "house," the world. He also included in this seminal work, from which Central European playwrights derived much of their expressionist fuel and flame, a general plea, implicit rather than explicit, for toleration. It is a plea for letting people alone and not compounding their sufferings with righteousness, interference, and hypocritical solicitude. It is the appeal of an inveterate individualist and of a man both endowed and cursed with uncommonly keen sensitiveness. Its fundamental tenderness for the innocent and compassion for bewildered and bedeviled humanity—Athena he treated with such masterly skill in *A Dream Play*—has more validity and is more genuinely felt than the rather tacked-on and operatically spectacular finale.

PERFORMANCE NOTES

The Ghost Sonata had its première on January 21, 1908, at Strindberg's own Intimate Theatre in Stockholm—the modern little theatre he had founded in association with August Falck the preceding year, and for which he wrote this and the four other so-called chamber plays with noteworthy concentration of action that allowed no intervals during which the audience might divert its attention.

Subsequently Reinhardt staged this work in Swedish at the

Lorensberg Theatre in Gothenburg in 1916 and on May 3, 1917, at the Royal Opera in Stockholm, when Paul Wegener acted Hummel and Gertrude Eysoldt was the Mummy.

Ingmar Bergman, known today as a brilliant film director, staged the play in the fall of 1941 at the Medborgarhuset Theatre in Stockholm. Despite certain difficulties, the production captured the play's essential mood and poetry and constituted an intelligent performance by young Strindberg enthusiasts. Bergman produced the play again in 1954 at the Malmö Civic Theatre; the première, on March 5, was distinctly successful.

In 1942 the play was staged at the Royal Theatre in Stockholm by Olof Molander, with Lars Hanson as Hummel and Märta Ekström as the Mummy. Molander also gave a very successful production of the work in 1946 at the Civic Theatre of Gothenburg.

The play was produced in Finland at the Kansanteatteri in Helsinki in 1949, and in Zurich, Switzerland in June 1952 by Steckel—in a new German translation by Willi Reich. *The Ghost Sonata*—titled *Die Gespenstersonate* in German—was set to music by Julius Weissman and presented as an opera in Munich in 1930 and at Duisburg and Dortmund in 1956.

Max Reinhardt's successful staging of the play in the German language on October 17, 1916, at the Kammerspiele Theater in Berlin gave this work an international reputation. Following that performance, the play was presented in other German cities and also in Vienna. Max Reinhardt's German company also presented *The Ghost Sonata* in Copenhagen in 1920. In that city the play was also staged in 1948 at the Royal Theatre with Olof Molander as guest director and was notably successful. Molander succeeded with the play again when he staged it in the fall of 1953 at the Norwegian Theatre in Oslo, where the play had been previously given at the Central Theatre in 1921 in a production showing Reinhardt's influence. The vogue of the play among the European intelligentsia was also attested by the success of the work in 1925 at Bragaglia's experimental theatre in Rome.

An avant-garde production in England in 1927 at the Globe and Strand theatres was a failure, because the London critics were hostile. Translated into French by Maurice Rémon from the German, the play was produced in Paris in the spring of 1933 and was revived in 1949 in celebration of the hundredth anniversary of Strindberg's birth. The reception in Paris was respectful rather than enthusiastic, but Parisians were able to see a masterly performance of the play by the Swedish Royal Theatre Company in 1962.

In New York, the Provincetown Players at the instigation of Strindberg's great American admirer Eugene O'Neill produced the play in Björkman's translation under the title of *The Spook Sonata* in 1924. New York newspaper critics were evidently confused and quite irritated by the presentation, but reviews in the periodicals were appreciative of the excellent production, which had twenty-four performances. Since then, there have been many university and little-theatre productions, perhaps most notably at the University of Wisconsin in 1940, at Vassar College (with an all-female cast) in the 1940's, and at Yale University in January 1950.

✤

CHARACTERS

HUMMEL
THE STUDENT (ARKENHOLZ)
THE MILKMAID (an apparition)
THE JANITRESS
THE DECEASED (THE CONSUL)
THE DARK LADY, daughter of the Janitress and the Consul
THE COLONEL
THE MUMMY, the Colonel's wife
THE YOUNG LADY (Adele, the Colonel's daughter; in reality
    Hummel's daughter)
THE ARISTOCRAT (BARON SKANSKORG; engaged to the Janitress's
    daughter)
JOHANSSON, Hummel's attendant
BENGTSSON, the Colonel's butler
THE FIANCÉE, once engaged to Hummel, now white-haired and
    old
THE COOK
THE SERVANT GIRL (on the second floor)
BEGGARS

✤

THE SETTINGS

SCENE 1. The façade of a modern apartment house.
SCENE 2. The Round Room.
SCENE 3. The Hyacinth Room.

462

SCENE 1. *The façade of a modern apartment house; only the corner and the two lower floors are visible. The house terminates in a circular wing, in which the Round Room is situated on the ground floor. Above it is a balcony with a flagstaff. The windows of the Round Room are open but the shades are drawn. When they are raised, the white marble figure of a young woman can be seen surrounded by palms and sharply illuminated by the sun's rays. In the window to the right are potted hyacinths of different colors, white, pink, and blue.*

On the balcony up above, a bedspread of blue silk and two white bed pillows are hung on the balustrade. Inside, the windows at the right are hung with white sheets. A green bench stands in front of the house, downstage.

On the left, in the foreground, a drinking fountain; on the right, a billboard in the shape of a column, with posters.

At the rear, right, is the main entrance to the house, showing the marble steps of the stairway with its railing of mahogany and its brass fixtures. On the sidewalk, flanking the entrance, are laurels in tubs.

On the extreme right the house faces a cross-street that may be presumed to lead to the rear of the stage.

At the right of the entrance door on the lower floor is a window with a reflector mirror.

When the curtain rises, church bells are heard ringing from several steeples a distance away.

The entrance doors are wide open, and on the steps stands, immobile, a woman dressed in black.

The Janitress is sweeping the vestibule; this done, she polishes the brass knobs and fixtures on the doors, and then waters the laurels.

Seated in a wheelchair by the billboard is old Hummel. His hair is white and he has a white beard and wears spectacles. He is reading a newspaper.

The Milkmaid enters from the street round the corner, downstage, right. She carries a wire crate with milk bottles, is dressed in a light, airy dress, black shoes and black stockings, and wears a white cap. She removes the cap and places it on the edge of the fountain, wipes the perspiration from

*her brow, fills the dipper attached to the fountain, and
drinks. Then she washes her hands, arranges her hair, and
gazes at her own reflection in the water.*

*The sound of a bell from a steamboat is heard; and now
and then the bass notes from the organ in a nearby church
penetrate the silence.*

*After a few moments of silence, and after the Milkmaid
has finished primping, the Student comes from the right.
He is unshaven and looks as if he had not had any sleep.
He goes straight to the fountain. There is a silence.*

STUDENT. May I have the dipper? *(The Milkmaid draws back
and holds on to the dipper.)* Won't you be through soon? *(The
Milkmaid stares at him in horror.)*

HUMMEL *(to himself)*. Whom is he talking to? I don't see anybody!—Can he be mad? *(He keeps regarding the Student with
extreme puzzlement.)*

STUDENT *(to the Milkmaid)*. What are you staring at? Do I
look so horrible? Yes—I had no sleep last night—and you think,
of course, that I spent the night having a good time, don't you?
. . . *(She keeps staring at him.)* . . . that I spent the night
drinking, I suppose? Don't you?—Do I reek of liquor, do I?
I'm unshaven, I know that . . . Let me have a drink of water,
girl—I think I deserve one. *(There is a pause.)* Well—in that
case, let me tell you that I've been up all night, looking after
the injured and dressing their wounds. . . . You see, I was at
the scene of that disaster last night—where the house collapsed.
. . . Now you know. . . . *(The Milkmaid rinses the dipper
and offers him a drink.)* Thanks! *(The Milkmaid does not
move. Somewhat timidly.)* Will you do me a great favor?
(There is a pause.) As you can see, my eyes are inflamed—and
I have touched so many injured, yes, even dead bodies, with
my hands—that I don't dare touch my eyes myself. . . . Would
you mind taking my clean handkerchief, dip it in the fresh
water and bathe my poor eyes with it?—Would you do that?—
Will you be the good Samaritan? *(The Milkmaid hesitates but
does what he asks.)* Thank you, my dear. *(He takes out his
wallet. The Milkmaid turns away with a deprecatory gesture.)*
Forgive me my thoughtlessness, but I am scarcely awake. . . .

HUMMEL *(to the Student)*. Excuse me for interrupting—but I
heard you say that you were at the scene of the disaster last
night. . . . I am just reading about it in the newspaper
here. . . .

STUDENT. Is it already in the newspapers?

HUMMEL. Yes—the whole story; and your picture is here, too . . . but they deplore the fact that they have been unable to learn the identity of the young student who was so helpful and self-sacrificing. . . .

STUDENT *(peers at the newspaper account)*. You don't say. . . . Why, yes, there's my picture! Well, well. . . .

HUMMEL. Whom were you talking with just now?

STUDENT. Didn't you see? *(There is a silence.)*

HUMMEL. Would it be impertinent to ask you—your name?

STUDENT. My name is of no account. I don't care for public acclaim. Once you are praised, it isn't long before criticism follows. Nowadays the habit of belittling has been developed to a considerable degree; besides, I am not looking for any reward. . . .

HUMMEL. Perhaps you are well provided for?

STUDENT. Not at all—quite the contrary!—I am poor as a church mouse.

HUMMEL. Tell me—your voice sounds strangely familiar to me. . . . In my youth I had a friend who had certain peculiarities of speech. . . . He is the only person I ever met who spoke that way—and you talk exactly like him. . . . Is it possible that you are related to a wholesale dealer by the name of Arkenholz?

STUDENT. He was my father.

HUMMEL. Wondrous are the ways of Fate. . . . I saw you when you were a little child—under circumstances that were very trying. . . .

STUDENT. Yes, I understand I was born in the midst of bankruptcy proceedings. . . .

HUMMEL. Yes—that's right.

STUDENT. Do you mind if I ask your name?

HUMMEL. My name is Hummel. . . .

STUDENT. Can it be . . . yes, I remember. . . .

HUMMEL. You have heard my name mentioned more than once in your home, haven't you?

STUDENT. Yes!

HUMMEL. And perhaps heard it mentioned with a certain aversion? *(The Student does not reply.)* Yes, I can well imagine! . . . And I presume you were told that I had ruined your father?—All who ruin themselves through brainless speculation always blame it on someone they haven't been able to cheat. *(There is a pause.)* However, the fact is that your father had done me out of seventeen thousand crowns—which at that time was all I possessed.

STUDENT. It's strange how a story can be told in two such entirely different ways.

HUMMEL. You don't mean to say I am not telling the truth, do you?

STUDENT. Whom do you expect me to believe? My father did not tell lies!

HUMMEL. You are quite right—one's father never lies. . . . But I, too, am a father, and therefore . . .

STUDENT. Just what are you driving at?

HUMMEL. I rescued your father from his unfortunate plight, and he repaid me with the unnatural hate that a debt of gratitude breeds . . . and he imbued his family with that same hate.

STUDENT. Perhaps you caused him to feel ungrateful by poisoning your generosity with needless humiliation?

HUMMEL. All help is humiliating, young man!

STUDENT. And what do you want of me now?

HUMMEL. I am not asking you to pay back the money—but if you will do me some little service now and then—then I shall feel that I have been well repaid, As you see, I am a cripple. . . . Some say that I myself am to blame for that; others say it's my parents' fault. My own feeling is that life—with its many snares and treacheries—is to blame. . . . For if you escape one snare, you rush head over heels into another. In any event, I can't climb stairs and I can't ring doorbells—and that is the reason I now ask you to help me. . . .

STUDENT. What can I do?

HUMMEL. First of all, push my chair over toward the billboard so that I can read the posters. . . . I want to see what is being given at the Opera this evening. . . .

STUDENT (pushes the chair over toward the billboard). You have no attendant to help you?

HUMMEL. Yes, but he is doing an errand for me just now—he'll be back any minute. . . . Are you studying medicine?

STUDENT. No, I am studying languages—but I really haven't made up my mind just what line to pursue. . . .

HUMMEL. Oho, oho—How are you at mathematics?

STUDENT. Oh, fairly good.

HUMMEL. Good!—Perhaps you would like to have some employment, would you?

STUDENT. Yes, why not?

HUMMEL. Good! (He studies the poster.) They are giving The Valkyrie at the matinée today. . . . Then the Colonel and his daughter are sure to be there; and as he always has

the end seat in the sixth row, I'll place you beside him. . . .
Will you go into that telephone booth over there and order a
ticket for seat number 82 in row six?

STUDENT. You want me to go to the Opera in the middle
of the day?

HUMMEL. Yes! And if you will listen to me, things will go
well with you. I would like to see you happy, rich, and honored. . . . Yesterday you made your debut as the heroic res-
cuer; tomorrow you will be a celebrity—and then your name
will be worth something.

STUDENT (goes toward the telephone booth). I must say this
is a mad adventure!

HUMMEL. Don't you ever take chances?

STUDENT. Yes—and it turned out to be my undoing. . . .

HUMMEL. But now we'll turn your misfortune into good luck
instead! Go and telephone now! (Hummel resumes reading
the newspaper. The Dark Lady comes out and stops on the
sidewalk where she engages in conversation with the Janitress.
Hummel listens to them; their conversation is inaudible to
the audience. The Student comes out of the booth.) Is it done?

STUDENT. It's all arranged.

HUMMEL (pointing to the apartment house). You see this
house?

STUDENT. Yes, indeed, I have been looking at it. . . . I passed
here yesterday, while the sun danced on the window panes. . . .
And I couldn't help thinking of all the luxury and beauty
that must be found within, and I said to my companion:
"Oh, if I could only have an apartment in this house—four
flights up—a beautiful young wife—two lovely little children—
and an income of twenty thousand. . . ."

HUMMEL. Is that what you said? Did you really? There you
see!—I'm in love with this house, too. . . .

STUDENT. You speculate in houses, do you?

HUMMEL. N-yes—but not the way you mean. . . .

STUDENT. Do you know the people who live here?

HUMMEL. I know them all. When one has reached my age,
one knows everybody and everybody's parents and their parents; and we are all related in one way or another. I was
eighty recently—but nobody knows me—not altogether. . . .
My interest is the destinies of human beings. (The window
shades in the Round Room on the ground floor are being
raised. The Colonel, in civilian attire, can be seen inside looking at the thermometer outside the window; then he walks
back into the room and stops before the marble figure. Hum-

mel continues speaking.) That's the Colonel you see standing there—you'll be sitting next to him at the Opera. . . .

STUDENT. Is that—the Colonel? I don't understand all this—it's like some fairy tale. . . .

HUMMEL. My whole life is like a succession of fairy tales, my dear young man. . . . But even though they read differently, they are bound together by a common thread, and the leading theme recurs in every tale throughout.

STUDENT. Whom does the marble figure in there represent?

HUMMEL. That's his wife, of course. . . .

STUDENT. Was she really that lovely?

HUMMEL. Why . . . yes!

STUDENT. Tell me about her!

HUMMEL. How can we really evaluate human beings, dear boy!—If I should tell you now that he beat her—that she left him—that she came back to him—that she married him again—and that she now sits in there as a living mummy, worshiping her own image—then you would say that I was out of my mind.

STUDENT. I just don't understand!

HUMMEL. I can well imagine. . . . Then we have the window with the hyacinths. There is where his daughter lives. She is out horseback riding—but she will soon be home. . . .

STUDENT. And who is the dark lady who is speaking with the Janitress?

HUMMEL. Well, now, that is a little complicated . . . but it has to do with the deceased—who lived up there where the white sheets are hung.

STUDENT. And—who was he?

HUMMEL. He was a human being like you or me—but the most conspicuous thing about him was his vanity. . . . If you were born on a Sunday, you would soon see him come out of the door over there and stand on the sidewalk, in order to satisfy himself that the consulate flag was flying at half-mast. You see, he was a consul, and he reveled in all sorts of insignia: royal crowns and coats of arms, plumed hats and fancy-colored ribbons and decorations.

STUDENT. You spoke of children being born on a Sunday. . . . I have been told that I was born on a Sunday. . . .

HUMMEL. Were you? Really? I might have known it. . . . I could tell by the color of your eyes. . . . Then you can see what others can't! Haven't you noticed that?

STUDENT. I don't know what others *can* or *cannot* see, but sometimes—well . . . but one doesn't talk about things like that. . . .

HUMMEL. I was almost certain of it! But you can tell me—for you see—I understand—such things. . . .

STUDENT. For example, take what happened yesterday. . . . I felt myself drawn to that dim little street where the house collapsed soon after. . . . The moment I got there I found myself stopping in front of the building—which I had never seen before. . . . Suddenly I noticed a crack in the wall—I heard the floor beams snap and break—I sprang forward and snatched up a little child that was toddling alongside the wall —and a second later the house caved in. . . . I was saved, but in my arms—where I thought I carried the child—was nothing. . . .

HUMMEL. Well, I must say. . . . I have heard of many things. . . . But tell me one thing: why did you gesticulate as you did a moment ago at the fountain? And why were you talking to yourself?

STUDENT. Didn't you see the milkmaid I talked to?

HUMMEL *(seems horrified)*. The milkmaid?

STUDENT. Certainly—the girl who handed me the dipper?

HUMMEL. Oh—so—so that's the way it is. . . . Well, now. . . . I haven't your sight—but I have something else. *(At this moment a white-haired woman can be seen seating herself at the window with the reflector mirror.)* Look at that old woman in the window! Do you see her?—Well—she was my betrothed once upon a time—sixty years ago. . . . I was twenty then. Have no fear, she won't recognize me! We see each other daily—and it doesn't affect me in the least, despite the fact that we once vowed to love each other eternally—eternally!

STUDENT. How silly people were in those days! It would never occur to us today to say such things to our girls.

HUMMEL. Forgive us, young man—we did not know any better. But can you imagine that this old woman was once young and beautiful, can you?

STUDENT. No, I see no trace of beauty. Yes—there is something about her gaze that is appealing . . . her eyes I can't see. *(The Janitress comes out with a basket of fir sprigs which she strews in front of the house.)*

HUMMEL. Yes—and the Janitress!—The Dark Lady is her daughter by the dead man—that's why her husband was given the position of janitor. . . . But the Dark Lady has a suitor who is highborn and has hopes of becoming rich. He is in the throes of being divorced from his wife. She is giving him a mansion as an inducement to get rid of him. This noble suitor is the son-in-law of the dead consul, it's his bedclothes you see being aired up there on the balcony. . . . It's a little involved, isn't it?

STUDENT. Yes—terribly involved!

HUMMEL. It is, indeed, whichever way you look at it—no matter how simple it may seem.

STUDENT. But exactly who was the dead man?

HUMMEL. You asked me that question a moment ago and I answered you. Now—if you could look round the corner, where the servants' entrance is, you would see a flock of poor people whom he used to help—when he felt like it.

STUDENT. Then he was a charitable man, wasn't he?

HUMMEL. Yes—sometimes.

STUDENT. He wasn't always?

HUMMEL. No-o-o! . . . People are like that! Now, will you please give my chair a slight push so that I can get a little sunshine. I am terribly cold—I'm freezing. That comes from being unable to move about—the blood congeals. I'm afraid I don't have long to live—I *know* I don't. . . . But before I die, I have a few things I want to do. . . . Feel my hand—feel how cold it is. . . .

STUDENT (*takes hold of Hummel's hand and shrinks back*). Yes—frightfully cold!

HUMMEL. Don't leave me! I am tired—I'm lonely—but I wasn't always like this, you understand. I have an enormously long life behind me—enormously long!—I have made people miserable, and people have made me miserable; the one thing offsets the other—but before I die, I would like to see you happy. Because of your father—and other circumstances—our fates have become linked. . . .

STUDENT. Let go of my hand—you are taking all my strength! You are freezing my blood! What is it you want of me?

HUMMEL. Have patience, and soon you'll both see and understand. . . . Here comes the Young Lady. . . .

STUDENT. The Colonel's daughter?

HUMMEL. His daughter, yes! Look at her! Did you ever see such a masterpiece?

STUDENT. She is the image of the marble figure in there. . . .

HUMMEL. Well, that's her mother. . . .

STUDENT. You are right! Never have I seen such a woman of woman born!—The man who is fortunate enough to get her for his wife will indeed be lucky!

HUMMEL. You appreciate her, don't you?—It isn't everybody who can see her beauty. . . . Well, so be it then. *(The Young Lady enters from the right. She is dressed in a modern English riding habit. Without looking at anyone, she walks slowly to the entrance door. There she stops, exchanging a few words with the Janitress. Then she goes into the house. The Student covers his eyes with his hand.)* Are you crying?

STUDENT. When you see the hopelessness of things—how can you feel anything but despair?

HUMMEL. I can open both doors and hearts, if I can only find an arm to do my will. . . . Serve me, and you will have power!

STUDENT. Is this some sort of pact? Am I to sell my soul?

HUMMEL. You sell nothing! You see—all my life I have done nothing but *take;* now I feel a desire to give. . . . But no one wishes to receive. . . . I am a rich man, a very rich man, but I have no heirs. . . . Yes—I have one, a scamp who is torturing the life out of me. . . . Be a son to me—and take your inheritance while I am still living—enjoy life—and let me look on—if only from a distance. . . .

STUDENT. What do you wish me to do?

HUMMEL. First, go and hear *The Valkyrie.* . . .

STUDENT. That we have already settled. What next?

HUMMEL. This evening you will be sitting in there in the Round Room.

STUDENT. How can I get in there?

HUMMEL. By going to *The Valkyrie.*

STUDENT. Just why have you chosen me for your purposes? Did you know me somewhere before?

HUMMEL. Why, of course. I have had my eye on you for a long time. . . . But look up there now—up on the balcony! See the maid hoisting the flag at half-mast out of respect for the consul!—Now she is turning the bedclothes. You see the blue bedspread? It was made for two to sleep under—but now it will cover only one. *(The Young Lady now appears in the window. She has changed into a different dress and is watering the hyacinths.)* And there is my little girl—look at her! —She talks with the flowers—and she herself is like a blue hyacinth, isn't she? She quenches their thirst—but with pure water only—and they convert the water into color and fragrance. Here comes the Colonel with his newspaper! He shows her the picture of the collapsed house—now he points to your photograph. . . . She is not unimpressed. She reads the description of your courageous act. . . . It looks as if it were going to rain.

. . . If it does, I'll be in trouble—unless Johansson comes back soon. . . . *(It is growing increasingly dark. The old woman at the window with the reflector mirror closes the window.)* Now my beloved is closing her window. Seventy-nine years old! —The reflector mirror is the only mirror she looks into—for there she doesn't see herself, only the world outside . . . and she can see it from two directions. But the world can see *her* —and that's something she doesn't realize. . . . Just the same, she is a good-looking old lady. *(At this moment, the deceased —wrapped in a winding sheet—comes out of the entrance door.)*

STUDENT. God in heaven! What's that I see!

HUMMEL. What is it you see?

STUDENT. Don't you see—there—in the entrance—the dead man?

HUMMEL. I don't see a thing—but I had a strange feeling this would happen! Tell me what you see!

STUDENT. He is coming out into the street. *(There is a silence.)* Now he turns his head . . . he is looking at the flag. . . .

HUMMEL. What did I tell you? And you may be sure he will count the wreaths, too, and read all the cards on them! And God help the one whose wreath is missing!

STUDENT. Now he is turning the corner. . . .

HUMMEL. He goes to count the poor standing outside the servants' entrance . . . the poor furnish such a decorative background: "Mourned and blessed by a multitude of people!" Well—but he won't get my blessing, no, sir!—Just between you and me, he was a great scoundrel!

STUDENT. But he was charitable, wasn't he? . . .

HUMMEL. A charitable rascal in whose mind dwelled uppermost a magnificent funeral. . . . When he felt the end was near, he cheated the state out of fifty thousand crowns. Now his daughter is having an affair with a married man, and her interest centers on his will. . . . The scoundrel—he can hear every word we say, and he is welcome to it!—There comes Johansson! *(Johansson enters from the right.)* Report! *(Johansson speaks to Hummel in an inaudible voice.)* So—he was not at home? You are an imbecile!—Did you go to the telegraph office? —No telegram! . . . What about the rest? . . . This evening at six? Good!—What's in the special news edition?—His name in full —Arkenholz—student—year of birth—his parents. . . . Excellent—I think it's starting to rain. . . . What did he answer? —Is that so? Is that so? He said he couldn't, eh?—Well, then I'll *make* him want to!—Here comes the Aristocrat. . . . Push me round the corner, Johansson, so I can hear what the beggars are saying. *(To the Student.)* And you, Arkenholz, you might wait for me here! Understand? *(To Johansson.)* Hurry up, hurry up, Johansson! *(Johansson pushes the wheelchair round the corner. The Student remains standing, gazing at the Young Lady, who is loosening the earth in the hyacinth pots.)*

ARISTOCRAT *(enters. He is dressed in mourning. He speaks to the Dark Lady, who has been strolling back and forth on the sidewalk).* Well—what can we do about it?—We just have to wait. . . .

DARK LADY. I can't wait!

ARISTOCRAT. You mean that? Then go to the country!

DARK LADY. No, I don't want to go to the country!

ARISTOCRAT. Come over here so they can't hear us. *(They walk over toward the billboard, where they continue their conversation in subdued tones.)*

JOHANSSON *(comes from the left. He goes to Arkenholz).* Mr. Hummel asked me to remind you, Mr. Arkenholz, about that other matter—so you won't forget. . . .

STUDENT *(slowly).* Tell me—tell me first—just who is your employer?

JOHANSSON. Well—he is so many things—and he has been everything. . . .

STUDENT. Is he quite right in his head?

JOHANSSON. Well— just what does that mean, exactly?—All his life he has been looking for a Sunday child, he says—but who can tell if that's true?

STUDENT. What is his purpose? Is he a miser?

JOHANSSON. What he wants is power. . . . The whole day long he rides about in his chariot like the god Thor himself. He looks at houses, tears them down, constructs new streets, builds new squares—but he also breaks into houses, steals his way in through windows, plays havoc with human destinies, kills off his enemies—and he never forgives. . . . Can you picture this shriveled lame cripple as having once been a Don Juan? But he always lost his women.

STUDENT. It's hard to believe. . . .

JOHANSSON. He is so sly, you see, that—once he is tired of a woman—he tricks her into leaving him. And now he acts just like a horse thief in the human market square: he steals human beings—and in more ways than one. He literally stole me from out of the hands of the law. You see—hm—I once committed a stupid blunder, and he was the only one who knew about it. So, instead of putting me behind bars, he made me his slave!

I wear myself out for him—and all I get for it is my food . . . and that's not too good.

STUDENT. What is he after here—in that house?

JOHANSSON. Well, now—that is something I can't tell you! It's altogether too involved!

STUDENT. I think I'll give up the whole thing.

JOHANSSON. Look! The young lady dropped her bracelet out of the window. . . .

(Timidly the Student steps forward, picks up the bracelet, and hands it to her. Her manner is reserved and rather cold. The Student rejoins Johansson.)

JOHANSSON. So—you are thinking of leaving. . . . That's not so easy as you may think—once *he* has you in his clutches. . . . And there is nothing between heaven and earth that he is afraid of. Yes, there is one thing—or rather, one person . . .

STUDENT. Wait a second—I think, perhaps, I know. . . .

JOHANSSON. Why, how could you? . . .

STUDENT. I'm simply guessing!—Is it—a little milkmaid he's afraid of?

JOHANSSON. Whenever he sees a milk wagon, he always turns his head the other way. . . . And sometimes he talks in his sleep! I think—at one time—he must have been in Hamburg. . . .

STUDENT. How can you trust a man like him?

JOHANSSON. You can trust him—to do *anything!*

STUDENT. What's he doing round the corner?

JOHANSSON. He is listening to the poor. Sowing a little word here and there, removing one stone at a time—until the structure falls apart—speaking metaphorically. You see—I am a man of education—I was once a book dealer. . . . Are you still bent on going?

STUDENT. I find it hard to be ungrateful. . . . This man once saved my father—and all he asks now is a small favor in return. . . .

JOHANSSON. What is it?

STUDENT. He wants me to go to *The Valkyrie.* . . .

JOHANSSON. There is something puzzling about that. . . . But he has so many ideas. . . . Look—now he is talking to the policeman. . . . He always keeps on good terms with the police; he uses them, embroils them in his interests, holds them in check with false promises and enticements—and all the while he is pumping them. You'll see that before the day is over he will be received in the Round Room.

STUDENT. What is it he is after? What does he want from the Colonel?

JOHANSSON. Well—I have a faint idea—but I don't know for certain. You'll find out yourself when you are there.

STUDENT. I'll never get in there!

JOHANSSON. That depends on yourself. Go to *The Valkyrie!*

STUDENT. Is that the way to get in there?

JOHANSSON. Yes, if he said so. . . . Look—look at him, standing erect in his battle chariot, drawn in triumph by the beggars—who get nothing but thin air for it—only a vague hope of something to eat at his funeral!

HUMMEL (*enters, standing up in his wheelchair, which is pulled by a Beggar. Other men in rags follow*). Hail! Hail to the noble youth who saved so many lives at the risk of his own at the disaster yesterday! Hail to Arkenholz! (*The Beggars uncover their heads but do not cheer. The Young Lady in the window waves her handkerchief. The Colonel is seen staring at the scene from his window. The old woman rises at hers. The Maid hoists the flag to the top of the flagstaff.*) Applaud, fellow citizens! Clap your hands! For even though this is a day of rest, the ass in the pit and the ears in the fields will give us absolution. Although I was not born on a Sunday, I have both the gift of prophecy and the power of healing; on one occasion I brought a drowned man back to life. . . . Yes—that happened in Hamburg—on a Sunday morning like this. (*The Milkmaid appears. She is seen only by the Student and Hummel. She raises her arms like a person drowning; all the while her eyes are fixedly on Hummel, who falls into his chair and shrinks with fear.*) Take me away, Johansson! As fast as you can! . . . Arkenholz—don't forget *The Valkyrie!*

STUDENT. What can be the meaning of all this?

JOHANSSON. We'll see, no doubt! We'll see!

SCENE 2. *The Round Room. In the rear, a white, mirrored, porcelain stove. On its ledge stands a pendulum clock, flanked by two candelabra.*

On the left is seen the entrance hall, and beyond it one glimpses a room in green with mahogany furniture. In the center of the left wall, a wallpapered door leads to a closet, in which the Mummy lives.

On the right, shadowed by palms, is the marble figure. It is so placed that it can be concealed by a curtain or drapery. At right, rear, a door leads to the Hyacinth Room, where the Young Lady is seated, reading. The Colonel sits in the

*Green Room. He is busy writing and has his back to the
audience.*

*Bengtsson, the butler, enters from the hall, left; he is in
livery. He is followed by Johansson, who wears a tailcoat
and black tie.*

BENGTSSON. Now, Johansson, you will do the serving, and
I'll take their wraps. Have you done it before?

JOHANSSON. You know I push a battle chariot all day long
—but at night I wait at private parties; and this is one house
I have always wanted to work in. Queer people in this house,
eh?

BENGTSSON. Well—I'd say they are a little unusual. . . .

JOHANSSON. Are they having a musicale tonight—or what?

BENGTSSON. No, it's the usual ghost supper—that's what we
call it. They sip their tea—and don't speak a word. . . . Or the
Colonel will be talking solo. . . . And then they nibble and
gnaw at their *petits fours*—all of them at the same time, so that
it sounds like rats in an attic.

JOHANSSON. Why do you call it "ghost supper"?

BENGTSSON. They look and act like ghosts. . . . And this has
been going on for twenty years!—And always the same people
—saying the same things—or saying nothing, afraid of tripping
themselves up. . . .

JOHANSSON. Has the house no mistress?

BENGTSSON. Oh yes—but she is touched in the head. She
lives in a closet—because her eyes can't bear the light. *(He
points to the wallpapered door in the left wall.)*

JOHANSSON. In there?

BENGTSSON. I told you they were a little unusual, didn't I?

JOHANSSON. What does she look like?

BENGTSSON. Like a mummy! Do you want to see her? *(He
opens the closet door.)* See—there she is!

JOHANSSON. God in heav—

MUMMY *(prattling away).* Why do you open the door,
haven't I told you to keep it shut?

BENGTSSON. Ta-ta-ta-ta! My little baby must be nice now—
and I'll give you something good to eat!—Pretty Polly!

MUMMY *(talking like a parrot).* Pretty Polly! Oh, Jacob,
where are you? *Currrr!*

BENGTSSON. She thinks she is a parrot—and perhaps she is.
(To the Mummy.) Polly! Whistle for us! *(The Mummy whistles.)*

JOHANSSON. I have seen many things in my day—but never
anything like this!

BENGTSSON. Well—you see, when a house gets old, it starts to be moldy and musty. And when people live together for any length of time, and keep tormenting one another, they eventually go mad. The lady of this house . . . Shut up, Polly! This mummy has been living here for forty years . . . with the same husband, the same relatives, the same friends, the same furniture. *(He closes the closet door.)* And what has taken place in this house—well, that's more than I can tell. . . . Take a look at this marble figure! That's she—when she was young. . . .

JOHANSSON. Good Lord! Is that really the mummy?

BENGTSSON. That's she! It's enough to make you weep! And —through the power of imagination or for some other reason —she has taken on some of the traits of the talkative bird. For instance, she has an aversion to cripples and sick people. She can't bear her own daughter because she is sick. . . .

JOHANSSON. Is the Young Lady sick?

BENGTSSON. Didn't you know?

JOHANSSON. No! And the Colonel—who is he?

BENGTSSON. You'll probably find out!

JOHANSSON *(regarding the marble figure).* It's horrible to think that . . . How old is she now?

BENGTSSON. That's something nobody knows . . . but they say that when she was thirty-five, she looked nineteen—and that's what she made the Colonel believe she was. . . . And here in this house . . . do you know what that black Japanese screen—next to the chaise longue—is used for? They call it the "death screen"—and whenever anyone is dying, it's placed in front of the deathbed, just as they do in hospitals.

JOHANSSON. What a terrible house. . . . And for this house the Student had a longing as for paradise!

BENGTSSON. Which student? Oh yes—I know! The one who is coming here this evening. . . . The Colonel and the Young Lady met him at the Opera and took a great liking to him. . . . Hm. . . . But now it's my turn to ask you a question: Who is your employer? The gentleman in the wheelchair?

JOHANSSON. Yes—yes! Is he coming here, too?

BENGTSSON. He is not invited.

JOHANSSON. If he wants to come, he'll come—invited or not. . . .

HUMMEL *(appears in the hall, dressed in frock coat and top hat. He steals forward on his crutches and can be seen listening to the two servants' conversation.)*

BENGTSSON. He is a regular old crook, isn't he?

JOHANSSON. There's none bigger!

BENGTSSON. He looks like the devil himself!

JOHANSSON. I think he knows something about sorcery, too, for he can go through locked doors. . . .

HUMMEL *(comes forward; he goes over to Johannson and pulls his ear).* Take care, you scoundrel! *(To Bengtsson.)* Tell the Colonel I have come to pay him a visit!

BENGTSSON. Yes, but—he is expecting guests this evening . . .

HUMMEL. I know that! But my visit is as good as expected— even if not exactly looked forward to. . . .

BENGTSSON. Oh!—What is the name? Mr. Hummel?

HUMMEL. Precisely. Yes! *(Bengtsson goes through the hall into the Green Room and shuts the door after him. To Johansson.)* Get out! *(Johansson hesitates.)* Get out! *(Johansson leaves by way of the hall. Examines the room; he stops before the marble figure in profound admiration.)* Amalia! . . . It's she! . . . She! *(He saunters through the room, and here and there he picks up and scrutinizes objects. Then he rearranges his wig in front of the mirror; this done, he returns to the figure.)*

MUMMY *(from the closet).* Pretty Polly!

HUMMEL *(shrinks back).* What was that? Is there a parrot in the room? I don't see it!

MUMMY. Is Jacob there?

HUMMEL. Spooks!

MUMMY. Jacob!

HUMMEL. This is frightening! . . . So—it is secrets of this kind they guard in this house! *(He goes over to look at a painting and stands with his back turned to the closet.)* There he is! . . . He!

MUMMY *(comes out of the closet and steals up behind Hummel, pulling at his wig.)* Currrr! Is it you—Currrr?

HUMMEL *(leaps, frightened out of his senses).* Lord in heaven! —What is it?

MUMMY *(in a normal human voice).* Is it Jacob?

HUMMEL. Yes—that's my name—actually, yes. . . .

MUMMY *(with deep emotion).* And my name is Amalia!

HUMMEL. No, no, no. . . . Oh God, oh God!

MUMMY. This is the way I look now! Yes!—And that is how I used to look! *(She points to the marble figure.)* Life teaches us many things, doesn't it? I am spending most of my life now in the closet there—not only not to see, but to avoid being seen. . . . And you, Jacob—what are you here for?

HUMMEL. My child! *Our* child!

MUMMY. There you see her. . . .

HUMMEL. Where?

MUMMY. There—in the Hyacinth Room. . . .

HUMMEL (gazing at the Young Lady). Yes—it's she! (There is a silence.) And what does her father think . . . the Colonel—I mean your husband?

MUMMY. Once—when he made me lose my temper—I told him everything. . . .

HUMMEL. And what did he . . . ?

MUMMY. He didn't believe me. He only said: "That's what all women say when they try to get rid of their husbands." But it was a dreadful thing to do just the same. His whole life has become perverted—yes, even his paternity and family tree! Sometimes, when I glance through the peerage, I can't help thinking to myself: "She is masquerading with a false birth certificate—just as some servant girls do!" And for such fraud they are sent to prison! . . .

HUMMEL. She is not the only one doing that! I seem to remember that you yourself had a false birth date on yours. . . .

MUMMY. It was my mother who made me change it! The blame was not mine! But it was you—it was you who had the greater share in our crime. . . .

HUMMEL. No!—It was your husband who was the cause of it when he stole you from me!—And I was born with the kind of nature that can't forgive until I have punished—it was nothing short of compulsion to me—a compelling duty! And I still feel that way!

MUMMY. Why have you come here—to this house? What is it you want? How did you get in?—Has your visit anything to do with my daughter?—If you so much as touch her, you shall die!

HUMMEL. I mean well by her.

MUMMY. And you must spare her father. . . .

HUMMEL. No!

MUMMY. Then you shall die—in this room—behind this screen. . . .

HUMMEL. So be it—but I can't let go, once I have started to bite. . . .

MUMMY. You plan to marry her to that student—why? He is nothing and has nothing!

HUMMEL. He will be rich—through me.

MUMMY. Have you been invited here this evening?

HUMMEL. No—but I intend to invite myself to your ghost supper.

MUMMY. Do you know who is coming?

HUMMEL. No—not exactly.

MUMMY. The Baron—who lives up above—his father-in-law was buried this noon. . . .

HUMMEL. He who is divorcing his wife in order to marry the janitor's daughter . . . and who was once your lover?

MUMMY. And then there will be your former fiancée—whom my husband seduced. . . .

HUMMEL. A choice gathering!

MUMMY. Oh God! If He would only let us die! If He would only let us die!

HUMMEL. Why do you continue to get together? Why?

MUMMY. Crimes and secrets and guilt are what bind us together. . . . Time after time we have broken apart and gone our own separate ways—but inevitably we are drawn together again. . . .

HUMMEL. I think the Colonel is coming now. . . .

MUMMY. Then I will go in to Adèle. *(There is a silence.)* Jacob—think of what you do! Spare him. *(Again there is silence. Then she goes out.)*

COLONEL *(enters. He is reserved and cold).* Please be seated! *(Hummel seats himself slowly. There is a pause. Gazes fixedly at Hummel.)* This letter was written by you, wasn't it? *(He shows Hummel a letter.)*

HUMMEL. Yes. *(There is a pause.)*

COLONEL. Your name is Hummel?

HUMMEL. Yes. *(Again there is a pause.)*

COLONEL. Now that I know that you have bought up all my unpaid, overdue promissory notes, I am consequently at your mercy. What do you want of me now?

HUMMEL. I want you to pay me—in one way or another!

COLONEL. How?

HUMMEL. It's very simple—forget about the money—simply welcome me in your home, as your guest. . . .

COLONEL. If that is all you desire, why . . .

HUMMEL. Thank you.

COLONEL. Anything else?

HUMMEL. Discharge Bengtsson!

COLONEL. For what reason? My faithful old servant—who has been with me for all these years—who has been given the Patriot's Medal for long and devoted service. . . . Why—tell me —should I discharge him?

HUMMEL. All the beautiful qualities you see in him are nothing but an illusion! Bengtsson is not the man he seems to be. . . .

COLONEL. Who is—for that matter?

HUMMEL *(with a start)*. That's true!—But Bengtsson must go!

COLONEL. Are you trying to run my household?

HUMMEL. Quite so—since everything here is my property: furniture, draperies, curtains, silver, linen, and the other things. . . .

COLONEL. What other things?

HUMMEL. Everything—everything you see here belongs to me!

COLONEL. Quite right, it is all yours! But there are two things you can't take from me: my ancestral escutcheon and my good name!

HUMMEL. Yes—even them! *(There is a silence.)* You are not a nobleman!

COLONEL. Have you no decency!

HUMMEL *(produces a document)*. If you will read this extract from the Heraldry Record, you will see that the line whose name you are using has been extinct for a hundred years.

COLONEL *(reads the document)*. I admit I have heard rumors to this effect—but I inherited the name from my father. *(He continues reading.)* Yes—yes—you are right! . . . I have no right to my noble name!—Not even my name is mine! . . . I must remove my crested ring. . . . Oh, of course it too belongs to you. . . . Here you are! . . .

HUMMEL *(puts the ring in his pocket)*. Now let us continue. . . . You are not a colonel!

COLONEL. I am not a colonel?

HUMMEL. No! You held at one time the temporary rank of colonel in the American Army of Volunteers; but all such temporary titles were abolished after the war in Cuba and the reorganization of the army.

COLONEL. Is this true?

HUMMEL *(fumbling in his pocket)*. Would you care to read?

COLONEL. No—it isn't necessary. . . . Who are you? What right have you to sit here and strip me naked?

HUMMEL. We'll come to that later . . . but as for stripping you naked—do you know who you are?

COLONEL. How dare you?

HUMMEL. Take off that wig and take a good look at yourself in the mirror. . . . And spit out your false teeth and shave off your mustache at the same time—let Bengtsson unhook your steel stays . . . then let us see if a certain lackey is able to recognize himself as the individual who used to visit the maids in a certain kitchen for the sake of getting a meal! *(The Colonel is about to ring for Bengtsson, but Hummel intercepts him.)* Don't touch that bell—and don't call Bengtsson! If you do, I shall have him arrested! *(The sound of voices is heard from the entrance hall.)* I hear the guests coming. . . . Keep calm now—let's play our roles as before. . . .

COLONEL. Who are you? Your voice and look seem familiar. . . .

HUMMEL. Stop prying! Just keep silent and do as I say!

STUDENT *(enters. He bows to the Colonel)*. Good evening, Colonel!

COLONEL. Welcome to my home, young man! I esteem it an honor to have you in my home because of your noble behavior at the great disaster. Everybody is talking about you . . . and I consider it a privilege to have you as my guest. . . .

STUDENT *(with the utmost respect; somewhat timidly)*. My humble birth, sir. . . . Your illustrious name. . . . Your noble birth. . . .

COLONEL. May I present you to Mr. Hummel—Mr. Arkenholz. . . . Perhaps you would like to join the ladies—they are in there. *(He points to the Hyacinth Room.)* Mr. Hummel and I are in the midst of a discussion. *(The Student is shown into the Hyacinth Room by the Colonel. The Student engages in timid conversation with the Young Lady. The Colonel continues.)* A superb young man. . . . He is musical, sings, writes poetry. . . . If he were wellborn and of equal station I would not hesitate to . . .

HUMMEL. To do what?

COLONEL. I was thinking of my daughter. . . .

HUMMEL. *Your* daughter!—Incidentally, why does she always sit in there?

COLONEL. Whenever she is not out-of-doors, she just *has* to sit in the Hyacinth Room. It's a peculiarity of hers. . . . Ah, here we have Miss Beate von Holsteincrown—a charming woman! She is active in her church—and has an income commensurate with her station and birth. . . .

HUMMEL *(to himself)*. My fiancée! *(The fiancée enters. She is white-haired and acts as if she were slightly deranged. She curtsies and seats herself. The Aristocrat enters. He looks enigmatic, secretive, and is in mourning. He takes a seat.)*

COLONEL *(introducing him)*. Baron Skanskorg. . . .

HUMMEL *(in an aside, without rising)*. Well, if it isn't the jewelry thief! *(To the Colonel.)* Usher in the Mummy—then the company will be complete. . . .

COLONEL *(in the doorway to the Hyacinth Room)*. Polly!

MUMMY *(enters)*. Currrr!

COLONEL. Would you like the young people to come in, too?

HUMMEL. No, not the young people! They must be spared!
(All are now seated in a circle, and all are silent.)

COLONEL. May we have the tea brought in now?

HUMMEL. What's the use? No one likes tea—so why the pretense? *(Silence.)*

COLONEL. Well—shall we engage in conversation?

HUMMEL *(holding on to his words, with a pause here and there)*. Talk about the weather—which we can see and feel; ask one another whether we are in good health—when we know what the answer will be. I prefer silence! For then one's thoughts can be heard, and one discovers the past. Silence conceals *nothing*—but words do. . . . I read the other day that the confusion of tongues owed its origin to the savages. It is their way of keeping tribal secrets from outsiders. Languages are, therefore, nothing but codes; and whoever discovers the key will understand them all. This, however, does not mean that secrets cannot be bared without any key—and this especially when a question of paternity has to be proved. Be that as it may, to prove such a thing to the satisfaction of a court of law—that's another matter. Two false witnesses can prove anything the law requires, as long as their testimony tallies. But the kind of venture I have in mind has no need of any witnesses. Nature itself has endowed human beings with a sense of modesty that instinctively hides what should be hidden; yet—against our will—we fall into precarious situations at one time or another when, by some chance, our innermost secrets are exposed . . . when the mask is torn from the impostor, and the villain exposed. *(There is silence. All regard one another in dumb show.)* What a deathlike hush! *(Prolonged silence.)* Here, for example, in this estimable house, this beautiful home, where you find beauty, culture, and wealth *(Another long silence.)* . . . all of us present here know who we are—don't we? So there is no need for me to mention it. . . . And you know who I am, although you profess you don't. On the other hand, in there sits my daughter *(He points to the Hyacinth Room.)* . . . *mine,* as you also know. . . . She has lost the desire to live, without knowing why . . . she has been withering away in this atmosphere charged with crime, falsehood, and deception of every kind. That is why I looked about for a companion for her, in whose company she could find a glint of light and warmth, kindled by noble acts. *(Again there is a long silence.)* And that is why I have come here: I have come here to pull up and kill off the weeds, to expose the crimes, to settle all accounts in order that these two young people shall be able to start a new life in this house, which I am giving to them. *(A long pause.)* And now I'll let you off scot-free—each and everyone of you, in due turn,—and then you will leave! Whoever remains I'll have arrested! *(There is another long silence.)* You hear the clock ticking—like the death-watch in a wall? Do you? Do you hear what it says? Time—time! Time—time! In a few moments—when it strikes—your time will be up—and then you may go—but not before. . . . But before it strikes, its hands point at you threateningly!—Listen—here comes the warning: "The clock is about to strike". . . . And I can strike, too. *(He hits the top of the table with his crutch.)* Do you hear what I say? *(Silence.)*

MUMMY *(goes over to the pendulum clock and stops it. Then —in a sane, normal tone—she says earnestly).* But I can stop time—I can wipe out the past and undo what has been done— but not with bribery and not with threats . . . but through suffering and repentance. *(She goes up to Hummel.)* We are miserable mortals—and we know it. We have erred, we, like other mortals. We are not what we seem, for at the bottom of our souls is something that is more noble than our own human selves, since we disapprove of our trespasses. And when you, Jacob Hummel—with your assumed name—mean to sit in judgment on us, you prove yourself worse than any of us miserable sinners. You are no more the one you seem to be than we are!—You are a thief of human souls—you stole mine once with your false promises . . . you took the life of the consul who was buried today . . . you strangled him with his unpaid promissory notes—you have bound the student with a spurious debt claim on his dead father—who never owed you a farthing. *(Hummel has tried to get up on his feet to say something. He sinks back in his chair, and—as the Mummy continues to expose him—he shrinks more and more.)* But there is one black spot in your life that mystifies me. While I can't quite see through it, I nevertheless have a vague idea what it is. . . . Perhaps Bengtsson can throw some light on it. *(She rings the bell.)*

HUMMEL. No! Not Bengtsson. Not Bengtsson!

MUMMY. Oh—then he does know! *(She rings again. The Milkmaid appears in the doorway to the hall; but the only one who sees her is Hummel. He shrinks back, frightened. When Bengtsson enters, she disappears.)* Do you know this man, Bengtsson?

BENGTSSON. Yes—I do. I know him—and he knows me. We all know that life has its ups and downs. I was once in his employ, and at another time he was in mine. For two whole years he came to our kitchen to see our cook and to get a free meal.

Because he had to leave for his work at three, the cook had dinner ready for him at two; and so my family had to eat warmed-up meals after that swine. But that was not all! He drank up the soup stock, too, and we had to eat watered-down soup! He sat in the kitchen like a vampire and sucked my home dry of all its pith and marrow until we looked like skeletons . . . and then he almost had us put in prison because we called the cook a thief!

Some years later I met this man in Hamburg. He had taken a different name, then. He was in the money-lending business —in short, a bloodsucker; but he was also accused of having enticed a young girl out on the ice with the intent of drowning her because she had witnessed a crime he had committed—and he was afraid she would expose him. . . .

MUMMY (*passes her hand across Hummel's face*). This is you! Now let us have the notes and your last will and testament! (*Johansson is seen in the doorway to the hall; he takes in the scene with visible interest, realizing that he is free from his slavery at last. Hummel produces a bundle of documents and papers that he throws down on the table. The Mummy goes up to him and strokes his back.*) Polly! Is Jacob there?

HUMMEL (*talking like a parrot*). Jacob is here! *Kaka-dora! Dora!*

MUMMY. Can the clock strike now?

HUMMEL (*with a clucking sound*). The clock can strike! (*He imitates a cuckoo clock.*) *Cuckoo—cuckoo—cuckoo.* . . .

MUMMY (*opens the door to the closet*). The clock has struck. Now get up and go into the closet, where I have lived for twenty years, weeping over our transgression. In there you will find a rope which you can think of, so to speak, as the one you strangled the consul with . . . and which it was your plan to use on your benefactor. . . . Now go! (*Hummel enters the closet. The Mummy closes the door after him.*) Bengtsson! Put up the screen—the death screen! (*Bengtsson places the screen before the door.*) Now it is done!—May God have mercy on his soul!

ALL. Amen! (*There is a prolonged silence. . . . In the Hyacinth Room the Young Lady is seen playing the harp, accompanying the Student, who recites.*)

STUDENT. As I gazed into the sunlight
'Twas as if I'd seen His spirit.
Man must reap what he has sown;
Blest be he whose deeds are worthy;
evil actions done in anger

are not purged by further wrongs. . . .
Comfort him you have brought sorrow—
Good brings good to you in turn. . . .
Righteous living exiles fear. . . .
Blessed be the pure in heart! . . .[1]

SCENE 3. *The Hyacinth Room. It is a room furnished in
a somewhat bizarre style, Oriental in effect. Hyacinths of
various colors are placed everywhere. In a recess on the
porcelain stove is a large figure of Buddha holding a bulb
in his lap. The stem of a shallot (Allium ascalonicum) rises
from it with its small white clustered flowers resembling stars.*

*In the rear, left, is a door leading to the Round Room,
where the Colonel and the Mummy are seated. They are
silent and do not move. The death screen is partly visible. At
right, a door to the pantry and kitchen.*

*The Student and the Young Lady (Adèle) are by the
table: she with her harp, he standing.*

YOUNG LADY. Now sing to my flowers. . . .

STUDENT. Is this the flower of your soul?

YOUNG LADY. My one and only. . . . And you—do you love
it, too?

STUDENT. I love the hyacinth above all other flowers: its
virginal shape, rising straight and slender from its bulb floating
on the surface, sending its pure, white roots down into the
pale water. I love its colors: the snow-white—pure as snow;
the yellow—sweet as honey; the pink—the color of youth; the
red—the sign of ripeness . . . but above all, the blue—blue as
the morning dew, with deepset eyes, steadfast and faithful.
. . . I love them all—more than gold and precious pearls. . . .
I have loved them since I was a child, have looked up to them
because they possess all the noble qualities I lack. . . . And
yet . . .

YOUNG LADY. And yet?

STUDENT. My love finds no response—these beautiful flowers
do not like me. . . .

YOUNG LADY. Why?

---

[1] The Song of the Sun, recited or sung by the Student, is not from the Poetic
Edda, as some Strindberg translators have maintained; it is a medieval Icelandic
poem of great length, originally containing perhaps more than the eighty-two stanzas
which have been handed down in written form. The poem as it occurs here is therefore an independent effort on Strindberg's part, paraphrasing several stanzas. The
original poem was undoubtedly written by an Icelandic cleric in the thirteenth
century. Its name in Icelandic is Sólarlióth.

STUDENT. Their fragrance—strong and pure as the early winds of spring that have swept across melting snow—seems to confuse my senses—it benumbs me, dazzles me, crowds me out of the room, assails me with poisoned arrows that bring pain to my heart and set my head afire. Do you know the legend of the hyacinth?

YOUNG LADY. Tell it to me!

STUDENT. First let me tell you what it symbolizes. The bulb is the earth which is cradled by water or rests in the soil. Then the stem shoots up, straight as the axis of the earth, and at its apex are the six-pointed, starlike flowers.

YOUNG LADY. Above the earth—the stars! Oh—how divine! Where did you get that thought? How did you unriddle it?

STUDENT. Let me think!—I looked into your eyes!—So it must be an image of the cosmos. . . . That is why Buddha is pictured holding the earth-bulb in his lap, his eyes brooding on it, waiting to see it grow and spread—in all directions—and transforming itself into a heaven. This is what Buddha is waiting for: that this poor, wretched earth shall some day become a heaven!

YOUNG LADY. I see it now!—Are not the snowflakes also six-pointed, like the Hyacinthus?

STUDENT. Yes, they are!—And so the snowflakes must be falling stars. . . .

YOUNG LADY. And the snowdrop a snow star—shooting out of the snow. . . .

STUDENT. But the narcissus—with its red-and-yellow cup and its six white rays—the narcissus is the Sirius of the flowers, the most beautiful and the greatest of all the stars in the heavens. . . .

YOUNG LADY. Have you ever seen a shallet in bloom?

STUDENT. Yes, indeed, I have. It cradles its flowers inside a ball—a globe resembling the celestial sphere, studded with white stars. . . .

YOUNG LADY. Oh, God, how wonderful! Who gave birth to your thoughts?

STUDENT. You!

YOUNG LADY. No—you!

STUDENT. We both! We gave birth to them together—we are one. . . .

YOUNG LADY. Not yet. . . .

STUDENT. What else remains?

YOUNG LADY. The long wait—pain and suffering—we must learn patience.

STUDENT. Well—put me to the test! *(There is a pause.)* Tell me—why do your parents sit in there so silently? They are not saying a single word.

YOUNG LADY. They have nothing to say to each other—because neither one believes what the other one says. My father once expressed it this way: "What good does it do to talk? We can't deceive each other anyhow!"

STUDENT. Isn't that horrible! . . .

YOUNG LADY. Here comes the Cook. Look at her—how big and fat she is! . . .

STUDENT. What does she want?

YOUNG LADY. She wants to ask me about the dinner. You see, I am looking after the household during my mother's illness.

STUDENT. Must we worry about the kitchen, too?

YOUNG LADY. Well—we have to eat. . . . Look at her—I just can't bear looking at her!

STUDENT. Who is this Gargantuan bulk of a woman?

YOUNG LADY. She belongs to the Hummel family of vampires. She is devouring us alive. . . .

STUDENT. Why don't you discharge her?

YOUNG LADY. She won't leave! We can't get her to do anything—she is a scourge for our sins. . . . Can't you see that we are wasting away?

STUDENT. Don't you get enough to eat?

YOUNG LADY. Yes—we get plenty of dishes—but there is no strength in them. She boils the life out of the meat, gives us nothing but fiber and water—and she herself eats the broth with all the nourishment. And whenever we have steak, she first boils out the marrow, eats the gravy, and drinks the broth. No matter what she touches, she takes the strength out of it. It is as if she had eyes to suck you dry with. When she gives us coffee, it's nothing but dregs; when she gives us wine, it is diluted with water. . . .

STUDENT. Send her packing!

YOUNG LADY. We can't. . . .

STUDENT. Why not?

YOUNG LADY. We don't know. She refuses to leave. And none of us can cope with her. You see, we haven't the strength! She has taken all our strength from us. . . .

STUDENT. Will you let me get rid of her?

YOUNG LADY. No! I think it has to be the way it is!—Here she is! She will ask me what I wish for dinner—I'll tell her—then she will come with objections and say what *she* would like—and in the end she does as she pleases. . . .

STUDENT. Well—let her take care of the household, then, by herself.

YOUNG LADY. She refuses that, too.

STUDENT. This certainly is a weird house!—This is witchcraft!

YOUNG LADY. Yes! She turned and left—as soon as she saw you. . . .

COOK *(in the doorway)*. No—that was not the reason. *(She grins a wide grin, showing her teeth.)*

STUDENT. Get out, you creature!

COOK. I go when I feel like it! *(There is a pause.)* I feel like it now. . . .   *(She leaves.)*

YOUNG LADY. Don't lose your temper! You must learn to be patient!—She is one of the trials we have to suffer in this house. But we have a chambermaid also who is a scourge: we always have to go over her work. . . .

STUDENT. No more! No more! *Cor in aethere!* Let's have some music!

YOUNG LADY. Wait!

STUDENT. Music!

YOUNG LADY. Patience!—This room is called the Room of Trials and Tribulations. . . . It is beautiful to look at, but it is full of imperfections. . . .

STUDENT. It is?—Well, but they have to be overlooked. It's really beautiful—but it's a little cold. Why don't you have a fire?

YOUNG LADY. Because the smoke comes into the room.

STUDENT. Why don't you have the chimney swept out?

YOUNG LADY. It doesn't help. You see the writing table there?

STUDENT. It's extraordinarily attractive!

YOUNG LADY. But it's wobbly. Every day I put a piece of cork under one of the legs, yet—when she sweeps—the chambermaid removes it, and so I have to cut a new piece. And every day I find my penholder smeared with ink—and my inkstand, too. Then I have to wash off the ink—and, upon my word, this I have to do every single day! *(There is a pause.)* What is the worst chore you can think of?

STUDENT. To count the wash! Ugh!

YOUNG LADY. That's one of the things I have to do! Ugh!

STUDENT. What else?

YOUNG LADY. To be waked up from my sleep and have to get up and fasten the window when it rattles—because the maid has forgotten to lock it.

STUDENT. And what else?

YOUNG LADY. To have to get up on a stepladder and fix the pull-cord on the damper which the maid has pulled off.

STUDENT. What else?

YOUNG LADY. Having to sweep up after her, to dust after her, and to make the fire in the parlor stove—for all she ever does is to put in the wood—to watch the damper, to wipe the glassware, to rearrange the dinner table, to uncork the wine bottles, to open the windows and air out the rooms, make up my bed, rinse out the greenish sediment in the water bottles, replenish matches and toilet soap—which we never seem to have in the house, keep the lamp chimneys clean and trim the wicks so that the lamps won't smoke—and to be sure that they won't go out when we have company, I have to fill them myself.

STUDENT. Music!

YOUNG LADY. Wait!—First the toil and drudgery—the pains of keeping the filth and mire of life away from us. . . .

STUDENT. But you are rich, and you have two servants!

YOUNG LADY. Even if we had three, it would not help. Life is hard, and I often tire. Then imagine having a nursery besides. . . .

STUDENT. What greater joy could you wish?

YOUNG LADY. The most dearly bought. . . . Is life really worth all this pain?

STUDENT. It depends, perhaps, upon what one expects for one's labor. . . . There is nothing I would not do to win you!

YOUNG LADY. Don't say that! I can never be yours!

STUDENT. Why?

YOUNG LADY. You must not ask. (*There is a silence.*)

STUDENT. Yet you dropped your bracelet out of the window. . . .

YOUNG LADY. Yes—because my hand has grown so thin. (*Another silence. The Cook appears in the doorway to the pantry, holding a Japanese bottle in her hand.*) There you see her—she who devours me and all of us.

STUDENT. What is it she has in her hand?

YOUNG LADY. It's the bottle with the coloring—labeled with scorpion letters! It's the soy liquid that turns water into broth— it's her substitute for gravy; and she makes cabbage soup with it, too— and mock-turtle soup. . . .

STUDENT (*to the Cook*). Out with you!

COOK. You sap our marrow—and we sap yours. We help ourselves to the blood and let you have water, with some coloring in it. (*She holds up the bottle.*) That's what is in this bottle!

I'm going now—but I am staying just the same—and as long as I want to! *(She goes out.)*

STUDENT. What did Bengtsson get a medal for?

YOUNG LADY. For his loyalty and his excellent service.

STUDENT. Is he so perfect, then?

YOUNG LADY. Oh no, he has his faults—some very great ones . . . but you don't get a medal for those! *(They both smile.)*

STUDENT. This house has many secrets. . . .

YOUNG LADY. So have other houses. . . . We like to keep ours to ourselves! *(There is a pause.)*

STUDENT. Do you like frankness?

YOUNG LADY. Yes—within reason.

STUDENT. Sometimes an uncontrollable desire comes over me to speak up and give vent to my every thought. . . . Yet I know that—if we were to be completely frank—the universe would collapse. *(Pause.)* The other day I went to a funeral— a church funeral: it was most solemn and beautiful. . . .

YOUNG LADY. Mr. Hummel's, you mean?

STUDENT. My spurious benefactor's, yes. At the foot of the coffin stood an elderly friend of the deceased; he carried the mace. The clergyman's dignified manner and his moving words made a deep impression on me. I wept—we all wept. When the service was over, we went to a tavern. . . . There I learned that the elderly friend who carried the mace had been in love with the dead man's son. *(The Young Lady gazes at him quizzically, not understanding what he means.)* I also learned that the dead man had borrowed money from his son's admirer. *(Pause.)* The next day the clergyman was arrested for embezzling church funds!—A nice story, isn't it?

YOUNG LADY. Oh! *(There is a pause.)*

STUDENT. Do you know how I think of you now?

YOUNG LADY. If you say it, I shall die!

STUDENT. I must say it—or I will die!

YOUNG LADY. People in an asylum say anything that comes to their mind. . . .

STUDENT. Yes, so they do!—My father ended his days in an asylum. . . .

YOUNG LADY. Was he sick?

STUDENT. No, he was not sick, but he had lost his reason. . . . It came upon him suddenly one day, and this is how it happened. . . . He was surrounded by a circle of acquaintances whom he—for the sake of brevity—called his friends. They were a pack of rascals, as most people are—but he had to have some sort of companionship; he couldn't bear to be alone. Well, you know that, as a rule, you don't tell people what you think of them; and my father didn't either. He knew quite well how false they were; he was thoroughly convinced of their deceitfulness . . . but he was a wise man, and a man of good breeding and therefore always courteous. But one day he gave a large party—it was in the evening. He was tired after a hard day's work—and partly from the strain of keeping his thoughts silent, partly from having to talk a lot of nonsense with his guests. *(The Young Lady seems horrified.)* Well, while at table he suddenly rapped for silence, raised his glass and began to speak. . . . And then he opened the sluices, and in a lengthy speech he stripped the whole company naked, one by one, and blurted out in detail their deceits and treacheries. Worn out by the effort he ended by seating himself squarely on the table, telling them all to get out of his house and go to hell!

YOUNG LADY. Oh!

STUDENT. I was there—and I shall never forget what happened then! . . . My parents came to blows—the guests couldn't get out fast enough—and Father . . . Father was taken to a hospital for the insane. There he died! *(There is a pause.)* To suppress and hold back one's thoughts is much like still water: it stagnates, becomes foul—and that is what has happened in this house. There is something unhealthy here! And yet—when I first saw you enter this house, I thought it was paradise itself!— That Sunday morning when I stood outside looking in, I saw a colonel who was not a colonel; I met a benefactor who turned out to be a crook and was forced to hang himself; I saw a mummy who was not a mummy—and a spinster . . . what about her virginity, by the way? And as for beauty—where do you find it? In nature, and in my own mind when it is dressed in its holiday best! Where do you find honor and faithfulness? At the theatre—in fairy tales and spectacles for children. . . . What do we find that truly lives up to what it promises? . . . Only things in our dreams, our imagination!—Here your flowers have poisoned me, and now I am in turn poisoning you. . . . I asked you to be my wife—we sang and played and made poetry—and then the cook appeared. . . . *Sursum corda!* Try once again to strike fire and sublimity from the golden harp. . . . Try, I beg of you, I implore you on my knees. *(She does not move.)* Well, then I shall try it myself! *(He takes the harp; but the strings are mute.)* It has lost its voice—it's mute!—To think that the most beautiful of flowers can be so poisonous— more poisonous than any other! A curse seems to have been placed on all life and all Creation. . . . Why did you refuse to be my wife?—Because your very well-spring of life is contaminated . . . and now I am beginning to feel the vampire in the kitchen—she is draining me of life—I believe she is a Lamia—one of the kind that sucks the blood of children. . . . It's always in the servants' quarters that the seed-leaves of the children are nipped—or else it happens in the bedroom. . . . There are poisons that blind, and there are poisons that make one see more clearly. . . . I must be one of those born with the latter, for I cannot look upon what is ugly and call it good, nor can I call evil good! I just cannot! Jesus Christ descended to hell—which was His stay on earth: this madhouse, this penal prison, this charnel house that we call the earth. And when He tried to set us free, the madmen killed Him; but they set free the thief. . . . The thief always gets the sympathy!—Woe, woe to us all! Saviour of the World, we are perishing! Save us! *(The Young Lady has shown signs of being in a state of collapse as the Student's speech draws to an end. Now she is visibly dying. She rings, and Bengtsson enters.)*

YOUNG LADY. Quick . . . bring the screen. . . . I am dying. *(Bengtsson brings the screen, which he places in front of the Young Lady.)*

STUDENT. The Deliverer is coming! Be welcomed, you pale and gentle one! Sleep, you lovely, innocent, unhappy soul, who unblemished suffers for the guilt of others! Sleep without dreaming . . . and when you wake again, may you be greeted by a sun that does not sting, in a house that gathers no dust, by friends without guile, by a love that is pure and ennobling! . . . You wise and gentle Buddha, waiting for a heaven to sprout from this earth of ours—grant us patience in our trying moments—give us purity of will, that your hope may not be in vain! *(The strings of the harp emit a sighing, whispering, murmuring sound, and a white light fills the room.)*
As I gazed into the sunlight
'Twas as if I'd seen His spirit.
Man must reap what he has sown;
Blest be he whose deeds are worthy;
Evil actions done in anger
Are not purged by further wrongs. . . .
Comfort him you have brought sorrow—
Good brings good to you in turn. . . .
Righteous living exiles fear. . . .
Blessèd be the pure in heart! . . .
(From behind the screen comes a moaning sound.) You poor little child—child of this world of illusion, of sin and suffering

and death—this world of never-ending change, of disappointments and pain! May the Father of Heaven be merciful to you
on your journey! . . . (*The room disappears. The image of
Böcklin's painting "The Isle of Death" is seen in the background, and from there are heard the soft strains of ecstatic
music, mournfully ending on a note of peace.*)

CHRONOLOGY OF EVENTS

IN AUGUST STRINDBERG'S LIFE*

His birth 1849
Death of his mother...................................... 1862
Student at Uppsala University............................ 1867
Public School substitute teacher (Stockholm) 1868
Medical student 1868
Student at the Royal Academy of Acting.................. 1869
Return to Uppsala....................................... 1870
His first published play *(The Freethinker)* 1870
His first play to be both published and produced *(In Rome)* .. 1870
University studies discontinued.......................... 1872
Editor of an insurance gazette........................... 1873
Assistant librarian at the Royal Library................. 1874
First meeting with Siri von Essen....................... 1875
His first journey to France.............................. 1876
His first marriage (to Siri von Essen) 1877
His first prolonged stay in France....................... 1883
Domicile in Switzerland.................................. 1884
Prosecuted for heresy in Sweden......................... 1884
Return to Stockholm to defend himself; his exoneration.... 1884
Return to Switzerland.................................... 1884
Domicile in France...................................... 1885
He moves to Switzerland.................................. 1886
Domiciled in Germany (Bavaria) 1887
He moves to Denmark.................................... 1887
He has plans for a Scandinavian experimental theatre..1887–1888
Return to Sweden....................................... 1889
His divorce from Siri von Essen......................... 1891
He moves to Germany (Berlin) 1892
His second marriage (to Frida Uhl) 1893
His trip to England..................................... 1893
He moves to Paris...................................... 1893
The beginning of his "Inferno" period................... 1894
Journeys to Ystad (Sweden), Austria, and Lund (Sweden)..... 1896
His separation (1894) and second divorce................ 1897
Return to Paris... 1897

Climax and end of his "Inferno" period......................1897
Domicile in Lund (Sweden)............................1896–1899
Return to Stockholm....................................... 1899
His third marriage (to Harriet Bosse) 1901
His third divorce.. 1904
Founding of the Intimate (Strindberg) Theatre............ 1907
Moves to his final domicile (the "Blue Tower") in Stockholm 1908
The Intimate Theatre closes................................ 1910
National subscription to the Swedish Strindberg Fund...... 1911
His death 1912

* As compiled by Erik Hedén in his biography *Strindberg*, with additional events and dates by the translator.

BIBLIOGRAPHICAL NOTE

The following is a selective list of books and articles that have particular reference to the plays in this volume. A larger bibliography will be found in the Bantam volume *Seven Plays by August Strindberg*, translated by Arvid Paulson, with introduction and prefaces by John Gassner.

Bentley, Eric, *The Playwright as Thinker*. New York, 1946. (See especially pp. 205-210.)

Björkman, Edwin, *Plays by August Strindberg*. First and Fourth Series. New York, 1926.

Dahlström, Carl E. W. L., "Situation and Character in *Till Damaskus*," *PMLA* (Publication of the Modern Languages Association), LIII, No. 3 (September 1938), 886–902.

——, *Strindberg's Dramatic Expressionism*. Ann Arbor, Mich., 1930.

Erdmann, Nils, *August Strindberg, Die Geschichte einer kämpfenden und leidenden Seele*. Leipzig, 1924, pp. 709–725.

Gassner, John, *A Treasury of the Theatre: From Ibsen to Ionesco*. New York, 1961. (See introductions to *There Are Crimes and Crimes* and *A Dream Play*.)

Gravier, Maurice, *Strindberg et le théâtre moderne I: L'Allemagne*. Lyon, 1949.

Lamm, Martin, *Strindbergs Dramer*. Stockholm, 1924, 1926, II, 52–76, 255–259.

Lewis, Allan, *Contemporary Theatre*. New York, 1962.

Liebert, Arthur, *August Strindberg, seine Weltanschauung und seine Kunst*. Berlin, 1920.

Marcus, Carl David, *August Strindbergs Dramatik*. Munich, 1918. (See especially pp. 231–289.)

McGill, V. J., *August Strindberg: The Bedeviled Viking*. London, 1930.

Ollén, Gunnar, *Strindbergs dramatik*. Stockholm, 1961.

Paulson, Arvid, *Strindberg's Pilgrimage Dramas*. In *The Chronicle* (American Swedish Historical Association). Philadelphia, 1954-1955.

Strindberg, August, *The Confession of a Fool*. New York, 1925.

——, *The Inferno*. New York, 1917.

——, *The Son of a Servant*. New York, 1913.

——, *Zones of the Spirit*. New York, 1913.

J.G.

PRINCIPAL WORKS

OF AUGUST STRINDBERG

PLAYS: *Mäster Olof (Master Olof)*, 1872/1880; *Gillets hemlighet (The Secret of the Guild)*, 1879–80/1880; *Lycko-Pers resa (Lucky Per's Journey)* 1881–2/1882; *Herr Bengts hustru (The Wife of Sir Bengt)*, 1882; *Kamraterna (Comrades)*, 1886–8/1888; *Fadren (The Father)*, 1887; *Fröken Julie (Miss Julie)*, 1888; *Fordringsägare (Creditors)*, 1888/1890; *Paria (Pariah)*, 1889/1890; *Den starkare (The Stronger)*, 1889/1890; *Samum (Simoon)*, 1889/1890; *Himmelrikets nycklar (The Keys of Heaven)*, 1890–2/1892; *Debet och kredit (Debit and Credit)*, 1892/1893; *Första varningen (The First Warning)*, 1892/1893; *Inför döden (In the Face of Death)*, 1892/1893; *Moderskärlek (Motherlove)*, 1892/1893; *Bandet (The Bond)*, 1892/1897; *Leka med elden (Playing with Fire)*, 1892/1897;*Till Damaskus, I-II (To Damascus, Parts I and II)*, 1898; *Advent (Advent)*, 1898/1899; *Brott och brott (Crimes and Crimes)*, 1898–9/1899; *Folkungasagan (The Saga of the Folk Kings)*, 1899, *Gustaf Vasa (Gustav Vasa)*, 1899; *Erik XIV (Erik XIV)*, 1899; *Gustaf Adolf (Gustav Adolf)*, 1899–1900/1900; *Dödsdansen (The Dance of Death)*, 1900/1901; *Kronbruden (The Crown Bride)*, 1900/1902; *Påsk (Easter)*, 1900/1901; *Till Damaskus, III (To Damascus, Part III)*, 1901/1904; *Engelbrekt (Engelbrekt)*, 1901; *Carl XII (Charles XII)*, 1901; *Svanevit (Swanwhite)*, 1901/1902; *Kristina (Queen Christina)*, 1901/1903; *Ett drömspel (A Dream Play)*, 1901–2/1902; *Gustaf III (Gustav III)*, 1902/1903; *Näktergalen i Wittenberg (The Nightingale of Wittenberg)*, 1903/1904; *Oväder (Stormclouds)*, 1907; *Brända tomten (The Burned Site)*, 1907; *Spöksonaten (The Ghost Sonata)*, 1907; *Pelikanen (The Pelican)*, 1907; *Svarta handsken (The Black Glove)*, 1908–9/1909; *Siste riddaren (The Last Knight)*, 1908; *Abu Casems tofflor (The Slippers of Abu Casem)*, 1908; *Riksföreståndaren (The Regent)*, 1908/1909; *Bjälbo-Jarlen (The Earl of Bjälbo)*, 1908/1909; *Stora landsvägen (The Great Highway)*, 1909.

NOVELS: *Röda rummet (The Red Room)*, 1879; *Hemsöborna (The Natives of Hemsö)*, 1887; *I havsbandet (By the Open Sea)*, 1890; *Götiska rummen (The Gothic Rooms)*, 1904; *Svarta fanor (Black Banners)*, 1904/1907; *Taklagsöl (The Rearing Feast)*, 1906/1907.

AUTOBIOGRAPHICAL NOVELS: *Han och hon (He and She)*, 1875–6/1919; *Tjänstekvinnans son (The Son of a Servant)*, 1886; *Jäsningstiden (Fermentation Time)*, 1886; *I röda rummet (In the Red Room)*, 1886/1887; *Författaren (The Author)*, 1887/1909; *Le*

498

Plaidoyer d'un Fou (The Confession of a Fool), 1887–8/1895;
Inferno (Inferno), 1897; Legender (Legends), 1897–8/1898; Fager-
vik och Skamsund (Faircove and Foulgut), 1902; Ensam (Alone),
1903; *Syndabocken (The Scapegoat),* 1906/1907.

SHORT STORIES: *Giftas I (Married, Part I),* 1884; *Giftas II (Married,*
Part II), 1885/1886.

HISTORICAL WRITINGS: *Svenska folket i helg och söcken (The Swedish*
People in Holiday and Everday Life), 1881–2/1882; *Svenska öden*
och äventyr (Swedish Destinies and Adventures), 1882–1891/1884,
1904; *Historiska miniatyrer (Historical Miniatures),* 1905; *Nya*
svenska öden (New Swedish Destinies), 1905/1906.

POETRY: *Dikter på vers och prosa (Poems in Verse and Prose),*
1883; *Sömngångarnätter (Sleepwalking Nights), I–IV,* 1883/1884;
V, 1889/1890; 1900, *etc.*

MISCELLANEOUS: *En blå bok (A Blue Book),* 1907–1912/1907, 1908,
1912; *Memorandum till Intima Teatern (Memorandum to the*
Intimate Theatre), 1908; *Tal till svenska nationen (Address to*
the Swedish Nation), 1910.

The English translations which follow the original titles of the
above works are for the convenience of the reader, and do not
necessarily indicate that the works have been translated into English.

The date of writing of each work is followed, after a slash, by the
date of original publication, except when the work was written and
published in the same year.

A.P.